THE ACTS OF THE GENERAL ASSEMBLIES OF THE CHURCH OF SCOTLAND FROM THE YEAR 1638 TO THE YEAR 1649

THE ACTS OF THE GENERAL ASSEMBLIES OF THE CHURCH OF SCOTLAND FROM THE YEAR 1638 TO THE YEAR 1649

GENERAL ASSEMBLY, CHURCH OF SCOTLAND

ISBN: 978-93-5342-625-5

First Published: -

LECTOR HOUSE LLP
E-MAIL: lectorpublishing@gmail.com

THE ACTS OF THE GENERAL ASSEMBLIES OF THE CHURCH OF SCOTLAND FROM THE YEAR 1638 TO THE YEAR 1649.

INCLUSIVE.

PRINTED IN THE YEAR 1682.

TO WHICH ARE NOW ADDED
THE INDEX OF THE UNPRINTED
ACTS OF THESE ASSEMBLIES;
AND THE ACTS OF THE GENERAL ASSEMBLY 1690.

PRINTED IN THE YEAR 1691.

TO THE READER.

It were long, neither do we now intend, to represent, what in the beginning, by the Mercies of our *God* and Ministry of his faithful Servants, was the reformation of this Kirk: what purity of Doctrine and Worship, what Order, what Authority, and what Unity continued for many years, by the Prayers and Labours of Ministers and Professors, what Novations and Corruptions have been introduced upon us of late, in the time of our Division and Detection, by such as have ever been enemies to the Cross of *Christ*, and who have minded earthly things: How manifold and how comfortable experience we have at this time of the care and compassions of our *Lord* and *Saviour* preventing the utter ruine of Religion, and the horrible vastation of this Kirk, by looking upon the afflictions of his people, by hearing their groans, mocked by the World: And by moving the Heart of our gracious and dread Soveraign the Kings Majesty to conveen a free national Assembly for redressing the wrongs done to Religion, and what undeniable testimonies, and notable manifestations of the divine presence and assistance of *Christ*, have accompanied this meeting and whole work. *Who so is wise and observeth these things will see the loving kindness of the Lord.*

For the present it seemed necessary that such of the Acts and Constitutions of the Assembly as are of most general concernment should be published in print; the correct writing of so many Copies as were called for, not being possible to be exped in due time, and the Kirk having resolved upon this course in former times, which, had it been keeped, our defection through the almost invincible ignorance of the proceedings of the Kirk, had not proven so dangerous and deplorable.

In these Acts and Constitutions special regard was had to our National Confession of Faith, as it was at first and diverse times after professed and is now of late sworn and subscribed, that all mens minds, who delight not to cavil, might rest satisfied in the true meaning thereof, found out by the diligent search of the Ecclesiastick Registers. Our care was also rather at this time to revive and bring to light, former laudable Acts, than to make any new ones, reflecting as little as might be upon the reformation of other Kirks, and choosing to receive our directions from our own Reformation, approven by the ample testimony of so many Forreign Divines: according to the example of the venerable Assembly at Dort, where special caution was, that the 30. and 31. article of the Confession of the Belgick Kirks touching Ecclesiastick Order should not be examined by Strangers, there being a Difference touching that point amongst Reformed Kirks, So many as were present can bear witness that all the Members of the Assembly were many times called on, and required to propone their Doubts, and to give their Judgments of every Article, before it was Enacted, that every one might receive Satisfaction, and from the full perswasion of his mind might give his Voice: Wherin the Unanimity and Harmony was the more admirable, that many parting from their preconceived Opinions, which had possessed their Minds, did most willingly receive the Light, which did now unexpectedly appear from the Records of the Kirk.

That this *Extract* shall stop the *Mouthes* of the malicious, is more than we can promise, or should be expected, We know there be some Incendiaries who would with great joy and content of mind, seek their lost penny in the ashes of this poor Kirk and Kingdom: And we have already found, that our *Laboures* and the grounds whereupon we have proceeded, before they be seen, are misconstrued by so many as finds their hopes blasted, and are come short of their earthly projects: but our comfort is that we have walked in the truth of our hearts as in the sight of God, That the Adversaries of the Kirk have not transformed themselves into Angels of light, nor can say they are doing *God* service, but are seen in their colours, and do seek themselves, and that so many as have erred before, not knowing the order and constitutions of this Kirk, will as absent Children to their mother speaking plainly and powerfully of old and now after long silence opening her mouth again, and uttering her mind in a free Assembly, hear her voice, and with that reverence that beseemeth under the supreme Majesty of *Christ*, obey her directions, that being all of one mind, peace may be upon us, and upon the Kirk of *God*; and the *God* of peace, and love may be with us. 1639.

CONTENTS

THE GENERAL ASSEMBLY, AT EDINBURGH, 1639.

THE GENERALL ASSEMBLY, CONVEENED AT ABERDENE, JULY 28. 1640.

THE GENERALL ASSEMBLY, HOLDEN AT ST. ANDREWS, AND EDINBURGH. 1641.

THE GENERALL ASSEMBLY, CONVEENED AT S. ANDREWS, JULY 27. 1642.

THE GENERALL ASSEMBLY AT EDINBURGH

THE GENERALL ASSEMBLY, AT EDINBURGH, 1644.

THE GENERALL ASSEMBLY MET AT EDINBURGH JUNII 3. 1646.

THE GENERALL ASSEMBLY, AT EDINBURGH 4. AUGUST. 1647.

26. AUGUST 1647. POSTMERIDIEM. SESS. 22.

THE GENERALL ASSEMBLY, AT EDINBURGH.

THE GENERALL ASSEMBLY, HOLDEN AT EDINBURGH, JULY 7. 1649.

THE PRINCIPAL ACTS OF THE GENERAL ASSEMBLY OF THE CHURCH OF SCOTLAND HOLDEN AT EDINBURGH THE 16TH DAY OF OCTOBER 1690.

INDEX

THE GENERAL ASSEMBLY, AT GLASGOW.

ACT SESS. 6. NOVEMBER 27. 1638.

The testimony of the Committy for tryall of the Registers, subscribed with their hands, being produced, with some reasons thereof in another paper, and publickly read; *My Lord Commissioner* professed that it had resolved him of sundry doubts, but desired a time to be more fully resolved.

The Moderatour desired that if any of the Assembly had any thing to say against the said testimonie for the books, that they would declare it, and finding none to oppon, yet be appointed the day following, to any to object any thing they could say; and if then none could object the Assembly would hold the Registers as sufficient approven.

ACT. SESS 7. NOVEMBER 28.

ACT. APPROVING THE REGISTERS.

Anent the report of the Assemblies judgement of the authority of the books of Assembly; The Moderatour having desired that if any of the Assembly had any thing to say, they would now declare it, otherwise they would hold all approved by the Assembly.

The Commissioner his Grace protested that the Assemblies approving these books, or any thing contained in them be no wayes prejudicial to his Majestie, nor to the Archbishops, and Bishops of this Kingdome, or any of their adherents; because he had some exceptions against these books. My Lord Rothes desired these exceptions to be condescended on, and they should be preferably cleared, and protested that these books should be claimed authentick and obligatorie hereafter.

The whole Assembly all in one voice approved these books, and ordained the same to make faith in judgement, and out with, in all time committit, as the true and authentick Registers of the Kirk of Scotland, conform to the testimonie subscribed by the Committie, to be insert with the reasons thereof in the books of Assembly: Whereof the tenour followeth.

We under-subscribers, having power and commission from the generall Assembly now presently convened, and sitting at *Glasgow*, to peruse, examine and cognosce upon the validity, faith and strength of the books and registers of the Assembly under-written, to wit: A register beginning at the Assembly holden the twentie day of *December* 1566. and ending at the fourth session of the Assembly held in the 28 of *December* 1566.

Item another register beginning at the generall Assembly, holden the second day of June 1567. and ending at the fourth session of the Assembly holden at *Perth* the ninth day of *August* 1572, which register is imperfect, and mutilate in the end, and containeth are no leaf nor page after that page which containeth the said inscription of the said fourth session, which two registers bears to be subscribed by *John Gray* scribe.

Item a register of the Assembly holden at *Edinburgh* the seventh day of *August* 1574, and ending with the twelfth session, being the last session of the Assembly 1579.

Item another register beginning at the Assembly holden at *Edinburgh* the tenth of *May* 1586. and ending in the seventeenth session of the Assembly holden in *March*, 1589.

Item another register being the fifth book, and greatest volume, beginning at the Assembly holden in *Anno* 1560, and ending in the year 1590.

Having carefully viewed, perused and considered the first registers, and every one of them, and being deeply and maturely advised, as in a matter of greatest weight and consequence, do attest before God, and upon our conscience declare to the world and this present Assembly, that the saids foure registers above expressed, and every one of them, are famous, authentick and good registers: which ought to be so reputed and have publick faith in judgement and out with ad validem it the records in all things, and that the said fifth & greatest book, beginning at the Assembly 1560. and ending 1590. being by the hand writs of the Clerk, cognosced, and tryed, and agreeable to the other four registers, in what is extant in them, ought be free of all prejudice and suspicion, and received with them. And in testimonie of our solemne affirmation, we have made these presents with our hands.

Subscribitur,
Master Andrew Ramsay.
Master John Adamson.
Master John Row.
Master Rohre Murray.
Master Alexander Gibson.
Master James Boner.
Master Alexander Peerson.
Master Alexander Wedderburn.

Reasons prooving the five Books and Registers produced before the Assembly to be authentick.

The books now exhibited unto us underscribers, which we have revised and perused by commission from the generall Assembly, are true registers of the Kirk: to wit, Five Volumes, whereof the first two contain the acts of the Assembly, from the year of God 1560. to the year 1572. all subscribed by John Gray Clerk. The third from the year of God 1574. to the year 1579. The fourth from the year of God 1586.

to the year 1589. At which time Master James Richie was Clerk, who hath frequently written upon the margine of the saids two last books, and subscribed the said margine with his hand-writing. And the fifth book being the greatest Volume, containing the acts of the generall Assembly, from the year of God 1560. to the year 1590. which agreeth with the foresaids other foure books and registers, in so far as is extant in them, and further recordeth, what is wanting by them, passing by what is mutilate in them, and which with the two Volumes produced by Master Thomas Sandilands from the year 1590. to this present, maketh up a perfect register.

I. For the first two Volumes subscribed by Ionn Gray, albeit it be not necessar in such antiquietie to proove that he was Clerk, seeing he designes himself so by his subscription, yet the same is manifest by an act mentioned in the third book, in the time of Master James Richie, who succeeded him in the said office, and his hand-writ was acknowledged by sundry old men in the ministery.

II. The uniformitie of his subscriptions through both Volumes, evident by ocular inspection above the ordinarie custome of most famous Notars, delivers the same from all suspicion in facto tam antiquo.

III. There be many coppies, specially of general acts, yet extant, which do not debord from the saids registers, but are altogether agreeable thereto.

IV. It is constant by the universal custome of this Kingdome, that all registers are transmitted from one keeper to his successour; and so comming by progresse and succession from the first incumbent to the last possessour, are never doubted to be the registers of that judicatorie, whereof the last haver was Clerk; and therefore it is evident, that these books comming successfulie from John Gray, Master James Richie, and Master Thomas Nicolson, who were all Clerks to the Assembly, into the hands of Master Robert Winrame, who was constitute Clerk depute by the said Master Robert Nicolson (as his deputation here present to show, will testifie) are the undoubted registers of the Assembly: like as Alexander Blair succeeded the said Master Robert in his place of Clerkship to the assignations and modifications of Ministers stipends; and during Master Robert his life-time, was his actual servant, and so had the said books by progresse from him, which the said Alexander's readie presently to testifie.

V. The two registers of Master James Richie, albeit not under his own hand, yet are frequently margined with his own hand-writ, and the same marginal additions subscribed by him, which hand-writ is seen and cognosced by famous men, who knoweth the same, and it is evident, being compared with his several writings and subscriptions yet extant.

VI. The said registers are more perfect, lesse vitiated, scored, and interlined, then any other authentick and famous registers of the most prime judicatories within this Kingdom:

VII. Master Thomas Sandilands, in name of his father, who was late Clerk by dimution of Master Thomas Nicolson, hath produced a Volume, which proveth the saids two registers of Master James Richie to be sufficient records; because that same Volume is begun by that same hand, whereby the said Master James Richie his registers are written, and is subscribed once in the margine by Master James

Richie his hand, and followed forth, and continued in the same book by Master Thomas Nicolson, who succeeded him in the place, and was known by most men here present to be of such approven worth and credit, that he would never have accomplished a register which had not been famous and true: and whereof the hand-write, had not then been known to him sufficiently.

VIII. That register produced by Master Thomas Sandilands, and prosecuted by Master Thomas Nicolson, proves the first part of that register to be true and famous, and that first part being by ocular inspection of the same hand writ, with Master James Richies registers, and subscribed in the margine with the same hand writ, proveth Richies two books to be good records, and Richies registers doth approve Grays books by the act of Assembly before written: specially considering the same hath come by progresse and succession of Clerks, in the hands of Alexander Blair, now living, and here present.

IX. The compts anent the thirds of benefices between the Regent for the time, and the Assembly, in the second volume, pag. 147. are subscribed by the Lord Regents own hand, as appeareth: for it is a royall-like subscription, and there is no hand writ in all the book like unto it, and beareth not Sic subscribitur, which undoubtedly it would do, if it were a coppie.

X. Master Iames Carmichell was commanded by the generall Assembly 1595, Sess. 9, in the book produced by Master Thomas Sandilands, to extract the generall acts forth of their books; and it is evident that these books are the same which he perused for that effect, because he hath marked therein the generall acts with a crosse, and hath designed the act by some short expression upon the margine, which is cognosed and known to be his hand writ, by famous and worthy persons: which is also manifest by the said Master James his hand and subscription, written with his own hand in the last leafe of the said books; as also acknowledged in the said book, produced by Master Thomas Sandilands, wherein the said Master James Carmichell granteth the receipt of these, with some other books of the Assemblies.

XI. The registers produced, are the registers of the Assembly, because in Anno 1586, the Assembly complaineth that their registers are mutilate: which hath relation to Richies third book, which is lacerat and mutilate in divers places without any interveening of blank paper, or any mention of hic deese.

XII. If these were not principall registers, the enemies of the puritie of Gods worship, would never have laboured to destroy the same which notwithstanding they have done; as appeareth by the affixing and battering of a piece of paper upon the margine, anent a condition of the commission not to exceed the established discipline of this Kirk; subscribed by the Clerk, book 3, pag. 147, and the blotting out the certification of the excommunication against Bishop Adamson, book 4, pag. 30, who in his Recantation generally acknowledgeth the same: but which, without that recantation, cannot be presupposed to have been done, but by corrupt men of intention to corrupt the books, which were not necessary, if they were not principall registers.

XIII. In the Assembly 1596, the Church complained upon the Chancelour his retention of their registers, & desired they might be delivered to their Clerk, which accordingly was done; as a memorandum before the beginning of the first book, bearing the redeliverie of these foure books to Master James Richie, clerk proporteth; which clearly evinceth that those foure books are the registers of the Assembly.

XIV. The said fifth book and greatest Volume, is also marked on the margine, with the hand-writ of the said Master James Carmichell; (which is cognosced) who was appointed to peruse the books of the Assembly as said is, and would not have margined the same by vertue of that command, nor extracted the general acts out of it, if it were not an approbation therof, as an authentick and famous book.

XV. The said fifth Volume doth agree with the other foure books; in all which is extant in them, and marketh the blanks, which are lacerate and riven out of the same; and compleateth all what is lacking in them.

XVI. In the book of Discipline pertaining to Master James Carmichel, superscribed by himself, and Master James Richie, there are sundry acts and passages quoted out of the said fifth great Volume, saying, It is written in such a page of the book of the Assembly, which agreeth in subject and quotation with the said fifth book, and cannot agree with any other; so that Master James Carmichel reviser of the Assembly books, by their command, would not alledge that book, nor denominate the same a book of the Assembly, if it were not an authentick famous book.

XVII. Though the corrupt nature of man hath been tempted to falsifie particular evidents, yet it hath never been heard that any whole register hath ever been counterfeited; neither can it bee presupposed that any will attempt that high wickednesse, seeing the inducements anwerable to that crime, can hardly be presupposed.

XVIII. It is certain, and notour to all these who are intrusted with the keeping of the publick records of the Kingdome, that the same are never subscribed by the Clerk, but only written and filled up by servants, and most frequently by unknown hands, yet they and the extracts thereof make publick faith, and the same are uncontrovertedly authentick registers; and when the most publick registers of the Kingdom shall be seen, and compared with these registers of the Assembly, it shall be found that these other registers of the most soveraigne judicatories ever unsubscribed are more incorrect, oftner margined, scored, and interlined, made up by greater diversitie of unknown hand writs, than these books of the Assembly, which by special providence are preserved so intire, that in the judgement of any man acquainted with registers, they will manifestly appear at the very sight to be true, famous, and authentick.

XIX. The fame and credit of ancient registers in this Kingdome, is so much reverenced that if any extract be different or discontinuous from the register, that extract albeit subscribed by the person who for the time had been of greatest eminence in the trust of registers, will be rectified, conform to the register, and have no force, so far as it debordeth therefrom; although the registers be written with an obscure, unknown hand, and unsubscribed.

ACT. SESS. 12. DECEMBER FOURTH.

THE SIX LATE PRETENDED ASSEMBLIES CONDEMNED.

Anent the report of the Committie, for trying the six last pretended Assemblies: They produced in writ sundrie reasons, clearing the unlawfulnesse and nullitie of these Assemblies; which were confirmed by the registers of the Assembly, the books of Presbyteries, the Kings Majesties own letters, and by the testimonie of divers old reverend Ministers, standing up in the Assembly, and verifying the truth thereof. The Assembly with the universall consent of all, after the serious examination of the reasons against every one of these six pretended Assemblies apart, being often urged by the Moderatour, to informe themselves thoroughly, that without doubting, and with a full perswasion of minde, they might give their voices, declared all these six Assemblies of *Linlithgow* 1606. and 1608, *Glasgow* 1610, *Aberdeen* 1616, St. *Andrews* 1617, *Perth* 1618. And every one of them to have been from the beginning unfree, unlawfull, and null Assemblies, and never to have had, nor hereafter to have any Ecclesiasticall authoritie, and their conclusions to have been, and to bee of no force, vigour, nor efficacie: Prohibited all defence and observance of them, and ordained the reasons of their nullitie to be insert in the books of the Assembly: *Whereof the tennour followeth.*

REASONS ANNULLING THE PRETENDED ASSEMBLY, HOLDEN AT LINLITHGOW, 1606.

I. From the indiction of it. It was indicted the third of December to bee kept the tenth of December. And so there was no time given to the Presbyteries, far distant, neither for election of Commissioners nor for preparation to those who were to be sent in Commission. The shortnesse of the time of the indiction is proved by the Presbyterie books of Edinburgh, Perth, and Hadingtonn, &c.

II. From the want of a lawfull calling, to these who went to the meeting, seeing they were not at all elected by their Presbyteries, but were injoyned to come by the Kings letters. This also is proved by the foresaids books of the Presbyteries, and by his Majesties letters.

III. From the nature of that meeting, which was only a private meeting, or convention, for consultation to be taken by some persons of sundry estates written for, as the Kings letters and the Presbyterie books do acknowledge.

IV. From the power of those ministers who were present. Their Presbyteries did limitate them: First, That they should give no suffrages in that meeting as a generall Assembly. Secondly, That they agree to nothing that may any wayes be prejudiciall to the acts of the generall Assemblies, or to the established discipline of the Kirk. Thirdly, That they should not agree to resolve or conclude any question, article, or mater whatsoever, the decision whereof is pertinent, and proper to a free generall Assembly. Fourthly, If any thing be concluded contrary thereunto, that they protest against it. These limitations are clear by the Presbyterie books.

V. The acts of this meeting were not insert in the book of Assemblies, as is evident by the register.

VI. The next pretended Assembly at Linlithgow, 1608, doth acknowledge the Assembly, Whereof Master Patrick Galloway was Moderatour, to have been the last immediate Assembly, preceding it selfe: and that Assembly whereof he was moderatour, was the Assembly holden at Halyroodhouse, 1602. So they did not acknowledge that meeting at Linlithgow, 1606. for any Assembly at all. This is clear by the registers of the Assembly, 1608, in the entrie thereof.

REASONS FOR ANNULLING THE PRETENDED ASSEMBLY AT LINLITHGOW, 1608.

I. Manie of the voters in that pretended Assembly had no lawfull commission from the Kirk, to wit, 42 Noble men, officers of state, councellours, and Barrons, also the Bishops, contrare to the act of Dundie, 1597. And one of their caveats, the Noble men, were as commissioners from the King, the Bishops had no commission at all from the Presbyterie, for every Presbyterie out of which they came, had their full number of Commissioners beside them, as the register of the Assembly beareth.

II. In a lawfull Assembly there should be none but Commissioners from Presbyteries, Burghs, and Universities, and but three ministers at most, with one Elder, Commissioners from every Presbyterie, according to the act made at Dundie, 1597. But in that pretended Assembly, there were foure ministers from the severall Presbyteries, of Edinburgh, and Cowper, five from the Presbyteries of Arbroth, as the roll of the said pretended Assembly beareth, whereas there were no ruling Elders sent from Presbyteries, according to the book of policie and act of Dundie.

REASONS FOR ANNULLING THE PRETENDED ASSEMBLY AT GLASGOW, 1610.

I. The Commission of the pretended Commissioners to the meeting was null. 1. Because the election of them was not free, seeing they were nominate by the Kings Letters, as the Presbyterie books of Edinburgh, Perth, and Hadingtoun declare. And the Bishop of St. Andrews in his letter to some Presbyteries required them to send such commissioners as the King had nominate: assuring them, that none other would be accepted. This the Bishops letter registered in the Presbyterie books of Hadingtoun doth cleare. 2. And whereas there were no ruling Elders sent from the Presbyteries to that pretended Assembly, as the roll of Commissioners sheweth; yet there were moe ministers from undue severall Presbyteries then three, as five from Brechen, five from Arbroth, five from Kirkenbright, seven from the Presbytery of Argyl, foure from the Presbyterie of Cowper, foure from Linlithgow, foure from Pasley, foure from Hammilton, foure from Drumfreis, foure from Dunkell: as the register of that Assembly beareth.

II. There where thirtie voters of Noble men and Barrons, beside the pretended Bishops, who had no commission from any Presbyterie. In the fourth Session of this pretended Assembly it is plainly said, That the Noble men and Barrons came to it by the Kings direction.

III. The voting of the commissioners was not free: for by the Kings Letter to the Assembly they were threatned, and it was declared that their content was not needfull to any act to be made there: The King might doe it by his own power, yet they were allured to vote by a promise that their good service in so doing should be remembred and rewarded thereafter.

IV. The principall acts which were made, were set down verbatim in the privie conference, which chiefly consisted of the Kings Commissioners and pretended Bishops, and only read to be ratified in the Assembly.

V. Sundrie ministers then present, doe now declare, that they knew the ministers who voted the wrong way, to have received their present reward, and that money was largely dealt unto them.

REASONS FOR ANNULLING THE PRETENDED ASSEMBLY AT ABERDENE, 1616.

I. There was no election of a Moderatour: but that place usurped by the pretended Bishop of Saint Andrews, as the Register beareth.

II. The indiction of that pretended Assembly was but twentie dayes before the holding of it: so that the Presbyteries and burghes could not be prepared for sending their commissioners: which caused the absence of many Presbyteries and fourtie foure Burghes.

III. There were twentie five noble-men, and gentle-men voters without commission from the Kirk. Ma. William Struthers voted for the Presbyterie of Edinburgh, yet had no commission there-from. The commission being given by that Presbyterie to other three, as the said Commission registrar in the books of the Presbytery beareth. And whereas there should be but one Commissioner from every burgh, except Edinburgh, to the Assembly; at this pretended Assembly, there were two Commissioners from Glasgow, two from Cowper, two from St. Andrews: whereas there were no ruling Elders having commission from their Presbyteries at that Assembly.

IV. When the acts of that pretended assembly were written, the Bishop of St. Andrews with his own hand did interline, adde, change, vitiate, direct to be extracted or not extracted, as he pleased: as the scrolls themselves seen, doe show; wherefore the Clerk did not registrat the acts of that Assembly, in the books of Assemblies, as may be easily seen by the blank in the register left for them remaining unfilled.

THE NULLITIE OF THE PRETENDED ASSEMBLY AT SAINT ANDREWS, 1617.

I. There is no mention of it in the register of the Assemblies, and so no warrand for their commissions, their Moderatour or Clerk.

II. The indiction of it was so unformall, that as the scroll declareth, a great part of the Commissioners from Synods, Burrows, and gentle-men, would not be present.

III. The Kings Majestie in his letter to Perths Assembly, acknowledged it was but a meeting, wherein disgrace was offered to his Majestie.

IV. The former corruptions of the foure preceding Assemblies had their confluence in this and the subsequent Assembly.

REASONS FOR ANNULLING THE PRETENDED ASSEMBLY, HOLDEN AT PERTH, 1618.

I. The Assembly was indicted but twentie dayes before the holding of it: and all parties requisit received not advertisement, as appeareth by their absence. The untimous indicting of it, is cleared by Presbyterie books.

II. There was no election of the Moderatour, as was accustomed to be in lawfull Assemblies; The register cleareth this.

III. No formall election of their new Clerk.

IIII. There were five whole Dioces absent, viz. Orknay, Cathnes, Rosse, Argyll, and Isles: and many Presbyteries had no Commissioners there, as the register of that pretended Assembly beareth.

V. There were nineteen noblemen and Barrons, eleven Bishops that had no Commission from the Kirk. Whereas the act for constitution of Assemblies, ordaineth every Burgh to have but one Commissioner, except Edinburgh, which may have two (Act at Dundie 1597) yet in that pretended Assembly, Perth had three Commissioners, Dundie, had two, Glasgow had two, and St. Andrews had two: Of the Burghes, there were there six absent: And for ruling Elders, there were none at all with commission from their Presbyteries. All these things are cleared by the records of that pretended Assemblie.

VI. The Commissioners from some Presbyteries exceeded their numbers prescribed in the act at Dundie, 1597, for the Presbyterie of Arbroth were foure Commissioners and three for the Presbyterie of Aughterardour: Beside these that were heard to vote, having no commission at all, and some who had commission were rejected, and were not enrolled, but others put in their place without commission.

VII. The pretended Bishops did practice foure of the articles to be concluded there, before the pretended Assembly, in Edinburgh, St. Andrews, and other cathedral Churches, by keeping festival dayes, kneeling at ye Communion. Thus their voices were prejudged by their practice of these services before condemned by the Kirk, and therefore they should have been secluded from voicing.

VIII. In all lawfull Assemblies, the voicing should be free: But in this pretended Assembly there were no free voicing; for the voicers were threatned to voice affirmative, under no lesse pain nor the wrath of authoritie, imprisonment, banishemnt, deprivation of ministers, and utter subversion of the state: Yea, it was plainly professed, that neither reasoning nor the number of voices should carie the matter away: Which is qualified by the declaration of many honest old reverend Brethren of the ministery now present.

IX. In all lawful Assemblies, the grounds of proceeding were, and used to be, the word of God, the confession of Faith, and acts of former general Assemblies. But in this pretended Assembly, the ground of their proceeding in voicing was the Kings commandment only: For so the question was stated: Whether the five articles, in respect of his Majesties commandement, should passe in act, or not: As the records of that pretended Assembly beareth. Where it is declared, that for the reverence and respect which they bear unto his Majesties Royal commandements, they did agree to the foresaids articles.

X. Many other reasons verifying the nullitie of all these Assemblies, were showen and proven before the Assembly, which needeth not here to be insert.

ACT. SESS. 13. DECEMBER 5. 1638.

AGAINST THE UNLAWFULL OATHS OF INTRANTS.

The six Assemblies immediately preceeding, for most just and weightie reasons above-specified, being found to be unlawful, and null from the beginning: The Assembly declareth the oathes and subscriptions exacted by the Prelates of the intrants in the ministerie all this time by past (as without any pretext of warrand from the Kirk, so for obedience of the acts of these null Assemblies, and contrare to the ancient and laudable constitutions of this Kirk, which never have been nor can be lawfully repealled, but must stand in force) to be unlawful, and no way obligatorie. And in like manner declareth, that the power of Presbyteries, and of provincial and general Assemblies, hath been unjustly surpressed, but never lawfully abrogate. And therefore that it hath been most lawful unto them, not withstanding any point unjustly objected by the Prelats to the contrare, to admit, suspend, or deprive ministers, *respectivè* within their bounds, upon relevant complaints sufficiently proven; to choose their own Moderatours, and to execute all the parts of ecclesiastical jurisdiction according to their own limits appointed them by the Kirk.

ACT. SESS. 14. DECEMBER 6. 1638.

CONDEMNING THE SERVICE-BOOK, BOOK OF CANONS, BOOK OF ORDINATION, AND THE HIGH COMMISSION.

I. The Assembly having diligently considered the Book of common prayer, lately obtruded upon the reformed Kirk within this Realme, both in respect of the manner of the introducing thereof, and in respect of the matter which it containeth, findeth that it hath been devised and brought in by the pretended Prelats, without direction from the Kirk, and pressed upon ministers without warrand from the Kirk, to be universally received as the only forme of divine service under all highest paines, both civill and ecclesiasticall, and the book it self, beside the *popish* frame and forms in divine worship, to contain many *popish* errours and ceremonies, and the seeds of manifold and grosse superstition and idolatrie. The Assembly therefore all in one voice, hath rejected, and condemned and by these presents doth reject and condemne the said book, not only as illegally introduced, but also as repugnant to the doctrine, discipline and order of this reformed Kirk, to the Confession of Faith, constitutions of generall Assemblies, and acts of Parliament establishing the true Religion; and doth prohibite the use and practice thereof: and ordaine Presbyteries to proceed with the censure of the Kirk against all such as shall transgresse.

II. The Assembly also, taking to their consideration the book of Canons, and the manner how it hath been introduced, findeth that it hath been devised by the pretended Prelats, without warrand or direction from the generall Assembly; and to establish a tyrannicall power in the persons of the pretended Bishops, over the worship of God, mens consciences, liberties and goods, and to overthrow the whole discipline and government of the generall and Synodall Assemblies, Presbyteries, and Sessions formerly established in our Kirk.

Therefore the Assembly all in one voice hath rejected and condemned, and by these presents doth reject and condemne the said book, as contrare to the confession of our Faith, and repugnant to the established government, the book of Discipline, and the acts and constitutions of our Kirk: prohibits the use and practise of the same; and ordains Presbyteries to proceed with the censure of the Kirk against all such as shall transgresse.

III. The Assembly having considered the book of consecration and ordination, findeth it to have been framed by the Prelats, to have been introduced and practised without warrand of authority, either civill or ecclesiasticall: and that it establisheth offices in Gods house, which are not warranded by the word of God, and are repugnant to the Discipline, and constitutions of our Kirk, that it is an impediment to the entrie of fit and worthie men to the ministery, and to the discharge of their dutie after their entrie, conforme to the discipline of our Kirk. Therefore the Assembly all in one voice hath rejected and condemned, and by these presents doe reject and condemne the said book; and prohibits the use and practise of the same: And ordaines Presbyteries to proceed with the censure of the Kirk against all such as shall transgresse.

IV. The generall Assembly, after due tryall, having found that the Court of high Commission, hath been erected without the consent or procurement of the Kirk, or consent of the Estates in Parliament, that it subverteth the jurisdiction and ordinarie judicatories and Assemblies of the Kirk-Sessions, Presbyteries, provinciall and nationall Assemblies, that it is not regulate by lawes civill or ecclesiasticall, but at the discretion and arbitrement of the Commissioners; that it giveth to ecclesiasticall persons, the power of both the swords, and to persons meerly civill, the power of the keys and Kirk censures: Therefore the Assembly all in one voice, hath disallowed and condemned, and by these presents doth disallow and condemne the said court, as unlawfull in it selfe, and prejudiciall to the liberties of Christ—Kirk and Kingdome, the Kings honour in maintaining the established lawes and judicatories of the Kirk; and prohibits the use and practise of the same; and ordaines Presbyteries to proceed with the censures of the Kirk, against all such as shall transgresse.

After the serious discussing of the several Processes, in many Sessions, from Sess. 14. (which are in the Clerks hands, and needeth not here to be insert) the following sentences were solemnly pronounced after Sermon by the Moderatour, in the Assembly of *Glasgow, Sess. 20 December 13, 1638.*

SENTENCE OF DEPOSITION AND EXCOMMUNICATION AGAINST MR. JOHN SPOTTISWOOD, PRETENDED ARCH-

BISHOP OF ST. ANDREWS; MR. PATRIK LINDSAY, PRETENDED ARCHBISHOP OF GLASGOW: MR. DAVID LINDSAY, PRETENDED BISHOP OF EDINBURGH: MR. THOMAS SIDSERFE, PRETENDED BISHOP OF GALLOWAY: MR. JOHN MAXWELL, PRETENDED BISHOP OF ROSSE: MR. WALTER WHYT-FOORD, PRETENDED BISHOP OF BRECHEN.

The general Assembly, having heard the libels and complaints, given in against the foresaids pretended Bishops to the Presbyterie of Edinburgh, and sundry other Presbyteries within their pretended Dyocies, and by the saids Presbyteries referred to the Assembly, to be tryed: The saids pretended Bishops being lawfully cited, often-times called, and their Procutour Doctour Robert Hammiltoun, and not compearing, but declining and protesting against this Assembly, as is evident by their declinatour, and protestation given in by the said Doctour Robert Hammiltoun minister at Glasfoord, which by the acts of Assembly is censurable with summar excommunication: Entered in consideration of the said declinatour, and finding the same not to be relevant, but on the contrare to be a displayed banner against the setled order and government of this Kirk, to be fraughted with insolent and disdainful speeches, lies and calumnies against the lawful members of this Assembly, proceeded to the cognition of the saids complaints, and libels against them; and finding them guiltie of the breach of the cautions, agreed upon in the Assembly holden at Montrose, Anno 1600. for restricting of the minister voter in Parliament, from incroaching upon the liberties and jurisdiction of this Kirk, which was set down with certification of deposition, infamie, and excommunication, specially for receiving of consecration to the office of Episcopacie, condemned by the confession of Faith, and acts of this Kirk, as having no warrand, nor foundament in the word of God, and by vertue of this usurped power, and power of the high Commission, pressing the Kirk with novations in the worship of God, and for sundrie other haynous offences, and enormities, at length expressed, and clearly proven in their processe, and for their refusal to underly the tryal of the reigning slander of sundrie other grosse transgressions and crymes laid to their charge: Therefore the Assembly moved with zeal to the glorie of God, and purging of his Kirk, hath ordained the saids pretended Bishops to be deposed, and by these presents doth depose them, not only of the office of Commissionaire to vote in Parliament, Councel, or Convention in name of the Kirk, but also of all functions whether of pretended Episcopal or ministerial calling, declareth them infamous. And likewise ordaineth the saids pretended Bishops to be excommunicate, and declared to be of these whom Christ commandeth to be holden by all and every one of the faithful as ethnicks, and publicanes; and the sentence of excommunication to be pronounced by Mr. Alexander Henderson, Moderatour in face of the Assembly in the high Kirk of Glasgow; and the execution of the sentence to bee intimat in all the Kirks of Scotland by the Pastours of every particular congregation, as they will be answerable to their Presbyteries and Synods, or the next general Assembly, in case of the negligence of Presbyteries and Synods.

SENTENCE OF DEPOSITION AND EXCOMMUNICATION,

AGAINST MR. ADAM BALLANTYNE, PRETENDED BISHOP OF ABERDEEN, AND MR. JAMES WEDDERBURN PRETENDED BISHOP OF DUMBLANE.

The generall Assembly, having heard the lybels and complaints given in against the foresaids pretended Bishops, of Aberdeen and Dumblane, to the Presbytery of Edinburgh, and sundry Presbyteries within their pretended Dioceses, and by the saids Presbyteries referred to this Assembly to be tryed: The saids pretended Bishops being lawfully cited, often-times called, and not compearing, proceeded to the cognition of the complaints and lybels against them, and finding them guilte of the breach of the cautions, agreed upon in the Assembly holden at Montrose, Anno 1600 for restricting the minister voter in Parliament, from encroaching upon the liberties and jurisdictions of this Kirk, which was set down with certification of deposition, infamie and excommunication, specially for receiving of consecration to the office of Episcopacie, condemned by the confession of Faith, and acts of this Kirk, as having no warrand nor foundament in the word of God, and by vertue of this usurped power, and power of the high Commission, pressing the Kirk with novations in the worship of God, and for sundry other haynous offences and enormities, and length expressed, and clearly proven in their Processe, and for their refusall to underly the tryall of the reigning slander of sundry other grosse transgressions and offences laid to their charge: Therefore the assembly moved with zeal to the glorie of God, and purging of the Kirk, hath ordained the saids pretended Bishops to be deposed, and by these presents doth depose them, not only of the office of Commissionary to vote in Parliament, Councell, or Convention, in name of the Kirk, but also of all functions, whether of pretended Episcopall or ministeriall calling, declareth them infamous: and likewise ordains the saids pretended Bishops to be excommunicate, and declared to be of these whom Christ commanded to be holden by all and every one of the faithfull as Ethnicks and Publicans; and the sentence of excommunication to be pronounced by Mr. Alexander Henderson Moderatour, in face of the Assembly after Sermon, in the high Kirk of Glasgow: and that the execution of the sentence be intimat in all the Kirks within this Realme, by the Pastours of every particular congregation, as they will be answerable to their Presbyteries and Synods, or the next generall Assembly, in case of the negligence of Presbyteries and Synods.

SENTENCE OF DEPOSITION AGAINST MASTER JOHN GUTHRY, PRETENDED BISHOP OF MURRAY: MR. JOHN GRAHAME, PRETENDED BISHOP OF ORKNAY, MR. JAMES FAIRLIE, PRETENDED BISHOP OF LISMOIR: MR. NEIL CAMBELL, PRETENDED BISHOP OF ISLES.

The generall Assembly having heard the lybels and complaints given in against the foresaids pretended Bishops, to the Presbyterie of *Edinburgh*, and sundrie Presbyteries within their Dyocies, and by the saids Presbyteries referred to this Assembly to bee tryed: the saids pretended Bishops being lawfully cited, often-times called, and not compearing, proceeded to the cognition of the complaints and lybels against them; and finding them guiltie of the breach of the cautions agreed upon in the Assembly at *Montrose, Anno* 1600. for restricting of the minister, voter in Parliament, from incroaching upon the liberties and Jurisdictions of this Kirk, which was set down with certification of deposition, infamie and excommunication; and especially for receiving consecration to the office or Episcopacie condemned by the confession of Faith, and acts of this Kirk, as having no warrand nor foundament in the word of God, and by vertue of this usurped power, and power of the high commission, pressing the Kirk with novations in the worship of God; and for their refusall to underly the tryall of the reigning slander of sundrie other grosse transgressions and offences, laid to their charge: Therefore the Assembly, moved with zeal to the glorie of God, and purging of this Kirk, ordaines the saids pretended Bishops, to bee deposed, and by these presents doth depose them, not only of the office of commissionarie, to vote in Parliament, Councel, or convention in name of the Kirk: but also of all functions, whether of pretended Episcopall, or ministeriall calling: And likewise in case they acknowledge not this Assembly, reverence not the constitutions thereof, and obey not the sentence, and make not their repentance, conforme to the order prescribed by this Assembly, ordaines them to be excommunicated, and declared to bee of these whom Christ commandeth to be holden by all and every one of the faithfull as Ethnicks and Publicanes: and the sentence of excommunication to be pronounced upon their refusall, in the Kirks appointed, by any of those who are particularly named, to have the charge of trying their repentance or impenitencie, and that the execution of this sentence bee intimate in all the Kirks within this Realme by the Pastours of every particular Congregation, as they will be answerable to their Presbyteries and Synods, or the next generall Assembly, in case of negligence of the Presbyteries and Synods.

SENTENCE OF DEPOSITION AGAINST MAISTER ALEXANDER LINDSAY PRETENDED BISHOP OF DUNKELL.

The generall Assembly having heard the complaint and lybel given in against Mr. Alexander Lindesay pretended Bishop of Dunkell, to the Presbytery of Edinburgh, and sundry Presbyteries of his pretended Dyocie, and by the Presbyteries referred to this Assembly to be tryed: The said pretended Bishop being lawfully cited, often-times called, & not compearing, but by a letter of excuse submitting himself to the Assembly, proceeded to the cognition of the complaint and lybell itselfe against him, and finding him guiltie of the breach of the cautions agreed upon in the Assembly holden at Montrose, Anno 1600 for restricting the minister voter in parliament, from encroaching upon the liberties and jurisdictions of this Kirk, which was set down with certification of deposition, infamie and excommunication, especially for receiving consecration to the office of Episcopacie condemned by the confession of Faith, and acts of this Kirk, as having no warrand nor foundament in the word of God, and by vertue of this usurped power, and power of the high Commission, pressing the Kirk with novations in the worship of God: Therefore the Assembly moved with zeal to the glory of God, and purging of this Kirk, hath ordained the said Mr. Alexander to bee deposed, and by these presents deposeth him, from the pretended Episcopall function, and from the office of commissionarie to vote in Parliament, Councel or Convention in name of the Kirk, and doth suspend him from all ministeriall function, and providing he acknowledge this Assembly, reverence the constitutions of it, and obey this sentence, and make his repentance conforme to the order prescribed, continueth him in the ministrie of St. Madoze; And likewise, if he acknowledge not this Assembly, reverence not the constitutions of it, and obey not the sentence, and make his repentance, conforme to the order prescribed by this Assembly, ordains him to be excommunicat, and declared to bee one of those whom Christ commandeth to bee holden by all and every one of the faithfull, as an Ethnick and Publicane, and the sentence of excommunication to be pronounced upon his refusall, in the Kirks appointed, by one of these who are particularly named, to have the charge of trying his repentance or impenitencie, and that the execution of this sentence be intimate in all the Kirks within this Realme, by the Pastours of every particular congregation, as they will be answerable to their Presbyteries and Synods, or the next generall Assembly, in case of the negligence of Presbyteries, and Synods.

SENTENCE OF DEPOSITION AGAINST MASTER JOHN AB-ERNETHIE PRETENDED BISHOP OF CATHNES.

The generall Assembly having heard the lybell and complaint given in against Mr. John Abernethie pretended Bishop of Cathnes to the Presbytery of Edinburgh, and sundry Presbyteries within his Dyocie: And by the saids Presbyteries, referred to this Assembly to be tryed: The said pretended Bishop being lawfully cited, of-ten-times called, and not compearing, but by his letter of excuse upon his sick-nesse, proceeded to the cognition of the complaint and lybell it selfe against him, and finding him guiltie of the breach of the cautions, agreed upon in the Assembly holden at Montrose, Anno 1600. for restricting the minister voter in Parliament, from encroaching upon the liberties and jurisdictions of this Kirk, which was set down with certification of deposition, infamie, and excommunication, specially for receiving consecration to the office of Episcopacie, condemned by the confession of Faith, and acts of this Kirk as having no warrand nor foundament in the word of God, and by vertue of the usurped power, and power of the high Commission pressing the Kirk with novations in the worship of God: Therefore the assembly moved with zeal to the glorie of God, and purging of this Kirk, hath ordaineth the said Mr. John to be deposed, and by these presents deposeth him from the pretended Episcopall function, and from the office of Commissionary to vote in Parliament, Councel, or convention, in name of the Kirk, and doth suspend him from the ministeriall function. And providing he acknowledge this Assembly, reverence the constitutions of it, and obey the sentence, and make his repentance conforme to the order prescribed by this Assembly, will admit him to the ministerie of a particular flok: and likewise, in case he acknowledge not this Assembly, reverence not the constitutions of it, and make his repentance conforme to the order prescribed by this Assembly, ordains him to be excommunicate, and declared to be one of these whom Christ commandeth to be holden by all and everyone of the faithfull as an Ethnick and Publicane: and the sentence of excommunication to be pronounced upon his refusall in the Kirks appointed, by one of these who are particularly named to have this charge of trying his repentance or impenitencie, and that the execution of this sentence be intimat in all the Kirks within this Realme, by the Pastours of every particular Congregation, as they will be answerable to their Presbyteries and Synods, or the next generall Assembly, in case of the negligence of Presbyteries and Synods.

ACT OF THE ASSEMBLY AT GLASGOW,

SESS. 16. DECEMBER 8. 1638.

DECLARING EPISCOPACIE TO HAVE BEEN ABJURED BY THE CONFESSION OF FAITH, 1580. AND TO BE REMOVED OUT OF THIS KIRK.

The Assembly taking to their most grave and serious consideration, first the unspeakable goodnesse, and great mercy of God, manifested to this Nation, in that so necessarie, so difficult, and so excelent and divine work of reformation, which was at last brought to such perfection, that this Kirk was reformed, not only in doctrine and worship, but also after many conferences and publick reasonings in divers nationall Assemblies, joyned with solemne humiliations and prayers to God, the discipline and government of the Kirk, as the hedge and guard of the doctrine and worship, was prescribed according to the rule of Gods word, in the book of Policie and Discipline, agreed upon in the Assembly 1578. and insert in the register 1581. established by the Acts of Assemblies, by the confession of Faith, sworn and subscribed, at the direction of the Assembly, and by continuall practise of this Kirk: Secondly, that by mens seeking their own things: and not the things of Jesus Christ; divers novations have been introduced to the great disturbance of this Kirk, so firmly once compacted, and to the endangering of Religion, and many grosse evils obtruded, to the utter undoing of the work of reformation, and change of the whole forme of worship and face of this Kirk; Thirdly, that all his Majesties Subjects both Ecclesiasticall and civil, being without consent of the Kirk, commanded to receive with reverence a new book of common prayer, as the only forme to be used in Gods publick worship, and the contraveeners to be condignely censured, and punished, and after many supplications and complaints, knowing no other way for the preservation of Religion; were moved by God, and drawn by necessitie, to renew the nationall Covenant of this Kirk, and Kingdome, which the Lord since hath blessed from heaven, and to subscribe the Confession of Faith, with an application thereof, abjuring the great evils wherewith they were now pressed, and suspending the practise of all novations formerly introduced, till they should bee tryed in a free generall Assembly, Lastly, that some of his Majesties Subjects of sundrie ranks, have by his Majesties commandement subscribed and renewed the confession of Faith, without the former application, and that both the one and the other subscribers have subscribed the said Confession of Faith in this year, as it was professed and according to the meaning that it had in this Kingdome, when it was first subscribed 1581. and afterward the Assembly therefore, both by the subscription of his Majesties high Commissioner, and of the Lords of secret Councel, Septem. 22. 1638. And by the acts of Councel, of the date foresaid, bearing that they subscribed the said Confession, and ordaining all his Majesties Liedges to subscribe the same, according to the foresaid date and tennour, and as it was then professed within this Kingdome, as likewise by the Protestation of some of the Senatours of the Colledge of justice, when they were required to subscribe, and by the many doubtings of his Majesties good Subjects, especially because the subscribers of the Confession in February 1635. are bound to suspend the approbation of the corruptions of the government of the Kirk, till they be tryed in a free generall Assembly; finding it proper for them, and most necessary and incumbent to them, to give out the true meaning thereof as it was at first professed. That all his Majesties Subjects in a matter so important; as is the publik Confession of Faith, so solemnely sworn and subscribed, may be of one minde, and one heart, and have full satisfaction to all their doubts, and that the posteritie afterward may be fully perswaded of the true meaning thereof, after earnest calling upon the name of God, so religiously attested in the said Confession; have entered into a diligent search of the registers of the Kirk, and books of the generall Assembly, which the greatest part of the Assembly had not seen before; and which by the speciall providence of God were preserved, brought to their hands, and publicly acknowledged to bee authentick, and have found that in the latter confession of the Kirk of Scotland: We profess, that we deteste all traditions brought into the Kirk without, or against the word of God, and doctrine of this reformed Kirk: Next, we abhorre and deteste all contrarie religion and doctrine, but chiefly, All kinds of papistry in generall & particular heads, as they were then damned & confuted by the word of God, and Kirk of Scotland, when the said Confession was sworn and subscribed, An. 1580. and 1581, 1590, and 1591. Thirdly, that we deteste the Romane Antichrist, his worldly monarchie, and wicked hierarchie: Fourthly, that we joyn our selves to this reformed Kirk in doctrine, Faith, Religion, & discipline, promising and swearing by the great name of GOD, that we shall continue in the Doctrine and Discipline of this Kirk, and defend the same according to our vocation and power all the dayes of our life.

But so it is that Episcopall government is abhorred and detested, and the government by Ministers and Elders, in Assemblies generall and provinciall, and Presbyteries was sworn to, and subscribed in subscribing that Confession, and ought to be holden by us, if we adhere to the meaning of the Kirk, when that Confession was framed, sworn to, and subscribed; unto which we are obliged by the nationall oath and subscription of this Kirk, as is evident by the acts of generall Assemblies, agreed upon both before, at, and after the swearing and subscribing of the said Confession, in the years above-mentioned, and the book of policie agreed upon in the Assembly which was holden at *Edinburgh* the twentie foure of *April*, and twentie foure of *October*, *Anno* 1578. Insert in the register of the Kirk, by ordinance of the Assembly holden at *Glasgow* 1581 and to be subscribed by all Ministers, that then did bear, or thereafter were to bear office in this Kirk, by ordinance of the Assembly holden the fourth of *August* at *Edinburgh* 1590. And at *Edinburgh* the second of *July* 1591. but specially in the 2. 3. 4. 6. 7. and 11, chapters of the said book.

The Bishops being tollerat from the year 1572, till the Assembly holden in August 1575. And all this time the Assembly being wearied with complaints made against them, did enter in search of the office it selfe, and did agree in this that the name of a Bishop is common to every one of them that hath a particular flock, over which he hath a particular charge, as well to preach the word, as to minister the

Sacraments.

At the next Assembly which was holden in April 1576. Such Bishops were censured as had not taken them to a particular flock. In the generall Assembly conveened in April the year of God 1578. Sess. 4. Intimation was made as followeth.

For so much as the heads of the policie being concluded and agreed upon in the last Assembly, by the most part of the brethren: certain of the brethren had some difficultie in the head de diaconatu, whereupon farther reasoning was reserved to this Assembly: It is therefore required, if any of the brethren have any reasonable doubt or argument to propone, that he be ready the morow, and then shall be heard and resolved. In the 6. Sess. April 26. According to the ordinance made the day before; all persons that had any doubt or argument to propone, were required to propone the same; but none offered to propone any argument on the contrare.

In the Assembly holden at *Edinburgh*, in *October* 1578. It was showen by the Moderatour thereof to the noble-men, who were present, viz. *My Lord Chancelour*, the Earle of *Montrose*, my Lord *Seaton*, and my Lord *Lindsay*, *What care and study the Assembly had taken to entertain and keep the puritie of the sincere word of God, unmixed with the inventions of their own heads, and to preserve it to the posteritie hereafter, and seeing that the true Religion is not able to continue nor endure long without a good Discipline and policie, in that part also have they imployed their wit and studie, and drawen forth out of the pure fountain of Gods word, to bee a Discipline as is meet to remain in the Kirk.*

In the same Assembly, the speciall corruptions were set down, which they craved such of the Bishops as would submit themselves to the Assembly to remove, with promise, that if the generall Assembly, hereafter shall finde further corruptions in the said estate, then hitherto are expressed that they be content to be reformed by the said Assembly according to the word of God, when they shall be required thereto. First, That they be content to bee Pastours and Ministers of one flock: That they usurpe no criminall jurisdiction, that they vote not in Parliament in name of the Kirk, without Commission from the Kirk: That they take not up for the maintenance of their ambition and rictousnesse, the emoluments of the Kirk, which may sustain many Pastours, the Schools, and the poore; but be content with reasonable livings according to their office: That they claime not to themselves the titles of Lords temporall, neither usurpe temporall jurisdictions, whereby they are abstracted from their office: That they empyre not above the particular Elderships, but be subject to the same: That they usurpe not the power of the Presbyteries.

The question being proponed by the Synod at Loutbian in the Assembly holden in July 1579. anent a generall order to be taken for erecting of Presbyteries in places where publick exercise is used, untill the time the policie of the Kirk be established by a law: It is answered, The exercise may be judged to be a Presbyterie. In the Assembly holden at Dundie in July 1580. Sess. 4, The office of a Bishop was abolished by a particular act; as appeareth by the tennour of the act following.

For so much as the office of a Bishop, as it is now used and commonly taken withen this Realme, hath no sure warrand authoritie, nor good ground in the Scriptures, but is brought in by the foly and corruption of mans inventions, to the great overthrow of the Kirk of God, the whole Assembly of the Kirk in one voice after libertie given to all men to reason in the matter, none opponing himself in defending the said pretended office, findeth and declareth the said pretended office, used and termed, as is above said, unlawfull in the selfe, as having neither foundament, ground, nor warrand in the word of God, and ordaineth that all such persons, as brook or shall brook hereafter the said office, shall be charged simply to dimit, quite, and leave off the same, as an office whereunto they are not called of God: and suchlike, to desist and cease from all preaching, ministration of the Sacraments, or using any way the office of pastours, while they receive de novo, admission from the generall Assembly, under the pain of excommunication to be used against them, wherein if they be found disobedient, or contradict this act in any point, the sentence of excommunication, after due admonition, to be execute against them.

In the same Assembly holden Anno 1580. Sess. 10. This article was appointed to be proponed to the King and Councel, that the book of policie might be established by an act of privie Councel, while a Parliament be holden, at which it might be confirmed by a law.

The extent of the act made at Dundie, was interpreted and explained in the Assembly, holden at Glasgow, in April, 1581. Sess. 6. as followeth.

Anent the Act made in the Assembly holden at Dundie against Bishops, because some difficultie appeareth to some brethren to arise out of the word (office) contained in the said act, what should be meaned thereby, The Assembly consisting for the most part of such as voted, and were present in the Assembly at Dundie, to take away the said difficultie, resolving upon the true meaning and understanding of the said act, declare that they meaned wholly to condemne the whole estate of Bishops, as they are now in Scotland, and that the same was the determination and conclusion of the Assembly at this time, because some brethren doubted, whether the former act was to be understood of the spiritual function only, and others alledged, that the whole office of a Bishop as it was used, was damnable, and that by the said act, the Bishops should be charged to dimit the same: This Assembly declareth that they meaned wholly to condemne the whole estate of Bishops, as they were then in Scotland, and that this was the meaning of the Assembly, at that time.

The Kings Commissioner presented to this Assembly the Confession of Faith, subscribed by the King, and his houshold, not long before, together with a plot of the Presbyteries to be erected, which is registrate in the books of the Assembly, with a letter to be directed from his Majestie to the noble-men and gentle-men of the Countrey, for the erection of Presbyteries, consisting of Pastours, and Elders, and dissolution of Prelacies, and with an offer to set forward the Policie untill it were established by Parliament. The Kings letter subscribed by his hand, to the Noble-men, and Gentle-men, was read in open audience of the whole Assembly.

This Assembly ordained the book of Policie to be insert in the register by the act following.

For as much as travels have been taken in the framing of the Policie of the Kirk, and diverse suits have been made to the Magistrat for approbation thereof, which yet have not taken the happie effect, which good men would wish, yet that the posteritie may judge well of the present age; and of the meaning of the Kirk; The Assembly hath concluded, that the book of Policie agreed to in diverse Assemblies before, should be registrat in the acts of the

Kirk, and remaine therein ad perpetuam rei memoriam: and the coppies thereof to be taken to every Presbyterie: of which book the tennour followeth, &c.

Immediatly after the inserting of the book of Policie, called there the book of Discipline, the Assembly ordained that the confession of Faith be subscribed as followeth.

Anent the confession of Faith lately set forth by the Kings Majestie, and subscribed by his highnesse. The Assembly in one voice, acknowledgeth the said Confession to be a true, Christian, and faithful confession, to be eagreed unto by such as truly professe Christ, and have a care of Religion, and the tennour thereof to be followed out efoldly as the samine is laid out in the said Proclamation, wherein that Discipline is sworn to.

In the general Assembly holden at Edinburgh in October 1581. Sess. 10. Mr. Robert Montgomery is accused for teaching that Discipline is a thing indifferent. Sess. 23. The Assembly gave commission to the Presbyterie of Stirling, to charge Mr. Robert Montgomerie, to continue in the ministerie of Stirling, and not to medle with any other office or function of the Kirk, namely in aspyring to the Bishoprick of Glasgow, against the word of God, and acts of the Kirk, under the pain of excommunication.

In the same Assembly it is acknowledged that the estate of Bishops is condemned by the Kirk, a commission for erection of moe Presbyteries was renewed: and a new ordinance made for subscribing the confession of Faith, and to proceed against whatsoever persons that would not acknowledge and subscribe the same.

In the Assembly holden in April 1582. there was a new commission for erection of Presbyteries, where none was as yet erected, Mr. Robert Montgomerie, pretending to be Bishop of Glasgow, was ordained to be deposed and excommunicat, except hee gave evident tokens of repentance, and promise to superseed, which he did not: and therefore he was excommunicat shortly after, according to the ordinance of this Assembly.

In the generall Assembly holden at Edinburgh, 1582. The generall Assembly gave commission to some Presbyteries, to try and censure such as were called Bishops, for the great slander arising by their impunitie. Commission was given at this Assembly to present some articles to the Councel and Estates, for approving and establishing by their authoritie the Presbyteries, the Synodall, and generall Assemblies. In the 19. Sess. The Assembly declared, that no Bishop may sit upon the Councell in name of the Kirk.

In the Assembly holden Anno 1586. These two articles were agreed upon. *First It is found that all such as the Scripture appointeth governours of the Kirk, to wit Pastours, Doctours, and Elders, may conveen to the generall Assemblies, and vote in Ecclesiasticall matters. Secondly: There are foure office bearers set down to us by the Scriptures, to wit Pastours, Doctours, Elders, and Deacons, and the name of Bishop ought not to be taken as it hath been in time of Papistrie, but is common to all Pastours, and Ministers.*

In the Assembly holden *Anno* 1587. Sess. 8. It was ordained that the admission of Mr. *Robert Montgomerie* by the Presbyterie of *Glasgow*, suppose to the temporalitie of the Bishoprick only, be undone and annulled with all possible diligence, to the effect slander might be removed from the Kirk. In Sess. 15. Mr. *Robert Pont* shewed the Kings presentation to the Bishoprick of *Cathnes*, & desidered the judgement of the Assembly. The Assembly in their letter to the Kings Majestie, declared that they judged the said *Mr. Robert* to be a Bishop already according to the Doctrine of St. *Paul*: But as to that corrupt estate or office, of these who have been termed Bishops heretofore, they found it not agreable to the word of God, and that it hath been damned in diverse Assemblies before.

In the instructions given to such as were appointed to wait upon the Parliament, it was ordained in the same Assembly Sess. 17. That they be careful that nothing be admitted prejudicial to the liberties of this Kirk, as it was concluded according to the word of God in the general Assemblies, preceeding the year 1584. but precisely to seek the same to be ratified in the Assembly holden in March 1589. where the articles were made for subscribing the confession of Faith with the generall band, it was ordained as followeth.

For so much as the neighbour Kirk in England, is understood to bee heavily troubled, for maintaining of the true Discipline and government: whose grieves ought to move us. Therefore the Presbytery of Edinburgh was ordained to comfort the said Kirk in the said matter.

In the Assembly holden 1590. when the confession of Faith was subscribed universally de novo, a ratification of the liberties of the Kirk, in her jurisdiction, discipline, Presbyteries, Synods, and generall Assemblies, and an abrogation of all things contrarie thereunto; was ordained to be sought both of the Councel and Parliament. In the next Session it was ordained that the book of Discipline, specially the controverted heads, should be subscribed by all Ministers that bear, or hereafter was to bear office in this Kirk, and that they be charged by the Presbyteries, under the pain of excommunication: Seeing the word of God cannot bee keeped in sincerity, unlesse the holy Discipline be preserved. The Presbyteries were ordained to get a coppie under the Clerks hand; there were sundrie coppies subscribed by the Ministers in the Presbyteries yet extant, as Hadingtoun, Dumfermling, &c. produced before the Assembly.

In the Assembly 1591. Sess. 4. The former act anent the subscription to the book of Policie is renewed, and a penaltie imposed upon the Moderatour, in case it be not put in execution.

In the Assembly 22. May 1592. Sess. 2. These articles were drawn up. That the acts of Parliament made 1584. against the Discipline, libertie and authoritie of the Kirk be annulled, and the samine discipline, whereof the Kirk hath been in practise, precisely ratified. That Abbots, Priors, and other Prelats pretending the title of the Kirk, be not suffered in time coming. In the 11. Session the number of the Presbyteries were given up, and insert in the Parliament immediatly following. The fifth of June 1592. The libertie, discipline, and jurisdiction of the true Kirk, in her Sessions, Presbyteries, Synodal and general Assemblies, is largely ratified, as the samine was used, and exercised within this Realme, and all the acts contrary thereto abrogat: The Kings prerogative declared not to be prejudicial to the same priviledges grounded upon the word of God, the former commissions to Bishops

1584. rescinded, and all Ecclesiastical matters, subjected to Presbyteries, according to the discipline of this Kirk. Anno 1595. The book of Policie with other acts is ratified and ordained to be printed.

It was also cleared that Episcopacie was condemned in these words of the Confession, HIS WICKED HEIRARCHIE. For the Popish Hierarchie doth consist of Bishops, Presbyters, and Deacons, that is baptizing and preaching Deacons: For so it is determined in the councel of Trent, in the 4. chap. De Sacramento ordinis, can. 6.

Censura propositionum quarundam ex Hibernia delatarum per sacram Facultatem Theologiæ Parisiensis facta.

Si quis dixerît in ecclesia Catholica non esse heirarchiam divina ordinatione institutam, quæ constat ex Episcopis. Presbyteris & ministris, anathema sit. Bellarmine likewise in his book De Clericis. cap. 11. saith, That there are three Hierarchies in the militant Kirk: The first of Bishops, the second of Priests, the third of Deacons, and that the Deacons are also Princes, if they be compared with the people: This proposition following; Hierarchia ecclesiastica constat ex Pontifice, Cardinalibus, Archiepiscopis, Episcopis & Regularibus, was censured by the Facultie of Theologie in the Universitie at Paris, as followeth, Inicta prima propositione enumeratio membrorum hierarchiæ ecclesiasticæ sen sacri principatus, divina ordinatione instituti est manca & redundaus atque, inducens in errorem contrarium determinationi sacræ Sinodi Tridentinæ: The proposition was defective, because it pretermitted the Presbyters and Deacons; it was censured as redundant, because it made the Hierarchie to consist of the Pope, Cardinals, Archbishops, and Regulars; the Pope is not within the Hierarchie of Primats, Metropolitanes, and Archbishops, but as they are Bishops. Furthermore, this Hierarchie is distinguished in the confession from the Popes monarchie. And howbeit this Hierarchie be called the Antichrists Hierarchie, yet it is not to distinguish betwixt the Hierarchie in the Popish Kirk, and any other as lawful: But the Hierarchie, wheresoever it is, is called his, as the rest of the Popish corruptions are called his: To wit, Invocation of Saints, canonisation of Saints, dedication of Altars, &c. are called his, not that there is another lawfull canonization, invocation, or dedication of altars: whatsoever corruption was in the Kirk, either in doctrine, worship, or government since the ministry of iniquitie began to work, and is retained, and maintained, by the Pope, and obtruded upon the Kirk by his authority, are his. A passage also out of the history of the councell of Trent was alledged, where it is related, that the Councell would not define the Hierarchie by the seven orders: we have in our confession of Faith the manifold orders set apart and distinguished from the Hierarchie, but as it is set down in the cannon above cited: We have in the book of Policie or second booke of Discipline, in the end of the second chapter, this conclusion agreed upon. Therefore all the ambitious titles invented in the kingdome of Antichrist, and in his usurped HIERARCHIE which are not of one of these four sorts, To wit, Pastours, Doctours, Elders, and Deacons, together with offices depending thereupon, in one word ought to be rejected.

All which and many other warrands being publickly read, and particularly at great length examined, and all objections answered in face of the Assembly, all the members of the Assembly being many times desired and required to propone their doubts, and scruples, and every one being heard to the full, and after much agitation as fully satisfied; the Moderatour at last exhorting every one to declare his minde, did put the matter to voicing in these termes: Whether according to the confession of faith, as it was professed in the year 1580. 1581. and 1590. There be any other Bishop, but a Pastour of a particular flock, having no preheminence nor power over his brethren, and whether by that Confession, as it was then professed, all other episcopacie is abjured, and ought to bee removed out of this Kirk. The whole Assembly most unanimously, without contradiction of any one (and with the hesitation of one allanerly) professing full perswasion of minde, did voice, that all Episcopacie different from that of a Pastour over, a particular flock, was abjured in this Kirk, and to be removed out of it. And therefore Prohibites underr ecclesiasticall censure any to usurpe accept, defend, or obey the pretended authoritie thereof in time coming.

ACT. SESS. 17. DECEMBER 10. 1638.

THE ASSEMBLY AT GLASGOW, DECLARING THE FIVE ARTICLES OF PERTH TO HAVE BEEN ABJURED AND TO BEE REMOVED.

The Assembly remembring the uniformity of worship which was in this Kirk, before the articles of Perth, the great rent which entered at that time, and hath continued since, with the lamentable effects, that it hath produced both against Pastours, and professours, the unlawfulnesse and nullitie of Perth Assembly already declared by this Assembly, and that in the necessarie renewing of the confession of Faith in February 1638. the practice of novations introduced in the worship of God, was suspended, till they should be determined in a free generall Assembly: and that in the same year at his Majesties command some had subscribed the confession of Faith, as it was professed when it was first subscribed: For these causes the Assembly entered into a diligent tryall of the foresaid articles, whether they be constant to the confession of Faith, as it was meaned and professed in the year 1580. 1581. 1590. and 1591. And findeth that first in generall: In the confession of Faith we professe, We willingly agree in our consciences to the forme of Religion, of a long time openly professed by the Kings Majestie, and Whole body of this Realme in all points, as unto Gods undoubted truth and verity, grounded only upon his written word, and therefore abhor and deteste all contrary Religion and Doctrine, but chiefly, all kinde of papistrie in generall and partrcular heads, even as they were then damned and confuted by the Word of God and Kirk of Scotland, and in speciall the Romane Antichrist his five bastard sacraments, with all rites, ceremonies and false doctrine, added to the ministration of the true Sacraments, without the word of God, his cruell judgement against Infants departing without the Sacrament, his absolute necessitie of baptisme, and finally, we deteste all his vain allegories, rites, signes, and traditions brought into the Kirk without, or against the word of God, and doctrine of this true reformed Kirk, to the which we joyne our selves willingly in Doctrine, Faith, Religion, Discipline, and use of the holy Sacraments, as lively members of the same in Christ our Head; promising and swearing, &c. And that these five articles are contrarie to the Religion then professed, were confuted by the word of God, and Kirk of Scotland, or are rites, and ceremonies, added to the ministration, of the true Sacraments, without the word God, or nourish the popish judgement against Infants departing without the Sacrament, or absolute necessitie, of Baptisme or rites, signes, and traditions brought in to the Kirk, with out or against the word of God, and doctrine of this true reformed Kirk.

And next in particular, concerning festivall dayes, findeth, that in the explication of the first head, of the first book of Discipline, it was thought good that the feasts of Christmas, Circumcision, Epiphanie, with the feasts of the Apostles, Martyres, and Virgine Mary, bee utterly abolished, because they are neither commanded nor warranded by Scripture, and that such as observe them be punished by civill Magistrats. Here utter abolition is craved, and not reformation of abuses only, and that because the observation of such feasts hath no warrand from the word of God. In the generall Assembly holden at Edinburgh Anno 1556. the large confession of Helvetia was approved, but with speciall exception against the same five dayes, which are now urged upon us. It was not then the Popish observation only, with the Popish opinion of worship and merit, which was disallowed; (for so the reformed Kirk in Helvetia did not observe them) but simpliciter all observation. For this end was read a letter in Latine, sent at that time by some of our divines to certaine divines in these parts to this purpose. In the Assembly holden 1575. in August, complaint was made against the Ministers and Readers beside Aberdene; because they assembled the people to preaching and prayers upon certane festival dayes: So that preaching and prayers upon festival dayes was judged rebukable. It was ordained likewise, that complaint be made to the Regent, upon the town of Drumfreis, for urging and convoying a Reader to the Kirk with Tabret and Whistle, to read Prayers, all the holy dayes of Christmas, upon the refusal of their own Reader. Among the articles directed by this Assembly to the Regent: It was craved that all holy dayes hereto-fore keeped holy, beside the Lords day, such a Yooleday, and Saints dayes, and such others may bee abolished, and a certain penaltie appointed for banqueting, playing, feasting upon these dayes. In the Assembly holden in April, Anno 1577. It was ordained that the visitors with the advice of the Synodal Assembly, should admonish Ministers, preaching or ministrating the Communion at Easter, or Christmas, or other like superstitious times, or Readers reading, to desist, under the paine of deprivation. In the ninth head of the first book of Discipline, the reason is set down against Easter Communion. Your honours are not ignorant how superstitiously the people run to that action at Pascheven; as if the time gave vertue to the Sacrament, and how the rest of the whole year, they are carelesse and negligent, as if it appartained not to them, but at that time only. And for this reason, other times were appointed by that book, for that holy action. In the Assembly holden 1596. begun in March 1595. at which time the Covenant was renewed, superstition and idolatrie breaking forth in observing festival dayes; setting out of bone-fires, singing Carols, are reakoned amongst the corruptions which were to be amended: And the Pulpits did sound from time to time, against all shew of observing any festival day whatsoever, except the Lords day.

Concerning kneeling at the Communion, findeth that in the confession of Faith prefixed before the Psalmes, and approved by our Kirk in the very beginning of the reformation, we have these words, Neither in the ministration of the Sacraments, must we follow men: but as Christ himself hath ordained, so must they be ministred. In the large confession of Faith chap. 23. It is required as necessary, for the right ministration of the Sacraments, that they bee ministred in such elements, and in such sort, as God hath appointed, and that men have adulterate the Sacraments with their own inventions: So that no part of Christs action abideth in the originall puritie. The judgement of our reformers, who drew up the large Confession, was by cleare evidents shewed to be contrary to this gesture in the act of receiving the Sacrament. In the order of celebrating the Lords Supper, prefixed before the Psalmes in meeter, sitting and distributing by the Communicants, are joined: as likewise by the second head of the first book of Discipline, as nearest to Christs own action, and to his perfect practise, and most convenient to that holy action, and all inventions devised by man are condemned, as alterations and accusations of Christs perfect ordinance: Ministers were enjoyned by act of Assembly in December 1562. To observe the order of Geneva: that is the English Kirk at Geneva: where Master Knox had been sometime Minister, in the ministration of the Sacraments. This act was renewed in the Assembly holden in December 1564. where Ministers are referred to the order set down before the Psalmes, for ministration of the Sacraments; which is all one with the former: for that was the order of the English Kirk at Geneva.

In the Parliament holden Anno 1567. It was declared that whosoever did not participate of the Sacraments, as they were then publickly administrat in this reformed Kirk ought not to be reputed members of this Kirk. The act for the Kings oath at his coronation, to maintain the due administration of the Sacraments, as they were then ministred, Anno 1567. Was ratified Anno 1581. At which time the short Confession, adhering to the use of the Sacraments, in the Kirk of Scotland, was subscribed: as also Anno 1592. after the second Subscription to the confession of Faith. In the Parliament 1572. an act was made against such as did not participat of the Sacraments as they were then rightly ministered: But the gesture of kneeling, in the act of receiving, putteth the ministration of the Sacraments used in this Kirk out of frame: whereby it is clear that whatsoever gesture or rite, cannot stand with the administration of the Sacraments as they were then ministred and were ministred ever since the reformation, till the year 1618. must bee condemned by our Kirk as a rite added to the true ministration of the Sacraments without the word of God, and as rite or tradition brought in without, or against the word of God, or doctrine of this reformed Kirk.

III. Concerning Confirmation; The Assembly findeth it to be comprehended in the clause of the Confession, where the five bastard Sacraments are condemned. And seeing Episcopacie is condemned, imposition of hands by Bishops falleth to the ground. And in all the acts for catechising or examination before admission to the communion, no inkling of imposition of hands.

IIII. Concerning the administration of the Sacraments in private places, or private baptisme, and communion; findeth that in the book of common order, set down before the Psalmes, it is said, That the Sacraments art not ordained of God to be used in private corners, as charmers and sorcerers use to doe, but left to the Congregation. In the Assembly holden at Edinburgh in October Anno 1581. the same year and Assembly, that the confession of Faith was subscribed: It was ordained, that the Sacraments be not administred in private houses, but solemnly according to good order hither to observed. The Minister of Tranent was suspended at that time, for baptizing an infant in a private house: but confessing his offence, he was ordained to make his publick repentance in the Kirk of Tranent, before he be released. Another Minister was to be tried, and censured, for baptizing privately, and celebrating the Communion upon Pasch-day, at the Assembly holden in October 1580. Which acts and censures make manifest, that our Kirk abhorred whatsoever fostered the opinion of the necessitie of Baptisme, and giving of the Sacrament, as a viaticum.

All which, and many other acts, grounds, and reasons, being at length agitated, and with mature deliberation pondered, and libertie granted to every man to speak his minde; what could be said further, for the full satisfaction of all men.

The matter was put to voicing, in these words: Whether the five articles of Perth, by the confession of Faith, as it was meaned and professed in the year 1580. 1581. 1590. 1591. ought to be removed out of this Kirk: The whole Assembly all in one consent, one onely excepted, did voice that the five articles above specified were abjured by this Kirk, in that Confession, and so ought to be removed out of it: And therefore prohibiteth and dischargeth all disputing for them, or observing of them, or any of them, in all time comming, and ordains Presbyteries to proceed with the censures of the Kirk against all transgressours.

ACT. SESS. 21. DECEMBER 17. 1638.

Concerning Kirk Sessions, provinciall and nationall Assemblies, the generall Assembly considering the great defection of this Kirk, and decay of Religion, by the usurpation of the Prelates, and their suppressing of ordinaire judicatories of the Kirk, and clearly preceiving the benefit which will redound to the Religion by the restitution of the said judicatories, remembring also that they stand obliged by their solemne oath, and covenant with God, to return to the doctrine and discipline of this Kirk; as it was profest 1580, 1581, 1590, 1591. which in the book of Policie, registrat in the books of the Assembly 1581. and ordained to be subscribed, 1590, 1591. is particularly exprest both touching the constitution of the Assemblies, of their members, Ministers, and Elders, and touching the number, power, and authority of these members, in all matters ecclesiastical.

The Assembly findeth it necessar to restore, and by these presents restoreth all these Assemblies unto their full integritie in their members, priviledges, liberties, powers, and jurisdictions; as they were constitute by the foresaid book of Policie.

ACT. SESS. 23, 24. DECEMBER 17. 18.

Anent the report of the Committie, appointed for considering what constitutions were to be revived, or made of new, they proponed the overtures following:

which were read and allowed by the whole Assembly, or by them referred to the consideration of the severall Presbyteries.

Anent Presbyteries which have been erected since the year 1586. It seemeth needfull, that they bee ratified by an act of this generall Assembly, and that other Presbyteries shall be erected, where they shall be found needfull, and especially now in the Synod of Lismore, according to the particular note given there anent.

The Assembly ratifieth these Presbyteries since 1486. and erected those in Lismore, conforme to the note registrat in the books of Assembly.

Anent the keeping of Presbyteriall meetings; It is thought fit that they be weekly, both in Sommer and Winter, except in places farre distant, who during the winter season, (that is between the first of October and the first of April) shall be dispensed with for meeting once in the fourteen dayes, and that all absents be censured, especially those who should exercise and adde, according to the Act of Assembly 1582. at St. Andrews, April 24. Sess. 12. and that some controverted head of doctrine bee handled in the presbyterie publikly, and disputed among the brethren, every first Presbyterie of the Moneth, according to the act of Assembly holden at Dundie 1598. Sess. 12.

The Assembly alloweth this Article.

Anent the visitation of particular Kirks within Presbyteries; It is thought expedient that it be once every year, wherein a care is to be had, among other things necessary, that it bee tryed, how domestick exercises of Religion be exercised in particular families, and to see what means there is in every Parish in Landward, for catechising and instructing the youth.

The Assembly alloweth this article.

IV. Anent the visitation of Kirks, Schooles, and Colledges: It is thought meet that the acts of Assembly holden at Edinburgh the 25. of Junie 1565. Sess. 2. be put in execution: that the Ministers of the parochin, the Principall, Regents, and professours within Colledges, and Masters, and Doctors of Schooles, be tryed concerning the soundnesse of their judgement in matters of Religion, their abilitie, for discharge of their calling, and the honesty of their conversation: as the act of Assembly at Edinburgh, Juni 21. 1567. Sess. 3. And the act of the Assembly holden at Montrose. 1595. Sess. 9. do import: and this visitation of Colledges to be by way of commission from the generall Assembly.

The generall Assembly alloweth this article.

V. Anent none residents: It is thought necessary, that every Minister be oblished to reside in his own Parochin at his ordinarie Manse, for the better attending of the duties of his calling, conforme to the Acts of Assemblies, viz. act of Assembly at Edinburgh, March 24. 1595. Sess. 7. as also act at Edinburgh, December 25. 1563. Sess. 5. and Assembly at Edinburgh, December 25. 1565. Sess. 4. Assembly at Edinburgh, March 6. 1572. Sess. 3.

The Assembly alloweth this article.

VI. Anent the planting of Schools in Landward, the want whereof doth greatly prejudge the grouth of the Gospel and procure the decay of Religion: The Assembly giveth direction to several Presbyteries for the setling of Schooles in every Landward Parochin, and providing of men able for the charge of teaching of the youth, publick reading and precenting of the Psalme, and the catechising of the common people, and that means be provided for their intertainment, in the most convenient manner that may be had, according to the abilitie of the Parochin.

The Assembly alloweth; and referreth the particular course unto the severall Presbyteries.

VII. Anent the late admission of Ministers by Presbyteries, and the choise of Moderatours, according to the ancient power of the said Presbyteries: The Assembly declareth they had power to doe the same, and ratifieth that what hath been done of late of that kinde upon warrantable grounds, that here after it be not called in question.

The Assembly alloweth this article.

VIII. Anent the competencie of Presbyteries and parochins, that some proportion may be keeped, both anent the number and distance of place: It would seem expedient that this generall Assembly should appoint a Commission for every Shyre, where there is such necessitie, that the particular Parochins and Presbyteries within the bounds be duely considered, and overtures be these of the same commission given in to the provinciall Synods, and by them to the generall Assembly, that there they may be advised, and ratified.

The Assembly referreth this to the care of the particular presbyteries.

IX. Anent the entrie and conversation of Ministers: It is expedient that the act of Assembly holden at Edinburgh, March 24. 1595. Sess. 7. be ratified, and put in execution in every Presbyterie, and to that end, that they get a coppie thereof, under the Clerks hand whereof the tennour followeth.

Act Sess. 7. March 26. of the Assembly at Edinburgh 1596.

"Concerning the defections in the ministerie, the same being at length read out, reasoned, and considered; The brethren concluded the same, agreeing therewith: and in respect that by Gods grace, they intend reformation, and to see the Kirk and ministery purged; to the effect the worke may have better successe, they think it necessar that this Assembly be humbled, for wanting such care as became in such points, as is set down; and some zealous and godly brethren in doctrine, lay them out for their better humiliation; and that they make solemne promise before the Majestie of God; and make new covenant with him for a more carefull and reverent discharge of their ministerie. To the which effect was chosen Mr. John Davidson; and Twesday next at nine houres in the morning appointed, in the new Kirk, for that effect: whereunto none is to resort, but the ministrie: the forme to bee advised the morne in privie conference."

The tennour of the advise of the brethren; depute for penning the enormities and corruptions in the ministerie, and remead thereof, allowed by the generall Assembly here conveened. 1596.

Corruptions in the office.

"For as much as by the too sudden admission and light tryall of persons to the ministrie, cometh to passe that many scandals fall out in the persons of ministers: it would be ordained in time comming, that more diligent inquisition and triall be used of all such persons as shall enter into the ministrie.

"As specially these points. That the intrant shall be posed upon his conscience, before the great God, (and that in most grave manner) what moveth him to accept the office and charge of the ministrie upon him.

"That it be inquired, if any by solistation, or moyen, directly or indirectly, prease to enter in the said office: And, if it bee found, that the solister be repelled; and that the Presbyterie repell all such of their number from voting in the election or admission as shall bee found moyeners for the soliciter, and posed upon their conscience to declare the truth to that effect.

"Thirdly, because by presentations, many forcibly are thrust into the ministery, and upon Congregations, that utter thereafter that they were not called by God: It would bee provided that none seeke presentations to Benefices without advice of the Presbyterie within the bounds whereof the benefice is, and if any doe in the contrarie, they to be repelled as rei ambitus.

"That the triall of persons to be admitted to the ministrie hereafter, consist not only in their learning and abilitie to preach, but also in conscience, and feeling, and spiritual wisedome, and namely in the knowledge of the bounds of their calling in doctrine, discipline, and wisedome, to behave himselfe accordingly with the diverse ranks of persons within his flock, as namely with Atheists, rebellious, weak consciences, and such other, wherein the pastoral charge is most suited, and that he be meet to stop the mouthes of the adversaries; and such as are not qualified in these points to be delayed to further tryal; and while they be found qualified. And because men may be found meet for some places who are not meet for other, it would be considered, that the principall places of the Realme be provided by men of most worthie gifts, wisedome and experience, and that none take the charge of greater number of people nor they are able to discharge: And the Assembly to take order herewith, and the act of the provinciall of Louthain, made at Linlithgow, to be urged.

"That such as shall bee found not given to their book and studie of Scriptures, not Carefull to have books, not given to sancification and prayer, that studie not to bee powerful and spiritual, not applying the doctrine to corruptions, which is the pastorall gift, obscure and too scholastick before the people, cold, and wanting of spiritual zeal, negligent in visiting of the sick, and caring for the poore; or indifferent in chosing of parts of the word not meetest for the flock, flatterers and dissembling at publick sins, and specially of great personages in their congregations, for flattery, or for fear, that all such persons bee censured, according to the degree of their faults, and continuing therein, bee deprived.

"That such as be slothfull in the ministration of the Sacraments and irreverent, as prophaners receiving the cleane and uncleane, ignorants and senselesse prophane, and making no conscience of their profession in their calling and families, omitting due tryall or using none, or light tryall, having respect in their tryall to persons, wherein there is manifest corruption; that all such bee sharply rebuked, and if they continue therein, that they be deposed.

"And if any be found a seller of the Sacraments, that hee bee deposed simpliciter: and such as collude with slanderous persons in dispensing and over-seeing them for money, incurre the like punishment. That every Minister be charged to have a Session established of the meettest men in his Congregation, and that Discipline strike not only upon grosse sins, as whoredome, blood-shed, &c. but upon sins repugnant to the word of God, as blasphemie of God, banning, profaning of the Sabbath, disobedient to parents, idle, unruly ones without calling, drunkards, and such like deboshed men, as make not conscience of their life and ruling of their families, and specially of education of their children, lying, slandering, and backbiting and breaking of promises: and this to be an universal order throughout the Realme, &c. and such like as are negligent herein, and continue therein after admonition, be deposed.

"That none falling in publick slanders, be received in the fellowship of the Kirk, except his Minister have some appearance and warrand in conscience, that hee hath both a feeling of sin, and apprehension of mercie, and for this effect, that the Minister travell with him, by doctrine, and private instruction to bring him here-to, and specially in the doctrine of repentance, which being neglected, the publick place of repentance is turned in a mocking.

"Dilapidation of benefices, dimitting of them for favour, or money, that they become laick patronages, without advise of the Kirk, and such like interchanging of benefices, by transaction and transporting of themselves by that occasion, without the knowledge of the Kirk, precisely to be punished: Such like, that setting of acts without the consent of the Assembly, be punished according to the acts: and that the dimitters in favours for money, or otherwise to the effect above-writen: bee punished as the dilapidators."

Corruptions in their persons and lives.

"That such as are light and wanton in their behaviour, as in gorgeous and light apparell; in speech, in using light and prophane companie, unlawfull gaming, as dancing, carding, dycing and such like; not beseeming the gravitie of a Pastour, bee sharply and gravely reproved by the Presbyterie, according to the degree thereof: and continuing therein after due admonition, that hee be depryved, as slanderous to the Gospel.

"That Ministers being found swearers, or banners, prophaners; of the Sabbath, drunkards, fighters, guiltie of all these or any of them, be deposed simpliciter; and suchlike, lyars, detracters, flatterers, breakers of promise, brawlers, and quarrellers, after admonition continuing therein, incurre the same punishment.

"That Ministers given to unlawful and incompetent trades and occupations for filthie gain, as holding of ostleries, taking of ocker beside conscience and good lawes, and bearing worldly offices in noblemen and gentlements houses, marchandise, and such like, buying of victuals, and keeping to the dearth, and all such worldly occupations, as may distract them from their charge, and may be slanderous to the pastorall calling, be admonished and brought to the acknowledging of their sins, and if they continue therein, to be deposed.

"That Ministers not resident at their flocks, be deposed according to the acts of the generall Assembly, and laws of the Realme: otherwise the burthren to be laid on the Presbyteries, and they to be censured therefore.

"That the Assembly command all their members, that none of them await on the court and afairs thereof without the advice and allowance of their Presbyterie. Item, that they intend no action civill without the said advice; except in small maters: and for remeding of the necessitie, that some Ministers hath to enter in plea of law, that remedie bee craved, that short processe bee devised, to bee used in Ministers actions.

"That Ministers take speciall care in using godly excercises in their families, in teaching of their wives, children, and servants, in using ordinarie prayers and reading of Scriptures, in removing of offensive persons out of their families, and such like other points of godly conversation, and good example, & that they at the visitation of their Kirks, try the Ministers families in these points foresaid, and such as are found negligent in these points, foresaid after due admonition, shall be adjudged unmeet to govern the house of God, according to the rule of the Apostle.

"That Ministers in all companies strive to bee spirituall and profitable, and to talke of things pertaining to godlinesse, as namely of such as may strengthen us in Christ, instruct us in our calling, of the means how to have Christs Kingdome better established in our Congregations, and to know how the Gospel flourisheth in our flocks, and such like others the hinderances, and the remeeds that we finde, &c. wherein there is manifold corruptions, both in our companying with our selves, and with others: and that the contraveeners thereof be tryed, and sharply be rebuked.

"That no Minister be found to contenance, procure, or assist a publick offender challenged by his own Ministers, for his publick offence, or to bear with him, as though his Minister, were too severe upon him, under pain of admonition and rebuking."

Anent generall Assemblies.

"To urge the keeping of the Acts anent the keeping of the Assembly, that it may have the own reverence and majestie—"

The Assembly having heard the whole act read, most unanimously alloweth and approveth this article.

X. Anent the defraying of the expenses of the Commissioners to the generall Assembly, referreth and recommendeth the same unto the particular Presbyterie, and especially to the ruling Elders therein, that they may take such courses whereby, according to reason and former acts of Assemblies, the Commissioners expenses to this Assembly, and to the subsequent, may be born by the particular parochins of every Presbyterie, who sendeth them in their name, and to their behalf, and for that effect, that all sort of persons able in land or moneys proportionally, may bear a part of the burthen, as they reap the benefit of their paines.

The Assembly referreth this unto the care of the particular Presbyteries.

XI. Anent the repressing of poperie and superstition; It seemeth expedient that the number and names of all the Papists in this Kingdome be taken up at this Assembly, if it may be conveniently done, and if not, that it be remitted to the next provincial Assemblies, that it may appear what grouth poperie hath had, and now hath through this Kingdome, what popish priests, and Jesuit there be in the land; and that all persons of whatsoever state and condition, be obliged to swear and subscribe the confession of Faith, as it is now condescended upon by this general Assembly, that they frequent the word and Sacraments in the ordinar dyets and places, otherwise to proceed against them with the censures of the Kirk, and that children be not sent out of the countrey without license of the Presbyteries or provinciall Synods of the bounds where they dwell.

The Assembly referreth this article to the severall Presbyteries.

XII. Anent order to be taken that the Lords Supper be more frequently administrat both in burgh and landward, then it hath been in the year by gone: It were expedient that the act at Edinburgh December 25. 1562. Sess. 5. bee renewed, and some course bee taken for furnishing of the elements, where the Minister of the Parish hath allowance only for once in the year.

The Assembly referreth this to the consideration of Presbyteries, and declareth that the charges be rather payed out of that dayes collection, then that the Congregation want the more frequent use of the sacrament.

XIII. Anent the entrie of Ministers to the ministrie: The Assembly thinks expedient that the act holden at St. Andrews, April 24. 1582. Sess. 7. Touching the age of twenty five years be renewed, and none to be admitted before that time, except such as for rare and singular qualities shall be judged by the general or provincial Assembly to be meet and worthie thereof.

The Assembly approveth this article.

XIV. Anent mercats on Monday and Saturday within Burghs, causing intollerable profanation of the Lords Day, by carying of loads, bearing of Burthens; and other work of that kinde: It were expedient for the redresse thereof, that the care for restraining of this abuse be recommended by the Assembly unto the severall Burghs, and they to bee earnestly entreated to finde out some way for the repressing of this evill, and changing of the day; and to report their diligence there anent to the next generall Assembly.

The Assembly referreth this article to the consideration of the Burrows.

XV. Anent the profanation of the Sabbath day in Landward, especially for want of divine service in the afternoone: The Assembly ordaineth the act of Assembly holden at Dundie, July 12. 1580. Sess. 10. for keeping both dyets, to be put in execution.

The Assembly alloweth this article.

XVI. Anent frequenting with excommunicat persons: The Assembly ordaineth that the act at Edinburgh, March 5. 1569. Sess. 10. to wit, That these who will not forbear the companie of excommunicat persons after due admonition, be excommunicat themselves, except they forbear, to be put in execution.

The Assembly alloweth this article.

XVII. Whereas the confession of the Faith of this Kirk, concerning both Doctrine and Discipline, so often called in question by the corrupt judgement and tyrannous authoritie of the pretended Prelats, is now clearly explained, and by this whole Kirk represented by this generall Assembly concluded, ordained also to bee subscribed by all sorts of persons within the said Kirk and Kingdome: The Assembly constitutes, and ordaines, that from henceforth no sort of person, of whatsoever quality and degree, be permitted to speak, or write against the said Confession, this Assembly, or any act of this Assembly, and that under the paine of incurring the censures of this Kirk.

The Assembly alloweth this Article.

XVIII. Anent voicing in Kirk Sessions: It is thought expedient that no Minister moderating his Session, shall usurpe a negative voice over the members of his Session, and where there is two or moe Ministers in one Congregation, that they have equall power in voicing, that one of them hinder not the reasoning or voicing of any thing, whereunto the other Minister or Ministers, with a great part of the Session inclineth, being agreeable to the acts and practise of the Kirk, and that one of the Ministers without advice of his colleague appoint not dyets of Communion nor examination, neither hinder his colleague from catechising and using other religious exercises as oft as he pleaseth.

The Assembly referreth this article to the care of the Presbyteries.

XX. Since the office of Diocesane, or lordly Bishop, is utterly abjured, and removed out of this Kirk: It is thought fit that all titles of dignitie, favouring more of poperie than of Christian libertie, as Chapters with their elections and consecrations, Abbots, Priors, Deans, Arch-deacons, Preaching-deacons, Chanters, Sub-chanters, and others having the like title, flowing from the Pope and canon law only, as testifieth the second book of Discipline, bee also banished out of this reformed Kirk, and not to bee usurped or used hereafter under ecclesiastical censure.

The Assembly alloweth this Article.

XX. Anent the presenting either of Pastours or Readers and School-masters, to particular Congregations, that there be a respect had to the Congregation, & that no person be intruded in any office of the Kirke, contrare to the will of the congregation to which they are appointed.

The Assembly alloweth this article.

XXI. Anent Mariage without proclamation of bans, which being in use these years by-gone hath produced many dangerous effects: The Assembly would discharge the same, conforme to the former acts, except the Presbyterie in some necessarie exigents dispense therewith.

The Assembly alloweth this article.

XXII. Anent the buriall in Kirks, the Assembly would be pleased to consider anent the act of Assembly at Edinburgh 1588. Sess. 5. if it shall be put in execution, and to discharge funeral sermons, as favouring of superstition.

The Assembly referreth the former part of this article anent buriall in Kirks to the care of Presbyteries, and dischargeth all funerall sermons.

XXIII. Anent the tryall of Expectants before their entrie to the ministrie, it being notour that they have subscribed the confession of Faith now declared in this Assembly, and that they have exercised often privatly, and publickly, with approbation of the Presbyterie, they shall first adde and make the exercise publickly, and make a discourse of some common head in Latine, and give propositions thereupon for dispute, and thereafter be questioned by the Presbyterie upon questions of controversie, and chronologie, anent particular texts of Scripture how they may be interpreted according to the analogie of Faith, and reconciled, and that they be examined upon their skill of the Greek & Hebrew, that they bring a testificat of their life and conversation from either Colledge or Presbyterie, where they reside.

The Assembly alloweth this article.

XXIV. The Assembly having considered the order of the provincial Assembly, given in by the most ancient of the Ministrie within every Province, as the ancient plate-forme thereof, ordained the same to be observed, conforme to the roll, registrat in the books of Assembly, whereof the tennour followeth.

The order of the Provincial Assemblies in Scotland, according to the Presbyteries therein contained.

1. The Provincial Assembly of Mers and Tividail.

The Presbyteries of
Dunce.
Chirnside.
Kelso.
Ersliltoun.
Fedburgh.
Melros.

The bounds.
Mers.
Tividail.
The Forrest.
Lauderdail.

To meet the first time at Fedburgh, the third Twesday of April.

2. The Provincial of Louthian.

The Presbyteries of
Dumbar.
Hadingtoun.
Dalkeeth.
Edinburgh.
Peebles.
Linlithgow.

The bounds.

east Louthian.
w. Louthian.
Tweeddail.

To meet the first time at Edinburgh the third Twesday of April.

3. The Provincial of Perth.

The Presbyteries of
Perth.
Dunkel.
Aughterardor.
Striviling.
Dumblane.

The bounds.
The Shyresdome of Perth and of Striviling Shire.

To meet the first time at Perth, the second Twesday of April.

4. The Province of Drumfrees.

The Presbyteries of
Dumfrees.
Penpont.
Lochmabane.
Middilbee.

The bounds.
Niddisdaill.
Annandaill.
Ewsdaill.
Eskdail.
Wachopdaill.
& a part of Galloway.

To meet the first time at Drumfrees, the second Twesday of April.

5. The Provincial of Galloway.

The Presbyteries of
Wightoun.
Kirkubright.
Stanraver.

The bounds.
The Shyresdome of Wigtoun, and Stemartie of Kirkubright.

To meet the first time at Wigtoun, third Twedsay of April.

The Provincial Synod of Aire or Irwing.

The Presbyteries of
Aire.
Irwing.

The bounds. The Shyresdome of Aire.

To meet with the Provincial Synod of Glasgow pro hac vice, the first Tuesday of April.

6. The Provincial Synod of Glasgow.

The Presbyteries of
Pasley.
Dumbartane.
Glasgow.
Hammiltoun.
Lanerik.

The bounds.
The Shyr. of Lennox, the Barrony of Renfrow, the Shy. of Clydsdail over and nether.

To meet with the Provinciall Synod Synod of Aire and Irwing at Glasgow, pro hac vice.

7. The Provincial Synod of Argyl, desired to bee erected in several Presbyteries, according to the note given in.

The Presbyteries of
Dunune.
Kinloch.
Inneraray.
Kilmoir.
Skye.

The bounds.
The Shyrisdomes of Argil & Boot, with a part of Loohabar.

To meet the first time at Innereray, the fourth Twesday of April.

8. The Provincial Synod of Fife.

The Presbyteries of
St. Andrews.
Cowper.
Kirkadie.
Dumfermling.

The bounds.
The Shyresdome of Fife.

To meet the first time at Cowper in Fife the first Twesday of April.

9. The Provincial Synod of Angus and Merns.

The Presbyteries of
Meegle.
Dundie.
Arbroth.
Forfair Brechen Merns.

The bounds.
The Shyresdomes of Forfair and Merns.

To meet the first time at Dundie, the third Tuesday of April.

10. The Provincial Synod of Aberdene.

The Presbyteries of
Aberdene.
Kincairdin.
All-foord.
Garioch.
Ellan Deer.
Turreffe.
Fordyce.

The bounds.
The Shyresdomes of Aberdene and Bamfe.

To meet the first time at new Aberdene the 3 Twesday of April.

11. The provincial Synod of Murray.

The Presbyteries of
Innernes.
Forresse.
Elgin.
Strabogie.
Abernethie.
Aberlower.

The bounds.
The Shyresdomes of Innernes in part, Nairn in part, Murray Bamf in part,
Aberden in part.

To meet the first time at Forresse the last Tuesday of April.

12. The provincial Synod of Rosse.

The Presbyteries of
Chanrie.
Taine.
Dingwall.

The bounds.
The Shyresdome of Innernes in part.

To meet the first time at Chanrie, the second Twesday of April.

13. The provincial Synod of Cathnes.

The Presbyteries of
Dornoch.
Weeke. or
Thurso.

The Bounds:
Cathnes.
Sutherland.

To meet the first time at Dornoch, the third Twesday of April.

14. The provincial Synod of Orkney and Zetland.

The Presbyteries of
Kirkwall.
Scalloway.

The Bounds:
The Shyresdome of Orkney and Zetland.

To meet the first time at Kirkwall, the second Twesday of April.

15. The Provinciall Synod of the Isles

All the Kirks of the North-west Isles, viz. Sky, Lewes, and the rest of the Isles, which were lyable to the Diocie of the Isles, except the South-west isles which are joyned to the Presbyteries of Argyll, To meet the first time at Skye the second Twesday of May.

That the Minister of the place where the Synodall Assembly meets shall preach the first day of their meeting, and give timouse advertisement to the rest of the Presbyteries.

It is remembred that of old the Synodall Assemblies that were nearest to others, had correspondence among themselves, by sending one or two Commissioners mutually from one to another, which course is thought fit to bee keeped in time comming: viz. The Provincials of Louthian, and Mers, &c. The Provincials of Drumfreis, Galloway, Glasgow, and Argyll, The Provincials of Perth, Fyfe, and Angus, &c. The Provincials of Aberdein and Murray. The Provincials of Rosse, Caithnes, and Orknay. The Commissioners for correspondence amongst the Synodals to be a Minister and a ruling Elder.

The Assembly recommendeth to the severall Presbyteries the execution of the old acts of Assemblies, against the break of the Sabbath-day, by the going of Milles, Salt-pans, Salmond-fishing, or any such-like labour, and to this end revives and renews the act of the Assembly, holden at Halyrudehouse 1602. Sess. 5 whereof the tennor followeth.

"The Assemblie considering that the conventions of the people, specially on the Sabbath-day, are verie rare in manie places, by distraction of labour, not only in Harvest and Seed-time, but also every Sabbath by fishing both of whyte fish and Salmond fishing, and in going of Milles; Therefore the Assemblie, dischargeth and inhibiteth, all such labour of fishing as-well whyte fish as Salmond fish, and going of Miles of all sorts upon the Sabbath-day, under the paine of incurring the censures of the Kirk. And ordains the Commmissioners of this Assemblie to meane the same to his Majestie, and to desire that a pecuniall paine may be injoyned upon the contraveeners of this present act."

ACT SESS. 14. DECEMBER 18. 1638.

The Assembly considering the great necessity of purging this land from by-gone corruptions, and of preserving her from the like in time coming, ordaineth the Presbyteries to proceed with the censures of the Kirk, to excommunication, against those Ministers who being deposed by this Assembly acquiesces not to their sentences, but exercise some part of their Ministerial function, refuseth themselves, and with-draw others from the obedience of the acts of the Assembly.

ACT. SESS. 25. DECEMBER 19. 1638.

AGAINST THE CIVIL PLACES AND POWER OF KIRK-MEN.

The generall Assembly, remembering that among other causes of the application of the confession of Faith to the present time, which was subscribed in *February* 1638. The clause touching the civill places and power of Kirk-men, was referred unto the tryal of this Assembly; entered into a serious search thereof, especially of their sitting on the bench, as Justices of peace, their sitting in Session and Councel, their riding and voting in Parlament: and considering how this vote in Parliament, was not at first sought nor requyred by this Kirk, or worthy men of the Ministerie, but being obtruded upon them, was disallowed for such reasons as could not well be answered (as appeareth by the conference, holden at *Halyrude-house* 1599. which with the reasons therein contained was read in the face of the Assembly) & by plurality of voices nor being able to resist that enforced favour, they foreseeing the dangerous consequences thereof, in the Assembly at *Montrose* did limitate the same by many necessare cautions: Considering also the protestation made in the Parliament 1606 by Commissioners from Presbyteries, and provincial Assemblies, against this restitution of Bishops to vote in Parliament, and against all civil offices in the persons of Pastors, separate unto the Gospel, as incompatible with their spiritual function; with the manifold reasons of that Protestation from the word of God, ancient Councels, ancient and moderne Divines, from the Doctrine, discipline and Confession of Faith of the Kirk of *Scotland*, which are extant in print, and were read in the audience of the Assembly: Considering also from their own experience the bad fruits and great evils, which have been the inseparable consequents of these offices, and that power in the persons of Pastors separate to the Gospel, to the great prejudice of the freedome and libertie of the Kirk, the jurisdiction of her Assemblies, and the powerful fruits of their spiritual Ministerie; The Assembly most unanimously in one voice, with the hesitation of two allanerly, declared, that as on the one part the Kirk and the Ministers thereof are oblidged to give their advise and good counsel in matters concerning the Kirk or the Conscience of any whatsomever, to his Majestie, to the Parliament, to the Councel, or to any members thereof, for their resolutions from the word of God, So on the other part, that it is both in-expedient, and unlawful in this Kirk, for Pastors separate unto the Gospel to brook civil places, and offices, as to be Justices of peace; sit and decerne in Councel, Session, or Exchecker; to ride or vote in Parliament, to be Judges or Assessors in any Civil Judicatorie: and therefore rescinds and annuls, all contrarie acts of Assembly, namely of the Assembly holden at *Montrose* 1600. which being prest by authority, did rather for an *interim* tolerat the same, and that limitate by many cautions; for the breach whereof the Prelats have been justly censured, then in freedome of judgement allow thereof, and ordaineth the Presbyteries to proceed with the Censures of the Kirk, against such as shall transgresse herein in time coming.

ACT SESS. 26. DECEMBER 20. 1638.

The Assembly considering the great prejudice which Gods Kirk in this land, hath sustained these years by-past, by the unwarranted printing of lybels, pamphlets, and polemicks; to the disgrace of Religion, slander of the Gospel, infecting and disquyeting the mindes of Gods people, and disturbance of the peace of the Kirk, and remembring the former acts, and custome of this Kirk, as of all other Kirks, made for restraining these and the like abuses, and that nothing be printed concerning the Kirk, and Religion, except it be allowed by these whom the Kirk intrusts with that charge: The Assembly *unanimously*, by vertue of their ecclesiastical authority, dischargeth and inhibiteth all printers within this Kingdome, to print any act of the former Assemblies, any of the acts or proceedings of this Assembly, any confession of Faith, any Protestations, any reasons *pro* or *contra*, anent the present divisions and contraversies of this time, or any other treatise whatsoever which may concerne the Kirk of Scotland, or Gods cause in hand, without warrand subscribed by Mr. *Archbald Johnston*, as Clerk to the Assembly, and Advocate for the Kirk; or to reprint without his warrand, any acts or treatises foresaids, which he hath caused any other to print, under the paine of Ecclesiastical censures to be execute against the transgressours by the several Presbyteries, and in case of their refusal, by the several Commissioners from this Assembly: Whereunto also we are confident, the honourable Judges of this land will contribute their civill authority: and this to be intimat publickly in pulpit, with the other generall acts of this Assembly.

ACT. SESS. 26. DECEMBER 20. 1638.

The generall Assembly ordaineth all Presbyteries and Provinciall Assemblies to conveen before them, such as are scandalous and malicious, and will not acknowledge this Assembly, nor acquiesce unto the acts thereof: And to censure them according to their malice and contempt, and acts of this Kirk: and where Presbyteries are refractarie, granteth power unto the severall Commissions to summond them to compear before the next generall Assembly to be holden at *Edinburgh*, the third Wedinsday of Julie, to abide their tryall and censure.

ACT SESS. 26. DECEMBER 20. 1638.

The Assembly considering the acts and practise of this Kirke in her purest times, that the Commissioners of every Presbyterie, Burgh, and Universitie, were both ordained to take, and really did take from the Clerk; the whole generall acts of the Assembly, subscribed by the Clerk: Whereby they might rule and conforme their judicatorie themselves, and all persons within their jurisdictions, unto the obedience thereof: Considering the great prejudices we have lately felt out of ignorance of the acts of Assembly, Considering also the great necessity in this time of reformation, beyond any other ordinarie time, to have an extract thereof: The Assembly ordaineth be this present act, that all Commissioners from Presbyteries, Burghes and Universities, presently get under the Clerks hand an Index of the acts, till the acts themselves be extracted, and thereafter to get the full extract of the whole generall acts, to be insert in their Presbyterie books, whereby all their proceedings may be regulate in time coming. Likeas the Assembly recommendeth unto every Kirk Session, for the preservation of their particular Paroch from the reentrie of the corruptions now discharged, and for their continuance in the Covenant, anent doctrine, worship and discipline now declared, to obtain an extract of these acts: especially if they be printed: Seeing their pryce will no wayes then be considerable: as the benefite both of the particular Parish, and the interest of the whole Kirk, in the preservation thereof from defection is undenyable: seeing Presbyteries are composed of sundry Parochins, and so must be affected, or infected as they are, as Provinciall and generall Assemblies are composed of Presbyteries, and so must be diposed as they are.

ACT SESS. 26. DECEMBER 20.

In the Assembly at Glasgow 1638. *concerning the confession of Faith renewed in Februar, 1638.*

The Assembly considering that for the purging and preservation of religion, for the Kings Majesties honour, and for the publick peace of the Kirk and Kingdome, the renewing of that nationall Covenant and oath of this Kirk and Kingdome, in Februar 1638. was most necessare, likeas the Lord hath blessed the same from Heaven with a wonderfull successe for the good of religion, that the said Covenant suspendeth the practise of novations already introduced, and the approbation of the corruptions of the present governement of the Kirk, with the civill places, and power of Kirk-men, till they be tryed in a free general Assembly, and that now after long and serious examination, it is found that by the confession of Faith, the five articles of Perth, and Episcopall governement are abjured and to be removed out of this Kirk, and the civill places and power of Kirk-men are declared to be unlawfull; The Assembly alloweth and approveth the same in all the heads and articles thereof, And ordaineth that all Ministers, Masters of Universities, Colledges, and Schooles and all others who have not already subscribed the said Confession and Covenant, shall subscribe the same with these words prefixed to the subscription viz., The article of this Covenant which was at the first subscription referred to the determination of the general Assembly being now determined at Glasgow, in December 1638. and thereby the five articles of Perth, and the governement of the Kirk by Bishops, being declared to be abjured and removed, the civill places and power of Kirk-men declared to be unlawful; We subscrive according to the determination, of the said free and lawfull generall Assembly holden at Glasgow: and ordaineth, ad perpetuam rei memoriam, the said Covenant with this declaration to be insert in the registers of the Assemblies of this Kirk; generall, Provinciall and Presbyteriall.

ACT SESS. 26. DECEMBER 20. 1638.

CONCERNING THE SUBSCRIBING THE CONFESSION OF FAITH LATELY SUBSCRIBED BY HIS MAJESTIES COMMISSIONER, AND URGED TO BE SUBSCRIBED BY OTHERS.

Seeing the generall Assembly, to whom belongeth properly the publick and judiciall interpretation of the confession of Faith, hath now after accurat tryall, and mature deliberation clearly found, that the five articles of Perth, and the governement of the Kirk by Bishops, are abjured by the confession of Faith, as the same was professed in the year 1580. and was renewed in this instant year 1638. And that the Marques of Hammiltoun his Majesties Commissioner, hath caused print a Declaration, bearing that his Majesties intention and his own, in causing subscribe the confession of Faith, is no wayes to abjure, but to defend Episcopall governement, and that by the oath and explanation set down in the act of Councel, it neither was nor possibly could be abjured, requiring that none take the said oath, or any other oath in any sense, which may not consist with Episcopall governement: which is in-directly repugnant to the genuine and true meaning of the foresaid Confession as it was professed in the year 1580. as is clearly now found and declared by the generall Assembly: Therefore the generall Assembly: Doth humbly supplicate, that his Majestie may be graciously pleased, to acknowledge and approve the foresaid true interpretation, and meaning of the generall Assembly, by his Royall warrand to his Majesties Commissioner, Councel, and Subjects, to be put in record for that effect, whereof we are confident, after his Majesty, hath received true information from this Kirk, honoured with his Majesties birth and baptisme, which will be a royal testimonie of his Majesties piety and justice, and a powerfull meane to procure the heartie affection and obedience of all his Majesties loyall Subjects: And in the meane time, least any should fall under the danger of a contradictorie oath, and bring the wrath of God upon themselves and the land, for the abuse of his Name and Covenant; The Assembly by their Ecclesiastical authority, prohibiteth and dischargeth, that no member or this Kirk swear or subscribe the said Confession, so far wreasted to a contrary meaning, under paine of all Ecclesiastical censure: but that they subscribe the confession of Faith, renewed in Februar, with the Declaration of the Assembly set down in the former act.

ACT. SESS. 26. DECEMBER 20. 1638.

CONCERNING YEARLY GENERALL ASSEMBLIES.

The Assembly having considered the reasons lately printed for holding of general Assemblies, which are taken from the light of nature, the promise of *Jesus Christ*, the practise of the holy Apostles, the doctrine and custome of other reformed Kirks, and the liberty of this national Kirk, as it is expressed in the book of Policie, and acknowledged in the act of Parlament 1592, and from recent and present experience; comparing the lamentable prejudices done to religion, through the former want of free and lawful Assemblies, and the great benefite arysing to the Kirk, from this one free and lawful Assembly; finde it necessary to declare, and hereby declares, that by Divine, Ecclesiasticall, and Civill warrands, this national Kirk hath power and liberty to Assemble and conveen in her year-ly generall Assemblies, and oftner, *pro re nata,* as occasion and necessity shall require. Appointeth the next Generall Assembly to sit at *Edinburgh* the third Weddinsday of Julie 1639. And warneth all Presbyteries, Universities, and Burghes, to send their Commissioners for keeping the same. Giving power also to the Presbytery of *Edinburgh, pro re nata*: and upon any urgent extraordinarie necessity (if any shall happen before the diet appointed in Julie) to give advertisement to all the Presbyteries, Universities, and Burghes, to send their Commissioners for holding an occasionall Assembly. And if in the meane time it shall please the Kings Majestie to indict a generall Assembly, ordaineth all Presbyteries; Universities, and Burghes, to send their Commissioners for keeping the time and place which shall be appointed by his Majesties Proclamation.

ORDAINING AN HUMBLE SUPPLICATION TO BE SENT TO THE KINGS MAJESTIE.

The Assembly, from the sense of his Majesties pietie and justice, manifested in the publick indiction of their solemne meeting, for the purging and preservation of Religion, in so great an exigent of the extreame danger of both, from their fears arising out of experience of the craftie and malicious dealing of their adversaries in giving sinistrous informations against the most religious and loyall designes and doings of his Majesties good Subjects, and from their earnest desire to have his Majestie truely informed of their intentions and proceedings, from themselves: who know them best, (which they are confident, will be better beleeved: and finde more credite with his Majestie, than any secret surmisse or private suggestion to the contrarie) that they may gaine his Majesties princely approbation and ratification in the ensuing Parliament to their constitutions: Hath thought meet and ordaineth, that an humble supplication be directed to his Majestie, testifying their most heartie thankfulnesse for so Royal a favour, as at this time hath refreshed the whole Kirk and Kingdome, stopping the way of calumnie, and humbly supplicating for the approbation, and ratification foresaid: That truth and peace may dwell together in this Land, to the increase of his Majesties glory, and the comfort of quietness of his Majesties good People: This the Assembly hath committed, according to the Articles foresaid, to be subscribed by their Moderatour and Clerk, in their name. The tennour whereof followeth.

To The Kings Most Excellent Majestie:

The humble Supplication of the general Assembly of the Kirk of Scotland, conveened at Glasgow, November 21. 1638.

Most gracious Soveraigne,

We your Majesties most humble and loyal Subjects, The Commissioners from all the parts of this your Majesties ancient and native Kingdome, and members of the National Assembly, conveened at Glasgow, by your Majesties special indiction, considering the great happinesse which ariseth both to Kirk and Common-wealth, by the mutual embracements of Religion and Justice, of truth and peace, when it pleaseth the Supreame Providence so to dispose, that princely power and ecclesiastical authoritie joyne in one, do with all thankfulnesse, of heart acknowledge, with our mouthes doe confesse, and not only with our pennes, but with all our power are readie to witnesse unto the world, to your Majesties never dying glorie, how much the whole Kingdome is affected, and not only refreshed, but revived, with the comfortable sense of your Majesties pietie, justice, and goodnesse, in hearing our humble supplications, for a full and free general Assembly: and remembring that for the present, a more true and real testimonie of our unfained acknowledgement, could not proceed from us your Majesties duetyful Subjects, then to walke worthie of so royal a favour: It hath been our greatest care and serious endevour, next unto the will of JESUS CHRIST, the great King of his Kirk redeemed by his own bloud, in all our proceedings, joyned with our hearty prayers to GOD, for a blessing from heaven upon your Majesties Person and government, from the first houre of our meeting, to carie our selves in such moderation, order and loyaltie, as beseemed the subjects of so just and gracious a King, lacking nothing so much as your Majesties personal presence: With which had we been honoured and made happie, we were confident to have gained your Majesties Royall approbation to our ecclesiastick constitutions, and conclusions, knowing that a truly Christian minde and royall heart inclined from above, to religion and piety, will at the first discern, and discerning be deeply possessed with the love of the ravishing beautie, and heavenly order of the house of God; they both proceeding from the same Spirit. But as the joy was unspeakable, and the hopes lively, which from the fountaines of your Majesties favour did fill our hearts, so were we not a little troubled, when wee did perceive that your Majesties Commissioner, as before our meeting, he did endevour a prelimitation of the Assembly in the necessarie Members thereof, and the matters to bee treated therein, contrarie to the intention of your Majesties Proclamation indicting a free Assembly according to the order of this Kirk, and laws of the Kingdome: So from the first beginnings of our sitting (as if his Lordship had come rather to crosse, nor to countenance our lawful proceedings, or as we had intended any prejudice to the good of Religion), or to your Majesties honour (which GOD knoweth was far from our thoughts) did suffer nothing, although most necessarie, most ordinarie, and most undenyable, to passe without some censure, contradiction, or protestation: And after some dayes debating of this kinde, farre against our expectation, and to our great griefe, did arise himself, commanded us, who had laboured in every thing to approve our selves to GOD, and to his Lordship, as representing your Majesties Person, to arise also, and prohibited our further meeting by such a proclamation, as will be found to have proceeded, rather from an unwillingnesse that we should any longer sit, then from any ground or reason, which may endure the tryal either of your Majesties Parliament, or of your own royall Judgement, unto which if (being conveened by indiction from your Majestie, and sitting now in a constitute Assembly) we should have given place, This Kirk and Kingdome, contrare to your Majesties most laudable intentions manifested in former proclamations, and contrarie to the desires and expectation of all your Majesties good people, had been in an instant precipitate in such a world of confusions, and such depths of miserie, as afterward could not easily have been cured. In this extreamitie we made choise rather of that course which was most agreeable to your Majesties Will revealed unto us, after so many fervent Supplications, and did most conduce for the good of Religion, your Majesties honour, and the well of your Majesties Kingdome; then to give way to any sudden motion, tending to the ruin of all: wherein wee are so far from fearing the light, least our deeds should be reproved, that the more accuratly that we are tryed, and the more impartially our using of that power, which God Almighty, and your sacred Majestie, his Vicegerent had put in our hands, for so good and necessarie ends, is examined, we have the greater confidence, of your Majesties allowance and ratihabition: and so much the rather, that being in a manner inhibited to proceed in so good a work, we doubled our diligence, and endevoured more carefully then before, when your Majesties Commissioner was present, in every point, falling under our consideration, to walke circumspectly, and without offence, as in the sight of God, and as if your Majesties eyes had been looking upon us, labouring to proceed according to the word of God, our confession of Faith, and nationall oath, and the laudable constitutions of the lawfull Assemblies of this Kirk; and studying rather to renew, and revive old acts made for the reformation of Religion, in the time of your Majesties Father, of happie memorie, and extant in the records of the Kirk, which divine providence hath preserved, and at this time brought to our hands; then either to allow of such novations, as the avarice and ambition of men, abusing authoritie for their own ends, had without order introduced; or to appoint any new order, which had not been formerly received, and sworn to be reteined, in this Kirk. In all which the members of the Assembly, found so clear and convincing light, to their full satisfaction, against all their doubts and difficulties, that the harmonie and unanimitie was rare and wonderfull, and that we could not have agreed upon other constitutions, except wee would have been found fighting against GOD. Your Majesties wise and princely minde knoweth, that nothing is more ordinary then for men, when they doe well, to bee evil spoken of, and that the best actions of men are many times misconstrued, and mis-reported. Balaam, although a false Prophet, was wronged: for in place of that which hee said, The Lord refuseth to give me leave to go with you: the princes of Moab reported unto Balack, that Balaam refused to goe with them. But our comfort is, That Truth is the daughter of time, and although calumnie often starteth first, and runneth before, yet Veritie followeth her at the heels, and possesseth her self in noble and royall hearts: where base calumnie cannot long finde place. And our confidence is, that your Majestie with that worthie King, will keep one eare shut against all the obloquies of men; and with that more wise King, who when he gave a proofe that the wisedome of GOD was in him to doe judgement, would have both parties to stand before him at once: that hearing them equally, they might speed best, and go out most chearfully from his Majesties face, who had the best cause. When your Majesties wisedome hath searched all the secrets of this Assembly, let us be reputed the worst of all men, according to the aspersions whith partialitie would put upon us, let us be the most miserable of all men to the full satisfaction of the vindictive malice of our adversaries, let us by the whole world bee judged of all men the most unworthie to breath any more in this your Majesties Kingdome, if the cause that we maintaine, and have been prosecuting, shall be found any other, but that we desire that the Majestie of GOD, who is our fear and our dread, be served, and his house ruled, according to his owne will; if we have not carried along with us in all Sessions of our Assemblie, a most humble and loyall respect to your Majesties honour, which next unto the honour of the living GOD, lyeth nearest our hearts; if we have not keeped our selves within the limits of our reformation, without debording or reflecting upon the constitution of other reformed Kirks, unto which wee heartily wish all truth and peace, and by whose sound judgement and Christian affection we certainly look to be approven; if we have not failed rather by lenitie then by rigour in censuring of delinquents, never exceeding the rules and lines prescribed, and observed by this Kirk, and if (whatsoever men minding themselves, suggest to the contrary) the government and discipline of this Kirk, subscribed and sworn before, and now acknowledged by the unanimous consent of this Assembly, shall not bee found to serve for the advancement of the Kindome of CHRIST, for procuring all duetifull obedience to your Majestie, in this your Kingdome, and great riches and glorie to your Crown, for peace to us, your Majesties loyall subjects, and for terrour to all the enemies of your Majesties honour and our happinesse: and if any act hath proceeded from us, so farre as our understanding could reach, and humane infirmitie would suffer which being duely examined according to the grounds laid by your Majesties Father, of everlasting memory, and our religious Progenitours, and which Religion did forbid us to infringe, shall merit the anger and indignation, wherewith wee are so often threatned: But on the contrare, having sincerely sought the glorie of GOD, the good of Religion, your Majesties honour, the censure of impietie, and of men who had sold themselves to wickednesse, and the reestablishment of the right constitution and government of this Kirk, farre from the smallest appearance of wronging any other reformed Kirk, we humbly beg, and certainly expect, that from the bright beames of your Majesties countenance shining on this your Majesties own Kingdome and people, all our stormes shall bee changed in a comfortable calme, and sweet Sun-shine, and that your Majesties ratification in the ensuing Parliament, graciously indicted by your Majesties Proclamation to bee keeped in May, shall setle us in such a firmnesse, and stabilitie in our Religion, as shall adde a further lustre unto your Majesties glorious Diadem, and make us a blessed people under your Majesties long and prosperous reigne; which we beseech him who hath directed us in our affaires, and by whom Kings reigne, to grant unto your Majestie, to the admiration of all the world, the astonishment of your enemies, and comfort of the godly.

Collected, visied, and extracted forth of the Register of the acts of the Assembly by me Mr A. Jhonston Clerk thereto, under my signe and subscription manuall.

Edinburgh, the 12. of Jan. 1639.

THE GENERAL ASSEMBLY, AT EDINBURGH, 1639.

SESS. 8. AUGUST 17. 1639.

MASTER GEORGE GRAHAME HIS RENOUNCING AND ABJURING OF EPISCOPACIE.

The which day was given into the Assembly, direct from Master George Grahame, sometimes pretended Bishop of Orknay, an abjuration of Episcopacie, subscribed with his hand, which was publickly read in audience of the Assembly; and thereafter they ordained the same to be registrat in the assembly Books ad perpetuam rei memoriam, whereof the tenor follows.

To all and sundry whom it effects, to whose knowledge these presents shall come, specially to the reverend and honourable Members of the future Assembly to be holden at Edinburgh, the twelfth day of August 1639. years: Me Master George Graham, sometime pretended bishop of Orknay, being sorry and grieved at my heart that I should ever for any wordly respect have embraced the order of Episcopacie, the same having no warrand from the Word of God, and being such an order, as hath had sensibly many fearful and evill consequences in many parts of Christendome, and particularly within the Kirk of Scotland, as by doleful and deplorable experience this day is manifest, to have disclaimed, like as I by the tenor hereof doe altogether disclaime and abjure all Episcopal power and jurisdiction, with the whole corruptions thereof, condemned by lawful Assemblies within the said Kirk of Scotland, in regard the same is such an order as is also abjured within the said Kirk, by vertue of that National Oath with was made in the years 1580. and 1581. promising and swearing by the great Name of the Lord our God, That I shall never whiles I live, directly or indirectly, exerce any such power within the Kirk, neyther yet shall I ever approve or allow the same, not so much as in my private or publike discourse: But on the contrary, shall stand and adhere to all the Acts and Constitutions of the late Assembly holden at Glasgow, the 21. of Novemb. 1638. last by-past, and shall concurre to the uttermost of my power, sincerely and faithfully, as occasion shall offer, in execution the said Acts, and in advancing the Work of Reformation within this Land, to the glory of God, the peace of the Countrey, and the comfort and and contentment of all good Christians, as God shall be my help. In testimony of the which premisses, I have subscribed thir presents with my hand at Breeknes in Stronnes, the eleventh day of February, the year of God 1639. years, before thir witnesses Master Walter Stuart, Minister at Shoutronnaldsay, Master James Heynd, Minister at Kirkwall, Master Robert Peirson, Minister at Firth, and Master Patrick Grahame, Minister at Holme, my Son.

SESS. 8. AUGUST 17. 1639.

ACT CONTAINING THE CAUSES AND REMEDIE OF THE BY-GONE EVILS OF THIS KIRK.

The Kings Majestie having graciously declared, That it is His Royal will and pleasure, that all questions about Religion, and matters Ecclesiastical be determined by Assemblies of the Kirk, having also by publike Proclamation indicted this free national Assembly, for setling the present distraction of this Kirk, and for establishing a perfect peace, against such divisions and disordres as have been sore displeasing to his Majestie, and grievous to all his good Subjects. And now his Majesties Commissioner John Earle of Traquair, intrusted and authorized with a full Commission, being present, and sitting in this Assembly, now fully conveened and orderly constitute in all the members thereof, according to the order of this Kirk, having at large declared His Majesties zeal to the reformed Religion, and His Royal care and tender affection to this Kirk, where His Majestie had both His Birth and Baptisme, His great displeasure at the manifold distractions and divisions of this Kirk and Kingdome, and His desires to have all our wounds perfectly cured with a fair and fatherly hand: And although in the way approven by this Kirk, tryal hath been taken in former Assemblies before from the Kirk registers, to our full satisfaction, yet the Commissioners Grace making particular enquiry from the members of the Assembly, now solemnly conveened, concerning the real and true causes of so many & great evils as this time past had so sore troubled the peace of this Kirk and Kingdome, It was represented to his Majesties Commissioner by this Assembly, That beside many other, the maine and most material causes were, First, The pressing of this Kirk, by the Prelates with a Service Book, or Book of Common Prayer, without warrand or direction from the Kirk, and containing beside the Popish frame thereof, diverse Popish errors and ceremonies, & the seeds of manifold grosse Superstitions and Idolatry, with a Book of Canons, without warrand or direction from the general Assembly, establishing tyrannicall power over the Kirk in the person of Bishops, and overthrowing the whole discipline & government of the Kirk by Assemblies, with a Book of Consecration and Ordination, without warrand of Authoritie, Civill or Ecclesiasticall, appointing offices in the house of God, which are not warranted by the word of God, and repugnant to the discipline and Acts of our Kirk, and with the high Commission, erected without the consent of the Kirk, subverting the jurisdiction and ordinary Judicatories of this Kirk, and giving to persons meerely Ecclesiasticall, the power of both swords, and to persons meerly Civill, the power of the Keys and Kirk-sensures. A second cause was the Articles of Perth, viz. the observation of Festivall dayes, kneeling at the Communion, Confirmation, Administration of the Sacraments in private places, which are brought in by a null Assembly and are contrary to the Confession of Faith, as it was meant and subscribed Anno 1580, and divers times since and to the order and constitutions of this Kirk. Thirdly, the changing of the government of the Kirk, from the Assemblies of the Kirk to the persons of some

Kirkmen, usurping prioritie and power over their Brethren by the way, and under the name of Episcopall government against the Confession of Faith, 1580 against the order set downe in the Book of Policy, and against the intention & constitution of this Kirk from the beginning. Fourthly the Civill places and power of Kirkmen, their sitting in Session, Councell and Exchequer, their Riding, Sitting, and voting in Parliament, and their sitting in the Bench as Justices of peace, which according to the constitutions of this Kirk are incompatible with their spiritual function, lifting them up above their Brethren in worldly pomp, and do tend to the hinderance of the Ministrie. Fiftly the keeping and authorizing corrupt Assemblies at Linlithgow, 1606. and 1608. At Glasgow, 1610. At Aberdene, 1616. At S. Andrews, 1617. At Perth, 1618. which ar null and unlawful, as being called and constitute quite contrary to the order and constitutions of this Kirk received and practised ever since the reformation of Religion, and withal laboring to introduce novations into this Kirk, against the order and religion established. A sixth cause is the want of lawful & free General Assemblies, rightly constitute of Pastors, Doctors, and Elders yearly, or oftner pro re nata, according to the libertie of this Kirk, expressed in the Book of Policy: and acknowledged in the Act of Parliament, 1592. After which the whole Assembly in one heart and voyce did declare, that these and such other, proceeding from the neglect and breach of the Nationall Covenant of this Kirk and Kingdome, made in Anno 1580. have been indeed the true and maine causes of all our evills and distractions. And therefore ordain, according to the constitutions of the Generall Assemblies of this Kirk: And upon the grounds respectivè above-specified, That the foresaid Service-Book, Books of Cannons, and Ordination, and the high Commission, be still rejected: that the Articles of Perth, be no more practised: That Episcopall Government, and the Civill places and power of Kirk-men be holden still as unlawfull in this Kirk: That the above named pretended Assemblies, At Linlithgow 1606. and 1608. At Glasgow 1610. At Aberdene 1616. At S. Andrews 1617. At Perth 1618. be hereafter accounted as null, and of none effect. And that for preservation of Religion, and preventing all such evill in time-coming, Generall Assemblies rightly constitute, as the proper and competent judge of all matters Ecclesiasticall, heereafter be kept yearly and oftner, pro re nata, as occasion and necessity shall require; The necessity of these occasionall Assemblies being first remonstrate to His Majestie by humble supplication: As also that Kirk Sessions, Presbyteries and Synodall Assemblies, be constitute and observed, according to the order of this Kirk.

After the voycing of the Act (anent the causes of our by gone evills) His Majesties Commissioner consented verbally to the said Act, and promised to give into the Clerk in writ, the Declaration of His consent, and that he should ratifie this Act in the ensuing Parliament.

SESS. 18. AUG. 26. 1639.

ACT APPROVING AN OLD REGISTER OF THE GENERALL ASSEMBLY.

The whole Assembly (upon the report made to them anent the old Register of the As-

sembly, gotten from Master John Rig) *all in one voice approved the said Register, And ordained the same to make faith in judgement, and outwith in all time coming: as a true and authentick Register of the Kirk of* Scotland, *conforme to the testimonie subscribed by the Committee, to be insert in the Books of Assembly: whereof the tenor followeth:*

We under subscribers, Forsameikle as the late Generall Assembly holden at Glasgow, gave power and Commission to us, To peruse, examine, and cognosce upon the validity, faith, and strength of the books and Registers of the Assembly, particularly set down in the Commission given to us thereanent: According where-unto we did carefully view, peruse, and consider the saids Registers, and gave our testimony thereof under our hands, of the validity and sufficience of the samine, to the said Generall Assembly. And now having a new Commission given to us from the Generall Assembly now presently conveened and sitting at Edinburgh. To peruse, examine, and cognosce upon the validity, faith and strength of another Register of the Assembly, which was not set down and recommended to us by the said former Commission, which Register beginneth at the Assembly holden at Edinburgh the sixt day of March 1572. and endeth at the Assembly likewise holden at Edinburgh 1573. we have carefully viewed, perused, and considered the said Register: And being deeply and maturely advised, as in a matter of greatest weight and consequence, do attest before God, and upon our consciences declare to the world, and this present Assembly, That the said Register above exprest, is a famous, authentick, and good Register, which ought to be so reputed, and have publike faith in judgement and outwith, as a valid and true Record in all things, And finds the same to be of the same handwrit, and subscribed by the same Clerk of the Generall Assembly as divers of the said other Registers (formerly perused by us) are. And in testimonie of our solemne affirmation we have subscribed these presents with our hand, at Edinburgh the 14. day of August 1639.

ACT SESS. 19. AUGUST 27. 1639.

ACT APPROVING THE DEPOSITION OF THE MINISTERS BY THE COMMITTEES.

The Assembly, after the receiving of the whole reports from the Committees, appointed for revising of the processes and sentences, led, deduced, and pronounced before, and by the several Commissions granted by the Assembly at Glasgow, All in one voice approved the saids whole Processes as orderly proceeded, and the whole sentences pronounced therein till, as just and lawful decrees, without prejudice of any favour that can be showne to any person or persons, against whom the said sentences are pronounced upon their supplications, or of Justice to such as complain of their processe, and offers to reduce the same upon whatsoever reason competent, by the Constitutions of this Kirk and Kingdome, before the General Assembly and the Commissioners thereof, they being appointed for that effect.

ACT SESS. 20. AUG. 28. 1639.

ACT ANENT RECEIVING OF DEPOSED MINISTERS.

The which day the General Assembly upon the report of the Committees anent these who are deposed by Synods, Doe make this General Act, recommending to the Synods all these who are deposed befor them for subscribing of the Declinator, & reading of the Service book and for no other grosse cause, That upon their true repentance & submission to the Constitutions of this Kirk & upon their purgation and clearnesse from any grosse Faults laid to their charge in any new processe against them, they may be found by the Synod as capable of the Ministrie, when God grants them an ordinary and lawful calling by admission from the Presbyterie, either in the Church they served in before, or in any other Church.

ACT SESS. 21. AUGUST 29. 1639.

ACT ANENT THE KEEPING OF THE LORDS DAY.

The General Assembly recommendeth to the several Presbyteries the execution of the old acts of Assembly, against the breach of the Sabbath Day, by going of Mylnes, Salt-Pannes, Salmond-fishing, or any such like labour; and to this end revives and renues the act of the Assembly holden at Haly-rude-house, 1602. *Sess. 5. whereof the tenor follows.*

The Assembly considering that the conventions of the People, specially on the Sabbath Day are very rare in many places, by distraction of labour not only in harvest and seed-time, but also every Sabbath, by fishing both of the white fish, and Salmond-fishing, and in going of Mylnes. Therefore the Assembly dischargeth and inhibiteth all such labour of fishing, as well white fish and Salmond-fish, and going of Mylnes of all sorts upon the Sabbath, under the pain of incurring the censures of the Kirk: And ordaines the Commissioners of this Assembly, to mean the same to His Majestie, and to desire that a pecunial paine may be injoyned upon the contraveeners of this present Act.

ACT SESS. 22. AUG. 29. 1639. A MERIDIE.

ARTICLES AND OVERTURES APPROVED BY THE ASSEMBLY.

That some Commissioners be appointed to visit and peruse the whole Acts of General Assemblies, and to marke such Acts as are for the use of the Kirk in General, To extract the same out of the Registers, to the effect that after they be tryed, they may be printed according to the old Acts of the Assembly at Edinburgh, March 7. 1574. Sess. 9.

The Assembly appoints the Presbyterie of Edinburgh, to have a care of this article, and to report their diligence to the next Assembly.

That course may be taken for restraining of people from passing to England to marry, which is the occasion of great in conveniences.

The Assembly alloweth this article, and recommends to the Parliament, that they would appoint a pecuniall summe to be payed by the contraveeners.

That the Acts for furnishing expences to Commissioners, sent by the Presbyteries to the General Assembly, and sent in Commission by Generall Assemblies, may be explained; And it be declared that all such Commissioners whatsoever, by their stipends may be furnished by the Kirks of the Presbyterie, according to the order, set down in the Act of the last Assembly, since the errand is common, and the benefit concerneth all: and that order may be taken, how that an expedient voluntarie course, thought fit by the Assembly, shall by advise of Parliament, have the force of a law, for compelling these to pay who are stented, both for the last and this Assembly and in time to come.

The Assembly allowes this article, and referres the same to the Parliament.

That the Session-books of every Paroche be presented once a year to the Presbyteries, that they may be tryed by them.

The Assembly alloweth this article.

That the Act of the 38. Assembly at Edinburgh, October 24, 1578. Sess. 8. ordaining Ministers who are deposed, to be charged under the pain of excommunication, to dimit their places, that they may be unquestionably vacand, may now be renewed.

The Assembly alloweth this article, and remits the same to the Parliament.

The Assembly would revive or renew all former Acts of Assembly against Papists, and excommunicate persons, against haunters with them and receivers of them.

The Assembly alloweth this article.

That an uniforme Catechisme may be appointed to be used throughout this whole Kingdome in the examinations before the Communion.

The Assembly alloweth this article.

That all Ministers or Intrants presented to Kirks, be tryed before their admission, if they be qualified for the places to which they are presented, besides the ordinary tryalls of Expectants before their entrie to the Ministerie.

The Assembly alloweth this article.

SESS. 23. AUGUST 30. 1639.

THE SUPPLICATION OF THE GENERAL ASSEMBLY TO THE KINGS MAJESTIES COMMISSIONER, CONCERNING THE BOOK, CALLED, THE LARGE DECLARATION.

We the Members of this present Assembly, for our selves, and in name of the severall Presbyteries, Burghs, and Universities, for which we are Commissioners resenting the great dishonour done to God, our King, this Kirk, and whole Kingdome, by the Book called, A large Declaration, have here represented the same to your Grace, and have collected some amongst many of false grosse and absurd passages; That from the consideration thereof, your Grace, perceiving the intolerable evills foresaids contained therein, may be pleased to represent the same to our gracious Soveraigne, and in our behalfs humbly to beseech his Majestie, so much wronged by the many foul and false relations, suggested and perswaded to him as trueths, and by stealing the protection of His Royal Name and Authoritie to the patrocinie of such a Book: To be pleased first to call in the said Book: and thereby to shew his dislike thereof: Next to give Commission and warrant, To cite all such parties as are either knowne or suspect to have hand in it, and to appoint such as His Majestie knowes to be either authors, informers, or any wayes accessarie, being Natives of this Kingdome, To be sent hither to abide their tryall and censure before the Judge Ordinary, and in speciall Master Walter Balcanquell, now Deane of Durham, who is known and hath professed to be the author, at least a vower and maintainer of a great part thereof; that by their examplar punishment, others may be deterred from such dangerous courses, as in such a way to raise sedition betwixt the King and His Subjects, Gods honour may be vindicate from so high contempt, His Majesties justice may appear, not only in cutting away such Malefactors, but in discouraging all such under-miners of His throne, His loyall and loving Subjects shall be infinitly contented to be cleared before the world of so false and unjust imputations, and will live hereafter in the greater securitie, when so dangerous a course of sedition is prevented, and so will have the greater and greater cause to pray for His Majesties long & prosperous Reigne.

His Majesties Commissioner in Councell having received the said supplication, promised to impart the same to His Majesty, and to report his diligence therein.

The Supplication of the Assembly to His Majesties High Commissioner, and the Lords of secret Councell.

Wee the Generall Assembly, considering with all humble and thankful acknowledgement, the many recent favours bestowed upon us by His Majestie, and that there resteth nothing for crowning of His Majesties incomparable goodnesse towards us, but that all the members of this Kirk and Kingdom be joyned in one and the same Confession and Covenant with God, with the Kings Majestie, and amongst ourselves: And conceiving the main lett and impediment to this so good a work, and so much wished by all, to have been the Informations made to his Majestie, of our intentions to shake off Civil and dutiful obedience due to Soveraignity, and to diminish the Kings greatnesse and authoritie, and being most willing and desirous to remove this and all such impediments which may hinder and impede so full and perfect an Union, and for clearing of our loyaltie, WEE in our own names, and in name of all the rest of the Subjects and Congregations whom we represent, do now in all humility represent to your Grace, His Majesties Commissioner, and the Lords of His Majesties most honourable privie Councel, and declares before God and the World, that we never had nor have any thought of with-drawing our selves from that humble and dutiful obedience to His Majestie, and to his Government, which by the descent & under the reign of 107 Kings is most chearfully acknowledged by us and our predecessors: And that we never had, nor have any intention nor desire to attempt any thing that may tend to dishonour of God, or the diminution of the Kings greatnesse and authoritie: But on the contrary, acknowledging our quietnesse, stabilitie and happinesse to depend upon the safety of the Kings Maj. Person, & maintenance of His greatnesse and Royal authority who is Gods Vice-gerent set over us, for the maintenance of Religion and ministration of Justice, We have solemnly sworn and do sweare, not only our mutual concurrence and assistance for the cause of Religion, and to the uttermost of our power, with our means and lives, to stand to the defence of our dread Soveraigne, his Person and authority, in preservation and defence of the true Religion, Liberties and Lawes of this Kirk and Kingdome, but also in every cause which may concerne His Majesties honour, shall according to the Lawes of this Kingdome, and the duties of good Subjects concurre with our friends and followers in quiet manner, or in armes, as we shall be required of His Majestie, His Councel, or any having his Authority. And therefore being most desirous to cleare our selves of all imputation of this kinde, and following the laudable example of our predecessors, 1589. do most humble supplicate your Grace, His Majesties Commissioner, and the Lords of His Majesties most honourable privie Councell, to enjoyn by Act of a Councel, that this Confession and Covenant, which, as a testimony of our fidelity to God, and loyaltie to our King, we have subscribed, be subscribed by all His Majesties Subjects, of what rank and quality soever.

THE ACT OF THE LORDS OF COUNCEL AT EDINBURGH, AUGUST 30. 1639. CONTAINING THE ANSWER OF THE PRECEDING SUPPLICATION.

The which day in presence of the Lord Commissioner and the Lords of privie Councel, compeired personally John Earle of Rothes, James Earle of Montrose, John Lord Lowdoun, Sir George Stirling of Keir Knight, Sir William Douglas of

Cavers Knight, Sir Henry Wood of Bonytoun Knight, John Smyth Burgesse of Edinburgh, Mr. Robert Barclay Provest of Irwing, Mr. Alexander Henderson Minister at Edinburgh, and Mr. Archbald Johnstoun Clerk to the General Assembly, and in the name of the present sitting General Assembly, gave in to the Lord Commissioner, and Lords of privie Councel, the Petition above written; which being read, heard, and considered by the saids Lords, they have ordained, and ordain the same to be insert and registrate in the books of Privie Councel, and according to the desire thereof, ordaines the said Confession and Covenant to be subscribed in time coming by all His Majesties Subjects of this Kingdome, of what ranke and quality soever.

THE KINGS MAJESTIES COMMISSIONERS DECLARATIONS.

The which day His Majesties Commissioner, and Lords of Councel, after the receiving of the Supplication of the General Assembly, anent the subscribing of the Covenant, having returned to the Assembly, His Majesties Commissioner in name of the Councel, declared; That he had received the Supplication of the Assembly, desiring that the Covenant might receive the force of an Act of Councel, to be subscribed by all His Majesties Subjects, that they had found the desire so fair and reasonable, that they conceived themselves bound in duety to grant the same; and thereupon have made an Act of Councel to that effect: And that there rested now the Act of Assembly. And that he himself was so fully satisfied, that he came now as his Majesties Commissioner to consent fully unto it: And that he was most willing that it should be enacted here in this Assembly, to oblige all his Majesties Subjects to subscribe the said Covenant, with the Assemblies explanation. And because there was a third thing desired, His subscription as the Kings Commissioner, unto the Covenant, which he behoved to do, with a Declaration in writ, and he declared as a Subject, he should subscribe the Covenant as strictly as any, with the Assemblies Declaration; but as His Majesties Commissioner in his name behoved to prefix to his subscription, the Declaration following, which no Scots Subjects should subscribe, or have the benefit of, no not himself as Earle of Traquair. The tenor whereof follows:

Seeing this Assembly, according to the laudable form and custome heretofore kept in the like cases, have in an humble and dutiful way, supplicate to us His Majesties Commissioner, and the Lords of His most honourable Privie Councel, That the Covenant, with the explanation of this Assembly, might be subscribed: And to that effect that all the Subjects of this Kingdome by Act of Councel be required to doe the same: And that therein for vindicating themselves from all suspitions of disloyaltie, or derogating from the greatnesse and authoritie of our dread Soveraigne, have therewith added a Clause, whereby this Covenant is declared one in substance with that which was subscribed by His Majesties Father of blessed memory 1580, 1581, 1590. and oftner since renewed. Therefore I as His Majesties Commissioner, for the full satisfaction of the Subjects, and for settling a perfect Peace in Church and Kingdome, doe according to my foresaids Declaration and Subscription, subjoyned to the Act of this Assembly of the date the 17 this instant, allow and consent that the Covenant be subscribed throughout all this

Kingdome. In witnes whereof I have subscribed the premisses.

LIKE AS HIS MAJESTIES COMMISSIONER, READ AND GAVE IN THE DECLARATION FOLLOWING, OF HIS CONSENT TO THE ACT OF THE ASSEMBLY 17. AUGUST, ANENT THE CAUSES OF OUR BY GONE EVILS.

I *John* Earle of *Traquair*, His Majesties Commissioner this present Assembly, doe in His Majesties Name declare, that nothwithstanding of His Majesties own inclination, and many other grave and weightie consideration yet such is His Majesties incomparable goodnesse, that for settling the present distractions, and giving full satisfaction to the Subject, He doth allow, like as I His Majesties Commissioner do consent to the foresaid Act, and have subscribed the premisses.

LIKE AS HIS MAJESTIES COMMISSIONER, READ AND GAVE IN THE DECLARATION FOLLOWING:

It is alwayes hereby declared by me His Majesties Commissioner, That the practise of the premisses, prohibited within this Kirk and Kingdome, outwith the Kingdome of Scotland shall never bind nor inferre censure against the practises outwith the Kingdome; which when the Commissioner required to be insert in the Register of the Kirk, and the Moderator in name of the Assembly, refused to give warrant for such practise, as not agreeable with a good conscience His Grace urged, that it should be recorded, at least that he made such a Declaration, whatsoever was the Assemblies Judgement in the contrair: And so it is to be understood to be insert here only recitative.

ACT ORDAINING THE SUBSCRIPTION OF THE CONFESSION OF FAITH AND COVENANT, WITH THE ASSEMBLIES DECLARATION.

The Generall Assembly considering the great happiness which may flow from a full and perfect Union of this Kirk and Kingdome, by joyning of all in one and the same Covenant with God, with the Kings Majestie, and amongst our selves, having by our great Oath declared the uprightnesse and loyaltie of our intentions in all our proceedings, and having withall supplicated His Majesties high Commissioner, and the Lords of His Majesties honorable Privie Councell, to injoyn by Act of Councell, all the Lieges in time coming to subscribe the Confession of faith and Covenant, which as a testimony of our fidelity to God and loyaltie to our King we have subscribed; And seeing His Majesties high Commissioner, and the Lords of His Majesties honorable Privie Councell, have granted the desire of our Supplication, ordaining by Civill authority, all His Majesties Lieges in time comming, to subscribe the foresaid Covenant, that our Union may be the more full and perfect, We by our Act and Constitution Ecclesiasticall, do approove the foresaid Covenant, in all the Heads and Clauses thereof and ordains of new, under all Ecclesiasticall censure, that all the Masters of Universities, Colledges, and Schooles, all Schollers at the passing of their degrees, all persons suspect of Papistry, or any other errour; and finally all the members of this Kirk & Kingdome, subscribe the same with these words prefixed to their subscription: The Article of this Covenant, which was at the first subscription referred to the determination of the General Assembly, being determined. And thereby the five Articles of Perth, the government of the Kirk by Bishops, the civill places and power of Kirkmen, upon the reasons and grounds contained in the Acts of the Generall Assembly declared to be unlawfull within this Kirk: we subscribe according to the determination foresaid. And ordains the Covenant, with this Declaration, to be insert in the Registers of the Assemblies of this Kirk, Generall, Provinciall, and Presbyteriall, ad perpetuam rei memoriam; and in all humility supplicates His Majesties high Commissioner, and the honourable Estates of Parliament, by their authority, to ratifie and injoyne the same, under all civill paines, which will tend to the glory of God, preservation of Religion, the Kings Majesties honour, and perfect peace of this Kirk and Kingdome.

ACT ANENT APPELLATIONS.

The Assembly appointed that in all time hereafter, no Appellations should be leaping over either Presbyterie or Synod, but to ascend by degrees as from the Kirk Session to the Presbytry, or from the Presbyterie to the Synod, and from the Synod to the Generall Assembly, except it be after the Synod be past, and immediatly before the Generall Assembly, or in the time thereof, and renews all former Acts made to this effect.

ACT ANENT ADVISING WITH SYNODS AND PRESBYTERIES BEFORE DETERMINATION IN NOVATIONS.

The Generall Assembly desiring that the intended Reformation being recovered, may be established, Ordains, that no Novation which may disturbe the peace of the Church, and make division, be suddenly proponed and enacted: But so as the motion be first communicate to the severall Synods, Presbyteries and Kirks, that the matter may be approved by all at home, and Commissioners may come well prepared, unanimously to conclude a solide deliberation upon these points in the Generall Assembly.

ACT ANENT MINISTERS CATECHISING, AND FAMILY EXERCISES.

The Assembly considering that the long waited-for fruits of the Gospel, so mercifully planted and preserved in this Land, and Reformation of ourselves, and Families, so solemnly vowed to God of late in our Covenant, cannot take effect, except the knowledge and worship of God be caried from the Pulpit to every family within each Parish, hath therefore appointed that every Minister, besides his paines on the Lords day, shall have weekly catechising of some part of the Paroch, and not altogether cast over the examination of the people, till a litle before the Communion. Also that in every Familie the worship of God be erected, where it is not both Morning and Evening, and that the Children & Servants be catechised at home, by the Masters of the Families, whereof account shall be taken by the Minister, and Elders assisting him in the visitation of every Family: And lest they fail, that visitation of the severall Kirks be seriously followed by every Presbyterie, for this end among others. The execution and successe whereof, being tried by the

Synods, let it be represented to the next Generall Assembly.

SESS. 24. AUG. 30. A MERIDE.

THE ASSEMBLIES SUPPLICATION TO THE KINGS MAJES-TIE.

Most Gracious Souveraigne.

Wee Your Majesties most humble and loyall Subjects, the Commissioners from all the parts of this your Majesties ancient & native Kingdome, and members of the Nationall Assembly, conveened at Edinburgh by your Majesties speciall indiction, and honoured with the presence of Your Majesties high Commissioner, have been waiting for a day of rejoycing, and of solemne thanksgiving to be rendred to God by this whole Kirk and Kingdome, for giving us a King so just and religious, that it is not only lawfull for us to be Christians under Your Majesties government, which sometime hath been the greatest praise of great Princes, but also that it hath pleased Your gracious Maj. to make known that it is Your Royall will and pleasure, that all matters Ecclesiasticall be determined in free Nationall Assemblies, and matters civill in Parliaments; which is a most noble and ample expression of Your Majesties justice, and we trust shall be a powerful mean of our common happinesse under your Majesties most blessed Reign. In the mean while we do most humbly, upon the knees of our hearts, blesse your Majesty for that happinesse already begun in the late Assembly at Edinburgh; in the proceedings whereof, next under God, we have laboured to approve our selves unto Your Majesties Vice-gerent, as if Your Majesties eyes had been upon us, which was the desire of our souls, and would have beene the matter of our full rejoycing, and doe still continue Your Majesties most humble supplicants for Your Majesties civill sanction and ratification of the constitutions of the Assembly in Parliament; That your Majesties Princely power, and the Ecclesiasticall Authority joyning in one, the mutuall embracements of religion and justice, of truth and peace may be seen in this Land, which shall be to us as a resurrection from the dead, and shall make us, being not only so farre recovered, but also revived, to fill Heaven and Earth with our praises, and to pray that King CHARLES may be more and more blessed, and His throne established before the Lord for ever.

The Assembly appoints the next Generall Assembly, to sit at Aberdene the last Tuesday of July next, 1640. years. And warneth all Presbyteries, Universities and Burrows, to send their Commissioners, for keeping the same. And thereafter the Assembly was concluded by giving of thanks by the Moderator, and singing of a Psalme, according to the custome.

THE GENERALL ASSEMBLY, CONVEENED AT ABERDENE, JULY 28. 1640.

SESS. 2. JULY 29. 1640.

The Assembly having past the first day before they would make any Act in attending of His Majesties Commissioner.

This day the Moderator openly asked in face of the Assembly, if there was any Commissioner come from His Majestie: And finding there was none, the Assembly proceeded according to their Liberties.

OVERTURES GIVEN IN BY THE COMMITTEE APPOINTED BY THE LAST ASSEMBLY, ANENT THE ORDERING OF THE ASSEMBLY-HOUSE: WHICH BEING READ IN AUDIENCE OF THE ASSEMBLY THEY APPROVED THE SAME.

I. The Assembly finds it expedient for the ordering of the House in all time coming, that the Commissioners sit together unmixt, and that the places where they sit be railed about, or some other way divided from the seats of others, and that places be provided without the bounds of the Commissioners seats to persons of respect, who are not Commissioners, and others according to their qualities, as the Magistrates of the Town shall find most convenient.

II. Also that the Commissioners, having received tickets from the Magistrates of the Burgh, at the delivery of their Commissions, whereby they may have ready accesse to the Assemblie-House and place appointed for them, do keep the hour of meeting precisely, and whosoever comes after the time, or shall be found absent at the calling of the Rols, to be censured as the Assemblie sees fitting: And whatsoever Presbyterie, Burgh, or Universitie, shall not send Commissioners, or Commissioners sent from them doe not come at all to the Assembly, be summond unto the next Assembly, and censured as the Assembly shall find reasonable.

III. That foure persons of respect have warrant from the Assembly to injoyne that there be no standing, no din, nor disorderly behaviour; And if any shall disobey them, or direct his speech to any, except to the Moderator, and that one at once with leave at first asked and given, to be rebuked publikely by the Moderator: And if he desist not be removed out of the Assembly for that Session.

IV. That no motion come in unto the Assembly but by the Committee appointed for matters of that nature: And if the Committee refused to answer the same, let it be proponed to the Assembly with the reasons thereof.

V. That the minutes of ilk Session be read before their rising, and if the matter concerne the whole Kirk, let it be drawn up in forme and read in the beginning of the next ensuing Session, that the Assembly may judge whether or not it bee according to their minde.

ACT ANENT THE DEMOLISHING OF IDOLATROUS MON-UMENTS.

Forasmuch as the Assembly is informed, that in divers places of this Kingdome, and specially in the North parts of the same, many Idolatrous Monuments, erected and made for Religious worship, are yet extant, Such as Crucifixes, Images of Christ, Mary, and Saints departed, ordaines the saids Monuments to be taken down, demolished, and destroyed, and that with all convenient diligence: And that the care of this work shall be incumbent to the Presbyteries and Provinciall Assemblies within this Kingdome, and their Commissioners to report their diligence herein to the next Generall Assembly.

ACT AGAINST WITCHES AND CHARMERS.

The Assembly ordaines all Ministers within the Kingdome, carefully to take notice of Charmers, Witches, and all such abusers of the people, and to urge the Acts of Parliament, to be execute against them: And that the Commissioners from the Assembly to the Parliament, shall recommend to the said supreme judicatory, the care of the execution of the Lawes against such persons in the most behoovefull way.

SESS. 5. AUG. 1. 1640.

ACT FOR CENSURING SPEAKERS AGAINST THE COVE-NANT.

The Assembly ordaines, that such as have subscribed the Covenant and speakes against the same, if he be a Minister, shall be deprived: And if he continue so, being deprived, shall be excommunicate: And if he be any other man, shall be dealt with as perjured, and satisfie publikely for his perjury.

SESS. 10. AUG. 5. 1640.

ACT AGAINST EXPECTANTS REFUSING TO SUBSCRIBE THE COVENANT.

The Assembly ordaines, that if any Expectant shall refuse to subscribe the Covenant, he shall be declared uncapable of a Pedagogie, teaching of a School, reading at a Kirk, Preaching within a Presbyterie, and shall not have libertie of residing within a Burgh, Universitie or Colledge: And if they continue obstinate, to be processed.

The Generall Assembly appoints the next Assembly, to be in St. Andrews *the third Tuesday of* July 1641. *And that the Moderator in a convenient way, by the secret Councell—or otherwise as may best serve, request the Kings Majestie to send his Commissioner to the said Assembly. And if any exigent fall out, that the Presbyterie of* Edinburgh *give advertisement for an Assembly* pro re nata.

THE GENERALL ASSEMBLY, HOLDEN AT ST. ANDREWS, AND EDINBURGH. 1641.

SESS. 1. JULY 20. 1641.

John Earle of Weymes, His Majesties Commissioner, presented His Majesties Letter to the Assembly, whereof the tenor followeth.

Charles R.

Trustie and welbeloved, Wee greet you well. It is no small part of Our Royall care and desires, that the true Reformed Religion, wherein by the grace of God, We resolve to live and dye, be settled peaceably in that Our ancient and native Kingdome of Scotland, and that the same be truly taught, and universally received and professed by Our Subjects there, of all degrees. For preventing of all division and trouble hereafter, We did intend in Our Own Royall Person, to have been present at this Assembly; but conceiving it to be unfitting, to detaine the Ministers from their particular charges, till the time of Our coming to the Parliament. We have resolved to make knowne unto you by these, and by Our Commissioner, That in the approaching Parliament, it is Our intention by Our authority, to ratifie and confirm the Constitutions of the late Assembly at Edinburgh, that they may be obeyed by all Our Subjects living in that Our Kingdome. And that We will take into Our Royall consideration, by what meanes the Churches belonging to Our presentation, when any of them shall happen to need, may be best provided with well qualified Preachers: Like as We are not unwilling, to grant presentations unto such as in these times of trouble have entred into the Ministerie, providing they have been examined by the Presbyteries, and approved by them: Because We want not Our own feares of the decay of Learning in that Church and Kingdome, We intend also to consider of the best meanes for helping the Scooles and Colledges of Learning especially of Divinity, that there may be such a number of Preachers there, as that each Parish having a Minister, and the Gospel being preached in the most remote parts of the Kingdome, all Our Subjects may taste of Our care in that kinde, and have more and more cause to blesse God that we are set over them. And finally, so tender is Our care, that it shall not be Our fault if the Churches and Colledges there flourish not in Learning and Religion: For which Royall testimonie of Our goodnesse, We require nothing upon your part, but that which God hath bound you unto, even that you be faithfull in the charge committed unto you, and care for the soules of the people: That you study Peace and Unity amongst your selves, and amongst the people, against all Schisme and Faction; and that you not only pray for Us, but that you teach the People, which We trust are not unwilling to pay that honour and obedience which they owe unto Us, as his Vicegerent set over them, for their good; wherein We expect you will by your good example goe before them. Which hoping you will doe, We bid you farewell. From Our Court at Whitehall, the 10. day of July 1641.

SESS. 3. JULY 28. 1641.

Act approving the Overtures of the Assembly at Aberdene, for ordering the Assembly-House.

The Overtures for ordering the Assembly-House, given in to, and approved by the Assembly of Aberdene the 29. July 1640. Act Sess. 2 were openly read, and again approved by this Assembly, and ordained to be kept the whole time thereof.

SESS. 5. JULY 30. 1641.

ACT ANENT OLD MINISTERS BRUIKING THEIR BENEFIC-ES.

The Assembly having considered the Supplication given in by Doctor Robert Howie, Provest of the new Colledge of S. Andrews, whereby he craved, that (notwithstanding of his admission of his charge) he should not be prejudged of his full provision and maintenance during his life time: The Assembly thinks it fit and necessary, that his provision and maintenance should not be diminished, but that he should injoy the same fully, as before during all the dayes of his life time, and craveth his dismission to be only but a cessation from his charge, because of his age and inability: And declares, that old Ministers and professors of Divinitie, shall not by their cessation from their charge, through age and inabilitie, be put from injoing their old maintenance & dignity. And recommends this and others the like things, concerning the estate of that Universitie of S. Andrews, to the Parliament, and the Visitation to be appointed from the Assembly & Parliament. And likewise the Assembly being informed, that the said Doctor Howie hath been very painfull in his charge, and that he hath divers papers which would be very profitable for the Kirk: Therefore they think fit, that the said doctor Howie be desired to collect these papers, which doeth concerne, & may be profitable for the use of the Kirk, that the samine may be showne to the Visitors of the said Universitie.

SESS. 8. AUG. 2. 1641. A MERIDIE.

ACT AGAINST SUDDEN RECEIVING MINISTERS DE-POSED.

The Assembly ordaines, that Ministers who are deposed either by Presbyteries, Synods, or Generall Assemblies, or Committees from Assemblies for the publike cause of the Reformation and order of this Kirk, shall not be suddenly received againe to the Ministerie, till they first evidence their repentance both before the Presbyterie and Synod, within the bounds where they were deposed, and thereafter the samine reported to the next ensuing Generall Assembly.

SESS. 9. AUG. 3. 1641.

The Overtures under-written, concerning the Universities and Colledges of this Kingdome to be represented by the Generall Assembly, to the Kings Majesty and Parliament, being openly read, the Assembly approved the saids Overtures, and ordained them to be recommended to the Parliament.

First, because the good estate both of the Kirk and Commonwealth, dependeth mainly upon the flourishing of Universities and Colledges, as the Seminaries of both, which cannot be expected, unlesse the poore meanes which they have, be helped, and sufficient revenues be provided for them and the same well imployed: Therefore that out of the rents of prelacies; Collegiat or Chapter-Kirks, or such like, a sufficient maintenance be provided for a competent number of Professors, Teachers, and Bursers in all faculties, and especially in Divinitie, and for upholding, repairing, and enlarging the Fabrick of the Colledges, furnishing Libraries, and suchlike good uses in every Universitie and Colledge.

II. Next for keeping of good order, preveening and removing of abuses, and promoving of pietie and learning, it is very needfull & expedient, that there be a communion and correspondencie kept betwixt all the Universities and Colledges. And therefore that it be ordained, that there be a meeting once every year at such times and places as shall be agreed upon, of Commissioners from every University and Colledge to consult and determine upon the common affairs, and whatsoever may concerne them, for the ends above-specified, and who also, or some of their number may represent what shall be needfull and expedient for the same effect, to Parliaments and Generall Assemblies.

III. Item, That special care be had that the places of the Professors, especially of Professors of Divinity in every University and Colledge. Be filled with the ablest men, and best affected to the Reformation and order of this Kirk.

SESS. 10. AUGUST 4. 1641.

ACT AGAINST IMPIETY AND SCHISME.

The Assembly seriously considering the present case and condition of this Kirk and Kingdome, what great things the Lord hath done for us, especially since the renewing of our Covenant, notwithstanding our former backsliding and desertion; and if we shall either become remisse in the dueties of Piety, or shall not constantly hold and keep our Religion, unto which we have bound ourselves so straitly and solemnly, what dishonour we doe unto the Name of God before men, who have their eyes upon us, and how great judgements we bring upon our selves, upon these and the like considerations, The Assembly doth finde it most necessary to stirre up themselves, and to provoke all others both Ministers and people of all degrees, not only to the religious exercises of publike worship in the Congregation, and of private worship in their families, and of every one by themselves apart, but also to the dueties of mutual edification, by instruction, admonition, exhorting one another to fordwardnesse in Religion, and comforting one another in whatsoever distresse; and that in all their meetings, whither in the way of civill conversation, or by reason of their particular callings, or any other occasion offered by divine providence, no corrupt communication proceed out of their mouth, but that which is good to the use of edifying, that it may minister grace unto the hearers: And because the best means have been, and may still be despised or abused, and particularly the duetie of mutual edification, which hath been so little in use, and so few know how to practise in the right manner, may be upon the one part subject to the mocking of ungodly and worldly men, who cannot endure that in others, which they are not willing to practise themselves, and upon the other part, to many errors and abuses, to which the godly through their weaknes may fall, or by the craftinesse of others may be drawn into, such as are Error, Heresie, Schisme, Scandal, Self-conceit, and despising of others, pressing above the common calling of Christians, and usurping that which is proper to the Pastoral Vocation, contempt or misregard of the publike means idle and unprofitable questions which edifie not, uncharitable censurings, neglect of duties in particular callings, businesse in other mens Matters and Callings, and many such others in doctrine, charity, and manners, which have dolefully rent the bowels of other Kirks, to the great prejudice of the Gospel.

Therefore the Assembly, moved with the zeal of God against all abuses and corruptions, and according to their manifold obligations, most earnestly desiring and thirsting to promove the work of Reformation, and to have the comfort and power of true godlinesse sensible to every soul, and Religion to be universally practised in every Family, and by every person at all occasions, Doth charge all the Ministers and Members of this Kirk whom they doe represent, that according to their several places and vocations, they endeavour to suppresse all impiety and mocking of religious exercises, especially of such as put foule aspersions, and factious or odious names upon the godly. And upon the other part, that in the fear of God they be aware and spiritually wise, that under the name and pretext of religious exercises, otherwayes lawful and necessary, they fall not into the aforesaid abuses; especially, that they eschew all meetings which are apt to breed Error, Scandall, Schisme, neglect of dueties and particular callings, and such other evils as are the works, not of the spirit, but of the flesh, and are contrary to truth and peace; and that the Presbyteries and Synods have a care to take order with such as transgresse the one way or the other.

SESS. 14. AUGUST 6. 1641. A MERIDIE.

ACT ANENT NOVATIONS.

Since it hath pleased God to vouchsafe us the libertie of yearly General Assemblies, It is ordained according to the Acts of the Assembly at Edinburgh 1639. and at Aberdene 1640. that no Novation in Doctrine, Worship, or Government, be brought in, or practised in this Kirk, unlesse it be first propounded, examined, and allowed in the General Assembly, and that transgressors in this kinde be censured by Presbyteries and Synods.

ACT. SESS. 15. AUGUST 7. 1641.

OVERTURES ANENT BURSARS, AND EXPECTANTS.

The Overtures under-written being openly read in audience of the Assembly, were approved, and declared by them to be Acts of the Assembly, in all time coming, to be observed respective, as the samine bears.

The Assembly thinks meet for maintaining of Bursars of Divinitie, that every Presbyterie that consists of twelve Ministers shall maintain a Bursar, and where the number is fewer nor twelve, shall be joyned with these out of another Presbyterie where their number exceeds; where this course is not already kept, it is to be begun without longer delay, and every Provincial is ordained to give an accompt of their number of Bursars, that is constantly to be entertained by their Province, at the next ensuing General Assembly.

II. No expectant shall be permitted to preach in publike before a Congregation, till first he be tryed after the same manner, howbeit not altogether with that accuracie which is injoyned by the act of the Assembly of Glasgow 1638. which prescribes the order and manner of tryall that is to be kept with these who are to be admitted to the holy Ministrie: and none so tryed shall preach in publike, without the bounds of the University or Presbyterie where he past his tryalls, till he first make it known to the other Presbyteries, where he desires to be heard, by a testimoniall from the Universitie or Presbyterie where he lived, that he hath bin of an honest conversation, and past his tryalls conform to the order here prescribed: Which being done in the meeting of the Province or Presbyterie, where he desires to be heard; he is to be allowed by them to preach within the bounds of that Province or Presbyterie, without any further tryall to be taken of him.

III. Expectants being educate in a Colledge that was corrupt, or under a corrupt Minister, if they themselves have been known to have been tainted with error, or opposite to our Covenant, and the blessed Work of Reformation within this Kirk, the same order is to be kept in admitting them to the holy Ministrie, or to any place in the Colledges or Schooles of this Kingdome, that was ordained to be kept in admission of these Ministers who fled out of the Countrey, and shew themselves opposite to our Covenant and Reformation.

ACT SESS. 17. AUGUST 9. 1641.

ACT AGAINST UNLAWFULL BANDS.

The Assembly taking to their consideration the question proponed unto them concerning the Band, the copy whereof was presented before them from the Parliament, doth find and declare that Bands of this and the like nature, may not lawfully be made: By which Declaration the Assembly doth not intend to bring any censure for what is past, and by the wisedome and care of the Committee of the Parliament is taken away, upon any person, who being required by the Moderator and the Clerk, shall under his hand declare before them, That as the Assembly doth finde that the subscribers are not astricted by their Oath to the tenor of the said Band, so he findeth himself not to be astricted by his Oath to the tenor thereof; but the intention of the Assembly is meerly to prevent the like in time coming.

SESS. 18. AUGUST 9. 1641. A MERIDIE.

A LETTER FROM SOME MINISTERS IN ENGLAND TO THE ASSEMBLIE.

Right Reverend and dear Brethren, now conveened in this Generall Assembly,

Wee most heartily salute you in the Lord, rejoycing with you in his unspeakable goodnesse, so miraculously prospering your late endeavours, both for the restoring and settling of your own Liberties and Priviledges, in Church and common wealth (which we heare and hope he is now about to accomplish) as also for the occasioning and advancing of the Worke of Reformation among our selves; for which as we daily blesse the highest Lord, sole Author of all one good, so doe we acknowledge your selves worthy Instruments thereof. And for that (besides all other respects) doe, and ever shall (by the help of God) hold you deare unto us, as our own bowels, and our selves obliged to tender unto you all due correspondence according to our power, upon all good occasions.

And now (dear Brethren) forasmuch as the Church of Christ is but one body, each part whereof cannot but partake in the weale and woe of the whole, and of Each other part; and these Churches of England and Scotland, may seem both to be imbarqued in the same bottome, to sink and swim together, and are so near conjoyned by many strong tyes, not only as fellow members under the same Head Christ, and fellow-subjects under the same King; but also by such neighbour-hood and vicinity of place, that if any evil shall much infest the one, the other cannot bee altogether free: Or if for the present it should, yet in processe of time it would sensibly suffer also. And forasmuch as evils are better remedied in their first beginning, then after they have once taken deep root; therefore we whose names are here under-written, in the behalf of our selves, and of many others, Ministers of the Church of England be bold to commend to your consideration; (being met together in this venerable Assembly) a difference of great concernment, which you may please (in brief) thus to understand. Almighty God having now of his infinite goodnesse raised up our hopes of removing the yoke of Episcopacie (under which we have so long groaned) sundry other forms of Church-government are by sundry sorts of men projected, to be set up in the roome thereof: One of which (amongst others) is of some Brethren that hold the whole power of Church-government, & all Acts thereunto appertaining (as Election, Ordination, and Deposition of Officers, with Admission, Excommunication & Absolution of Members) are by divine Ordinance in foro externo, to be decreed by the most voices, in, and of every particular Congregation, which (say they) is the utmost bound of a particular Church: endued with power of Government, & only some Formalities of solemne execution to be reserved to the Officers (as servants of the saids Church) if they have any, or if none, then to be performed by some other members, not in office, whom the said Church shal appoint thereunto, And that every of the said particular Congregations (whether they consists of few or many Members, and be furnished with Offices or not) lawfull: may & ought to transact, determine & execute all matters pertaining to the government of themselves amongst & within themselves without any authoritative (though not consulatory) concurrence or interposition of any other persons or Churches whatsoever, condemning all imperative and decisive power of Classes, or compound Presbyteries and Synods, as a meere usurpation. Now because we conceive that your judgement in this case may conduce much by the blessing of God, to the settling of this question amongst us; Therefore we doe earnestly intreat the same at your hands, and that so much the rather, because we sometimes hear from those of the aforesaid judgement, that some famous and eminent Brethren, even amongst your selves, doe somewhat encline unto an approbation of that way of government. Thus humbly craving pardon for our boldnesse, leaving the matter to your grave considerations, and expecting answer at your convenient leasure, We commit you, and the successe of this your meeting, to the blessing of the Almighty, in whom we shall ever remain.

London, 12 Ju'y. 1641.

Your faithfull Brethren to serve you in all offices of love.

THE ASSEMBLIES ANSWER TO THE ENGLISH MINISTERS LETTER.

Right reverend and dearly beloved Brethren in our Lord and common Saviour Jesus Christ.

Wee the Ministers and Elders met together in this Nationall Assembly, were not a little refreshed and comforted by the good report which we heard of you, and others of our Brethren of the Kirk of England, by some of our Ministers, who by the good providence of our Lord had seen your faces, and conversed with you. But now yet more comforted by your Letters which we received, and which were read in the face of the Assembly, witnessing your Christian love, and rejoycing with us in God for his great and wonderfull Work in the Reformation of this Kirk, and in the beginning of a blessed Reformation amongst your selves, and that you are so sensible of your communion and fellowship with us, and to desire to know our minde and judgement of that which some Brethren amongst you hold, concerning Kirk-government.

We doe with our hearts acknowledge and wonder at the great and unspeakable wisedome, mercie, and power of our God, in restoring unto us the truth and puritie of Religion, after many Back-slidings and defection of some in this Kirk, & desire not only to confesse the same before the world, and all other Christian Kirks, but also doe pray for grace to walk worthy of so wonderful a love: We have been helped by your prayers, in our weak endeavours, & you have mourned with us, (we know) in the dayes of our mourning; and therefore is it that you doe now rejoyce and praise God with us. Neither are we out of hope, but the same God shall speedily perfect that which he hath begun amongst you, that your joy may be full, which is the desire of our soule, and for which we doe now pray, and in our severall Congregations will be instant at the throne of grace, for this and all other spirituall and temporall blessings upon the Kirk and Kingdome of England, by name, expecting the like performance of mutuall love from you and others equally minded with you, for your parts, till a common consent may be obtained, even that you will recommend the Kirk of Scotland by name in your prayers to God. Thus shall we be as one people, mourning and rejoycing, praying and praising together; which may be one meane of the preservation of Unity, and of many other blessings to us both.

We have learned by long experience, ever since the time of the Reformation, and specially after the two Kingdomes have been (in the great goodnesse of God to both) united under one Head and Monarch, but most of all of late, which is not unknown to you, what danger and contagion in matters of Kirk-government, of divine worship, and of doctrine, may come from the one Kirk to the other, which beside all other reasons make us to pray to God, and to desire you, and all that love the honour of Christ, and the peace of these Kirks and Kingdomes, heartily to endeavour, that there might be in both Kirks, one Confession, one Directory for publicke worship, one Catechisme, and one Forme of Kirk-government. And if the Lord who hath done great things for us, shall be pleased to hearken unto our desires, and to accept of our endeavours, we shall not only have a sure foundation for a durable Peace, but shall be strong in God, against the rising or spreading of Heresie and Schisme amongst our selves, and of invasion from forraine enemies.

Concerning the different Formes of Kirk-government, projected by sundrie sorts of men, to be set up in place of Episcopall Hierarchie, which we trust is brought near unto its period, we must confesse, that we are not a little grieved that any godly Ministers and Brethren should be found, who doe not agree with other Reformed Kirks in the point of government as well as in the matter of Doctrine and worship; and that we want not our own feares, that where the hedge of Discipline and Government is different, the Doctrine and Worship shall not long continue the same without change: yet doe not marvell much, that particular Kirks and Congregations which live in such places, as that they can conveniently have no dependencie upon superiour Assemblies, should stand for a kind of independencie and supremacie in themselves, they not considering that in a nation or Kingdome, professing the same Religion, the government of the Kirk by compound Presbyteries and Synods is a help and strength, and not a hinderance or prejudice to particular Congregations and Elderships, in all the parts of Kirk-government; and that Presbyteries and Synods are not an extrinsecall power set over particular Kirks, like unto Episcopal dominion, they being no more to be reputed extrinsecal unto the particular Kirks, nor the power of a Parliament, or Convention of Estates, where the Shires and Cities have their own Delegates, is to be held extrinsecal to any particular Shire or City.

Our unanimous judgement and uniforme practice, is, that according to the order of the Reformed Kirks, and the ordinance of God in his Word, not onely the solemne execution of Ecclesiastical power and authoritie, but the whole acts and exercise thereof, do properly belong unto the Officers of the Kirk; yet so that in matters of chiefest importance, the tacite consent of the Congregation be had, before their decrees and sentences receive final execution, and that the Officers of a particular Congregation, may not exercise this power independently, but with subordination unto greater Presbyteries and Synods, Provincial and National: Which as they are representative of the particular Kirks conjoyned together in one under their government; so their determination, when they proceed orderly, whether in causes common to all, or many of the Kirks, or in causes brought before them by appellations or references from the inferiour, in the case of aberation of the inferiour, is to the several Congregations authoritative and obligatorie and not consultatory only: And this dependencie and subordination, we conceive not only to be warranted by the light of nature, which doth direct the Kirk in such things as are common to other societies, or to be a prudential way for Reformation, and for the preservation of Truth and Peace, against Schisme, Heresie, and Tyranny, which is the sweet fruits of this government wheresoever hath place, and which we have found in ancient and late experience; but also to be grounded upon the Word of God, and to be conforme to the paterne of the Primitive and Apostolical Kirks: And without which, neither could the Kirks in this Kingdome have been reformed, nor were we able for any time to preserve Truth and Unity amongst us.

In this forme of Kirk-government, our unanimity and harmony by the mercy of God, is so full and perfect, that all the Members of this Assembly have declared themselves to be of one heart, and of one soule, and to be no lesse perswaded, that it is of God, then that Episcopal government is of men; resolving by the grace of God, to hold the same constantly all the dayes of our life, and heartily wishing that God would blesse all the Christians Kirks, especially the famous Kirk of England, unto which in all other respects we are so nearly joyned with this divine Forme of government. Thus having briefly and plainly given our judgement for your satisfaction, and desiring and hoping that ye will beleeve against all mis-reports, that we know not so much as one man, more or lesse eminent amongst us, of a different judgement, we commend you unto the riches of the grace of Christ, who will perfect that which he had begun amongst you, to your unspeakable comfort. Subscribed by our Moderator and Clerk.

Edinburgh 9. August, 1641.

THE ASSEMBLIES ANSWER TO THE KINGS MAJESTIES LETTER.

Most gracious Soveraign,

Beside the conscience of that duetie which we owe to supreme Authority, we are not only encouraged, but confirmed by the Royal favour and Princely munificence, expressed in Your gracious Majesties Letters, which filled our hearts with joy, and our mouths with praise, to offer up our prayers with the greater fervencie to God Almightie for your Majesties happinesse, our selves for our own parts, and for the whole Kirks of this your Majesties Kingdome, which we doe represent, to serve Your Majestie in all humble obedience, our faithful labours for preserving Trueth and Peace amongst all Your Majesties Subjects, and our example (according to Your Majesties just commandments laid upon us) to be a presedent to others in paying that honour, which by all Lawes divine and humane, is due unto Your sacred Majestie, being confident that your Majestie shall finde at your coming hither much more satisfaction and content then can be expressed by

Your Majesties most humble Subjects and faithful Servants, the Ministers and Elders met together in the vonerable Assembly at St. Andrews, July 20, and Edinburgh, July 27. 1641.

ACT ANENT THE KIRK OF CAMPHEIR.

The which day a motion was made in the Assembly, that it seemed expedient for correspondencie that might be had from forraigne parts, for the weal of this Kirk, That the Scots Kirk at Campheir were joyned to the Kirk of Scotland, as a Member thereof: Which being seriously thought upon and considered by the Assembly, they approved the motion, and ordained Master Robert Baillie Minister at Cilwinning, to write to Master William Spang Minister at Campheir, and Kirk-Session thereof, willing them to send their Minister, and a ruling Elder, instructed with a Commission to the next General Assembly to be holden at St Andrews, the last Wednesday of July 1642. at which time they should be inrolled in the Books of the General Assembly, as the Commissioners of the General Assembly of Scotland, from the Scots Kirk at Campheir.

The Assembly appoints the next General Assembly to be holden at St. Andrews, the last Wednesday of July next, 1642.

THE GENERALL ASSEMBLY, CONVEENED AT S. ANDREWS, JULY 27. 1642.

ACT SESS. 1. JULY 27. 1642.

THE KINGS LETTER TO THE GENERALL ASSEMBLY, PRE-SENTED BY HIS MAJESTIES COMMISSIONER, THE EARLE OF DUMFERMLING, JULY 27. 1642.

Charles R.

In the midst of Our great and weighty affaires of Our other kingdoms, which God Almighty, who is privie to Our Intentions, and in whom We trust, will in his own time bring to a wished and peaceable conclusion, We are not unmindfull of that duetie which we owe to that Our ancient and native Kingdome, and to the Kirks there, now met together by their Commissioners in a Nationall Assembly. God whose Vice-gerent We are, hath made Us a King over divers Kingdomes, and We have no other desire, nor designe, but to govern them by their own Lawes, and the Kirks in them by their own Canons and Constitutions. Where any thing is found to be amisse, We will endeavour a Reformation in a fair and orderly way; and where a Reformation is settled, We resolve, with that authoritie where with God hath in vested Us, to maintain and defend it in peace and libertie, against all trouble that can come from without, and against all Heresies, Sects, and Schismes which may arise from within. Nor do We desire any thing more in that Kingdom (and when We shall hear of it, it shall be a delight and matter of gladnesse unto Us) then that the Gospel be faithfully preached throughout the whole Kingdom, to the outmost skirts and borders thereof. Knowing that to be the mean of honour to God, of happinesse to the people, and of true obedience to Us. And for this effect, that holy and able men be put in places of the Ministery, and that Schooles and Colledges may flourish in Learning and true Pietie. Some things for advancing of those ends, We did of Our own accord promise in Our Letters to the last Assembly, and We make your selves Judges, who were witnesses to Our Actions, while We were there in Person, whether we did not perform them both in the point of presentations which are in our hands, and in the liberall provision of all the Universities and Colledges of the Kingdome, not only above that which any of Our Progenitors had done before Us, but also above your owne hopes and expectation. We doe not make commemoration of this Our Beneficence, either to please Our-selves, or to stop the influence of Our Royal goodnesse and Bountie for afterward, but that by these reall demonstrations of Our unfained desires and delight to do good, you may be the more confident to expect from Us, whatsoever in Justice We can grant, or what may be expedient for you to obtaine. We have given expresse charge to Our Commissioner, to see that all things be done there orderly and peaceably, as if We were present in Our Own Person; not doubting but in thankfulnesse for your present estate and condition, you will abstaine from every thing that may make any new disturbance, and that you will be more wise then to be the enemies of your own peace, which would but stumble others, and ruine your selves. We have also commanded Our Commissioner to receive from you your just and reasonable desires, for what may further serve for the good of Religion, that taking them to Our consideration, We may omit nothing which may witnesse Us to be indeed a nursing Father of that Kirk, wherein We were born and baptized, and that if ye be not happy, you may blame not Us, but your selves. And now what doe We again require of you, but that which otherwise you owe to Us as your Soveraigne Lord and King, even that ye pray for Our prosperitie and the peace of Our Kingdomes, that ye use the best meanes to keep Our People in obedience to Us and Our Lawes, which doth very much in Our personall absence from that Our Kingdom depend upon your preaching, and your owne exemplary loyaltie and faithfulnesse, and that against all such jealousies, suspitions, and sinister rumors as are too frequent in these times, and have been often falsified in time past, by the reality of the contrary events: Ye judge Us and Our professions by Our actions, which we trust through God in despight of malice shall ever go on in a constant way for the good of Religion, and the weal of Our People, which is the Chiefest of Our intentions and desires. And thus We bid you farewell. Given at Our Court at Leicester, the 23. of July, 1642.

To Our trusty and wel beloved the Generall Assembly in our Kingdom of Scotland conveened at S. Andrews.

ACT SESS 3. JULY 29. 1642.

ACT FOR BRINGING IN OF THE SYNODE BOOKS YEERLY TO THE GENERAL ASSEMBLIES.

The Moderator calling to minde that which was forgotten in the preceeding Sessions, the examination of the Provincial Books, caused call the Roll of the Provinciall Assemblies, And the Assembly finding very few Provinces to have sent their Books to this Assembly, notwithstanding of the ordinance of the former Assembly thereanent, for the more exact obedience of that ordinance hereafter, the Assembly in one voyce ordaines, That the Books of every Provincial Assembly shall be brought and produced to every General Assembly: And that this may be performed, ordaines that every Clerk of the Provincials, either bring or send the said Books yearly to the General Assemblies, by the Commissioners sent to the Assemblies, from these Presbyteries where the Clerks reside. Which charge the Assembly also layes upon the said Commissioners, sent from the saids Presbyteries where the Clerks reside, may and while some meanes be provided, whereby the Clerks charges may be sustained for coming with the saids Books themselves: And that under the pain of deprivation of the Clerk, in case of his neglect, and of such censure of the saids Commissioners, in case of their neglect as the Assembly shall think convenient.

ACT SESS 5. AUGUST 1. 1642.

ACT ANENT THE CHOOSING OF KIRK SESSIONS.

Anent the question moved to the Assembly, concerning the election of Kirk Sessions, The Assembly ordaines the old Session to elect the new Session both in Burgh and Land. And that if any place shall vaik in the Session chosen, by death or otherwise, the present Session shall have the election of the person to fill the vacand roome.

SESS 6. AUGUST 2. 1642.

THE REPORT OF THE INTERPRETATION OF THE ACT AT EDINBURGH, ANENT TRYAL OF MINISTERS.

The meaning of the foresaid Act, is not that an actual Minister to be transported, shall be tried again by the tryals appointed for trying of Expectants, at their entry to the Ministery, according to the Acts of the Kirk; but only that he bringing a Testimonial of his former tryals, and of his abilities, and conversation, from the Presbyterie from whence he comes, and giving such satisfaction to the Parochiners Presbyterie whereto he comes in preaching, as the Presbyterie finds his gifts fit and answerable for the condition and disposition of the Congregation, whereto he is presented. Because, according to the Act of the Assembly 1596. renewed at Glasgow, some that are meet for the Ministery in some places, are not meet for all alike: And Universities, Towns and Burghs, and places of Noblemens residence, or frequencie of Papists, and other great and eminent Congregations, and in sundry other cases, require men of greater abilities, nor will be required necessarily in the planting of all private small Paroches, the leaving of the consideration of these cases unto the judgement and consideration of the Presbyterie, was the only intention of the Act.

The Assembly approves the meaning and interpretation foresaid: And appoints the said Act, according to this interpretation, to stand in force, and to have the strength of an Act and ordinance of Assembly in all time coming.

ACT SESS. 7. AUGUST 3. 1642.

ACT ANENT THE ORDER FOR MAKING LISTS TO HIS MAJESTIE, AND OTHER PATRONS FOR PRESENTATIONS; THE ORDER OF TRYAL OF EXPECTANTS, AND FOR TRYING THE QUALITY OF KIRKS.

Forsameikle as His Majestie was graciously pleased in His Answer to the Petition, tendred by the Commissioners of the late Assembly to His Majestie, to declare and promise, for the better providing of vaiking Kirks at His Majesties Presentation with qualified Ministers, to present one out of a list of six persons, sent to His Majestie from the Presbyteries wherein the vaiking Kirk lyeth, as His Majesties Declaration, signed with his Royal hand at White-hall, the 3. of January last, registrate in the books of Assembly, this day at length beares. And suchlike whereas the Lords of Exchequer upon a Petition presented to them by the Commissioners of the Generall Assembly, and the Procurator and Agent for the Kirk representing two Prejudices; one, that gifts obtained from His Majestie of Patronages of Kirks, at His Presentation were passing the Exchequer, without the qualification and provision of a List, wherewith His Majestie was pleased to restrict himself; and the other, that some were seeking gifts of patronage of Bishop-Kirks, which we declared to belong to Presbyteries, to be planted by two Acts of the late Parliament, The saids Lords have ordained that no signatory containing gifts of patronages from His Majestie, shall passe hereafter, but with a speciall provision that the same shall be lyable to the tenor of His Majesties said Declaration. Ordaining also the Procurator & Agent of the Kirk to be advertised, & to have place to see all signaters whatsoever, containing any patronage, to the effect they may represent the interest of the Kirk therein; as the said Act of the date the 27 of June last, registrate also in the Books of Assembly, this day at length beares. Therefore that the saids Kirks which now are, or which were at his Majesties presentation the sayd third day of January last, may be the better provided with able Ministers, when the samine shall vaik, The Assembly ordaines that hereafter every Presbyterie shall give up yearly a Roll of the ablest of their Expectants, to their Synods; and that the Synods select out of these Rolls such persons whom they in certain knowledge judge most fit for the Ministrie and worthiest of the first place, With Power to the Synods to adde or alter these Rolls given by the Presbyteries, as they thinke reasonable: And that the Synods shall send the Rolls made by them in this manner, to the next Generall Assembly, who shall also examine the Rolls of the Synods, and adde or alter the same as shall be thought expedient. Which Roll made by the Generall Assembly, shall be sent to every Presbyterie & that the Presbyterie, with consent of the most or best part of the Congregation, shall make a List of six persons willing to accept of the presentation out of that Roll of the Assembly, upon every occasion of vacation of any Kirk within their bounds, and shall send the samine together with a blank presentation: The which (if His Majesty be Patron to the vacant Kirk) shall be sent by the said Procurator and Agent, to such as the Commissioners of the Generall Assembly, or in their absence the Presbyterie of Edinburgh: shall direct and think at that time most able and willing to obtain the presentation, to be signed and filled up by His Maj. choise of one of the List. And if the vacant Kirk be of a Patronage disponed by His Majesty since the 3. of January, in that case either the Presbyteries themselves shall send a List of six persons in maner aforesaid, with a blank presentation to the Patron, to be filled up by his choise, & subscribed or send the samine to the saids Officers of the Kirk, to be conveyed by them to the Patron of the vaiking Kirk, as the Presbyterie shall think most expedient. It is always declared, that this order shall be without prejudice to the Presbyteries, with consent foresaid, to put actual Ministers upon the said List of six persons, to be sent to the Patron of the said vaiking Kirks, if they please. And least that the nomination of Expectants by Presbyteries, Synods, or Assemblies, in their Rolls or Lists foresaid, be mis-interpreted, as though the Expectants nominated in these Rolls and Lists, were thereby holden & acknowledged to be qualified, which is not the intention of the Assembly, who rather think, that in respect of this Order, there should be a more exact tryal of Expectants then before: Therefore the Assembly ordaines, that no Expectants shall be put on the Rolls or Lists above-mentioned, but such as have been upon the publike exercise, at the least by the space of half a year, or longer, as the Presbyterie shall finde necessary. And suchlike ordaines, that hereafter none be admitted to the publike exercise, before they be tried according to the tryal appointed for Expectants, at their entrie to the Ministerie in the late Assembly at Glasgow, in the 24. Article of the Act of the 23. Session thereof: which tryall of the Assembly appoints to be taken of every Expectant, before his admission to the publike exercise. And suchlike ordaines, That the samine tryall shall be again taken immediatly before their admission to the Ministerie, together with their triall mentioned in the advice of some Brethren deputed for penning the corruptions of the Ministery, approven in the said Act of the Generall Assembly at Glasgow. And because that Kirks of the patronages foresaids, will vaik before the Rolls and Lists be made up by the Presbyteries, Synods, and General Assemblies, in manner foresaid: Therefore in the interim the Assembly ordains the Commissioners of every Presbyterie here present, to give in a List of the ablest Expectants within their bounds, the morn, to the Clerk of the Assembly, that the Assembly may out of these Rolls, make a List to be sent to every Presbyterie: Out of which the Presbyteries shall make a List of six persons, with consent foresaid, and send the samine upon vacancie of any Church within their bounds, together with a presentation to His Majestie, or any other patron, in manner foresaid. And because the Procurator and Agent of the Kirk cannot get sufficient information to the Lords of Exchequer anent the Right and Interest of the Kirk, and Presbyteries in Kirks, whereof gifts of patronages may be presented to the Exchequer: Therefore the Assembly ordaines for their better information hereanent, that every Presbyterie, with all diligence, use all meanes of exact tryall of the nature and qualitie of all Kirks within their bounds, as what Kirks belong to the Kings Majesties patronage, what to other Laick patronages, what Kirks of old were planted by the Presbyteries, and what by Prelates, and Bishops, before the Assembly at Glasgow 1638. what hath been the way and time of the change of the planting and providing of the Kirks, if any have been changed or any other thing concerning the nature and qualitie of every Kirk within their bounds, and to send the same to the Procurator of the Kirk with all diligence.

ACT ANENT LISTS FOR THE KIRKS IN THE HIGH-LANDS.

The Assembly considering that in Argyle, and in other places of the Irish language, there will not be gotten six expectants able to speak that language, And therfore the Assembly is hopefull, that in these singular cases, His Majestie will be pleased for Kirks vacand in the Highlands, to accept of a List of so many expectants as can be had, able to speak the Irish language. And the Commissioners Grace promiseth to recommend it to His Majestie.

OVERTURES AGAINST PAPISTS, NON-COMMUNICANTS,

AND PROFANERS OF THE SABBATH.

The Assembly would draw up a Supplication to be presented by the Commissioners of the Presbyterie of Edinburgh to the Councell at their first meeting, for the due execution of the Acts of Parliament and Councell against Papists, wherein it will be specially craved, that the Exchequer should be the Intromettors with the Rents of these who are excommunicate, and that from the Exchequer the Presbyterie may receive that portion of the confiscate goods, which the Law appoints to be imployed ad pios usus.

II. Every Presbyterie would conveen at their first meeting, all known Papists in their bounds, and require them to put out of their company, all friends and servants who are Popish within one moneth: Also within that same space, to give their children, sons and daughters, who are above seven yeers old, to be educate at their charges, by such of their Protestant friends, as the Presbyterie shall approve, and finde sufficient caution for bringing home within three moneths such of their children who are without the Kingdom, to be educate in Schooles and Colledges at the Presbyteries sight; to finde caution likewise of their abstinence from Masse, and the company of all Jesuits and Priests.

III. That all, of whatsoever rank or degree, who refuse to give satisfaction in every one of the foresaid Articles, shall be processed without any delay; but those who give satisfaction shall be dealt with in all meeknesse, after this manner: The Presbyteries shall appoint such of their number as they shall find fittest to confer with them so frequently as the Brethren are able to attend, until the midst of October next, against which time, if they be not willing to go to Church, they shall give assurance to go and dwell in the next adjacent University Town, whether Edinburgh, Glasgow, St. Andrews, or Aberdene, from November 1. to the last of March, where they shall attend all the diets of conference which the Professor and Ministers of the bounds shall appoint to them: By which, if they be not converted, their obstinacy shall be declared in the Provincial Synods of April, and from thence their Processe shall go on to the very closure without any farther delay.

IV. That every Presbyterie, as they will be answerable to the next General Assembly, be careful to do their dutie in all the premisses.

V. That there be given presently by the Members of this present Assembly unto the Commissioners of the Presbyterie of Edinburgh, a List of all excommunicate Papists they know, and of all Papists who have children educate abroad, that they may be presented, together with our Supplication to the Councel, at their first sitting.

VI. That the Councel may be supplicate for an Act, that in no Regiment which goes out of the Kingdom, any Papists bear office, and that the Colonel be required to finde caution for this effect, before he receive the Councels warrant for levying any Souldiers: Also that he finde caution for the maintaining of a Minister, and keeping of a Session in his Regiment.

Item, The Assembly would enjoyn every Presbyterie to proceed against Non-communicants, whether Papists or others, according to the Act of Parliament made thereanent. And suchlike, that Acts of Parliament against prophaners of the

Sabbath be put to execution.

The Assembly approves the Overtures foresaid, and ordains Presbyteries to put the samine to execution with all diligence: And that the Commissioners of every Presbyterie give in a List of the excommunicate Papists within their bounds, and of Papists children out of the countrey to the Clerk, that the same may be presented to the Councel by the Commissioners of this Assembly.

ACT ANENT THE JOYNING OF THE PRESBYTERIE OF SKY TO THE SYNODE OF ARGYLE.

The General Assembly having considered the whole proceedings of the Commissioners of the late General Assembly holden at Edinburgh, anent the reference made to them concerning the Presbyterie of Sky, together with the whole reasons pro & contra in the said matter, after mature deliberation have ratified and approved, and by these presents ratifie and approve the Sentence of the saids Commissioners thereintil. And further ordains the said Presbytery of Sky, and all the Ministers and Elders thereof, to keep the meetings of the Provincial Assembly of Argyle, where they shall happen to be appointed in all time coming, suchlike as any other Presbyterie within the bounds of the said Province of Argyle uses to do: And that the samine Presbyterie be in all time hereafter within the Jurisdiction of the said Provincial Assembly, without any further question to be made thereanent.

SESS. 8. AUGUST 3. POST MERIDIEM.

THE SUPPLICATION OF THIS ASSEMBLY TO THE KINGS MAJESTIE.

To the Kings most Excellent Maj. the hearty Thanksgiving, and humble Petition of the General Assembly of the Kirk of Scotland, met at St. Andrews, July 27. 1642.

Our hearts were filled with great joy and gladnesse at the hearing of Your Majesties Letter, which was read once and again in face of the Assembly, every line thereof almost either expressing such affection to the Reformed Religion, and such Royal care of us, as we could require from a Christian Prince; or requiring such necessary duties from us, as we are bound to performe as Ministers of the Gospel, and Christian Subjects: For which, as solemne thanks were given by the Moderator of the Assembly, so do we all with one voice in all humility, present unto Your Majestie the thankfulnesse of our hearts, with our earnest prayers to God for your Majesties prosperity, and the peace of Your Kingdoms, that Your Majestie may be indeed a nursing Father to all the Kirks of Christ in Your Maj. Dominions; & especially to the Kirk of Scotland honoured with Your Birth and Baptisme: Promising our most serious indeavours by doctrine and life, to advance the Gospel of Christ, & and to keep the people in our charge in Unity and Peace, and in all loyalty and obedience to Your Majestie and Your Laws. Your Majesties commands to Your Commissioner, the Earle of Dumfermling, to receive from us our just and reasonable desires for what may further serve for the good of Religion here, the favours which we have received already, and Your Maj. desires and delight to do good, expressed in Your Letter, are as many encouragements to us, to take the boldnesse in all humility to present unto Your Majestie (beside the particulars recommended to Your Majesties Commissioner) one thing, which for the present is the chiefest of all Our desires, as serving most for the glory of Christ, for Your Majesties Honour and Comfort; and not onely for the good of Religion here, but for the true happinesse and peace of all Your Majesties Dominions; which is no new motion, but the prosecution of that same by the Commissioners of this Your Majesties Kingdom in the late Treatie, and which Your Majestie, with advice of both houses of Parliament, did approve in these words: To their desire concerning unitie in Religion and uniformitie of Church government, as a speciall meanes of conserving of Peace betwixt the two Kingdoms, upon the grounds and reasons contained in the Paper of the 10 of March, given in to the Treaty and Parliament of England: It is answered upon the 15 of June, That his Majestie, with advice of both Houses of Parliament, doth approve of the affection of His Subjects of Scotland, in their desire of having the conformity of Church-government, betwixt the two Nations, and as the Parliament hath already taken into consideration the reformation of Church government, so they will proceed therein in due time, as shall best conduce to the glory of God, the Peace of the Church, and of both Kingdoms, 11 of June 1641. In Our answer to a Declaration sent by the now Commissioners of this Kingdom from both Houses of Parliament, we have not onely pressed this point of unity in Religion and Uniformity of Church government, as a meane of a firme and durable union betwixt the two Kingdomes, and without which former experiences put us out of hope long to enjoy the puritie of the Gospel with Peace, but also have rendred the reasons of our hopes and confidence, as from other considerations, so from Your Majesties late Letter to this Assembly, that Your Majestie in a happy conjunction with the Houses of Parliament, will be pleased to settle this blessed Reformation, with so earnestly desired a Peace in all Your Dominions. And therfore we Your Majesties most loving Subjects, in name of the whole Kirks of Scotland, represented by us, upon the knees of our hearts, do most humbly and earnestly beg, that Your Majesty in the deep of Your Royall Wisdom, and from Your affection to the true Religion, and the Peace of Your Kingdoms, may be moved to consider, that the God of Heaven and Earth is calling for this Reformation at Your hands, and that as you are his Vice-gerent, so You may be his prime Instrument in it. If it shall please the Lord (which is our desire and hope) that this blessed unitie in Religion and Uniformity in Government shall be brought about; Your Majesties Conscience, in performing of so great a dutie: shall be a well-spring of comfort to Your Self, Your memory shall be a sweet favour, and Your name renowned to all following generations. And if these unhappy commotions and divisions shall end in this peace and unity; then it shall appeare in the Providence of God, they were but the noyse of many waters, and the voyce of a great thunder before the voyce of harpers harping with their harps, which shall fill this whole Iland with melodie and mirth, and the name of it shall be, THE LORD IS THERE.

THE DECLARATION OF THE PARLIAMENT OF ENGLAND, SENT TO THE ASSEMBLY.

The Lords and Commons in this present Parliament assembled, finding to their great grief, that the distractions of this Kingdome dayly increase, and that the wicked Counsels and practises of a malignant party amongst us (if God prevent them not) are like to cast this nation into bloud and confusion, To testifie to all the World how earnestly they desire to avoid a Civill Warre, they have addressed themselves in an humble Supplication to His Majestie, for the prevention thereof. A Copy of which their petition, they have thought fit to send at this time to the National Assembly of the Church of Scotland, to the intent that that Church and Kingdome (whereunto they are united by so many and so near bounds and tyes, as well Spiritual as Civil) may see that the like minde is now in them, that formerly appeared to be in that Nation. And that they are as tender of the effusion of Christian bloud on the one side, as they are zealous on the other side of a due Reformation both in Church and State. In which work, whilest they were labouring, they have been interrupted by the plots and practises of a malignant party of Papists, and ill affected persons, especially of the corrupt and dissolute Clergy, by the incitement and instigation of Bishops and others, whose avarice and ambition being not able to bear the Reformation endeavoured by the Parliament, they have laboured (as we can expect little better fruit from such trees) to kindle a flame, and raise a combustion within the bowels of this Kingdom: Which if by our humble supplication to His Majesty it may be prevented, and that according to our earnest desire therein, all Force and Warlike preparations being laid aside, we may returne to a peaceable parliamentary proceeding, We do not doubt, but that by the blessing of Almighty God upon our endeavours, we shall settle the matters both in Church and State, to the encrease of His Majesties honour and State, the peace and prosperitie of this Kingdome, and especially to the glory of God, by the advancement of the true Religion, and such a Reformation of the Church, as shall be most agreeable to Gods Word. Out of all which, there will also most undoubtedly result a most firme & stable Union between the two Kingdomes of England and Scotland, which according to our Protestation, we shall by all good wayes and meanes, upon all occasions, labour to preserve and maintain.

Subscribitur
John Brown, Cler. Parl.

THE ASSEMBLIES ANSWER TO THE DECLARATION OF THE PARLIAMENT OF ENGLAND.

The Generall Assembly of the Kirk of Scotland having received a Declaration sent unto them by the Commissioners of this Kingdome, now at London, from the Honourable Houses of the Parliament of England expressing their care to prevent the effusion of Christian bloud in that Kingdome, and their affections to Reformation both in Kirk and State, and having taken the same to such consideration as the importance of so weighty matters, and the high estimation they have of so wise and honourable a meeting as is the Parliament of England, did require; have with universall consent resolved upon this following Answer.

I. That from the recent sense of the goodnesse of God, in their own late deliverance, and from their earnest desire of all happinesse to our native King and that Kingdome, they blesse the Lord for preserving them in the midst of so many unhappy divisions and troubles from a bloudy Intestine War, which is from God the greatest Judgement, and to such a nation the compend of all calamities. They also give God thanks for their former and present desires of a Reformation, especially of Religion, which is the glory and strength of a Kingdome, and bringeth with it all temporall blessings of prosperity and peace.

II. That the hearts of all the Members of this Assembly, and of all the wel-affected within this Kingdome, are exceedingly grieved and made heavy, that in so long a time, against the professions both of King and Parliament, and contrary to the joynt desires and prayers of the godly in both Kingdomes, to whom it is more deare and precious then what is dearest to them in the world, the Reformation of Religion hath moved so slowly, and suffered so great interruption. They consider that not only Prelates, formall Professours, profane and worldly men, and all that are Popishly affected, are bad councellours and workers, and do abuse their power, and bend all their strength and policies against the Work of God; but the God of this world also, with Principalities and powers, the rulers of the darknesse of this world, and spiritual wickednesse in high places, are working with all their force and fraud in the same opposition, not without hope of successe, they having prevailed so farre from the beginning, That in the times of the best Kings of Juda of old, and the most part of the Reformed Kirks of late, a through and perfect Reformation of Religion hath been a work full of difficulties, Yet doe they conceive, that as it ought first of all to be intended so should it be above all other things, with confidence in God, who is greater then the World, and he who is in the World, most seriously endeavoured. And that when the supream providence giveth opportunity of the accepted time & day of salvation, no other work can prosper in the hands of his servants, if it be not apprehended, & with all reverence & faithfulnesse improved. This Kirk and Nation, when the Lord gave them the calling, considered not their own deadnesse, nor staggered at the promise through unbelief, but gave glory to God. And who knoweth (we speak it in humility and love, and from no other mind then from a desire of the blessing of God upon our King and that Kingdome) but the Lord hath now some controversie with England, which will not be removed, till first and before all, the worship of his name and the government of his house be settled according to his own will? When this desire shall come, it shall be to England after so long deferred hopes, a tree of life, which shall not only yeeld temporell blessings unto themselves, but also shall spread the branches so far, that both this nation and other reformed Kirks shall finde the fruits thereof to their great satisfaction.

III. The Commissioners of this Kingdome in the late Treaty of peace, considering that Religion is not only the meane of the service of God and saving of Souls, but is also the base and foundation of Kingdomes and Estates, and the strongest band to tye Subjects to their Prince in true loyaltie, and to knit the hearts of one to another in true unity and love, They did with preface of all due respect and reverence, far from arrogancy or presumption, represent in name of this Kingdome, their serious thoughts and earnest desires for unity of Religion, That in all His Majesties Dominions, there might be one Confession of Faith, one directory of worship, one publike Catechisme, and one form of Kirk Government. This they conceived to be acceptable to God Almighty, who delighteth to see his People walking in truth and unity, to be a speciall meanes for conserving of peace betwixt the Kingdomes, of easing the Kings Majesty, and the publike government of much trouble, which ariseth from differences of Religion, very grievous to Kings and Estates, of great content to the King himself, to his Nobles, his Court, and all his people, when (occasioned to be abroad) without scruple to themselves, or scandal to others; all may resort to the same publike worship, as if they were at their own dwellings; of suppressing the names of Heresies, and Sects, Puritans, Conformists, Separatists, Anabaptists, &c. Which do rent asunder the bowels both of Kirk and Kingdome, of despaire of successe to Papists and Recusants, to have their profession, which is inconsistent with the true Protestant Religion, and authority of Princes, setup again, and of drawing the hearts and hands of Ministers, from unpleasant and unprofitable Controversies, to the pressing of mortification, and to Treatises of true pietie, and practical Divinity. The Assembly doth now enter upon the labour of the Commissioners, unto which they are encouraged, not only by their faithfulnesse in the late Treaty, but also by the zeale and example of the Generall Assemblies of this Kirk in former times, as may appeare by the Assembly at Edinburgh, Decemb. 25. in the year 1566. which ordained a Letter to be sent to England against the Surplice, Tippet, Cornercap, and such other Ceremonies as then troubled that Kirk, that they might be removed. By the Assembly at Edinburgh, April 24. 1583. humbly desiring the Kings Majesty to command his Ambassadour, then going to England, to deale with the Queen, that there might be an Union and Band betwixt them & other Christian Princes & Realmes, professing the true Religion for defence and protection of the Word of God, and Professors thereof, against the persecution of Papists and confederates joyned and united together by the bloudy league of Trent: as also that his Majesty would disburden their brethren of England of the yoke of Ceremonies, imposed upon them, against the liberty of the Word: And by the Assembly at Edinburgh March 3. 1589. ordaining the Presbyterie of Edinburgh to use all good and possible means for the relief and comfort of the Kirk of England, then heavily troubled for the maintaining the true discipline and government of the Kirk, and that the Brethren in their private and publike prayers, recommend the estate of the afflicted Kirk of England to God, While now by the mercy of God the conjunction of the two Kingdomes is many wayes increased, the zeale of the Generall Assembly towards their happinesse ought to be no lesse. But besides these, the Assembly is much encouraged unto this duetie, both from the Kings Majesty and his Parliament, joyntly, in their Answer to the proposition, made by the late Commissioners of the Treaty, in these words: To their desire concerning unity of Religion, and uniformity of Kirk government as a speciall meanes for conserving of peace betwixt the two Kingdomes, upon the grounds and reasons contained in the paper of the 10 of March, and given in to the treatie and Parliament of England: It is answered upon the 15. of June, That his Majestie with advise, of both Houses of Parliament doth approve of the affection of His Subjects of Scotland in their desire of having conformitie of Kirk government between the two Nations, and as the Parliament hath already taken into consideration the Reformation of Kirk government, so they will proceed therein in due time, as shall best conduce to the glory of God, the peace of the Kirk, and of both Kingdomes. And also severally: for His Majestie knoweth that the custodie and vindication, the conservation and purgation of Religion, are a great part of the duetie of Civill authority and power. His Majesties late practise while he was here in person, in resorting frequently to the exercises of publike worship, His Royall actions, in establishing the worship and government of this Kirk in Parliament, and in giving order for a competent maintenance to the Ministery and Seminaries of the Kirk, and His Majesties gracious Letter to the Assembly (seconded by the speech of His Majesties Commissioner) which containes this religious expression: Where any thing is amisse, we will endeavour a Reformation in a fair and orderly way, and where Reformation is settled, we resolve with that authority wherewith God hath vested us, to maintain and defend it in peace and liberty, against all trouble that can come from without, and against all Heresies, Sects, and Schismes, wich may arise from within. All these doe make us hopeful that His Majestie will not oppose, but advance the work of Reformation. In like manner the Honourable Houses of Parliament, as they have many times before witnessed their zeale, so now also in their Declaration sent to the Assembly, which not only sheweth the constancy of their zeale, but their great grief that the worke hath been interrupted by a malignant party of Papists and evill affected persons, especially of the corrupt and dissolute Clergie, by the incitement and instigation of Bishops and others, their hope according to their earnest desire, when they shall returne to a peaceable and Parliamentary proceding, by the blessing of God, to settle such a Reformation in the Church, as shall be agreeable to Gods word, and that the result shall be a most firm and stable union between the two Kingdoms of England and Scotland, &c. The Assembly also is not a little encouraged by a Letter sent from many reverend Brethren of the Kirk of England, expressing their prayers and endeavours against every thing which shall be found prejudiciall to the establishment of the Kingdome of Christ, and the Peace of their Soveraigne. Upon these encouragements, and having so patent a doore of hope, the Assembly doth confidently expect, that England will now bestirre themselves in the best way for a Reformation of Religion, and do most willingly offer their prayers and utter-endeavours for furthering so great a Work, wherein Christ is so much concerned in his glory, the King in his honour, the Kirk and Kingdome of England in their happinesse, and this Kirk and Kingdome in the purity and peace of the Gospel.

IV. That the Assembly also from so many reall invitations, are heartened to renew the Proposition made by the aforenamed Commissioners of this Kingdome, for beginning the Work of Reformation, at the uniformity of Kirk-government. For what hope can there be of Unity in Religion, of one Confession of Faith, one Form of Worship, & one Catechisme, till there be first one Forme of Ecclesiasticall Government? Yea, what hope can the Kingdome and Kirk of Scotland have of a firme and durable Peace, till Prelacie, which hath been the main cause of their miseries and troubles, first and last, be plucked up, root and branch, as a plant which God hath not planted, and from which, no better fruits can be expected then such sower grapes, as this day set on edge the Kingdome of England?

V. The Prelaticall Hierarchie being put out of the way, the Work will be easie, without forcing of any conscience, to settle in England the government of the

Reformed Kirks by Assemblies. For although the Reformed Kirks do hold, without doubting, their Kirk Officers, and Kirk government by Assemblies higher and lower, in their strong and beautifull subordination, to be jure divinio, and perpetuall: yet Prelacie, as it differeth from the Office of a Pastor, is almost universally acknowledged by the Prelates themselves, and their adherents, to be but an humane ordinance, introduced by humane reason, and settled by humane Law and Custome for supposed convenience: which therefore by humane authority, without wronging any mans conscience, may be altred and abolished upon so great a necessity, as is a hearty conjunction with all the Reformed Kirks, a firm and well grounded Peace betwixt the two Kingdomes, formerly divided in themselves, and betwixt themselves by this partition wall and a perfect Union of the Kirks in the two Nations: which although by the providence of God in one Hand, & under one Monarch, yet ever since the Reformation, and for the present also, are at greater difference in the point of Kirk-government, which in all places hath a more powerfull influence upon all the parts of Religion, then any other Reformed Kirks, although in Nations at greatest distance, and under divers Princes.

VI. What may be required of the Kirk of Scotland for furthering the Work of Uniformitie of Government, or for agreeing upon a common Confession of Faith, Catechisme, and directory for Worship, shall according to the order given by this Assembly, be most willingly performed by Us, who long extreamly for the day when King and Parliament shall joyn for bringing to passe so great, so good a Work, That all Warres and Commotions ceasing, all Superstition, Idolatry, Heresie, Sects, and Schismes being removed, as the Lord is one, so his name may be one amongst us; and mercy and truth, righteousnesse and peace meeting together, and kissing one another, may dwell iñ this Iland.

ACT SESS. 8. AUG. 3. 1642.

Overtures for transplantation of Ministers; and provision of Schools, ordained by the late Assembly at Edinburgh to be sent to Synods, and reported to this Assembly.

ACT SESS. 11. EDINB. AUGUST 5. 1642.

These Overtures underwritten, anent the transporting of Ministers and Professors to Kirks and Colledges, being read in audience of the Assembly, and thereafter revised by a Committee appointed for that effect, The Assembly appoints them to be sent to the severall Synods, to be considered by them, and they to report their judgements thereof to the next Generall Assembly.

I. No transportation would be granted hereafter without citation of parties having interest (viz. the Minister who is sought and his Parish) to hear what they can oppose, and the matter is to come first to both the Presbyteries (viz. that wherein the Minister dwels, whose transportation is sought, and the other Presbyterie to which he is sought if the Kirks lye in several Presbyteries) and if the Presbyteries agree not, then the matter is to be brought to the Synod, or Generall Assembly (which of them shall first occure after such transportation is sought) and if the Synod (occurring first) agree not; or if there be appeale made from it, then the matter is to come to the Generall Assembly.

II. A Minister may be transplanted from a particular Congregation (where he can onely doe good to a part) to such a place, where he may benefit the whole Kirk of Scotland because, in reason the whole is to be preferred to a part, such as Edinburgh.

1. Because all the great Justice Courts sit there, as Councell, Session, Justice Generall, Exchequer, &c. and it concerns the whole Kirk, that these Fountains of Justice be kept clean, both in the point of Faith, and Manners.

2. Because there is great confluence to Edinburgh, from time to time, of many of the chief Members of the whole Kingdome, and it concerns the whole Kirk to have these well seasoned, who (apparantly) are to be the Instruments of keeping this Kirk and Kingdome in good temper.

That this may be the more easily done, the Assembly first recommends to Edinburgh, that some young men of excellent spirits may be (upon the charges of the said Town) trained up, at home or abroad, toward the Ministery from time to time. Secondly we meane not, that all the places of the Ministrie of Edinburgh be filled with Ministers to be transported by Authority of this Act, but only till they be provided of one Minister (transplanted by the Authority of the Assembly) for every Kirk in Edinburgh, and that the rest of the places be filled either according to the Generall Rules of transportation for the whole Kingdome, or by agreement with actuall Ministers, and their Parishes, with consent of the Presbyterie or Synod, to the which they belong.

III. In the next roome, we finde, that it is a transporting of Ministers for publike good, that Colledges, (having the profession of Divinitie) be wel provided of professors.

Wherin the Colledge of Divinitie in S. Andrews is first to be served without taking any Professors or Ministers out of Edinburg, Glasgow, or Aberdene, and then the rest of the Colledges, would be provided for, as their necessity shal require: yet (in respect of the present scarcity) it were good for the Universities to send abroad for able and approved men, to be Professors of Divinitie, that our Ministers may be kept in their pastoriall charge as much as may be.

Towns also wherein Colledges are, are very considerable in the matter of transportation.

IV. Also Congregations, where Noblemen have chief residence are to be regarded, whether planted or unplanted, and a care is to be had, that none be admitted Ministers where Popish Noblemen reside, but such as are able men (especially for controversies) by sight of the Presbyterie: and moreover it is necessary, that such Minesters as dwell where Popish Noblemen are, and are not able for controversies, that they be transported.

V. They who desire the transportation of a Minister should be obliged to give reasons for their desire: Neither should any Presbyterie or Assembly, passe a sentence for transportation of any Minister, till they give reasons for the expediencie of the same, both to him and his Congregation, &c. to the Presbyterie whereof he is a member. If they acquiesce to the reasons given, it is so much the better: if they doe not acquiesce, yet the Presbyterie, or Assembly, (by giving such reasons before the passing of their sentence) shal make it manifest, that what they doe is not pro arbritratu, vel imperio onely, but upon grounds of reason.

VI. Because there is such scarcity of Ministers having the Iris tongue, necessity requires, that when they be found in the Low-lands, they be transported to the High-lands: providing their condition be not made worse, but rather better by their transportation.

VII. In the point of voluntary transportation, no Minister shal transact and agree with any Parish, to be transssported thereto, without a full hearing of him, and his Parish, before the Presbyterie to which he belongs in his present charge, or superiour Kirk judicatories, if need shall be.

VIII. The planting of vacant Kirks, is not to be tyed to any (either Ministers, or Expectants) within a Presbyterie: but a free election is to be; according to the order of our Kirk, and Lawes of our Kingdome.

IX. The chief Burghs of the Kingdome are to be desired to traine up young men of excellent spirits for the ministery, according to their power, as was recommended to Edinburgh: Which course will in time (God willing) prevent many transplantations.

The Overtures under-written anent the Schooles being likewise read in audience of the Assembly, they recommend the particulars therein mentioned, anent the providing of the maintenance for School-masters to the Parliament: And ordaine the rest to be sent to the Synods, to be considered by them, and they to report their judgements thereof to the next General Assembly, as said is.

I. Every Parish would have a Reader and a Schoole, where Children are to be bred, in reading, writing, and grounds of Religion, according to the laudable Acts, both of Kirk and Parliament, made before.

And where Grammar Schooles may be had, as in Burghs, and other considerable places, (among which all Presbyterial Seats are to be reputed) that they be erected, and held hand to.

II. Anent these Schooles, every Minister with his Elders shall give accompt to the Presbyteries at the visitation of the Kirk: The Presbyteries are to make report to the Synode, and the Synode to the General Assembly, that Schools are planted, as above said, and how they are provided with men and means.

III. And because this hath been most neglected in the High-lands, Ilands, and borders. Therefore the Ministers of every Parish are to instruct by their Commissioners, to the next General Assembly, that this course is begun betwixt and then: and they are further to certifie from one General Assembly to another, whether this course is continued without omission, or not.

IV. And because the means hitherto named or appointed for Schooles of all sorts, hath been both little, and ill payed, Therefore, beside former appointments, (the execution whereof is humbly desired, and to be petitioned for at the hands of His Majestie and the Parliament) the Assembly would further supplicate this Parliament that they (in their wisdome) would finde out how meanes shall be had for so good an use, especially that the Children of poore men, being very capable of learning, and of good engines, may be trained up, according as the exigence and necessity of every place shall require. And that the Commissioners, who shall be named by this Assembly, to wait upon the Parliament may be appointed to represent this to his Majestie, and the Parliament, seeing His sacred Majestie, by his gracious Letter hath put us in hope hereof, wherewith we have been much refreshed.

V. The Assembly would supplicate the Parliament, that for youths of the finest and best spirits of the High-lands, and borders, maintenance may be allotted (as to Bursars) to be bred in Universities.

VI. For the time and manner of visitation of Schooles, and contriving the best and most compendious and orderly course of teaching Grammar, we humbly desire the Assembly to appoint a Committee for that effect, who may report their diligence to the next General Assembly.

The Overtures and Articles above-written being reported to this Assembly, after reading and serious consideration thereof, the Assembly approves the same, and ordaines them to have the strength of an Act and ordinance of Assembly, in all time-coming.

SESS. 11. AUGUST 5. 1642.

ACT ANENT CONTRARY OATHS.

The Generall Assembly finding the inconvenience of contrary Oaths in trying of Adulteries, Fornications, and other faults and scandals, do therefore for eviting there of, discharge Synods, Presbyteries and Sessions, to take Oath of both parties in all time hereafter, Recommending to them in the mean time all other order and wayes of tryall used in such cases: And that there may be a common order and course kept in this Kirk of trying of publike scandals, The Assembly ordains the Presbyteries to advise upon some common order hereintill, and to report their judgements to the next Assembly.

OVERTURES ANENT FAMILY EXERCISES, CATECHISING, KEEPING OF SYNODS AND PRESBYTERIES, AND RESTRAINT OF ADULTERIES, WITCH-CRAFTS, AND OTHER GROSSE SINS.

The Committee supplicates the Assembly,

I. To urge the severall Synods and Presbyteries, especially these of the North, that Family Exercise in Religion, visitation of the Churches, Catechising, keeping of the Presbyteriall and Provinciall meetings (both by Preaching and Ruling Elders) be more carefully observed.

II. That the Clerk at least subscribe every Book before it come to the Assembly, and that every Act be noted on the Margent, for a directory of expedition.

III. That the Assembly would seriously studie by all meanes and wayes how to procure the Magistrates concurrence to curb and punish these notorious vices which abound in the Land, especially in the Northern parts.

The Assembly approves the Overtures foresaids, and ordains them to be observed: and for the last, the Assembly being confident of the readinesse of the Judge Ordinar to restrain and punish these faults, Do therefore ordain all Presbyteries to give up to the Justice, the names of the Adulterers, incestuous persons, Witches and sorcerers and others guilty of such grosse and fearfull sins within their bounds that they may be Processed and punished according to the Laws of this Kingdom; and that the Presbyteries and Synods be carefull herein, as they will answer to the Generall Assemblies, And because that Witch craft, Charming, and such like proceeds many times from ignorance, Therefore the Assembly ordains all Ministers, especially in these parts where these sins are frequent, to be diligently Preaching, Cathichising, and conferring, to inform their people thereintill.

SESS. 11. AUG. 5. 1642.

ACT AGAINST PETITIONS, DECLARATIONS, & SUCHLIKE IN NAME OF MINISTERS, WITHOUT THEIR KNOWLEDGE AND CONSENTS.

The Generall Assembly being informed, that after the Petition presented to the Lords of His Majesties Privie Councell by the Noblemen Burgesses, and Ministers, occasionally met at Edinburg the 31. day of May last by-past, had received a very gracious Answer, There was another Petition given in to their Lordships upon the 2 day of June last, entituled, The Petition of the Nobilitie, Gentrie, Burrows, Ministers, and Commons: which as it was not accompanied with any one Minister to the Lords of Privie Councell, so all the Ministers of this Assembly, disclaimes and disavoweth any knowledge thereof, or accession thereto, And the Assembly conceiving that the Kings Majestie Himself, and all the Courts and Judicatories of this Kingdome may be deluded and abused, and the Kirk in Generall, and Ministers in particular injured and prejudged by the like practises hereafter, Do therefore prohibite and discharge all and every one to pretend or use the name of Ministers to any Petition, Declaration, or suchlike at any time hereafter, without their knowledge consent and assistance: And if any shal doe the contrary, ordaines Presbyteries and Provinciall Assemblies to proceed against them with the highest censures of the Kirk.

SESS 11. AUG. 5. 1642.

ACT ANENT THE ASSEMBLIES DESIRES TO THE LORDS OF COUNSELL, AND CONSERVATORS OF PEACE.

The Assembly being most desirous to use all, and to omit no lawful meane or occasion to testifie their zeale by dealing with God and man, for furtherance of their desires of Unity in Religion and uniformity of Kirk-government, And considering the great necessity, that the Kirk and State contribute joyntly their best endeavours to this happy end: Therefore enjoynes the Moderator, and the commissioners from the Assembly, to supplicate with all earnestnesse and respect, the Lords of his Majesties Honourable Privie Councel, and likewise the Commissioners appointed by His Majestie, and the Parliament, for conservation of the Peace, that they may be pleased to concur with the Kirk in the like desires to His Majesty and the Parliament of England, and in the like directions to the Commissioners of this Kingdome, at London for the time, that by all possible means, Civill, and Ecclesiastick, this blessed Worke may be advanced, and a happy settling betwixt His Majestie and His Parliament, may be endeavoured, and the common Peace betwixt the Kingdomes continued and strengthened.

SESS. 11. AUG 5. 1642.

THE ASSEMBLIES HUMBLE DESIRE TO THE KINGS MAJESTIE FOR THE SIGNATOR OF 500 L. STERLING AND RECOMMENDATION THEREOF TO THE KINGS COMMISSIONER.

The Generall Assembly having received the Report of the proceedings of the Commissioners of the late Assembly, and specially that His Majesty was graciously pleased, upon their humble Petition, solemnly to promise and declare under his Royall hand, his pious resolution and dedication of 500. l. sterling, out of the readiest of his Rents and revenues, to be imployed yearly on publike necessary and pious uses of the Kirk, at the sight of the Generall Assembly, as his Majestie gracious answer of the 3. of January, 1642. registrate in their books at His Majesties own desire, for their further assurance of his Majesties pious zeale, doth more fully proport. Likeas being informed that His Majestie was gratiously pleased to signe and send down to the Kirk the Signator of the said 500. l. yearly to have past the Exchequer, albeit the samine is not as yet delivered; And considering His Majesties pious directions to them by his Majesties Letter to plant and visit the utmost skirts and borders of the Kingdome, as most necessary for the glory of God, the good of the Kirk, and His Majesties honour, and service, which is only stopped by the want of charges for publike visitations, And withall to remonstrate to His Majestie by His Commissioner, their just and necessary desires for what may further serve to the good of Religion, whereunto His Majesties Commissioner promised his best endeavours and assistance. Therefore the Assembly doth most earnestly recommend to His Majesties Commissioner to represent to His Majestie, with his best assistance, the humble and necessary desires of the whole Assembly, that His Majestie will be graciously pleased to command that Signator, already signed by His Royall hand (or to signe another of the samine tenor, whereof they deliver the just double to his Maj Commissioner for that effect) to be sent to this Kingdom, and delivered to the Commissioners from this Assembly, who are to sit at Edinburgh, or to the Procurator of the Kirk, whereby his Majestie shall more and more oblige this whole Kirk to pray for a blessing from Heaven upon His Royal Person and Government.

SESS. 11. AUG. 5. 1642.

THE ASSEMBLIES LETTER TO THE COMMISSIONERS OF THIS KINGDOM AT LONDON.

Right Honourable,

We have received your Lordships Letter, with the Declaration of the Parliament of England, and have sent this Noble bearer to His Majesty with our humble Supplication, and to your Lordships with our Answer earnestly desiring Unity of Religion, and Uniformity of Kirk-government, to be presented by your Lordships, and this Noble bearer to the Honourable Houses of Parliament. Your Lordships will perceive by the inclosed Copies, and by our desires to His Majesties honourable Privie Councel and Commissioners for the conservation of the Peace, to joyn their best endeavours with his Majestie and the Parliament, and their directions to your Lordships, by our leaving a Commission behinde us, to concur with them in all Ecclesiastick wayes, and by our appointing publike Prayers, and a solemn Fast through this Kirk, for the furtherance of this great work of Reformation, and continuance of the common Peace, that this Unity in Religion and uniformity of Kirk-government is the chiefest of our desires, prayers and cares: Where unto as we have been encouraged by the faithful labors of the Commissioners of this Kingdom in the late Treaty, and continued and renewed by your Lordships; so we are assured, that your Lordships will omit no lawful mean, argument, or occasion of seconding the same there, And advertising our Commissioners at Edinburgh, wherein they may further concur with your Lordships, for the furtherance of the Work, which tends so much to the glory of God, advancement of Christs Kingdom, increase of the honour and happinesse of our Soveraign, and the peace and welfare of these Kingdoms, whereby your Lordships will oblige this Kirk more and more to pray for a blessing on your persons and travels, and to rest.

Yours in the Lord
The Commissioners of the General Assembly.

S. Andrews 5. Aug. 1642.

A LETTER FROM SOME MINISTERS OF ENGLAND.

Reverend and wel-beloved in our Lord and Saviour.

We received with much joy and satisfaction the Answer which your General Assembly vouchsafed us to our Letters of the last yeer. Some of us in the name of our Brethren, thought it then fit by Mr. Alexander Henderson (a Brother so justly approved by you, and honoured by us) to return our deserved thanks. And we now further think it equall upon this occasion, to make a more publike acknowledgement of such a publike favour. You were then pleased to give us fair grounds, to expect that brotherly advice and endeavours, which the common cause of Christ, and the mutual interest of the united Nations, command us now again to ask, if not to chalenge. We doubt not but your experience, together with your intelligence, abundantly informes you of our condition, what various administrations of providence we have passed through and we still lye betwixt hopes and feares, a fit temper for working; the God of all grace enable us to improve it. As our hopes are not such as may make us fear, so neither doe our Feares prevail, to the casting away our confidence. Your own late condition, together with this Declaration of ours present, may acquaint you with the certain, though subtil, authors & fomentors of these our confused conflicts: which we conceive to be the Hierarchical faction, who have no way to peace & safety, but through the trouble & danger of others. Our prayers and endeavours, according to our measure, have been and shall be for the supplanting and rooting up whatsoever we finde so prejudicial to the establishment of the Kingdome of Christ, and the peace of our Soveraigne. And that this Declaration of ourselves may not leave you unsatisfied, we think it necessary further to expresse, That the desire of the most godly and considerable part amongst us, is, That the Presbyterian Government, which hath just and evident Foundation both in the Word of God, and religious reason, may be established amongst us, and that (according to your intimation) we may agree in one confession of Faith, one directorie of Worship, one publike Catechisme and form of Governement: Which things, if they were accomplished, we should much rejoyce in our happy subjection to Christ our Head, and our desired association with you our beloved brethren. For the better effecting whereof, we thought it necessary, not only to acquaint you with what our desires are in themselves, but likewise to you, that is, That what way shall seem most fit to the wisedom of that grave and religious Assembly, may be taken for the furtherance of our indeavours in this kind. We understand that our Parliament hath been before hand with us in this intimation, and it cannot but be our duty, who are so much concerned in the businenesse, to adde what power the Lord hath given us with you to the same purpose. This designe and desire of ours hath enemies on the Left-hand; and dissenting brethren on the Right; but we doubt not, that as our hearts justifie us that our intentions are right, and such as we conceive tend most to the glory of God, and the peace of the Churches of the Saints; so (by your brotherly concurrence in the most speedy and effectuall way you can find out) the Work will in Gods due time receive a prayed for, hoped for issue. We shall not need by many arguments from mutuall Nationall interest (though we know you will not overlook them) to inforce this request, the firme bond wherewith we are all united in our Lord Jesus Christ, we are assured will alone engage your faithfull endeavours in this businesse. To him we commit you, with these great and important affairs you have in hand. Be pleased to accept of these as the expression of the mindes of our many godly and faithfull Brethren, whose hearts we doubt not of, neither need you, though their hands in regard of the suddennesse of this opportunity could not be subscribed together with ours, who are.

Your most affectionate Friends and Brethren in the work of the Lord.

London, 22. July, 1642.

ANSWER TO THE MINISTERS LETTER.

Right Reverend and beloved in the Lord Jesus.

By our Answer to the Declaration sent unto us from the honourable Houses of Parliament, ye may perceive that your Letter which came into our hands so seasonably, was not only acceptable unto us, but hath also encouraged us to renew both to the Kings Majestie and the Houses of Parliament, The desires of the late Commissioners of this Kingdome for Unity in Religion, in the four particulars remembred by you, we cannot be ignorant but the opposition from Satan and worldly men in Kirk and Policy, will still be vehement as it hath been already, But we are confident through our Lord Jesus Christ, that the prayers and indeavours of the godly in both Kingdoms, will bring the work to a wished, and blessed Issue. This whole national Kirk is so much concerned in that Reformation and Unity of Religion in both Kingdomes, that without it we cannot hope for any long time to enjoy our puritie and peace, which hath cost us so dear, and is now our chiefest comfort and greatest treasure: Which one cause (beside the Honour of God, and the happinesse of the People of God in that Kingdome, more desired of us then Our lives) is more then sufficient to move us, To contribute all that is in our power for bringing it to passe. And since we have with so great liberty made our desires and hopes known both to King and Parliament, it is a duety incombent both to you and us, who make mention of the Lord, and are Watch-men upon the Walls of Jerusalem, never more to keep silence nor to hold our peace day nor night, till the Righteousnesse of Sion go forth as brightnesse, and the salvation thereof as a lamp that burneth. And if it shall please the Lord to move the hearts of King and Parliament, to hearken unto the motion, for which end we have resolved to keep a solemne Fast and Humiliation in all the Kirks of this Kingdome, the mean by which we have prevailed in times past, we wish that the Work may be begun with speed, and prosecuted with diligence by the joint labours of some Divines in both Kingdoms, who may prepare the same for the view and examination of a more frequent Ecclesiastick meeting of the best affected to Reformation there, and of the Commissioners of the General Assembly here, that in end it may have the approbation of the Generall Assembly here, and of all the Kirks there, in the best way that may be, we wish & hope at last in a nationall Assembly; Our Commissioners at Edinburgh, shall in our name receive and returne answers for promoving so great a Work, which we with our heart and our soule recommend to the blessing of God, we continue,

Your loving brethren and fellow-labourers.

ACT FOR THE LORD MAITLANDS PRESENTING THE ASSEMBLIES SUPPLICATION TO HIS MAJESTIE, AND FOR GOING TO THE COMMISSIONERS AT LONDON, WITH THE ANSWER TO THE PARLIAMENT OF ENGLANDS DECLARATION.

The General Assembly considering the necessity of sending some person of good worth & quality for to present their humble Supplication to His Majestie, and to deliver their directions to the Commissioners of this Kingdom, now at London, with their Declaration to the Parliament of England, and Answer to some wel-affected Ministers of that Kirk: And having certain knowledge of the worth, ability, and faithfulnesse of John Lord Maitland, one of their number, who being witnesse to all their intentions and proceedings, can best relate their true loyaltie and respect to their Soveraign, and brotherly affection to the Kirk and Kingdom of England therein; Therefore do unanimously require his Lordships pains, by repairing to Court and to London for the premisses, which hereby they commit to this diligence and fidelity, willing his Lordship to make account of his proceedings herein to their Commissioners appointed to sit at Edinburgh.

SESS. 11. AUGUST 5. POST MERIDIEM.

COMMISSION FOR PUBLIKE AFFAIRS OF THIS KIRK, AND FOR PROSECUTING THE DESIRES OF THIS ASSEMBLY TO HIS MAJESTIE, AND THE PARLIAMENT OF ENGLAND.

The General Assembly considering the laudable custome of this Kirk for to appoint some Commissioners in the interim betwixt Assemblies, for presenting of Overtures and prosecuting the other desires of the Kirk to His Majestie, the Lords of His Councell, and the Estates of Parliament; And taking to their consideration the present condition of the Kirk of England, with the Declaration thereof sent down from the Parliament, and some Reverend Brethren of the Ministery there, with their own Answer to the Parliament and Ministery, and their humble Supplication to His Majestie for Unity of Religion and Uniformity of Kirk-government. And withall remembring their desires to the Honourable Lords of His Majesties secret Councell, and to the Commissioners appointed by the King and Parliament, for conservation of the common Peace, That they would joyn their concourse in their desires to His Majestie and Parliament, and directions to the Commissioners of this Kingdom at London for the time. And likewise considering their good hopes from Gods gracious favour to this Island, that by his good providence he will in his own way and time settle this great Work through this whole Ile; And that it is both our earnest desire and Christian duty to use all lawfull means and Ecclesiastick wayes for furtherance of so great a Work, continuance of the common peace betwixt these nations, and keeping a brotherly correspondence betwixt these Kirks. Therfore the Assembly thinks it necessary before their dissolving, to appoint, and by these Presents do nominate and appoint, Masters Andrew Ramsay, Alex Henderson, Robert Dowglas, William Colvill, William Bennet Ministers at Edinburgh. Mr. William Arthur Minister at St. Cuthbert, Mr. James Robertson, John Logan, Robert Lighton, Commissioners from Dalkeith Assembly: Masters, Andrew Blackhall, James Fleeming, Robert Ker, Commissioners from Hadingtoun to the Assembly. Masters, George Hamilton, Robert Clair, Arthur Mortoun, David Dalgleish, Andrew Bennet, Walter Greg, John Moncreff, John Smith, George Gillespie, John Row, John Duncan, Walter Bruce, Commissioners for the Presbyteries within the Province of Fyffe: Mr. David Calderwood Minister at Pencait and Mr. John Adamson Principall of the Colledge of Edinburgh, Mr. John Strang Principall of the Colledge of Glasgow. Mr. David Dikson, Mr. James Bonar, Mr. Robert Bailie, Mr. John Bell, Mr Robert Ramsay, Mr. George Young, Mr Henry Guthrie, Mr. Samuel Oustein, Mr. John Robertson Minister at St. Johnstoun, Mr. John Robertson Minister at Dundie, Mr. John Hume Minister at Heckills, Mr. Andrew Cant, Mr William Guild, Mr. Samuel Rutherfurd, Mr. James Martin, Mr. Alexander Monroe, Mr. Robert Murray, Mr. John Maclellan, Mr. Andrew Doncanson, Mr. Silvester Lambie, Mr. Gilbert Ross, Ministers: Marquesse of

Argile, Earles of Lauderdaile, Glencarne, Kingborne, Eglintoun, Weemes, Cassils: Lords Gordoun, Maitland, Balcarras, Sir Patrick Hepburne of Wauchtoun, Sir David Hum of Wedderburne, Sir David Creightoun of Lugtoun, Sir David Barclay of Cullearnie, John Henderson of Fordell, Mr. George Winrame of Libertoun, Sir Robert Drummond, Sir William Carmichaell, John Binnie, Thomas Paterson, John Sempill, John Kennedy of Air, John Leslie from Aberdene, William Glendinning Provest of Kirkubrigh, John Colzear, Ruling Elders with the concurse of the Procurator of the Kirk: and grants to them full Power and Commission in this interim, betwixt and the next Assembly, for to meet and conveen at Edinburgh upon the 17. day of this moneth of August, and upon any other day, or in any other place, as they shall think convenient: And being met and conveened, or any fifteen of them, there being always twelve Ministers present: With full power for to consider and performe what they finde necessary for the Ministerie, by preaching, supplicating, prepairing of draughts of one Confession, one Cathechisme, one directory of publike Worship (which are alwayes to be revised by the next Generall Assembly) and by all other lawfull & Ecclesiastick wayes, for furtherance of this great Work in the Union of this Iland in Religion and Kirk-government, and for continuance of our own peace at home, and of the common peace betwixt the Nations, and keeping of good correspondence betwixt the Kirks of this Iland. Like as if it shall please God to blesse the prayers and endeavours of his Saints for this blessed Union, and that if either the Lords of Councell, or Commissioners for the Peace shall require their concurse at home or abroad, by sending Commissioners with theirs to His Majesty and Parliament for that effect, or that they themselves shall finde it necessary; The Assembly grants full power to them, not only to concurre by all lawfull and Ecclesiastick wayes, with the Councell and Conservators of the Peace at home, but also to send some to present and prosecute their desires and humble advice to His Majesty and the Parliament, and the Ministerie there, for the furthering and perfecting of so good and great a Worke. Like as, with power to them to promove their other desires, overtures and recommendations of this Assembly, to the Kings Majestie, Lords of Councell, Session, Exchequer, and Commissioners of Parliament, for plantation of Kirks, for common burdens, or conservation of the common peace, and to the Parliament of this Kingdom, in case it fall out pro re nata before the next Assembly. And such like, with as full power to them to proceed, treat and determine in any other matters to be committed to them by this Assembly, as if the samine were herein particularly insert, and with as ample power to proceede in the matters particularly or generally above-mentioned, as any Commissioners of Generall Assemblies have had, and have been in use of before: They being alwayes comptable to, and censurable by the next Generall Assembly, for their proceedings thereanent.

SESS. 13. AUG. 6. 1642.

A PETITION FROM SOME DISTRESSED PROFESSORS IN IRELAND.

To the reverend and right Honourable the Moderator and remanent members of the Generall Assembly of Scotland, conveened at S. Andrews, July 1642.

The humble Petition of the most part of the Scottish Nation in the North of Ireland, in their own names, and in name of the rest of the Protestants there.

Humbly sheweth,

That where your Petitioners, by the great blessing of the Lord, enjoyed for a little while a peaceable and fruitfull Ministerie of the Gospel, yet through our own abuse of so rich a mercy, and through the tyrannie of the Prelates, we have been a long time spoiled of our Ministers (a yoke to many of us heavier then death) who being chased into Scotland, were not altogether un-usefull in the day of your need; And we having been since oppressed and scattered, as sheep who have no shepherd, now at last the wise and righteous hand of the Lord, by the sword of the Rebels, hath bereft us of our friends, and spoiled us of our goods, &c. left us but a few, and that a poor handfull of many, and hath chased from us the rest that were called our Ministers; the greatest part whereof we could scarce esteem such as being rather Officers to put the Prelats Injunctions in execution, then feeders of our souls: So that now being visited with sword and sicknesse, and under some apprehension of famine, if withall we shall taste of the sorest of all plagues, to be altogether deprived of the Ministery of the Word, we shall become in so much a worse condition then any Pagans, as that once we enjoyed a better: Neither know we what hand to turn us to for help, but to the Land so far obliged by the Lords late rare mercies, and so far enriched to furnish help of that kinde; a Land whence many of us drew our blood and breath and where (pardon the necessary bold-nesse) some of our own Ministers now are, who were so violently plucked from us, so sore against both their own and our wills; yea, the Land that so tenderly in their bosoms received our poor out-casts, and that hath already sent us so rich a supply of able and prosperous Souldiers to revenge our wrong.

Therefore, although we know that your zeale and brotherly affection would urge you to take notice without our advertisement, yet give us leave in the bowels of our Lord Jesus Christ, to intreat, if there be any consolation in Christ, if any com-fort of love, if any fellowship of the spirit, if any bowels of mercy, that now in this nick of time, when the sword of the Enemie making way for a more profitable en-tertaining the Gospel, having also banished the Prelates, and their followers, when our extremity of distreste, and the fair hopes of speedy settling of peace, hath opened so fair a doore to the Gospel, you would take the cause of your younger sister, that hath no brests, to your serious consideration, and pity poore Macedo-nians crying to you that ye would come over and help us, being the servants of the God of your Fathers, and claiming interest with you in a common Covenant, that according to the good hand of God upon us, ye may send us Ministers for the house of our God. We do not take upon us to prescribe to you the way or the number, but in the view of all, the finger of the Lord points at these, whom though persecution of the Prelats drew from us, yet our interest in them could not be taken away, wherein we trust in regard of severall of them, called home by death, your bounty will super-adde some able men of your own that may help to lay the foundation of Gods house, according to the Pattern. But for these so unjustly reft from us, not only our necessity, but equity pleads, that either you would send them all over, which were a Work to be parallelled to the glories of the Primitive times, or at least that ye would declare them transportable, that when Invitators shall be sent to any of them, wherein they may discerne a call from God, there may be no difficultie in their loosing from thence, but they may come back to perfect what they began, and may get praise and fame in the Land, where they were put to shame. Neither are you to question your power over us so to doe, or crave a president of your own practise in that kind, for our extraordinary need calling on you, furnisheth you with a power to make this a president for the like cases hereafter: herein if you shall lay aside the particular concernment of some few places, which you may easily out of your rich Nurseries plant again, and make use of your publike spirits, which are not spent, but increases by your so many noble designes; you shall leave upon us and our posteritie the stamp of an obligation that cannot be delete, or that cannot be expressed; you should send to all the neighbouring Churches a pattern, and erect for after-ages a monument of self-denying tender zeale; you shall disburden the Land of the many outcasts, who will follow over their Ministers; and you shall make it appear, that the churlish bounty of the Prelats, which at first cast some of these men over to us, is not comparable with the cheerful liberalitie of a rightly constitute General Assembly, to whom we are perswaded, the Lord will give seed for the loane which you bestow on the Lord; yea, the day may come, when a General Assembly in this Land may returne to you the first fruits of thanks, for the plants of your free gift. And although you were scant of furniture of this kinde your selves, or might apprehend more need then formerly, yet doubtlesse, your bowels of compassion would make your deep povertie even in a great tryal of affliction, abound to the riches of your liberalitie. But now seeing you abound in all things, and have formerly given so ample a proof of your large bestowing on Churches abroad in Germanie and France, knowing that you are not wearied in well-doing, we confidently promise to our selves in your name, that we will abound in this grace also, following the example of our Lord and the Primitive Churches, who alwayes sent out Disciples in paires. But if herein our hopes shall faile us, we shall not know whether to wish that we had died with our Brethren by the Enemies hand; for we shall be as if it were said unto us, Goe serve other Gods; Yet looking for another kinde of Answer at your hands, for in this you are to us as an Angel of God, we have sent these bearers, M. John Gordoun, and M. Hugh Campbell our brethren, who may more particularly in-forme you of our case, and desire that at their returne, they may refresh the bowels of

Your most instant and earnest Supplicants.

COMMISSION TO SOME MINISTERS TO GO TO IRELAND.

The Assembly having received a Petition, subscribed by a considerable number in the North of Ireland, intimating their deplorable condition, through want of the Ministerie of the Gospel, occasioned by the tyrannie of the Prelats, and the sword of the Rebels, and desiring some Ministers, especially such as had been chased from them, by the persecution of the Prelats, and some others to be added, either to be sent presently over to reside amongst them, or declared transportable, that upon invitation from them they might goe and settle there; together with some particular Petitions, desiring the returne of some particular Ministers, who had laboured there before: All which the Assembly hath taken to their serious consideration, being most heartily willing to sympathize with every member of Christs Body, although never so remote; much more with that Plantation there, which for the most part was a Branch of the Lords Vine, planted in this Land. In which sollicitude, as they would be loath to usurpe without their own bounds or stretch themselves beyond their oun measure; so they dare not be wanting, to the enlargement of Christs Kingdome, where so loud a cry of so extreame neccesitie, could not but stirre up the bowels of Christian compassion. And although they conceive that the present unsettled condition both of Church, and State, and Land, will not suffer them as yet to loose any to make constant abode there; yet they have resolved to send over some for the present exigent till the next Gen. Assembly, by courses to stay there four moneths allanerly: And therefore doe hereby authorize and give Commission to the persons following, to wit, M. Robert Blair, Minister at S. Andrews, and M. James Hamilton, Minister at Dumfreis for the first four moneths: M. Robert Ramsay, Minister at Glasgow, and M. John Mac'elland, Minister at Kirkudbright, for the next four moneths: And to M. Robert Baillie, Professor of Divinitie in the Universitie of Glasgow, and M. John Levistoun, Minister of Stranaire, for the last four moneths: To repair into the North of Ireland, and there to visit, comfort, instruct and encourage the scattered flocks of Christ, to employ to their uttermost with all faithfulnesse and singlenesse of heart, in planting and watering, according to the direction of Jesus Christ, and according to the doctrine and discipline of this Church in all things, And if need be (with concurrence of such of the Ministers of the Army as are there) to try and ordain such as shall be found qualified for the Ministerie, Giving charge unto the persons foresaid in the sight of God, that in Doctrine, in Worship, in Discipline, and in their dayly conversation, they studie to approve themselves as the Ministers of Jesus Christ, and that they be comptable to the General Assembly of this Kirk, in all things. And in case if any of the above-mentioned Ministers be impeded by sickness or otherwise necessarily detained from this service, the Assembly ordaines the Commissioners residing at Edinburgh, for the publike affairs of the Church, to nominate in their place well qualified men, who hereby are authorized to undertake the foresaid imployment, as if they had been expressely nominate in the face of the Assembly. And this, although possibly it shall not fully satisfie the large expectation of the Brethren in Ireland, yet the Assembly is confident they will take in good part at this time, that which is judged most convenient for their present condition, even a lent mite out of their own, not very great plenty, to supply the present necessity; requiring of them no other recompence, but that they in all cheerefulnesse may embrace and make use of salvation, and promising to enlarge their indebted bounty at the next Assembly, as they shall finde the Worke of the Lord there to require. In the meane while, wishing that these who are sent, may come with the full blessing of the Gospel and peace, and recommending them, their labours, and these to whom they are sent, to the rich blessing of the great Shepherd of the flock.

SESS. 13. AUGUST 6. 1642.

ACT AGAINST SLANDERING OF MINISTERS.

The General Assembly considering the malice of divers Persons in raising calumnies and scandals against Ministers, which is not onely injurious to their persons, and discreditable to the holy calling of the Ministerie, but doth also prove often a great prejudice and hinderance to the promoving of the Gospel: Doe therefore ordain Presbyteries and Synods to proceed diligently in processe against all persons, that shall reproach or scandal Ministers, with the censures of the Kirk, even to the highest, according as they shall finde the degree or quality of the scandal deserve.

ACT ANENT ORDERING OF THE ASSEMBLY HOUSE.

The Assembly for better order in time coming ordains the Act of the Assembly at Aberdene for ordering the House of the Assembly to be kept hereafter punctually. And for that effect, that the samine be reade the first Session of every Assembly.

ACT FOR REMEMBRING IN PUBLIKE PRAYERS THE DESIRES OF THE ASSEMBLY TO THE KING AND PARLIAMENT, AND INDICTION OF A PUBLIKE FAST.

The General Assembly being desirous to promove the great work of Unity in Religion, and Uniformity in Church government, in all thir three Dominions, for which the Assembly hath humbly supplicate the Kings Majestie, and remonstrate their desires to the Parliament of England, lest they should be wanting in any meane that may further so glorious and so good a work: Doe ordain, that not only the said Declaration to the Parliament, and supplication to the Kings Majestie, shall be accompanied with the earnest Petition, and prayers of the whole brethren in private and publike, for the Lords blessing hereunto, according to the laudable custome of our predecessors, who in the year of God 1589. ordaines that the Brethren in their private and publike prayers, recommend unto God the estate of the afflicted Church of England: But having just cause of fear, that the iniquities of the Land, which so much abount may marre this so great a Work, doe also ordain a solemne Fast to be kept on the second Lords Day of September and the Wednesday following throughout the whole Kingdome for the causes after specified.

I. Grosse ignorance and all sort of wickedness among the greater part, security, meer formality and unfruitfulnesse among the best, and unthankfulnesse in all.

II. The sword raging throughout all Christendome, but most barbarously in *Ireland*, and dayly more and more threatned in *England*, through the lamentable division betwixt the King and the Parliament there, tending to the subversion of Religion and Peace in all the three Kingdomes.

III. That God may graciously blesse the Supplication of the Assembly to the Kings Majesty, and their motion to the Parliament of *England*, for Unitie in Religion, and Uniformity of Kirk-government, and all other meanes which may serve for the promoving of so great a Worke, and advancement of the Kingdome of Christ every where.

IV. That God may powerfully overturne all wicked plots and designes of Antichrist and his followers, and all divisive motions against the course of Reformation, and the so much longed for Union of the King and Parliament.

V. That God may blesse the harvest.

REFERENCE FROM THE PRESBYTERIE OF KIRKCALDIE.

Anent the Acts of Assemblies, for observation of the Lords Day, profaned by going of salt-pannes, That this Assembly would declare the limits of the Sabbath, during which the pannes should stand.

The Assembly referres the Answer of this Question, to the Acts of former Assemblies.

REFERENCE FRROM THE SYNODE OF FYFFE.

That the Provinciall of Angus keep their meeting on the same day with the Synod of Fyffe, which breakes the correspondence between them, appointed by the General Assembly of Glasgow.

ANSWER.

The Assembly ordaines the Provinciall Assembly of Angus to keep their first meeting upon the third Tuesday of April, comforme to the Act of the said Assembly of Glasgow.

OVERTURES TO BE ADVISED BY PRESBYTERIES AGAINST THE NEXT ASSEMBLY.

How Appeals shall be brought into the Generall Assemblies, and by what sort of citation.

What shall be the prescription of scandalls, within what space of time shall they be challenged, whether after three years, the Minister having been allowed and approved in life and doctrine by Synods, Presbyteries, and Visitations.

What order shall be taken for keeping general Assemblies, when Presbyteries send not the full number of Commissioners: Or when the Commissioners abide not until the conclusion and dissolving of the Assembly.

Order to be advised for Testimonials.

The Assembly appoints the next Generall Assembly to hold at Edinburgh, *the first Wednesday of August, 1643.*

THE GENERALL ASSEMBLY AT EDINBURGH

SESS. 1. AUGUST 2. 1643.

THE KINGS LETTER TO THE GENERAL ASSEMBLY.

Presented by his Majesties Commissioner Sir Thomas Hope of Craighall Knight, His Majesties Advocate.

Charles R.

Trustie and welbeloved, We greet you well. The time now approaching for the holding of the Generall Assembly of Our Kirk of Scotland, and We having appointed Sir Thomas Hope Our Advocate to be Our Commissioner there; We thought good to present him there with these Our Letters, and to take this occasion to minde you of the duty which you owe to Us your Soveraigne, and to the peace of that Our Native Kingdome. How far We have lately extended Our grace and favour towards satisfaction of your humble desires, there is not any amongst you but may well remember: And therefore in this conjuncture of Our affairs, it is but reasonable that We expect from you such moderation in the dutifull proceedings of this Assembly, as may concurre with our Princely inclinations and desires, to preserve that Kirk and that our Kingdome in peace; having wel observed that alterations in points of Religion, are often the inlets to civill dissentions, and the hazard, if not overthrow of both Kirk and Kingdomes. Therefore of Our great affection and speciall tendernesse to your peace (who of all Our Dominions are yet happie therein to the envy of others) We conjure and require you in the fear of God, and obedience of Us his Vicegerent, that your endeavours and consultations tend onely to preserve peace and quietnesse among you. And so We bid you farewell. Given at Our Court at Oxford the 22. day of July, 1643.

To our right trusty and welbeloved Counsellour, Sir Thomas Hope Knight, our Advocate general, and Our Commissioner at the generall assembly of the Kirk in Our Kingdome of Scotland, and to the rest of the said Assembly now conveened.

SESS. 2. AUGUST 3. 1643.

OVERTURES ANENT BILLS, REFERENCES, AND APPEALES.

I. That all Bills whatsoever of particular concernments whereunto all parties having interest are not cited, should be rejected.

II. That all Bills be first presented to the inferiour Judicatories of the Kirk, who may competently consider of them, and from them be orderly and gradatim brought to the Assembly, according to the order prescribed for Appellations in the Assembly of Edinburgh, 1639. in the 24. Sess. August 30.

III. That the said Act of Assembly 1639. anent Appelations, be also extended to References.

IV. In Appellations and References of particular concernment, if all parties having interest, have been present in the inferiour Judicatorie when the Appeal and Reference was made, then there is no necessitie of citation. But in case of their absence, citation of parties is so necessar, that if it be wanting, Appellations and References should not be received.

V. That conform to former Acts of Assemblies; Appellations post sententiam be made within ten dayes after the sentence, and otherwise not to be respected.

The Assembly ordaines their Overtures to be given to the severall Committees for their direction.

SESS. 3. AUGUST 4. 1643.

ACT FOR ELECTION OF PROFESSOURS TO BE COMMISSIONERS TO ASSEMBLIES BY PRESBYTERIES.

The Assembly thinks, if Professours of Divinitie in Universities be Ministers, that they may be chosen Commissioners to the Generall Assembly, either by the Presbyterie as Ministers or by the Universitie as Professours of Divinitie.

SESS. 4. AUG. 5. 1643.

THE PETITION OF THE DISTRESSED PROFESSOURS IN IRELAND FOR MINISTERS.

To the reverend and honourable Moderatour and remanent Members of the General Assembly of Scotland, conveened at Edinburgh, Aug. 1643.

The humble Petition of the distressed Christians in the North of Ireland.

Humbly sheweth,

That whereas you were pleased the last Year to take notice of our Petition, and conceived so favourable an act in our behalf, from our hearts we blesse the Lord God of our Fathers, who put such a thing as this in your heart to begin in any sort to beautifie the House of the Lord amongst us: Doubtlesse you have brought upon your selves the blessing of them who consider the poor; the Lord will certainly deliver you in the time of trouble. We trust no distance of place, no length of time, no pressure of affiction, yea, nor smiling of prosperity, shall delete out of our thankfull memories the humble acknowledgement of your so motherly care: in drawing out your breasts, yea, your souls to satisfie the hungrie: although we have been beaten with the sword, bitten with famine, our own wickednes correcting us, our back-slidings reproving us, yet we have not so farre forgotten the Lords ancient love, but that our hearts were brought to a little reviving in the midst of our bondage, by the Ministery of these, who at your direction made a short visit amongst us. We know you did not conceive it expedient at that time, to loose any for full settling here, till the waters of the bloudy inundation were somewhat abated, and prohability might be of some comfortable abode, which we through the Lords revenging hand, pursuing our enemies, and the vigilancie of your victorious Army, is in a great measure attained unto. Whatsoever might have detained some of these whom ye directed to us, whose stay made our expectation prove abortive, we shall ascribe it to our own abuse of such treasure, and want of spirituall hunger, occasioned justly through the want of food; And yet that same dis-appointment, together with your faithfull promise of inlarging your indebted bountie, which is put upon record in all our hearts, hath made us conceive the seed of a lively expectation, that you will now no more put your bountie, and the means of our life, into the hazard of such frustrations, but will once for all, bestow an ample and enduring blessing. And of this we are so much the more confident, because our former suit was not denyed but delayed: only we fear, if a new delay be procured, till all things be fully settled, that the observing of winde and clouds, shall hinder both sowing and reaping. And in the mean time, the Prelates and their Faction may step in and invest themselves of their old tyrannie over our consciences, who if they once shall see us possessed of our own Inheritance, those Canaanites dare not offer to thrust us out. By all appearance, if the Jesuites had any hope to finde welcome amongst us, they had provided us fully ere now with their poysoned plants, Our hearts abhorre the checking or suspecting of your proceedings, yet it is lawfull to learn sometime from our enemie: But in this you have begun before, not only to do, but also to be forward a year ago, and thereby have ingaged your selves to perfect your own beginnings, and bring us out of our orphan condition. We are fallen in your lap, this ruine must be under your hand; you cannot pretend want of bread or cloathing, you must be healers: We have chosen you curators to your little young sister that wants breasts; there is none in earth to take her out of your hand, for we will not, nor cannot hide it from your Honours and Wisedome, that we want bread, and must not only, as before, have a bit for our present need, but also seed to sow the Land.

It is therefore our humble and earnest desire, that you would yet again look on our former Petition, and your own obligatorie Act, and at least declare your consent, that a competent number of our own Ministers may be loosed to settle here, and break bread to the children that lye fainting at the head of all streets, which although it may be accounted but a restoring of what we lost, and you have found, yet we shall esteem it as the most precious gift that earth can affoord. When they are so loosed, if they finde not all things concurring to clear Gods calling, it will be in their hand to forbear and you have testified your bountie. But oh for the Lords sake, do not kill our dying souls, by denying these our necessar desires. There are about twelve or fourteen waste congregations on this nearest coast: let us have at least a competent number that may erect Christs throne of discipline, and may help to bring in others, and then shall we sing, that the people who were left of the sword, have found grace in the wildernesse. We have sent these our brethren, Sir Robert Adair of Kinhilt Knight, and William Mackenna of Bel fast merchant, to attend an answer from you, who have attained that happinesse to be lenders and not borrowers, and to present the heartie longing affections of

Your most obliged and more expecting brethren and servants.

Subscribed by very many hands.

SESS. 6. AUGUST 8, 1643.

ACTS FOR SUBSCRIBING THE COVENANT.

The General Assembly considering the good and pious advice of the Commissioner of the last Assembly, upon the 22 of September, 1642 post meridiem, recommending to Presbytries, to have Copies of the Covenant to be subscribed by every Minister at his admission, doth therefore ratifie and approve the samine. And further ordaines, that the covenant be reprinted, with this Ordinance prefixed thereto, and that every Synod, Presbyterie, and Paroch, have one of them bound in quarto, with some blank paper, whereupon every person may be obliged to subscribe: And that the Covenants of the Synod and Presbyterie be keeped by their Moderatours respectivè of Universities by their Principals, of Paroches by their Ministers, with all carefulnesse. And that particular account of obedience to this Act, be required hereafter in all visitations of Paroches, Universities, and Presbyteries, and all trialls of Presbyteries and Synod books.

The General Assembly considering that the Act of the Assembly at Edinburgh 1639. August 30. injoyning all persons to subscribe the Covenant, under all Ecclesiastical censure, hath not been obeyed: Therefore ordaines all Ministers to make intimation of the said Act in their Kirks, and thereafter to proceed with the censures of the Kirk against such as shall refuse to subscribe the Covenant. And that exact account be taken of every Ministers diligence hereintil by their Presbyteries and Synods, as they will answer to the General Assembly.

SESS. 7. AUGUST 9. 1643.

ACT FOR SEARCHING BOOKS TENDING TO SEPARA-TION.

The Generall Assembly considering the recommendation of the Commissioners of the late Assembly at S. Andrews, upon the 12 of May last, to every Minister within their several bounds; especially to Ministers upon the coasts, or where there is Harbourie and Ports, to try and search for all books tending to Separation: And finding the same most necessar, do therefore ordain that recommendation to have the strength of an ordinary Act of Assembly: And that every Minister be careful to try and search if any such books be brought to this Countrey from beyond seas, and if any shall be found, to present the samine to Presbyteries, that some course may be taken to hinder the dispersing thereof: And earnestly recommend to the Civil Magistrates, to concurre with their authoritie in all things, for effectual execution hereof.

APPROBATION OF THE PROCEEDINGS OF THE COMMIS-

SIONERS OF THE LAST ASSEMBLY.

The Generall Assembly having heard the report of the Committee appointed to consider the proceedings of the Commissioners of the late Assembly at S. Andrews; after mature deliberation, and serious consideration thereof, findes the whole Acts, Conclusions and Proceedings of the saids Commissioners, contained in a Book and Register subscribed by Master Andrew Ker their Clerk, and by Master David Lindsay Moderatour, and Master James Hamilton Clerk to the said Committe, to declare much wisedome, diligence, vigilancie, and every way commendable zeal and fidelitie in doing and discharging every thing according to their Commission.

SESS. 8. AUGUST 10. 1643.

PROPOSITIONS GIVEN BY THE COMMISSIONERS OF THE PARLIAMENT OF ENGLAND TO A COMMITTEE, TO BE PRESENTED BY THEM TO THE ASSEMBLY.

We the Commissioners appointed by both Houses of the Parliament of England, desire your Lordships, and the rest of this reverend Committee, to represent to the reverend the Generall Assembly of the Church of Scotland, that we are commanded.

To acknowledge with all thankfulnesse to God, their zeal for purging and reforming Religion, and care not only to prevent the grouth, but utterly to extirpate the Reliques of Popery: And also the great blessing of Almighty God upon their so constant and faithful endeavours, thus far establishing them in truth and peace, together with their labour of love, to procure the like happinesse to our Church and Nation.

To give them an account of their earnest desire and endeavour to see the same Work promoted and perfected among our selves; which though it hath been opposed and retarded by the industrious malice of the Popish, Prelaticall, and malignant partie, yet through Gods goodnesse it hath so far prevailed, as to produce the removeall of the High Commission, the making void the coercive power of the Prelates and their Courts, The ejection of the Bishops from the House of Peers, the turning out of many scandalous Ministers, Besides that they have passed and presented to his Majestie diverse Bills, viz. For the suppressing of Innovations, For the more strict observation of the Lords Day, against Pluralities and non-residencie, For the punishment of the scandalous Clergie, For the abolition of Episcopacie, and the calling an Assembly: The true Copies of which, we herewithall deliver. Which Bills, through the underminning of the Papists, Prelates, and their party (the constant enemies of Reformation) have not yet obtained his Majesties Royall assent. And yet considering the urgent necessity of purging and settling the Church (as hath been often pressed and presented to the Parliament of England, by pious and frequent exhortations and Declarations from that reverent Assembly) they have been constrained by an Ordinance of both Houses, to call an Assembly of Divines, and others, now fitting, to consider and prepare what may conduce thereunto, which by the assistance of some godly and learned Divines sent from this Nation (as is earnestly desired) we hope may through the blessing of God, bring it to perfection.

And yet notwithstanding to let them know that by reason of the prevailing of the Papists, Prelaticall Faction, and other malignant enemies to this so much desired Reformation, (all of them being now in arms against the Parliament) these hopefull beginnings are likely, not onely to be rendred ineffectuall, but all the former evils, superstitions, and corruptions (which for the present, through the blessing of God, are in a good measure removed) to be re-introduced by strong hand which if once they should take root again in the Church and Kingdome of England, will quickely spread their venome & infection into the neighbour Church and Kingdome of Scotland the quarrell of the enemies of this Work being not so much against the persons of men, as the power of Godlinesse, and purity of Gods worship, wheresoever it is professed. Both Houses do therefore desire that reverent Assembly to lay seriously to heart the state and condition of their sister Church and Kingdome, and not only by their prayers to assist in these straits, but also by such seasonable and effectuall means as to them shall seem meet, to further and expedite the present aid and assistance demanded by both Houses.

And lastly, to make known unto them, that we are designed and sent by both Houses of Parliament to the Generall Assembly of the Church of Scotland, to propound to them and consult with them concerning such things as may conduce to our own Reformation, and our so much desired conjunction with this Church, which they have more fully expressed in a Declaration of their own, which here withall we present.

August 10. 1643,
William Bond,
Secr. Commiss.

A DECLARATION OF THE LORDS AND COMMONS IN THE PARLIAMENT OF ENGLAND, TO THE GENERALL ASSEMBLY OF THE CHURCH OF SCOTLAND.

The Lords and Commons in Parliament acknowledging with humble thankfulnesse to Almighty God, the disposer of hearts, the Christian zeal and love which the Generall Assembly of the Churches of Scotland, have manifested in their pious endeavours for the preservation of the true reformed Protestant Religion, from the subtle practices and attempts of the Popish and Prelaticall party, to the necessary Reformation of Church discipline and Government in this Kingdome, and the more near union of both Churches, do earnestly desire that reverend Assembly to take notice, that the two Houses of Parliament fully concurring with them in these pious Intentions; for the better accomplishment thereof, have called an Assembly of diverse godly and learned Divines, and others of this Kingdome, unto the City of Westminster, who are now sitting and consulting about these matters, And likewise have nominated and appointed John Earle of Ruthland, Sir William Armine Baronet, Sir Henry Vane the younger, Knight, Thomas Hatcher, and Henry Darley Esquires. Committees and Commissioners of both Houses, to the Kingdome and States of Scotland, who beside their Instructions in matters concerning the

Peace and Common weal of both Kingdomes, have received Directions to resort to the General Assembly of the Church of Scotland, and propound and consult with them, or any Commissioners deputed by them, in all occasions which may further the so much desired Reformation in Ecclesiastical matters in this Church and Kingdome, and a nearer conjunction betwixt both Churches. In performance whereof, Master Stephen Marshal, and Master Philip Nye, Ministers of Gods Word, and men of approved faithfulnesse and abilities in their Function, both Members of this Assembly of Divines here congregated, and sitting, are appointed to assist and advise the same Committee in such things as shall concerne this Church. And the two Houses do hereby recommend the Commitees and divines afore-mentioned, to the reverend Assembly of the Church of Scotland, to be by them received with favour, and credited in those things, which they, or any three, or more of them shall propound to them.

It is likewise desired, that that reverend Assembly will according to their former promise and resolution, send to the Assembly here, such number of godly and learned Divines, as in their wisedome they think most expedient for the furtherance of this work, which so much concernes the honour of God, the prosperity and peace of the two Churches of England and Scotland; and which must needs have a great influence in procuring more safe and prosperous condition to other reformed Churches abroad. And that their endeavours may be more effectual, the two Houses do make this request to them, with their authority, advice and exhortation, so far as belongs to them, to stir up that Nation to send some competent Forces in aid of this Parliament and Kingdome, against the many Armies of the Popish and Prelatical party, and their adherents, now in arms for the ruine and destruction of the reformed Religion, and all the Professours thereof. In all which they shall do that which will be pleasing to God, whose cause it is, and likewise safe and advantageous to their own Church and Kingdome, who cannot securely enjoy the great blessings of Religion, Peace, and Libertie in that Kingdome, if this Church and Kingdome, by the prevailing violence of that partie, shall bee brought to ruine and destruction.

Jo. Browne, Cleric. Parliamentorum.
Henr. Elsynge, Cler. Parliamentorum.

A LETTER FROM SOME BRETHREN OF THE MINISTERIE IN THE KIRK OF ENGLAND, TO THE ASSEMBLY.

Reverend and beloved;

The experience which we have had of your forwardnesse in receiving, and faithfulnesse in weighing our former addresses, hath given us abundant encouragement to take hold upon this present opportunitie of breathing out something of our sorrowes, which your love and our necessity, command us to represent to your consideration and compassion. Much we know we may commit to the wisedome and fidelity of our Brethren these messengers, to impart unto you concerning our miserable condition, and unto them shall leave the most. Your own Nationall, but specially Christian interest, will not permit you to hide your eyes from the bleeding condition of your poor distressed Brethren in England, should neither Letters, nor Messengers be sent unto you; But Messengers coming, we should at once neglect our selves, should we not thus a little ease our burdened hearts, by pouring them out into your bosomes, and seem ungrateful to you, of whose readinesse to suffer with us, and do for us, we have had so great & ample testimonies.

Surely if ever a poor Nation were upon the edge of a most desperate precipice, if ever a poor Church were ready to be swallowed up by Satan and his Instruments, we are that Nation, we are that Church. And in both respects by so much the more miserable, by how much, we expected not a Preservation onely, but an augmentation also, of happinesse in the one, and glory in the other. We looked for Peace, but no good came, and for a time of healing, and behold trouble! Our GOD who in his former Judgements was a moth & rottenesse (and yet had of late begun to send us health and cure) is now turned into a Lion to us: and threatens to rend the very cawle of our hearts: From above he hath sent a fire into our bones, and it prevails against us; From our own bowels he hath called forth, and strengthened an adversarie against us, a generation of brutish hellish men, the rod of his anger, and the staff of his indignation, under whose cruelties we bleed, and if present mercy step not in, we die. Righteous art thou, O LORD, and just are all thy Judgements! But O the more then barbarous carriages of our enemies, where ever GOD gives any of his hidden ones up into their hands, we need not expresse it unto you, who knows the inveterate and deadly malice of the Antichristian faction against the Members of our Lord Jesus. And it is well we need not expresse it unto you, for in truth we cannot. Your own thoughts may tell you better then any words of ours, what the mercie of Papists is, toward the Ministers and Servants of our Lord Jesus Christ. But the Lord knows we are not troubled so much with their rage against us, or our own miseries and dangers; but that which breaks our hearts is, the danger we behold the Protestant Religion, and all the Reformed Churches in at this time, through that too great and formidable strength the Popish Faction is now arrived at. If our GOD will lay our bodies as the ground, and as the street under their foot, and poure out our bloud as dust before their fury, the wil of the Lord be done, might our bloud be a sacrifice to ransome the rest of the Saints or Church of Christ from Antichristian fury, we would offer it up upon this service gladly. But we know their rage is insatiable, and will not be quenched with our blouds, immortall, and will not die with us, armed against us, nor as men, but as Christians, but as Protestants, but as men desiring to reform our selves, and to draw our selves and others yet nearer unto God. And if God gave us up to be devoured by this rage, it will take the more strength and courage (at least) to attempt the like against all the Protestant and Reformed Churches. In a deeper sense of this extream danger, threating us and you, and all the Churches then we can expresse, we have made this addresse unto you; in the bowels of our Lord Jesus Christ, humbly imploring your most fervent Prayers to the GOD that hears Prayers; who (should we judge by providences) seems to be angry with our Prayers (though we trust he doth but seem so, and though he kill us, yet will we trust in him) Oh, give us the brotherly aide of your re-inforced tears and payers, that the blessings of truth and peace which our prayers alone have not obtained, yours combined, may. And give us reverend and much honoured in our Lord your advices, what remains for us further to doe, for the making of our own and the Kingdomes peace with GOD.

We have lien in the dust before him; we have poured our hearts in humiliation to him, we have in sincerity, endeavoured to reform our selves, and no lesse sincerely desired, studied, laboured the publick Reformation, Neverthelesse the Lord hath not yet turned himself from the fiercenesse of his anger. And be pleased to advise us further, what may be the happiest course for the uniting of the Protestant partie more firmly? That we may all serve GOD with one consent, and stand up against Antichrist as one man, that our GOD who now hides himself from his people may return unto us, delight in us scatter and subdue his and our enemies, and cause his face to shine upon us. The Lord prosper you and preserve us for that the great work of these latter ages may be finished to his honour, and our own and the Churches happinesse through Christ Jesus.

Subscribed by very many hands.

SESS. 9. AUGUST 11. 1643.

ACT AGAINST BURIALS AND HINGING OF HONOURS, &C. IN KIRKS.

The Generall Assembly considering the great abuse of burying within Kirks, wherein GODS publick worship is exercised, notwithstanding diverse Acts of this Kirk, prohibiting the same. And that through toleration thereof, other abuses in hinging of Pensils and Brods, affixing of Honours and Arms, and such like scandalous Monuments in the Kirk, hath crept in. Therefore for remedy hereof, do hereby ratifie and approve the former Acts and Constitutions made against burials in Kirks. And inhibites and discharges all persons of whatsoever qualitie, to bury any deceased person within the body of the Kirk, where the people meet for hearing of the Word, and administration of the Sacraments. And inhibites them to hing Pensils or Brods, to affixe Honours or Arms, or to make any such like Monuments, to the honour or remembrance of any deceased person upon walls, or otherplaces within the Kirk, where the publick worship of God is exercised, as said is.

SESS. 10. AUGUST 12. 1643.

ACT ANENT REPOSITION OF MINISTERS, DEPOSED BY SUPERIOUR JUDICATORIES.

The Generall Assembly considering that sentences of Superiour Judicatories of the Kirk should stand effectuall, while they be taken away by themselves, and that they should not be made void and ineffectuall by Inferiour Judicatories: Therefore discharges all Provinciall Assemblies to repone any Minister deposed by the Generall Assembly. And all Presbyteries to repone any Ministers deposed either by General or Provincial Assemblies; And declares and ordains, that all such sentences of reposition by these Inferiour Judicatories respectivè, shall be null in themselves; And that the sentences of deposition by the Superiour Judicatories respectivé shall stand valid and effectual notwithstanding thereof.

SESS. 11. AUG. 14. 1643.

ACT AGAINST MASTERS WHO HAVE SERVANTS THAT PROPHANE THE LORDS DAY.

The Generall Assembly declares, that the Acts made against Salmond fishing upon the Sabbath, or against any other labour upon the Lords day, to be not only against servants who actually work: But also that the samine should be extended against masters, whose hired servants they are.

SESS. 12. AUG. 15. 1643.

ACT FOR PREPARING THE DIRECTORIE FOR THE WORSHIP OF GOD.

The Assembly considering how convenient it is, that all the Ministers of the particular Kirks within this Kingdome, in their administration, keep unity and uniformity in the substance and right ordering of all the parts of the publick worship of God, and that all the particular Kirks by the same unity and uniformity, testifie their unanimous consent against all schisme and division, unto which these times, through the working of Satan and his instruments, against the propagation of the Gospel of peace are so inclinable: Doth ordain, that a Directorie for divine worship, with all convenient diligence be framed and made ready in all the parts thereof, against the next Generall Assembly, to be held in the year 1644. And for this end that such as shall be nominate by this Assembly, shall immediatly after the rising of the Assembly, set themselves apart (so far as may be) from their particular callings, and with all diligence and speed, go about this so publick, so pious and so profitable a work. And when they have brought their endeavours and labours about this Directorie to an end, that it be put into the hands of the Commissioners of the Generall Assembly, to be revised, and thereafter by them sent in severall Copies to all the particular Synods to be held in April and May, that the famine being reported with their observations, notes, and animadversions to the Generall Assembly, it may in end, after their full triall and approbation, by order and authority from them be received, and practiced by all the Ministers and particular Kirks. And for preserving of peace and brotherly unity, in the mean while, till the Directorie by universall consent of the whole Kirk be framed, finished, and concluded, The Assembly forbiddeth under the pain of the censures of the Kirk, all disputation by word or writing, in private or publick, about different practices in such things, as have not been formerly determined by this Kirk, And all condemning one of another in such lawfull things as have been universally received, and by perpetuall custome practised by the most faithfull Ministers of the Gospell, and opposers of corruptions in this Kirk, since the first beginning of Reformation to these times. And doth exhort and command that all endeavour to keep the unity of the spirit, in the bond of peace, that all beginnings of Separation, all scandall and division, be by all means avoided; And that against envying, and strife, and faction, and glorying in men, every one go before another in the duties of love, and so fulfill the Law of Christ; That continuing in one spirit and one minde, & fighting together through the faith of the Gospel, we may mutually aide, strengthen and comfort one another in all Pastorall and Christian emploiments, better resist the common adversaries, edifie one another in the knowledge and fear of God, and the more acceptably, and with the greater blessing serve the Lord who hath done so great things for us.

PROPOSITIONS FROM THE ENGLISH COMMISSIONERS PRESENTED THIS DAY TO THE ASSEMBLY.

We the Commissioners appointed by both Houses of the Parliament of England, being commanded by them (as we have already declared) to desire the reverend Assembly of Scotland, seriously to lay to heart the present Estate of their Sister Church and Kingdome of England, and not onely to assist with their Prayers in their straits, but also by such reasonable and effectuall means as to themselves shall seem meet to further and expedite the assistance now desired by both Houses from the Kingdome of Scotland, and a more strict union with them, Have thought fit in Pursuance of the commands received from both Houses of Parliament, to communicate to this Assembly the paper which to this purpose we have lately delivered to the Honourable Convention of Estates, in this Kingdome, that so this reverend Assembly might be the better enabled, to contribute their best assistance toward the furthering and expediting of the same. Wherein we assure our selves of their ready and willing affections, considering the great service they may do to God, and the great honour may redound to themselves in becoming the Instruments of a glorious Reformation, not onely through this Iland, but from thence possibly to be spread to other Churches now oppressed under the Antichristian bondage, and tyrannie of the Popish and prelatical Faction. We will not say there lies any obligation upon this Church and Kingdome, to comply with the desires of the two Houses of Parliament; though we might call to minde that God by the hand of the Church and Kingdome of England, did once reach forth assistance and aid unto this Nation, and hath since used them as a help to that blessed Reformation it now enjoyes. And who knoweth whether the wise providence of God hath not suffered this Church and Kingdome to be tempted thereby, to make them the more feasible of the present miseries of their brethren, and likewise given them a good issue, with the tentation, that they might be made a means of our deliverance? We shall not need to offer any grounds of prudence to invite them hereunto, who have already prevented us in the acknowledgement of what might be said of that kinde in the advice presented by the Commissioners of the General Assembly. July 6. 1643. unto the Convention of Estates, expressing as one remedie of the present dangers of this Church and Kingdome, their earnest desire of renewing the league and association with England, for the defence of Religion against the common enemie, and of further extending the same against Prelacie, and Popish Ceremonies, for Uniformity in externall worship and Church-government. And we hope that the same God who hath put these desires into the hearts of both Kingdomes, will make use of this present opportunity to knit them both to himself, and each other in a most strict and durable Union, and thereby the more firmly to establish truth and peace in both Nations. Howsoever this which we have done in discharge of our duty, will afford the comfort of a good conscience in our greatest distresses, and give us ground to expect deliverance some way or other from the manifold wisedome and power of God, who though men and means fail, will not cast off his people, nor forsake his inheritance. We have onely this to adde further, that we are commanded by both Houses to let this reverend Assembly know that it is their earnest desire, that what other Propositions may be thought fit to be added and concluded by this Assembly, whereby the assistance and Union betwixt the two Nations, may be made more beneficiall and effectuall for the securing of Religion and Libertie, should be offered to us, and taken to our speedy consideration,

August 15. 1643.

William Bond. Secr. Com.

THE PAPER BEFORE-MENTIONED, DELIVERED AUGUST 12. TO THE CONVENTION, AND THIS DAY TO THE ASSEMBLY

We the Commissioners appointed by both Houses of the Parliament of England, are by our instructions commanded to put their brethren of Scotland in minde, that the Popish and prelaticall Faction that began with them, about the year 1638. and 1639. and then intended to make way to the ruine of the Kingdome of England by theirs, have not abated any part of their malice toward the Nation and Church of Scotland, nor are at all departed from their designe of corrupting and altering Religion through the whole Iland, though they have inverted the manner of their proceeding, conceiving now that they have an easier way to destroy them, if they may first prevail over the Parliament and Kingdome of England. In which respect it is the desire of both Houses, that the two Nations may be strictly united, for their mutuall defence against the Papists and prelaticall Faction, and their adherents in both Kingdomes, and not to lay down arms till those their implacable enemies shall be dis-armed, and subjected to the authority and justice of Parliament in both Kingdomes respectively. And as an effectual mean hereunto, they desire their brethren of Scotland to raise a considerable force of Horse and Foot, for their aide and assistance, to be forthwith sent against the Papists, prelatical Faction, and malignants now in arms in the Kingdome of England.

And for the better encouragement of the Kingdome of Scotland to this necessary and so much desired Union, we are by both Houses of Parliament authorized to assure their brethren, that if they shall be annoyed or endangered by any Force or Army, either from England or any other place, the Lords and Commons of England will assist them with a proportionable strength of Horse and Foot, to what their Brethren shall now affoord them to be sent into Scotland for the defence of that Kingdome. And they will maintain a guard of Ships at their own charge upon the coast of Scotland for the securing of that Kingdome, from the invasion of Irish Rebels or other enemies, during such time as the Scotish Army shall be employed in the defence of the Kingdome of England, And to the end that nothing might be wanting in the Parliament and Kingdome of England to facilitate this work (wherein the true reformed Religion, not onely in these two Kingdomes, but throughout all Europe is so highly concerned) We are farther authorized to consider with their brethren the Estates and Kingdome of Scotland, of what other Articles or propositions are fit to be added and concluded, whereby this assistance and Union betwixt the two Nations, may be made more beneficial and effectual for the security of Religion and Libertie in both Kingdomes.

All which being taken into the serious and Christian consideration of the right honourable the Lords and others of the Convention of the Estates of Scotland, we hope there will not need many arguments to perswade and excite them to give their consent, and that with all convenient speed, to these desires of both houses of the Parliament of England; seeing now they have so fully declared, as by what they have done already, so by what they are yet desirous to do, that the true state of this cause and quarrel is Religion, in the Reformation whereof they are, and have been so forward and zealous, as that there is not any thing expressed unto them by their brethren of Scotland, in their former or latter Declarations, which they have not seriously taken to heart, and seriously endeavoured to effect, (notwithstanding the subtle malicious and industrious oppositions) that so the two Kingdomes might be brought into a near conjunction in one form of Church-government, one directorie of worship, one Catechisme, &c. and the foundation laid of the utter extirpation of Popery and prelacie out of both Kingdomes. The most ready and effectual means whereunto, is now conceived to be, that both Nations enter into a strict Union and league, according to the desires of the two Houses of Parliament.

And to induce the perswasion of this (if there were cause) we might observe, that, in the many Declarations made by the General Assembly or States of Scotland, to their Brethren of England, there have been sundry expressions, manifesting the great necessitie that both Kingdomes for the securitie of their Religion and Liberties, should joyn in this strict Union against the Papists, Prelats, and their adherents: As also in the endeavour of a near conjunction between the Churches of both Nations. The apprehension and foresight of which, hath caused the Popish and Prelatical Faction in forreigne parts as well as in his Majesties Dominions, strictly and powerfully to combine themselves to the hinderance of this so necessary Work, and the universal suppression of the true protestant Religion in Europe: A course not much different from that which they took in the year 1585. when the wisedome and zeal of this Nation to counter-myne so wicked a conspiracie, and from the due sense of the mutual interest of these two Kingdomes in Religion and Libertie, found a necessity of entring into a league of this nature, as well considering, that thereby no lesse safetie might be expected to both Nations, then danger by forbearing the same. And though we doubt not but in so necessary and so good a Work, many difficulties may arise to interrupt and retard the same; yet we are as confident, that the heartie and brotherly affection of this Nation to the Parliament and Kingdome of England, will easily break through them; and the rather because in the like cases of difficultie and danger, not only at the time of the league above-mentioned, but before, and likewise since, when any opportunity hath offered it self particularly, during the sitting of this present Parliament, the Kingdome of England hath been very forward and ready to lay to heart the dangers of the Kingdome of Scotland as their own, and to decline no means within the reach of their power for the redresse or prevention of the same.

August 12. 1643.

William Bond Secr. Com.

SESS. 13. AUG. 16. 1643.

RECOMMENDATION TO THE PRESBYTERIES AND UNIVERSITIES ANENT STUDENTS THAT HAVE THE IRISH LANGUAGE.

The Assembly considering the lamentable condition of the people in the Highlands, where there are many that gets not the benefite of the Word in respect there are very few Preachers that can speak the Irish language, Do for remeid thereof think good, that young Students who have the Irish tongue, be trained up at Colledges in Letters, especially in the studies of Divinitie, And to this effect recommend to Presbyteries and Universities to preferre any hopefull Students that have the language aforesaid, to Bursaries, that they by their studies in processe of time attaining to knowledge, and being enabled for the Ministerie, may be sent forth for preaching the Gospel in these Highland parts, as occasions shall require.

SESS. 14. AUGUST 17. 1643.

THE LETTER FROM THE ASSEMBLY OF DIVINES IN THE KINGDOME OF ENGLAND.

To the right reverend the Generall Assembly of the Church of Scotland.

Right reverend and dearly beloved in our Lord Jesus Christ,

We the Assembly of Divines and others, called and now sitting by authority of both Houses of Parliament, to be consulted by them in matters of Religion; have received from the honourable Houses of Commons, a speciall order (dated the 3. of this instant August) recommending it to us to write a Letter to the Generall Assembly of the Church of Scotland, taking notice of the pious and good expeditions to this Church and State, certified in the late Answer of the Commissioners of the Generall Assembly of the Kirk of Scotland, from their meeting at Edinburgh the 17. of July 1643. And further to desire them to possesse the people of that Kingdome with our condition, and to encourage them to our assistance in this cause of Religion. And having with that order received and read the said Answer directed to the honourable Houses of the Parliament of England, we cannot sufficiently expresse the great content and comfort, unto which it hath raised us in the midst of the sad and calamitous condition under which we lie.

It is no small refreshing to our mourning spirits to finde, that yet our God hath not left us wholly comfortlesse, nor cast us so far out of his sight, as having made us sick with smiting that should be verified of us, Lover and friend hast thou put far from us, and that no man should turn aside to ask how we do: but that we finde so many of the Churches of Christ, and above them all, our dearest Brethren of Scotland, so far to take to heart our extremities, as to sit in the dust with us, and so to look upon our adversities, as being themselves also in the body.

And as we cannot render thanks sufficient unto our God for remembring such mercie in the midst of so much wrath; so we embrace with all chearfulnesse this opportunitie of thankfull acknowledgement of the great debt which your love doth continually lay upon, not us alone, but upon this whole Kingdome, in the free and full expressions of your care, piety and zeal, and of like affections of that whole Nation, to assist and concurre with the Parliament here, by all good and lawfull means, for sending of Religion in godly unity and uniformitie throughout all his Majesties Dominions, against all the designes, power and malice of bloudie Papists, and the Prelaticall Faction, with all their malignant adherents, the common enemies of Reformation, truth and peace.

We are likewise much ingadged to the great vigilancie and travels of the honourable Convention of the Estates of Scotland, in contributing their brotherly advice, and for their readinesse to give assistance for recovering and settling the peace of this Kingdome, against the devices, power and practices of the enemies of Religion, and the publick Good, whereof some hints are given in that Answer and of which we doubt not but the honourable Houses or Parliament will be so sensible as to give such a return as becomes them: for they, better knowing then we do, the depth of the evils under which this Nation now groaneth, and the further dangers imminent, will be more able to value and improve the great affection and wisedome of their Brethren, in points of so high and generall concernement, for the safetie and glory of the Kings Majestie, and of all his Kingdomes, and are more fit to take notice of advices of that kinde, in reference to the civil State, which therefore we wholly leave with them.

But as for the many prudent, pious, and reosonable admonitions which concerne our Assembly, the good Lord reward (for we cannot) seven fold into your bosomes all the good, which you have laboured to procure unto the House of our GOD, and blessed be his Name who hath put such a thing as this into the hearts of our Parliament, to cleanse the House of the Lord of all the uncleannesse that is in it, by impure Doctrine, Worship, or Discipline.

Nor can we in the depth of all our sufferings and sorrows, withhold our hearts from rejoycing in the wonderful goodnes of God toward this Kingdome, in that he hath let us see the gracious fruit of your effectuall prayers and teares, as well as of our own endeavours this way: In bringing together this Assembly, although in a very troublous time, whereby we may have better opportunity more fully to poure out our soules jointly and together to our GOD, for healing of this now miserable Church and Nation: To consider throughly, for what more especially the Land mourneth, and how we may be most usefull to our great GOD and Master JESUS CHRIST; In contributing somewhat to the vindicating of his precious truth, many wayes corrupted through the craft of men that have lyen in wait to deceive: In the seeking out of a right way of worshipping our GOD according to his own heart: In promoting the power of Godlinesse: in the hearts and lives of all his people, and in laying forth such a Discipline as may be most agreeable to Gods holy Word, and most apt to procure and preserve the peace of this Church at home, and nearer agreement with the Church of Scotland (highly honoured by us) and other the best reformed Churches abroad, That so to the utmost of our power, we may exalt him that is the only Lord over the Church, his own House, in all his Offices, and present this Church as a chast virgin unto Christ.

It is a timely and savourie prayer which you have put up at the throne of

Grace, touching the due managing of the proceedings in this Assembly, and that with straigth intentions we may all seek the truth in every thing, which by the blessing of God upon our labours, must needs produce all those blessings which your worthie Commissioners mention. And now, for your comfort as well as our own encouragement, we desire you to take notice of the gracious answer of the God that heareth prayer, unto your fervent cryes. For beside our own particular addresses and secret vows to our God to be faithful (with disdain of all baits of avarice and ambition) it hath pleased the Divine Providence so to direct both the honourable Houses of Parliament, to take care of preventing all obliquitie in our proceedings, and to stop the mouthes of all that watch for their and our haltings, and are apt maliciously to traduce both, (as if we were so restrained by them, in our votes and resolutions, as to be bound up to the sense of others, and to carry on private designes in a servile way) that the Houses have tendered to us, and we have most readily taken a solemne and serious Protestation in the presence of Almighty God, to maintain nothing in this Assembly touching Doctrine, but what we are perswaded in our consciences to be the truth; nor in matters of Discipline, but what we conceive to conduce most to the glory of God, and the good and peace of his Church; which doth not only secure the Members against fettering of their judgements or votes, but engage them to the use of all freedome, becoming the integrity of conscience, the weight of the Cause, the gravitie and honour of such an Assembly. It is likewise a great consolation, that our GOD hath put it into your hearts to designe some godly and learned Brethren to put in their sickles with us into this Harvest, which is so great, and requires so many Labourers; for which, as we heartily return thanks, so we earnestly pray the Lord to open a way to their timely coming hitherto and do assure them of all testimonies of respect, love, and the right hand of fellowship, who shall under-take a journey so tedious, and now so perillous, to joyne with us in the Work, when it shall please the honourable Houses of Parliament to invite them thereunto.

It remaines that we should now spread before you our calamities, dangers and fears of further evils, not only drawing toward us, but even threatning you also; and crave your passionate aids in all wayes becoming the Servants of Jesus Christ. But your Commissioners have so fully declared your certain knowledge and deep sense of them, that they have left us no room for inlarging ourselves in this particular, to Brethren so full of bowels and zeal. And they have sufficiently intimated unto the honourable Houses, that you are well aware how often the common enemies of both Kingdomes have consulted together with one consent to cut off both the one and the other from being a Nation, and that the Tabernacles of Edom, and the Ishmaelites of Moab, and the Hagarens, Geball, Ammon, and Amalek, the cursed Papists, and their implacable and bloudy Abettors here, do still retain the same malice, and carry on the same designe against Religion, and perfect Reformation even in your Kingdome, happily rescued from their former tyrannies, as well as in this of scorched England, now in the furnace: Only they have varied the Scene, pouring out all their fury upon us at the present: That so, having once troden us under as mire in the streets, they may afterward more easily; (which God avert) set their proud and impure feet upon your necks also. Wherefore the good leave and favour of the honourable Houses of Parliament, we shall now spare the further exciting of you to that which we doubt not of your forwardnesse by all lawfull and meet means to promote with all your might; namely, the possessing the good people of that Kingdome; (of whose willing minde and readinesse you have already given ample testimony) touching our condition, and to encourage them to our assistance in this Cause of Religion.

And now remembring without ceasing your work of faith, and labour of love, and patience of hope in our Lord Jesus Christ, with all due acknowledgments of the precious effects of your prayers; We most humbly and earnestly desire, that the same breathings of the spirit in you may still continue, and (if possible) more frequently and fervently ascend to your God, and our God, not only for removall of outward pressures, and the visitation of the sword, that hath already learned to eat much of our flesh, but also for the special assistance and protection of the Father of lights, in this great Work unto which we are now called, and wherein we already finde many and potent adversaries: that seeing the plummet is now in the hands of our Zerubbabels, all mountaines may become plains, and they may bring forth the capstone of the Lords House with shoutings, crying, Grace, grace unto it: and that how weak and contemptible builders soever we be, the Lord would enable us to build with them, that none may have cause to despise the day of our small beginnings, nor to stop our progresse in the work which he hath given us to do, And as for us, who cannot but take notice of the extraordinary employments unto which you are called in your great Assembly, now also sitting: God forbid that we should sin against the Lord, in ceasing to pray for you, that the Lord may enable you to be wise masterbuilders, preserve your peace alwayes by all means, and make you stedfast, unmoveable, alwayes abounding in the work of the Lord, to the praise of the glory of his grace, and to the further benefit and comfort of the whole Church of God, but more especially of this our afflicted Ark, now wafted into the midst of a sea of miseries, and tossed with tempests, untill our wise and gracious God, by the furtherance of your prayers and brotherly endeavours, shall cause it to rest upon the mountains of Ararat, which may take away our fears, as well as put an end to our present sufferings and give you to rejoyce with us, that now mourn for us.

Westminster, August 4. 1643.

Subscribed by your most loving Brethren, highly prisyng the graces of God in you, and that are your Servants for Jesus sake, in the name of the whole Assembly.

William Tuisse, Prelocutor.
John White, Assessor.
Cornelius Burges, Scribe of the Assembly.
Henry Roborough, Scribe of the Assembly.
Adonirum Byfield, Scribe of the Assembly.

THE RESULT OF THE DEBATES AND CONSULTATIONS OF THE COMMITTEES OF THE CONVENTION OF ESTATES AND GENERAL ASSEMBLY, APPOINTED TO MEET WITH THE COMMISSIONERS OF THE PARLIAMENT OF ENGLAND.

August 17. 1643.

The Committees of the Convention of Estates of Scotland, and of the General Assembly, being appointed to meet with the Commissioners of the two Houses of the Parliament of England, upon the Papers delivered in by the said Commissioners, unto the Convention of Estates, and unto the General Assembly, upon the 12. and 15, of this instant 1643. Concerning the desires of both Houses, for a near and strict Union to be entered into by the two Kingdomes. And it being declared at the said meeting, with what sensible affections the General Assembly and Convention, did receive the desires above-mentioned: And how beneficial it would be for the more firme settlement of the said union, that a Covenant should be entred into by both Nations: And this forme thereof being by all the foresaid persons taken into most serious debate and consideration, and agreed unto: It was thereupon resolved by them, that it should be presented to the General Assembly, to the Convention of Estates of Scotland, and to the two Houses of the Parliament of England, by their respective Committees and Commissioners, that it might with all speed receive their respective resolutions.

Subscribed

Ja. Primerose.
A. Ker.
William Bond Sec. Com.

The League and Covenant above-mentioned, being sent with the Commissioners of this Assembly, to the Parliament of England, and Assembly of Divines in that Kingdome, to be received and approven there, is to be printed at the return thereof.

APPROBATION OF THE LEAGUE AND COVENANT ABOVE MENTIONED.

The Assembly having recommended unto a Committee, appointed by them to joyne with the Committee of the Honourable Convention of Estates, and the Commissioners of the Honourable Houses of the Parliament of England, for bringing the Kingdomes to a more near conjunction and Union, received from the aforesaid Committees, the Covenant above mentioned, as the result of their consultations: And having taken the same, as a matter of so publick concernment, and of so deep importance doth require, unto their gravest consideration, Did with all their hearts, and with the beginnings of the feelings of that joy which they did finde in so great measure upon the renovation of the National Covenant of this Kirk and Kingdome, All with one voice approve and embrace the same, as the most powerfull meane, by the blessing of GOD, for settling and preserving the true Protestant Religion, with perfect Peace in his Majesties Dominions, and propagating the same to other Nations, and for establishing his Majesties throne to all ages and generations. And therefore with their best affections recommend the same to the Honourable Convention of Estates, that being examined and approved by them, it may be sent with all diligence to the Kingdome of England: that being received and approven there, the same may be with publick humiliation, and all Religious and answerable solemnitie, sworn and subscribed by all true Professours of the reformed Religion, and all his Majesties good Subjects in both Kingdomes.

SESS. ULT. AUGUST 19. 1643.

THE ASSEMBLIES HUMBLE DESIRES TO HIS MAJESTIE ANENT THE LISTS FOR PRESENTATIONS: WITH A RECOMMENDATION TO PRESBYTERIES.

The Assembly considering the difficultie of obtaining six able and well qualified Persons to be put into a List to his Majestie, for every vaiking Kirk at his Majesties Presentation: Therefore do most earnestly recommend to his Majesties Commissioner, to represent their humble desires to his Majestie, that he would be pleased to accept of a List of three: As also conform to the desire of the last Assembly at S. Andrews, that his Majestie would be pleased to accept of any one qualified man, who shall be able to speak the Irish Language for Kirks vaiking in the Highlands: Which the Commissioners Grace promised to do with the first conveniencie.

And with all his Grace representing to the Assembly, that he conceived his Majestie had already done more, and yet would do more for satisfaction to the desires of this Kirk, anent Patronages, nor any other Patron: And therefore that it were convenient that all other Patrons were earnestly desired to follow his Majesties example; And the Assembly thinking it very necessary that some General course were set down for providing and planning of vaiking Kirks, whereby all occasions of contests and differences amongst Patrons, Presbyteries, and Paroches may be removed, Therefore the Assembly recommend to every Presbyterie, to consult and advise upon the best wayes and means for effectuating hereof, And to report the results of their consultations herein till to the next Assembly.

OVERTURES ANENT WITCH-CRAFT, AND CHARMING, &C.

The abundance and increase of the sin of Witch-craft, in all the sorts and degrees of it in this time of Reformation, is to be taken to heart by this reverend Assembly, who would to that end consider.

I. Of the occasions thereof, which are found to be these especially, extremity of grief, malice, passion, and desire of revenge, pinching povertie, solicitation of other Witches and Charmers; for in such eases the devill assails them, offers aide, and much prevails.

II. Of the reasons and causes of Satans prevailing; which are grosse ignorance, infidelitie, want of the love of the truth (which GOD hath made so long and clearly to shine in our Land) and profanesse of life.

III. Of the means and wayes to bring them to a confession and censure, which we conceive to be, that a standing Commission for a certain time be had from the Lords of Secret Councel, or Justice Generall, to some understanding Gentlemen and Magistrates within the bounds of Presbyteries that shall crave it, giving them power to apprehend, try, and execute justice against such personares are guilty of

Witch-craft within these Presbyteries; For many Paroches want the concurrence of civill Magistrates.

IV. Of the grounds of apprehending them, Which may be a reigning brute of Witch craft, backed with dilations of confessing Witches, being confronted with them; for it is found that the dilations of two or three confessing Witches, hath ordinarily proved true: Also depositions of honest persons, anent malefices committed, or cures used by them, may be a ground of apprehending them.

V. Being apprehended, there would be honest and discreet persons appointed to watch them; for being left alone they are in danger to be suborned and heardened by others, or of destroying themselves.

VI. Ministers would be careful at all times, especially Morning and Evening, to deal with them, by Prayer and Conference, whiles they are in prison or restraint.

VII. The means to prevent the grouth of this wickednesse, are:

That Ministers be every way careful and painful in warning people of the danger thereof, and of Satans temptations, both privately and publickly, and to instruct them in the knowledge of the Gospell, and grounds of Religion, by plain cathechesing, to urge lively faith in Christ, which faith Witches bestow otherwise; Also to presse holinesse of life, and fervent prayes in private, and in Families, and in publick, that they be not led into temptation; And to use the censures of the Kirk against profane persons, such as Cursers, Whoores, Drunkards, and such like, for over such like, he gets great advantage. Finally, it is requisite for preventing of this hainous sin, that people seek knowledge studie to beleeve, walk in holinesse, and continue constant and instant in prayer.

And because Charming is a sort and degree of Witch-craft, and too ordinary in the Land; It would be injoyned to all Ministers to take particular notice of them, to search them out, and such as consult with them, and that the Elders carefully concurre in such search; And this Assembly would think on an uniforme way of censuring these Charmers, and such as employ them, or consult with them, primo quoque tempore.

The Assembly approves the articles and Overtures aforesaid, And ordaines every Presbyterie to take to their further consideration by what other wayes or means, the sins aforesaid of Witch craft, Charming, and consulting with Witches, or Charmers, & such like wickednes, may be tried, restrained, and condignely censured and punished ecclesiastically and civilly: And to report their judgementt herein to the next Assembly.

COMMISSION FOR MINISTERS TO GO TO IRELAND.

The General Assembly having received a Petition subscribed by a very great number in the North of Ireland, intimating their deplorable condition through want of the Ministery of the Gospel, occasioned by the tyrannie of the Prelats, and the sword of the Rebels, and desiring some Ministers, especially such as had been chased from them by the persecution of the Prelats, and some others to be added, either to be sent presently over to reside among them, or declared transportable, that upon invitation from them, they might go and settle there: Together with a

Letter from the Vicount of Airds to that same effect. All which the Assembly hath taken to their serious consideration, being most heartily willing to sympathize with every Member of Christ his body, although never so remote, much more with that plantation there, which for the most part was a branch of the Lord his vine, planted in this Land. In which solicitude, as they would be loath to usurpe without their own bounds, or stretch themselves beyond their own measure, so they dare not be wanting to the inlargement of Christs Kingdome, where so loud a cry of so extreme necessity, could not but stir up the bowels of Christian compassion. And although they conceive, that the present unsettled condition both of Church and State in that Land, will not suffer them (as yet) to loose any, to make any constant abode there; yet they have resolved to send over some for the present exigent, till the next general Assembly, by courses, to stay three moneth allanerly. And therefore do hereby authorize and give Commission to the persons following, to wit, Master William Cockburne Minister at Kirkmichell, and Master Matthew Mackaill minister at Carmanoch, for the first three moneths, beginning upon the 8. of September next. Master George Hatchison Minister at Calmonell, and Master Hugh Henderson Minister at Darly, for the next three moneths, beginning the 8. of December. Master William Adair Minister at Air, and Master John Weir Minister at Dalserfe, for the third three moneths, beginning the 8. of March, 1644. And Master James Hamilton Minister at Drumfreis, and Master John Macclellane Minister at Kirkubright for the last three montths, beginning the 8. of June, the said year 1644. To repair unto the North of Ireland, and there to visit, instruct, comfort, and encourage the scattered flocks of Christ. To employ themselves to their uttermost with all faithfulnesse and singlenesse of heart in planting and watering, according to the direction of Jesus Christ, and according to the Doctrine and Discipline of this Kirk in all things. And if need be (with the concurrence of such of the Ministers as are there) to try and ordain such as shall be found qualified for the Ministery; Giving charge unto the persons foresaids in the sight of God, that in Doctrine, in Worship, in Discipline, and in their daily conversation, they study to approve themselves as the Ministers of Jesus Christ; And that they be countable to the Gener. Ass. of this Kirk in all things. And in case of any of the above-mentioned Ministers be impeded by sicknes, or otherwayes necessarily detained from this service; The Assembly ordains the Commissioners residing at Edinb. for the publick affairs of the Kirk, to nominate in their place well qualified men, who hereby are authorized to underrake the forefaid imployment, as if they had been expresly nominate in the face of the Assemb. And this although possibly it shall not fully satisfie the large expectation of their Brethren in Ireland: yet the Assembly is confident they will take in good part at this time that which is judged most convenient for the present condition, even a mite out of their own, not very great plentie to supply the present necessity: Requiring of them no other recompence, but that they in all chearfulnesse may embrace and make use of the Message of Salvation, and promising to inlargre their indebted bountie at the next Assembly, as they shall finde the Work of the Lord there to require, in the mean while wishing that these who are sent, may come with the full blessing of the Gospel of peace, recommends them, their labours, and these to whom they are sent, to the rich blessing of the great Sheepherd of the flock.

ACT AGAINST MINISTERS HAUNTING WITH EXCOMMU- NICATE PERSONS.

If any Minister haunt the company of an excommunicate person, contrair to the Lawes of this Kirk; The said Minister for the first fault shall be suspended from his Ministerie by his Presbyterie, during their pleasure: And for the second fault be deprived. And in case the Presbyteries be negligent herein, the Provincial Assembly shall censure the Presbyterie thus negligent.

ACT ANENT AN ORDER FOR USING CIVIL EXECUTION AGAINST EXCOMMUNICATE PERSONS.

The Assembly taking to their consideration an Article, in the Heads and Propositions sent to the Assembly held at Edinburgh, in August, 1573. by the Lord Regents Grace, and allowed by that Assembly: Whereof the tenour followes. It is resolved that the Executions of the sentence of Excommunication against Persons excommunicate; after the space of fourtie dayes past, shall be presented to the Lord Thesaurer or his Clerk, who thereupon shall raise Letters by deliverance of the Lords of Session, to charge the Persons Excommunicate, to satisfie the Kirk and obtain themselves absolved under the pain of Rebellion: And in case they passe to the Horne, to cause their Escheits be taken up; and also to raise and cause execute Letters of Caption against them; And these to be done at the Kings Majesties charges: Do ratifie and approve the said Article, And farther that the intention of the said Article may be the better effectuate, doth also ordain, that every Presbyterie cause send to the Procurator, or Agent of the Kirk, the foresaid Execution, that is, an minute or note of the sentences of Excommunication within their bounds, bearing the time and cause thereof: And that under the hands of the Moderatour or Clerk of the Presbyterie, or of the Minister who pronounced the sentence; That the samine may be delivered to his Majesties Thesaurer, Advocate, or Agent. To cause Letters of Horning and Caption be raised and execute, and other diligence to be used against the Excommunicat Persons in manner foresaid. And that all other civil action and diligence may be used against them, warranted and provided by Acts of Parliament, or secret Counsel made thereanent: And that particular account be craved hereof in every General Assembly.

TO THE KINGS MOST EXCELLENT MAJESTIE,

The humble Answer of the National Assembly of the Kirk of Scotland.

Although the many and ample testimonies of Your Majesties Royal favour and bountie towards this Kirk and Kingdome be living and lasting Monuments to hold all Your Majesties good Subjects and us most of all, in remembrance of that duty, which we owe to Your Majestie our great Benefactour, never by any length of time to be deleted out of our minds: Yet when we remember even of conscience we owe honour and subjection unto Your Majestie as our dread Soveraigne, as well in Your Majesties absence as presence, We finde our obligation to be Religious, and thereby much increased: And therefore have we at this time in all our consultations and conclusions, of which some have been of more then ordinary weight and concernment, in answer to certain Propositions, made unto us by the Commissioners of the Houses of Parliament of Your Majesties Kingdome of England, and some Reverend Divines assisting them, fixed our eyes and thoughts upon Your Majesties honour and happinesse, with no other and with no lesse intention, then if we had been honoured by Your Majesties Royal Person in our Assembly. And in like manner have given such Instructions to some Ministers and others, to be sent unto the Assembly of Divines now in England, as next unto the honour of God, and the good of Religion, may most serve for Your Majesties preservation, and the peace of Your Kingdomes: Concerning which, the Commissioners of the last General Assembly have so fully exprest their humble thoughts and desires in their Supplication and Remonstrance sent unto Your Majestie, that we need not adde any thing, and Your Majesties times and affairs forbid all repetition. We do onely in all humilitie beseech Your Majestie to judge of us and our proceedings, by the nature and necessity of our vocation, and the rules prescribed in the word of God for our direction, and not by uncertain rumours, and ungrounded reports of such men as have not the fear of God before their eyes. And do earnestly pray to God Almighty, in whose hands are the hearts of Kings, to incline Your Majesties heart to the counsels of truth and peace, to direct Your Government for the good of your People, the punishment of male-factours, and praise of well-doers, that this fire of unnatural and unchristian warre being extinguished, the People of God, Your Majesties good Subjects may lead a quiet and peaceable life, in all godlinesse and honestie.

THE ANSWER OF THE GENERAL ASSEMBLY OF THE CHURCH OF SCOTLAND, TO THE DECLARATION OF THE HONOURABLE HOUSES OF THE PARLIAMENT OF ENGLAND.

The General Assembly of the Church of Scotland, having received a Declaration from the honourable Houses of the Parliament of England, by their Committees and Commissioners now residing here; have thought good to make knowne unto the Lords and Commons in Parliament, that all the Members of this Assembly, and others well-affected here, do with most thankful respects, take special notice of the expressions which they have been pleased to make in the afore-named Declaration, not only concerning their approbation of the desires and endeavours of the General Assembly of this Kirk, for the Reformation of the Church of England, and the union of both Churches in Religion and Church-government; but also concerning the resolution of both Houses, fully to concurre with them in these pious intentions. With the same thankfulnesse and due reverence, they acknowledge the high respects expressed towards them by both Houses, in directing unto them their Committees and Commissioners, assisted by two reverend Divines, and in desiring some of the godly and learned of this Kirk to be sent unto the Assembly sitting there.

The Assembly doth blesse the Lord, who hath not only inspired the Houses of Parliament with desires and resolutions of the Reformation of Religion, but hath advanced by several steps and degrees that blessed Work; By which, as they shall most approve themselves to the Reformed Churches abroad, and to their Brethren of Scotland, so shall they most powerfully draw even from Heaven the blessings of prosperity and peace upon England. And as it is the earnest wish of their Brethren here, that the true state and ground of the present differences and controversies in England may be more and more cleared to be concerning Religion, and that both Houses may uncessantly prosecute that good Work first and above all other matters, giving no sleep to their eyes, nor slumber to their eye-lids, until they finde out a place for the Lord, an habitation for the mighty GOD of Jacob, whose favour alone can make their mountain strong, and whose presence in his own ordinances shall be their glory in the midst of them: So it is our confidence, that the begun Reformation is of GOD, and not of man, that it shall increase, and not decrease; and that he to whom nothing is to hard, who can make mountaines, valleyes, crooked things, straigth, and rough wayes, smooth, shall lead along and make perfect this most wonderful Work, which shall be remembred to his glory in the Church throughout all generations.

And lest through any defect upon the General Assemblies part, the Work of Reformation (which hitherto to the great grief of all the Godly hath moved so slowly) should be any more retarded or interrupted, they have according to the renewed desires of both Houses of Parliament, and their own former promises, nominated and elected Master Alexander Henderson, Mr Robert Douglas, Mr Samuel Rutherfoord, Mr Robert Balzie, Mr George Gillespie, Ministers of Gods Word; and John Earle of Cassels, John Lord Maitland, and Sir Archbald Jonhstuon of Warritoun, ruling Elders, all of them men much approved here; With Commission and power to them, or any three of them, whereof two shall be Ministers, to repair unto the Assembly of Divines, and other of the Church of England, now sitting at Westminster, to propound, consult, treat, and conclude with them, and with any Committees deputed by the Houses of Parliament; (if it shall seeme good to the honourable Houses in their wisedome to depute any for that end) in all such things as may conduce to the utter extirpation of Popery, Prelacie, Heresie, Schisme, Superstition and Idolatrie, And for the feeling of the so much desired Union of this whole island in one forme of Church government, one Confession of Faith, one common Catechisme, and one Directorie for the Worship of GOD, according to the Instructions which they have received, or shall receive from the Commissioners of the Generall Assembly appointed to meet at Edinburgh from time to time, with the Assemblies power for that end. And as the Generall Assembly doth most gladly and affectionatly receive and fully trust the Committees and Divines sent hither, so do they hereby commend the afore-named Commissioners, not only to the like affection and trust of the Assembly there, but also to the favour and protection of both Houses of Parliament.

And for the further satisfaction and encouragement of their Brethren of England, the whole Assembly in their own name, and in name of all the particular Churches in this Kingdome, whom they represent; Do hereby declare, that from their zeal to the glory of GOD, and propagation of the Gospell, from their affection to the happinesse of their native King, and of the Kingdome of England, and from the sense of their own interest in the common dangers of Religion, Peace, and Libertie, They are most willing and ready to be united and associated with their Brethren in a nearer League and solemne Covenant for the maintenance of the truly reformed Protestant Religion, against Popery and Prelacie, and against all Popish and Prelatical corruptions, in doctrine, discipline, worship, or Church-government, and for the settling and holding fast of unity and uniformity betwixt the Kirks of this Iland, and with the best reformed Churches beyond sea. Which Union and Covenant, shall with Gods assistance be seconded by their cooperating with their Brethren in the use of the best and most effectall meanes that may serve for so good ends; For the more speedy effectuating whereof, to the comfort and inlargement of their distressed Brethren (whose hope deferred might make their hearts to faint) the whole Assembly with great unanimity of judgement, and expressions of much affection have approved (for their part) such a draught and forme of a mutuall Leagu and Covenant betwixt the Kingdomes, as was the result of the joint debates and consultations of the Commissioners from both Houses, assisted by the two reverend Divines, and of the Committees deputed from the Convention of the Estates of this Kingdome, and from the Genrall Assembly:

Expecting and wishing the like approbation thereof by the right honourable the Lords and Commons in Parliament, and by the reverend Assembly there, That thereafter it may be solemnely sworne and subscribed in both Kingdomes, as the surest and straitest obligation to make both stand and fall together in that cause of Religion and Libertie.

As the Estates of this Kingdome have often professed in their former Declarations, the integritie of their Intentions against the common enemies of Religion and Libertie in both Kingdomes, and their great affection to their Brethren of England, by reason of so many and so near relations: So doubtlesse now in this time of need they will not fail to give reall proof of what before they professed. A friend loveth at all times, and a brother is born for adversitie. Neither shall the Assembly, or their Commissioners be wanting in exhorting all others to their duty, or in concurring so far as belongeth to their place and vocation, with the Estates now conveened, in any lawful and possible course which may most conduce to the good of Religion and Reformation, the honour and happinesse of the Kings Majestie, the deliverance of their Brethren of England from their present calamitous condition, and to the perpetuating of a firme and happy peace betwixt the Kingdomes.

THE ASSEMBLIES ANSWER TO THE RIGHT REVEREND THE ASSEMBLY OF DIVINES IN THE CHURCH OF ENGLAND.

Right reverend and dearly beloved,

As the sufferings of Christ abound in you, So our heartie desire to God is, that your consolations may much more abound by Christ. The perusing of your Letter, produced in every one of us such a mixture of affections, as were at the laying of the foundation of the second Temple, where there was heard both shouting for joy, and weeping aloud; We rejoyced that Christ our Lord had at last in that Land created a new thing, in calling together, not as before of a Prelaticall Convocation to be task-masters over the people of the Lord, but an Assembly of godly Divines, minding the things of the Lord, whose hearts are set to purge the defiled House of GOD in that Land: yet this our joy was not a little allayed by the consideration of the sad and deplorable condition of that Kingdome, where the high provocations of so many years, the hellish plots of so many enemies in a nick of time, have brought in an inundation of over-flowing calamities: We know you are patiently bearing the indignation of the Lord, because you have sinned against him, till he throughly plead your cause, and disquiet the inhabitants of Babylon, who now laugh among themselves, while you are fed with the bread of tears, and get tears to drink in great measure, being on the mountains like the doves of the valleyes, all of you mourning every one for his iniquitie.

It is now more nor evident to all the Kirks of Christ, with what implacable fury and hellish rage, the bloud-thirstie Papists, as Babylon without, and the Prelaticall Faction, the children of Edom within, having adjoyned to themselves many malignant adherents, of time-serving Atheists, haters of holinesse, rejecters of the yoke of Christ, (to whom the morning light of Reformation is as the shadow of death) have begun to swallow up the inheritance of the Lord, and are not easily satisfied in making deep and long furrowes on your backs. We cannot say that the loudnesse of your cry surpasseth the heavinesse of your stroake; but though the Lord hath delivered the men, every one into his neigbours hand, and into the hand of his King, and they have smitten the Land, yet the rod of the wicked shall not not rest upon the lot of the righteous: This cloud shall speedily passe away, and a fair sun-shine shall appear.

As for us, though your extreme calamitie did not threaten the ruine of our Religion, Peace, and Liberties, as it doth most evidently, we would hate our selves, if we did not finde our hearts within us melting with compassion over you: You are engraven on the tables of our hearts to live and die with you: we could desire that our heads were waters, and our eyes a fountain of tears, that we might weep day and night for the slain of the daughter of the Lords people; So calamitous a condition of any of the Kirks of Christ, could not but be very grievous unto us; How much more shall not we stoup and fall down in the dust to embrace our dearest Brethren of England, to whom we are tied in to near and tender relations. When we were but creeping out of the deep darknesse and bondage of Popery, and were almost crushed with the fury of Foreigne Invaders, joined with intestine enemies, pretending the name and warrand of authority, as now your oppressours do; Then did the Lord by your Fathers send us seasonable assistance against that intended and begun bondage both of soul and body: The repayment of which debt, the Divine Providence seemeth now to require at our hands. And whereas of late through our security we had fallen into a wofull relapse, and were compassed about with dreadfull dangers on all hands, while we aymed at the recovery of our former puritie and libertie: Then we wanted not the huge supply of your fervent Prayers, and other brotherly assistance of that Nation, while those who are now your malignant enemies, would have swallowed us up.

These strait bonds of your ancient and late love, do so possesse our hearts, that when the motions of the Commissioners of honourable House of Parliament, and your Letters did challenge our advice and aid for defence of Religion, and advancement of Reformation, our desires for a more strict Union and Uniformitie in Religion betwixt both the Nations, did break forth into a vehement flame, in such sort, as when the draugt of a League and Covenant betwixt both Kingdoms for defence of Religion, &c. was read in open audience, it was so unanimously and heartily embraced, with such a torrent of most affectionate expressions, as none but eye or ear witnesses can conceive whereof the two reverend Divines sent from you to us being then present, no doubt will give you an account. Neither was it so onely with us, but also the honourable Convention of Estates here, with the like harmony of affectionate expressions, did entertain the same; So that we hope to be reall and constant in prosecuting the contents of this Covenant. When we in our straits fled to the Lord, and entred in Covenant with him, he owned us and our Cause, rebuked and dissipated our enemies, and hitherto hath helped us, and blessed our entreprises with successe from heaven, notwithstanding our great weaknesse and unworthinesse. We trust in the Lord, that as once it was prophesied of Israel & Judah, So shall Scotland & England shall become one stick in the hand of the Lord, they shall ask the way to Sion, with their faces thitherward, saying, Come, let us joyne our selves to the Lord in a perpetual Covenant, that shall not be forgotten; And so shall it come to passe, that the Lords Jerusalem in this Island, shall be a cup of trembling, and a burthensome stone to all their enemies roundabout. Though now it be the time of Jacobs trouble, the Lord will deliver him out of it. Reverend and dear Brethren, we conceive your case, and of all the Faithful in that Land to be no other then of a woman crying, travelling in birth, and pained till she be delivered. The great red Dragon, (under whose standard the sons of Belial are fighting) is your Arch enemy, This cannot but be a time of fear and sorrow; But when the male childe shall be brought forth, the pain shall cease, and the sorrow shall be forgotten. We are very confident in the Lord, that you will be faithful to Jesus Christ, in the work committed to you by him in all his ordinances, and taking neither foundation, corner stone, nor any part of the rubbish of Babel to build the City that is called, The Lord is there: But measuring all with the golden reed of the Sanctuary, you may more closely be united to the best Reformed Kirks, in Doctrine, Worship, and Government, that you may grow up in him in all things which is the head, even Christ.

And now Reverend and dear Brethren, though we know that you abound in all gifts and graces, the Spirit of Jesus Christ being plentifully powred out upon you, yet according to your desire and the motion made by the Commissioners of the Honourable Houses of Parliament, to testifie our hearty sympathie with you in the work of the Lord, We have nominate and elected some Godly and learned of this Church to repair to your Assembly. We doubt nothing of your hearty embracing them in the Lord, and their diligent concurrance with you in advancing that great work.

Not onely the common danger we are under, but the conscience of our duty to his suffering people, layeth bonds on us frequently to present you, and that blessed Work of Reformation, in your hands, to the throne of Grace, that the GOD of all Grace, who will call you into his eternal glory by Christ Jesus, after that you have suffered and a while may make you perfect, stablish, strengthen, settle you.

Edinburgh, August 19. 1643.

Subscribed in name of the Assembly of the Church Scotland, by the Clerk, of the Assembly.

THE ASSEMBLIES ANSWER TO THE REVEREND THEIR BE-LOVED BRETHREN, MINISTERS IN THE CHURCH OF EN-GLAND.

Reverend and beloved,

We acknowledge with thankfulnesse to GOD, that this is one of the good blessings bestowed upon our Kirk of late, and a pleasant fruit of our free Assemblies, That a way is opened for keeping communion with our sister Kirks abroad, and correspondence with you our dear Brethren, in whose joy and sorrow we have so near interest, and whose cause and condition we desire to lay to heart as our own.

All your former Letters were most acceptable, and full of refreshment unto us, being taken as the earnest of a more full and constant fellowship, longed after and hoped for: And this your last, although full of sadnesse and sorrow, yet accounted of us all most worthy of our tenderst affection and best respects, both for your cause who sent it, and for these worthy witnesses which did attest it: Wherein as you have given unto us no small evidence, not only of your love, but also of trust and friendly respect, by choosing to poure out your grieved souls in our bosome; so we shall with, and Godwilling endeavour, that you may really finde some measure of brotherly compassion in our receiving thereof. For these your sad expressions of deep sorrow, being as you have given us to conceive but a part of your complaint, and a lamentation lesse then the causes doth require, cannot but melt every heart, wherein there is any the least warmnesse of the love of Christ and his Saints: And what Childe of the Bridegrooms chamber, can hear the voice of so many friends of the Bridegroom, lamenting for the evils which have befallen Christs Bride in England, in the very night before her expected espousals, and not sit down and mourn with them except his heart be fallen asleep and frozen within him? This pitiful condition of our sister Church in England hes matter enough we confesse to move, yea, to rend our bowels.

If we should weigh this your heavie grief in the scales of common reason, we behoved either to stand aloof from your plague as men astonished, or sink down in heavinesse and be swallowed up of sorrow: but when we ponder your sad condition in the Ballance of the Sanctuary, we finde that nothing hath as yet befallen unto you, save that which hath been the exercise of the Saints in former times, who have been made to sit down for a while in the shadow of death before the day of their deliverance. We finde nothing but that which may be a fit Preparation for a comfortable out-gate from all your troubles. What if it was necessary in the wise dispensation of Almighty GOD, that a People in great estimation for wisedome and power, such as England, should be thus farre humbled, as you declare, to the end that your deliverance maybe seen hereafter to be of the Lord, and not of your selves? What if the Lord would not draw back his hand from the Wine-presse wherein you now lye, till he should draw forth from you these pitiful expressions of your low estate, and so provide himself witnesses against the day to come, that he may have the greater and purer glory in your salvation, and your gloriation may be in the Lord alone! Dear Brethren, comfort your selves in the Lord; this sowing in tears, doth promise a reaping in joy, and who knoweth how soon he will give to you who are mourners in Zion, beauty for ashes, the oyle of joy for mourning, the garment of praise for the spirit of heavinesse; That you may be called the trees of righteousness, the planting of the Lord, that he may be glorified.

Though weeping be in the evening of this begun Reformation and purging of the Lords House among you, yet in the morning when the discovered filthinesse and sweepings of the Temple shall be orderly cast out, joy shall come with thanksgiving and praise. Though a fire be kindled in the Land, yet it is not to consume any of the mettal, for the Lord is sitting down as a Refiner amongst you, and especially to purifie the sons of Levi, that he may have a more pure oblation of spiritual worship and service in all his holy ordinances throughout all the Land, which is no token of wrath, but of loving kindnesse towards you. No wonder that Satan doth thus rage, as you relate, foreseeing his casting out: No wonder he stirre up all the children of disobedience, and kindle their natural malice against the children of God with the inspiration of hellish fury: No wonder the spirit of Antichrist be mad, when the morsel half swallowed down, is like to be pulled out of his throat, the fat morsel of the rich Revenues of England: No wonder he be cruell against you the servants of Christ, who are consuming him by the breath of the Lords mouth.

You do well to expect no mercy, if Papists and Prelats prevail over you, neither desire we to deceive our selves with hopes to be free from what the power and malice can do against us; for they will not do to us if they get the upper-hand, as we have done, and must do, if God bring them low again under us; as they were before; for we and they are led by the contrary spirits of Christ, and Anti-Christ: We have laboured, and must labour for their conversion, but they (except in so far as God shall bridle them) will not rest without our destruction; for their fury against our persons is much more fierie then our zeal is fervent against their abominations: Let them follow the spirit of lying and murthering, we must take us to our refuge, and joyne our selves with all that are sensible of the danger of the reformed Religion in prayer and supplication. The Lord of Hosts is with us, the God of Jacob is our refuge.

Now for advice, what can we say to you who are upon your watch tower, wherein is the spirit of wisedome and counsel; who lye thus as humble Disciples under the Lords foot, who did never forsake them that sought him. Go on in the Name of our Lord Jesus Christ, against all opposition, without fear of whatsoever dangers, to purge the House of the Lord, to repair the breaches thereof, to set up all his Ordinances in their full beautie and perfection, to the uttermost of your power, according to the pattern of the Word of GOD, and zeal of the best reformed Kirks; And let these two Kingdomes be knit together as one man in maintaining and promoving the truth of the Gospel, Let us enter in a perpetual Covenant for our selves and our posterity, to endevour that all things may be done in the House of GOD according to his own will, and let the Lord do with us what seemeth good in his eyes. Only wait upon the lord, be of good courage, and he shall strengthen your heart. Let your hands be ever at your Masters Work, and hold your faces resolutely to his Cause. Watch ye, stand fast in the faith, quite your selves like men, be strong, for ye shall see the salvation of the Lord, and your labour shall not be in vain.

Subscribed in name of the Generall Assembly of the Church of Scotland, by the Clerk of the Assembly.

COMMISSION OF THE GENERALL ASSEMBLY, FOR THESE THAT REPAIR TO THE KINGDOME OF ENGLAND.

The Generall Assembly of the Church of Scotland, finding it necessary to send some Godly and learned of this Kirk to the Kingdome of England, to the effect under-written. Therefore gives full Power and Commission to Master Alexander Henderson, Master Robert Douglas, Master Samuel Rutherfoord, Master Robert Bailzie, and Master George Gillespie, Ministers, John Earl of Cassills, John Lord Maitland, and Sir Archbald Johnstoun of Waristoun Elders, or any three of them, whereof two shall be Ministers, to repair to the Kingdome of England, and there to deliver the Declaration sent unto the Parliament of England and the Letter sent unto the Assembly of Divines now sitting in that Kingdome. And to propone, consult, treat and conclude with that Assembly or any Commissioners deputed by them, or any Committees or Commissioners deputed by the Houses of Parliament, in all matters which may further the Union of this Island in one forme of Kirk-government, one confession of Faith, one Catechisme, and one Directorie for the Worship of GOD, according to the Instructions which they have received from the Assembly, or shall receive from time to time hereafter from the Commissioners of the Assembly deputed for that effect. With power also to them to convey to his Majestie, the humble Answer sent from this Assembly to his Majesties Letter, by such occasion as they shall think convenient; And suchlike to deliver the Assemblies Answer to the Letter sent from some wel-affected Brethren of the Ministry there. And generally authorizes them to do all things which may further the so much desired Union, and nearest conjunction of the two Churches of Scotland and England, conform to their Instructions aforesaid.

REFERENCE TO THE COMMISSION, ANENT THE PERSONS DESIGNED TO REPAIR TO THE THE KINGDOME OF ENGLAND.

The Assembly having this day approven the nomination made by the Commissioners of the late Assembly, of persons to repair to the Synod of Divines in England: And having of new elected and nominated all the same Persons, except Master *Eleazar Borthwick*, who is now with GOD. Therefore gives power to the Commissioners to be appointed by this Assembly for the publick affairs of this Kirk, to nominate and appoint any other whom they shall think meet in his place. And suchlike the Assembly refers to the said Commission, to consider whether it be convenient to send now at this present time to the Kingdome of England, all the Persons appointed to go thither, and to designe the Persons whom they think meet to go at this present occasion, to determine the time of their dispatch, and to give unto them their Instructions. And further in case of sicknesse or death of any of the Persons appointed for that employment, or in the case of any other necessary impediment of their undertaking the samine; Gives power to the said Commission, to nominate others in their place if the Commission shall finde it convenient.

COMMISSION FOR THE PUBLICK AFFAIRS OF THIS KIRK.

The General Assembly, considering the laudable costome of this Kirk, in appointing Commissions betwixt Assemblies for the publick affairs of the Kirk, and the commendable practice of the late Assembly at Saint Andrews, in appointing their Commission for prosecuting the blessed Work, for uniting the Kirks of this Island in Religion and Kirk-government, by all lawfull and Ecclesiastick wayes, for continuance of our own peace at home, and of the common peace bytwixt the two Nations, and for other good ends, as at length is exprest in that Commission: And finding that the painful endevours and proceedings of that Commission, unanimously approven in this Assembly, though they have much advanced that glorious Work of Unity in Religion and Government; Yet has not brought the samine to full perfection and a finall accomplishment: And the Assembly being now much animate and encouraged to prosecute that Work by the Parliament of England their Bills past against Episcopacie, and sundry other corruptions, and the good hopes of a solemne Covenant betwixt the Nations, And conceiving that in their times of danger there may be some occasions for conveening the Assembly, before the time indicted for their next meeting. Therefore the Assembly finding it necessary to appoint a new Commission, By these presents, nominates and appoints Mr Andrew Ramsay, Mr Alexander Henderson, Mr Robert Douglas, Mr William Colvil, Mr William Bennet, Mr George Gillespie, Mr John Adamson, Mr John Sharpe, Mr James Sharpe, Mr William Dalgleish, Mr David Calderwood, Mr Andrew Blackhall, Mr James Fleeming, Mr Robert Ker, Mr John Macghie, Mr Oliver Colt, Mr Hugh Campbell, Mr Adam Penman, Mr Richard Dickson, Mr Andrew Stevinson, Mr John Lauder, Mr Robert Blair, Mr Samuel Rutherfoord, Mr Arthur Morton, Mr Robert Traill, Mr Frederick Carmichell, Mr Mungo Law, Mr John Smith, Mr Patrick Gillespie, Mr John Duncan, Mr John Hume, Mr Robert Knox, Mr William Jameson, Mr Robert Mura, Mr Henry Guthrie, Mr James Hamilton, Mr Bernard Sanderson, Mr John Leviston, Mr James Boner, Mr Evan Cameron, Mr David Dickson, Mr Robert Bailzie, Mr James Cunninghame, Mr George Youngh, Mr Andrew Auchinleck, Mr David Lindsay, Mr Andrew Cant, Mr John Oiswald, Mr William Douglas, Mr Murdoc Mackenzie, Mr Coline Mackenzie, Mr John Monroe, Mr Walter Stuart, Ministers: Marquesse of Argyle, Earle Marshell, Earle of Sutherland, Earle of Eglintoun, Earle of Cassils, Earle of Dumsermling, Earle of Lawderdail, Earle of Lindsay, Earle of Queensberrie, Earle of Dalhouse, Lord Angus, Vicount of Dudhope, Lord Maitland, Lord Elcho Lord Balmarinoch, Lord Cowper, Sir Patrick Hepburne of Wauchtoun, Sir Archbald Johnstoun of Waristoun, Sir David Hume of Wedderborne, Sir Alexander Areskine of Duns, Sir William Cockburne of Langtoun, Sir Thomas Ruthven of Frieland, Sir James Arnos of Fernie, Sir Walter Riddell of that Ilk., Sir Lodonick Houstoun of that Ilk, Sir William Carmichael Fiar of that Ilk, Laird of Bonjedburgh, Laird of Libbertoun, Laird of Brodie, Sir John Smith, James Dennistoun, Master Barclay, John Rutherfoord, William Glendinning, John Sempill, John Kennedie, Master Alexander Douglas, To meet at Edinburgh the 21. day of August next, and upon any other day thereafter, and in any other place they shall think good. And gives and grants unto them, or any fifteen of them, there being twelve Ministers present, full power and Commission, to consider and performe what they finde necessary by Praying and

Preaching, by supplicating his Majestie and all the Judicatories of this Kingdome, by Declarations and Remonstrances to the Parliament of England, to the Synod of Divines in that Kingdome, by Informations, Directions, Instructions to, and continual correspondence with the Commissioners, now designed by this Assembly to go to the Synod of Divines in England, or by any other lawful Ecclesiastick wayes, for furtherance of this great Work, in the Union of this Island in Religion and Kirk-goverment, and for continuance of our own Peace at home, and of the common Peace betwixt the Nations, and keeping of good correspondence betwixt the Kirks of this Island. With power also to them to concurre with the Lords of Councel, Commissioners of Peace, or with the Honourable Estates assembled in Convention or Parliament, or with their Committees and Commissioners, in prosecuting this good Work at home or abroad by all Ecclesiastick wayes. And suchlike with power to them to prevent the dangers conteined in the Remonstrance, presented unto the Convention of Estates by the Commissioners of the late Assembly in June last, and to prosecute the remedies of these dangers conteined in another Remonstrance, presented by the aids Commissioners to the Convention the 6. of July last by admonitions, directions, censures, and all other Ecclesiastick wayes. And further in case their Brethren of England shall agree to the Covenant betwixt the Kingdomes, the draught and frame whereof is now so unanimously approven in this Assembly Gives also unto the Persons foresaid, or the Quorum above-written, full Power and Authoritie to command and enjoyn the samine to be subscribed and sworn by all the members of this Kirk: And that in such order and manner, and with such solemnities as they shall think convenient for so great and glorious a Work; And to send their directions to Sessions, Presbyteries and Synods, for execution of their orders thereanent. And with power to proceed against any Person whatsoever, that shall refuse to subscribe and swear the said Covenant, with all the censures of the Kirk, or to refer the tryall and censures of such delinquents to Presbyteries or Synods as they shall think convenient. And such like gives unto the persons foresaids power and libertie, to call a General Assembly pro re nata, in case they shall finde the necessity of the Kirk, and this great Work to require the same: With full power also to them to give Answers in name of the Assembly, to all Letters sent to the Assembly from the Kirks of Holland, Zealand, or any other forraigne Reformed Kirks. And further gives power to them to promove the other desires, Overtures and recommendations of this, or of any former Assemblies to the Kings Majestie, Parliament or Convention of Estates, to the Lords of Councel, Session, Exchequer, Commissioners of Parliaments, for plantation of Kirks, for the common burdens, and for conserving the Peace. And suchlike gives as full power and Commission to them to treat and decerne in any other matters referred, or to be referred to them by this Assembly, as if the samine were herein particalarly insert. And generally gives unto the Persons foresaids, or the Quorum abovementioned full power and Authoritie, to do and performe all things which may advance, accomplish, and perfect the great Work of Unity of Religion, and Uniformity of Kirk-government in all his Majesties Dominions, and which may be necessary for good order in all the publick affairs of this Kirk, untill the next Assembly, ne quid detrimenti capiat Ecclesia. With als ample power in all matters particularly or generally above-mentioned, as any other Commission of General

Assemblies, has had or been in use of before; They being alwayes countable to, and censurable by the next General Assembly, for their proceedings thereintill.

The General Assembly appoints the meeting of the next General Assembly, to be at Edinburgh the last Wednesday of May, in the year 1644.

THE GENERALL ASSEMBLY, AT EDIN-BURGH, 1644.

DIE JOVIS PENULT. MAII, SESS. 2.

THE LETTER FROM THE PRESBYEERIE WITH THE ARMY IN ENGLAND, TO THE GENERALL ASSEMBLY.

Right reverend,

Having the opportunity of the sitting of this Venerable Assembly, we thought our selves obliged to render some accompt of the state of our Affairs. It hath pleased the Lord to exercise us since our out-coming, with many straits and difficulties, yet in the mids thereof he hath wonderfully upheld and carried us through. The depth of his wisedome hath suspended us for a time from any great action, to make us walk humbly before him, and to keep us in a continual dependance upon himself: And yet he hath by his own power scattered before us the great Popish Army, and much diminished the number thereof, so that they do not now appeare against us in the Fields; That all may learne to trust in GOD, and not in Man. It was farre from our thoughts and intentions to have come this length at that instant when the course of Divine Providence pointed out our way unto us, which led us on by some long and speedie marches to joyne with my Lord Fairfax and his Sonne their Forces. The City of York, wherein a swarme of obstinate Papists have taken sanctuary, is blocked up; Now and then God favoureth us with successe in some enterprises about it, and wee look for more if the time be come which he hath appointed for the deliverance of this People.

Our Soules do abhorre the treacherous attempts of our disnatured Countrey-men, that have endeavoured to make their native Kingdome a seat of Warre, and our bowels within us are moved to think upon the maine mischiefs, if not timeously prevented, that may follow upon the unatural Warres there; Like unto these under which this Kingdome hath groaned for a long time. We have found none more malicous and cruel against us than these of our own Nation, and we measure those at home, by these here; Cursed be their rage, for it is fierce, and their anger for it is cruell. The present danger calls upon all to lay out of their hands what ever may hinder their haste, as one Man to come together for saving the Vine-yeard that the wilde Boares would lay waste, and taking the Foxes that would destroy the Vines. You are, Right Reverend, now set upon the highest Watch-tower, from whence you may discover the dangers that threaten on all coasts, and we need not put you in minde to give warning to the Watch-men in their severall stations;

To rouze up the People from their too great security; To call them to unfeigned Humiliation, and to stirre them up to wrestle with GOD by prayer; that hee would preserve Truth and Peace at home against the machinations of Malignants; That hee would prepare the People here, and make them more fit to embrace the intended Reformation; And that hee would command these unnaturall and bloudy Warres to cease, that Religion and Righteousnesse may flourish through the three Dominions, Praying GOD to send upon you the Spirit of truth, who may lead you in all truth. We remaine

Middle-thorp, 20. May, 1644.

Your loving Brethren, The Presbyterie of the Scottish Army in England,

Master Robert Douglas, Moderator in their name.

THE PETITION FROM THE DISTRESSED CHRISTIANS IN THE NORTH OF IRELAND.

To the Reverend and Honourable Moderator and remanent Members of the Generall Assembly of Scotland, conveened at Edinburgh in May 1644.

The humble Petition of the distressed Christians in the North of Ireland.

Humbly sheweth,

That whereas your former enlarged bounty, and our present overflowing straits would require a gratefull acknowledgement of the one, and a serious representation of the other: Our case is such, as neither can be expected at our hands, being stricken with astonishment, and full of the furie of the Lord. We are these indeed who have seen affliction by the rod of his wrath: So that it were more fit, we had a Cottage in the Wildernesse amongst the Owles to mourn out our imbittered Spirits, then that by word or writ we should compeere before any of his People: Although you cannot be wearied in wel-doing, yet we shall up way think it strange, if now you shall give over any more care of us; Seeing the Lord hath testified against us, and the Almighty hath afflicted us. Your judgement is with the Lord, and your reward is with God, not onely for your two years visiting and watering a barren vineyard, but also for your zeale and care to have your Reformation spred amongst other opprest and borne-down Churches, whereof you have given an ample and famous testimony in sending hither that blessed League and Covenant which wee much desired and longed for, as by our Petitions to the Church & State of our Native Kingdome is knowne unto you; which hath had a wished and gracious successe by the favour and blessing of God, accompanying the pains of these to whom the tendering thereof was intrusted by you. And we conceiving a chief part of our miserie to consist in our want of opportunitie to joyne our selves with the People of God in the foresaid Leagues; Esteeming our selves rejected of God and unfit to be joyned in any comfortable fellowship in the Gospel with them, when the said League and Covenant was presented to the Regiments; Wee made bold to lay hold upon the opportunity (though aflicted abjects) and cheerfully and unanimously joyned our selves thereunto: That if wee peerish in our misery, wee may die a Covenanted People: and, if our miserable life be prolonged, we may finde shelter and refreshment under the shadow thereof in our fierie trials, confidently expecting from the Lord by our neerer conjunction with you than before, an accomplishment of what is agreed into the Covenant, which ye bountifully expressed before we were one with you, to your never-dying-commendation. We are nothing shaken in our minds with the odious aspersions of sedition, combination against the King: and overthrow of Muncipal Laws, &c. (wherewith our Covenant is branded) nor with the threats of these who should be comfortable to us in our troubles: But are the more encouraged to beleeve that God shall raise up the Tabernacle of David that is fallen, and repair the breaches thereof: For since we Covenanted with God, and united our selves together, our dying Spirits have revived, and we sing like those who have come forth from their Graves, for God hath had mercy on Jacob: In testimony whereof he hath opened the bowels of the Churches of Holland, who were strangers to us, and yet dear Brethren, and tender Sympathizers with our afflictions and sorrows, who, when these who were left of the Sword were in danger to dye by famine, did plentifully relieve us in our straits, not onely by comfortable encouragements to walk humbly with God, and wait for him who hides his face from the house of Jacob for a season; but also by their rich supply in Victuals and others necessar for our relief and comfort, which we humbly desire our Lord to repay seven-fold in their bosome, and become your Supplicants to joyne with us in a grateful acknowledgement of their singular favours: And upon the heels of these favours you have continued your unparalled compassions in keeping your forces and enabling them, together with the other Forces, for avenging the cruel murders, and effusion of Christian blood in this Land, notwithstanding of your owne multiplied difficulties. The Lord hath begun to delight into us, and in a day of salvation hath helped us (So happy are the people who are in Covenant with God.) We are these (indeed) who may justly be burnt up for our unfruitfulnesse in the dayes of our plenty, & stubbornesse in the dayes of our affliction, which has brought us so low, that where we once enjoyed a blessed plenty, we must now beg of the crumbs that fall from your Table: We cannot dissemble, but so farre as we can discern our owne hearts, we would preferre the joyful sound of the Gospel to our much wished Peace and precious lives: But it may be discerned, your Consultations of before have been guided by the Spirit of the Lord; in that when wee twice in our forward hasting desires begged the present loosing and planting of some Ministers amongst us, you judged it more convenient to supply us by turnes, as foreseeing that our Captivity was likely to endure: Our hopes are so far revived, that we trust to see the day when he shall take the Cup of trembling out of our hands, and put it in the hands of them that afflicted us.

And therefore, if you account us fellow-partners of the Purchased Inheritance, Yet again suffer our necessitie to plead with you, that as it hath been by the Committee of Bils already advised, that a competent number of Ministers may be gifted to us by your Commission when they shall set the Calling cleared, the same may be granted as a testimony of your confidence, and expectation of our delivery; And in the meane time some others may be sent by turnes to keep in the dying lives of above twenty foure desolate Congregations, who are in danger to perish for want of Vision: And although we do proteste, we count not our selves worthy of such favours, yet as we have resolved to dye with the cry of hope in our mouthes to the Lords Throne; So in obedience of the use of the means by him appointed, we stretch out our hearts and our hands to you for help, and have sent our Brother William Mackenna Merchant at Belfast, to attend what answer it shall please the Lord by you to returne unto

Your distressed Brethern and Supplicants.

Subscribed by very many hands.

3. JUNII 1644. ANTEMERIDIEM. SESS. 5.

ACT FOR THE PRESENT ENTRIE OF THE NEW ERECTED PRESBYTERIE AT BIGGAR.

The which day anent the Supplication subscribed and given in to the General Assembly to the Ministers and ruling Elders of the Kirks of Biggar, Skirling, Brochton, Glenquhome, Kelbocho, Culter, Lamyngtoun, Symontoun, Covingtoun Quothquen, Welstonn, and Dolphingtoun making mention, That the General Assembly at Edinburgh in August 1643. years, by their Act of the date of the twelfth day of the samine moneth and year, did upon good grounds, and after tryal and hearing of all Parties to the full, erect a Presbyterie seat at Biggar, to consist of the Kirks above-written, And granted to their Presbyterie full power of jurisdiction and exerceing Discipline, with all other Liberties and Priviledges belonging to any other Presbyterie; but suspended the entrie and possession of this new erected Presbyterie, during the pleasure of the Assembly; And therefore desiring the said Generall Assembly to ordaine and appoint the entrie and possession of the foresaid Presbyterie at Biggar now presently; And to declare, that it is their pleasure, that the entrie and possession thereof shall be no longer suspended, as the Supplication proports. Which Supplication being read in audience of the Generall Assembly, and thereafter the Commissioners from the Presbyteries of Lanerk and Peebles, and all others having entresse to oppose the desire foresaid being publickly called, and the saids Commissioners for Peebles and Lanerk personally present, being at length heard in what they could say or alledge therein: And the said the Supplication and desire thereof, with the Alledgeances and Objections made against the samine, being taken to consideration by the Assembly, and they therewith being fully and ripely advised: The Assembly after removing of the Parties, and after consideration of the premisses and voycing of the foresaid desire, Ordaines the entrie and possession of the foresaid Presbyterie of Biggar, consisting of the particular Kirks above-mentioned, to begin now presently; And appoints and ordaines all the Ministers and Ruling Elders of the foresaids Kirks above specified, whereof the said Presbyterie consists, to meet and conveene as a Presbyterie, with all convenience, at the said Kirk of Biggar, which is the Place and Seat of the samine Presbyterie. And the Assembly refers to the Commissioners to be appointed by them for the publick affairs of the Kirk, to determinn to what Synod the said new erected Presbyterie shall be subordinate; As also to prescribe the order and solemnities that shall be necessar for entring and possessing the Ministers and Elders in the said Presbyterie.

JUNII 3. 1644 SESS.

ACT CONCERNING THE DECLARATION SUBSCRIBED BY THE SCOTTISH LORDS AT OXFORD.

The Generall Assembly having received a Copy of a Declaration, made and subscribed at Oxford, sent unto them from the honourable Convention of Estates, and having seriously considered the tenour thereof, doth finde the same to be a perfidious Band and unnaturall confederacy, to bring this Kirk and Kingdome to confusion; and to be full of blasphemies against the late solemne League and Covenant of the three Kingdomes, of vile aspersions of Treason, Rebellion and Sedition, most falsly and impudently imputed to the Estates and the most faithfull and loyall Subjects of these Kingdomes, And seeing it is incumbent to the Assembly to take notice thereof, and to stop the course of these malicious intentions, in so farre as concernes them, Declare that the subscribers of this or the like Declaration or Band, or any that have been accessory to the framing, or that has been, or shall be accessory to the execution thereof, deserve the highest censure of the Kirk: And therefore gives power to the Commissioners of this Assembly appointed for the publick affairs, to proceed against them to the sentence of Excommunication, unlesse they make humble confession of their offence publickly, in such manner, and in such places as the Commission shall prescribe; Or otherwise to refer the tryall and censure of such Delinquents to Presbytereries or Synods as they shall think convenient. And when the sentence of Excommunication shall be pronounced, discharges Presbyteries or Synods to relax any from the sentence, without the advice of the Generall Assembly, or their Commissioners, nisi in extremis. And in respect of the atrocicite of this Fact, the Assembly in all humility, do seriously recommend to the right honourable the Estates of Parliament to take such course, as the persons that shall be found guilty, may be exemplary punished, according to the merit of so unnaturall and impious an offence: And that some publick note of ignominie be put upon the Declaration and Band it self, if their Honours shall think it meet.

ACT AGAINST THE REBELLS IN THE NORTH AND SOUTH.

The Generall Assembly considering the just sentence pronounced against the principall Actors in that Rebellion in the North and South, by ordinance of the Commissioners of the late Assembly; And finding it most necessary, that such as assisted or joyned with them in that impious and unnaturall Fact, be likewise censured; Therefore ordains Presbyteries and Synods respectivè, to proceed against them with the highest Censures of the Kirk, if they give not satisfaction by publick repentance; And when the sentence of Excommunication shall be pronounced, The Assembly discharges the said Judicatories to relax any of them from the sentence, without the advice of the Generall Assembly, or their Commissioners, nisi in extremis: To whom also the saids Presbyteries and Synods, shall be answerable for their diligence in the premisses as they shall be required. And the Assembly doth humbly recommend to the Honourable Estates of Parliament, to take such course as the Persons that shall be found guilty may be exemplarly punished according to the merit and degree of their offence.

ACT AGAINST SECRET DISAFFECTERS OF THE COVE-

NANT

The Generall Assembly understanding that divers Persons dis-affected to the Nationall Covenant of this Kirk, and to the Solemne League and Covenant of the three Kingdoms, do escape their just censure, either by their private and unconstant abode in any one Congregation, or by secret conveyance of their malignant speeches and practises; Therefore ordains all Ministers to take speciall notice when any such Person shall come within their Paroches, and so soon as they shall know the same, that without delay they cause warn them to appear before the Presbyteries within which their Paroches lyes, or before the Commissioners of this Assembly appointed for publick affairs, as they shall finde most convenient, which warning the Assembly declares shall be a sufficient citation unto them: And als that all Ministers and Elders declare to the saids Judicatories respectivè, every such disaffected person, although without their own Paroch, so soon as they shall hear and be informed of them. And the Assembly ordains the said Commissioners not only to proceed to Tryal and Censure of such disaffected Persons, but also take a special account of the diligence of Ministers, Elders, and Presbyteries herein respectivè.

ACT FOR SENDING MINISTERS TO THE ARMIE.

The Assembly understanding that Ministers are not duly sent forth to the Regiments of the Army, neither such as are sent duly relieved, which neglect falleth out oftimes, by reason of questions among Presbyteries interested in the Regiments: Therefore for remedy hereof, thinks it convenient that this order be keeped hereafter; That a List be made of three Ministers by the Colonels, or in their absence by the chief Officers of every Regiment, with advice and consent of the Presbyterie at the Army, and sent to Presbyteries here, or if the list be of Ministers in divers Presbyteries to the Commissioners of the General Assembly, that they may appoint one out of that list to be sent to the Regiment, to attend them for performing Ministeriall duties 3 Moneths: And that the relief of Ministers already sent or to be sent hereafter shall be in the same manner, And the Assembly ordains Ministers who shall be thus appointed by Presbyteries or the Commissioners of the Assembly respectivè, to repair to the Armie with all diligence, under the paine of suspension: And humbly recommends to the Honourable Estates of Parliament, to provide some way whereby these Ministers may have due and ready payment of their allowance, from the time of their going from their charges here. And it is declared that this order shall be also keeped for sending forth of Ministers to the Regiments in the second expedition.

RENOVATION OF THE COMMISSION FOR THE PUBLICK AFFAIRS OF THE KIRK.

The Generall Assembly considering that the Commissioners appointed by the last Assembly upon the ninteenth day of August 1643. years, the last Session thereof to sit at Edinburgh, for the Publick affairs of the Kirk, have not yet fully perfected that great Work for Unity of Religion, and Uniformitie of Kirk-government in his Majesties Dominions; And that now in respect of the present condition of affairs in this Kingdome, their proceedings cannot be examined at this time:

Therefore finding it necessar that the said Commission be renewed unto the Commissioners therein mentioned, and to the Persons afternamed now thought, fit to be added for the better expediting of the businesse, Do hereby appoint the Persons particularly nominate in the said Commission, viz. Masters Andrew Ramsay, Alexander Henderson, Robert Douglas, William Colvill, William Bennet, George Gillespie, John Oiswald, Mungo Law, John Adamson, John Sharp, James Sharp, William Dalgleish, David Calderwood, Andrew Blackball, James Fleeming, Robert Ker, John Mackenzie, Oliver Cole, Hugh Campbell, Adam Penman, Richard Dickson, Andrew Stevinson, John Lawder, Robert Blair, Samuel Rutherfurd, Arthur Mortoun, Robert Traill, Frederick Carmichael, John Smith, Patrick Gillespie, John Duncan, John Hume, Robert Knox, William Jameson, Robert Murray, Henry Guthrie, James Hamilton, in Dumfreis, Bernard Sanderson, John Levingstoun, James Bonar, Evan Camron, David Dickson, Robort Bailzie, James Cuninghame, George Youngh, Andrew Affleck, David Lindsay, Andrew Cant, William Douglas, Murdo Mackenzie, Coline Mackenzie, John Monroe, Walter Stuart Ministers; Archbald Marquesse of Argyle, William Earle Marshall, John Earle of Sutherland, Alexander Earle of Eglingtoun, John Earle of Cassils, Charles Earl of Dumfermeling, John Earle of Lauderdale, John Earle of Lindsay, James Earle of Queensberry, William Earle of Dalhousie, Archbald Lord Angus, James Vicount of Dudhope, John Lord Maitland, David Lord Elcho, John Lord Bahnerinoch, James Lord Cowper, Sir Patrick Hepburne of Waughtoun, Sir Archbald Johnstoun of Waristoun, Sir David Hume of Wedderburne, Sir Alexander Areskine of Dun, Sir William Cockburne of Langtoun, Sir Thomas Ruthven of Frieland, Sir James Arnot of Fernie, Sir Walter Riddall of that Ilk, Sir Ledovick Houstoun of that Ilk, Sir William Carmichael Fiar of that Ilk, Mr George Douglas of Bonjedburgh, Mr George Winrame of Libertoun, Laird of Brodie, Sir John Smith, James Dennistoun, Master Robert Barclay, John Rutherford, William Glendunning, John Sempill, John Kennedy and Master Alexander Douglas Elders: And also Masters, David Dalgleish, Andrew Bennet, John Moncreiff, Alexander Carse, Thomas Wilkie, James Gushrie, Henry Levingstoun, David Drummond at Creiff, John Hay at Renfrew, John Strang, Richard Inglis, William Falconer, John Paterson, Gilbert Rosse, Richard Maitiand, George Cumming, William Campbel Ministers, And William Earle of Glancairne, William Earle of Louthian, James Lord Murray of Gask, John Lord Yester, Robert Maitland, Frederick Lyon of Brigtoun, James Macdowell of Garthland, David Beton of Creich, Sir James Stuart Sheriff of Buit, Sir John Weemes of Bogie, Mr William Sandilands Tutor of Torphichin, Archbald Sydserfe, Laurence Henderson, James Stuart, Thomas Paterson, and Alexander Jaffrry Elders now added by this Assembly, to meet at Edinburgh upon the fifth day of this instant moneth of June, and upon the last Wednesday of August next, the last Wednesday of November next, and upon the last Wednesday of February next; and upon any other day, or in any other place they shall think meet: Giving and granting unto them, or any fifteen of them, there being twelve Minister present, full power and commission to prosecute the said work of unitie in Religion, and uniformitie of Kirk government in all his Majesties Dominions, and to do and performe all things particularly or generally contained in the said Commission of the preceeding Assembly, or in an Act of the said Assembly upon the said 19. day of August, intituled, A Reference to the

Commission anent the Persons designed to repair to the Kingdome of England, and to treat and determine therin, and in all other matters referred unto them by this Assembly, siclike, and as freely, as if all these were herein expressed, and as the persons nominat in that said former Commission might have done by vertue of the said Act and former Commission at any time by-gone, and with as ample power as any Commission of former General Assemblies hath had, or been in use of before, they being alwayes comptable and censurable for their whole proceedings hereintill by the next General Assembly.

RENOVATION OF THE COMMISSION GRANTED TO THE PERSONS APPOINTED TO REPAIR TO THE KINGDOME OF ENGLAND.

The General Assembly, finding that the great Work of unity in Religion, and uniformity of Kirk-government in all his Majesties Dominions is not yet perfected, Do therefore renew the Commission granted for that effect by the preceeding Assembly, unto the Persons appointed to repair to the Kingdome of England upon the 19. day of August 1643. in the last Session thereof, Giving and granting to the Persons therin mentioned, the same power, to do all and every thing particularly or generally contained in the said Commission, in the same manner, and as fully, as if the same were herein expressed, and as they might have done at any time by gone by vertue of the former Commission.

THE ASSEMBLIES ANSWER TO THE PRESBYTERIE WITH THE ARMIE.

Reverend and loving Brethren in the LORD,

We received yours of the 17 and 20 of May, and were much refreshed with the knowledge you gave unto us therein, of your sense of our condition here, and of the Lords dealing with yourselves there in your straits and difficulties: We rejoyce exceedingly to see you make such a blessed use of the Lords delayes, for your further Humiliation and Dependence upon him: That Sanctuary, your Enemies, and the Enemies of your GOD hath taken, shall not save them: You have found by experience in your marches and maintenance, that events are not ordered by the propositions of men, but by the Providence and purpose of GOD. There is a time for every purpose under Heaven, and the Cup of the Amorites must be filled: Which being now full of every abomination, yea of the blood of the Saints, the cry whereof cannot but be heard in Heaven, and answered on Earth, presageth no lesse to us, than that the Lords time of his deliverance of his own, and destruction of his Enemies draweth near.

We are not unsensible of your present estate, and by the Lords grace shall be careful, both here and with our Congregations at home, to make all take the same to heart. As for our condition here remembred with such pious affection by you, we doubt not but ye have heard what the Lord hath done for us; these happy beginnings of the Lords scattering our unnatural Enemies in the North, gives us confidence of his assistance in the midst of difficulties against these that assault us in the South: It is nothing with the Lord to help whether with many, or with them that have no power.

The security of this Nation indeed is great, it is our part to blow the Trumpet to give warning to the People, and to rouze them from that fearful condition which threatneth so much desertion. And to this end we have injoyned a solemne Fast, the causes whereof being more particularly considered by our Commissioners here, will no question be sent unto you, that if the Lord please, you may joyne with us there in that Action.

We have set down an order to be kept hereafter, for sending Ministers unto the Armie, which the Clerk will send herewith unto you. Now the Lord our GOD, in whose Name his people go forth against his Enemies, help and assist them, and cover their heads in the Day of Battel, and be their Refuge; and blesse your travels and endeavours, for the good of their souls and his own glory.

Edinburgh, 3. June 1644.

Subscribed in name of the Generall Assembly by the Moderator.

4. JUNE 1644. SESS 7.

THE LETTER FROM THE COMMISSIONERS AT LONDON TO THE GENERAL ASSEMBLY.

Right Honourable, Reverend and beloved in the LORD,

It was the earnest desire of our hearts to have come unto you at this time, and to have brought with us the desireable fruits of our weighty imployments and labours, to our common rejoycing in the mids of so many troubles both here and there: but our Lord in his wisedome hath not judged it fitting, that this should be the time of our joyful harvest, and of bringing our sheaves, to be matter of sacrifice to himself, and of shouting to us. Both Nations as yet do but go forth weeping and bearing their precious seed; yet are we confident through JESUS CHRIST, that as it is a seed time, if the Labourers (although other men before us have laboured and we are entred into their labours) prove faithful unto the end, the harvest shall come in due time, and in great plenty.

The common Directory for publick Worship in the Kirks of the three Kingdomes is so begun (which we did make known to the Commissioners of the General Assembly) that we could not think upon any particular Directory for our own Kirk, and yet is not so far perfected, that wee could present any part thereof unto your view: for although wee have exhibited unto the Grand Committee (which is composed of some of the Members of both Houses, and of the Assembly, with our selves) the materials of the publick prayers of the Kirk, the method of Preaching, and the order of administration of both Sacraments, and have the Catechisme in hand; yet are they not throughly examined by the Committee, nor at all by the Assembly or Parliament, which we cannot impute to any neglect or unwillingnesse, but to the multiplicity and weight of their affairs, by which they are sore pressed, and above their power.

The Directory for Ordination of Ministers (which upon the extreme exigence of this Kirk was much pressed by the Parliament) is agreed upon by the Committee and Assembly, and some dayes past is presented to both Houses, but hath not yet passed their Vote. The Assembly hath been long in debate about the Officers and Government of the Kirk (concerning which, we offered the two Papers which wee drew up, according to the practice of our own, and other Reformed Kirks, and so neere as we could conceive, to the minde of the General Assembly, and did send to the Commissioners of the General Assembly) and hath passed many votes about the one and the other, but hath turned their thoughts to such ripenesse and perfection, that they could think upon the publishing of them, or presenting them to your sight, nor is it in their power to do so, without warrant of Parliament. Your wisedome will consider that they are not a General Assembly, but some select Persons, called by Authority to give their advice in matters of Religion, that they walk in a way which hath not been troden by this Nation before this time, that many things seeme new unto them, and cannot obtain their assent, till they see them clearly warranted by the Word of GOD; That matters of the Government of the Kirk have been much controverted here, and the prejudices against Presbyteriall Government are many and great; That the two extremes of Prelacie and Independencie, which latter is the general claime of all Sects and Sectaries, have prevailed most in this Kirk, and no other thing known by the multitude but the one or the other; That such as look toward the Government of the Reformed Kirks, finde a mighty party within and without opposing them; And that Reformation and Uniformitie must therefore be a work to full of difficulty, that the hand of the most high GOD, which is now begun to be streched out in this Land, must bring it to passe.

There was also presented to the Assembly, a new Paraphrase of the Psalmes in English Meeter, which was well liked of, and commended by some of the Members of the Assembly; But because we conceived that one Psalme Book in all the three Kingdomes was a point of Uniformity much to be desired, we took the boldnes (although we had no such expresse and particular Commission) to oppose the present allowing thereof, till the Kirk of Scotland should be acquainted with it; and therefore have we now sent an essay thereof in some Psalmes. We have also sent another Specimen, in Print, done by some Ministers of the City. Your wisedome has to consider, whether it be meet to examine them by your Commissioners there, that their judgements be sent up unto the Assembly here, both about the generall of Uniformity in this point, and about the particular way of effecting it, whether by either of these two, or by any other Paraphrase, or by changing some expressions in the Books now in use, which is aymed at by the first of these two.

As we cannot but admire the good hand of GOD in the great things done here already, particularly; That the Covenant (the foundation of the whole Work) is taken, Prelacie and the whole train thereof, extirpated; The Service-Book in many places forsaken, plain and powerful preaching set up; Many Colledges in Cambridge provided with such Ministers, as are most zealous of the best Reformation; Altars removed; The Communion in some places given at the Table with sitting; The great Organs at Pauls and of Peters in Westminster taken down; Images and many other Monuments of idolatry defaced and abolished; The Chappel-royal at

Whitchal purged and reformed; and all by authority in a quiet manner at noon day, without tumult: So have we from so notable experience, joyned with the promises of the Word sufficient ground of confidence that GOD will perfect this Work against all opposition, and of encouragement for us all to be faithfull in the Work of God, which is carried on by his mighty Hand, that no man can oppose it, but he must be seen fighting against GOD, It is unto us no small matter of comfort, that we have heard of no Minister of the Gospel (except such as the Kirk hath rejected) joining with the Malignants there, in their ungodly and unnaturall afflicting of that Kingdome, while they are endeavouring the relief of the afflicted in this Kingdome; and we pray and hope, that they may carefully keep the unity of the Spirit in the bond of peace, and walk worthy both of their holy calling, and of the great Work, which the Lord is working by his own weak servants in Kirk and Policy.

Be pleased to receive a Letter from the Assembly, unto which you will return such an answer as shall seem good unto your wisedome, and withall (which is our humble desire) some word of your thankfull acknowledgement of the respect and favours done by them unto us.

We have at all occasions since our coming hither, acquainted the Commission with our proceedings, and by the help of God, shall be industrious in obeying your directions and theirs, during our abode here, which through the power and blessing of God, bringing the affairs of his own Church to a peaceable and blessed successe, wee wish may be for a short time, and unto which your fervent prayers through Christ maybe very effectuall, which therefore is the humble and earnest desire of

Worcester house,
London May 20. 1644.

Your affectionate fellow-labouring and fellow feeling Brethren in the Work of the Lord.

JO. MAITLAND.

Alex Henderson. Sam. Rutherfurd. Robert Baillie. George Gillespie.

THE LETTER FROM THE SYNOD OF DIVINES IN THE KIRK OF ENGLAND, TO THE GENERALL ASSEMBLY.

Right Honourable, right Reverend, and dearly beloved Brethren in Jesus Christ,

The blessing and comfort of that inviolable Union which our gracious GOD hath vouchsafed to both Churches and Nations, gave us opportunity the last year, to breath out some of our sighs into your compassionate bosomes; And such have been the soundings of your bowels, as have offered violence to Heaven by your effectuall fervent prayers, and brought many sweet refreshing to our languishing spirits by your pious and comfortable Letters, in answer to ours.

This makes us studious of all means of acknowledging your tender Sympathie, and of laying held on all opportunities of repaying again to the same streams of consolation: for which end, as we canno but confesse, that in the midst of those boysterous waves wherein we have been daily tossed, wee have met with many gracious and unexpected encouragements, so we must needs renew our former mournings, and rend our hearts afresh unto you, with greatest instance for all the assistance that your Prayers, Tears, Learning, Piety, and Largenesse of heart can possibly contribute to your poor afflicted and still-conflicting Brethren: And this we the rather beg of you, who, having bin first in the furnace of affliction, and are come out of great tribulation, are meetest to commiserate, and best able to comfort others in any trouble, by the comforts wherewith you your selves have been comforted of GOD.

It was in our desires to have presented to your Venerable Assembly, some of our dearest respects in writing, by that eminently learned and much honored Commissioner of yours, the Lord Waristoun: But his departure hence was so sudden to us, and unexpected by us that we could not have time (as his Lordship can inform you) to tender by him such a testimony of our Brotherly & intimate affections, as may in some measure suite with your manifold and most affectionate expressions toward us, when our sighings were many, and our hearts faint: For such hath been your love, that no waters can quench it, and such the undertakings of the whole Kingdome of Scotland through your furtherance, that we already begin to reap the fruits of all that Piety, Prudence, and Valour, which at this day render your Nation worthily renowned in the Christian World; and us, exceedingly straitned and restlesse in our selves, untill God please to open a way for our endeavours, to make some more answerable returns.

Toward this, our thoughts and hopes were to have made, ere now, some proceedings of our Assembly legible in yours, But such are the continued distractions which lye upon our spirits, by means of the sad and bleeding condition of this Kingdome, as have cast us much behinde our own expectations, and hindred that expedition which the necessities of this Nation, and the desires of our Brethren abroad, do earnestly call for at our hands.

Sometimes through GODS goodnesse wee have a prosperious Gale, Sometimes againe, we saile like Paul and his company, very slowly many dayes. And even then, when wee draw near the fair Havens, some contrary Windes put us out into the Deep again. We walk in paths that have hitherto been untrodden by any Assembly in this Church: We therefore are inforced to spend more time in our inquiries, and in seeking of GOD a right way for us, that at length we may put into that high way, the way of holinesse, wherein Wayfaring men, though fools, shall not erre: And we will wait upon our GOD (before whom we have been this Day humbling of our souls) untill he lead us into all these Truths which we seek after; and we shall labour to be yet more vile in our own eyes, as finding by experience that it is not in man to direct his way.

Those Winds which for a while do trouble the Aire, do withall purge and refine it: And our trust is that through the most wise Providence and blessing of GOD, the Truth by our so long continued agitations, will be better cleared among us, and so our service will prove more acceptable to all the Churches of Christ, but more especially to you, while we have an intentive eye to our peculiar Protestation, and to that publick Sacred Covenant entred into by both the Kingdomes, for Uniformity in all his Majesties Dominions.

Which Work we carry on (against what ever difficulties are cast in our way) with more ease and comfort, by the great sedulity and seasonable assistance wee daily receive from your Noble and Reverend Commissioners sitting among us: Their Prudence will (we doubt not) sufficiently furnish you with more particular information touching our affairs; And here, we cannot but acknowledge that the assidious presence of these our learned and highly-esteemed Brethren among us, and their free and faithfull contributing of their counsels to us, doe oblige us much to a double duty; the one of Thanks, which we now heartily render to you, for sending to us such excellent Helpers; the other of Request, which wee earnestly make for their continuance with us, untill the Work bee brought up to the finishing Cubite.

Now, the Great Master-Builder (without whose Almighty concurrence, the Builders labour but in vain) accomplish and perfect all his own glorious Work in your hands, and in ours, also, to his own Glory, the peace and edification of all the Churches, and the comfort of our selves over all our travels and sufferings.

Westminster, May 17. 1644.

Your most affectionate Brethren and servants in the Lord, by the direction, and in the Name of this whole Assembly,

William Twiffe, Prolocutor.
Cornelius Burges, Assessor.
Henry Robrough, Scriba.
Adoniram Byfield, Scriba.

THE GENERALL ASSEMBLIES ANSWER TO THE RIGHT REVEREND THE ASSEMBLY OF DIVINES IN THE KIRK OF ENGLAND.

Right Honourable, right Reverend, and most dearly beloved in our Lord,

We do thankfully acknowledge your respectfull remembrance of us by your Letters at all occasions; and not a little rejoyce to see that happie correspondence and Christian communion so sweetly entertained amongst us, which is so acceptable in the sight of the Lord, so pleasant and profitable, especially when kept and entertained betwixt Kirks and Kingdomes about affairs of highest and most publick concernment and interest: We have nothing more in our desires than to entertain that harmonious correspondence, that Christian sympathie and compassion, that sounding and resounding of bowels, which well beseemeth Kirks and Nations, United by a solemn League & sacred Covenant, for mutuall endeavours, by all lawfull means to a further unitie in that Faith once delivered to the Saints, and greater Uniformitie in Divine Worship, Discipline, and Government, according to the Paterne.

The case and condition of your bleeding Kingdome is no lesse sensible to us, than if our selves were in affliction with you; but we trust all is working to your best, and to our Lords glory: That some of you hes fallen, it is to try you, purge you, and make you white: If the Lord by those means be with that Reformation of his Ordinances, bringing also alongst that other Reformation of hearts and lives should it not be welcomed with all joy, although it bee upon the expence of blood and lives? The Lord will turn the bygone rage of Man to his glory and your spiritual good the remnant of rage will hee restraine. The Lord delivereth his owne by degrees, he is with them in trouble, and delivereth them, and honoureth them; He who hath been sensibly with you hitherto, and upholden you in your trouble, will we trust, yet deliver you, and honour you: The more ye sow in tears, the greater shall be your harvest of peace and joy, when the Lord according to the dayes wherein he hath afflicted you, and the years wherein yee have seen evill, shall make you glad, and his Work to appeare unto you, and his glory unto your children, and the beautie of the Lord your God to be upon you, and shall establish the work of your hands; yea, even establish the work of your hands.

We should prove both unthankfull to God, and unfaithfull to men, did wee not hold out unto you the Lords gracious and powerfull dealing with us in the like condition, and comfort you with the consolations wherewith wee our selves have been comforted: We were involved in the like difficulties; we had the strong opposition of highest Authoritie set over two powerfull Kingdoms, beside this of ours; and the unhappy providence of our wickedly wise and wary Prelates, had done what in them lay, to make the Ministery of this Land sworn Enemies to the intended Reformation: So that we walked in a very wildernesse, in a labyrinth, and as upon deep waters, wherein not onely did our feet lose footing, but also our eyes all discovering or discerning of any ground; yea; wee were ready to lose our selves: Yet the Lord hath graciously rid us, and recovered us out of all these difficulties, and set our feet upon a rock, and ordered our goings. The experience wee have had in our own persons, affoordeth us confidence and hope concerning your affaires; and wee trust this hope shall not be disappointed; it is our duety to hope upon experience, and it is the Lords word and promise, that such an hope shall not be ashamed. It cannot choose but beget confidence in you, when ye shall consider, that ye have seen before your eyes your neighboring Ship of this Kirk and Kingdome, having (as it were) loosed from your side, in the like or self-same storme, notwithstanding all tossing of windes and waves, yet (not by might, nor by power, but by the Spirit of the Lord of hosts) to have arrived safe and sound to the Port and Harberie; yea, and to have dared to put out again unto the storm, to contribute her weak endeavours for your help.

We acknowledge your impediments to be great and many, the sufferings of your Brethren, the People of GOD, cannot choose but both damp your spirits, and divide your thoughts: Your walking in an untroden and unknown way, must put you (though never so willing to go on speedily, yet) to take time and leisure to ask for the right way, and ye want nor the opposition of some amongst your selves, to whom notwithstanding we trust the Lord will reveale his truth in his own time. Never the lesse (much honoured and dear Brethren) go on couragiously against the stream of all opposition; every Mountain in the way of Zerubbabel, the Lord shall make plain; and as many of you as are perfect, be thus minded, that forgetting the things that are behinde, and looking to the things that are before, you presse hard towards the mark, as having before you, not onely the prize of the high calling and recompence of reward, but also at the end of this race, these two precious Pearls and inestimable Jewels of Truth and Unity, and all the Reformed Churches beholding and looking on, not onely as witnesses, but also being ready to congratulate and embrace you.

We were greatly refreshed to hear by Letters from our Commissioners there with you, and by a more particular relation from the Lord Waristoun now with us, of your praise-worthy proceedings, and of the great good things the Lord hath wrought among you and for you: Shall it seem a small thing in our eyes, that the Covenant (the foundation of the whole Work) is taken? That that Antichristian Prelacy with all the traine thereof is extirpate? That the door of a right entrie unto faithful Shepherds is opened; many corruptions, as Altars, Images, and other Monuments of Idolarry and Superstition removed, defaced and abolished; the Service-book in many places forsaken, and plaine and powerfull preaching set up; the great Organs at Pauls and Peters taken down; That the Royal Chappell is purged and reformed, Sacraments sincerely administrate, and according to the paterne in the Mount, That your Colledges, the Seminaries of your Kirk, are planted with able and sincere Professors? That the good hand of GOD hath called and kept together so many pious, grave, and learned Divines for so long a time, and disposed their hearts to search his Truth by their frequent Humiliations, continuall Prayers, and learned and peaceable debates? Should not all and each one of these stir up our souls to blesse the Lord, and render both you and us confident, that he who hath begun the good Work, will perfect it, and put the Copestone upon it; That the beauty of a perfected Worke may shine to all Nations, and we may say and shout, Grace, Grace, unto it; That the time may be when full liberty and leasure shall be to all the Builders of the House of GOD, to give themselves with both their hands to the building up and edifying the People of GOD in these things that belong to life and Godlinesse, to the making of them wise to salvation, and throughly furnished to every good work, and when the Lord shall delight to dwell more familiarly, and to work more powerfully in, and by his throughly purified Ordinances? That you afflicted and tossed with tempests and not comforted, shall have your stones laid with fair Colours, your foundation with Saphires, your Children shall be taught of GOD, and shall have great peace, and no Weapon framed against you shall prosper, and every tongue that riseth against you in Judgement shall bee condemned; That the Lord will awake as in the ancient dayes, as in the generation of old; That the Redeemed of the Lord shall come unto Zion with singing, and sorrow and mourning shall flee away.

And as we are confident that the Lord who heareth Prayer, and hath promised to guide his Servants in all truth, will bring your labours to a comfortable Conclusion: So do all the Reformed Kirks, and the Kirk of Scotland above all others extreamly long for the taste of the fruits of their pious labours and continual pains: And so much the more, that we have suspended some material determinations amongst our selves, upon expectation of Uniformity; And that in the meane time so many scandalous Papers come to our view, and to the hands of the People here, for libertie of Conscience, toleration of Sects, and such Practices as are contrary to the Doctrine, Goverment, and Peace of all the Reformed Kirks. For stopping and suppressing whereof, as wee doubt not, but your wisedome, and the Authority of the honourable Houses of Parliament will use some more effectual means; So do we hope that your Determinations shall carry such evidence of Divine Truth, and demonstration of the Spirit, that those unhappy Clouds of darknesse shall be so scattered, that they shall be no more gathered nor appear hereafter, to the dishonour of God, the prejudice of his Truth, and the scandalizing of so many Souls for which Christ hath dyed.

We do with hearty thankfulnesse resent all the kindnesse and respect you have shown to our Commissioners, and your high esteeme of them in love for the Works sake; Although their presence here would be very comfortable unto us, very steedable to the publick, and necessar in respect of their great and important particular charges and Stations; yet do we willingly dispense with all, yea nothing shall be too dear unto us, so that this Work be finished with joy, and Jerusalem made the glory and praise of the whole Earth: Because of the house of the Lord our God we will feel her good: For our Brethren and Companions sake, we will now say, Peace be within her Walls, prosperity within her Palaces.

Edinburgh 4 June 1644,

Subscribed in name of the Generall Assembly of the Kirk of Scotland, by the Moderator of the Assembly.

THE ASSEMBLIES ANSWER TO THEIR COMMISSIONERS AT LONDON.

Reverend and Beloved Brethren,

It would have been the rejoycing of our hearts, and the lightning of our countenances, to have seen your faces, and injoyed your presence here with us, especially, should yee have arrived unto us loaden with the spoils of Antichrist, the Trophees of the Kirk of Christ, and the long longed-for fruits of your painfull labours: But seeing it hath pleased the Lord whose Interest in the businesse is main and principall otherwise to dispose, it doth become us with all humility to submit to his good pleasure, with faith & patience to attend his leasure, for he that beleeveth maketh not haste, and with more frequency and fervencie in prayer seek to him who will be sought for these things and having begun the good work will perfect it, and double the benefit by bestowing it in a more seasonable time unto us.

We have not been a little refreshed with your Letters sent unto us and the Commissioners of the preceeding Assembly, and with these from the Reverend Synod of Divines, the answer whereof you will be pleased to present unto them: by all which and more particularly by a full Relation from the Lord Waristoun a faithfull witnesse and a fellow labourer with you there, we see and acknowledge that by the Lords blessing, the Progresse of the Work is already more, than we can overtake in the course of our thankfulness; that your labours are very great, your pains uncessant, your thoughts of heart many, that ye endure the heat of the day; but being confident of your patient continuance in wel-doing, and that your labours shall not be in vaine in the Lord, wee have renewed your Commission, and returned the Lord Waristoun unto you, according to your desire, that ye may prosecute that great Work which the Lord hath blessed so farre in your hands.

When the Ordination and entry of Ministers shall be conformable to the Ordinance of God, there is to be expected a richer blessing shall be powred out from above, both of furniture and assistance upon themselves, and of successe upon their labours; for which end as our earnest desire is, that the Directory for it may be established: so doe we exceedingly long to see the common Directory for worship perfected, which may prove an happy meane of that wished for Uniformity in the Kirks of the three Kingdomes, shall (we trust) direct by all Rocks of offence and occasions of stumbling, and shall remove all these corruptions wherewith the Lords sacrifice and service hath been defiled.

That point concerning a change of the Paraphrase of the Psalmes in Meeter, we have referred to the Commissioners here, whose power and Commission granted by the preceding Assembly, we have renewed and continued. That there be difficulties concerning Kirk-Government, wee think it not strange for these reasons you lay our before us; yet because the minds of men are still in suspense upon the successe of the determination of that Reverend Assembly on the one hand, and upon the successe of the Warre on the other: which doth not a little faint their hearts and feeble their hands, both you and we must be instant with God and man for a finall determination of all these debates, and a happy and speedy conclusion of this great affaire, so much concerning his own glory and the good of his Kirk. Now the Lord lead you in all truth, and give you understanding in all things.

Edinburgh 4. June 1644.

Subscribed in name of the Generall Assembly by the Moderator.

THE ASSEMBLIES LETTER TO THE KIRKS IN THE NETHERLANDS.

Fratres in Domino plurimum colendi.

Quæ Anno superiore Ecclesiarum Zelandicarum nomine, missæ sunt ad nos Literæ, ut eas communis totius Ecclesiæ vestræ Religicæ voluntatis restes suisse interpretaremur, effecit benevolentia vestra tot tantisque officiis nobis spectata: Quam sententiam nobis confirmarunt ea quæ copiosè clarissimus Eques D. Archibadus Jonsto nus Varistonus in soro supremo Judex, à reliquis tum Ordinum cum Ecclesiæ hujus Regni Delegate Londine nonita pridem remissus, in hac ipsa Synodo Nationali de eximio vestro erga nos syudio commemoravit: Præfertim quanta fid, quam solicita diligentia nofsram, vel Domini potius nostri Jesu Christi causam, quæ nunc Londini agitur & promoveriitis, & promovers etiamnum fatagatis. Quo in negotio, ex iis, quorum ab eo resitata audivimus nomina, de propensa reliquorum voluntate & cura, ut conciliandæ Ecclesiarum Britannicarum unionis fæliciter suscepta consilia, vestra ope & opera prosperum mature fortiantur exitum, minime obscura fecimus indicia. Sunt hæc tam illuseria benevolentiæ vestræ testimonia, & in omnium bonorum oculis adeo perspicua ut eorum memoriam nulla unquam delere potuerint oblivia. Laboris autem & jam inpensi & porrò suscepti ad controversias in Synodo Londinensi suborientes fœliciter expediendas

& decidendas nequando pœniteat ex eo quem per divinam jam benedictionem fructum cepistis, optima quæque in posterum sperare consentaneum est.

Huic tam honorifice beneficiorum vestrorum commemorationi à D. Varistonio factæ supervenerunt ex partibus Hiberniæ aquilonaribus Literæ multorum Chirographis subsignatæ; Qui singularis gratiæ in illam Ecelesiam divinitus effusæ, ex quo tempore in societatem fœderistrium unitorum sub Rege nostro Regnorum admissi sunt, "mentione facta, hujus inquiunt divinæ benedictionis amplissimum nuper habuimus testimonium. Sanctorum in Belgio liberalitatem eximiam; Qui nobis, ignotis licet & poregrinis, fratres se nostri amantissimos, & malorum nostrorum sensu tenerrima compunctos aperte demonstrârunt. Pauculos enim nos gladis superstites, & fame propediem interituros, omnibus extremis circumventos, in ipso articulo sublevarunt: Nec tantum oratione ad consolationum composita nobis animos confirmârunt, hortantes ut humiliter incedentes Deum liberatorem expectemus, qui non nisi ad breve tempus aciem suam à domo Jacob abscondere solet, sed subsidio insuper opulento cum annonæ tum aliarum rerum ad nostram intantis angustis relaxationem & solatium necessarium copiose nos refocillârunt. Tantum munificentiam cum supplices a Deo contendimus, ut septuplam ipsis in sinum rependat tum demisse vos etiam atque etiam rogamus ut in tanti beneficii agnitione Ecclesiis Belgicis, nobi eum gratias agatis. Hæc illi. In quo quidem officio si illis desimus, in nos pariter & illos graviter peccemus."

Agnoscimus igitur illustrissimorum & potentissimorum Hollandiæ, Zelandiæ, aliorumque Ordinum Belgicorum tam eximiam beneficenciam: Quibus non conniventibus modo & permittentibus (quod ipsum non vulgare beneficium habendum esset) sed authoribus etiam modumque & rationem ræscribentibus, exemplo qnoque præunitibus in subsidium fratrum nostrorum Hiberne collecta per Ecclesias facta ad ipsos mature deportata sit: Agnoscimus piorum in iisdem Ecclesiis Belgicis tam expromptam: volantatem & liberalitatem; tantum beneficium non in ipsos magis fratres nostres, quam in illorum persona in nosinet ipsos esse collatum: Vosque (fratres Reverendi) obnixè rogatos volumus, ut quemadmodum nos ad omnem grati animi significationem prompti semper erimus, ita quâ potissimum ratione commodum videbitur, illustrissimis & potentissimis Ordinibus nostre nomine gratias agatis populo autem Christiano curæ vestræ commisso tum publice universo, tum privatim singulis, ut occasio tulerit, demonstretis quam honorifice de ipsis sentiamus, & quanti faciamus tam eximiam benevolentiam & charitatem, quâ in Ecclesiarum Hibernicarum consolatione viscera nostra refocillaverunt. Quæ autem vestræ fuerint partes, fratres charissimi, quam pio studio & labore, quam assidua diligentia tantæ charitatis semen in segetem & maturam tandem messem provexeritis, cum nos libentes agnoscimus, tum res ipsa loquitur, & fructus opimus abunde testatur. Inprimis autem (quod caput est) tantæ gratiæ authorem & largitorem nos una cum Ecclesiis Hibernicis laudamus & celebramus: comprecantes ut in vos universos, in Ecclesias a Domino vobis commissas, in illustrissimos Belgii vestri Ordines Spiritum suum copiose effundat, ut quemadmodum in Rep. vestra adversus hostem potentissimum defendenda, & inter tantas bellorum moles indies amplificanda, in Evangelii luce & veritate incontaminatâ contra inferorum portas in vestris Ecclesiis propugnandâ, atque inde latius propagandâ, immensa

Dei vobis excubantis potentia, multiformis sapientia, & eximia beneficentia, per universum terrarum orbem hactenus celebrata est; ita bonis omnibus vos deinceps cumulare pergat idem fons omnis bonitatis, ut frementibus religionis & libertatis vestræ hostibus, sapientiæ & optimarum artium juxta ac armorum triumphorum-que gloriâ inter nobilissimas gentes Resp. vestra fœderata quotidie magis emineat, Ecclesia sacrorum puritate, & cælestis veritatis splendore perspicua refulgeat; eoque prosperè vobis cedant vestra prudentissima & saluberrima consilia, quibus certissimum ad fælicitatem publicam compendium vos capessure demonstratis, nec vobis tantum consulitis, sed de vicinis etiam Ecclesiis soliciti, quâ operâ, quâ consilio opibusque vestris eas sublevatis & confirmatis omnes, & quasi de specula unversis prospicientes de periculis imminentibus commonefacitis, & ad ruinam ab hostibus dolosè machinatam maturè precavendam armatis.

Ergo quod anno superiori, veluti signo dato, Reformatas omnes Ecclesias, missis ex Zelandia literis commonuistis, ut cum impostores, Jesu nomen impudenter ementiti, cæterique Antichristi satellites, quo securius in populum erroribus Pontificiis fascinatum grassari, & puriores Christi Ecclesias funditus extirpare queant, arctissimâ conjuratione Sociati ad impia consilia patranda sese accinxerunt, Ita Ecclesiæ quoque Reformatæ sine mora consilia in medium alacriter conferant, & animos ac vires conjungant, ut perniciem sibi omnibus intentatam in hostium capita retorqueant: ni fecerint, tam pudendæ ignaviæ excusatione apud posteritatem carituri: consilium non minus prudens & fidum, quam fælix & salutare libenter & tum agnovimus & nunc ipso etiam eventu comprobamus.

Principio autem ad hoc consequendum necessarium videtur, ut sine morâ convolemus omnes ad Deum nostrum clementissimum, qui postquam Ecclesiarum Reformatarum mores minimè reformatos multis annis longanimitate suâ pertulisset, ferulam primum, mox etiam gladium vibratum interminata, tandem rubentem & madidum suorumque sanguine calentem & spumantem per regiones plurimas jam diu circumtulis; in nos denique reliquos nunc intentat, nisi mature resipuerimus, & de domo ipsius amplius purgandâ, de gratia Domini nostri Jesu Christi pluris facienda, de cultu Dei ipsiusque institutis religiosius habendis, de Sabbatho ejus sanctificando, a quo nimium oculos nostros avertimus, & de moribus ad pietatis normam componendis magis serio quam hactenus a nobis factum est, nobiscum statuentes cum populo Dei sub Nehemia, Josia, reliquisque piis Gubernatoribus, religioso fœdere percusso, tanquam firmissimo vinculo Deo obstricti, nos internes arctius adversus hostes univerimus, ut avertat Deus jam fumantem & capitibus nostris imminentem iram, quam peccata nostra plurima & maxima adversus nos prevocerunt & accenderunt.

Non tantum nobis deferimus, nondum eos renovato cum Deo fœdere, & votis nuncupatis dignos edidimus fructus, ut nostrum exemplum vobis proponere libeat: Quod tamen experti fumus, de Dei erga nos gratia, quod gratitudo erga Deum, quod gloria ipsius a nobis flagitat, celare non audemus. Quecunque nostra male merita sunt in conspectu Dei & hominum; certe ex quo die nos de religìoso fœdere cum Deo & inter nos ineundo cogitavimus, a portis inferorum revocari, & res nostræ omnes in Deum nostrum necessario conjectæ melius habere cæperunt, & fæliciore hactenus successu processerunt. Quod si de fœderis huiusmodi religiosa societate cocunda (quod rerum veltrarum & Religionis in Britannia nostra ex fœdere nuper inito perpurgandæ & stabilandæ commodo fieri possit) vestræ prudentiæ visum fuerit cogitare, & ex consilio eorum quorum interest statuere, ac eum aliis Reformatis Ecclesiis agere (proea qua apud omnes valetis gratia) ut eandem vobiscum ineant rationem, non dubium est, per Domini ac Dei nostri benignissimi Jesu Christi in Ecclesias suas gratiam, fore, ut non modo, quod certissimum adversus impendentia mala persugium anno superiore missis ex Zelandia literis denunciastis: Ecclesiæ Reformatæ arctioris Societatis vinculo inter se unita ad hostium conatus impetusque frangendos corroberentur & confirmantur; sed disiecti etiam lapides Dómus Dei per Germaniam ex rudere & cineribus ridevivi recolligantur, ac gloriosum Domini nostri Templum ibidem instauretur: & purioris Religionis Professores in istis Ecclesiis, per resipiscentiam ad eum qui percussit eos, reversi, & quod nullis canescat sæculis fœdere, Domino nobiscum coadunati, malis, sub quorum pondere tot annos gemiscunt, tandem subleventur. Qui Dies longe optatissimus si per Dei gratiam semel illuxerit: de consiliorum communione inter Reformatarum Ecclesiarum Synodos per Legatos & Literas concilianda redivivi possit ratio, per quam Ecclesiæ hostes compescantur, hæreses opprimantur, & schismata retarciantur, pax cum Deo & inter Ecclesias firma conservetur, & gloriosum Dei opus in Evangelio per orbem terrarum propagando, & Antichristi regno abolendo promoveatur. Quod ut optandum, & sperandum, piis & prudentibus vestris meditationibus, ut bonnum semen fæcundissimo solo commendamus.

Edinburgi. 4 Junii 1644.

Vestræ Dignitati & Fraternitati addictissimi, Pastores & Seniores Nationalis Synodi Scoticanæ, &c. nostro omnium nomine ac mandato.

DIRECT.

Ecclesiis Dei, qua sunt in unitis Hollandiæ, Zelandiæ, aliisque fœderati Belgii Provinciis.

ORDINANCE CONCERNING BURSARS.

The Assembly understanding that the Overture for maintaining Bursars, in the Assembly holden in the year 1641. upon the 7. of August, Sess. 15 is never yet put in practice: Do therefore Ordain Presbyteries to put the same in practice with all diligence, and to make account thereof to the next Assembly.

ORDINANCE FOR UP LIFTING AND IMPLOYING PENAL-TIES CONTAINED IN ACTS OF PARLIAMENT, UPON PI-OUS USES.

The Assembly understanding that the executing of some laudable Acts of Parliament, made against Non-Communicants and Excommunicate persons, and of divers other Acts containing pecuniall pains for restraining of Vice, and advancing Piety, is much neglected by the slownesse of Presbyteries and Ministers, in seeking Execution thereof: Therefore ordains Presbyteries and Ministers respectivè, to be diligent hereafter by all means, in prosecuting full and exact Execution of all such Acts of Parliament, for lifting the saids Penalties contained in the same, and for faithfull imployment thereof, upon pious uses, and that every Presbyterie report their diligence herein yearly to Generall Assemblies.

AN OVERTURE CONCERNING PROMISES OF MARRIAGE MADE BY MINORS, TO THOSE WITH WHOM THEY HAVE COMMITTED FORNICATION.

Forsameikle as it is found by experience, that some young men being put to Colledges by their wel-affected Parents, that they may be instructed in the knowledge of Arts and Sciences, to the intent they may bee more able for publick Imployments in the Ecclesiastick and Civill state, that the said Children hes committed Fornication. And the Woman and her friends hes seduced the foresaid Schollers being Minors, to make promise of Marriage to the party with whom they have committed Fornication; And thereupon intends to get the benefite of Marriage with the said young men, not onely without the consent of their Parents, but to their great grief, and to the great appearance of the ruine and overthrow of their estate: Which may be the case of Noblemen and Gentlemens children, as welas of these of other estates and degrees within the Kingdom. Wherefore if the Assembly think it expedient, it would be declared that all such promises be made null and of none effect, especially where the maker of the promise is Minor, and not willing to observe the samine; because his Parents will not consent, but oppose and contradict, threatning to make him lose not onely his favour but both blessing and birth-right. This Ordinance shal not onely be very expedient for many good civill causes, but is very consonant and agreeable to the Word of God, and will be very comfortable to many Godly Parents, who otherwise may be disappointed of their pious intentions, and have the comfort they expected, turned to an heavy and grievous crosse.

The Generall Assembly thinks it convenient at this time to delay any determination in the matter above-written untill the next assembly, That in the meane time every Presbterie may take the same to their serious consideration, and report their judgements to the Assembly.

ACT CONCERNING DISSENTING VOICES IN PRESBYTERIES AND SYNODS.

The Assembly thinks it necessar, if any Member of Presbyteries or Synods shall finde in matters depending before them, that the Moderator shall refuse to put any thing of importance to voices; Or if they finde any thing carried by plurality of voices to any determination which they conceive to be contrary to the Word of God, the Acts of Assembly, or to the received order of this Kirk, That in either of these cases they urge their dissent to be marked in the Register; And if that be refused, that they protest as they would desire to be free of common censure with the rest: And the Assembly declares the dissenters to be censurable, if their dissent shall be found otherwise nor they conceived.

ACT CONCERNING THE ELECTION OF A MODERATOR IN PROVINCIALL ASSEMBLIES.

The General Assembly understanding that some Provincial Assemblies in choosing their Moderator, tye themselves to these Persons who have been before named and designed in particular Presbyteries, which is against the libertie of the Provincial Assembly: Therefore discharges Presbyteries to make any such nomination hereafter; And ordain Provincials in their first meeting, to elect their Moderator, and to make their own List for that effect without any such prælimitation.

ACT FOR KEEPING OF THE FAST BY THE CONGREGATIONS IN THE TOWNE WHERE THE ASSEMBLY HOLDS.

The Assembly judge it most necessar and comely, seeing the first day of the meeting of Generall Assemblies, is by the laudable practice of this Kirk a day of Fasting and Humiliation, for craving the Lords blessing to that Meeting; That not onely the Members of the Assembly, but that all the Congregations also of the Town where the Assembly holds bee so exercised: And that publick Worship bee in all the Kirks thereof that day for that effect.

MEETING ANNOUNCEMENT.

The Generall Assembly appoints the meeting of the next Assembly, to be upon the last Thursday of May, in the Yeer 1645. at Edinburgh.

LETTER.

Right Honourable, Reverend, and beloved in the Lord,

As we are not without the knowledge, so are we not without the feeling of the distresses of our Native Countrey, and of the troubles of our dear Brethren, specially that the hand of the Lord is stretched out against you, not only by Invasion from without of the basest of the children of men, but also by the unnatural treachery of some within; who have dealt perfidiously in the Covenant and Cause of God: They hisse and gnash the teeth; they say, Wee have swallowed her up: certainly this is the day that wee looked for: Wee have found, wee have seen it; the Lord hath caused thine Enemy to rejoice over thee, he hath set up the horn of thine Adversaries: Yet (saith the Lord, who is thy Maker and thy Husband, the Lord of hosts is his name, and thy Redeemer the holy One of Israel) for a small moment have I forsaken thee, but with great mercies will I gather thee. In a little wrath I hide my face from thee, for a moment; but with everlasting kindnesse will I have mercy on thee: For this is as the waters of Noah, the Covenant of my peace shall not be removed, saith the Lord that hath mercy on thee. When the foundation of the House of the Lord was laid, the Priests and Levites sung together in praising and giving thanks to the Lord; Because he is good, for his mercy endureth for ever, And we hope at this time upon the coming of our reverend Brethren, and the sight of that which they bring with them, the noise of the shout of joy; shall be louder then the noise of the weeping of the People. This we may say, that not many years ago many of us would have been content to have losed our lives, that we might have obtained that which the Lord, if not in a miraculous, yet in a marvellous and merciful providence, hath brought to passe in this Iland, in these dayes, which many before us, have desired to see, & have not seen. God forbid that it should seeme a small thing in your eyes which is done here already, as it is expressed in a Paper from the Parliament, and Letters from the Assembly. Ye are best acquainted with the tentations and difficulties which ye meet with there, which are also very sensible unto us; And when we consider how the Lord hath carried on his work here at the first taking of the Covenant, and since, against much learning and contradiction, against much Policie, power, and all sorts of opposition (such as Reformation useth to encounter) we are ravished with admiration of the right hand of the Almighty. For our part, we may confidently avouch in the sight of GOD and before you, whom next unto GOD we do respect and reverence, and to whom as your servants we are accomptable, that in all our proceedings we had first of all the word of GOD before our eyes for the Rule; and for our Patern the Church of Scotland, so much as was possible; and no lesse (if not more) then if all this time since we parted from you, we had been sitting in a National Assembly there, and debating matters with our Brethren at home: Where we were not able to get every thing framed to our minde, we have endeavoured as much as we could, to preserve our own Reformation and practice, of which our Brethren will give you accompt in the particulars, we hope, to your satisfaction. That an Uniformitie in every thing is not obtained in the beginning, let it not seem strange; The levelling of the high Mountain of Prelacie, The laying aside of the Book of Common Prayer, The Directory of Worship concluded in both Houses of Parliament, and the principall Propositions of Church-government passed in the Assembly, all of them according to the solemne League and Covenant, the greatest of all, are three or foure witnesses to prove, that the Lord hath done great things for us, whereof we are glad, and which make us like them that dream: And we are sure, that not onely the Reformed Kirks, but the Papists will say, The Lord hath done great things for them.

All that we desire, is: 1. That the Directory of Worship may be returned by our Brethren with all possible expedition, that it may be published here, and put in practise, as that which is extreamely longed for by the good People, and will be a remedy of the many differences and divisions about the Worship of God in this Kingdome, esspecially in this place: If there be any thing in it that displeaseth, let it be remonstrate upon irrefragable and convincing reason, otherwise ye will in your wisedome give approbation to it. 2. If there be any particular differences among some Brethren; which are not determined, but passed over in silence in the Directory, and yet hinted at in the Letter from the Assembly, we hope that in your wisedome ye will so consider of them, that they may be layde aside in due time, and that in the mean while, till the Directory be concluded and put in practice, there be no trouble about them, for that were as Snow in Summer, and as Rain in Harvest. We know nothing of that kinde, that all of us who love Unitie, Order, and Edification, may not perfectly agree in, without scandall or disturbance: And we beseech the Lord to keep that Kirk free of such Sects and Monsters of opinions, as are daily set on foot and multiplied in this Kingdome, through the want of that Church-government by Assemblies, which hath preserved us, and we hope, through the blessing of God, shall cure them. 3. Because Nationall Assemblies cannot frequently conveene, we humbly desire, that such a Commission may be settled as we may at all occasions till the Work be finished, have our recourse unto, for our direction and resolution: for we know both our own weaknesse: and the greatnesse of the Work: wherein we can promise no more but to be faithfull in obeying your commandments, as in the sight of God, whom with our Souls we pray, to grant you his Spirit, to guide you into all truth, And thus continue.

Worcester house, Jan. 6. 1646.

Your humble and faithfull Servants.

Subscrib.
Alex. Henderson.
Jo. Maitland.
Sam. Rutherfurd.

DIRECT.

For the Right Reverend the Generall Assembly of the Kirk of Scotland.

THE LETTER FROM THE SYNODE OF DIVINES IN EN-GLAND, TO THE GENERALL ASSEMBLY.

Right honourable, right reverend, and dearly beloved in the LORD JESUS,

As cold waters to a thirsty soul, so is good news from a far Countrey. We your Brethren, yet remaining in the Furnace of affliction, and still labouring in the very fire, Have at length, by the good Hand of GOD upon us, attained so far toward the Mark at which we all aime, that we shall now send you, by two of your Reverend and Faithful Commissioners Mr Robert Bailie, and Mr George Gillespie (our much honoured Brethren) some good news of that great Work, after which your zeal for Truth and Peace hath so much thirsted, and for which you have not loved your lives unto the death.

Our progresse therein hath not been so expeditious as was desired and expected. This, unto such as either know not, or consider not, The weight and greatnesse of the Work, nor The manifold difficulties which have occurred to obstruct our proceedings in this day of darknesse and calamity (too sad to be expressed) hath been like unto hope deferred; which makes the heart sick: Howbeit, we trust, That when their desire (namely that which we have prepared, and are further in travell with) shall come unto them, It will be, through God, a Tree of life, as to our great comfort and encouragement, we already perceive it to be to both the honourable Houses of Parliament.

Touching this severall Papers brought to us from your Honourable and Reverend Commissioners, by the hands of the Committee appointed to treat with them in matters of Religion (one of the Papers, being given in the 10. of November 1643. Concerneth the severall sorts of Church-officers and Assemblies: Another, bearing date the 24. of January 1643. Concerneth Congregationall Elderships, and Classicall Presbyteries: The other, being presented the 15. of August last, representeth the necessity of making greater speed in settling the intended Uniformity in Religion, according to the late solemne Covenant:) We hold it our duty, in regard both of the act and inseparable Union, which the Lord hath happily and seasonably made between you and us, and of your indefatigable and inestimable labour of love to this afflicted Kingdom, to give your Lordships and the rest of that Venerable Assembly, some brief account.

Concerning one Confession of Faith, and Forme of Catechisme, we make no question of a blessed and perfect harmony with you. The publick Doctrine, held out by our Church to all the World (especially when it shall be reviewed, which is in great part done) concurring so much with yours, may assure you of your hearts desire in those particulars, so soon as time and opportunity may give us liberty to perfect what we have begun.

The chief reason of laying aside the review of our publick Doctrine, after the happy and much desired arrivall of your Reverend Commissioners here, was, The drawing up and accelerating of a Directory for Worship, and of a Forme of Church-Government; in both of which we stood at a greater distance from other Reformed Churches of Christ, and particularly from yours (which we very much honour) with whom our solemne sacred Nationall Covenant requireth us to endeavour the nearest Conjunction and Uniformity, that we and our posterity after us, may as Brethren live in Faith and Love, and the Lord may delight to dwell in the midst of us.

Nor have our labours there in been frustrate: For we have perfected and transmitted a Directory for Worship, to both Houses of Parliament; where it hath received such acceptance, that it is now passed in both the Honourable Houses of Parliament; which we hope will be to the joy and comfort of all our godly and dear Brethren in all His Majesties Kingdoms and Dominions.

We have not advised any imposition which might make it unlawfull to vary from it in any thing; Yet we hope, all our Reverend Brethren in this Kingdom, and in yours also, will so far value and reverence that which upon so long debate and serious deliberation hath been agreed upon in this Assembly (when it shall also passe with you, and be settled as the common publick Directory for all the Churches in the three Kingdomes) that it shall not be the lesse regarded and observed. And albeit we have not expressed in the Directory every minute particular, which is or might be either laid aside or retained among us, as comely and usefull in practice; yet we trust—that none will be so tenacious of old customs not expressely forbidden, or so averse from good examples although new, in matters of lesser consequence, as to insist upon their liberty of retaining the one, or refusing the other, because not specified in the Directory; but be studious to please others rather then themselves.

We have likewise spent divers moneths in the search of the Scriptures, to finde out the minde of Christ concerning a Forme of Church-government, wherein we could not but expect the greatest difficulty: For our better Progresse herein, wee have with all respect considered the severall Papers of your Honourable and Reverend Commissioners, touching this Head; and do with all thankfulnesse, acknowledge their great zeal, judgement, and wisdom expressed therein (as also, the excellent assistance and great furtherance of your Reverend Commissioners in this great Work; which now, through GODS goodnesse, is very near to a period also).

In pursuit whereof, we made a strict survey and scrutinie of every Proposition, that we might finde it agreeable to, and warranted by the Word of God, in a method of our own; without resting upon any particular modell or frame whatsoever already constituted: What we have performed, and how farre we have proceeded therein, we leave to the information of your Reverend Commissioners, who have been eye and ear witnesses of all that hath past, and we doubt not but you will shortly receive a satisfactory answer from hence, so soon as it shall be passed in the Honourable Houses of Parliament.

And now, Right Honourable, and right Reverend Brethren, let it not seem grievous that we have this long delayed the satisfying of your earnest and just expectation: It is the Lot of Jerusalem, to have her Wals built in troublous times, when there are many adversaries. Nor let it offend, that (albeit we acknowledge the many, great, and inestimable expressions of your love zeal, and helpfulnesse unto us every way in the day of our distresse, to be beyond all that we can in words acknowledge) we professe plainly to you, That we do most unwillingly part with those our Reverend and dear Fellow-labourers, your Commissioners, whom now you have called home, to render an account of their imployment here; which hath been so managed both by them and the rest of their Honourable and Reverend Colleagues, as deserveth many thanks, and all Honourable acknowledgement, not onely from us, but from you also.

Give us leave to adde, that the long experience we have had of the great sufficiency, integrity, and usefulnesse of them all, in the great Work of Christ our common Lord and Master, inforceth us (next to our greatest sute, continuance of your fervent prayers) to be earnest suiters, not onely for the continuance of these excellent helpers, Mr. Alex Henderson, and Mr. Sam. Rutherfurd, yet remaining with us, but also for the speedy return hither of our Reverend Brethren that are now going hence, for the perfecting of that Work which yet remains. And this sute we trust, you will the rather grant, because of the great and joint concernment of both Churches and Kingdoms in these matters.

Now the spirit of wisdom and of all grace rest upon you in all your great consultations, as at all times, so especially now when you shall be gathered together in the Name of the Lord Jesus, for the further building up and polishing of his Church; and cause the fruit of all your labour to be to the praise and glory of GOD, and the comfort and rejoycing of the hearts of all the Israel of God: He reward all our dear Brethren of that Sister Church and Nation manifold into their bosome, all the labours, love, and sufferings which they have afforded, and still do, cheerfully continue, for our sakes and the Gospels, in this distracted and bleeding Kingdom; suppresse all commotions and bloody practices of the common Enemy, in both, yea in all the three Kingdoms; set up the Throne of Jesus Christ, and make all the Kingdoms to be the Lords, and our Jerusalem to be a praise upon Earth, that all that love her and mourn for her, may rejoyce for joy with her, and may suck and be satisfied with the breasts of her consolation.

Westminster, Jan 6. 1644.

Subscribed by Your most loving Brethren, and fellow labourers in the Work of the Lord, in the name of this whole Assembly,

William Twisse, Prolocutor.
Cornelius Burges, Assessor.
John White, Assessor.

Henry Robrough, Scriba.

Adoniram Byfield, Scriba.

DIRECT.

To the Right Honourable, and right Reverend, the Generall Assembly of the Church of Scotland, these presents

28 JAN. 1645. POST MERIDIEM. DIE MARTIS. SESS. 5.

APPROBATION OF THE PROCEEDINGS OF THE COMMIS-SION OF THE TWO PRECEDING ASSEMBLIES.

The Generall Assembly, having heard the report of the Committee appointed to consider and examine the Proceedings of the Commissioners of the two last Generall Assemblies, viz. Of the Assemblies held in Edinburgh in the yeers 1643 and 1644. And after mature deliberation, and serious consideration thereof, Finding that the whole Acts, Proceedings, and Conclusions of the saids Commissioners contained in a Book and Register, subscribed by Mister Andrew Ker their Clerk, and by Master George Leslie Moderator, and Master William Jaffray, Clerk to the said Committee; Declare much wisedome, diligence, vigilancie, and commendable zeal; And that the saids Commissioners have orderly and formally proceeded in every thing according to their Commissions; Do therefore Ratifie and Approve the said whole Acts, Proceedings, and Conclusions of the Commissioners of the two Assemblies aforesaid.

3. FEBRUAR. 1645. DIE LUNÆ, POST MERIDIEM. SESS. 10.

ACT OF THE GENERALL ASSEMBLY OF THE KIRK OF SCOTLAND, FOR THE ESTABLISHING AND PUTTING IN EXECUTION OF THE DIRECTORY FOR THE PUBLICK WORSHIP OF GOD.

Whereas an happy Unity and Uniformity in Religion amongst the Kirks of Christ in these three Kingdoms; united under one Soveraigne, hath been long and earnestly wished for by the godly and well-affected amongst us, was propounded as a main Article of the large Treaty, without which Band and Bulwark no safe well-grounded and lasting Peace could be expected; And afterward with greater strength and maturity, revived in the Solemne League and Covenant of the three Kingdomes; whereby they stand straitly obliged to endeavour the neerest Uniformity in one forme of Church-government, Directory of Worship, Confession of Faith, and forme of Catechising: Which hath also before and since our entring into that Covenant, been the matter of many Supplications and Remonstrances and sending Commissioners to the Kings Majestie, of Declarations to the Honourable Houses of the Parliament of England, and of Letters to the Reverend Assembly of Divines, and others of the Ministerie of the Kirk of England, being also the end of our sending Commissioners, as was desired from this Kirk, with Commission to treat of Uniformitie in the foure particulars afore-mentioned, with such Committees as should be appointed by both Houses of the Parliament of England, and by the Assembly of Divines sitting at Westminster: And beside all this, it being in point of conscience the chief motive and end of our adventuring upon manifold and great hazards, for quenching the devouring flame of the present unnaturall and bloody Warre in England, though to the weakning of this Kingdome within it self, and the advantage of the Enemy which hath invaded it, accounting nothing too dear to us, so that this our joy be fulfilled. And now this great Work being so far advanced, that a Directory for the publick Worship of GOD in all the three Kingdomes, being agreed upon by the Honourable Houses of the Parliament of England, after consultation with the Divines of both Kingdomes there assembled, and sent to us for our Approbation, that being also agreed upon by this Kirk and Kingdome of Scotland, it may be in the name of both Kingdomes presented to the King, for his Royal consent and Ratification. The General Assembly having most seriously considered, revised, and examined the Directory afore mentioned, after several publick readings of it, after much deliberation, both publickly, and in private Committees, after full liberty given to all to object against it, and earnest, invitations of all who have any scruples about it to make known the same; that they might be satisfied, Do unanimously, and without a contrary Voice, Agree to, and Approve the following directory, in all the Heads thereof, together with the Preface set before it: And doth require, decerne, and ordain, That according to the plain tenour and meaning thereof, and the intent of the Preface, it be carefully and uniformly observed and practised by all the Ministers and others within this Kingdome, whom it doth concerne; which practice shall be begun, upon Intimation given to the several Presbyteries, from the Commissioners of this General Assembly, who shall also take special care for the timeous Printing of this Directory, that a printed Copy of it, be provided and kept for the use of every Kirk in this Kingdome; Also that each Presbyterie have a printed Copy thereof for their use, and take special notice of the Observation or neglect thereof in every Congregation within their bounds, and make known the same to the Provincial or General Assembly, as there shall be cause. Provided alwayes, that the Clause in the Directory, of the Administration of the Lords Supper, which mentioneth the communicants sitting about the Table, or at it, be not interpreted, as if in the judgement of this Kirk, it were indifferent and free for any of the Communicants, nor to come to, and receive at the Table; or as if we did approve the distributing of the Elements by the Minister to each Communicant, and not by the Communicants among themselves. It is also provided, That this shall be no prejudice to the order and practice of this Kirk, in such particulars as are appointed by the Books of Discipline, and Acts of General Assemblies, and are not otherwise ordered and appointed in the Directory,

Finally, the Assembly doth with much joy and thankfulnes acknowledge the rich blessing and invaluable mercy of God, in bringing the so much wished for uniformity in Religion, to such a happy Period, that these Kingdoms once at so great distance in the form of Worship, are now by the blessing of GOD brought to a neerer Uniformity than any other Reformed Kirks, which is unto us the return of our Prayers, and a lightning of our Eyes, and reviving of our hearts, in the midst of our many sorrows and sufferings, a taking away in a great measure, the reproach of the People of GOD, to the stopping of the mouthes of Malignant and dis-affected persons, and an opening unto us a door of hope, that GOD hath yet thoughts of Peace towards us, and not of evil, to give us an expected end: In the expectation and confidence whereof we do rejoyce, beseeching the Lord to preserve these Kingdomes from Heresies, Schismes, Offences, Prophanesse, and whatsoever is contrary to sound Doctrine, and the power of Godlinesse, and to continue with us and the generations following, these his pure and purged Ordinances, together with an increase of the power and life thereof, To the glory of his great Name, the enlargement of the Kingdom of his Son, the corroboration of Peace and Love between the Kingdoms, the unity and content of all his People, and our edifying one another in love.

The Directory for Worship, mentioned in the preceeding Act, needs not to be here printed, because it is to be printed in a Book by it self.

7. FEBRUARY, 1645. POST MERIDIEM. SESS. 14.

OVERTURES FOR ADVANCEMENT OF LEARNING AND GOOD ORDER IN GRAMMAR SCHOOLS AND COLLEDGES.

I. That every Grammar School be visited twice in the year by Visitors, to be appointed by the Presbyterie and Kirk-Session in Landward Parishes, and by the Town-Councel in Burghs, with their Ministers; and where Universities are, by the Universities, with consent alwayes of the Patrons of the School, that both the fidelitie and diligence of the Masters, and the proficiencie of the Schollars in Pietie and Learning may appear, and deficiencie censured as well; And that the Visitors see that the Masters be not attracted by any other imployments, which may divert them their diligent attendance.

II. That for the remedie of the great decay of Poesie, and of abilitie to make Verse, and in respect of the common ignorance of Prosodie, no School-master be admitted to teach a Grammar School, in Burghs, or other considerable Paroches, but such as after examination, shall be found skilfull in the Latine Tongue, not only for Prose, but also for Verse; And that after other trials to be made by the Ministers, and others depute by the Session, Town, and Paroch for this effect, that he be also approven by the Presbyterie.

III. That neither the Greek Language, nor Logick, nor any part of Philosophie be taught in any Grammar School, or private place within this Kingdom, to young Schollers, who thereafter are to enter to any Colledge, unlesse it be for a preparation to their entrie there: And notwitstanding of any progresse, any may pretend to have made privately in these studies, yet in the Colledge hee shall not enter to any higher Classe, then that wherein the Greek Language is taught, and being entred, shall proceed orderly through the rest of the Classes, until he finish the Ordinary course of four years: Unlesse after due triall and examination, he be found equall in Learning, to the best or most part of that classe, to which he desires to ascend, by over-leaping a mid-Classe, or to the best or most part of those who are to be gradu-at, if he supplicate to obtain any degree before the ordinary time. And also, That there be found other pregnant reasons to move the faculty of Arts to condescend thereto; And otherwise that he be not admitted to the Degree of Master of Arts.

IV. That none be admitted to enter a Student of the Greek tongue in any Colledge, unlesse after triall he be found able to make a congruous Theame in Latine, or at least, being admonished of his errour, can readily shew how to correct the same.

V. That none be promoved from an inferiour Class of the ordinary course to a superiour, unlesse he be found worthy, and to have sufficiently profited: otherwise, that he be ordained not to ascend with his con-disciples, and if he be a Burser, that he lose his Burse. And namely, it is to be required, That those who are taught in Aristotle, be found well instructed in his Text, and be able to report in Greek, and understand his whole definitions, divisions, and principall precepts, so far as they have proceeded.

VI. Because it is a disgrace to Learning, and hinderance to Trades and other Callings, and an abuse hurtfull to the Publick, that such as are ignorant and un-worthy, be honoured with a Degree or publick Testimony of Learning; That there-fore such triall be taken of Students, specially of Magistrands, that those who are found unworthy, be not admitted to the Degree and honour of Masters.

VII. That none who have entred to one Colledge for triall or studie, be admit-ted to another Colledge, without the Testimonial of the Masters of that Colledge wherein he entred first, both concerning his Literature, and dutifull behaviour, so long as he remained there: at least, untill the Masters of that Colledge from whence he cometh, be timely advertised, that they may declare if they have any thing lawfully to be objected in the contrary. And that none be admitted, promoved, or receive Degree in any Colledge, who was rejected in another Colledge for his unfitnesse and unworthinesse, or any other cause repugnant to good Order, who leaves the Colledge where he was for eschewing of Censure, or chastising for any fault committed by him; or who leaves the Colledge because he was chastised, or for any other grudge or injust Quarrell against his Masters.

VIII. That none of those who may be lawfully received in one Colledge, after he was in another, be admitted to any other Classe, but to that wherein he was or should have been in the Colledge from whence he came, except upon reasons mentioned in the third Article preceding.

IX. That at the time of every Generall Assembly, the Commissioners directed thereto, from all the Universities of this Kingdom, Meet and consult together, for the establishment and advancement of Pietie, Learning, and good Order in the Schools and Universities, and be carefull that a correspondence be kept among the Universities, and so farre as is possible, an Uniformitie in Doctrine and good Order.

The Generall Assembly, after serious consideration of the Overtures and Ar-ticles above written, Approves the same, and ordains them to be observed, and to have the strength of an Act and Ordinance of Assembly in all time-coming.

THE HUMBLE PETITION THE GENERALL ASSEMBLY OF THE KIRK OF SCOTLAND.

To the Honourable and High Court of Parliament.

According to the constant and commendable practice of the Generall Assemblies of this Kirk, Wee judge it incumbent to us, Right Honourable, when the displeasure of the Almighty, and the extream danger of this Kirk and Kingdome is so undenyably demonstrate to the eyes of the whole World, by the Invasion, Increase, and Successe of these Barbarous Irishes, and treacherous Countrey-men joyned with them (Not onely out of conscience of the trust committed unto us), To proceed with the censures of the Kirk, against these who have joyned, or shall happen to joyne themselves with these Enemies of GOD and his Cause, To appoint a Solemne Fast and Humiliation through the Kingdom, and to give Warning to all the Ministers and Members of this Kirk of the dangers and duties of the time; But also, out of respect to your Honours, who judge not for man, but for the Lord: Who is with you in the Judgement: and standeth in the Congregation of the mighty: Humbly to present your Honours with our thoughts and desires concerning the duties which the exigency of this time expecteth from your hands.

The impunity of known Incendiaries and Malignants, as by the course of Divine providence (permitting those who have formerly escaped the hand of Justice to be the prime instruments of our present Troubles) it is held forth for a cause of the Wrath which yet burneth more and more; So hath it been acknowledged before GOD in our publick Humiliations, to be a maine cause of GODS Controversie with the Land, and an accession to the guiltinesse of the cruelty, villainy, and other mischiefs committed by them and their followers: And to lye still under the guilt after solemne Confession, were an high provocation of GOD, and an heavy aggravation of our sinne; And on the one part, doth grieve the Godly, discourage their hearts, and weaken their hands, On the other part, doth harden them who are already engaged, to persist in their unnaturall and bloudy practices, heartneth others, who have not hitherto avowed their Malignancy, openly to declare themselves, and is laid hold upon by the disaffected, who lye in wait to finde occasions, as fitting to work the People to an unwillingnesse of undergoing necessary Burthens imposed for publick good.

Although the Lord hath shewn unto us great and sore Troubles, and our heart may be broken with reproach, shame, and dishonour, put upon us by the vilest among men; Yet hath he made known unto us the power of his working amidst these manifold troubles, bringing forward the much desired Work of Uniformity in Worship and Government to a greater perfection then was expected (as your Honours and wee did see the other day with joy of heart) which is a Testimony from Heaven, That the Lord hath not left us in the fiery Furnace, but dwelleth still in the midst of the burning Bush, and should rouze up our drouping spirits to follow GOD fully, and quicken our slownesse to hasten and help the Lord against the mighty. In delay there is perill of strengthening the arme of the intestine Enemie, making faint the hearts of our Neighbours and Friends, and disabling us for reaching help unto those who are wrestling against much opposition to perfect the Work of Reformation. The reproach under which we lye almost buried, should bee so farre from retarding proceedings, that it should insend the Spirit into a higher degree of desire, and expede the hand to speedier action for vindicating our own name, and that Name which is above all names from the daily reproach of the foolish.

May it therefore please your Honours, in the zeal of the Lord, To proceed with some speedy course of Justice against such persons as are known to have joyned themselves, either actually in Arms, or by their counsell, supplies, encouragements, have strenghtened the hands of the bloody Enemies, whereby a cause of the Controversie shall be removed, the Land cleansed of the blood that is shed therein, the cruell and crooked generation disheartned, the fainting hearts of the Godly refreshed, and their feeble knees strengthened; And cheerfully and unanimously to resolve upon, and put in execution all lawfull and possible wayes of speedy and active pursuing and extirpating these barbarous and unnaturall Enemies within the Kingdom: Whereby your thankfulnesse to GOD for promoving his owne Work, and your endeavours of uniformity, shall be testified; your sense of the dishonour of this Nation, and of the danger of delay expressed; and your conscience of the Oath of God upon you manifested. Wee are confident of your Honours conscience, and care, onely we exhort you in the Lord, to unite your Spirits and accelerate your counsels and endeavours: And pray the Lord of Hosts to prosper your enterprises, according to the engagement of his Name, interest of his Work, and necessity of his People, to his own glory, the establishment of the Kings Throne in righteousnesse, the comfort of his Saints, and the conversion or confusion of Enemies. Be of good courage, and behave your selves valiantly, for our people, and for the cities of our God. Arise, and the Lord be with you.

OVERTURES PROPOUNDED BY THE COMMITTEE, APPOINTED BY THIS VENERABLE ASSEMBLY, FOR ORDERING OF THE BURSARS OF THEOLOGIE, AND MAINTAINING OF THEM AT SCHOOLS OF DIVINITIE.

I. That every Bursar have yearly payed him for his maintenance 100. l. at the least.

II. That the said maintenance be taken forth of the Kirk penalties, according to the intention of the first Act for maintaining of Bursars.

III. That every Presbyterie consisting of twelve Kirks in number, maintain a Bursar yearly at the University.

IV. And where the Presbyteries are fewer in number, that they joyne with other Presbyteries to make up their number: And the superplus of the number to be ordered and disposed by the Presbyteries and Synods: And that their Books bear Records thereof.

V. That the Kirks of these Presbyteries be proportionally stented according to the number of the communicants in each Parochin.

VI. That the said maintenance be collected by the Moderatour of every Presbyterie, by equall divided portions, and the one half to be brought in to the Winter Synod, and given to the said Bursars, and the other half at the Summer Synod, to be sent unto them: And that the severall Synods take an exact compt hereof, and see that all be rightly done, and that their Books bear the report hereof to the Generall Assembly.

VII. That the time of Bursars abode at the Schools of Divinity exceed not foure years: which being expired, or in case before the expiring of the said time, any be removed either by death, or by some Calling to a particular Charge, another be presented to the said Benefit.

VIII. That in case any prove deficient in payment of the said maintenance for the time to come, That it shall be carefully exacted by the Synods, and sent over to the General Assembly, to be disposed upon by them, as they shall finde expedient; that no Person may have benefit in their slacknesse and neglect.

IX. That all Bursars of Theologie bring sufficient Testimonies yearly from the Universities where they are bred, of their proficiencie and good behaviour: And that they be also ready to give a proof of their labours at the severall Synods, if it shall be required. And if they be found deficient, that they be denuded of the said benefit, and others more hopefull placed in their rooms.

The General Assembly approves these Overtures above-written, And Ordains the same to be observed in all time coming. And that Presbyteries (who have not already done it) begin and enter to the maintaining of their Bursars, in manner foresaid, in this present year 1645. And recommends to Presbyteries, to make choice of such for the Burse, as are of good report, inclined to Learning, and have past their course of Philosophie, And to try their qualifications before they send them to Universities.

THE OPINION OF THE COMMITTEE FOR KEEPING THE GREATER UNIFORMITIE IN THIS KIRK, IN THE PRACTICE AND OBSERVATION OF THE DIRECTORY IN SOME POINTS OF PUBLICK WORSHIP.

I. It is the Humble Opinion of the Committee for regulating that Excercise of reading and expounding the Scriptures read upon the Lords Day, mentioned in the Directory, That the Minister and People repair to the Kirk, half an hour before that time at which ordinarily the Minister now entreth to the publick Worship; And that, that Exercise of reading and expounding, together with the ordinary Exercise of Preaching, be perfected and ended at the time which formerly closed the Exercise of publick Worship.

II. In the Administration of Baptisme, it will be convenient, That, that Sacrament be administred in face of the Congregation, that what is spoken and done, may be heard and seen of all, and that it be administred after the Sermon, before the Blessing.

III. In the Administration of the Lords Supper, it is the judgement of the Committee.

1. That Congregations be still tried and examined before the Communion, according to the bygone practice of this Kirk.

2. That there be no reading in the time of communicating; but the Minister making a short Exhortation at every Table, that thereafter there be silence during the time of the Communicants receiving, except onely when the Minister expresseth some few more sentences, sutable to the present condition of the Communicants in the receiving, that they may be incited and quikned in their Meditations in the Action.

3. That distribution of the Elements among the Communicants be universally used: And for that effect, that the Bread be so prepared, that the Communicants may divide it amongst themselves, after the Minister hath broken, and delivered it to the nearest.

4. That while the Tables are dissolving, and filling, there be alwayes singing of some portion of a Psalme, according to the custome.

5. That the Communicants both before their going to, and after their coming from the Table, shall only joyne themselves to the present publick Excercise then in hand.

6. That when the Communion is to be celebrate in a Paroch, one Minister may be imployed for assisting the Minister of the Paroch, or at the most two.

7. That there be one Sermon of Preparation delivered in the ordinary Place of publick Worship, upon the day immediatly preceeding.

8. That before the serving of the Tables, there be onely one Sermon delivered to those who are to communicate, and that in the Kirk where the Service is to be performed. And that in the same Kirk there be one Sermon of Thanksgiving, after the Communion is ended.

9. When the Parochiners are so numerous, that their Paroch Kirk cannot contain them, so that there is a necessity to keep out such of the Paroch as cannot conveniently have place, That in that case the Brother who assists the Minister of the Paroch, may be ready, if need be, to give a word of Exhortation in some convenient place appointed for that purpose, to those of that Paroch, who that day are not to Communicate; which must not be begun until the Sermon delivered in the Kirk be concluded.

10. That of those who are present in the Kirk where the Communion is celebrate, none be permitted to go forth while the whole Tables be served, and the blessing pronounced, unlesse it be for more commodious order, and in other cases of necessity.

11. That the Minister who cometh to assist, have a special care to provide his own Paroch, lest otherwise while he is about to Minister comfort to others, his own Flock be left destitute of preaching.

12. That none coming from another Paroch, shall be admitted to the Communion, without a Testimonial from their own Minister: And no Minister shall refuse a Testimonial to any of his Paroch, who communicates ordinarily at their own Paroch Kirk, and are without scandal in their life for the time. And this is no wayes to prejudge any honest Person, who occasionally is in the place where the Communion is celebrate; or such as by death, or absence of their own Minister,

could not have a Testimonial.

IV. It is also the judgement of the Committee, That the Ministers bowing in the Pulpit; though a lawful custome in this Kirk, be hereafter laid aside, for satisfaction of the desires of the reverend Divines in the Synod of England, and uniformity with that Kirk so much endeared to us.

The Assembly having considered seriously the judgement of the Committee above-written, Doeth approve the same in all the Articles thereof, and Ordains them to be observed in all time hereafter.

10. FEBRUARY, 1645. POSTMERIDIEM SESS. 16.

ACT OF THE GENERALL ASSEMBLY OF THE KIRK OF SCOTLAND, APPROVING THE PROPOSITIONS CONCERNING KIRK GOVERNMENT AND ORDINATION OF MINISTERS.

The General Assembly, being most desirous and solicitous, not onely of the establishment and preservation of the Form of Kirk-government in this Kingdome, according to the Word of GOD, Books of Discipline, Acts of Generall Assemblies, and Nationall Covenant; But also of an Uniformity in Kirk-government betwixt these Kingdomes now more straitly and strongly united by the late Solemne League and Covenant: And considering, That as in former times there did, so hereafter there may arise through the neernesse of Contagion, manifold mischiefs to this Kirk from a corrupt Form of Government in the Kirk of England: Like as the precious opportunity of bringing the Kirks of Christ in all the three Kingdoms, to an Uniformity in Kirk-government, being the happinesse of the present times above the former; which may also by the blessing of God, prove an effectuall meane, and a good foundation to prepare for a safe and well-grounded Pacification, by removing the cause from which the present Pressures and bloodie Wars did originally proceed: And now the Assembly having thrice read, and diligently examined the Propositions (hereunto annexed) concerning the officers, Assemblies, and Government of the Kirk; and concerning the Ordination of Ministers, brought unto us as the results of the long and learned Debates of the Assembly of Divines sitting at Westminster, and of the Treaty of Uniformity with the Commissioners of this Kirk there residing; After mature deliberation, and after tymous calling upon and warning of all who have any exceptions against the same, to make them known, that they might receive satisfaction, Doth Agree to, and Approve the Propositions aforementioned touching Kirk-government and Ordination, and doth hereby Authorize the Commissioners of this Assembly who are to meet at Edinburgh, to agree to, and conclude in the name of this Assembly, an Uniformitie betwixt the Kirks in both Kingdoms in the aforementioned particulars, so soon as the same shall be ratified, without any substantiall alteration, by an Ordinance of the Honourable Houses of the Parliament of England: Which Ratification shall be timely intimate and made known by the Commissioners of this Kirk residing at London. Provided alwayes, That this Act shall be no wayes prejudiciall to the further discussion and examination of that Article, which holds forth, that the Doctor or Teacher, hath power of the administration of the Sacraments as well as the Pastor;

As also of the distinct Rights and Interests of Presbyteries and People in the calling of Ministers: But that it shall be free to debate and discusse these points as GOD shall be pleased to give further light.

The Propositions of Government, and Ordination mentioned in the preceding Act, are not to be here Printed: but after the Ratification thereof by the Parliament of England, they are to be Printed by warrant of the Commissioners of this Assembly.

12. FEB. 1645. POST MERIDIEM SESS. 18.

The Generall Assembly, after mature deliberation, having found it most necessary that this whole Nation be timely Warned, and duly Informed of their present Dangers, and the Remedies to be used, and Duties to be done for preventing and removing thereof, Doth ordain this Warning to be forth with Printed and Published, and sent to all the Presbyteries in this Kingdom, as also to the Presbyteries that are with our Armies. And that each Presbyterie immediately after the receipt hereof, take speedy course for the Reading of it in every Congregation within their bounds, upon the Lords day after the forenoons Sermon, and before the blessing: and that they give account of their diligence herein to the Commissioners of the Generall Assembly; Who have hereby Power and Warrand to try and censure such as shall contemne or slight the said Warning, or shall refuse or neglect to obey this Ordinance.

A SOLEMNE AND SEASONABLE WARNING TO THE NOBLEMEN, BARONS, GENTLEMEN, BURROWS, MINISTERS, AND COMMONS OF SCOTLAND; AS ALSO TO OUR ARMIES WITHOUT AND WITHIN THIS KINGDOM.

The Cause of GOD in this Kingdom, both in the beginnings and Progresse of it, hath been carried, through much craft and mighty opposition of Enemies, and through other perplexities and dangers; GOD so disposing, for the greater glory of his manifold and marvellous Wisedome and his invincible Power, and for our greater tryall.

These dangers both from without and from within, together with the remedies thereof, have been from time to time represented and held forth, in the many publick Supplications of this Kirk and Kingdom to the King, and in their many Declarations, Remonstrances, Letters, Acts, and other publick Intimations: Particularly by a necessary Warning published by the Commissioners of the Generall Assembly in January 1643; And by the Remonstrance of the same Comissioners to the Convention of Estates in July thereafter concerning the Dangers of Religion, and Remedies of these Dangers: which Warning and Remonstrance at that time had, by the blessing of GOD, very good and comfortable effects. And now the General Assembly itself, being by a speciall Providence, and upon extraordinary occasions called together, while GOD is writing bitter things against this Land in great Letters, which he that runs may read: and knowing that we cannot be answerable to GOD, nor our own consciences, nor the expectation of others, if from this chief Watch Tower we should give no Seasonable Warning to the City of GOD:

While we think of these things, For Sions sake we will not hold our peace, and for Jerusalems sake we will not rest: trusting that GOD will give, though nor to all, yet to many, a seeing Eye, a hearing Ear, and an understanding Heart: For who is wise and he shall understand these things, prudent and he shall know them; For the Waves of the Lord are right, and the just shall walk in them, but the transgressors shall fall therein, and the wicked shall do wickedly and none of the wicked shall understand.

That which we principally intend, is to hold forth (so farre as the Lord gives us light) how this Nation ought to be affected with the present Mercies and Judgements; What use is to be made of the Lords dealings: And, what is required of a people so dealt with.

Had we been timely awaked, and taken warning, either from the exemplary judgement of other Nations; or from Gods threatnings by the mouths of his servants amongst our selves; or from our owne former visitations, and namely, The Sword, threatned and drawn against us, both at home and from abroad, but at that time through the forbearance of GOD, put up in the Sheath again, wee might have prevented the miseries under which now we groane. But the Cup of trembling, before taken out of our hands, is again come about to us, that wee may drink deeper of it: And although when these bloody Monsters, the Irish Rebels, together with some degenerate, unnaturall, and perfidious Countreymen of our own, did first lift up their heads, and enter this Kingdome in a hostile way, it was looked upon as a light matter, and the great judgement which hath since appeared in it, not apprehended: yet now wee are made more sensible, that they are The rod of Gods wrath, and the staffe in their hand, which hath stricken us these three times, is his indignation. He hath shewed his people hard things, and made us to drink the wine of astonishment. Take we therefore notice of the hand that smiteth us, for affliction cometh not forth of the dust, neither doth trouble spring out of the ground. There is no evil in the City nor Countrey which the Lord hath not done. He it is that formeth the light, and createth darknesse; Who maketh peace, and createth evill: He it is that hath given a charge to the Sword, so that it cannot be still: He it is that hath his other Arrows ready upon the string to shoot at us, the Pestilence and Famine.

In the next place let us apply our hearts to know, and to search, and to seek out wisdome, and the reason of things, and to understand the language of this present judgment, and Gods meaning in it, For though the Almighty giveth not an accompt of any of his matters, and hath his way in the sea, and his path in the deep waters which cannot be traced; Yet he is pleased by the light of his Word and Spirit, by the voice of our own consciences, and by that which is written and ingraven upon our judgement, as with the point of a Diamond and a Pen of iron, to make known in some measure his meaning unto his servants. God hath spoken once, yea twice, yet man perceiveth not; Therefore now hath he made this rod to speak aloud the third time, that we may hear the voice of the rod, and who hath appointed it. That which the rod pointeth at, is not any guilt of Rebellion or disloyaltie in us, as the Sons of Belial do slander and belye the Solemne League and Covenant of the three Kingdoms, which we are so farre from repenting of, that we cannot remember or mention it without great joy and thankfulnesse to God, as that which hath drawn many blessings after it, and unto which God hath given manifold and evident testimonies, for no sooner was the Covenant begun to bee taken in England; but sensibly the condition of affairs there was changed to the better; and though a little before the Enemy was coming in like a Flood, yet as soon as the Spirit of the Lord did lift up the Standard against him, from that day forward the Waters of their Deluge did decrease.

And for our part, our Forces sent into that Kingdom, in pursuance of that Covenant, have been so mercifully and manifestly assisted, and blessed from Heaven (though in the mids of many dangers and distresses, and much want and hardship) and have been so farre instrumentall to the foyling and scattering of two principal Armies; First, the Marquesse of Newcastle his Army, And afterward, Prince Ruperts and his together; And to the reducing of two strong Cities, York and Newcastle, that we have what to answer the Enemy that reproacheth us concerning that businesse, and that which may make iniquitie it self to stop her mouth. But which is more unto us than all Victories, or whatsomever temporal Blessing, the Reformation of Religion in England, and Uniformity therein between both Kingdoms (a principal end of that Covenant) is so far advanced, that the English Service-Book, with the Holy-dayes, and many other Ceremonies contained in it, together with the Prelacy, the fountain of all these, are abolished and taken away by Ordinance of Parliament; and a Directory for the Worship of God in all the three Kingdoms, agreed upon in the Assemblies and in the Parliaments of both Kingdoms, without a contrary voice in either; the Government of the Kirk by Congregational Elderships, Classical Presbyteries, Provincial and National Assemblies, is agreed upon by the Assembly of Divines at Westminster, which is also voted and concluded in both Houses of the Parliament of England: And what is yet remaining of the intended Uniformitie is in a good way; So that let our Lot fal in other things, as it may, the Will of the Lord be done; In this we rejoyce, and will rejoyce, that our Lord Jesus Christ is no loser, but a Conquerour, that his Ordinances take place, that his Cause prevaileth, and the work of purging and building his Temple goeth forward, and not backward. Neither yet are we so to understand the voice of the rod which lyeth heavy upon us, as if the Lords meining were to pluck up what he hath planted, and to pull down what he hath builded in this Kingdom, to have no more pleasure in us, to remove our Candlestick, and to take his Kingdom from us: nay, before that our God cast us off, and the glory depart from Israel, let him rather consume us by the Sword, and the Famine, and the Pestilence, so that he will but keep his own great Name from reproach and blasphemy, and own us as his people in Covenant with him. But now there is hope in Israel concerning this thing, we will beleeve that we shall yet see the goodnesse of the Lord in the Land of the living: We will not cast away our confidence of a blessed peace, and of the removing of the scourge and casting it in the Fire, when the Lord, hath by it performed his whole Work upon mount Sion and Jerusalem, much more will wee be confident of the continuance of the blessings of the Gospel, that glory may dwell in our Land. This is the day of Jacobs trouble, but he shall be saved out of it: And the time is comming, when a new Song shall be put in our mouths, and we shall say, This is our God, we have waited for him, and he hath saved us. Though the

Lord smite us, it is the hand of a Father, not of an Enemy, he is not consuming us, but refining us, that we may come forth as Gold out of the Fire. We are troubled on every side; yet not distressed; we are perplexed, but not in despaire; persecuted, but not forsaken; cast downe, but not destroyed. We know assuredly there is more mercy in emptying us from Vessell to Vessell, then in suffering us to settle on our Lees, whereby our taste should remain in us, and our scent not be changed.

These things premised, we come to the true language of this heavy judgement, and to the reall procuring causes thereof. For the transgression of Jacob is all this, and for the sins of the house of Israel. God is hereby shewing to great and smal in this Land their work and their transgression, that they have exceeded. He openeth also their eare to discipline, and commandeth that they return from iniquity. We leave every Congregation in the Land, every Family in every Congregation, & every Person in every Family to examine their own hearts and wayes, & to mourn for Congregationall, Domesticall, and Personall sinnes: Cursed shall they be who have added fuell to the fire, and now bring no water to extinguish it, who had a great hand in the provocation, and bear no part in the humiliation.

Let every one commune with his own conscience, and repent of his own wickednesse, and say, What have I done? Wee shall here touch onely the Nationall sinnes, or at least more publick ones, then those of a Family or Congregation, which we also intend for chief causes of a publick Fast and Humiliation. If among our Nobles, Gentrie and Barons, there have been some studying their own private interests more then the publick, and Seeking their own things more then the things of Christ, or oppressing and defrauding the poore sort and the needie, because it was in the power of their hand: and if among our Ministrie there have been divers Time-servers, Who have not renounced the hidden things of dishonesty, whose hearts have not been right before God, nor stedfast in his Covenant, who have been secretly haters of the Power of Godlinesse, and of Mortification; shall not GOD search all this out? who will bring to light the hidden things of darknesse, and will make manifest the counsels of the hearts. In these also leaving all men to a judging and searching of themselves, there are many other provocations which are apparent in all or many of this Nation, from which, though they wash with nitre, and take much sope, yet they cannot make themselves clean: Because of these the Land mourneth, and at these the Sword striketh.

As first, the contempt, neglect, and dis-esteem of the glorious Gospel; our unbelief, unfruitfulnesse, luke-warmnesse, formality, and hardnesse of heart, under all the means of Grace; our not receiving of Christ in our hearts, nor seeking to know him, and glorifie him in all his Offices. The power of Godlinesse is hated and mocked by many to this day, and by the better sort too much neglected, and many Christian duties are not minded: as, The not speaking of our own words, nor finding of our own pleasure upon the Lords day: Holy and edifying conference both on that day, and at other occasions: The instructing, admonishing, comforting, and rebuking one another, as Divine Providence ministreth occasion. In many Families almost no knowledge nor worship of GOD to be found: yea, there are among the Ministers who have strenghtened the hearts and hands of the profane more then of the godly, and have not taken heed to the ministrie which they have received of the Lord to fulfill it.

Next, GOD hath sent the Sword to avenge the quarrel of his broken Covenant: For besides the defection of many of this Nation under the Prelats from our first Nationall Covenant, a sinne not forgotten by GOD, if not repented by men as well as forsaken, our latter Vows and Covenants have been also foully violated, by not contributing our uttermost assistance to this Cause, with our Estates and Lives; by not endeavouring with all faithfulnesse, the discovery, triall, and condigne punishment of Malignants, and evil Instruments; yea, by complying too much with those, who have not onely born Armes, and given their personall presence and assistance, but also drawn and led on others after them in the shedding of our Brethrens blood: Therefore is our sinne made our punishment, and We are filled with the fruit of our own wayes. These horns now push the sides of Judah and Jerusalem, because the Carpenters when they ought and might, did not cut them off: And yet so this day the course of Justice is obstructed: The Lord himself will execute justice if men will not. But above all, let it bee deeply and seriously thought of, that our Covenant is broken by the neglect of a reall Reformation of our selves and others under our power: let every one ask his own heart what lust is mortified in him, or what change wrought in his life since, more then before the Covenant? Swearing, Cursing, Profanation of the Lords day, Fornication, and other uncleannesse, Drunkennesse, Injustice, Lying, Oppression, Murmuring, Repining, and other sorts of Prophanenesse still abound too much both in the Countrey & in our Armies: yea, there is no Reformation of some Members of publick Judicatories, which is a great dishonour to God, and foul scandall to the whole Nation.

Thirdly, we have not glorified God according to the great things which he hath done for us, nor made the right use of former mercies: Since he loved us (a Nation not worthy to be beloved) he hath made us precious and honourable, but we have not walked worthy of this love: We waxed fat and kicked, forsaking God who made us, and lightly esteeming the Rock of our salvation. And this great unthankfulnesse filleth up our Cup.

Forthly, Notwithstanding of so much guiltinesse, we did send forth our Armies, and undertake great services presumptuously, without repentance, and making our peace with God, like the Children of Israel, who trusting to the goodnesse of their cause, minded no more, but Which of us shall goe up first.

It is now high time, under the feeling of so great a burden both of sinne and wrath to humble our uncircumcised heart, to put our mouth in the dust, if so be there may be hope, to wallow our selves in ashes, to clothe our selves with our shame as with a garment, to justifie Gods righteous judgements, to acknowledge our iniquitie, to make our supplication to our Judge, and to seek his face, that he may pardon our sinne, and heal our Land. The Lord roareth, and shall not his children tremble? The God of glory thundereth, and the Highest uttereth his voice, hailstones and coales of fire, who will not fall down and fear before him? The fire waxeth hot, and burneth round about us, and shall any sit still and be secure? The storm bloweth hard, & shall any sluggard be still asleep? This is a day of trouble, and of rebuke, and of blasphemy; who will not take up a lamentation? Let the Watchmen rouze up themselves and others, and strive to get their own, and their peoples hearts deeply affected, and even melted before the Lord: Let every one turn from his evill way, and cry mightily to God, and give him no rest till he repent of the evill, and smell a savour of rest, and say, It is enough. He hath not said to the seed of Jacob, Seek ye me in vain. Wee do not mourne as they that have no hope, but we will bear the indignation of the Lord, because wee have sinned against him, untill he plead our cause, and execute judgement for us. And what though our Candles be put out? So that our Sun shine: What though our honour be laid in the dust? So that GOD work out his own honour, yea, our happinesse out of our shame. In vain have we trusted to the arm of flesh: In the Lord our GOD is the Salvation of Israel. No flesh must glory before him, but he that glorieth, must glory in the Lord.

These duties of Humiliation, Repentance, Faith, Amendment of life, and Fervent Prayer, though the principal, yet are not all which are required at the hands of this Nation, but men of all sorts and degrees, must timely apply themselves to such other Resolutions and Actions as are most suteable and necessary at this time: Which that all may the better understand, and bee excited and encouraged to act accordingly, let it be well observed, that the present state of the Controversie and Cause is no other but what hath been formerly professed before GOD and the world, that is, The Reformation and Preservation of Religion, The Defence of the Honour and Happinesse of the King, and of the authority of the Parliament, together with the maintenance of our Lawes, Liberties, Lives, and Estates. We are not changed from our former principles and intentions, but these who did fall off from us to the contrary party, have now made it manifest, that these were not their ends when they seemed to joyn with us: Therefore are they gone out from us, because they were not of us. And as our Cause is the fame, so the danger thereof is not lesse, but greater then before, and that from two sorts of Enemies. First, from open Enemies, we mean those of the Popish, Prelatical, and Malignant Faction, who have displayed a Banner against the Lord, and against his Christ, in all the three Kingdoms, being set on fire of Hell, and by the special inspiration of Satan, who is full of fury; because he knowes he hath but a short time to reigne. The Cockatrice before hatched, is now broken forth into a Viper. The danger was before feared, now it is felt; before imminent, now incumbent; before our division, now our destruction is endeavoured; before the Sword was fourbished and made ready; now the Sword is made fat with Flesh, and drunk with Bloud, and yet it hungreth and thirsteth for more. The Queen is most active abroad, using all means for strengthening the Popish, and suppressing the Protestant party; insomuch that Malignants have insolently expressed their confidence, that her journey to France shall prove a successeful Counsel, and that this Island, and particularly this Kingdome, shall have a greater power to grapple with before the next Summer, then any which yet we have encountred with. The Irish Rebels have offered to the King to fend over a greater number into both the Kingdomes: The hostile intentions of the King of Denmark, if God be not pleased still to divert and disable him, do plainly enough appear from his own Letters, sent not long since to the Estates of this Kingdome. In the mean time, the hellish crue under the conduct of the excommunicate and forefaulted Earle of Montrose, and of Alaster Mac-Donald, a Papist and an Outlaw, doth exercise such barbarous, unnaturall, horrid, and unheard of cruelty, as is above expression: And (if not repressed) what better usage can others not yet touched expect from them, being now hardened and animated by the successe which God hath for our humiliation and correction, permitted unto them: and if they shall now get leave to secure the High-Lands for themselves, they will not onely from thence infest the rest of this Countrey, but endeavour a diversion of our Forces in England, from the prosecution of the ends expressed in the Covenant of the three Kingdoms, toward which ends, as their service hath already advantageous, so their continuance is most necessary.

The second sort of Enemies, from which our present dangers arise, are secret Malignants and Dis-covenanters, who may be known by these and the like Characters: Their slighting or censuring of the publick Resolutions of this Kirk and State: Their consulting and labouring to raise Jealousies and Divisions, to retard or hinder the execution of what is ordered by the publick Judicatories: Their slandering of the Covenant of the three Kingdomes and expedition into England, as not necessary for the good of Religion, or safety of this Kingdome, or as tending to the diminution of the Kings just power and greatnesse: Their confounding of the Kings Honour and Authority, with the abuse and pretense thereof, and with Commissions, Warrants, and Letters, procured from the King, by the Enemies of this Cause and Covenant, as if we could not oppose the latter, without encroaching upon the former: Their whetting of their tongues, to censure and slander those whom GOD hath honoured as his chief Instruments in this Work: Their commending, justifying, or excusing the proceedings of James Grahame, sometime Earle of Montrose, and his Complices: Their conversing or intercommuning by word of writ, with him, or other excommunicate Lords, contrary to the nature of that Ordinance of Christ, and to the old Acts of General Assemblies: Their making merry, and their insolent carriage, at the News of any prosperous successe of the Popish and Malignant Armies in any of these Kingdomes: Their drawing of Parties and Factions, to the weakning of the common Union: Their spreading of Informations, That Uniformitie in Religion, and the Presbyterial Government, is not intended by the Parliament of England: Their Endeavours, Informations, & Sollicitations, tending to weaken the hearts & hands of others and to make them withold their assistance from this Work.

Let this sort of bosome Enemies, and dis-affected Persons, be well marked, timely discovered, and carefully avoided, lest they infuse the poison of their seducing counsels into the mindes of others: Wherein let Ministers be faithful, and Presbyteries vigilant and unpartial, as they will answer the contrary to GOD, and to the General Assembly, or their Commissioners.

The cause and the dangers thereof being thus evidenced, unlesse men will blot out of their hearts the love of Religion, and the Cause of GOD, and cast of all care of their Countrey, Lawes, Liberties, and Estates, yea, all naturall affection to the preservation of themselves, their Wives, Children, and Friends, and whosoever is dearest to them under the Sun (all these being in the visible danger of a present ruine and destruction) they must now or never appear actively, each one stretching himself to, yea beyond his power. It is not time to dally, nor go about the businesse by halfes, nor by almost, but altogether zealous: Cursed be he that doth the

Work of the Lord negligently, or dealeth falsly in the Covenant of God. If we have been so forward to assist our Neighbour Kingdomes, shall we neglect to defend our own? Or shall the Enemies of GOD be more active against his Cause: than his People for it? GOD forbid. If the Work being so far carried on, shall now mis-carry, and fail in our hands, our own consciences shall condemne us, and posterity shall curse us: But if wee stand stoutly and stedfastly to it, the pleasure of the Lord shall prosper in our hands, and all Generations shall call us blessed.

Let Ministers stir up others by free and faithful preaching, and by admonishing every one of his duty, as there shall be occasion: And if it shall be the lot of any of them to fall under the power of the Enemy, let them through the strength of Christ, persevere in their integrity, choosing affliction rather then sin, glorifying GOD, and not fearing what Flesh can do unto them.

Let our Armies beware of ungodlinesse, and worldly lusts, living godly, soberly, and righteously, avoiding all scandalous carriage, which may give occasion to others to think the worse of their Cause and Covenant, and remembring that the eyes of GOD, Angels, and Men are upon them: Finally, renouncing all confidence in their own strength, skill, valour, and number, and trusting only to the God of the Armies of Israel, who hath fought, and will fight for them.

Let all sorts both of high and low degree in this Kingdome, call to minde their Solemne Covenants, and pay their vows to the most High; and namely, that Article of our first Covenant, which obligeth us not to stay nor hinder any such Resolution, as by common consent shall be found to conduce for the ends of the Covenant, but by all lawfull means to further and promove the same; Which lyeth as a Bond upon peoples consciences, readily to obey such orders, and willingly to under go such burdens, as by the publick and common resolution of the Estates of Parliament, are found necessary for the prosecution of the War; considering that the Enemy cannot bee suppressed without a competent number of Forces, and Forces cannot be kept together without maintenance, and maintenance cannot be had without such publick Burdens; Which however for the present, not joyous, but grievous, yet it shall be no grief of heart afterwards, even unto the common fort, that they have given some part of their necessary livelyhood, for assisting so good a work. It is far from our thoughts, that the pinching of some, should make others superfluously to abound: It is rather to bee expected of the richer sort, that they will spare and defalk, not onely the pride and superfluity, both of apparel and diet, but also a part of their lawful allowance in these things, to contribute the same as a free will offering, beside what they are obliged to, by Law or publick Order, after the example of godly Nehemiah, who for the space of twelve years, while the walls of Jerusalem were a building, did not eat the bread of the Governour, that hee might ease by so much the Peoples Burthens and Bondage.

In our last Covenant, there is another Article which (without the oblivion or neglect of any of the rest) we wish may be well remembred at this time; namely, That we shall assist and defend all that enter into this League and Covenant, in the maintaining and pursuing thereof and shall not suffer our selves, directly or indirectly, by whatsoever Combination, Perswasion, or Terror, to be divided and withdrawne from this blessed Union and Conjunction, whether to make defection to the contrary part, or to give our selves to a detestable indifferency or neutrality in this Cause: According to which Article, mens Reality and integrity in the Covenant, will be manifest and demonstrable as well by their omissions, as by their commissions; as well by their not doing good, as by their doing of evil; He that is not with us, is against us, and he that gathereth not with us, scattereth. Whoever he be that will not, according to publick order and appointment, adventure his person, or send out these that are under his power, or pay the Contributions imposed for the maintenance of the Forces, must be taken for an Enemie, Malignant, and Covenant-breaker, and so involved both into the displeasure of GOD, and Censures of the Kirk, and no doubt into civil punishments also to be inflicted by the State.

And if any shall prove so untoward and perfidious, their iniquitie shall be upon themselves, and they shall bear their punishment: Deliverance and good successe shall follow those who with purpose of heart cleave unto the Lord, and whose hearts are upright toward his glory. When wee look back upon the great things which GOD hath done for us, and our former deliverances out of several dangers and difficulties which appeared to us insuperable, experience breeds hope: And when we consider how in the midst of all our sorrows and pressures, the Lord our God hath given us a naile in his holy place, and hath lightned our eyes with the desireable and beautiful sight of his own glory in his Temple, we take it for an argument that he hath yet thoughts of peace, and a purpose of mercy toward us; Though for a small moment he hath forsaken us, yet with great mercies he will gather us as Hee hath lifted up our Enemies, that their fall may be the greater, and that he may cast them downe into desolation for ever. Arise, and let us be doing; The Lord of Hosts is with us, the God of Jacob is our Refuge.

ACT AGAINST LYKWAKES.

Whereas the corrupt Custome of Lykwakes hath fostered both Superstition and Profanitie through the Land, This present Assembly Discharges the same in time comming, And appoints Presbyteries To take speciall care for trying and censuring the Transgressors of this Act within their several Bounds.

ACT RECOMMENDING TO SESSIONS TO HAVE THE PRINTED ACTS OF ASSEMBLIE.

The General Assembly, considering how necessar it is, That every Session in a Parish have the Acts of the Assembly for their use, Doth therefore seriously recommend to every Parish and Session To buy the Printed Acts of the Assembly; and Ordains Presbyteries To crave account hereof from every Minister, before their going to Provinciall Assemblies: And likewise, That every Provinciall Assembly, crave account from Presbyteries in their trials, if every Session be so provided, and that they try the diligence, of Presbyteries and Ministers used for that effect.

13. FEBRUAR. 1645. POSTMERIDIEM. SESS. ULT.

ACT FOR CENSURING THE OBSERVERS OF YULE-DAY, AND OTHER SUPERSTITIOUS DAYES, ESPECIALLY IF

THEY BE SCHOLLARS.

The General Assembly taking to their consideration, The manifold Abuses, Profanitie, and Superstitions, committed on Yule-day and some other superstitions dayes following, Have unanimously concluded, and hereby Ordains, That whatsoever Person or Persons hereafter shall be found guilty in keeping of the foresaid superstitious dayes, shall be proceeded against by Kirk Censures, and shall make their publick Repentance therefore in the face of the Congregation where the offence is committed: And that Presbyteries and Provinciall Synods Take particular notice how Ministers try and censure Delinquents of this kinde, within the severall Parochines. And because Schollars and Students give great scandal and offence in this, That they (being found guilty) be severely disciplined and chastised therefore by their Masters: And in case the Masters of Schools or Colledges be accessorie to the said superstitious profanitie, by their connivence, granting of liberty of Vacance to their Schollars at that time, or any time thereafter, in compensation thereof, That the Masters be summoned by the Ministers of the Place to compeir before the next ensuing Generall Assembly, there to be censured according to their trespasse; And if Schollars (being guilty) refuse to subject themselves to Correction, or be Fugitives from Discipline, That they be not received in any other Schoole or Colledge within the Kingdom.

ACT FOR ENCOURAGEMENT OF SCHOLLARS TO PROFESSIONS IN SCHOOLES.

In respect of the paucitie of men, fit and willing to professe Divinitie in the Schooles, by reason that few frame their studies that way, The Generall Assembly thinks it fit, That the Provincials diligently consider and try who within their Bounds most probably may bee for a Profession in the Schooles, And report their names to the following Generall Assembly, that such may be stirred up and encouraged by the General Assembly, to compose and frame their studies, that they may be fit for such places.

ACT FOR RESTRAINING ABUSES AT PENNIE BRYDALS.

The Generall Assembly, considering the great profanitie and severall Abuses which usually fal forth at Pennie-Brydals proving fruitful Seminaries of all lasciviousnesse and debausherie, as well by the excessive number of people conveened thereto, as by the extortion of them therein, and licentiousnesse thereat, To the great dishonour of God, the scandall of our Christian Profession, and prejudice of the Countreys welfare; Therefore they Ordain every Presbyterie in this Kingdome, To take such special care for restraining these Abuses flowing from the causes foresaid, as they shall think fit in their severall bounds respectivè: And to take a strict accompt of every Minister and Session of their obedience to the Ordinance of the Presbyteria theyeanent, at the Visitation of every Parish Kirk in their Bounds.

ACT DISCHARGING DEPOSED MINISTERS TO BE REPONED TO THEIR FORMER PLACES.

The Generall Assembly, considering the manifold prejudices redounding to the Kirk in Generall, and private Congregations in particnlar; through the restoring of Ministers once deposed to the same places wherein formerly they served: As also, how derogatorie it would prove to the weight of that sentence of Deposition; Do therefore ordain, that no Minister deposed, shall be restored again into that place where formerly he served.

RENOVATION OF THE COMMISSION FOR THE PUBLICK AFFAIRS OF THE KIRK.

The General Assembly taking to their consideration, That in respect the great Work of Uniformitie in Religion in all his Majesties dominions, is not yet perfected, (though by the Lords blessing there is a good progresse made in the same) there is a necessity of renewing the Commissions granted formerly for prosecuting and perfecting that great Work; Doe therefore Renew the Power and Commission granted for the publick Affairs of the Kirk by the Generall Assembly, held in S. Andrews in the year 1642. upon the fifth day of August post meridiem, Sess, 12. And by the Generall Assembly held in Edinburgh in the year 1643 upon the 19. day of August, Sess. ult. And by the late Generall Assembly held at Edinburgh in the year 1644. upon the third of June, Sess. 6. to the Persons afternamed, viz. Mr Andrew Ramsay, Mr Alexan. Henderson, Mr Robert Douglas, Mr William Colvil, Mr William Bennet, Mr George Gillespie, Mr John Oswald, Mr Mungo Law, Mr Robert Lawrie, Mr John Adamson, D. John Sharp, Mr George Leslie, Mr Andrew Fairfowle, Mr David Calderwood, Mr Andrew Blackhall, Mr James Fleeming, Mr Robert Ker, Mr John Macghie, Mr John Dalyell, Mr Andrew Stevenson, Mr Robert Lander, Mr James Robertson, Mr Patrick Sibbald, Mr Robert Carson, Mr Alex. Spittall, Mr Alex. Dickison, Mr James Smith, Mr John Gibbison, Mr James Symton, Mr Ephraim Melvill, Mr Alex. Somervell, Mr Robert Eliot, Mr George Bennet, Mr Robert Blair, Mr David Forret, Mr Arthur Mortoun, Mr Samuel Rutherfurd, D. Alex. Colvill, Mr Andrew Bennet, Mr James Wedderburn, Mr Walter Greg, Mr John Moncreiff, Mr John Smith, Mr Frederick Carmichaell, Mr Patrick Gillespie, Mr John Duncan, Mr James Sibbald, Mr Robert Bruce, Mr John Hume at Eccles, Mr Mungo Dalyell, Mr Alex. Kinneir, Mr Thomas Ramsay, Mr William Turnbull, Mr James Guthrie, Mr Thomas Donaldson, Mr William Jameson, Mr David Fletcher, Mr Andrew Dunkison, Mr Robert Murray, Mr David Weemes, Mr John Hall, Mr John Freebairn, Mr David Drummond at Creist, Mr George Murray, Mr Henry Guthrie, Mr Robert Wright, Mr Andrew Jaffray, Mr Bernard Sanderson, Mr Alex. Iran, Mr Thomas Chalmers, Mr Andrew Lawder, Mr Hugh Henderson, Mr John Levingstoun, Mr James Blair, Mr James Bonar, Mr John Burne, Mr John Bell, Mr Hugh Mackale, Mr Matthew Birsbane, Mr David Elphingstoun, Mr David Dickson, Mr George Young, D. John Strang, Mr Robert Baillie, Mr Patrick Sharp, Mr Robert Birnie, Mr Evan Camron, Mr George Symmer at Megle, Mr Andrew Fleck, Mr Patrick Lyon, Mr John Lindsay, Mr Sylvester Lammie, Mr George Fogo, Mr David Strachan, Mr Andrew Cant, Mr William More, Mr William Davidson, Mr John Paterson, Mr William Jaffray, Mr Thomas Mitchell, Mr George Cummin, Mr Joseph Brodie, Mr William Lawder, Mr David Rosse, Mr Ferquhard Mackleman, Ministers; And Archbald Marquesse of Argyle, John Earle of Crawfurd-Lindsay, Alexander Earle of Eglintoun, William Earle of Glencarne, John Earle of Cassils, Charles Earle of Dumfermling, James Earle of Tullibarein, John Earle of Lauderdale, James Earle of Annandale, William Earle of Lothian, James Earle of Queenesberry, William Earle of Dalhousie, William Earle of Lanerick, Archbald Lord Angus, Vicount of Arbuthnet, James Vicount of Frendraught, Alexander Lord Carleys, James Lord Johnstoun, John Lord Yester, John Lord Balmerino, Alexander Lord Balcarras, John Lord Loure, John Lord Barganie, Sir Patrick Hepburn of Wauchtoun, Sir John Hope of Craighall, Sir Archbald Johnstoun of Waristoun, Sir David Hume of Wedderburn, Sir Frederick Lyon of Brigtoun, Sir Alexander Areskine of Dun, Sir Alexander Fraser of Phillorth, Sir William Baillie of Lammingroun, Hadding of Glennegies, Sir Thomas Ruthven of Freeland, James Macdougall of Garthland, Sir Alexander Murray of Blackbarronie, William Drummond of Rickartoun, Sir William Scot of Hardin, Sir Andrew Ker of Greenhead, Sir William Stuart, Sir Alexander Schaw of Sauchie, Alexander Brodie of that Ilk, Mr George Hume of Kimmerjame, Sir John Smith, Mr Alexander Colvill Justice Depute, John Binnie, Archbald Sydsers, Laurence Henderson, James Stuart Gilbert Sommernell, John Semple, Mr Robert Barclay, Patrick Leslie, James Law, Mr Robert Cuninghame, George Gardin, William Glendunning Elders. And for discharging the said Commission, Appoints the persons aforesaid, or any ninteene of them, whereof fifteen shall be Ministers, to meet at Edinburgh upon the 14. of this moneth of February and upon the second Wednesday of May, August, November, and of February next to come, and upon any other day, or in any other Place they shall think meet. Giving unto them full power and Commission to do all and every thing for prosecuting, advancing, perfecting, and bringing the said Work of Uniformity in Religion in all his Majesties Dominions to an happy conclusion, conforme to the former Commissions granted by the saids Assemblies thereanent: And further, Renewes to the Persons afore-named, the power contained in the Act of the said Assembly, 1643 Intituled, A reference to the Commission anent the Persons designed to repair to the Kingdom of England, As also the power contained in two several Acts of the said late Assembly 1644. Sess. 16. made Against secret dis-affecters of the Covenant, and, For sending Ministers to the Army. With full power to them, to treat and determine in the matters aforesaid, & in all other matters referred unto them by this Assembly, as fully and freely, as if the same were here particularly expressed, and with as ample power as any Commission of former General Assemblies hath had, or been in use of before; They being alwayes for their whole proceedings countable to, and censurable by the next General Assembly.

RENOVATION OF THE COMMISSION TO THE PERSONS APPOINTED TO REPAIR TO THE KINGDOM, OF ENGLAND, FOR PROSECUTING THE TREATY OF UNIFORMITIE IN RELIGION.

The Generall Assembly, Taking to their consideration, that the Treaty of Uniformity in Religion in all his Majesties Dominions is not yet perfected, though by the Lords blessing there is a good progresse made in the same, Do therefore Renew the Power and Commission granted to the Persons formerly nominate by the two preceding Assemblies, and by their Commissioners sitting at Edinburgh, for prosecuting the said Treatie of Uniformitie with the Honourable Houses of the Parliament of England, and the Reverend Assembly of Divines there, or any Committees appointed by them. Giving unto them full power to do all and every thing which may advance, perfect, and bring the said Treatie to an happy conclusion conforme to the former Commissions granted to them thereanent.

THE GENERAL ASSEMBLIES ANSWER TO THE RIGHT REVEREND THE ASSEMBLY OF DIVINES IN THE KIRK OF ENGLAND.

Right Reverend and welbeloved in the Lord Jesus,

Amidst the manifold troubles in which this Kingdome hath been involved, and under which it still laboureth, we greatly rejoyced when it was testified unto by us our reverend Brethren, and under your hands in your Letter, and these Papers by them presented to us from you, what progresse you had made in the much desired Work of Uniformities and acknowledge that the same hath comforted us concerning our work and toile of our hands, and seemeth to us as an olive branch, to prognosticate the abating of the waters, which overflow the face of the Earth.

When we consider, that you have walked in pathes unusuall, which have not been haunted by Travellers there, as the publick way, though pointed out as the good old way by the Reformed Kirks, we do not wonder that you have carefully adverted in every step to set foot upon sure ground; When we behold that strong and high tree of Episcopacie so deeply rooted by continuance of time not loosed of the Branches, and the stumpe of the root left in the Earth, with a band of iron and brasse, but pluckt up by the roots; We do confesse that the Carpenters, though prepared have a hard task, requiring time to hew it down, and root it up: And when we call to minde how much the Service-Book hath been cryed up as the only way of GODS Worship, how many thereby have had their wealth, and how difficult it is to forgoe the accustomed way; We admire the power and wisdom of the good GOD who hath prospered you in your way, and led you this length, through so many straits, and over so many difficulties in so troublous a time.

We do for our part not only admit and allow, but most heartily and gladly embrace the Directory of Worship, as a common Rule for the Kirks of GOD in the three Kingdoms, now more straitly and firmly united by the solemne League and Covenant; And we do all in one voice blesse the Lord, who hath put it in the hearts, first, of the Reverend, Learned, and Pious Assembly of Divines and then, of the Honourable Houses of Parliament. To agree upon such a Directory as doth remove what is none of Christs, and preserve the purity of all his Ordinances, together with Uniformity and Peace in the Kirk. Only we have thought necessary, to declare and make known, That the Clause in the Directory for the administration of the Lords Supper, which appointeth the Table to be so placed that the Communicants may orderly sit about it, or at it, is not to be interpreted as if in the judgement of this Kirk it were indifferent for any of the Communicants not to come to and receive at the Table; or as if we did approve the distributing of the Elements by the Ministers to each Communicant, & not by the Communicants among themselves: In which particulars, we still conceive and believe the order & practice of our own Kirk, To be most agreeable & sutable to the Word of GOD, the example of our Lord Jesus Christ, and the nature of that Heavenly Feast and Table. Neverthelesse, in other particulars we have resolved, and do agree, to do as ye have desired us in your Letter, That is, not to be tenacious of old Customs, though lawfull in themselves, and not condemned in this Directory, but to lay them aside for the nearer Uniformitie with the Kirk of England, now nearer and dearer to us than ever before; A Blessing so much esteemed, and so earnestly longed for among us, that rather than it faile on our part, we do most willingly part with such practices and customs of our own, as may be parted with safely, and without the violation of any of Christs Ordinances, or trespassing against Scripturall Rules, or our solemne Covenants.

We do in like manner agree to, and approve the Proportions touching Kirk-government and Ordination; and have given power to our Commissioners who are to meet in Edinburgh, to agree to, and conclude in our Name an Uniformitie therein, betwixt the Kirks in both Kingdoms, so soon as the same shall be without any substantiall alteration Ratified by an Ordinance of the Honourable Houses of the Parliament of England according to our Act of Approbation sent to our Commissioners with you.

As for the returning of our Commissioners; though the counsel and assistance of our Reverend Brethren might be of good use to us in these difficult times, and their particular stations and imployments importune the stay of these who are come unto us, and the returne of these who stay with you, yet preferring the publick good, and looking upon the profit may redound unto all by their continuing with you, we have satisfied your desire, & renewed their Commission; Praying GOD they may (as we are confident they shall) prove answerable to our trust, and to your expectation.

Concerning one Confession of Faith, and Forme of Catechisme, we apprehend no great difficultie: And to that which remains to be perfected in the matter of Kirk-government, we do believe, and both you and we know by experience, that there is no word impossible with our God. He that hath begun a good work among you, will also perform it of his good pleasure. Go on in the Lord your strength, and the Spirit of truth lead you in all truth: The God of all grace and peace that brought again from the dead our Lord Jesus that great Shepherd of the sheep through the blood of the everlasting Covenant, & by him hath called us unto his eternall glory, make you perfect in every good work to do his will, working in you, and by you, and among you, that which is well pleasing in his fight, stablish, strengthen, settle you, through Jesus Christ our Lord.

Edinburgh 13. Feb. 1645.

Subscribed in name of the Generall Assembly of the Kirk of Scotland, by the Moderator of the Assembly.

THE HUMBLE REMONSTRANCE OF THE GENERALL ASSEMBLY OF THE KIRK OF SCOTLAND, MET AT EDINBURGH THE 13. DAY OF FEBRUARY, 1645.

TO THE KINGS MOST EXCELLENT MAJESTIE.

As our Record is on high, and our conferences within us bear us witnesse, so the many former Supplications and Remonstrances to your Majestie, from this Kirk and Kingdome, our solemne Covenants, and the whole course of our proceedings from time to time in the prosecution of this Cause; Do make known to the World, and we trust also to your own consience, our loyaltie and faithful subjection, and how far our intentions are from the diminution of your Majesties just Power and Greatnesse; And although the successe of many of our humble addresses to your Majesty, hath been such as did frustrate our desires and hopes, yet this hath not blotted our of our hearts our loyaltie, so often professed before God and the World; but it is still our Souls desire, and our Prayer to God for you, that your Self and your Posterity may prosperously reigne over this your antient and Native Kingdome, and over your other Dominions. And now as we have published a solemn and free Warning to the Noblemen, Barons, Gentlemen, Burrons, Ministers, and Commons of this Kingdome, concerning the present affliction of this Nation, and their sins procuring the same; So when we call to minde, that God accepteth not the persons of men, and that the greatest are not to be winked at in their sins; We assure our selves, that the best and most reall testimony which we can give at this present of the tendernesse and uprightnesse of our affection to your Majesties true Happinesse is this our humble and faithfull Representation of your Majesties great and growing dangers, and the causes thereof. Of which, if we should be silent, our consciences would condemne us, and the stones themselves would immediatly cry out.

The troubles of our hearts are enlarged, & our fear increased in your Majesties behalf, perceiving that your Peoples patience is above measure tempted, & is like a cart prest down with sheaves, and ready to break, while as beside many former designes and endeavours to bring desolation and destruction upon us, (which were (and we trust all of that kinde shall be) by the marvellous and mercifull providence of God discovered and disappointed). Our Countrey is now infested, the blood of divers of our Brethern spilt, and other acts of most barbarous and horrid cruelty exercised, by the cursed crew of the Irish Rebels and their Complices in the Kingdome, under the conduct of such as have Commission and Warrant from your Majestie. And unless we prove unfaithfull both to God and to your Majestie, we cannot conceale another danger which is infinitely greater than that of your Peoples displeasure: Therefore we the servants of the most high GOD, and your Majesties most loyall Subjects in the humility and grief of our hearts, fall down before your Throne, and in the Name of our Lord and Master JESUS CHRIST, who shall judge the world in righteousnesse, both great and small, and in the Name of this whole Nationall Kirk, which we represent, We make bold to warn your Majesty freely, that the guilt which cleaveth fast to your Majesty and to your Throne, is such, as (whatsoever flattering preachers, or unfaithfull counsellours may say to the contrary) if not timely repented, cannot but involve your Self and your Posterity under the wrath of the ever-living GOD, For your being guiltie of the shedding of the blood of many thousands of your Majesties best Subjects; For your permitting the Masse, and other Idolatry, both in your own Family and in your Dominions; For your authorizing by the Book of Sports the profanation of the Lords Day; For your not punishing of publick scandals, and much profanenesse in, & about your Court; For the shutting of your eare, from the humble and just desires of your faithfull Subjects; For your complying too much with the Popish party in many wayes, and namely, by concluding the Cessation of Armes in Ireland, and your embracing the counsels of those who have not set GOD nor your good before their eyes; For your resisting and opposing this Cause, which so much concerneth the glory of GOD, your own honour and happinesse, and the peace and safetie of your Kingdomes; and for what other causes your Majesty is most conscious, and may best judge and search your own conscience (nor would we have mentioned any particulars, if they had not been publike and knowne.) For all which it is high time for your Majesty to fall down at the footstool of the King of Glory, to acknowledge your offence to repent timely, to make your peace with GOD through JESUS CHRIST, (whose blood is able to wash away your great sinne) and to be no longer unwilling that the Son of GOD reign over you and your Kingdoms in his pure Ordinances of Church-government and Worship. These things if your Majesty do, it shall be no grief of heart unto you afterward; a blessing is reserved for you, and you shall finde favour with GOD, and with your People, and with all the Churches of Christ; But if your Majesty refuse to hearken to this wholsome counsell (which the Lord forbid) we have discharged our own consciences, we take GOD and Men to witnesse That we are blamelesse of the sad Consequences which may follow, and we shall wait upon the Lord, who, when he maketh inquisition for blood, will not forget the cry of the humble. In the mean while, beseeching your Majesty to take notice That we are not staggering or fainting through diffidence of the successe of this Cause and Covenant of the three Kingdoms, unto which, as GOD hath already given manifold Testimonies of his favour and blessing; so it is our stedfast and unshaken confidence, that this is the Work and Cause of GOD, which shall gloriously prevail against all opposition, and from which, with the assistance of the grace of GOD, we shall never suffer our selves to be divided or withdrawn, but shall zealously and constantly in our severall Vocations, endeavour with our Estates and Lives, the pursuing and promoving thereof.

That which we have concluded concerning Uniformity in Religion between both Kingdoms, is to be humbly offered to your Majestie from the Commissioners of this Kingdom, for your Royall Consent and Ratification. Although your Majestie was not pleased to vouchsafe us the presence of your Commissioner, according to the supplication of the Commissioners or the preceeding Generall Assembly, yet we have proceeded with as much respect to your Majesties honour, and as much remembrance of our duty, as if your Royall Person had been present in the mids of us: And we shall still continue our Prayers for you, that GOD would graciously incline your heart to the counsels of Truth and Peace, and grant unto your Majestie a long and happy Raign, that we may live under you a peaceable and quiet life, in all Godlinesse and Honestie.

THE ASSEMBLIES ANSWER TO THEIR COMMISSIONERS AT LONDON.

Reverend and beloved Brethren,

These sweet Fruits of your long continued Labours in the Work of the Lord entrusted to you, brought to us at this time by these two of your number, whom you were pleased to send, were received by us with no small joy and rejoycing, as being, in great part, the satisfaction of our Souls desire, in that so much longed for, so much prayed for happy Uniformity of these Kirks and Kingdoms: And an evident Demonstration to us, that the Lord hath not, even in this time of his seen and felt displeasure, so covered himself with the cloud of his anger, that our Prayers should not passe through.

The great and main difficulties through which the Lord hath carried this Work, as we do acknowledge, ought mainly to be made use of, for the praise and glory of his power, who is the great Worker of all our works for us; So your overcoming of them is to us no small Demonstration of your zeal, wisdom, and faithfulnesse, which without great Injurie both to the Lord the prime Worker, and to you his instruments, we cannot but acknowledge, hath been much manifested in the whole managing of this work in your hands.

The full answer to all the particulars you write of in your Letters, we leave to the Relation of those that come from you, and are now appointed to return to you: And as with much thankfulnesse we acknowledge your fidelity in what ye have done already; so we have again renewed your Commission for the continuance of your Imployment there, for the perfecting of the Work so happily begun: For the furthering whereof, as we shall not be wanting in our prayers to GOD for his blessing upon your labours, so for your help and assistance, we have appointed a commission to sit at Edinburgh, to which at all occasions you may have your recourse, as the exigence of the Work shall require.

How satisfactory that Directory of Worship presented to us by our Brethren from you, was to us, we leave it rather to their relation at their return; being ear and eye witnesses to the manifold expressions of our joy and gladnesse, then offer to represent it to you in a Letter: The Act herewith sent, and ordained to be prefixed unto the Directory, will sufficiently declare our hearty approbation of it: Our judgement also concerning the proportions of Government and Ordination, and our earnest desire to have the Work of Uniformity promoved and perfected in that particular also, will appear to you by the other Act which herewith you will receive: Our zeal and desire to have that Work fully closed with so much harmonie as becometh the work of GOD, will appear to you in our resolution and answer to that particular in the point of Excommunication, concerning which you write.

These particular differences hinted in the Assemblies Letter, for uniformitie with that Kirk so much endeared to us, we have resolved to lay aside, and have taken course for preserving harmonie amongst our selves, whereof our Brethren will give you more particular account. Anent your desire of Mr Alexander Henderson his attending the Treatie, we are confident ere this you have received our resolution.

Amidst the many difficulties wherewith it pleaseth the Lord to presse us, as we thought it necessar to publish and send forth a Warning to all sorts of Persons in this Kirk and Kingdom, concerning the present affliction of this Nation, and their sins procuring the same; So we thought it incumbent to us in duty, as the best Testimony which we can give at this present to his Majesty, to remonstrate unto him faithfully The great and growing dangers his Majesty is now under, and the causes thereof. This Remonstrance we have sent to you, to be presented to his Majesty, by such means, and at such time, as you who are there upon the place shall judge fittest.

And now dear Brethren go on with cheerfulnesse in the Work of the Lord: Let no discouragement or opposition make your heart to faint, or your hands wax feeble: Perswade your self the Lords hand shall still be made known toward his servants, and his indignation against his Enemies. Remember the Work is his, who useth not to begin, but also to make and end, and is abundantly able to supply all your need according to the riches of his glory. Be confident therefore of this thing, that he who hath begun this good Work by you, will also in due time accomplish it to his own praise. To his gracious assistance we heartily recommend you.

Postscript.

Edinburgh 13. Feb. 1645.

It is earnestly desired That the Directorie for Worship be sent to Ireland, and that you recommend to the honourable Houses of the Parliament, To think upon the best way for the establishment & practice of it in that Kingdom. And that the like course may be taken with the government, and other parts of the Uniformity, so soon as they shall be agreed upon.

Subscribed in name of the Generall Assembly of the Kirk of Scotland by the Moderator of the Assembly.

The General Assembly Recommends to Presbyteries, To consider these matters referred to their consideration by preceding Assemblies; and to report their judgement therein to the next Assembly.

The Generall Assembly Appoints the meeting of the next Assembly to be at Edinburgh the first Wednesday of June, in the yeer 1646.

THE GENERALL ASSEMBLY MET AT EDINBURGH JUNII 3. 1646.

EDINB. 4. JUNII 1646. SESS. 2.

THE KINGS LETTER TO THE ASSEMBLY, PRESENTED BY M. ROBERT DOUGLAS MINISTER AT EDINBURGH.

Charles R.

Right trustly and welbeloved, We greet you well. Having lately written to Our Houses of Parliament at Westminster, and the Commissioners from Our Kingdom of Scotland at London, and likewise to the Committees of Estates of that our Kingdom; Shewing Our great sense and grief for the sad effects have flowed from the unhappy differences betwixt Us and Our Subjects; with Our reall resolutions to comply with the desires of Our Parliaments of both Kingdoms, and those entrusted by them for settling of Trueth and Peace in all Our Dominions: And now being informed of your meeting, We have thought fit hereby (since We could not conveniently send a Commissioner) to give you the same assurances; And withall, that it shall be Our constant endeavour to maintain Religion there, as it is established, in Doctrine, Worship, and Church-government, and leave no good means unassayed for setling an universall Peace in that our native and ancient Kingdom, with the Reformation and Religion, and settling Peace in England and Ireland: And after the return of an answer to Our late Message to Our Houses of Parliament heer, We shall more particularly acquaint you, or your Commissioners, with Our further resolutions. In the mean time, We seriously recommend Our selves and distracted condition of Our Kingdoms, to your most earnest Prayers to God in our behalf, expecting from you faithfulnesse in your severall Charges and Callings, with that Loyaltie and obedience which becometh the Ministers of the Gospel. We bid you very heartily farewell, from New-castle, the 28, of May 1646,

DIRECT.

For Our right trustie and welbeloved, The Moderatour and other Members of the Generall Assembly of the Kirk of Our Kingdom of Scotland.

6. JUNII 1646. ANTEMERIDIEM. SESS. 4.

ACT CONCERNING THE REGISTERS AND ACTS OF PROVINCIALL ASSEMBLIES.

The Assembly recommends to Provinciall Assemblies, that hereafter they cause read all their Acts, before the dissolving of every Assembly; And that their Registers be written formally, and in a good hand writing, with the severall Leafes or Pages thereof marked by ciphers according to their number.

11. JUNII 1646. ANTEMERIDIEM SESS. 7.

ACT CONCERNING THE PUBLIKE SATISFACTION OF MARRIED PERSONS, FOR FORNICATION COMMITTED BEFORE MARRIAGE.

The Generall Assembly understanding that in many places the publike scandals of Fornication committed before Marriage, are not taken notice of and removed by publike confession according to the order of this Kirk; Therefore for remedie thereof do Ordain, That all Married persons under publike scandall of Fornication, committed before their Marriage (although the scandall thereof hath not appeared before the Marriage) shall satisfie publikely for that sin committed before their Marriage, their being in the estate of Marriage notwithstanding, And that in the same manner as they should have done if they were not Maried.

13. JUNII 1646. ANTEMERIDIEM. SESS. 10.

ORDINANCE FOR EXCOMMUNICATION OF THE EARLE OF SEAFORT.

The Generall Assembly having taken to their serious consideration, that perfidious Band made and contrived lately in the North, under the name of *An humble Remonstrance*, against our Nationall Covenant, and the League and Covenant of the three Kingdoms; Which tendeth to the making of division and fomenting of Jealousie within this and between both Kingdoms, to the prolonging of these unnaturall Warrs, to the impeding of the intended Uniformity in Religion, and to the subversion of all the happie ends of our covenants: And finding that *George* Earle of Seafort hes not only most perfidiously himself subscribed the said wicked Band, contrary to his solemne Oaths in the Covenants aforesaid, and most arrogantly, owned the same under his owne hand writing in his letters to the Committee of Estates, and to the Commissioners of the preceding Assemblie; But also hes seduced and threatned others to subscribe that divisive Band, and to joyne with him in prosecution of his treacherous and wicked designes, therein masked with the pretences of Religion and libertie; boasting also the pursuance of that his Remonstrance against all deadly the opposers thereof, whether King or Parliament. And having also considered another wicked and treacherous Band of Union which the said Earle formerly entred into with that excommunicate Rebell *James Grahame*, after the sentence of forfalture and the dreadfull sentence of excommunication were pronounced against him, Oblieging himself therein under solomne Oaths to joyne with that forfaulted Rebell against this Kirk and Kingdome, and to oppose all their publike resolutions for pursuance of the happie ends of our said Covenants. All which, with his vile reproachfull aspersions and most false calumnies against this

Kirk and State, and their publike and lawfull endeavours and resolutions, with his other wicked and perfidious practises at length discovered in the Proclamation of the Committee of Estates, and the Declaration of the Commission of the Assembly against the said perfidious Band and Remonstrance, being gravely pondered and considered; Together with his base treachery to the Estates, being intrusted by them with ample Comission, and encouraged and enabled for discharging thereof, with Mony Ammunition and Arms in a good measure; Notwithstanding whereof contrary to that great trust reposed in him. It is notour that not only he did not joyne with the Forces raised for the defence of this Kingdome, But rather on the contrary, actually joining himself and his Forces with that excommunicate Rebel *James Grahame*, and these unnatural bloody Rebels his followers, did beleager Invernesse, a Towne Garrisoned by the Estates for the Defence of that part of the Country. And the Assembly, having also found that fair means have been used for reclaiming of the said Earle from that wicked and perfidious course, by publike Declarations and Proclamations, and particular Letters sent to himself from those that had power in that behalf, And that notwithstanding thereof and of Summonds direct against him to answer to the premisses, often called, he doth not appear, but still remains obstinate in his wicked courses. And after mature deliberation having found his frequent fearful and grosse perjuries, his perfidious and wicked conspiracies by Band and Oath, with the publike Enemies of this Kirk and Kingdom, and his other treacherous and wicked practises contemptuously and pertinaciously persisted into, To be heinous offences against God, and high contempt of all Ecclesiastical and Civil authority. Therefore the Assembly moved with the Zeal of God, do without a contrary voice Decerne and Ordain the said *George* Earle of Seafort to be summarly excommunicate, and declared to be one whom Christ commandeth to be holden by all and every one of the Faithful as an Ethnik and Publicane, and appoints the sentence of excommunication to be pronounced by Matter *Robert Blair* Moderator in the east Kirk of this Citie, upon the next Lords day, being the 14 of this Moneth; And that thereafter publike intimation be made thereof upon a Sabbath day before noone in all the Kirks of this Kingdom so soon as advertisement shall come unto them.

ENORMITIES AND CORRUPTIONS OBSERVED TO BE IN THE MINISTERY, WITH THE REMEDIES THEREOF.

ENORMITIES.

The first and main sin, reaching both to our personall carriage and callings, we judge to be, Not studying how to keep Communion and Fellowship with God in Christ, but walking in a naturall way without imploying of Christ, or drawing vertue from him, to inable us unto sanctification, and Preaching in spirit and power.

In our Lives.

1. Much fruitlesse conversing in companie, and complying with the sins of all sorts, not behaving our selves as becomes the men of God.

2. Great worldlinesse is to be found amongst us, minding and speaking most about things of this life, being busied about many things, but forgetting the main.

3. Slighting of Gods worship in their families, and therefore no cordiall urging of it upon others: yea, altogether a wanting of it in some, if it be credible.

4. Want of gravity in carriage and apparell, dissolutenesse in haire, and shaking about the knees, lightnesse in the apparrell of their wives and children.

5. Tippling and bearing companie in untimous drinking inn Tavernes and Ale houses, or any where else, whereby the Ministerie is made vile and contemptible.

6. Discountenancing of the godly; speaking ill of them, because of some that are unanswerable to their profession.

7. The Sabbath not sanctified after Sermons, which maketh people think that the Sabbath is ended with the Sermon.

8. There are also to be found amongst us, who use small and minced oaths.

9. Some so great strangers to Scripture, that except in their publike Ministerie, though they read many things, yet they are little conversant in the Scripture, and in meditation thereof. A dutie incumbent to all the people of God.

In our Callings.

1. Corrupt entry into the Ministrie in former times, and following the course of defection, though forsaken, yet never seriously repented: as also present entring into the Ministery, as to a way of living in the world, and not as to a spirituall calling.

2. Helping in, and holding in of insufficient and suspected men, who favour the things of this life and keeping the door straiter on them whom God hath sealed, then upon these who have lesse evidence of the power of grace and holinesse.

3. Partiality in favouring, and speaking for the scandalous, whether Ministers or other persons, teaching them how to shift and delay censures.

4. Silence in the publike cause, not labouring to cure the disaffection of people, not urging them to constancie and patience in bearing of publike burdens, nor to forwardnesse in the publike Cause; whereby Malignants are multiplied: yea some are so grosse herein, that even in publike Fasts little or nothing is to be heard from them sounding this way.

5. Some account it a point of wisdome to speak ambiguously: some incline to justifie the wicked cause, uttering words which favour of disaffection: and all their complaining of the times, is in such a way as may steal the hearts of people from liking of good Instruments in this work, and consequently from Gods Cause: yea, some reading publike Orders, are ready to speak against them in their private conferences.

6. Idlenesse, either in seldome Preaching, as once on The Lords day, or in preparation for publike duties, not being given to reading and meditation: others have but fits of paines, not like other Tradesmen continually at their work.

7. Want of zeal, and love to the conversion of souls, not being weighted with the want of success in reclaiming of sinners, nor searching in themselves the cause of not profiting, preaching ex officio; nor ex conscientia officii.

8. Self-seeking in preaching, and a venting rather of their wit and skill, then a Shewing foorth of the wisdome and power of God.

9. Lifelesnesse in preaching, not studying to be furnished by Christ with power; and so the ordinance of God teacheth not to the conscience: and thereto belongeth the not applying of the doctrine unto the auditory and times.

10. The indiscreet curing of the indiscretion of pious people and Ministers, whereby godlinesse hath gotten a deep wound, and profanitie hath lifted up the head, contrary to that wise and gracious order set foorth in the Generall Assembly holden at Edinburgh, 1641.

11. Little care to furnish our Armie, either abroad or at home with Ministers; One of our grievous sins and causes of our calamity.

12. Last, it is to be feared that Ministers in secret are negligent to wrestle in Prayer, for a blessing to be poured out upon their labours, contenting themselves with their publike performances.

Remedies.

1. First, That Presbyteries make great conscience to have all vacant places within their several bounds filled with godly and able men, where ever they be to be found: and that under pretence of being a helper, or second to another, none be taken in, but such as are able for the same charge.

2. Whereas it is known, that private tryall in Presbyteries are for the most part perfunctorious, the Brethren are hereby exhorted to be more serious, and faithfull herein, as they will be answerable to Christ, the Chief Shepherd: and in a way previous thereto, that Brethren be free, in loving admonition one of another secretly, from time to time; and that whosoever keeps not the Presbyterie or Synod, after grave admonitions may come under further censures.

3. That accuracie be used as visitation of Kirks, and that the Elders one by one (the rest being removed) be called in, and examined upon oath upon the Ministers behaviour in his calling and conversation.

4. That course be taken to divide Congregations in parts, and by the help not only of Elders in their severall parts, but of neighbors also, the evils, and neglect of persons and families, may be found out and remedied.

5. That every Minister be humbled for his former failings, and make his peace with God, that the more effectually he may preach repentance, and may stand in the gap, to turne away the Lords wrath: runing between the Porch and the Altar, fighing and crying for all the abominations of the land.

6. Speciall care would be had, that Ministers have their conversation in heaven, mainly minding the things of God, and exercising faith for drawing life out of Jesus Christ the fountain of life, arming themselves thereby with power against the contagion and wickednesse of the world.

7. Care would be had of godly conference in Presbyteries, even in time of their refreshment, and the Moderator is to look to it, that good matter be furnished thereto.

8. It is also very necessary for every Minister that would be fruitfull in the work of the Lord, to bring home the Word of God to his own heart and conscience, by Prayer and Meditation, both before and after the publike ordinance.

9. Use would be made of the roll of the Parish, not onely for examination, but also for considering the severall conditions and dispositions of the people, that accordingly they may be admonished, and particularly prayed for by the Ministers in secret.

10. It is very expedient that Ministers have more communion among themselves for their mutuall stirring up, and strengthening of their hands in the Lords work, and rectifying of these who are not incorrigible.

11. That Ministers in all sorts of companie labour to bee fruitfull, as the Salt of the earth, seasoning them they meet with, not only forbearing to drink healths (Satans snare, leading to excesse) but reproving it in others.

12. All Ministers would be carefull to cherish the smoaking flax of weak beginnings in the wayes of God, and ought couragiously to oppose all mockers and revilers of the godly.

13. As at all times, so specially now when the Lord is calling us all to an account; it becomes the Ministers of Christ, with all diligence and faithfulnesse, to improve their Ministerie to the utmost, to be instant in season and out of season; yea, even singally to imploy their time in private, in reading of, and meditating on Scripture, that the word of God may dwell plentifullie in them.

14. That the providing the Armies with Ministers be preferred to any congregation, and these who are appointed to attend the same, and are deficient, be without delay severelie censured according to the Act of the General Assembly; And that all Ministers not only in publike, pray for our Armies, specially these that are to incounter with the bloody enemie within the land, but also continually bear them up before the Lord, that their lives being reformed, their hearts and hands may be strengthned, and their undertaking at last blessed of GOD; with successe.

15. That beside all other scandals, silence or ambiguous speaking in the publike cause, much more detracting and disaffected speaches be seasonablie censured; and to this effect, all honest hearted Brethren would firmlie unite themselves in the Lord, the younger honouring the elder, and the elder not despising the younger.

16. And finallie, both for the corruption of the Ministerie and remedies thereof, we refer the brethren to the Act of the Generall Assemblie at Edinburgh 1596. revived in the late Assemblie at Glasgow 1638. to bee found in the printed Act concerning the same.

The Generall Assembly Ordains the Enormities above specified to be tryed and restrained, and that the Remedies thereof for that purpose be seriously observed and practised: Recommending especially to Presbyteries and Provinciall Assemblies, that use be made of the same in visitation of Kirks and tryall of Presbyteries.

COMMISSION OF THE APPROBATION OF THE PROCEEDINGS OF THE PRECEDING ASSEMBLY.

The General Assembly having heard the report of the Committee appointed to consider and examine the proceedings of the Commissioners of the late General Assembly holden at Edinburgh in the yeer 1646. And after serious consideration thereof, finding that the whole Acts, Proceedings, and Conclusions of the saids Commissioners, contained in the Register subscribed by Mr Andrew Ker their Klerk, and by Mr Robert Ramsay Moderator to the said Committee, do declare much Wisdom, Diligence, Vigilancie, and commendable Zeal; And that the said Commissioners have orderly and formally proceeded in every thing, according to their Commission: Do therefore ratifie and approve the said whole Acts, Proceedings, and Conclusions of the Commissioners of the said Assembly.

15. JUNII 1646. POSTMERIDIEM. SESS. 11.

ACT FOR JOYNING OF THE PRESBYTERIES IN ORKNEY AND ZETLAND TO THE PROVINCIAL OF CATHNES.

The General Assembly, considering that the Presbyterie of Kirkwall in Orkney and the Presbyterie of Schalloway in Zetland have never met in any Provincial Assembly, where through great abuses and disordres are there committed, Therefore the Assembly hereby joyns the said two Presbyteries to the Provincial of Cathnes and Suterland, And appoints all the Ministers and Elders of the said Presbyteries hereafter, to meet at the said Provincial Assembly, and to have place to reason and vote therein as Members of the said Provincial. And suchlike ordains the saids two Presbyteries to be of subordinate Jurisdiction to the said Provincial Assembly, Declaring hereby, that the said Provincial shall consist of the Presbyteries of Cathnes, Sutherland, Orknay, and Zetland in all time coming. And appoints them to meet onely once in the yeer, in respect of their great distance and interjection of seas; And that the first meeting be at Thurso in Cathnes upon the third Tuesday of August next, and thereafter as shall be appointed by the said Provinciall Assembly.

17. JUNII 1646. POSTMERIDIEM. SESS. 14.

ACT CONCERNING EXPECTANTS PREACHING IN PUBLIKE.

The General Assembly discharges any Person to preach in publike under the name and notion of an Expectant or under any other pretence whatsoever, except such as shall be tryed and found qualified according to the Acts of the General Assembly; Recommending to Presbyteries and Provincials to take special notice thereof, and to censure the Transgressors accordingly.

ACT FOR CENSURING THE COMPLYERS WITH THE PUBLIKE ENEMIES OF THIS KIRK AND KINGDOM.

The General Assembly taking to their serious consideration the great and scandalous provocation and grievous defection from the publike Cause, which some have beene guiltie of, by complying with the Rebels the publike Enemies of this Kirk and Kingdom: And judging it a dutie incumbent to them to bring such notorious Offenders to publike satisfaction, that the Wrath of God may be averted, and the publike scandal removed; Do therefore Require, Decern, and Ordain, that such as after lawfull tryall shall be found to have been in actuall Rebellion and to have carried charge with the Rebels, To have accepted Commissions for raising Horse or Foot unto them, To have been seducers of others to joyn in that Rebellion, To be the Penners or contrivers of James Grahames Proclamation for indicting a pretended Parliament, or of any other his Proclamations or Declarations, To have beene prime Instruments in causing publish the said Proclamations and Declarations; That all and every one of such offenders shal humbly acknowledge their offence upon their knees, first before the Presbyterie, and thereafter before the Congregation upon a Sabbath, in some place before the Pulpit; And in the mean time that they be suspended from the Lords Supper: And in case they do not satisfie in manner foresaid, that they be processed with Excommunication. And likewise Ordains; that such as shall be found to have procured Protections from the Rebels, To have execute their orders, To have invited them to their houses, To have given them intelligence, To have drunk James Grahames health or to be guilty of any other such grose degrees of complyance, shall acknowledge their offences publikely before the Congregation, and be suspended from the Communion, and while they doe the same. And further Decernes and Ordains, that all persons in any Ecclesiastick office guilty of any degrees of complyance before mentioned, shall be suspended from their office & all exercise thereof, for such time as the quality of the offence and condition of the offenders shall be found to deserve; And the Assembly hereby declares than Presbyteries have a latitude and liberty to agreadge the censures above specified, according to the degrees and circumstances of the offences; And gives in like maner the same latitude and liberty to the Commissioners of this Assembly for publike affairs, who have also power to try and censure the offenders in manner above exprest, and to take account of the diligence of Presbyteries thereintill.

ACT CONCERNING JAMES GRAHAMS PROCLAMATION.

The General Assembly having considered a copie of a Proclamation published by order of that excommunicat Traitor *James Graham*, for indicting of a pretended Parliament, and finding the same to be full of Blasphemies against the solemn League and Covenant of the three Kingdoms, and of vile aspersions of Treason, Rebellion, and Sedition most falsly and impudently imputed to the Estates, and most faithfull and loyall Subjects of this Kingdome: Doe therfore declare, That such as have bin prim Instruments of the publishing of that or the Proclamation and Declaration, deserve the highest censures of the Kirks, unlesse they make humble confession of their offence publickely, in such manner as is prescribed by this Assembly; And humbly Recommends to the Committee of Estates to take some course for their exemplary civill punishment, and that some publike note of ignominie be put upon that Proclamation as their Honors shall think meet.

18. JUNII 1646. ANTERMERIDIEM. SESS. ULT.

ACT AGAINST LOOSING OF SHIPS AND BARKS UPON THE LORDS DAY.

The Generall Assembly understanding how much the Lords day is profaned by Skippers and other Seafaring men, Do therefore discharge and inhibite all Skippers and Sailers to begin any voyage on the Lords day, or to loose any Ships, Barks or Boats out of Harbery or Road upon that day, And who shall do in the contrary hereof, shall be censured as profaners of the Sabbath: Recommending to Presbyteries and others whom it may concerne to see both of the Acts of Assembly and Parliament made for censuring and punishing profanation of the Lords day, to be put in execution against them.

ACT ANENT CHILDREN SENT WITHOUT THE KINGDOM.

Whereas divers Children have been sent without the Kingdom to be bred abrord, and have been or in time coming may be exposed to the temptations of seducers, and drawn away from the Trueth established and professed within this Church to errour of Poperie, or other Sects and Heresies: Therefore the Assembly Ordains, that the Parents or Friends of Children and Minors, shall before they send them without the Kingdom, first acquaint the Presbytery where they reside, that they may have their Testimoniall directed to the Presbytery or Classe within the Kingdom of *France*, or *England*, or *Ireland*, and at the time of these Childrens return from any of the saids Kingdoms, to report ane Testimoniall from the Presbytery or Synode where they lived without the Kingdom of their breeding there (and to shew the same to the Presbytery within the Kingdom who gave them a Testimoniall at their way going). Likeas the Assembly Ordains all Presbyteries to try if any Children have been sent to Popish Schooles or Colledges Without the Kingdom; And if any be found, that their names be given to the Presbytery or Commissioners of the Assembly, that the same may be presented to the Honourable Lords of Secret Councell, or Committee of Estates, that their Lordships may be humbly desired by their authority to recal them, that after return to this Kingdom course may be taken according to the former Ordinances of Generall Assemblies, for their breeding in the true Religion.

OVERTURES PRESENTED TO THE ASSEMBLY.

That correspondence be keeped among Presbyteries constantly by letter without prejudice of personall correspondence when need requires, whereby one Presbyterie may understand what many are doing, and they may be mutually assisting each to other.

II. That for the better breeding of young men to the Ministerie who are not able to furnish themselves in charges to attend in the Universities, that the Presbyteries where they reside appoint some to direct their studies.

III. That it be recommended to all the Universities to condiscend upon the best Overtures for the most profitable teaching of Grammar and Phylosophy, and as they may meet at the Commission of the Generall Assembly to make the matter ripe for the next Assembly.

The Assembly approves these Overtures, and recommends accordingly.

IV. That to the intent the knowlege of God in Christ may be spread through the Highlands and Islands (for in lack whereof the land hath smarted in the late troubles) these courses be taken: 1. Let an order be procured, that all Gentlemen who are able, at least send their eldest sons to be bred in the Inland. 2. That a Ministerie be planted amongst them, and for that effect that Ministers and expectants who can speak the Irish language be sen to imploy their talents in these parts, and that the Kirks there be provided as other Kirks in this Kingdome. 3. That Scots Schools be erected in all Parishes there, according to the Act of Parliament, where conveniently they can be had. 4. That Ministers and ruling Elders that have the Irish language be appointed to visit these parts.

The Assembly approves this Overture, and recommends this purpose to further consideration, that more Overtures may be prepared thereanent against the next Assembly.

V. That for keeping the Universities pure, and provoking the Professors of Divinitie to great diligence, each Professor in the Universities of this Church and Kingdom, bring with him or send with the Commissioner who comes to the General Assembly, ane perfit and well written copie of his Dictates, to be revised by the General Assembly, or such as they shall appoint for that work ilk year.

The Assembly continues the determination of a constant and perpetuall order herein untill the next Assembly, but in the mean time desires the professors of Divinity to present to the next Assembly their Dictates of Divinity whereof the professors present are to give intimation to the professors absent.

VI. The great burdens Intrants undergoes when they enter the Ministery, which holds many of them long at under, would crave the Assemblies judgement and authority, that Ministers Manses and Stipends may be all made free to the Intrant.

The Assembly refers and recommends to the Commissioners for publike affairs to seek redresse in this matter from the Honorable Houses of Parliament, and to consider of some fitting Overtures to be presented to their Honours for that effect.

RENOVATION OF THE COMMISSION FOR THE PUBLIKE AFFAIRS OF THE KIRK.

The Generall Assembly taking to their consideration that in respect the great work of Uniformity in Religion in all his Majesties Dominions is not yet perfited, (though by the Lords blessing there is a good progresse made in the same) there is a necessity of renewing the Commissions granted formerly for prosecuting and perfiting that great work, doe therefore renew the power and Commission granted for the publike affairs of the Kirk by the Generall Assemblies held in S. Andrews in the year 1642. and in Edinburgh 1643. 1644. and 1645. unto the persons following, viz. Masters Alexander Henderson, Robert Douglas, Willliam Colvil, William Bennet, George Gillespie, John Oswald, John Adamson, William Dalgleish, David Calderwood, James Fleeming, Robert Ker, John Dalyell, James Wright, John Knox, Adam Penman, Robert Lightoun, Alexander Dickeson, Patrick Fleeming, John

Hay, Richard Dickeson, Thomas Vasse, David Drummund, Alexander Somervill, Robert Eliot, Robert Blair, James Bruce, Robert Traile, Samuel Rutherfurd, Alexander Colvall, Walter Greg, Alexander Balfour, George Thomson, John Mencreiff, John Smith, Patrick Gillespie, John Duncan, James Sibbald, Alexander Casse, John Hume, Alexander Kinneir, Walter Swintoun, Robert Knox, William Penan, James Guthrie, Thomas Donaldson, William Jameton, Thomas Wilkie, John Knox, Robert Murray, John Freebairn, Robert Wright, David Auchterlonie, William Maior, Samuel Justein, John Leirmont, Andrew Lauder, James Irving, Alexander Turnbull, James Bonar, William Adair, John Neve, Patrik Colvil, Matthew Birsbane, John Hamiltoun, Allan Ferguson, Robert Ramsay, Geo. Young, David Dickson, Robert Bailie, James Nasmith, John Lindsay, John Weir, Evan Cameron, James Affleck, John Robison, Andrew Eliot, Silvester Lambie, Lawrence Skinner, William Rate, David Campbel, Andrew Cant, William Douglas, David Lindsay, Gilbert Anderson, Alexander Garrioch, William Jaffray, Thomas Caw, William Campbell, Walte Stewart Ministers; And Archibald Marquesse of Argle, John Eearle of Crawfurd-Lindsay, William Earle Marshall, William Earle of Glencairn, John Earle of Cassils, Charles Earle of Dumfermling, James Earle of Tullibardine, Francis Earle of Bacleugh, John Earle of Lauderdale, William Earle of Lothian, William Earle of Lanerk, Archibald Lord Angus, John Lord Balmerino, Robert Lord Burleigh, John Master of Yesteir, Sir Patrick Hepburn of Waughtoun, Sir John Hope of Craighall, Sir Archibald Johnston of Wariston, Sir David Hume of Wedderburn, Sir Robert Innes of that ilk, Sir William Baily of Lemington, Sir John Muncreiffe of that ilk, James Macdougal of Garthland, Patrick Cockburn of Clarkington, Sir Hugh Campbel of Cesnock, Sir William Cunningham of Cunninghamhead, John Hume of Blackader, Sir James Dundas of Arniston, Alex Forbes Tutor of Pitsligo, Mr Geo. Winrham of Libberton, David Weemes of Fingask, Mr Francis Hay of Balhousie, Alex. Brodie of that ilk, Mr Alex. Colvill of Blair, Geo. Dundas of Dudiston, William Moor of Glanderston, Sir James Nicolson of Colbrandspaith, John Edgar of Wedderlie, William Hume of Lenthill, James Ruchhead, Laurence Henderson and James Stuart Bailes of Edinburgh, George Porterfield Provest of Glasgow, Wil. Hume there, Ro. Arnot Provest of Perth, John Semple Provest of Dumbarton, John Kennedie Provest of Air, Mr David Weems, Geo. Gardine, John Johnstoun, Tho. Paterson, Tho. White, John Sleigh Elders. Giving unto them full power and Commission To do all and every thing for prosecuting, advancing, perfecting, and bringing the said work of Uniformity in Religion in all His Majesties Dominions to a happy conclusion, conform to the former Commissions granted by preceding Assemblies thereanent. And to that effect appoints them, or any seventeen of them, whereof thirteen shall be Ministers, To meet at Edinburgh the 19 of this Moneth, and thereafter upon the second Wednesdais of August, November, Februar and May next to come, and upon any other day and in any other place they shall think meet. And further, renews to the persons before named, the power contained in the Act of the said Assembly 1643. Intituled, A reference to the Commission anent the persons designed to repair to the Kingdom of England; As also the power contained in two several Acts of the said Assembly 1644. Sess. 6 made against secret disaffecters of the Covenant, and for sending Ministers to the Armie, with full power to them to treat and determine in the matter aforesaid, and in all others matters referred unto them by this Assembly, as fully and freely as if the same were here particularly expressed, and with as ample power as any Commission of former General Assemblies hath had, or been in use of before; They being alwayes for their whole proceedings comptable to, and censurable by the next Generall Assembly.

RENOVATION OF THE COMMISSION FOR PROSECUTING THE TREATY FOR UNIFORMITY IN ENGLAND.

The Generall Assembly, Taking to their consideration that the Treatie of Uniformity in Religion in all His Majesties Dominions is not yet perfected, Therefore renews the power & Commission granted by preceding Assemblies for prosecuting that Treatie, unto these persons after named, viz. Mr. Alexander Henderson, Mr. Robert Douglas, Mr. Samuel Rutherfurd, Mr. Robert Bailie, Mr. Geo. Gillespie Ministers; And John Earle of Lauderdale, John Lord Balmerino, and Sir Archibald Johnston of Wariston Elders; Authorising them with full power to prosecute the said Treatie of Uniformity with the Honourable Houses of the Parliament of England, and the Reverend Assembly of Divines there, or any Committees appointed by them: And to do all and every thing which may advance, perfect and bring that Treatie to an happy conclusion, conform to the former Commissions given thereanent.

THE ASSEMBLIES ANSWER TO THE KINGS MAIESTIE.

May it please your Majestie,

Having received your Majesties Letter with thankfulnesse, we thought it our dutie to send some of our number to wait upon your Majestie and present our humble desires more particularly then at this time could be expressed by writ; And we are confident your Majestie will interpret our freedom and plain dealing by them, to be a reall testimonie of our unfained affection, who have constantly laboured to approve our selves in all fidelity to our Lord and Master Jesus Christ, and in all loyaltie to your Majestie; And are resolved to walk still after the same rule in our severall stations and vocations, continuing our Prayers for you, that God may multiply all sorts of Mercies upon your Royall Person and Posterity, and more and more incline your heart to the speedie following of the Counsels of Trueth and Peace and grant unto your Majestie along and happy Reign, that we may live under you a peaceable and quiet life, in all godlinesse and honesty.

Edinburgh, 18. Junii 1646.

Subscribed in name of the Nationall Assembly of the Kirk of Scotland by the Moderator.

THE ASSEMBLIES LETTER TO THE RIGHT HONORABLE THE LORDS AND COMMONS IN THE PARLIAMENT OF ENGLAND ASSEMBLED AT WESTMINSTER.

Right Honourable,

The report of the great things which the Lord hath done for your Honours, hath gone forth into many Lands, and it becometh us least of any either to smother or extenuate the same; We desire to be enlarged in the admiration of the Power & Mercie of God the Author, & to diminish nothing of that praise that is due unto you as Instruments. When the Lord set your Honours upon the Bench of Judgment, both the Kirk and Common wealth of England were afflicted with intestine and bosome evills, the cure whereof could not but be very difficult; because they were not only many, but for the most part Universall and deeply rooted, sheltred under the shadow of Custome and Law, and supported with all the wisdom and strength of the Malignant and Prelatical partie; who rather chose to involve the Land in an unnatural and bloody Warre, then to fail of their ambitious and treacherous designes, against Religion, the priviledges of Parliament, and the Lawes and Liberties of the Kingdom: Neither hath that miserable crew been wanting to their owne ends but for many years together hath desperatly pursued their resolutions in Arms; And was likely to have prevailed, if the Lord had not put himself in the breach, and furnished you with much Patience, Wisdom, Courage, and Constancy, in the midst of many difficulties and distresses; and at last with so glorious and triumphing a successe, that the Enemy hath fallen every where before you, and there is none left to appear against you. These things as they be the matter of our refreshment and of your glory, so doe they lay a strong obligation upon your Honours to walke humbly with your God, and to improve the power he hath put into your hands for the advancement of the Kingdom of his Son, and bringing forth of the head-Stone of his House. The slow progresse of the work of God hath alwaies been the matter of our sorrow, which is now increased by the multiplication of the spirits of errour and delusion, that drowne many souls into perdition, and so strengthen themselves that they shall afterward be laboured against, with more pains then successe, if a speedy and effectuall remedie be not provided. And therefore as the servants of the living God, who not onely send up our supplications daily for you, but have hazarded our selves in your defence, We do earnestly beseech your Honors in the bowels of Jesus Christ, to give unto him the glory that is due unto his Name, by a timous establishing all his Ordinances in the full integritie and power thereof, according to the League and Covenant. As long as the Assembly of Divines was in debate, & an enemy in the fields, we conceived that these might be probable grounds of delay, which being now removed out of the way, we do promise to our selves from your Wisdom, Faithfulnesse, and Zeale, the perfiting of that which was the main ground of our engagement, and a chief matter of consolation unto us in all our sad and heavy sufferings, from the hand of a most cruell Enemy. We know that there is a generation of men who retard the work of Uniformity, and foment jealousies betwixt the Nations, studying if it were possible, to break our bands asunder; But we trust, that he that sits in the Heaven will Laugh, and that the Lord shall have them in derision, that he shall speak to them in his wrath and vex them in his sore displeasure, and notwithstanding of all that they can do, set his King upon his holy hill of Sion, and make these Nations happy in the sweet fruits of Unity in Truth and Peace. The searcher of hearts knows that we desire to hold fast the band of our Covenant, as sacred and inviolable; being perswaded that the breach of so solemne a tye could not but hasten down upon our heads a curse and vengeance from the righteous Judge of the world, and involve these Kingdoms in sader calamities then they have yet seen,

And we abhor to entertain any other thought of you: Nay we are confident that your Honours will seriously indeavour the prosecution of all these ends designed in the Covenant, and the bringing these Nations unto the neerest conjunction both in judgement and affection, especially in these things that concern Religion, which with out all controversie, is the readiest and surest way of attaining and securing the Peace and Prosperity of both Kingdoms.

Edinburgh 18 Junii 1646.

Subscribed in name of the Generall Assembly by the Moderator.

THE ASSEMBLIES LETTER TO THE RIGHT HONORABLE THE LORD MAJOR ALDERMEN, AND COMMON-COUNCEL OF THE CITY OF LONDON.

Your late and seasonable testimony given to the Truth of the Gospel, and your affection to the Peace of the Kingdoms, manifested in your humble Remonstrance and Petition to the Honorable Houses of Parliament, hath so revived the remembrance of your former Faith and Zeal, and proclaimed you the worthy seed of so noble ancestors in that famous City, As we cannot but acknowledge with all thankfulnesse the grace of God bestowed on you, and stirre you up to take notice, how since you were precious in the Lords sight, you have been ever Honurable, The Lord hath loved you, given men for you, and people for your life: What an honour was it in the dayes of old, when the fire of the Lord was in Zion, and his furnace in your Jerusalem (even in Queen Maries dayes) that there were found in you men that loved not their lives unto the death? What a glory in after time, when Satan had his Throne and Antichrist his Seat in the midst of you, that there were still found not a few that kept their Garments clean? But the greatest praise of the good hand of God upon you hath been in this, That amidst the many Mists of Errour and Heresie which have risen from the bottomlesse pit, to bespot the face and darken the glory of the Church, (while the Bride is a making ready for the Lamb) you have held the Trueth, and most piously endeavoured the setling of Christ upon his Throne. We need not remember how zealous you have been in the Cause of God, nor how you have laid out your selves and estates in the maintenance thereof, nor how many acknowledgements of the same you have had from the Honourable Houses, nor how precious a remembrance will be had of you in after ages for your selling of all to buy the Pearl of price: We only at this time do admire, and in the inward of our hearts do blesse the Lord for your right and deep apprehensions of the great and important matters of Christ in his Royall Crown; and of the Kingdoms in their Union, while the Lord maketh offers to bring our Ship (so much afflicted and tolled with tempest) to the safe Harbour of Trueth and Peace. Right memorable is your Zeal against Sects and Sectaries; your care of Reformation, according to the word of God, and the example of the best Reformed Churches; your earnest endeavours and noble adventures, for preserving of the rights and priviledges of Parliament, and Liberties of the Kingdomes, Together with his Majesties just power and greatnesse; and your high profession, that it is not in the power of any humane authority to discharge or absolve you from adhearing unto that our (so solemnly sworn) League and Covenant, or to enforce upon you any sense contrary to the letter of the same, Besides your other good services done unto the Lord and to us, in the strengthening of the hands of the reverend Assembly of Divines, and of our Commissioners in their asserting of the government of Christ, (which the more it be tried will be ever found the more precious Truth), and vindicating of the same from the usurpation of man, and contempt of the wicked. These all as they are so many testimonies of your Pietie, Loyaltie, and undaunted resolution to stand for Christ; So are they and shall ever be so many obligations upon us your Brethren, to esteem highly of you in the Lord, to bear you on our brests before him night and day, and to contribute our best endeavours, and to improve all opportunities for your encouragement. And now we beseech you in the Lord, Honorable and welbeloved, go on in this your strength, and in the power of his might who hath honoured you to be faithful, stand fast in that liberty wherewith Christ hath made you free; And in the pursuance of this truth, we are confident, as you have, so you will never cease to study the Peace and neerer conjunction of the Kingdoms, knowing that a threefold cord is not easily broken. Now the Lord Jesus Christ himself, and God even our Father, which hath loved and honoured you, and given you everlasting consolation, & good help through grace, comfort your hearts, and stablish you in every good word and work.

Edinburgh 18 Iunii 1646.

Subscribed in name of the General Assembly by the Moderator.

THE ASSEMBLIES LETTER TO THE RIGHT REVEREND THE ASSEMBLY OF DIVINES IN THE KIRK OF ENGLAND ASSEMBLED AT WESTMINSTER.

Much Honoured and right Reverend.

Amongst other fruits of this our precious liberty, after such dissipation by Sword and Pestilence, to meet again, we account it not the least, to have the opportunity of making a publike Declaration of our earnest affection to all our brethren of that Nation, and especially your selves of the Reverend Assembly at Westminster. When we were lately in a very low condition, we may say that our own sufferings and fears, although imbittered with the sense of the Lords displeasure against our luke warmneese and unfaithfulnesse; yet they did not so take up our heart, but that room was left to congratulate with the Lords people there in all their successes, and to condole with them in all their dangers; And if at any time any here seemed to be more jealous then godly jealousie would allow, we know not how it can be imputed to any thing else, but to the vehemencie of ardent affection, and impatient desire to have our brethren there and us joyned neerer to Christ, and neerer to one another in all his Ordinances; and especially is Presbyterial Government, so well warranted by the Word, and approven by experience of our own and other reformed Churches; Wherein your long and unwearied endeavours have been blessed with a large increase, which yet hath proved still a seed unto a further and more glorious expected harvest. There could not be wished by mortal men a fairer opportunity then is cast in your laps, being invited and charged by so high an authority, to give so free and publike a testimony to those truths, which formerly many of the Lords precious ones by tongue and pen, by tears and blood have more privately asserted; The smallest of Christs truths (if it be lawful to call any of them small) is of greater moment, then all the other businesses that ever have been debated since the beginning of the world to this day; But the highest of honours and heaviest of burdens is put upon you, to declare out of the sacred records of Divine Truth, what is the prerogitive of the Crown and extent of the Scepter of Jesus Christ, what bounds are to be set between Him ruling in his House, and powers established by God on Earth, how and by whom his House is to be governed, and by what wayes a restraint is to be put on those who would pervert his Truth, and subvert the faith of many. No doubt mountains of oppositions arise, and gulfs of difficulties open up themselves in this your way; But you have found it is God that girdeth you with strength and maketh your way perfect and plain before you, who hath delivered, and doth deliver, and will yet deliver. We need not put you in minde that as there lyeth at this time a strict eye on all, so in a special manner both you and we are ingaged to interpose our selves between God and these Kingdomes; between the two Nations, between the King and the People, for averting of deserved wrath, for continuing and increasing of a well grounded Union, for procuring as far as in us lyeth a right settling of Religion and Church-Government; That when we shall sleep with our fathers the Posterity here and abroad may be reaping the fruits of our labours.

We are fully assured of your constant and sedulous promoving of this blessed Work, and of the Lords assisting and carrying you on therein: And are confident that your late experience and present sense of the great danger and fearfull confusion flowing from the rife and grouth of Sects and Sectaries not suppressed, hath stirred up in your hearts most fervent desires, and careful endeavours for remedying the same, wherein we exhort you to continue and abound; knowing that your labours shall not be in vain in the Lord, to whose rich grace we commend you, and the work in your hands.

Edinburgh 18 Juny 1646.

Subscribed in name of the General Assembly by the Moderator.

RECOMMENDATION TO PRESBYTERIES AND PROVINCIAL ASSEMBLIES.

1. The Assembly recommends to the several Presbyteries and Provincial Assemblies, to consider the interests of particular congregations, in the calling, and admission of Ministers, with all these questions that usually fall out upon that occasion; And to report their opinions to the next Assembly, with some fit Overtures for preventing all contests in that matter.

2. The Assembly recommends to Presbyteries and Provincial Assemblies to consider all the matters referred by preceding Assemblies to the consideration of Presbyteries, And to report their opinions therein to the next Assembly.

ACT FOR A PUBLIKE FAST BEFORE THE NEXT ASSEMBLY.

The Assembly having considered an Act of the Assembly 1644. Sess. Ult. enjoyning a publike Fast to be keeped in all the Kirks of the City where the General Assembly holds upon the first day of the meeting of the Assembly; And finding some inconveniencies therein, Therefore at this time until the matter be further considered, Appoints a publike Fast and Humiliation for the Lords blessing to the meeting of the next Assembly, to be universally observed in all the congregations of this Kirk upon the Sabbath next except one preceeding the said next Assembly; The exercises for the members of the Assembly at their first meeting, being still observed according to the ancient and laudable practise of this Kirk, This appointment not withstanding.

The Assembly appoints the meeting of the next General Assembly to be at Edinburgh upon the first Wednesday of August 1647.

THE GENERALL ASSEMBLY, AT EDINBURGH 4. AUGUST. 1647.

AUGUST. 16. 1647 POSTMERIDIEM. SESS. 2.

ACT ALLOWING THE HALF OF THE MINISTERS IN THE PRESBYTERIE OF ZETLAND ONLY, WITH THEIR RULING ELDERS, TO KEEP THE PROVINCIAL ASSEMBLY.

The General Assembly, Understanding that the whole Members of the Presbyterie of *Zetland*, joyned to the Provincial of *Caithnes* and *Sutherland* upon weighty considerations by the preceeding Assembly, cannot be by present at the meetings of that Provincial, without great prejudice to the particular Congregations within that Presbyterie, and many other inconveniences; That Isle being of great distance from Land, and the passage from and to the same being uncertain and dangerous: Doe therefore Declare and Ordaine, That the whole Ministers and Elders of the Presbyterie of *Zetland* shall not be tyed hereafter to come to meetings of their said Provincial; But that the half of the number of the Ministers with their Ruling Elders, shall be onely oblieged to keep the meetings of the said Provincial Assembly in time coming.

20. AUGUST 1647. ANTEMERIDIEM. SESS. 15.

A DECLARATION, AND BROTHERLY EXHORTATION OF THE GENERAL ASSEMBLY OF THE CHURCH OF SCOTLAND, TO THEIR BRETHREN OF ENGLAND.

The conscience of our dutie to God obliging us to give a testimony to his Truth, and to the Kingdom of his Sonne Jesus Christ, now so much resisted and opposed by many, and so little owned by others: The laudable custome and example of correspondency between Neighbouring Churches, exhorting, encouraging, and (in case of publike scandal) admonishing in love one another, as well as single Brethren ought to admonish one another in love, in the case of private offence: Our neerer relation and more special affection to our Brethren of England, making us to sympathize with them in their danger and affliction as our own, both Kingdomes being united as one entire Body in one Covenant, for pursuing the common cause and ends therein expressed: Yea, common reason and experience it self teaching us that we have no cause to conceive our Religion, the liberties of this Church, or our selves to be in a condition of safety, when ever the enemies of our Religion and Liberties are growing to a prevalency in the Neighbour Kingdom. Any one of these considerations, much more all of them together, cry aloud upon us to break our silence in this present Juncture of Affaires; yet we hope to expresse our selves both concerning the present Dangers and present Duties, as in a conscionable and Brotherly freedome, so in, a fair and in offensive way; for we have no pleasure nor purpose to provoke any Person or Party whatsoever, not to encrease, but to endeavour the allaying and composing of the present unhappy differences. If any shall offend at our discharging our conscience & doing our duty, yet we shall rather chose to take our hazard of that, then of displeasing God by neglect of duty. But we hope better things, then to be mis-understood, or mis-interpreted by such as desire a candide interpretation of their own actions or expressions.

First of all, whatsoever the present discouragements, difficulties or dangers are, or whatsoever for the future they may be, we cannot but commemorate to the glory of God, and we doubt not it shall be remembred to his glory in the Church throughout all ages, How great a salvation his Mighty Hand and Outstretched Arme hath wrought for these three Kingdomes; How he stirred up the Spirits of his People in this Kingdome ten yeares agoe, to begin to shake off the Yoke of Prelatical tyrannie, and of Popish Ceremonies obtruded upon us, contrary to the Lawes of God and Men; How he led us on from so small beginnings, & from one degree to another, till we were United in a National Covenant; How he gave us a Banner to be displayed for the Truth, and so blessed us in the prosecution of that Covenant, that the Kings Majesty was graciously pleased upon the humble Petitions of his Loyal Subjects in this Nation, to indict a General Assembly and Parliament for healing the grievances of Church and State respectively, As likewise to grant his Royal consent for Confirming and Ratifying by Acts of Parliament our National Covenant, & the Government and Liberties of this Church. After which the new Troubles raised against us by the malice and treachery of our enemies, did occasion the first expedition of this Nation into *England,* (upon which followed the calling of the Parliament there, and the large Treaty) and in the issue, the return of that Army was with an Olive branch of Peace, and not without the beginnings of a Reformation in *England*: In which work while the Parliament was interrupted and opposed, and a bloody War begun with great successe on that side which opposed the Parliament and the begun Reformation, from whence also did accrew great advantage to the Popish Party (whereof the Cessation of Arms concluded in *Ireland* may be in stead of many testimonies;) Commissioners were sent hither from both Houses, earnestly inviting and perswading to a nearer Union of the Kingdomes, and desiring Assistance from this Nation to their Brethren in that their great distresse; And this by the good Hand of God produced the solemne League and Covenant of the three Kingdomes, to the terrour of the Popish and Prelatical party our common Enemies, and to the great comfort of such as were wishing and waiting for the Reformation of Religion; and the recovery of just Liberties. And although for the conjunction of the Kingdomes in Covenant, and Armes (being a speciall means tending to the extirpation of Popery) and strengthening the true Reformed Religion; this Kingdome hath been invaded and infested by the bloody *Irish* Rebels aided and strengthened by some degenerate and perfidious Countrey-men of our owne: Although also in *England* there were not wanting incendiaries, who hating and envying nothing more then the Union of the Kingdomes in such a Covenant, were very vigilant to catch, and active to improve all occasions of making divisive motions, and creating Nationall Differences; Yet God hath been graciously pleased to break our Enemies strength at Home when it was greatest, and to guide us through these Jealousies and Differences fomented by disaffected Persons between the Kingdomes; So that in stead of a splitting upon these Rocks (the thing hoped for by our Enemies) there was a peaceable and friendly parting: Since which time God hath further blessed our Army at Home, to the expelling of the Enemie out of our own Borders. Nor can we passe in silence the happy progresse which hath been made in the Reformation of the Church of *England*; He that hath brought the Children to the birth, can also give strength to come forth; And hee whose hand did cast out Prelacie and the Book of Common Prayer (although strongly rooted in standing Lawes;) and who enclined the Parliament of *England* to owne no other Church Government but the Presbyterial, (Though it bee not yet fully settled according to the Word of God, and the example of the best Reformed Churches) can as easily encline when hee thinks good both the King and them, and the body of that Kingdome to a thorow and perfect Reformation. He that made the Assemblies and Parliaments of both Kingdomes to agree upon one directory for the Publike Worship of God, can also when he will make an agreement in the other Parts of Uniformitie, Confession of Faith, form of Church Government, and Catechisme; In all which there hath beene also a good progresse made in the Reverend and Learned Assemblie of Divines through the good hand of God so long upon them.

Having now seen so much of God both in the beginning and progresse of this his great Work, And his Hand having done so wondrous things for his People in their greatest extremities of danger, and having discovered and defeated the plots of Enemies, making them fall even by their own Counsels; These things wee resolve to keep still fixed in our hearts, and as memorials before our eyes, that remembring the Works of the Lord, and the Years of the Right Hand of the most High, wee may neither want matter of Praies and thanksgivings, nor experience to breed hope. Although the building of the House of the Lord in *England* be not yet, after so long expectation, finished, and now also the work ceaseth, Yet wee doe from our hearts blesse the Lord for the laying of the Foundation, and for so much progresse as hath been made in the Work; Having still confidence in the Almighty, to whom nothing is impossible or too hard, that every Mountaine which doeth or shall stand in the way shall become a plaine, and that the Head-stone shall bee brought forth with shoutings of Joy, *Grace, Grace unto it.*

Neverthelesse, we are also very sensible of the great and imminent dangers into which this Common Cause of Religion is now brought by the growing and spreading of most dangerous errours in *England,* to the obstructing & hindering of the begun Reformation, as namely (beside many others) Socinianisme, Arminianisme, Anabaptisme, Antinomianisme, Brownisme, Erastianisme, Independency, and that which is called (by abuse of the word) Liberty of Conscience, being indeed Liberty of Errour, Scandall, Schisme, heresie, dishonouring God, opposing the Truth, hindering Reformation; and seducing others; Whereunto we adde those Nullifidians, or men of no Religion, commonly called Seekers: Yea, wee cannot

but look upon the Dangers of the true Reformed Religion in this Island, as greater now then before; Not onely for that those very principles & fundamentals of
Faith which under Prelacy, yea, under Popery it self, were generally received as
uncontroverted, are now by the Scepticisme of many Sectaries of this time either
oppugned, or called in question; But also, because in stead of carrying on the Reformation towards perfection, that which hath beene already built is in part cast
down, and in danger to be wholly overthrowne through the endeavours of Sectaries to comply with many of the Prelaticall and Malignant, and even the Popish
party; and their joyning hand in hand, and casting in their lots, and interweaving
their interests together in way of Combination, against the Covenant and Presbyteriall Government; Yea, the unclean spirit which was cast out, is about to enter
againe with seven other spirits worse then himselfe, and so the latter end like to be
worse then the beginning.

We are extremely sorry that we have cause to aggravate these evils from the
crying sin of breach of Covenant, Whereof if we should hold our peace, yet according to the Word of the Lord; other Nations will say, and many among them do say,
Wherefore hath the Lord done thus unto this People? and what meaneth the heat
of this great anger? And they answer one another, *Because they have forsaken the
Covenant of the Lord their God.* We would not be understood as if we meant either
to Justifie this Nation, or to charge such a sin upon all in that Nation. We know the
Covenant hath been in divers particulars broken by many in both Kingdomes, the
Lord pardon it, and accept a Sacrifice; And wee doe not doubt but there are many
seven thousands in *England* who have not onely kept themselves unspotted, and
retained their integrity in that businesse, but doe also mourne and groane before
the Lord for that sin of others. Yet we should but deny our own sence and betray
the Truth, if we should not resent so great a sinne and danger, as is the breach of
a solemne Covenant, sworn with hands lifted up to the most High God: Which
breach however varnished over with some colourable and handsome pretexts, one
whereof is the Liberty & Common Right of the free People of *England*, as once
Saul brake a Covenant with the Gibeonites, *In his Zeal to the Children of Israel and
Iudah*: Yet God could not then, and cannot now be mocked; Yea, it is too apparent
and undeniable, that among those who did take the Covenant of the three Kingdomes, as there are many who have given themselves to a detestable indifferency
or neutralitie, so there is a Generation which hath made defection to the contrary
Part; Persecuting as far as they could that true Reformed Religion, in Doctrine,
Worship, Discipline, and Government, which by the Covenant they ought to preserve against the common Enemies; hindering and resisting the Reformation and
Uniformity, which by the Covenant ought to bee endeavoured; preserving and
tolerating those cursed things which by the Covenant ought to be extirpate, especially Heresie and Schisme, encroaching upon, yea offering violence unto the
Rights, Priviledges, and Authority of Magistracie, Protecting and assisting such as
by the Covenant ought to have been brought to condigne triall and punishment,
and persecuting those who by the Covenant ought to be assisted and defended;
Endeavouring also a breach in stead of a firme Peace and Union between the Kingdomes: So that there is not any one Article of the Solemne League and Covenant
which hath not been sinfully and dangerously violated before God, Angels, and

Men. Now if a Covenant for the preservation and Reformation of Religion, the Maintenance and Defence of Liberties was justly thought a *fit and excellent mean*, not only to *strengthen and fortifie* the Kingdomes against the common Enemie of the true Reformed Religion, publike Peace and Prosperity; But also *to acquire the favour of Almightie GOD towards the three Kingdomes, of England, Scotland, and Ireland,* as is expressed in the Ordinance of the Lords and Commons for the taking of the Covenant, dated *February 2. 1643.*

Surely then the Authors and chief Instruments of the breach of that Covenant, are to be looked upon as those who strengthen the hands of the common Enemie, and provoke the wrath of Almighty God against these Kingdomes. Yea, if this Covenant was the *Soveraigne and onely meanes of the recovery* of these embroiled bleeding Kingdoms, as is expressed in the exhortation of the Assembly of Divines to the taking of the Covenant, approved and ordered to be Printed by the House of Commons; The despising, refusing, and casting aside of that remedy, must needs render the disease much more desperate. And if by the Declaration of both Kingdomes joined in Arms, *Anno 1643.* such as would not take the Covenant, were declared *to be publike Enemies to their Religion and Countrey, and that they are to be censured and punished as professed Adversaries and Malignants.* Who seeth not now a strange falling away from these first Principles and Professions, among these who either magnifie and cry up, or at least connive at and comply with such as have not taken the Covenant, yea, are known Enemies to it, and cry down such as are most zealous for it?

In this case, while in the Neighbour Kingdom, the staves of Beauty and Bands, Covenant & Brother-hood are broken by many, the home of Malignants and Sectaries exalted, the best affected born down, Reformation ebbing, Heresie and Schisme flowing; It can hardly be marvelled at by any Person of prudence and discretion, if we be full of such feares and apprehensions as use to be in those who dwell near a House set on fire, or a Family infected, especially being taught by the sad experience of these Prelatical times, how easily a Gangrene in the one half of this Island may spread through the whole; Knowing also the inveterate and insatiable malice of the Enemies of this Cause and Covenant against this Church and Kingdome; which we cannot be ignorant of, unlesse we would shut our eyes & stop our ears.

Our present purpose leadeth us to touch somewhat of the proceedings of the Army in *England* this Summer, so far as Religion is therein concerned; As we are confident, divers have gone a long with them in the simplicity of their hearts, & we presume not to judge the thoughts & intentions of any, it being Gods owne prerogative, to bring to light the hidden things of darknes, and to make manifest the counsels of the hearts; So it cannot be denied, that upon these passages and proceedings hath followed the interrupting of the so much longed for Reformation of Religion, of the setling of Presbyteriall government, and of the suppressing of heresies and dangerous errors, (which works the Parliament had taken in hand) the retarding and delaying the relief of *Ireland*, the sowing of the seeds of another War in *England*, the strengthning of the hand of the Malignant & Episcopall party, the weakning and wounding both of Magistracy and Ministery: In all which, whether the Army bee blamelesse and innocent, from ministring occasion to so great evils, or whether there be not cause for them to repent and do the first works, and to practise more of that love, moderation, and meeknesse of Spirit, and of that zeal against Malignants and Prelaticall persons, which they have from the beginning professed, and the want whereof (when suspected in others) they did so much censure; or whether there be such a thing among them, as adjoyning with those against whom, and against whose with whom the Covenant was taken; We leave them in all these to the search and examination of their own consciences, that they may stand or fall unto God. For our part, we cannot conceive how the Proposals of that Army for setling of a Peace, do in point of Religion consist with the solemn League and Covenant, or with the Propositions of peace, formerly agreed upon by both Kingdomes; there being so considerable omission of divers materiall desires contained in those former Propositions, concerning the abolition of Prelacy; concerning the injoyning of the taking of the Covenant by all his Majesties Subjects, under such penalties as the Parliaments should agree upon; concerning the setling of Religion in *England* and *Ireland*, according to the Covenant, in such manner as both Houses of Parliament shall agree on, after advice had with the Assembly of Divines, concerning the setling of uniformity between the Churches of God in both Kingdomes, according to the Covenant, in such manner as shall be agreed on by both Houses of the Parliament of *England*, and by the Church, and Kingdome of *Scotland*, after advice had with the Divines of both Kingdomes; Also concerning an Act of Parliament to confirm the calling and sitting of the Assembly of Divines: All which, with some other particulars concerning Religion, expressed in the former Propositions, if they should now be omitted in the setling of a Peace, the progresse already made, not only in the Assembly of Divines, but in the Houses of Parliament, in setling Presbyteriall Government, with the Confession of Faith, yea the Directory of publike Worship (though agreed upon by the Assemblies and Parliaments of both Kingdomes) shall bee but so much lost labour. But beside these omissions it may be justly doubted whether there be not in the Proposals of the Army, somewhat for Episcopocy, and against the Covenant; For wee cannot understand the eleventh Proposall, in any other sense, but that it supposeth the continuance of the Ecclesiastical office of Bishops or Prelats, as well as of any other Church Officers, and taketh no more from the Prelats, but coercive power or jurisdiction extending to civil penalties, which indeed belongeth to no Ecclesisticall Officers. In the twelfth Proposall, wee do not see, how it can avoid or shun the toleration of Popery, Superstition, Heresie, Schisme, Profannesse, or whatsoever works of darknesse shall be practised by such as dispise the publicke Worship of God in the Church, & have the most unlawful and wicked meetings else where under a profession of Religious duties, exercises or ordinances. From the thirteenth Proposall, we can make no other result, but that in stead of enjoyning the taking of the Covenant, under such penalties as the Parliaments in their wisdome shall agree upon, the former ordinance of Parliament enjoyning the taking of it, is desired to be repealed: and then what may bee the danger of those that have taken, or shall take an oath of that kinde, not enjoyned nor ratified by authority, wee leave it to be judged by those who know best the Lawes of that Kingdome.

One thing more wee Cannot passe, that whereas in the Armies Declaration, or

Representation to the Parliament, dated June 14 1647. they mention their Brethren of *Scotland* as having proceeded in the vindication and defence of their just rights and liberties, much higher then that Army hath done; Wee are necessitated to say this much for clearing of these proceedings in this Nation reflected upon: They of this Church and Kingdom who joyned together and associated themselves in this Cause, first by humble Petitions, and afterwards by Covenant, were so far from slighting or breaking that Covenant which was taken, that it was the special visible character by which the friends of the Cause were distinguished from the enemies thereof and they were so far from crying down the Ministery and Ecclesiasticall Assemblies, or from disobeying any Orders or Commands of Parliament, that a Generall Assembly of the Church, and a Parliament, were two chief Heads of their Petitions and desires, at that time when they had neither; And when they had obtained a Generall Assembly and Parliament, they chearfully submitted to both respectively.

And now the dangers of Religion in this Illand being so great, as there hath been lately a Solemne Humilitation throughout this Land, upon occasion of these great and growing dangers; so we cannot but still look upon them as matters of frequent Prayer and Humiliation to our selves, as well as our Brethren in *England*, there being much sin in both Kingdomes procuring all this evill, and justly deserving these, and heavier judgements. And as wee desire in the first place to be humbled for our own sins, and the sins of this Nation, so we trust, our Brethren will bee willing to be put in minde of the necessity of their Humiliation and Repentance for the Nationall sins of the Kingdome; which wee shall wish rather to be sadly considered by them, then expressed by us. One thing wee are confident of, that God hath had a speciall controversie against his People of old for the sin of a broken Covenant, and unwillingnesse to bee Reformed and Purged according to the Word of the Lord; and that till their sinnes were acknowledged and repented, his controversie did not take an end.

And here is the wisdome and patience of the Saints, to choose affliction rather then iniquity, to do duety in the worst of times, and to trust God with events and in so doing, to hope to the end and wait upon the Lord, untill hee plead their cause and execute judgement for them: So shall they bee more purified and not made blacker (as, alas, some are) but whiter in times of tryall.

More particularly, wee do desire that Presbyteriall Government may be setled and put in practice through out that Kingdom, according to the Word of God, and example of the best Reformed Churches: for without this wee know no other proper and effectuall remedy against the present dangers of Religion there, or for purging the Church from scandals, which are destructive either to sound Doctrine, or to Godlinesse: And herein we are confident, the experience of all the Reformed Churches will bear witnesse with us. Nor do we doubt but in *England* also, time and experience will more and more commend, not only the beautifull order, but the great utility, yea, necessity of this Government, and dispell all the clouds of aspersions and prejudices which it lieth under among such as know it not, who ought therefore to beware of speaking evill of the things they understand not. Yet we would not have our zeal for Presbyteriall Government mis-understood, as if it tended to any rigour or domineering over the flock, or to hinder and exclude that instructing in meeknesse them that oppose themselves, which the Apostolicall rule holds forth; or as if wee would have any such to bee intrusted with that Government, as are found not yet purged, either from their old profannesse, or from the Prelaticall principles and practices which were but to put a piece of new cloath unto an old garment, and so to make the rent worse; or to put new wine into old bottles, and so to lose both wine and bottles. Yea who knows whether this may not be one of the causes, (and not the least) why the present Reformation succeeds the worse, even because of so little repentance, either for the profannesse, or Prelaticall errours and corruptions of divers who have acted in it: Neverthelesse, the right hand of fellowship is to bee given to all such as bring forth fruits meet for repentance, whatsoever their former errours of failings were. And to our great joy, we understand that there are many learned, able, godly, and prudent ministers in that Kingdome, fit to be imployed in that government, together with such able and pious men, as are to be joyned with them in the capacity of ruling Elders. It shall be a part of our prayers, that the Lord of the Harvest may send forth many more labourers in that Kingdome, where the Harvest is so great and the Labourers so few proportionably; and in the meane while, that such as he hath already thrust out, may not be unemployed, as to the point of discipline and Government.

Nor lastly, doth our zeal for the Covenant and Presbyteriall Government abate or diminish any thing at all from our Loyalty and Duety to the Kings Majesty, although Incendiaries and Enemies spare not to reproach this Church and Kingdome with Disloyaltie: Yet such calumnies will easily be repudiate by all who will examine the whole course of the publike proceedings in this Nation, in reference to the King, and particularly the Declaration of the Parliament of this Kingdome, dated *January 16. 1647.*

Wherefore passing all such calumnies, whiche cannot but be hatefull to God and good Men, wee do clearly and candidly professe, That the Covenant and Presbyteriall Government are so far from hindering or excluding our duety to the King, that it is thereby very much strengthened and supported; for our giving to God what is Gods doth not hinder us, but help us, to give unto Cæsar what is Cæsars. And wee earnestly wish his Majesties Royall Heart may bee graciously inclined to the just desires of his good Subjects in both Kingdomes, and to that happy settlement of Truth and Peace, Religion and Righteousnesse, which may be as well for the establishment of his own Throne, as for the good of his people.

Now the Prince of Peace Himself, grant his afflicted People, tossed with tempests and not comforted, a safe and wel-grounded Peace, bring light out of the present darknesse, and order out of all these confusions, give unto all who are waiting for the consolation of Israel *good hope through grace, comfort their hearts, stablish them in every good word and work,* make his Cause to triumph at last over all opposition, and the enemies foot to slide in due time, and so put a new Song of praise in the mouths of his people. Amen.

24. AUGUST 1647. ANTEMERIDIEM. SESS. 19.

ACT FOR OBSERVING THE DIRECTIONS OF THE GENERALL ASSEMBLY FOR SECRET AND PRIVATE WORSHIP, AND MUTUALL EDIFICATION, AND CENSURING SUCH AS NEGLECT FAMILIE WORSHIP.

The General Assembly, after mature deliberation, doth approve the following Rules and Directions, for cherishing Piety and preventing Division and Schisme, and doth appoint Ministers and Ruling Elders in each Congregation to take speciall care that these directions be observed and followed; As likewise that Presbyteries and Provincial Synods enquire and make tryall whether the saids Directions bee duely observed in their bounds, and to reprove or censure (according to the quality of the offence) such as shall bee found to be reproveable or censurable therein. And to the end that these Directions may not be rendred ineffectuall and unprofitable among some through the usuall neglect of the very substance of the duty of Family Worship, The Assembly doth further require and appoint Ministers and Ruling Elders, to make diligent search and enquiry in the Congregations committed to their charge respectively, whether there bee among them any Family or Families which use to neglect this necessary duty; And if any such Family be found, the head of that Family is to be first admonished privately to amend this fault; And in case of his continuing therein, he is to be gravely and sadly reproved by the Session. After which reproof, if he be found still to neglect Familie Worship, Let him be for his obstinacy, in such an offence, suspended and debarred from the Lords Supper, as being justly esteemed unworthy to communicate therein till he amend.

THE DIRECTIONS OF THE GENERALL ASSEMBLY, FOR SECRET AND PRIVATE WORSHIP & MUTUALL EDIFICATION, FOR CHERISHING PIETY, FOR MAINTAINING UNITIE, AND AVOIDING SCHISME AND DIVISION.

Besides the publike Worship in Congregations, mercifully established in this Land, in great purity; It is expedient and necessary, that Secret Worship of each person alone, and Private Worship of Families be pressed and set up: That with Nationall Reformation the profession and power of Godlinesse both Personall and Domestick bee advanced.

I. And first for Secret Worship; It is most necessar, that every one apart and by themselves be given to Prayer and Meditation, The unspeakable benefit whereof is best known to them who are most exercised therein: This being the meane whereby in a special way communion with God is entertained, and right preparation for all other duties obtained; And therefore it becometh not onely Pastors, within their severall Charges, to presse Persons of all sorts to performe this dutie Morning and Evening, and at other occasions, but also it is incumbent to the head of every Family, to have a care that both themselves & all within their charge be daily diligent herein.

II. The ordinar duties comprehended under the exercise of Pietie, which should be in Families when they are conveened to that effect, are these: First, Prayer and Praises performed, with a speciall reference as well to the publike condition of the

Kirk of God and this Kingdome, as to the present case of the Familie, and every member thereof. Next, Reading of Scriptures with Catechizing in a plaine way, that the understandings of the simpler may be the beter enabled to profit under the publike Ordinances, and they made more capable to understand the Scriptures when they are read? Together with godly conferences tending to the edification of all the members in the most holy faith: As also, admonition and rebuke upon just reasons from these who have Authority in the Familie.

III. As the Charge and Office of interpreting the holy Scriptures, is a part of the Ministeriall calling, which none (howsoever otherwise qualified) should take upon him in any place, but he that is duely called thereunto by God and his Kirk: So in every Familie where there is any that can read, The holy Scriptures should be read ordinarily to the Familie; And it is commendable that thereafter they confer, and by way of conference make some good use of what hath beene read and heard: As for example, if any sin be reproved in the Word read, use may bee made thereof, to make all the Familie circumspect and watchfull against the same; Or, if any judgement be threatned or mentioned to have beene inflicted in that Portion of Scripture which is read, use may bee made to make all the Familie fear, lest the same or a worse judgement befall them, unlesse they beware of the sin that procured it: And finally, if any duety be required, or comfort held forth in a promise, use may bee made to stirre up themselves to imploy Christ for strength to enable them for doing the commanded duty, and to apply the offered comfort; In all which the Master of the Familie is to have the chief hand, And any member of the Familie may propone ane question or doubt for resolution.

IV. The head of the Family is to take care that none of the Familie withdraw himself from any part of Familie Worship: And seeing the ordinar performance of all the parts of Family worship belongeth properly to the head of the Family, The Minister is to stirre up such as are lasie, and traine up such as are weak to a fitnesse for these exercises. It being alwayes free to persons of qualitie to entertain one approven by the Presbyterie for performing Familie Exercise; And in other families where the head of the Familie is unfit, that another constantly residing in the Familie approven by the Minister and Session, may be imployed in that service; Wherein the Minister and Session are to be countable to the Presbyterie. And if a Minister by divine providence bee brought to any Familie, It is requisite, that at no time he conveen a part of the Familie for Worship secluding the rest; Except in singular cases, specially concerning these parties, which (in Christian prudence) need not, or ought not to bee imparted to others.

V. Let no Idler who hath no particular calling, or vagrant Person under pretence of a calling, be suffered to perform worship in Families, to or for the same: Seeing persons tainted with errours or aiming at division, may be ready (after that manner) to creep into houses and lead captive silly and unstable souls.

VI. At Family Worship a speciall care is to be had, that each Familie keep by themselves: Neither requiring, inviting, nor admitting persons from divers Families; Unlesse it be these who are lodged with them or at meal, or otherwise with them upon some lawfull occasion.

VII. Whatsoever hath been the effects and fruits of meetings of persons of divers Families in the times of corruption or trouble (in which cases many things are commendable, which otherwise are not tolerable), Yet when God hath blessed us with Peace and the purity of the Gospel, such meetings of persons of divers Families (except in the cases mentioned in these Directions) are to be disapproved, as tending to the hinderance of the Religious exercise of each Familie by it self, to the prejudice of the publike Ministery, to the renting of the Families of particular Congregations, and (in progresse of time) of the whole Kirk: besides many offences which may come thereby, to the hardning of the hearts of carnall men, and grief of the godly.

VIII. On the Lords Day, after every one of the Family apart, and the whole Family together have sought the Lord (in whose hands the preparation of mens hearts are) to fit them for the publicke Worship, and to blesse to them the publike Ordinances; The Master of the Familie ought to take care that all within his charge repair to the publike Worship, that he and they may joyne with the rest of the Congregation; And, the publike Worship being finished, after prayer, he should take an account what they have heard, And thereafter to spend the rest of the time which they may spare, in Catechising and in spirituall conferences upon the Word of God; Or else (going apart) they ought to apply themselves to reading, meditation, and secret prayer, that they may confirme and increase their Communion with God; That so the profit which they found in the publike Ordinances may bee cherished and promoved, and they more edified unto eternall life.

IX. So many as can conceive prayer; ought to make use of that gift of God: Albeit these who are rude and weaker may begin at a set form of prayer; But so, as they bee not sluggish in stirring up in themselves (according to their daily necessities) the spirit of prayer, which is given to all the children of God in some measure. To which effect, they ought to bee the more fervent and frequent in secret prayer to God, for enabling of their hearts to conceive, and their tongues to expresse convenient desires to God for their Familie. And in the mean time, for their greater encouragement, let these materialls of prayer be meditated upon, and made use of, as followeth.

Let them confesse to God how unworthy they are to come in his presence, and unfit to worship his Majesty; And therefore earnestly ask of God the spirit of prayer.

They are to confesse their sins, and the sins of the Family accusing, judging, and condemning themselves for them, till they bring their souls to some measure of true humiliation.

They are to pour out their souls to God, in the Name of Christ, by the spirit, for forgivinesse of sins, for Grace to repent, to believe, and to live soberly, righteously, and godly, and that they may serve God with joy and delight in walking before him.

They are to give thanks to God for his many mercies to his people, and to themselves, and especially for his love in Christ, and for the light of the Gospel.

They are to pray for such particular benefits, Spirituall and Temporall, as they stand in need of for the time, (whether it be Morning or Evening) as health or sicknesse, prosperitie or adversitie.

They ought to pray for the Kirk of Christ in general, for all the Reformed Kirks, and for this Kirk in particular, and for all that suffer for the Name of Christ for all our Superiours, The Kings Majesty, the Queene, and their Children, for the Magistrates, Ministers, and whole body of the Congregation whereof they are members, as well for their Neighbours absent in their lawfull affaires, as for those that are at home.

The prayer may be closed with an earnest desire, that God may be glorified in the comming of the Kingdome of his Son, and in the doing of his wil; And with assurance that themselves are accepted, and what they have asked according to his will shall be done.

X. These exercises ought to be performed in great sinceritie without delay, laying aside all Exercises of worldly businesse or hinderances, Notwithstanding the mockings of Atheists, and profane men; In respect of the great mercies of God to this Land, and of his severe Corections wherewith lately he hath exercised us. And to this effect, persons of eminency (and all Elders of the Kirk) not onely ought to stir up themselves and their Families to diligence herein; But also to concurre effectually, that in all other Families, where they have Power and Charge, the said exercises be conscionably performed.

XI. Besides the ordinary duties in Families which are abovementioned, extraordinary duties both of humiliation and thanksgiving are to bee carefully performed in Families, when the Lord by extraordinary occasions (private or publike) calleth for them.

XII. Seeing the Word of God requireth, That wee should consider one another to provoke unto love and good works, Therefore, at all times, and specially in this time wherein profanitie abounds, and mockers walking after their own lusts think it strange that others run not with them to the same excesse of riot, Every member of this Kirk ought to stir up themselves and one another to the duties of mutuall Edification, by instruction, admonition, rebuke, exhorting one another to manifest the Grace of God, in denying ungodlinesse and worldly lusts, and in living godly, soberly, and righteously in this present world, by comforting the the feeble minded, and praying with, or, for one another; Which duties respectively are to be performed upon speciall occasions offered by divine providence; As namely, when under any calamity, crosse, or great difficultie, counsel or comfort is sought, Or when an offender is to bee reclaimed by private admonition, and if that bee not effectuall, by joyning one or two more in the admonition, according to the rule of Christ; that in the mouth of two or three witnesses every word may be established.

XIII. And because it is not given to every one to speak a word in season to a wearied or distressed conscience, It is expedint, that a person (in that case) finding no ease after the use of all ordinary means private and publike, have their addresse to their own Pastour, or some experienced Christian, But, if the person troubled in conscience be of that condition, or of that sex, that discretion, modestie of fear of scandall, requireth a godly grave and secret friend to be present with them in their said addresse, It is expedient that such a friend be present.

XIV. When persons of divers Families are brought together by divine providence, being abroad upon their particular Vocations, or any necessary occasions, As they would have the Lord their God with them whithersoever they go, they ought to walk with God, and not neglect the duties of Prayer and Thanksgiving, but take care that the same be performed by such as the company shall judge fittest: And that they likewise take heed that no corrupt communication proceed out of their mouth, but that which is good, to the use of edifying, that it may minister grace to the hearers.

The drift and scope of all these Directions is no other, but that upon the one part, the power and practice of godlinesse among all the Ministers and Members of this Kirk, according to their severall places and vocations, may be cherished and advanced, and all impietie and mocking of Religious Exercises suppressed; And upon the other part, that under the name and pretext of Religious Exercises; no such meetings or practices be allowed, as are apt to breed Error, Scandall, Schisme, contempt or mis-regard of the publike Ordinances and Ministers, or neglect of the duties of particular Callings, or such other evils as are the works not of the Spirit but of the Flesh, and are contrary to Truth and Peace.

ACT AGAINST SUCH AS WITHDRAW THEMSELVES FROM THE PUBLIKE WORSHIP IN THEIR OWN CONGREGATION.

Since it hath pleased God of his infinite goodnesse to blesse his Kirk within this Nation, with the riches of the Gospel, in giving to us his Ordinances in great purity, liberty, and withall, a comely and well-established order: The Assembly, in the zeal of God, for preserving Order, Unitie and Peace in the Kirk, for maintaining the respect which is due to the Ordinances and Ministers of Jesus Christ, for preventing Schisme, noisome Errours, and all unlawfull Practices, which may follow on the Peoples withdrawing themselves from their own Congregations, Doth charge every Minister to bee diligent in fulfilling his Ministerie, to be holy and grave in his conversation, to be faithfull in Preaching, declaring the whole counsell of God, and as he hath occasion from the Text of Scripture to reprove the sins and errours, and presse the duties of the time; and in all those, to observe the rules prescribed by the Acts of Assembly; wherein if he be negligent, he is to be censured by his own Presbytery. As also Ordains every Member in every Congregation to keep their own Paroch Kirk, to communicate there in the Word and Sacraments; And if any person or Persons shall hereafter usually absent themselves from their own Congregations, except in urgent cases made known to, and approven by the Presbytery, The Ministers of these Congregations whereto they resort, shall both in publike by Preching, and in private admonition, shew their dislike of their withdrawing from their own Minister; That in so doing, they may witnesse to all that heare them, their due care to Strengthen the hands of their fellow labourers in the work of the Lord, and their detestation of any thing that may tend to separation, or any of the abovementioned evils; Hereby their own Flock will be confirmed in their stedfastnesse, and the unstable spirits of others will be rectified. Likeas the

Minister of that Congregation from which they do withdraw, shall labour first by private admonition to reclaim them; And if any after private admonition given by their own Pastour do not amend, in that case the Pastour shall delate the foresaid persons to the Session, who shall cite and censure them as contemners of the comely order of the Kirk; And if the matter be not taken order with there, It is to bee brought to the Presbytery: For the better observing whereof, the Presbyteries at the Visitation of their severall Kirks, and Provincial Assemblies, in their censure of the several Presbyteries, shall enquire hereanent: Which inquirie and report shall be registrate in the Provincial Books, that their diligence may be seen in the General Assembly.

26. AUGUST 1647. POSTMERIDIEM. SESS. 22.

APPROBATION OF THE PRECEEDINGS OF THE COMMIS-SION OF THE PRECEEDING ASSEMBLY.

The General Assembly after mature deliberation do ratifie and approve the whole Acts and Conclusions of the Commissionners of the preceeding Assembly for publike affaires now tryed and examined; Declaring that they have proceeded therein with much zeal, wisdome, vigilance, and according to ther Commission.

27. AUGUST 1647. ANTEMERIDIEM. SESS. 23.

APPROBATION OF THE CONFESSION OF FAITH.

A Confession of Faith for the Kirks of God in the three Kingdomes, being the chiefest part of that Uniformity in Religion which by the solemne League and Covenant we are bound to endeavour; And there being accordingly a Confession of Faith agreed upon by the Assembly of Divines sitting at Westminster, with the assistance of Commissioners from the Kirk of Scotland; Which Confession was sent from our Commissioners at London to the Commissioners of the Kirk met at Edinburgh in January last, hath been in this Assembly twice publikely read over, examined and considered; Copies thereof being also Printed, that it might be particularly perused by all the Members of this Assembly, unto whom frequent intimation was publikely made, to put in their doubts and objections if they had any; And the said Confession being upon due examination thereof found by the Assembly to bee most agreable to the Word of God, and in nothing contrary to the received Doctrine, Worship, Discipline, and Government of this Kirk. And lastly, it being so necesary and so much longed for, That the said Confession be with all possible diligence and expedition approved and established in both Kingdoms, as a principal part of the intended Uniformity in Religion, and as a special means for the more effectual suppressing of the many dangerous errours and heresies of these times; The General Assembly doth therefore after mature diliberation agree unto and approve the said Confession as to the truth of the matter (judging it to be most orthodox and grounded upon the Word of God) and also as to the point of Uniformity. Agreeing for our part that it be a common Confession of Faith for the three Kingdomes. The Assembly doth also blesse the Lord; and thankfully acknowledge his great mercy, in that so excellent a Confession of Faith is prepared, and thus far agreed upon in both Kingdomes; which we look upon as a great strengthning of the true Reformed Religion against the common enemies thereof. But lest our intention and meaning be in some particulars misunderstood, It is hereby expresly Declared and Provided, that the not mentioning in this Confession the several sort of Ecclesiastical Officers and Assemblies, shall be no prejudice to the Truth of Christ in these particulars to be expressed fully in the Directory of Government. It is further Declared, that the Assembly understandeth some parts of the second Article of the thirty one Chapter, only of Kirks not settled or constituted in point of Government, And that although in such Kirks, a Synod of Ministerrs and other fit persons may be called by the Magistrates authority and nomination without any other Call, to consult and advise with about matters of Religion; And although likewise the Ministers of Christ without delegation from their Churches, may of themselves, and by vertue of their Office meet together Synodically in such Kirks not yet constituted; Yet neither of these ought to be done in Kirks constituted and setled: It being always free to the Magistrate to advise with Synods of Ministers and ruling Elders meeting upon delegation from their Churches, either ordinarly, or being indicted by his Authority occasionally and pro re nata; It being also free to assemble together Synodically, as well pro re nata, as at the ordinary times upon delegation from the Churches, by the intrinsical power received from Christ, as often as it is necessary for the good of the Church so to assemble, in case the Magistrate to the detriment of the Church withhold or deny his consent, the necessity of occasionall Assemblies being first remonstrate unto him by humble supplication.

EDINBURGH 28. AUGUST 1647. POSTMERIDIEM.
SESS. 25.

ACT FOR REVISING THE PARAPHRASE OF THE PSALMES BROUGHT FROM ENGLAND, WITH A RECOMMENDATION FOR TRANSLATING THE OTHER SCRIPTUALL SONGS IN MEETER.

The General Assembly having considered the report of the Committee, concerning the Paraphrase of the Psalmes sent from England: And finding that it is very necessary, that the said Paraphrase be yet revised; Therefore doth appoint Master John Adamson to examine the first fourty Psalmes, Master Thomas Craufurd the second fourty, Master John Row the third fourty, and Master John Nevey the last thirty Psalms of that Paraphrase; and in their Examination they shall not only observe what they think needs to be amended, but also to set downe their own essay for correcting thereof; And for this purpose recommends to them, to make use of the travels of Rowallen, Master Zachary Boyd, or of any other on that subject, but especially of our own Paraphrase, that what they find better in any of these Works may be chosen: and likewise they shall make use of the animadversions sent from Presbyteries, who for this cause are hereby desired to hasten their observations unto them; And they are to make report of their labours herein to the Commission of the Assembly for publike affaires against their first meeting in February next: And the Commission after revising thereof, shall send the same to Provincial Assemblies, to bee transmitted to Presbyteries, that by their further consideration, the matter may be fully prepared to the next Assembly: And because some Psalmes in that Paraphrasie sent from England are composed in verses which do not agree with the Common-tunes, Therefore it is also recommended that these Psalms be likewise turned in other verses which may agree to the Common-tunes, that is, having the first line of eight syllabs, and the second line of six, that so both versions being together, use may bee made of either of them in Congregations as shall bee found convenient: And the Assembly doth further recommend, That M. Zachary Boyd be at the paines to translate the other Scriptural Songs in meeter, and to report his travels also to the Commission of Assembly, that after their Examination thereof, they may send the same to Presbyteries to be there considered untill the next Generall Assembly.

ACT RECOMMENDING THE EXECUTION OF THE ACT OF PARLIAMENT AT PERTH, FOR UPLIFTING PECUNIALL PAINES TO BEE IMPLOYED UPON PIOUS USES, AND OF ALL ACTS OF PARLIAMENT MADE AGAINST EXCOMMU-NICATE PERSONS.

The Generall Assembly doth seriously Recommend and Ordain That Presbyteries diligently endeavour, that the ninth Act of the Parliament holden at Perth, Anno 1645. Concerning the uplifting of pecunial paines to bee imployed upon pious uses, may bee put to due execution within their several bounds; And also that the Acts of Parliament against excommunicate Persons, especially the twentieth Act of Parliament in March last, be also carefully execute: And that they cause use all diligence to that effect, and account hereof shall be required in Provinciall and Generall Assemblies.

ULT. AUGUST 1647. ANTEMERIDIEM. SESS. 26.

ACT DISCHARGING THE IMPORTING, VENTING OR SPREADING OF ERRONIOUS BOOKS OR PAPERS.

The General Assembly considering how the errours of Independency and Separation (have in our Neighbour Kingdome of England) spread as a Gangræn, and do daily eat as a Canker; In so much that exceeding many Errours. Heresies, Schismes, and Blaspemies, have issued therefrom, and sheltered thereby; And how possible it is, for the same evils to invade, and overspread this Kirk and Kingdome, (lying within the same Island) by the spreading of their erronious Books, Pamphlets, Lybels, and Letters, and by conversing with them that are infected with these errours, except the same bee timeously prevented; Doe therefore, in the Name of God, Inhibit and Discharge all Members of this Kirk and Kingdome, to converse with Persons tainted with such errours; Or to import, sell, spread, vent, or disperse such erronious Books or Papers: But that they beware of, and abstain from Books maintaineing Independencie or Separation, and from all Antinomian, Anabaptisticall, and other erronious Books, and Papers; Requiring all Ministers to warne their flocks against such Bookes in generall, and particularly such as are most plausible, insinuating, and dangerous: And to try carefully from time to time if any such Bookes be brought into this Countrey from England, or from byond Seas (which is especially recommended to Ministers on Sea Coasts, or Towns where any Stationers are) and if any shall be found, to present the same to the Presbyterie, that some course may be taken to hinder the dispersing thereof: And hereby all Presbyteries, and Synods, are ordained to try and Processe such as shall transgresse against the premisses or any part of the same. And the Assembly also doth seriously recommend to Civill Magistrates, that they may be pleased to be assisting to Ministers and Presbyteries in execution of this Act, and to concurre with their authority in every thing to that effect.

ACT FOR DEBARRING OF COMPLYERS IN THE FIRST CLASSE FROM ECCLESIASTICK OFFICE.

The Generall Assembly Declares and Ordaines, That no Person who is guilty of Compliance in the first Classe mentioned in the Act of the preceeding Assembly, shall bee received in any Ecclesiasticall charge, untill the evidence of his repentance before the Presbyterie and Congregation be reported to the Synode to which he belongs, and to the Generall Assembly, and their consent obtained for his bearing office. And if any such Person be already received unto the Eldership of any particular Congregation, yet he shall not be admitted to be a Member of any Presbyterie, Synode, or Generall Assemblie, untill (upon the evidence of his repentance) the consent and approbation of these judicatories respectively bee obtained thereto.

ACT FOR PRESSING AND FURTHERING THE PLANTATION OF KIRKS.

The Generall Assembly considering how the Work of Provision, Plantation, convenient Dividing, Dismembring, better uniting or enlarging of Parish Kirks is hitherto foreslowed, to the great prejudice of many Ministers, many good People, and hinderance of the Work of Reformation; Doth therefore Ordaine, That all Presbyteries have speciall care that the present opportunity bee diligently improved by all their Members, as need is, before the Commission for Plantation of Kirks, as they would not be found censurable for neglect. And that every Presbytery send in to the next Generall Assembly the names of all their Parishes, with declaration which of them have Ministers, which not, what is the largenesse of the bounds, commodious or incommodious situation of each Parish Kirk, what is the number of Communicants, what Kirks are under Patrons, what not, who are the severall Patrons, what is the nature and quantitie of the present provision, or possible ground of further provision for competent Maintence, where the same is not sufficiently provided already: As also, what Parishes are united or disunited or bettered already, and in what measure by the said Commission, that the Generall Assembly being acquaint therewith, may doe accordingly both for censuring Neglecters, and finding out Overtures for better furtherance of the Work for time to come. Moreover it is hereby Ordained, That the next ensuing Provinciall Synodes, crave account of the severall Presbyteries their diligence, And presse that they have it ready in writ to present to the Provinciall Synodes in April next to come, that so all may be in readinesse and the full account made at the next General Assembly.

ACT FOR CENSURING ABSENTS FROM THE GENERALL ASSEMBLY.

The Generall Assembly considering the absence of many Commissioners in this and other preceeding Assemblies, and that many of those present have gone from the Assembly before the dissolving thereof: Therefore, for remedie hereof in time coming Doth Ordaine, that hereafter Every Commissioner from Presbyteries and Universities who shall be absent from the Assembly without a reasonable excuse notified to the Assembly, Or who being present shall goe from the Assembly before the dissolving thereof without a licence, shall be suspended by the Assembly untill the Provinciall Synode next thereafter following.

RENOVATION OF FORMER ACTS OF ASSEMBLY FOR TRIALL AND ADMISSION OF EXPECTANTS TO THE MINISTRIE.

The Generall Assembly, doth hereby renew and confirme all former Acts and Ordinances for triall and admission of Expectants to the Ministery; Especially the Articles thereanentt allowed by the Generall Assembly 1596, and approven in the Assemblie at Glasgow 1638. The thirteenth Article concerning the age of intrants to the Ministery and the twentie fourth Article concerning the triall of Expectants, Of an Act of the said Assembly at Glasgow, Sess. 23 And the Act of the Assembly at St Andrews 1642. Sess. 7, concerning Lists for presentations from the King, and the trial of Expectants, &c. Ordaining Presbyteries to observe the same carefully in all time coming.

EODEM DIE, SESS. 28. POSTMERIDIEM.

RENOVATION OF THE COMMISSION FOR PROSECUTING THE TREATY FOR UNIFORMITY IN ENGLAND.

The Generall Assembly, Taking to their consideration that the Treaty of Uniformity in Religion in all his Majesties Dominions is not yet perfected; Therefore, Renews the Power and Commission granted by preceeding Assemblies for prosecuting that Treaty, unto the Persons afternamed, viz. Master Robert Douglas Master Samuel Rutherford, Master Robert Baillie, Master George Gillespie, Ministers: And John Earle of Lauderdaill, John Lord Balmerino, and Sir Archibald Johnstoun of Waristoun Elders; Authorizing them with full Power to prosecute the said Treaty of Uniformity with the Honourable Houses of the Parliament of England, and the Reverend Assembly of Divines there, or any Committees appointed by them: And to doe all and every thing which may advance, perfit, and bring that Treaty to an happy conclusion, conforme to the Commissions given thereanent.

RENOVATION OF THE COMMISSION FOR THE PUBLIKE AFFAIRES OF THE KIRK.

The Generall Assembly taking to their consideration, that in respect the great Work of Uniformity in Religion in all his Majesties Dominions is not yet perfected, (though by the Lords blessing there is a good progresse made in the same) there is a necessity of renewing the Commissions granted formerly for prosecuting and perfecting that great Work; Doe therefore renew the Power and Commission granted for the publike Affaires of the Kirk by the Generall Assmblies held in St. Andrews 1642. and at Edinburgh 1643. 1644. 1645. and 1646. unto the Persons following, viz. Masters, Alexander Casse, Samuel Douglas, Robert Knox, William Penman, James Guthrie, Robert Cuninghame, David Fletcher, Robert Lawder, Andrew Stevenson, Robert Davidson, David Calderwood, James Fleming, Robert Ker, James Fairlie, Oliver Colt, Patrick Sibbald, Andrew Ramsay, John Adamson, Robert Douglas, William Colvill, George Gillespe, Mungo Law, Andrew Fairfoul, George Lesly, Robert Lawrie, Alexander Spittle, Alexander Dickson, John Hay, Thomas Vassie, Ephraim Melvill, Patick Scheill, Alexander Simmervail, George Bennet, Alexander Levingstoun, Robert Murray, Alexander Rollock, William Menzies, Alexander Ireland, John Friebairn, George Murray, Henrie Guthrie, William Justice, Robert Wright, Henrie Livingstoun, James Hammiltoun, George Gladstanes, Bernard Sanderson, Andrew Lawder, George Rutherfurd, John Levingston, George Hutheson, John Bell, Heugh Mackaile, John Nevey, Matthew Brisbane, John Hammiltoun, Allan Ferguson, David Dickson, Zachary Boyd, Robert Ramsay, Robert Bailie, James Nesmith, Francis Aird, Robert Birnie, Thomas Kirkaldie, Evan Cameron, Robert Blair, Coline Adam, George Hammiltoun, Samuel Rutherford, Alexander Colvill, John Ramsay, James Martein, William Levingstoun, Thomas Melvill, John Smith, Fredrick Carmichaell, Patrick Gillespie, Alexander Moncreif, John Duncan, James Sibbald, Walter Bruce, George Pittillo, Andrew Affleck, John Barclay, Thomas Peirson, William Rait, David Srachan, Andrew Cant, William Douglas, John Forbes, George Sharp, William Chalmer, Joseph Brodie, Alexander Simmer, Gillbert Anderson, William Smith Ministers; And Archibald Marques of Argile, John Earle of Crawford, Alexander E. of Eglintoun, William E. of Glencairne, John E. of Cassils, James E. of Home, James E. of Tullibairdine, Francis E. of Bukeleuch, John E. of Lawderdaill, William E. of Lothian, James E. of Finlatour, William E. of Lanerk, James Earle of Callendar, Archibald Lord Angus, George L. Brichen, John L. Yester, John L. Balmerino, James L. Cowper, John Lord Bargenie, Sir Archibald Johnstoun of Waristoun, Sir John Hope of Craighall, Arthur Areskine of Scotiscraig, Alexander Fraser of Phillorth, Frederick Lyon of Brigtoun, James Mackdougall of Garthland, Sir William Cockburne of Langton, Sir Andrew Ker of Greinheid, Sir Heugh Campbell of Cesnock, Sir James Levingstoun of Kilsyth, Sir Thomas Ruthven of Freeland, Sir Gilbert Ramsay of Balmayne, John Henderson of Fordell, Walter Dundas younger of that ilk, Sir William Scot younger of Harden, Sir Lodovick Gordoun, Master George Winthame of Libertoun, Alexander Levingstoun of Saltcoats, John Birsbane of Bishoptoun, Sir Robert Douglas of Tilliquhillie, James Pringle of Torwoodlie, Sir Iames Nicolsone of Colbrandspath, William Ker of Newtoun, William Forbes younger of Lesly, John Kennedy of Carmucks, Robert Arburthnot of Findowrie, Alexander Brodie of Letham, Master Robert Narne younger of Strathurd, Master James Schoneir of Caskeberrie, James Ruchheid, Lawrence Hendersone, James Stewart, David Douglas, John Jaffray, George Porterfield, John Semple, John Kennedy, William Glendinning, Master John Cowan, John Mill Elders: Giving unto them full Power and Commission, to doe all and every thing for prosecuting, advancing, perfecting, and bringing the said Work of Uniformity in Religion in all his Majesties Dominions to a happy conclusion, conform to the former Commissions granted by preceding Assemblies thereanent. And to that effect, Appoints them or any seventeene of them, whereof thirteene shall bee Ministers, to meet heer in this City in the afternoone at four hours, and thereafter upon the last Wednesdayes of November, February, and May next, and upon any other day, and in any other place they shall think fit. Renewing also to the Persons before named, the Power contained in the Act of the Assembly 1643. intituled, A reference to the Commission anent the Persons designed to repaire to the Kingdome of England; As likewise the Power contained in the Act of Assemblie 1644. Sess. 6. for sending Ministers to the Armie. And further, in case Dilinquents have no constant residence in any one Presbyterie; Or if Presbyteries be negligent or overawed, in these cases, The Assemblie gives to the Persons before named, full power of censuring Complyers and Persons disaffected to the Covenant according to the Acts of Assemblie; Declaring always and Providing, that Ministers shall not bee deposed but in one of the Quarterly meetings of this Commission; With full power to them to treat and determine in the matters aforesaid, and in all other matters referred unto them by this Assemblie, as fully and freely as if the same were here particularly expressed, and with as ample power as any Commission of any former Generall Assemblies hath had, or been in use of before; They being alwayes for their whole proceedings countable to, and censurable by the next Generall Assembly.

DESIRES AND OVERTURES FROM THE COMMISSIONERS OF UNIVERSITIES, AND THE ASSEMBLIES ANSWER THERETO.

1. The Commissioners of Universities represents to the Assembly: First, That the Overtures of the Assembly 1643. for the visitation of Schools and advancement of Learning are very much neglected.

The Assembly recommends to Synodes to take account of the observation of these Overtures.

2. That it were good to exhort all the Universities, to be careful to take account of all their Schollers on the Sabbathday of the Sermons, and of their lessons or the Catechisme.

The Assembly approves this Overture, and recommends accordingly.

3. That all the Universities bee exhorted to send their commissioners instructed with answers to the Overtures agreed upon by the Commissioners of Universities, and which from this meeting or their Commissioners shall bee communicate to them, and this to bee when their Commissioners come in Februar or March to the Commission of the Kirk.

The Assemblie reccommends to Universities to bee carefull hereof.

4. That the Overtures concerning the providing of Bursars for Divinity be rec-

ommended to Presbyteries and Synodes, and that they report their diligence to the next Assembly.

The Assembly allowes this Article, and recommends accordingly.

EDINBURGH 1. SEPTEMBER 1647. SESS. ULT.

THE ASSEMBLIES LETTER TO THEIR COUNTREYMEN IN POLELAND, SWEDLAND, DENMARKE, AND HUNGARIE.

Unto the Scots Merchants and others our Countrey People scattered in Poleland, Swedland, Denmark, and Hungary; The General Assembly of the Kirk of Scotland wisheth Grace Mercy & Peace from God our Father, and from the Lord Jesus Christ.

Although this Kirk of Scotland, whiles spoiled of her Liberties under the Prelatical tyrannie, had much difficultie and wrestling to preserve the true reformed Religion from being quite extinguished among ourselves; yet since the mighty & out-stretched arme of the Lord our God hath brought us out of that Egypt, and hath restored to us well constituted and free national Synods, It hath been our desire and endeavour to set forward the Kingdom of our Lord Jesus Christ and the purity of his Ordinances, not only throughout this Nation, but in other parts also so far as God gave us a call and opportunity and opened a way unto us. And among other things of this nature we have more particularly taken into our serious thoughts the sad and lamentable condition of many thousands of you our Country-men who are scattered abroad as sheepe having no shepherd, and are through the want of the meanes of knowledge grace and salvation, exposed to the greatest spirituall dangers, whether through ignorance or through manifold tentations to errors and false Religions, or through the occasions and snares of sinne.

Wee have therefore thought it incumbent to us to put you in minde of the one thing necessary, while you are so carefull and troubled about the things of the world. And although we do not disallow your going abroad to follow any lawfull calling or way of lively hood, yet seeing it cannot profit a man although he should gain the whole world and lose his own soul, and seeing you have travelled so farre, and taken so much pains to get uncertain riches which cannot deliver in the day of the wrath of the Lord, and which men know not who shall inherit; We doe from our affection to the salvation of your immortall souls most earnestly beseech and warn you to cry after knowledge and lift up your voyce for understanding, seeking her as silver, and searching for her as for hid treasures, and so play the wise Merchants in purchasing the Pearl of Price, and in laying up a sure foundation for the time to come, by acquainting your souls with Jesus Christ, and by faith taking hold of him whose free grace is now offered and held out to sinners, excluding none among all the kindreds of the earth who will come unto him. God forbid that you should let slip the time and offers of grace, or neglect any warning of this kinde sent to you in the name of the Lord. We shall hope better things of you, and that knowing the acceptable time and the day of salvation will not alwayes last, but the Lord Jesus is to be revealed from heaven with his mighty Angels, in flaming fire taking vengeance on them that know not God and obey not the Gospel, you will the rather bestirre your selves timely and with all diligence to seek the Lord while he may bee found, to endeavour that you may have among you the ordinary means of grace and salvation, to pray that God would give you Pastors according to his heart, who shall feede you with knowledge and understanding, to consult also and agree among your selves with consent of your Superiors under whom you live (whose favour and good will we trust will not be wanting to you in so good and necessary a work) for setting up the worship of God and Ecclesiasticall Discipline among you according to the form established and received in this your mother Kirk, and for a way of settled maintenance to Pastors and Teachers, Which if you do, our Commissioners appointed to meet from time to time in the intervall betwixt this and the next Nationall Assembly, will bee ready (upon your desire made known to them) to provide some able and godly Ministers for you, as likewise to communicate to you our Directory for the publike worship of God, and our form of Ecclesiastical Government and Discipline; together with the Confession of Faith and Catechisme.

And in the meane time we exhort you that you neglect not the Worship of God in secret and in your families, and that ye continue stedfast in the Profession of that faith in which yee were baptised, and by a godly, righteous, and sober conversation adorn the Gospel; and with all, that distance of place make you not the lesse sensible of your Countries sufferings, both in respect of the just judgements of God for the sinnes of the land, and in respect of the malice of Enemies for the Common Cause & Covenant of the three Kingdoms, of which happie conjunction, notwithstanding we do not repent us, but by the grace of God shall continue faithful and steadfast therein.

This Letter wee have thought fit to bee Printed and published, that it may be with the greater ease and conveniency conveyed to the many several places of your habitation or traffique. Consider what we have said, and the Lord give you understanding in all things. The grace of our Lord Jesus Christ be with you all, Amen.

Edinburgh, August 31. 1647.

Subscribed in name of the Generall Assembly of the Kirk of Scotland

Mr Robert Douglasse Moderator.

ACT CONCERNING THE HUNDRED AND ELEVEN PROPOSITIONS THEREIN MENTIONED.

Being tender of so great an ingagement by Solemn Covenant, sincerely, really, and constantly to endeavour in our Place, and Callings, the preservation of the Reformed Religion in this Kirk of Scotland, in Doctrine, Worship, Discipline, and Government, the Reformation of Religion in the Kingdomes of England, and Ireland, in Doctrine, Worship, Discipline, and Government, according to the Word of God, and the example of the best Reformed Kirks, and to endeavour the nearest Conjunction and Uniformity in all these, together with the extirpation of Heresie, Schisme, and whatsoever shall bee found contrary to sound Doctrine: And considering withall that one of the speciall meanes which it becometh us in our Places and Callings to use in pursuance of these ends, is in zeal for the true Reformed Religion, to give our publike testimony against the dangerous Tenents of Erastianisme, Independencie, and which is falsely called Liberty of Conscience, which are not only contrary to sound Doctrine, but more speciall lets and hinderances, as well to the preservation of our own received Doctrine, Worship, Discipline, and Government, as to the Work of Reformation and Uniformity in England and Ireland. The Generall Assembly

Not that they are to be heer Printed, but because they being to be Printed severally, this Act is to be prefixed to them.

upon these considerations, having heard publikely read the CXI following Propositions exhibited and tendered by some Brethren, who were appointed to prepare Articles or Propositions for the vindication of the Trueth in these particulars, Doth unanimously approve & agree unto these eight generall Heads of Doctrine therein contained and asserted, viz. 1. That the Ministery of the Word and the Administration of the Sacraments of the New Testament, Baptisme and the Lords Supper, are standing Ordinances instituted by God himself to continue in the Church to the end of the World. 2. That such as Administer the Word and Sacraments, ought to be duely called and ordained thereunto. 3. That some Ecclesiasticall censures are proper and peculiar to be inflicted onely upon such as bear Office in the Kirk; Other censures are common and may bee inflicted both on Ministers and other Members of the Kirk. 4. That the censure of suspension from the Sacrament of the Lords Supper, inflicted because of grosse ignorance, or because of a scandalous life and conversation, As likewise the censure of Excommunication or calling out of the Kirk flagitious or contumacious offenders, both the one censure and the other is warranteble by and grounded upon the Word of God, and is necessary (in respect of divine institution) to be in the Kirk. 5. That as the Rights, Power, and Authority of the Civill Magistrate are to bee maintained according to the Word of God, and the Confessions of the Faith of the Reformed Kirks; So it is no lesse true and certaine, that Jesus Christ, the onely Head and onely King of the Kirk, hath instituted and appointed a Kirk Government distinct from the Civill Government or Magistracie. 6: That the Ecclesiastical Government is committed and intrusted by Christ to the Assemblies of the Kirk, made up of the Ministers of the Word and Ruling Elders. 7. That the lesser and inferiour Ecclesiasticall Assemblies, ought to bee subordinate and subject unto the greater and superiour Assemblies. 8. That notwithstanding hereof, the Civill Magistrate may and ought to suppresse by corporall or Civill punishments, such as by spreading Errour or Heresie, or by fomenting Schisme greatly dishonour God, dangerously hurt Religeon and disturbe the Peace of the Kirk. Which Heads of Doctrine (howsoever opposed by the authors and fomenters of the foresaid errours respectively) the Generall Assembly doth firmely beleeve, own, maintaine, and commend unto others, as Solide, True, Orthodoxe, grounded upon the Word of God, consonant to the judgement both of the ancient and the best Reformed Kirk; And because this Assembly (through the multitude of other necessary and pressing bussinesse) cannot now have so much leisure, as to examine and consider particularly the foresaid CXI. Propositions; Therefore, a more particular examination thereof is committed and referred to the Theologicall faculties in the four Universities of this Kingdome, and the judgement of each of these faculties concerning the same, is appointed to bee reported to the next Generall Assembly. In the meane while, these Propositions shall bee Printed, both that Copies thereof may bee sent to Presbyteries, and that it may be free for any that pleaseth to peruse them, and to make known or send their judgement concerning the same to the said next Assembly.

DESIRES AND OVERTURES PRESENTED FROM PRESBYTERIES AND SYNODS, WITH THE ASSEMBLIES ANSWER THEREUNTO.

It is humbly presented to the Assembly, that the children of many of the ordinary beggars want baptisme, Themselves also living in great vilenesse, and therefore desire that some remedie may be provided for these abuses.

The Assembly doth seriously recommend to Presbyteries to consider of the best remedies, and to report their opinions to the next Assembly.

That all Students of Philosophie at their entry and at their Lawreation, bee holden to subscribe the League and Covenant and be urged thereto, and all other Persons as they come to age and discretion before their first receiving the Sacrament of the Lords Supper.

The Assembly approves this Overture.

Whereas divers Ministers want Mansses and Gleebs, and others have their Gleeb so divided in parcells, or lying so Farre from their Charges the Ministers are thereby much prejudged; We desire that this Generall Assembly will recommend it to bee helped by the Parliament, or Committee for planting of Kirks, in the best manner that their Lordships can advise.

Whereas divers Kirks were incommodiously united in corrupt times, we desire that the same be now dismembered and adjoyned to other Kirks, or erected in Kirks by themselves alone, and when the present incumbents agrees thereto, we desire the same to bee recommend to the Parliament and Committee for plantation of Kirks, Provided alwayes, that the present Ministers who have laboured and indured the heat of day, may enjoy the benefit of such parcells as are taken from them during their life.

The Assembly doth approve these two Articles, and Recommends to the Commissioners for publike Affaires to assist any interested in the particulars for prosecuting the same before the Honourable Estates of Parliament, or the Commission appointed by them for plantation of Kirks.

The Generall Assembly, Doe yet againe recommend to Presbyteries and Provinciall Assemblies, to consider all matters formerly referred unto them by preceding Assemblies, and desires that their opinions concerning the same, be reported in writ to the next Generall Assembly.

It is this day appointed, that the next Generall Assembly shall meet at Edinburgh the second Wednesday of July 1648.

A. Ker.

THE GENERALL ASSEMBLY, AT EDIN-BURGH.

IULY 12. 1648. POST MERIDIEM, SESS. 1.

THE LETTER FROM THE SYNOD OF DIVINES IN ENGLAND TO THE GENERALL ASSEMBLY.

Right Honourable, right Reverend, and dearly beloved brethen in JESUS CHRIST,

As we have great cause to blesse God for the brotherly Union of these two Nations in the common Cause of Religion and Liberty, and for that good hand of blessing which hath accompanied the joynt endeavours of both, in the prosecution thereof: So we cannot but be sadly and deeply sensible of those many obstructions and difficulties, wherewith God in his wisdom hath seen good to exercise his Servants in both Kingdoms in the carrying on of that work, wherein they stand so much ingaged. Herein he hath clearly manifested his own power, wisdom, and goodnesse for our encouragement to trust him in the managing of his own Work, and our utter inability to effect it of our selves, thereby to train us up to a more humble and faithfull dependency upon him to do all, when we by our own wisdom and strength can do nothing. Our perplexities we must confesse, are and have been many, and yet in the midst of them all we cannot but thankfully acknowledge it is a token for good, and that which hath bin and still is a great comfort and refreshing to our hearts, that God hath given you wisdom timely to foresee approaching dangers, but especially to behold, as the stedfastnesse of your Faith, in that both formerly you have been and at present are able to trust God in straits and to appear for him in greatest dangers, so your eminent faithfulnesse and integrity in your firm adhering to your first principles, and chiefly in your constancy and zeal for the preservation and prosecution of the Solemn League and Covenant, so Religiously ingaged in by both Kingdoms: In your vigorous pursuance whereof, with much thankfulnesse to God, We are very sensible more particularly of your steering so steady, and even a course between the dangerous rocks of Prophanesse and Malignancie on the one hand, and of Errour, Schisme, Heresie and Blasphemy on the other hand; as also of your constant desires and endeavours to preserve the Peace and Union between the two Nations so nearly and so many wayes United. In all which we humbly acknowledge the mercy and faithfulnesse of God in guiding you so graciously hitherto; and through his assistance we shall still be ready to afford you the best help & incouragement of our prayers and praises to God on your behalf; having this confidence that he who hath already vouchsafed you and us so many blessed pledges of his favour, will in his own time and way accomplish his own Work, which so much concerneth his own Glory and his Peoples good. To his most gracious protection & guidance in these doubtfull and dangerous times we humbly commend you and all your holy endeavours, and rest.

Westminster June 7. 1648.

Subscribed in the name and by the apointment of the whole Assembly by us.

Direct

To the Right Honourable, Right Reverend, the Generall Assembly of the Church of Scotland, or their Commissioners.

Charles Harle, Prolocutor.
William Gouge, Assessor.
Henry Robrough, Scribe.
Adoniram Byfield, Scribe.

IULY 15 ANTEMERIDIEM, SESS. 4.

ACT CONCERNING COMMISSIONS FROM BURGHS.

It is resolved by the Generall Assembly, untill the matter concerning Commissioners from Burghs be further thought upon, that in the mean time according to the ordinary practice no Commission to the Generall Assembly be admitted from Burghs, but such as shall be consented to, and approven by the Ministry and Sessions thereof, the persons elected being always Elders.

IULY 18. 1648. ANTEMERIDIEM. SESS 6.

ACT CONCERNING THE EXAMINING OF THE PROCEED-INGS OF THE COMMISSIONERS OF ASSEMBLIES.

The Generall Assembly renews and revives the Act of the Assembly holden at Bruntiland Anno 1601. concerning the examination of the proceedings of the Commission of the Generall Assembly, tenour whereof follows. The Assembly hath Ordained that in every Assembly to be conveened in all time coming such as shall happen to be appointed Commissioners from the Generall Assembly, to endure while the Assembly next thereafter, shall give an account of their proceedings during the whole time of their Commission in the beginning of the Assembly, before any other cause or matter be handled and their proceedings to be allowed or disallowed as the Assembly shall think expedient.

IULY 18. 1648. POSTMERIDIEM. SESS. 7.

APPROBATION OF THE PROCEEDINGS OF THE COMMIS-SION OF THE PRECEEDING ASSEMBLY,

The Generall Assembly having examined the proceedings of the Commission of the preceeding Assembly, especially their Declarations, Remonstrances, Representations, Petitions, Vindication, and other Papers relating to the present Engagement in War, Do unanimously finde that in all their proceedings, they have been zealous, diligent and Faithfull in discharge of the trust committed to them; And therefore ratifie and approve the whole proceedings, Acts and conclusions of the said Commission: and particularly their Papers relating to the said Engagement, and their judgement of the unlawfulnesse thereof, Appointing Mr John Moncreiff Moderator pro tempore to return them hearty thanks in name of the Assembly for their great pains, travells & fidelity in matters of so great concernment to the Cause of God and to this Kirk, admidst so great and many difficulties.

JULY 20. 1648. POSTMERIDIEM, SESS. 10.

APPROBATION OF THE LARGER CATECHISME.

The Generall Assembly having exactly examined and seriously considered, the larger Catechisme agreed upon by the Assembly of Divines sitting at Westminster with assistance of Commissioners from this Kirk, Copies thereof being Printed, and sent to Presbyteries for the more exact tryall thereof, and publick intimation being frequently made in this Assembly, that every one that had any doubts or objections upon it, might put them in; Do finde upon due examination thereof, That the said Catechisme is agreeable to the Word of God, and in nothing contrary to the received Doctrine, Worship, Discipline and Government of this Kirk, a necessary part of the intended Uniformity in Religion, and a rich treasure for increasing knowledge among the People of God, and therefore the Assembly, as they blesse the Lord that so excellent a Catechisme is prepared, so they Approve the same as a part of Uniformity; Agreeing for their part, that it be a common Catechisme for the three Kingdoms, and a Directory for Catechising such as have made some proficiency in the knowledge of the grounds of Religion.

JULY 21. 1648. ANTEMERIDIEM, SESS. 11.

ACT AGAINST SUDDEN ADMITTING DEPOSED MINISTERS TO PARTICULAR CONGREGATIONS.

The General Assembly considering the danger of sudden receiving of deposed Ministers at this time when Malignancy is likely to spread; Therefore finding it necessary untill the ends of the Solemn League and Covenant be setled and secured to restrain the suddenness of admitting deposed Ministers to particular charges, Do Ordain that notwithstanding any License to be granted for opening the mouths of deposed Ministers yet they shall not be actually admitted to any particular Congregations without consent of the Generall Assembly, Declaring for such as have already their mouths opened before the time, that if any calling to a particular charge offer unto them before the next Assembly, it shall be sufficient for them to have the consent of the Commissioners of this Generall Assembly.

JULY 25. 1648. ANTEMERIDIEM. SESS. 14.

THE ASSEMBLIES ANSWER TO THE PAPER SENT FROM THE COMMITTEE OF ESTATES OF THE 24. JULY.

The Generall Assembly having considered the Paper of the 24. July delivered to them from the conference, and having compared it with the other Paper of the 17. of July presented from the Honourable Committee of Estates whereunto it relates, and with the Declaration lately emitted by the Committee to the Parliament and Kingdom of England, finde that it is supposed by their Lordships, that we may be satisfied in point of the security of Religion according to the Covenant; notwithstanding of the present engagement in war; The Assembly do therefore in answer to the said Paper declare, That we see no possibility of securing Religion, as long as this unlawfull Engagement is carried on, Religion being thereby greatly endangered,

1. Because none of the just and necessary desires of the Commission of the late General Assembly for securing Religion have been granted or satisfied; More particularly it was represented to the High and Honourable Court of Parliament, that for securing of Religion, it was necessary that the Popish, Prelaticall and Malignant party, be declared Enemies to the Cause upon the one hand, as well as Sectaries upon the other, and that all Associations, either in Forces or Councels with the former as well as the latter be avoided. That his Majesties Concessions and offers concerning Religion, sent home from the Isle of Wight, be declared by the Parliament to be unsatisfactory, That before his Majesties restitution to the exercise of his Royall power assurance be had from his Majesty by his solemn Oath under his hand and Seal for settling Religion according to the Covenant, That their Lordships should keep themselves from owning any quarrel concerning his Majesties Negative voice, That the managing of the publike affairs, might be intrusted onely to such persons as have given constant proof of their integrity, and against whom there is no just cause of exception or jealousie, and that there might be no Engagement without a solemn Oath, wherein the Kirk ought to hand the same interest they had in the solemn League and Covenant; All which are more particularly expressed in the Papers given in by the Commission of the late Assembly to the Parliament; notwithstanding the Engagement hath been carried on without satisfaction to these and the like desires, and so without giving security in the point of Religion, but with great and manifest danger to the same.

2. As the happy Union of the Kingdoms, by the solemn League and Covenant hath been justly looked upon as a speciall means for preserving and strengthening the true Reformed Religion in this Island, So it is no lesse weakened & hurt by endeavouring a breach between these Kingdoms; Which howsoever disclaimed, is yet manifest from the reality of the publike proceedings in this Engagement, and namely from the neglect of endeavouring a Treaty between the Kingdoms for preventing of War and bloodshed as was earnestly desired, from their associating and joyning with known Malignants and Incendiaries, and such as have been declared Enemies to this Cause, from their entring the Kingdom of England with an Army, upon the grounds of the Declaration of the Parliament, which cannot but infer a National quarrel against the Parliament and Kingdom of England, and from their garrisoning the frontire Towns of that Kingdom.

3. The Engagement is carried on by such means and ways, as tend to the destroying of Religion, by ensnaring and forcing the consciences of the people of God with unlawfull Bands and Oathes, and oppressing the Persons and Estates of such as have been most active and zealous for Religion and the Covenant. All which is strengthened and authorized by Acts of Parliament, appointing that all that do not obey, or perswade others not to obey the Resolutions of Parliament and Committee anent this Engagement, or who shall not subscribe the Act and Declaration of the 10. June, 1648. imposed upon all the Subjects, shall be holden as enemies to the Cause and to Religion, and have their persons secured, and their Estates intromitted with.

4. The Engagement is carried on, not without great encroachments upon the Liberties of the Kirk, as we are ready to clear in many particulars.

Wherefore the security of Religion, and carrying on of the present Engagement being inconsistent, We do propose for the necessary security and safety of Religion, that all the dangers thereof may be taken to consideration, and amongst the rest the said Engagement as one of the greatest which yet being established and authorized by Act of Parliament, we leave it to their Lordships to think of what remedies may be provided for redressing grievances which flow from such Acts and Ordinances. This we are sure of, the publike desires of the Kirk will abundantly witnesse for us, that such things as were necessary for the security of Religion, were in due season represented, & yet not granted by them that had greater power & authority at that time when it was much more easie to give satisfaction therein then now; So that the blame cannot lye upon the General Assembly or their Commissioners that Religion is not secured.

JULY 28. 1648. ANTEMERIDIEM, SESS. 18.

ACT AND DECLARATION AGAINST THE ACT OF PARLIAMENT & COMMITTEE OF ESTATES ORDAINED TO BE SUBSCRIBED THE 10. AND 12. OF JUNE, AND AGAINST ALL NEW OATHES OR BANDS IN THE COMMON CAUSE IMPOSED WITHOUT CONSENT OF THE CHURCH.

The Generall Assembly taking to consideration a Declaration and Act of Parliament, of the date 10. of June, 1648. highly concerning Religion, and the consciences of the People of God in the Land, and one Act of the Committee of Estates, of the date 12. of June, 1648. both published in Print, whereby all Subjects are Ordained by subscription to acknowledge as just, and oblige themselves to adhere unto the said Act and Declaration, containing an obligation upon their honours and credits, and as they desire to be, and to be holden, as lovers of their Country, Religion, Laws and Liberties, to joyn and concur with their Persons and Estates in the assistance of the execution, and observation of the Acts and Constitutions of this Parliament, as the most fit and necessary remedies of the by-gone and present evils and distractions of this Kirk and Kingdom, and for the preservation of Religion, Laws and Liberties and of his Majesties authority, with certification that such as refuse or delay to subscribe the same, shall be holden as Enemies and Opposites to the

Common Cause, consisting in the maintenance of the true reformed Religion, of the Laws and Liberties of the Kingdom and of his Majesties authority. Which subscription the Assembly cannot otherwise look upon, then as a snare for the People of God to involve them in guiltinesse, and to draw them from their former Principles and Vows in the solemn League and Covenant. For that subscription were an approving of some Acts of Parliament, which they have never yet seen nor known, they not being all published, were an agreeing to Acts of Parliament, highly concerning Religion and the Covenant, made not onely without, but expresly against the advise of the Kirk, were an acknowledging of this present Engagement in War, in all the means and ways for promoving the same, to be the most fit and necessary remedies of the by-gone and present evils, whereas so many Petitions to the Parliament, from Committees of War, Synods, Presbyteries and Paroches have made it appear, that they are no way satisfied therewith in point of conscience; were an ascribing of a power to the Parliament, to declare these to be enemies to the true Religion, whom the Kirk hath not declared to be such but rather friends; were an approving of an Act made for the restraining the liberty of printing from the Kirk, yea and of all the Acts of the Committee of Estates, to be made in time coming, till March 1650. which by Act of Parliament are ordained to be obeyed; were an allowing of Acts for securing of the persons, and intrometting with the Estates of such as themselves shall not obey, or perswade others not to obey resolutions concerning this Engagement, and for protecting persons under Kirk Censures, and so an infringing and violating of the Liberties and Discipline of the Kirk established by the Laws of the Land, and sworn to in the Nationall Covenant to be defended, under the pains contained in the Law of God, And in all these, such as do subscribe, do binde themselves not only to active obedience in their own persons, but to the urging of active obedience upon all others, and so draw upon themselves all the guiltinesse and sad consequences of the present engagement; Yea, such as are Members of Parliament, and have in the Oath of Parliament sworn not to Vote or consent to any thing, but what to their best knowledge is most expedient for Religion, Kirk and Kingdom, and accordingly have reasoned against, and dissented from divers Acts of this Parliament, These by the subscription of this Act, cannot eschew the danger of perjury, in obliging themselves to active obedience to these Acts, which according to their Oath, they did judge unlawfull. Neither can the 38. Act of the Parliament 1640. wherein such a kinde of Band was enacted to be subscribed by any precedent or Warrant for subscribing of this Act; For it plainly appears by the narrative of that Act omitted in this Band, how great a difference there is between the condition of affairs then & now. Then the Kings Commissioner had left and discharged the sitting of the Parl. then the Parl. for sitting was declared Traitors, and Armies in England and Ireland prepared against them, then not only the Act, but the very authority of Parliament was called in question, then Kirk and State were united in the Cause against the Malignant party, then nothing was determined in Parliament in matters of Religion without, much lesse against the advice of the Kirk; But beside that, it was not thought expedient by the State, that that Band should be pressed through the Kingdom. The case now not onely differs from what was then, But is in many things just contrary, as is evident to all who will compare the two together. And therefore the Generall Assembly professing in all tender respect to the high and Honourable Court of Parliament and Committee of Estates, but finding a straiter tye of God lying upon their Consciences, that they be not found unfaithfull watchmen, and betrayers of the souls of these committed to their charge, Do unanimously Declare the foresaid subscription to be unlawfull and sinfull. And do warn, and In the Name of the Lord Charge all the members of this Kirk, to forbear the subscribing of the said Act and Declaration, much more the urging of the subscription thereof, as they would not incur the wrath of God, and the Censures of the Kirk. And considering how necessary it is that according to the desire of the Commissioners of the Assembly to the Parliament, the Kirk might have the same interest in any new Oathes in this Cause, as they had in the solemn League and Covenant, and what dangers of contradictory Oathes, perjuries and snares to mens consciences may fall out otherwise: Therefore they likewise enjoyn all the members of this Kirk, to forbear the swearing, subscribing or pressing of any new Oathes or Bands in this Cause, without advice and concurrence of the Kirk, especially to in any way limit or restrain them in the duties whereunto they are obliged, by nationall or solemn League and Covenant, and that with certification as aforesaid. And such as have already pressed or subscribed the foresaid Act and Declaration, The Generall Assembly doth hereby exhort them most earnestly in the bowels of Christ, to repent of that their defection. And Ordains that Presbyteries, or in case of their negligence, or being overawed the provinciall Synods or the Commission of the Assembly, which of them shall first occur, and in case of the Synods negligence, that the said Commission be carefull to proceed against, and censure the contraveeners of the Act according to the quality and degree of their offences as they will be answerable to the Generall Assembly; and that therefore this Act be sent to Presbyteries to be republished in the several Kirks of their bounds.

EODEM DIE POSTMERIDIEM. SESS. 19.

APPROBATION OF THE SHORTER CATECHISME.

The Generall Assembly having seriously considered the shorter Catechisme, agreed upon by the Assembly of Divines sitting at *Westminster*, with assistance of Commissioners from this Kirk. Doe finde upon due examination thereof, That the said Catechisme is agreeable to the Word of God, and in nothing contrary to the received, Doctrine, Worship, Discipline and Government of this Kirk, And therefore Approve the said shorter Catechisme as a part of the intended Uniformity, to be a Directory for Catechising such as are of weaker capacitie.

ACT DISCHARGING A LITTLE CATECHISME PRINTED AT EDINBURGH, 1647.

The Generall Assembly having found in a little Catechisme, printed at Edinburgh, entituled, The A. B. C. with the Catechisme, That is to say, an instruction to be taught and learned of young children, very grosse errours in the point of Universall Redemption, and in the number of the Sacraments, Therefore doe discharge the venting or selling of the said Catechisme of the foresaid impression, or of whatsoever other impression the same be of, and all use thereof in Schools or Families, Inhibiting also all Printers to reprint the same, And recommends to Presbyteries to take speciall care that this Act be obeyed.

ULT. IULY 1648. POSTMERIDIEM, SESS. 21.

A DECLARATION OF THE GENERALL ASSEMBLY CONCERNING THE PRESENT DANGERS OF RELIGION, AND ESPECIALLY THE UNLAWFULL ENGAGEMENT IN WAR, AGAINST THE KINGDOM OF ENGLAND; TOGETHER, WITH MANY NECESSARY EXHORTATIONS AND DIRECTIONS TO ALL THE MEMBERS OF THE KIRK OF SCOTLAND.

It cannot seem strange to any that considereth the great trust that lyeth on us, comparing the same with the eminent dangers wherewith the Cause of God is invironed in this Land, if at this time We declare our sense thereof, and warn the people of God from this watch-tower of the present duties incumbent to them; Our witnesse is in heaven, and our record on high, that we doe not this from any disrespect to the Parliament whom we have honoured and will ever honour and also obey in all things which are agreeable to the Word of God, to our Solemn Covenants: And to the duties of our Callings, Not from any disloyalty or undutifulnesse to the Kings Majestie to whom we heartily wish, and to his posterity after him, a happy Reigne over these Dominions, Nor from any factious disposition or siding with this or that party whatsoever, Nor from any contentious humour about light or small matters, Nor from any favour to or complyance with Sectaries, against whose cursed opinions and ungodly practises, we have heretofore given ample testimony, and are still obliged by Solemn Covenant to endeavour the extirpation of Heresie and Schism; But from the Conscience or our duty when the glory of God, the Kingdom of his Son, his Word, Ordinances, Government, Covenant, Ministery, Consciences of People, Peace and Liberties of the Kirk are incompassed and almost overwhelmed with great and growing dangers.

How freely and faithfully the servants of God of old have rebuked sin in persons of all ranks, not sparing Kings, States nor Kingdoms, the Scripture maketh it most plain to all that looks thereon; Neither want we domestick examples, if we look back a little upon the behaviour of our zealous Ancestours in this Kirk, who not only in their Sermons severally with great gravity and freedom reproved the sins of the time, But more especially in the Kirk Judicatories plain and downright dealing was most frequent and familiar, as appears in the Assemblies holden in June and in October 1582. in October 1583. in May 1592. in May 1594. and in March 1595. And not only the Generall Assembly by themselves, but also by their Commissioners faithfully and freely laboured to oppose all the steps of defection; as at other times, so in the yeer 1596. wherein four or five severall times they gave most free admonitions to the King, Parliament and Councell, with a Protestation at the last before God, that they were free of their blood, and of whatsoever judgement should fall upon the Realm, and that they durst not for fear of committing High Treason against Jesus Christ the onely Monarch of his Kirk, abstain any longer from fighting against their proceedings with the spiritual armour granted to them of God, and mighty in him for overthrowing all these bulwarks set up against his Kingdom; And in their Declaration then emitted to the Kingdom, they shew that it was a main design to have the freedom of the Spirit of God in the rebuke of Sin by the mouthe of his Servants restrained and therefore they warne all Pastours of their duty in applying Doctrine and free preaching. Like as the Assembly, 24. March 1596, reckons up amongst the corruptions of the Ministery to be censured with deprivation, if continued in, the not applying their Doctrine against the corruptions of the time, which was renewed in our late Assembly at Glasgow 1638. What hath been done since that Assembly is in recent memory; and the Papers to that purpose have been published in Print, and are in the hands of all, Therefore being warranted by the Word of God, and encouraged by the forementioned examples, as after exact examination, we have approven the proceedings of the Commissioners of the last Generall Assembly, and specially their Declarations, Desires, Representatations, Remonstrances, Supplications, Vindication and other Papers relating to the present engagment in War, wherein they have given good proof of their fidelity, wisdom and zeal in the cause of God, So we finde our selves necessitate to make known unto all the People of God in this Nation our sense concerning the dangers and duties or this present time.

The cry of the insolencies of this present Army from almost all the parts of this Kingdom, hath been so great that it hath gone up to heaven, and if we should be silent, we could not be reputed faithfull in the performance of our duty. We do acknowledge that it is incident unto all Armies to be subject unto some disorders, and the Ministers of the Kingdom have not been deficient in former times to represent the same as they come unto their knowledge, calling for the redresse of them at their hands who had power: But the Commissioners of this present Assembly from the severall Provinces have exhibited great variety or abominable scandals and heinous impieties and insolencies committed by persons imployed in this service, whereof we think fitting here to give you a touch.

As if liberty had been proclaimed to the lusts of lewd men, These that have been imployed in very many places of Land have used horrible extortion of Moneys at their pleasure, and beside the taking of victuals as they would for their own use, they have in severall places wilfully destroyed the same, and have plundred many houses, taking all away they could and destroying what they could not carry away; in this great oppression & spoil of goods as the sufferers were many so choise hath been made of those who Petitioned the High and Honourable Court of Parliament for satisfaction to their Consciences before the Engagement, or who were known to make conscience of the worship of God in their families, on whom they might exercise their raging wrath and unsatiable convetousnesse; Nor stayed their rage here, but as though the war had been against God, publick Fasts have not only been neglected, but profaned by riotous spending and making merry, Divine Worship have been in many parts disturbed, some Ministers and people impeded from coming together, others scattered when they were met, some taken out of Kirks in time of worship, others apprehended at their coming out at the Kirk doors and carryed away; Besides these Ministers in performing the worship of God have been menaced, contradicted, not without blasphemous Oathes, yea their persons in Pulpit assaulted, not to speak of the spoiling of their goods, taking, beating, carrying away their persons and detaining them for a time. And finally that which excedes all the rest and is more immediately and directly against God, there hath also been many cruell mockings of his Worship, and horrid blasphemies; And it is not to be marvelled that such insolencies have been committed, since there hath been admitied upon this service some Papists, some bloody Irish Rebels, some non Covenanters, and very many fugitives from Kirk Discipline, Finally, even those who have been upon the late Rebellion, and these not onely common Souldiers but Commanders, beside many voluntiers who have no speciall command & trust.

Besides all these, the Liberties of the Kirk have been grievously encroached upon; 1. By emitting Declarations from the Parliament and Committee of Estates, containing severall things highly concerning Religion without the advice or consent of the Generall Assembly or their Commissioners, which was a ground of protestation to divers Members of Parliament who have been most zealous and active in the Cause. 2. The Article of Religion as expressed in the Declaration of Parliament hath in it many dangerous expressions, which are particularly instanced in the Representation of the Commissioners of the Generall Assembly; And the same Article of Religion in the late Declaration of the Committee of Estates to England is more unsatisfactory then the former: Like as in the said late Declaration there is a totall omission of some most materiall things pretended to in the Declaration of Parliament as satisfactory in point of securing Religion, viz. the clause concerning security to be had from his Majesty by his solemn Oath under his hand and Seal, that he shall for himself and his Successors give his Royall assent, and agree to such Act or Acts of Parliament, and Bills as shall be presented to him by his Parliaments of both and either Kingdoms respectively for enjoyning Presbyteriall Government, Directory of Worship and Confession of Faith in all his Majesties Dominions, and that his Majestie shall never make opposition to any of those, nor endeavour any change thereof; also the clause against association with any that refuse to take the Covenant is omitted: From all which it may appear in how great danger the liberties of the Kirk and even Religion it self are left. 3. In the close of the Declaration of Parliament, there is a new and unsound glosse put upon the Covenant and Acts of General Assembly, contrary to the sense of the General Assembly itself, as is more fully expressed in the Representation of the late Commission. 4. No redresse by the Parliament of certain injuries complained of to their Lordships by the Commissioners of the preceeding Generall Assembly. 5. Endeavours to weaken and frustrate Kirk-Censures by making provisions for securing the stipends of such as shall be censured for their concurring in, or preaching for this present Engagement. 6. A misrepresentation of the proceedings of the Commission of the Generall Assembly by the Parliaments Letter of May 11. to the severall Presbyteries, endeavouring to incense them against the Commission of the late Assembly and to pre-ocupie their Commissioners to this Assembly. 7. Whereas there were many Petitions presented to the High and Honourable Court of Parliament from the Commissioners of the General Assembly, Synods & Presbyteries against the present Engagement as stated in the Parliaments Declaration, yet notwithstanding of the said Petitions, and notwithstanding of many free & frequent warnings given by faithful Ministers in their Sermons, notwithstanding also that it was not unknown how much the generality of the wel affected in the Kingdom were unsatisfied in their consciences with the grounds and way of the said Engagement, yet good people are not onely left unsatisfied in their and our desires, but compelled and forced either to sin against their consciences or to be under heavy pressures & burdens. 8. Yea in the late Band injoyned to be subscribed by all the Subjects of this Kingdom, men are put to it to joyn and concur with their Persons & Estates, in the advancement, furtherance and assistance of the execution obedience & observation of the Acts and constitutions of the late Parliament; & consequently, as many as think the Engagement unlawful shall bind themselves not onely for their own part against their consciences, but to inforce the same upon others who refuse, and so not onely be oppressed, but turn oppressours of others. 9. This all the subjects are required by the Act and Declaration of Parliament to subscribe, as they desire to be holden true lovers of Religion; It being further affirmed in the said Act and Declaration, that the Acts and Constitutions of the late Parliament, are the most fit and necessary remedies for preservation of Religion; Where the Parliament assume to themselves, without the advice and consent of the Assemblies of the Kirk, to judge and determine such things wherein, (if in any thing) the ecclesiastical Assemblies have undoubtedly a special interest, viz. who are to be holden lovers of Religion, and what are the most fit and necessary remedies for preservation of Religion: Yea it is ordained by the fourth Act of Parliament, 1640. that for preservation of Religion, G. Assemblies rightly constitute, as the proper & competent judge of all matters Ecclesiastical, be keeped yearly and oftner pro re nata. The Coronation Oath doth also suppose the antecedent Judgement of the Kirk, as the proper and competent judge who are enemies to true Religion & who not; for his Majesty obliged himself by that Oath, that he should be carefull to root out all Hereticks and enemies to the true Worship of God, who shall be convict by the true Kirk of God, of the aforesaid crimes. 10. The General Assembly and their Commissioners are now deprived of their liberty of Printing, confirmed and ratified by Act of Parliament, there being an inhibition to the contrary upon the PRINTER, under the pain of Death by the Committee of Estates.

Whereas the desires of the Commissioners of the last Assembly, for the safety and security of Religion, and the right manner of proceeding to war, together with the supplications of Provinciall Assemblies and Presbyteries, all tending to the composing of the present unhappy differences, and to the begetting of a right understanding, have not produced the desired and wished-for effect; but on the contrary our just grievances being still more and more heightned, iniquity established by a law; and that law put in execution; We cannot chuse but declare and give warning to all the people of GOD in this land, concerning the sinfulnesse and unlawfulnesse of the present Engagement: which may be demonstrate by many reasons, as namely.

1. The Wars of GODS people, are called the Wars of the LORD, Numb. 21, 14. 2 Chron 20. 15. and if our eating and drinking, much more our engaging in war must be for God and for his glory; 1 Cor. 10. 31. whatsoever we do in word or deed, we are commanded to do all in the name of the Lord Jesus, and so for his glory, Col. 3.

17. The Kingdom of GOD and the righteousnesse thereof is to be sought in the first place and before all other things, Matth. 6. 33. It was the best flower and garland in the former expeditions of this Nation, that they were for God and for Religion principally and mainly. But if the principal end of this present Engagement were for the glory of GOD, How comes it to passe that not so much as one of the desires of the Kirk, for the safety and security of Religion in the said Engagement, is to this day satisfied or granted; But on the contrary such courses taken as are destructive to Religion. And if Gods glory be intended what meaneth the employing and protecting in this Army so many blasphemers persecutors of Piety, disturbers of divine worship, and others guilty of notorious and crying sins. Again, how can it be pretended that the good of Religion is principally aimed at, when it is proposed and declared that the Kings Majestie shall be brought to some of his houses in or near London, with Honour, Freedom and Safety, before ever there be any security had from him, or so much as any application made to him for the good of Religion. What is this but to postpone the honour of God, the liberties of the Gospel, the safety of Gods people to an humane interest, and to leave Religion in a condition of uncertainty, unsetlednesse and hazard, while it is strongly endeavoured to settle and make sure somewhat else.

2. Suppose the ends of this Engagement to be good (which they are not) yet the meanes and ways of prosecution are unlawfull, because there is no ane equall avoiding of rocks on both hands, but a joyning with malignants to suppresse Sectaries, a joyning hands with a black devill to beat a white devil; They are bad Physicians who would so cure one disease as to breed another as evil; or worse. That there is in the present Engagement a confederacy and association in war with such of the English who according to the solemn League and Covenant and Declarations of both Kingdoms, 1643. can be no otherwise looked upon but as Malignants and enemies of Reformation and the Cause of God, is now made so manifest before Sun and Moon, that we suppose none will deny it; And tis no lesse undeniable, that not only many known Malignants, but diverse who joyned in the late rebellion within this Kingdom are employed, yea, put into places of trust; All which how contrary tis to the Word of God, no man can be ignorant who will attentively search the Scriptures, for we finde therein condemned confederacies and associations with the enemies of true Religion, whether Canaanites, Exod. 23. 32. and 24. 12. 15. Deut. 7. 2. or other heathens 1 King 11. v. 1, 2. such was Asa his Covenant with Benhadad, 2 Chron. 16. to v. 10. Ahaz his confederacy with the King of Assyria 2 King. 16. 7. 10. 2 Chron. 28. 16. to v. 23. or whither the association was with wicked men of the seed of Abraham, as Jehoshaphats with Achab 2 Chron. 18. 2. compared with chap. 19. 2. also his association with Ahaziah 2 Chron, 20. 35. and Amaziachs associating to himself 100000. of the ten Tribes when GOD was not with them, 2 Chron. 25. 7, 8, 9, 10. The sin and danger of such associations may further appear from Isaiah 8. 12. 15. Jer.. 2. 18. Psal. 106. 35. Hos. 5. 13. and 7. 8, 11. Cor. 6. 14, 15. and if we should esteem Gods enemies, to be our enemies and hate them with perfect hatred, Psal. 139. 21 how can we then joyn with them as confederates and associates, especially in a cause where Religion is so highly concerned; and seeing they have been formerly in actuall opposition to the same cause.

3. We are commanded if it be possible and as much as lieth in us to have peace with all men, Rom. 12. 18, to seek peace and pursue it, Psal. 34. 14. war and blood-shed is the last remedy after all the wayes and means of peace have been used in vain. The intended war of the nine Tribes and a half against the two Tribes and half was prevented by a Message and Treaty of Peace Josh. 22; The like means was used by Jepthah (though not with the like success) for the preventing of war with the King of Ammon Judg. 11. The very light of nature hath taught Heathens not to make war till first all amicable wayes of preventing bloodshed were tried; yet this war hath been driven on without observing any such method of proceeding except by a message wherein not so much as one breach was represented. Yea though these two Kingdoms are straitly united in Covenant, yet these who have carried on this war did not only neglect to desire a Treaty, but also slight an offer of a Treaty made from the Parliament of England upon the Propositions of both Kingdoms.

4. There are many clear and ful testimonies of Scriptures against the breach and violation of Covenants, although but between man and man, Psal. 55. 20. Rom. 1, 31. 2 Tim. 3. 3, Especially where the name of God was interposed in Covenants by any of his people, Jer. 34. 8, 10, 11, 18. Ezek. 17. 18. 19. How much more the violation of a Solemn Covenant between God and his people. Lev. 26. 15. 25. Deut. 17. 2. and 29. 21, 14, 25. Jer. 22. 8, 9. 1 King. 19. 10. Dan. 11. 32. Hos. 6. 7. If therefore the present Engagement be a breach of our solemn League and Covenant, then they who have before taken the Covenant, and have now joyned in this Engagement, must grant by necessary and infailible consequence, either that the Covenant it self which they took was unlawful, and such as they cannot perform without sin (which yet they cannot professe) or otherwise, that the Engagement is unlawfull and sinfull, as being a breach of Covenant, and so contrary to the Word of God; that the present Engagement is a breach of Covenant may appear by comparing it with each of the Articles, for it is against all the six Articles of the Covenant.

Against the first, because in stead of the preservation of the Doctrine, Wor-ship, Discipline and Government of this Kirk; there is not onely a great quarelling by those that do Engage, at the present doctrine, and free preaching, a disturbing of and withdrawing from the Worship, and namely from the late solemn humil-iation: But also a refusall of such things as were desired by the Commission of the late Assembly and Provincial Synods, as necessary to the preservation of the true Reformed Religion: And we have just cause of fear that the Reformation of Religion in Doctrine, Worship, Discipline and Government is not intended to be sufficiently maintained and preserved, when we finde such a limitation and re-striction in the late Declaration of the Committee of Estates to the Parliament and Kingdom of England, That they will maintain and preserve the Reformation of Religion, Doctrine, Worship, Discipline and Government, as is by the mercy of GOD, and his Majesties goodnesse established by Law among us; but as there is no such limitation in the Covenant, so we have not had such proof of his Majesties goodnesse as to establish by Law all that hath been by the mercies of God inacted in Generall Assemblies. As to the rest of the first Article, concerning the Refor-mation of England and Ireland, and the Uniformity, as there was some hopefull beginnings thereof, and a good foundation laid, during the late War against the

Popish Prelaticall and Malignant party, so the state and ground of the War being now altered, and these chosen for confederates, and associates in the War, who are known enemies to that Reformation, and Uniformity, how can the Covenant be kept in that point as long as such a War is carried on.

The second Article is violated because in stead of indeavouring to extirpate Popery and Superstition without respect of persons (as is exprest in the Covenant) there is in the late Declaration of the Committee of Estates a desire of the Queens return, without any condition tending to the restraint of her Masse or exercise of Popery; We do also conceive there is a tacit condescending to the toleration of Superstition and the Book of Common prayer in His Majesties family, because as it was reserved by himself in his concession, brought home by the Commissioners of this Kingdom, So these concessions were never plainly declared by the Parliament to be unsatisfactory to their Lordships, howbeit it hath been often and earnestly desired: neither can we conceive how the clause concerning the extirpation of Prelacy, can consist with indeavouring to bring His Majesty with Honour, Freedom and Safety to one of his Houses in or about LONDON, without any security had from him, for the abolition of Prelacy; it being his known principle (and publickly declared by himself shortly after he went to the Isle of Wight) that he holds himself obliged in conscience, and by his Coronation Oath to maintain Archbishops, Bishops, &c. Can it be said that they are endeavouring to extirpate Prelacy, who after such a Declaration would put in His Majesties hand an opportunity to restore it?

As for the third Article we cannot conceive how the preserving of the Priviledges of Parliament, and asserting the Kings negative voice can consist; And we are sorrowfull that under the colour, of the Priviledges of Parliament, the liberties of the Subjects are overthrown, and the persons and Estates of such as have been best affected to the Cause and Covenant are exposed to most grievous injuries, crying oppressions: And whereas the duty in preserving and defending his Majesties Person and Authority, is by the third Article of the Covenant qualified with, and subordinate unto the preservation and defence of the true Religion and Liberties of the Kingdoms, There is no such qualification, nor subordination observed in the present Engagement, but on the contrary, it is so carried on, as to make duties to God and Religion conditionall, qualified, limited; and duties to the King absolute and unlimited.

The fourth Article of the Covenant is so foully broken, that they who were by that Article declared Enemies, Incendiaries, Malignants, and therefore to be brought to condigne tryall and punishment, are now looked upon as friends and associates, and are the men who get most favour and protection, and sundry of them imployed in places of trust, in the Army and Committees.

For the fifth Article, instead of endeavouring to preserve Peace and Union, a breach is endeavoured between the Kingdoms, not only by taking in and garrisoning their frontire Towns, but also entering the Kingdom of England with an Army, and joyning with the common enemies of both Kingdoms, notwithstanding of an offer of a Treaty upon the Propositions of both Kingdoms made by the Parliament of England to the Parliament of this Kingdom. And whether the way of this Engagement can consist with the large Treaty between the Kingdoms, we shall with the Honourable Committee of Estates may yet take it into their serious second thoughts.

The sixth is also manifestly broken, for we are thereby obliged to assist and defend all those that entered into this League and Covenant, in maintaining and pursuing thereof: Whereas the Army now entered into England, is to assist and defend many who have not entered into that League and Covenant: And for those who took the Covenant in that Nation. and continue faithfull in it, what they may expect from this Army, may be collected not onely from their carriage towards their Brethren at home; but also from that clause toward the close of the late Declaration of the Committee of Estates, And that we will do prejudice or use violence to none (as far as we are able) but to such as oppose us, or such ends above mentioned. It cannot be unknown that many of the English Nation who are firm and faithfull to the Covenant, and Presbyteriall Government do, and will according to their places and callings oppose some of those ends above mentioned in that Declaration, as namely, the restoring both of King and Queen without any condition or security first had from them; And so by that rule in the Declaration they must expect to be used as enemies, not as friends. That sixth Article is also broken by a departing from the first principles and resolutions: and by dividing, and withdrawing from those that adhere thereunto, which hath been before cleared by the Commission of the late Generall Assembly in their Declaration in March, Representation, and other Papers published in Print.

5. We leave it to be seriously pondered by every one who is truely conscientious, whether it be any ways credible or probable, or agreeable to Scripture rules, that the generality of all that have been most faithfull and cordiall to the Covenant and cause of God should be deceived, deluded and darkened in this businesse, and that they who for the most part were enemies to the work of God in the beginning, and have never brought forth fruits meet for Repentance, should now finde out the will of God more than his most faithfull Servants in the Land, and who, that fears God, will believe that Malignants are for the ends of the Covenant and that they who are most instrumental in the Reformation, are against the ends of the Covenant.

All which considered, as we could not, without involving our selves in the guiltinesse of so unlawfull an Engagement, yeeld to the desire of the Army for Ministers to be sent by us to attend them; So we do earnestly exhort, and in the name and authority of Jesus Christ, charge and require all and every one of the Members of this Reformed Kirk of Scotland.

I. That they search narrowly into the sins which have Procured so great judgements and so sad an interruption of the work of God, that they examine themselves, consider their wayes, be much in humiliation and prayer, study a reall and practicall Reformation, That they also mourn and sigh for the abominations of the Land, and stand in the gap to turn away the wrath, Among all these fearfull sins, the violation of the Solemn League and Covenant, would not be forgotten but seriously laid to heart, as that which eminently provoketh the Lord and procureth his judgements to be powred forth not onely upon persons and families, but also upon States and Kingdoms. Covenant-breakers through in common things, are reckoned by the Apostle in that Catalogue of the abominations of the Gentiles: But among the people of God, where his great name is interposed, the breach of Covenant even in meaner matters, such as the setting of servants at liberty provoketh the Lord to say, Behold I proclaim a liberty for you (saith the Lord) to the sword, to the pestilence, and to the famine, and I will give the men that hath transgressed my Covenant, and (not excepting, but expressly mentioning Princes) he addes, I will give them into the hands of their enemies, The History of the Gibeonites, who surreptitiously procured the Covenant made to spare them, and whom Saul some ages thereafter in his zeal to the children of Israel and Judah sought to slay, as being cursed Canaanites, evidenceth with what vengeance, the LORD followeth Covenant-breakers, whereof there wants not in prophane History also both forreign and domestick examples: Therefore let all the inhabytants of the Land of whatsoever rank, seriously ponder how terrible judgements the violation of a Covenant so recently, so advisedly, so solemnly made, and in so weighty matters, may draw on, if not timously prevented by speedy repentance.

II. That they so respect and honour Authority, as that they be not the servants of men, nor give obedience to the will and authority of Rulers in any thing which may not consist with the word of God, but stand fast in the liberty wherewith Christ hath made them free, and obey God rather then men.

III. That they carefully avoid the dangerous rocks and snares of this time, whereby so many are taken and broken. Upon the one hand the sowre leaven of Malignancy where ever it enters, spoileth and corrupteth the whole lump, postponing Religion, and the Cause of God to humane interest, what ever be pretended to the contrary, and obstructing the work of Reformation, and propagation of Religion out of false respects and creature interest. As this hath formerly abounded in the land, to the prejudice of the Cause and Work of God, so of late it is revived, spreading with specious pretences of vindicating wrongs done to his Majesty. We desire not to be mistaken, as if respect and love to his Majesty were branded with the infamous mark of Malignancy; But hereby we warn all who would not come under this soul stain, not onely in their speech and profession, but really & in their whole carriage not to prefer their own, and the interest of any creature whatsoever, before the interest of CHRIST and Religion. The characters of these have been fully given in former Declarations, specially in the Declaration of the Commissioners of the Generall Assembly in March last, which we hold as here repeated; onely adding this, that they ordinarily traduce Kirk Judicatures, as medling with civill affairs, which as it is no new calumny, but such as hath been cast upon the servants of GOD in former times; so the whole course of proceedings doth manifestly confute the same.

Upon the other hand Sectarisme hath no lesse hindered the blessed and glorious work of Reformation in our neighbour Kingdom, against the venome whereof, lest it approach and infect this Kirk, we have need to watch diligently to avoid all the beginnings and dangerous appearances thereof. The many faithfull testimonies from godly Ministers in severall parts of England, against the vile errours, and abominable blasphemies abounding there, as they are to us matter of rejoicing before the Lord; so they ought to be looked on as warnings to all sorts of people, especially that regard Religion, to beware of Sathans snares, craftily set to catch their souls. And because such gangreens creep insensibly, all that love the Honour of GOD, and welfare of Religion, would seriously consider the following points, both by way of marks to discern; and meanes to escape the danger of this infection.

1. Whosoever are misprises of the blessed work of Reformation established within this Land, and do not shew themselves grieved for the impediments and obstructions it hath met with in our neighbour Kingdom, these are even on the brink of this precipice, ready to tumble down in this gulf whensoever occasion is offered: All therefore that love the Lord Jesus, would stir up their hearts in the light and strength of the Lord highly to prize, and thankfully to acknowledge what the right hand of the most High hath done among us, as also to thirst fervently after the advancing and perfecting of the LORD's work among our neighbours.

2. Disrespect to the publick Ministery and Ordinances is a symptome of a dangerous inclination to that disease: And therefore as all Christs Ministers ought to stir up themselves, to walk as becometh their high and holy calling lest they be stumbling blocks to the people of God; so all the people of God ought most carefully to stir up themselves unto a precious estimation of the Ordinances of God, & highly to esteem the Stewards thereof for their works sake. A duty at all times needful but now especially, when Sathan by all means endevours the contrary.

3. Indifferency in points of Religien, and pleading for Toleration to themselves or others how far soever different among themselves, is not to be forgotten among the characters of Sectaries, and therefore ought the more carefully to be avoided and opposed by all who desire to hold fast the profession of their faith without wavering.

4. They who are glorying in, and seeking after new lights, or under the pretext of them are self-conceited in singular opinions, or who affect new and strange expressions, are entring into the snare ready to be carried about with every winde of Doctrine. And therefore albeit we ought always as Disciples of the Lord to set ourselves as in his sight to be taught by his Spirit according to his Word, yet in this time so fertil of errours; it becommeth all the lovers of truth to hold fast what they have received, that no man take their Crown.

5. Whosoever brings in any opinion or practise in this Kirk contrary to the confession of Faith, Directory of Worship or Presbyterian Government may be justly esteemed to be opening the door to Schisme and Sects: And therefore all depravers or misconstructers of the proceedings of Kirk-Judicatories, especially the Generall Assembly would take heed least by making a breach upon the walls of Jerusalem they make a patent way for Sectaries to enter.

6. They who separate the Spirit from the Word, and pretend the Spirit, when they have no ground or warrant from the Word, are already taken in an evill snare, And therefore tis necessary to try the Spirits whither they are of God, for many false Prophets are gone out into the world, if they speak not according to the word it is because there is no light in them.

Besides the former, these are also marks of a Sectary; If any commend, and recommend to others, or spread and divulge the erroneous books of Sectaries, If any allow, avow, or use Conventicles or private meetings forbidden by the Acts of the Generall Assembly 1641. and 1647. last past, If any be unwilling, and decline to reckon Sectaries among the enemies of the Covenant, from whom danger is to be apprehended, And (though we disallow the abusing and Idolizing of learning to the patrocinie of Errour or prejudice of piety) if any contemn literature as needlesse at best, if not also hurtfull to a Minister.

When we thus expreste our selves for preventing the dangers of Sects and Schismes, it is far from our intention to discourage any from the duties of piety, and mutuall edification, according to the directions of the last Assembly published in Print, and seriously recommended by them, or to give any advantage to Malignants and Prophane persons, with whom it is frequent to cast upon all those who adhere to former principles, and cannot approve the present Engagement, the odious nick-names of Sectaries and Independents. For the beter discovery of such prophane mockers, we give these markes and characters. 1. They do prophanely and tauntingly abuse the name of the Spirit, under that name deriding the work of Grace and sanctification. 2. They esteem and speak of exercises of conscience, as fancies, or fits of melancholy. 3. They mock at Family-worship and the means of mutuall edification so much recommended by the last Assembly in their directions. 4. They do usually calumniate godly Ministers, and professors who follow holinesse, with the names of Sectaries, or the like odious names, without any just cause: As we account all such to be enemies to the practise and power of godlinesse; So we do exhort all the lovers of truth to hold on in the way of holinesse through good report and ill report, being stedfast, immovable, alwayes abounding in the work of the Lord, forasmuch as they know their labour is not in vain in the Lord.

IV. That they do not concur in, nor any way assist this present Engagement, as they would not partake in other mens sins, and so receive of their plagues, but that by the grace and assistance of Christ they stedfastly resolve to suffer the rod of the wicked, and the utmost which wicked mens malice can afflict them with, rather then to put forth their hand to iniquity.

V. That they suffer not themselves to be abused with fair pretences and professions usuall in the mouths of those that carry on this designe, and often published in their Papers, But remember that the foulest actions have not wanted specious pretences; And if they who killed the Apostles did both pretend and intend to do God good service, what marvell that they who engage against the Covenant pretend to engage for it. Neither is it to be forgotten, That after the first subscription of our Nationall Covenant, these who had the chief hand in managing publick affairs, and had subscribed the Covenant, especially the Duke of Lenox, and Captain James then Earl of Arran, in the years 1581, 1582, 1583, 1584. when their designe was to subvert both the Doctrine and Discipline of this Kirk, yet gave great assurances by promises and Oaths to the contrary. At the Assemblies 1598, 1599, 1600. It was declared with many vows and attestations by the King, Statesmen, and these Ministers who were aspiring to Prelacy, That they intended no such thing as a change of the Government of the Kirk, or an introducing of Episcopacy, yet they were really doing what they disclaimed and professed not to do. And suppose that some who have an active hand in carrying on the present publick affairs, have no design either to destroy Religion, or utterly to sleight it: yet the way they are on, and work they are about as it is contrived, doth of its self, and in its own nature tend to the endangering, if not to the utter subversion of Religion, for it cannot be denyed, but the very undertaking of this War, sets the once suppressed Malignants on work again, and successe therein puts them in a capacity to set up according to their principles abolished and abjured corruptions; which will be the more hardly hindered, considering his Majesties propension, and professed resolution that way, Especially seeing His Majesties concessions (though it hath been often desired) have never been plainly declared unsatisfactore by the Parliament. And who in reason can think that any more then His Majesties concessions sent from the Isle of Wight will be required of him, by them who thereupon have proceeded to this Engagement. The Kings negative voice (asserted in the Papers of the Commissioners of this Kingdom unto England, which are owned in the late Declaration to the Kingdom of England, as the sense of this Kingdom) considered in relation to Religion makes the danger yet the greater and more palpable, yea, may reach further to shake and unsettle Religion established in this Land; If to the premises this be added which is not only often declared, but also demanded, That his Majestie be brought to one of his houses in Honour, Freedom and Safety, which may infer the admitting of his Maj. to the free exercise of his Royall power before security had from him for Reeligion, or Application made to him for the same, who sees not now what hazard Religion runs, certainly greater then a good intention can salve,

VI. That they do not mistake, or misunderstand the nature of the true Reformed Religion and of the Government of JESUS CHRIST, as if thereby either the Prerogative of Kings, Privileges of Parliaments or Liberties of Burghs, and other Corporations were any wayes hurt or weakened: whereas indeed Religion is the main pillar and upholder of civill authority, or Magistracie, and it is the resisting, and not the receiving of the Government of CHRIST, which hath overturned civill powers. If the Throne be established by righteousnesse (as we are plainly taught by the Word of God) then it is overthrowne by unrighteousnesse and iniquity.

VII. That they beware of all things which may ensnare their consciences, as evill councell, evill company, false informations, rash promises, and especially that they beware of taking any Oathes, subscribing any Bonds, which may relate to the Covenant and Cause of God, unlesse such Oaths or Bonds be approved by the General Assembly or their Commissioners for the publique affairs of the Kirk.

VIII. That they do not cast away their confidence, nor sink into despair, because of the present dangers and difficulties, but live by faith, waite for better times, and continue stedfast as seeing him who is invisible, firmly beleeving that such a course as is not of God but against him, will come to naught.

IX. To remember, that as the violation of the Covenant by some in England doth not set us free from the observation thereof, and as no laws nor authority on earth can absolve us from so solemn an obligation to the most High God (which not onely hath been professed by this Kirk but in a Petition of the City of London, and in publique Testimonies of many of the Ministery of England). So we are not acquited and assoiled from the obligation of our solemn Covenant, because of the troubles and confusions of the times; But that in the worst of times all those duties, whereunto by Covenant we oblige ourselves, do still lie upon us, for we have sworn (and must perform it) concerning that Cause and Covenant wherein we solemnly Engaged, That we shall all the dayes of our lives zealously and constantly continue therein against all opposition, and promove the same according to our power against all lets and Impediments whatsoever. And if against all lets and impediments whatsoever, then the altering of the way of opposition, or of the kinde of impediments doth not alter the nature, or the Joye of the Covenant, but we are obliged to all the duties therein contained.

We doe also exhort and charge in CHRISTS Name the Prince of Pastors, all the Ministers within this Kirk, that in no wayes they be accessary to this sinful Engagement, but in all their conferences and reasoning especially, in their publick Doctrine, they declare themselves freely, and faithfully, as they would eschew the wrath of GOD, due for a violated Covenant, and as they would escape the censures of the Kirk; and let all Presbyteries be watchful within their bounds, and carefully, wisely, and zealously to inflict Ecclesiastick censures.

Finally, we exhort all civil Iudicatories, and every one intrusted with power to manage the present affairs, That they would seriously remember the strict account they are to give before the Iudge of the quick and the dead, Considering deeply how fearful a thing it is to oppresse the consciences of their Brethren, either by pressing them to act where they finde no satisfactory warrant or by putting heavy pressures upon them for not acting according to their injunctions, and especially that they offer not to insnare by new Oaths, or Bonds those that make conscience of the great Oath of their Solemn Covenant, and hitherto have proven faithful and constant in promoving joyntly all the ends thereof.

If this our faithful warning finde favourable acceptance, so that the grievous things already enacted, be no more prosecuted and pressed, we shall blesse God who reigns in the Kingdoms and Councels of men: But if it fall out otherwise (as God forbid) we have liberate our souls of the guiltinesse of this sinful way of Engagement, and of all the miseries that shall ensue thereby upon this Kirk and Kingdom, And shall lament before the Lord that our labours have not as yet had the desired successe. In the meantime, we dare not cast away our confidence, but trusting in the name of the Lord, and staying upon our God, shall by his grace and assistance continue stedfast in our Solemn Covenants, and faithful in all the duties of our Calling.

AUGUST. 1. 1648. ANTEMERIDIEM. SESS. 22.

THE GENERAL ASSEMBLIES ANSWER TO THE PAPER PRESENTED FROM THE HONOURABLE COMMITTEE OF ESTATES OF THE DATE IULY 28. 1648.

The General Assembly having considered the Paper of the 28. of July, delivered to them from the Honourable Committee of Estates, Do finde that the first part thereof concerning the great Offers made by the Parliament and Committee of Estates for the security of Religion, is no other but what was fully answered in our last Paper of the 25. of July, delivered to their Lordships, wherein it was plainly demonstrat by Theologicall reasons (though their Lordships are pleased to call them Politick) that the present Engagement is inconsistent with the safety and security of Religion. Next whereas it is affirmed in their Lordships Paper, that the grounds and reasons are the same which were fully answered before, we wish it had been instanced when and where they were answered, for we know no such thing.

Another reflection upon that former Paper of ours is thus expressed, That the Generall Assembly hath proceeded to such a Declaration before they had in an Ecclesiaslick way from clear testimonies out of the Word of God or convencing of our consciences, demonstrate the unlawfulnesse of the undertaking: Where we can see no reason why it should seem so very strange to the Honourable Committee that the Generall Assembly hath so proceeded to a Declaration of their judgement concerning this businesse, For as it hath been no unusuall thing, but very ordinary that approved Synods, both Provinciall, Nationall, and Oecumeniall have declared their judgement without publishing the particular grounds & reasons thereof from Scripture (a work more proper for full Tractates then for Synodicall Decrees or Cannons.) So if their Lordships had been pleased to attend (for many attended not) the late Parliament-Sermons mainly intended for their Lordships information, and had with mindes unprejudiced, hearkened thereunto, and searched in to all the Papers lately published in Print by the Commission of the last Assembly, they might have been by the blessing of God convinced from the Word of God of the unlawfulnesse of the present Engagement.

There are three things which may justly seem to us more strange: One is, That the Declaration of Parliament having given assurance in this manner, We are re-solved not to ingage in any War before the necessity and lawfulnesse thereof be cleared, so as all who are wel-affected may be satisfied therewith, yet now they have ingaged in War without any such clearing of the necessity and lawfulnesse thereof, or satisfaction given to the wel-affected.

Another is, that although there are so great professions and offers in the gen-erall to satisfie what can be desired for the security of Religion, yet none of those particulars desired by the late Commission of the Kirk for the security of Religion have been granted. We shall here onely give instance in one of those desires, which was, that his Majesties concessions and offers concerning Religion, sent home from the Isle of Wight, having been found by the said Commission unsatisfactory and destructive to the Covenant, might be by the Parliament declared unsatisfactory to their Lordships.

In this great point there hath been no satisfaction given, onely it was light-ly touched in one clause of the Parliaments Declaration, and so ambiguously ex-pressed, as might suffer many interpretations, and although this ambiguity was clearly laid open by the Commissioners of the last Generall Assembly in their Representation; yet to this day there hath been nothing published neither by the Parliament nor Committee of Estates to give any clearer satisfaction, by disclaim-ing those offers and concessions as unsatisfactory to the parliament: So that this (if there were no more) gives us great cause to apprehend that there is a greater mystery latent in that businesse then yet appeareth.

A third thing which seemeth strange to us is, That their Lordships desire of arguments from Scripture to prove the unlawfulnesse of this Engagement was not propounded to the Commissioners of the last Assembly, before the emitting of the Declaration of Parliament, and before the Levies (when it had been most orderly & seasonable) but is now propounded after publick resolutions and Declarations, yea not till those resolutions are put in actuall execution.

However seeing their Lordships do now desire proofs from Scripture for the unlawfulnesse of the Engagement.

We answer, That as joyning and concurring in this Engagement is unlawfull to all the wel-affected in this Kingdom, their consciences being altogether unsatisfied in the lawfulnesse thereof; and as it is unlawfull in the manner of putting it in execution, being accompanied with so many injuries, oppressions, and crying abominations, and with so much persecution of piety; so it is unlawfull in the own nature of it, and as it is stated upon the grounds of the Declarations of Parliament, and Committee of Estates. And this unlawfulnesse of the Engagement in it self, we have demonstrate in the Declaration herewith communicate to their Lordships, unto which we remit them for satisfaction in that point, and do nor doubt but their Lordships may be convinced thereby of the evill of their way, and that it is so far from being a pious and necessary Engagement (as their Lordships are pleased to call it) that it is a most unlawfull and sinfull Engagement to be repented of, and forsaken by all that have any hand in it, as they desire to make their peace with God, And we heartily wish that their Lordships subsequent proceedings may be reall testimonies, that their calling for Scripture proofs was from a reall desire to be informed and edified.

As to their Lordships other desire of our demonstrating from the Word of God, that the Kirk hath interest in the undertakings and Engagements in War, and what that interest is, We had thought this point to be without controversie in this Kingdom, not onely in respect of Kirk and State, their joyning and co-operating (each in their proper sphere,) in the former Expeditions of this Kingdom into England, but also because the very Conferences which have been between Committees of Kirk and State concerning this undertaking and Engagement, doth plainly suppose an interest of the Kirk in such affairs.

If their Lordships mean any politick interest in such undertakings, we claim no such thing, if the meaning be of a Spirituall interest and so far as concerneth the point of Conscience, there can be no doubt thereof made by such as do with David make the testimonies of the Lord their Counsellers, Psalm 119. 24. And consult with God as he used to do in undertaking War: It is also to be remembred that Joshua and all the Congregation of Israel were commanded to go out and in at the word of Eliazer the priest, who was to aske councell of the Lord for them, Numb. 27. 28. Hath not the Word of God prescribed to the Christian Magistrate the Rules of a Lawfull War, And doth it not belong, to particular Ministers, much more to the Assemblies of the Kirk, to declare the minde of God from Scripture, for all sorts of duties, and against all sorts of sins. And if the present War be a case of conscience, and alledged to be the most fit and necessary means for preservation of Religion, who seeth not that the Kirk hath an undoubted interest in resolving and determining such a case of Conscience from the word of God. This we shall onely adde, that whereas in the Parliaments Letter to the Presbyteries there instances were adduced by way of reflection upon the proceedings of the late Commission, as medling with Civill matters in which they had no Interest, The Commission did in their Printed Vindication so clear from Scripturall grounds their Interest in such things as their Lordships might have been easily satisfied in that point. We shall here onely mention one passage containing a good and safe rule for such Cases, The Duties of the second Table, as well as of the first, as namely, The Duties between King and Subject, Parents and Children, Husbands and Wives, Masters and Servants, and the like being contained in, and to be taught and cleared from the Word of God, are in that respect, and so far as concerneth the point of Conscience, a subject of Ministeriall Doctrine, and in difficult cases a subject of cognizance and Judgement, to the Assemblies of the Kirk.

EODEM DIE POSTMERIDIEM, SESS. 23.

A DECLARATION AND EXHORTATION OF THE GENERALL ASSEMBLY OF THE CHURCH OF SCOTLAND, TO THEIR BRETHREN OF ENGLAND.

As the necessity of preserving a right understanding and mutuall confidence betwixt the Churches of Christ in both Kingdoms constrain us, so the good acceptance and the suitable affections that the Declaration of the last Generall Assembly met with in England from the Lovers of the Covenant and present Reformation, together with the many Testimonies that have of late been given unto the Truth in that Land, invites and incourages us to make known unto our Brethren there, our sense of the present condition of publick affairs, so far as concerns Religion and the point of Conscience.

The dispensation of God in ruling of the Nations, and in the revolutions of his Providence towards them, is full of wonder in all the earth; And we, who live in this Island, have cause to look upon it with speciall observation, in regard of that which concerns our selves. For many generations these two Kingdoms stood at odds and were the instruments of many sufferings and calamities one to another, untill at last the Lord having compassion upon both, did unite them under one King; which great and long desired Blessing hath received such increase from our being united together in one League and Covenant as doth adde much to the good and happinesse of both Nations: Therefore is it to be looked upon by all the Lovers of Truth and Peace in these Lands as a just ground of much thanksgiving & many praises unto GOD, even in the day of our greatest calamity and affliction what ever befall, as we know no cause why we should forget so a great a mercy or repent of so good a work.

But as the common Enemies of these Kingdoms studied by all means to keep them from entring into that Covenant, so hath all their power and Policy, now, for five years past, been imployed to bring it to nought. As soon as it had being the

Popish, Prelaticall and Malignant Party did bend all their forces against it; and when by the mighty hand of GOD they were scattered and brought to confusion, in their stead stood up in England a generation who have perverted the Truth, and by turning aside into Errour have obstructed the work of Reformation; and by forsaking of the Covenant, and forgetting of the Oath of GOD, have brought a great reproach upon his Name, and made the Enemy to blaspheme; whose un-thankfulnesse and unstedfastnesse, with the many provocations of these Lands, hath provoked the Lord again to raise out of the dust the horn of Malignants, and to arm them with such power as is terrible to his People, and threatenes his Work with ruine. And albeit, we acknowledge our selves bound and are still resolved to preserve and defend his Majesties Person and Authority in the preservation and defence of the true Religion and Liberties of the Kingdoms: Yet it is unto us mat-ter of very great sorrow and grief that so many in our Land should so far joyn in Malignant Designes, and that there should be found amongst us who have under-taken and are now putting in execution an unlawfull War promoving their ends and opposing and making void (so far as in them lies) the Ends of the Covenant: Neverthelesse in this we cannot but rejoyce that they went not without a Witnesse and a Warning disswading them to go.

And we desire our Brethren of England to know, that as a very considerable number of the Members of the Parliament did dissent from and protest against the proceedings of the major part in reference to this Engagement so all the particular Synods and Presbyteries in this Kingdom, excepting some few, who by reason of their remotenesse and shortenesse of time had not the opportunity, have most harmoniously joyned with and seconded the Desires of the Commissioners of the General Assembly for preventing so unlawful a War: And now the Commission-ers out of all the Provinces conveened in this National Assembly, as after an exact examination they have unanimously approved the proceedings of the Commis-sioners of the former Assembly against that Engagement; so have they emitted a Declaration to all the People of GOD in this Land, shewing it to be contrary to GODS Word and to the solemn League and Covenant. Neither have Ministers onely by their preaching, and Kirk Iudicatories by their Petitions and Declara-tions given testimony against it; but many others in this Land also by supplicating the High and Honourable Court of Parliament for satisfaction to their Conscience thereanent: And when it could not be obtained many have chosen rather to suffer the spoiling of their goods with joy, then to sin against GOD by complying with an evil course. And many of the Officers of our former Army, who are of special note for their good carriage and deserving in the Cause of GOD, have rather choosed to quit their charges then to joyn in it: Nay, the well-affected, both Ministers and People, as they do bear testimony against it before men, so groan under it before GOD. So that this character may justly be put upon it by all who shall speak of it now or in after Ages, That as it is a foul breach of the Covenant under a pretence and profession of being for the ends of the Covenant, so being carried on against the Consciences of the people, and contrary to the most harmonious and universal Testimonies of many Presbyteries and Synods that have been given against it, it is a sinning with many witnesses. A paralel will hardly be found in this or in any other Land wherein a publick sinful course hath been carried on with so high a hand against the Consciences of the People of GOD, and against so many Warnings of the Servants of GOD, and general opposition from the Judicatories of the Kirk; which yet is the less to be wondred at, because the greatest part of those who have been most active in contriving and carrying on of the fame, were either once open Enemies, or always secret underminers, or indifferent and neutral in the Cause of GOD.

But whatsoever be the falling away of such, we shall desire and do expect that our Brethren in England, who continue faithful, may rest confident of the generality of all such of this Kingdom as were at first active in promoting the Covenant and Work of Reformation, that they are also still faithful in adhering thereunto, and walking after their former principles do resolve to abide stedfast and to hold fast the bands of Brotherhood and union between these Kingdoms: Neither are we lesse confident of the like Resolutions and Affections of our Brethren in England: The many Testimonies which the Truth and Cause of CHRIST, the Covenant and Presbyterial Government have lately received from that cloud of Witnesses of the Ministery in several Provinces and Countries of that Kingdom, after the example of the worthy Ministery of the City of London, against the Errours of Independency, Anabaptism, Antinomianisin, Arminianism, Socinianism, Faminism, Libertinism, Sceptism, Erastianism, and other new and dangerous Doctrines spred and received amongst many in that Nation; As they are unto us matter of great praise and hearty thanksgiving unto GOD, so also an evidence of the stedfastness of many in England, and a token for good, and a wide door of hope that the Lord will perfect his Work and bring forth the headstone of his House in that Land. It shall be the wisdom of each Nation to keep the golden path of truth and righteousnesse betwixt the crooked wayes of Malignants upon the one hand and Secteries upon the other, and for each of the Nations so to look upon another, as to distinguish betwixt the prevalent part and the better part, and betwixt friends and foes.

We conceive it to be high time for both Nations to search and try their ways and turn again to the LORD, that he who hath wounded us may heal us, and he who hath broken us may binde us up. The sin of both hath been the departing from the rule of the Covenant, and that we did not trust God for the prefecting of his Work, walking by the rule of piety, but took ourselves to humane polices, and endeavoured to carry it on by carnal and worldly means. For as Scotland did to much connive at and comply with Malignants, which is the immediate and neerest cause of all our present troubles and distractions; so England neglecting to hold fast the truth and to submit themselves to the Government of Jesus Christ, so clearly held forth by the pious and learned Assembly of Divines, did connive at many abominable Blasphemies and Errors, and complying with Sectaries, gave way to their wicked Toleration. Neither is it the least part of the sin of both Lands, that they have more minded the outward then the inward Reformation, the erecting of the outward Fabrick of GODS House, then the providing furniture for it by advancing the power of the Gospel, that his glory may be seen in his Temple. Because of these things is there great wrath from the LORD against these Kingdoms, and this controversie shall be continued until we really turn away from our crooked paths. Therefore as we wish that none of this Land may flatter themselves in their evil wayes, but repent and amend, so we desire our Brethren of England to consider what hath been the bitter fruits of their slow progresse in and neglect of the Work of Reformation, and of their connivance at and complying with Sectaries, and to do no more so, but that whatsoever is commanded by the God of Heaven, it be diligently done for the House of the God of Heaven.

We trust that the Parliament of England will be wise to remember and consider the great mercies of GOD towards them in delivering them from all their Enemies, & the many opportunities put into their hands for advancing and establishing the work of Reformation; for neglect whereof God hath now again threatned to lift up their Enemies above them, that he may once more prove what they will do for his Name, and for setling the order of his House. God forbid that they should run from one extream to another, from compliance with Sectaries to compliance with Malignants, and hearken to terms of an unsafe and sinful Peace, We cannot but abhor the purposes of any who minde the subversion of Monarchical Government, which we heartily wish to be preserved and continued in his Majesties Person, and Posterity; and we do no lesse dislike the Practises of those who deal so hardly with his Majesties Person, earnestly desiring that he were in the condition he was into by the advice of both Kingdoms before he was taken away by a party of Sir Thomas Fairfax Army; Nor are we against the restoring of the King to the exercise of his power in aright order and way. Yet considering what great expence of blood and pains these Kingdoms have been at for maintaining their just liberties and bringing the Work of Reformation this length; And considering his Majesties great aversnesse from setling Reformation of Religion, and his adhering still to Episcopacy; We trust that security will be demanded and had from his Majesty for Religion, before he be brought to one of his Houses in or neer about London, with honour, freedom and safety. And considering of what importance the solemne League and Covenant is unto all the interests of both Kingdoms concerning their Religion, Liberties and Peace, to make an agreement without establishing of it, were not only to rob these Nations of the blessings they have already attained by it, but to open a door to let in all the corruptions that have been formerly in the Kirks of God in these lands, & all the abuses and usurpations that have been in the civil government, & again to divide these two Kingdoms that are now so happily united and conjoyned: & therefore as we wish that all mis-understanding betwixt the Nations, & betwixt the King & People may be removed, that there may be a happy & lasting Peace, so that there may be no agreement without establishing and enjoyning the Covenant in all these three Kingdoms; and that for this end God would give wisdom to all that are intrusted in the managing of publick Affairs that they may seasonably discover and carefully avoid all snares which may be laid either by Sectaries, or Malignants, or both, under colour of a Treaty of Peace. And we are confident, through the Lord, that all the obstructions and oppositions, by which his work has been retarded and interrupted in this Island, shall not onely be taken out of the way, but shall turn to the advantage and furtherance of it at last. The onely wise God can and will bring about his holy purposes by unlikely, yea by contrary means: And God forbid that either our Brethren in England or our selves should give way to despondency of Spirit, and cast away the hopes of that so much prayed for and so much wished for Reformation of Religion, and Uniformity in all the parts thereof according to the Covenant: And now it is our hearts desire and prayer to God, that amidst the many tryals and tentations of these times, none of the Servants of God and witnesses of Jesus Christ may be deserted, or left to themselves to comply either with the Malignant party upon the one hand, or with Sectaries upon the other. Brethren pray for us, and the God of all grace, who hath called us unto his eternal glory, after that ye have suffered a while, make you perfect, stablish strengthen and settle you.

AUGUST. 2. 1648. ANTEMERIDIEM, SESS. 26.

ANSWER TO THE LETTER OF THE REVEREND ASSEMBLY OF DIVINES IN ENGLAND.

Right Honourable, Right Reverend and Wel beloved in our LORD,

We cease not to give thanks to the Father of our Lord Jesus, by whose strength you keep the Word of his patience now in these times, when many depart from the Faith, giving heed to seducing Spirits; As also, that he who hath founded Zion, hath been pleased, by our Covenant sworn to the most high God, to lay the hopefull foundation of a glorious Work in these three Kingdoms, to unite his People therein, as one stick in the hand of the LORD.

We cannot but acknowledge to the Honour and Glory of the Lord, Wonderfull in counsell and excellent in working, that hee hath strongly united the spirits of all the godly in this Kingdom, and of his Servants in the Ministery, first in the severall Presbyteries and Synods, and now in this Nationall Assembly, in an unanimous and constant adhering to our first Principles and the Solemn League and Covenant, And particularly in giving a testimony against the present unlawfull Engagement in War: Yet it semeth good to the LORD who hath his Fire in Zion and Furnace in Jerusalem, for the purging of the vessels of his house to suffer many adversaries to arise with violence to obstruct and stop this great and effectuall door, which the Lord hath opened unto us. But we know that he openeth, and no man shutteth, and shutteth, and no man openeth: yea, he will cause them who say they are for the Covenant and are not, but are Enemies thereto, and do associate with Malignants or Sectaries, to acknowledge that God hath loved us, and that his truth is in us and with us. And now dearly beloved, seeing the Lord hath kept you together so many years, when the battel of the Warriour hath been with confused noise, and garments rolled in blood, the Lord also sitting as a refiner to purifie the Sons of Levi, and blessing you with unity and soundnesse in the Faith, we are confident you will not cease to give a publick testimony for Christ, both against Sectaries and all Seducers, who prophecie lies in the name of the LORD, and against Malignants and Incendiaries (the Prelaticall and Popish Faction) who now again bestir themselves to hold up the rotten and tottering throne of Antichrist, and are (whatever they pretend) the reall enemies of Reformation: As also, that as the Embassadors of Jesus Christ and his Watchmen, you will give seasonable warning to the Honourable Houses of Parliament, that now (after the losse of the opportunity of so many years) they would, in their places, repair the Houses of the LORD, that lyeth so long desolate, and promove the work of Reformation and Uniformity according to the Covenant.

For if the Honourable Houses of Parliament had timely made use of that power, which God hath put in their hands for suppressing of Sectaries, and had taken a speedy course for setling of Presbyterial Government, (a speciall and effectuall means appointed by God to purge his Church from all scandals in Doctrine and Practise) Then had not the insolencie of that party arisen to such a height, as to give occasion to the Malignants of both Kingdoms to justifie and blesse themselves in their old opposition to the work of Reformation, and to encourage one another, to new and more dangerous attempts; Neither had the Malignant party ever grown so strong in this Kingdom, if the Sectaries had not been connived at in ENGLAND; For their prime pretence (for their present rising in Armes) is, that they may suppress the Sectaries, and vindicate the King from that base condition, unto which he is brought by that party: Yet these do not wisely, nor well, who avoiding or opposing Sectarisme, split themselves upon the rock of Malignancy, and by taking that party by the hand how, do own all the cruelty, bloodshed and other ungodly and unjust Acts, which they have done since the beginning of this Reformation. And as we take thankfully your testimony of your steering so steady & even a course between the dangerous rocks of Prophanesse and Malignancy on the one hand, and of Errours, Schisme, Heresie and Blasphemy on the other hand; So we trust ye will not cease to give testimony against both these evils, and represent the same to the Honourable Houses of Parliament, as you shall have fit occasion; And that you will gravely warne your dissenting Brethren what a door they keep open for Errors, and Heresies, by their tenet of Independency; Whereby they leave no means of Authoritative Ecclesiastick Suppression of Errours; If an Independent Congregation will please to own them. We also are confident that you will be remembrancers to that famous City of London, and the whole Kingdom, of their Engagement to the LORD, in the solemn League and Covenant: Nor will we suffer our selves to believe that the wel-affected in the Houses of Parliament, In the City of London, and throughout that whole Kingdom will agree or harken to the motions of any such Treaty of Peace, as leaves out the best security for Religion, the Cause of GOD, and the solemn League and Covenant. Thus desiring the continuance of your Prayers to God for us, in this hour of temptation; and promising (through his grace and strength) to continue in prayers for you, We commit you to the infinite Wisdom, Power, Goodnesse, and Faithfulnesse of our blessed God and Father in Christ, in whom we are,

2. August 1648.

Your very loving and affectionate Brethren to serve you,

DIRECT

To the Right Honourable, And Right Reverend the Assembly of Divines in England now assembled at Westminster.

The Ministers and Elders conveened in the Generall Assembly of the Kirk of Scotland.

EODEM DIE POSTMERIDIEM, SESS. 25.

THE HUMBLE SUPPLICATION OF THE GENERALL ASSEMBLY, TO THE RIGHT HONOURABLE THE COMMITTEE OF ESTATES.

Whereas the High and Honourable Court of Parliament and your Lordships were pleased to injoyn the subscription of a Declaration and Band of the date June 10. 1648. And we having found after such examination and tryal, as is competent to the Servants of God in an Ecclesiastick way, that the same is a snare to the Consciences of the People of GOD in this Land to involve them in guiltinesse, and to draw them from their former principles and Vows in the solemn League and Covenant, as doth more fully appear in our Act concerning the same herewith presented unto your Lordships. Therefore from our zeal to the glory of GOD and tender care of the souls committed unto us; and for our exonoration, As we do seriously exhort that your Lordships would be sensible of the guilt that you have already brought upon your selves and others, by injoyning and urging that subscription, So we do earnestly and in the bowels of Jesus Christ intreat, That your Lordships would take such order and course as that it may be no further pressed upon the people of GOD throughout the Land.

And because the people groan under the violence and oppression of Officers and Souldiers in their Quarterings of otherwise throughout all the corners of the Countrey (which as it hath ascended into the ears of the Lord of Hosts, so we doubt not but it is come to your knowledge) We conceive it to be incumbent to us to represent the same to your Lordships, beseeching and obtesting you that as you would not desire that the Lord should visit because of these things, you would think upon an effectuall remedy for punishing and redressing what is past, and preventing the like in time coming.

And whereas by an Act and inhibition of your Lordships The Liberty of Printing being one of the Kirks Priviledges confirmed by Parliament is restrained, Therefore we intreat that the inhibition upon the Printers may be taken off.

And now having condiscended upon a Declaration to all the Members of this Kirk concerning present dangers & duties, We do in all humility offer the same to your Lordships (together with our Answer to the Paper last sent to us from your Lordships) professing in the sight of GOD (whose Servants we are) that we have walked herein according to the rule of his Word, and have nothing before our eyes but his Glory, and the well of his People, And therefore intreats your Lordships, that you would seriously ponder the same without prejudice, and as you desire to be comforted in the day of your accompts, to make right use of the light that is holden forth therein from Gods Word.

AUGUST 3. 1648. ANTEMERIDIEM, SESS. 26.

ACT FOR CENSURING MINISTERS FOR THEIR SILENCE, AND NOT SPEAKING TO THE CORRUPTIONS OF THE TIME.

The Generall Assembly, taking to their serious consideration, the great scandals which have lately encreased, partly through some Ministers their reserving and not declaring of themselves against the prevalent sins of the times, partly through the spite, Malignity, and insolency of others against such Ministers as have faithfully and freely reproved the Sins of the times without respect of persons, Do therefore for preventing and removing such scandals hereafter, Appoint and Ordain, that every Minister do by the word of Wisdom apply his Doctrine faithfully against the publick Sins and Corruptions of these times, and particularly against the Sins and Scandals in that Congregation wherein he lives, according to the Act of the Generall Assembly 1596. revived by the Assembly at Glasgow, 1638. Appointing that such as shall be found not applying their Doctrine to corruptions, which is the Pastorall gift, cold, and wanting of Spirituall zeal, flatters and dissembling of publick sins, and especially of great Personages in their Congregations, that all such persons be censured according to the degree of their faults and continuing therein be deprived; And according to the Act of the Generall Assembly 1646. Sess. 10. That beside all other scandals, silence, or ambiguous speaking in the publike Cause much more detracting and disaffected speeches be seasonably censured; As therefore the Errours and exorbitancies of Sectaries in England are not to be passed in silence, but plain warning to be given of the danger of so near a contagion, that people may beware of it, and such as neglect this duty to be Censured by their Presbyteries, So it is thought fit and Appointted by the Assembly, conform to the foresaid Acts. That the main current of applications in Sermons may run along against the evils that prevail at home, and namely against the contempt of the Word, against all profanesse, against the present defection from the League and Covenant, against the unlawful Engagement in War, against the unlawful Band and Declaration of the Date of the 10. of June ordained to be subscribed by all the Subjects, and other unjust Decrees established by Law, against the Plots and Practises of Malignants, and against the Principles and Tenents of Erastianism, which spread among divers in this Kingdom; For the better confutation whereof, it is hereby Recommended to the Ministery to study that point of controversie well, that they may be the more able to stop the mouths of gainsayers: Tis also hereby Recommended to the several Presbyteries and Provincial Synods, that they make special enquiry and trial concerning all the Ministery in their bounds, And if any be found too sparing general, or ambiguous in the foresaid applications and reproofs that they be sharply rebuked, dealt with, and warned to amend under the pain of suspension from their Ministery; And if after such warning given they amend not, that such be suspended by Presbyteries, and in case of their negligence by the Synods till the next General Assembly; But if there be any, who do neglect and omit such applications and reproofs, and continue in such negligence after admonition and dealing with them, they are to be cited, and after due triall of the offence to be deposed, for being pleasers of men rather then servants of Christ, for giving themselves to a detestable indifferency or neutrality in the Cause of God, &c. for defrauding the souls of people, yea for being highly guilty of the blood of souls in not giving them warning: Much more are such Ministers to be censured with Deposition from their Ministry who preach for the lawfulnes or pray for the success of the present unlawfull Engagement, or that go along with the Army themselves, or who subscribe any Bands or take any Oaths not approved by the General Assembly or their Commissioners, or by their counsel, countenance or approbation make themselves accessory to the taking of such Bands and Oaths by others: It is to be understood that if any Minister preach in defence of or pray for the successe of the Sectaries in England, he is likewayes to be censured by deposition. And this we adde as a generall rule to be observed on both hands, but not as if we had found any of the Ministery of this Kingdom to be favourers of the Sectaries in England:

And in case any Minister for his freedom in preaching, and faithfull discharge of his conscience shall be in the face of the Congregation or elsewhere upbraided, railed at, mocked, or threatened, or if any injury or violence be done to his person, or any stop and disturbance made to him in the exercise of his Ministeriall calling, The Presbyterie of the bounds shall forthwith enter in processe with the offender, and whoever he be Charge him to satisfie the Discipline of the Kirk by publick Repentance, which if any do not, or refuse to do, That then the Presbyterie proceed to Excommunication against him; In all which Presbyteries and Synods are to give an account of their diligence: And the Assembly Appoints this Act to be intimate in the several Congregations of this Kirk.

AUGUST 4. 1648. POSTMERIDIEM, SESS. 21.

OVERTURES CONCERNING THE EDUCATION OF THE HIE-LAND BOYS IN THE PROVINCE OF ARGYLE.

This day the report following being made from the Committee concerning the education of Hie-land Boys in Argyle, viz.

The Committee considering the Bill remitted by the Generall Assembly to us concerning the Hie-land Boys (who are given up to be fourty in number of good spirits and approven by the Province of Argyle) Do humbly think, that four of them who are ready for the Colledge should be recommended to the Universities to get Burses on in every Colledge. As for the rest of the 40, who are to be brought up at Grammar Schools, The Committee thinks that if the said Boys should be scattered through the Kingdom they should lose the Irish Language, and so the Assembly shall fail of their purpose to make them usefull for the Hie-lands: And therefore do humbly conceive that it were fitting that every Congregation pay yearly fourty Shillings Scots for maintaining the said Boys at Schools in Glasgow, or in other places where many of them may be together accepted of, and that the money be brought in yearly to the General Assembly by the Commissioners of Presbyteries, and that Presbyteries augment or diminish the said proportion according to the ability of every Congregation.

The Assembly having considered the foresaid Report, Approves the first Overture, And recommends *Colin Campbell* to the University of *Aberdeen*, *Duncan Campbell* to *Edinburgh*, *Patrick Campbell* to *Glasgow*, *Zachary Maccullum* to St. *Leonards* Colledge in St. *Andrews*: As also Approve the second Overture, seriously Recommending to Presbyteries, That the said fourty shillings be collected carefully and sent to *Glasgow*, And the Ministers of *Glasgow* shall appoint some sufficient man in that Town to receive the said Collection from Presbyteries, And to take charge of the boording and entertainment of the saids Boys in *Glasgow* at Schooles, and they shall send in the names of the Boys with a Certificate of their proficiency yearly to the Generall Assembly: And this Collection shall onely endure for the space of twelve years.

AUGUST 5. 1648. ANTEMERIDIEM, SESS. 30.

EXPLANATION OF THE FIFTH ARTICLE OF THE OVER-TURES CONCERNING APPEALS PAST IN THE ASSEMBLY, 1643.

The Generall Assembly for clearing the sense of the fifth Article of the Over-tures concerning Appeals in the Assembly, *1643. Sess.* 2 Declare, that if Appella-tions, *Post latam sententiam* be not presented to the Judicatory when the sentence is pronounced: The party shall then immediately after the sentence protest for liberty of Appeal, as he shall see cause; And accordingly within ten dayes shall give in his Appeal in writ under his hand, either to the Judicatory or the Moderator thereof, otherwise the Appeal is not to be respected.

EODEM DIE 1648. ANTEMERIDIEM, SESS. 30.

ACT DISCHARGING DEPOSED OR SUSPENDED MIN-ISTERS FROM ANY EXERCISE OF THE MINISTERY, OR MEDLING WITH THE STIPEND.

The Generall Assembly considering that according to the ancient practise and order of this Kirk, the Censure of Suspension and Deposition of Ministers is both ab officio and â beuoficio, as is also acknowledged by the 20. Act of the Parliament, Anno 1644. And that the continuance of suspended or deposed Ministers in the exercise of the Ministery or in the possession of their stipend hath been & ought to be accompted and censured as a great contempt of the Authority and Censures of the Kirk, Considering also that the continuance of deposed Ministers in the possession of the stipend, is a great prejudice and obstruction to the planting of the vaiking Kirk, and to the service of God there. Therefore do declare and Or-dain, That whosoever after the sentence of Deposition pronounced against them, Do either exercise any part of the Ministeriall calling in the places they formerly served in; or elsewhere, or do possesse, meddle, or intromet with the stipend or other benefits whatsoever belonging to these Kirks they served at, They shall be proceeded against with Excommunication; And if any suspended Minister during his suspension, either exercise any part of the Ministeriall Calling, or intromet with the Stipend, That he be Deposed, And after deposition, continuing in either of these faults, That he be processed with Excommunication; But prejudice always to them of their stipend resting for by-gone service and of any recompence due for building or repairing of the Manse according to the ordinary practise. And the Assembly recommends to Presbyteries seriously to be carefull of the putting of this Act in execution.

AUGUST 7. 1648. ANTEMERIDIEM. SESS 31.

THE ASSEMBLIES DECLARATION OF THE FALSEHOOD AND FORGERIE OF A LYING SCANDALOUS PAMPHLET PUT FORTH UNDER THE NAME OF THEIR REVEREND BROTHER MASTR ALEXANDER HENDERSON AFTER HES DEATH.

The Generall Assembly of this Kirk having seen a Printed Paper, Intituled, The Declaration of Mr. Alexander Henderson principall Minister of the Word of GOD at Edinburgh and chief Commissioner from the Kirk of Scotland to the Parliament and Synod of England made upon his death-bed. And taking into their serious consideration how many grosse lies and impudent calumnies are therein contained; Out of the tender respect which they do bear to his name (which ought to be very precious to them and all posterity, for his faithfull service in the great Work of Reformation in these Kingdoms, wherein the Lord was pleased to make him eminently instrumentall) and lest through the malice of some, and ignorance of others the said Pamphlet should gain belief among the weaker sort, They have thought fit to make known and declare concerning the same as followeth.

That after due search and tryall they do finde that their worthy brother Master Alexander Henderson did from the time of his coming from London to Newcastle til the last moment of his departure out of this life upon all occasions manifest the constancy of his judgement touching the Work of Reformation in these Kingdoms; Namely, in all his discourses and conferences with his Majesty, and with his Brethren who were employed with him in the same Trust at Newcastle, In his Letters to the Commissioners at London, and particularly in his last discourse to his Majestie at his departing from Newcastle, being very weak and greatly decayed in his Naturall strength. When he was come from Newcastle by sea to this Kingdom, he was in such a weak worn and failed condition, as it was evident to all who saw him, that he was not able to frame any such Declaration, for he was so spent that he died within eight dayes after his arrivall; And all that he was able to speak in that time did clearly shew his judgement of, and affection to the Work of Reformation and Cause of God to be every way the same then, that it was in the beginning and progresse thereof, as divers Reverend Brethren who visited him have declared to this Assembly, and particularly two Brethren, who constantly attended him from the time he came home till his breath expired. A further testimony may be brought from a short Confession of Faith under his hand found amongst his Papers, which is expressed as his last Words, wherein among other mercies he declareth himself most of all obliged to the grace and goodnesse of God for calling him to believe the Promises of the Gospel, and for exalting him to be a Preacher of them to others, and to be a willing though weak instrument in this great and wonderful work of Reformation, which he earnestly beseecheth the Lord to bring to a happy conclusion. Other reasons may be added from the levity of the stile and manifest absurdities contained in that Paper. Upon confederation of all which this Assembly doth condemn the said Pamphlet as forged, scandalous, and false, And further Declare the author and contriver of the same void of charity and a good conscience, and a grosse lyar and calumniator led by the Spirit of the accuser of the Brethren.

ACT FOR TAKING THE COVENANT AT THE FIRST RECEIVING OF THE SACRAMENT OF THE LORDS SUPPER, & FOR THE RECEIVING OF IT ALSO BY ALL STUDENTS AT THEIR FIRST ENTRY TO COLLEDGES.

The Generall Assembly according to former recommendations, Doth Ordain that all young Students take the Covenant at their first entry to Colledges; And that hereafter all Persons whatsoever take the Covenant at their first receiving the Sacrament of the Lords Supper: Requiring hereby Provinciall Assemblies, Presbyteries and Universities to be carefull that this Act be observed, and accompt thereof taken in the visitation of and particular Kirks, and in the tryall of Presbyteries.

EODEM DIE POSTMERIDIEM, SESS. 32.

ACT CONCERNING PRESBYTERIES MAINTAINING OF BURSARS.

The Generall Assembly Understanding that the frequent Recommendation of preceding Assemblies for maintaining Bursars, is by many Presbyteries neglected, Do therefore Ordain Synods to crave accompt thereof from Presbyteries at every Provinciall meeting, Which with the Presbyteries answer, shall be put upon record, That so the part both of Presbyteries and Synods and their negligance or diligence in so pious a work may be known by the examination of the Provinciall books to each Generall Assembly.

AUGUST 9. 1648. ANTEMERIDIEM SESS. 25.

ACT FOR DIS-JOYNING THE PRESBYTERIES OF ZETLAND, FROM THE PROVINCIALL SYNOD OF ORKNEY AND CATHNES.

The Generall Assembly now after exact tryall, finding that the Presbytery of Zetland cannot meet with the Provinciall of Cathnes and Orknay to which it was adjoyned by an Act of the Assembly 1646. Sess. 11. And that the allowance and dispensation granted in the preceding Assembly for the halfe of their number to keep the meetings of the said Provinciall cannot be observed in respect of the great distance of that Isle by sea from the land, and the dangerousness of the seas there, and of the passage through them, Therefore after hearing the parties interested and serious deliberation of the matter, The Assembly doth hereby Dis-joyn the Presbytery of Zetland from the Provinciall of Cathnes and Orknay, And declares for these reasons, That the said Presbytery is to be hereafter subordinate immediately to the Generall Assembly, For which cause, their Commissioners are to be sent to each Generall Assembly the more carefully, And it is hereby recommended to them that they send to the next Assembly a particular information of the quality and condition of all their Kirks according to the direction of the act of the preceding Assembly Sess. 27. Entituled an act for pressing and furthering the planting of

Kirks.

AUG. 10. 1648. POSTMERIDIEM, SESS. 38.

OVERTURES FOR THE REMEDIES OF THE GRIEVOUS AND COMMON SINS OF THE LAND IN THIS PRESENT TIME.

The Sins of the Land and the Causes and occasions thereof being considered, The following Remedies of these Sins were propounded.

Civill Remedies.

For the present, untill the Overtures prepared to be presented to the Parliament, It is to be Recommended to every Congregation to make use of the 9. Act of the Parliament 1645. at Perth, for having Magistrates and Justices in every Congregation, and of the 8. Act of the said Parliament against Swearing, Drinking and mocking of Piety, and all other Acts of Parliament for restraining or punishing of Vice; particularly for the better restraining of the sin of Whoredom that each Magistrate in every Congregation exact and make compt to the Session of fourty Pounds for each Fornicatour and Fornicatrix, of an hundred Merks for each one of their relapse in Fornication, of an hundreth Pounds for each Adulterer and Adulteress according to express Acts of Parliament which is to be exacted of these who may pay it, and the discretion of the Magistrate is to modifie it according to the ability or inability of each Delinquent.

Domestick Remedies.

1. Let care be taken of concionable receiving of Servants, that they have testimonials of their honest behaviour: And let all such as give testimonials take heed that these to whom they give them, be free of scolding, swearing, lying and such like more common sins, as well as fornication, adultery, drunkenesse, and other grosse and hainous evils; Let the ordinary time of giving Testimonials be in face of Session: And if an extraordinary exigent be: Let it be given by the Minister with consent of the elder of the bounds, wherein the person craving the Testimonial hath resided; If they have fallen or relapsed in scandalous sins, let their Testimonial bear both their fall and Repentance.

2. Let care be had that the Worship of God be practised, and Discipline exercised in Families, according to the Directory for Family Worship in all things as was appointed in the General Assembly 1647. especially in the Ministers constant Catechizing of the Family, and in the performance of the Duties of the Sabbath by all the Members thereof.

3. Let Persons to be married, and who have Children to be baptized, who are very rude and ignorant, be stirred up and exhorted, as at all times, so especially at that time, to attain some measure of Christian knowledge in the grounds of Religion, that they may give to the Minister, before the Elder of the Bounds wherein they live, some accompt of their knowledge that so they may the better teach their family and train up their Children.

4. Let every Family that hath any in it than can read, have a Bible and a Psalm-

book, and make use of them; and where none can read, let them be stirred up to traine up their children in reading, and use any other good remedie the Minister and Session can fall on.

General Ecclesiastick Remedies.

1. Let the Remedies which were given at Perth 1645. and are mentioned in the General Assembly 1646. anent the Sins of Ministers be put in execution.

2. Let suspension from the Lords Sacrament be more carefully executed.

3. Let Persons relapse in Adultery (or above) quadrilapse in fornication (or above) or often guilty of other grosser scandals, be Excommunicat somewhat more summarly nor in an ordinary processe (except there be more nor ordinary signes, and an eminent measure of Repentance made known to the Session and Presbyterie) both for the hainousness of the sins and continuance therein, and also for terrour to others; And these not to be relaxed from the sentence of Excommunication without evidence, and undeniable signes of Repentance.

4. Let unpartial proceeding be used against men of all quality, for their scandalous walking, and in particular for drunkenesse, swearing, and other scandalous sins. And this to be tryed at the Visitation of Kirk.

Particular Ecclesiastick Remedies.

And 1. against ignorance.

1. Let Ministers Catechise one day every week (whereon also they may Baptise and Lecture or Preach) and let them preach every Lords Day both before and after noon, according to former Acts of General Assemblies, Let Presbyteries and Synods be very careful of this; And let every Provincial Book, contain an exact accompt thereof.

2. Let Ministers examine all of every quality of whose knowledge they have no certain notice.

3. Let young Persons be Catechized by the Minister from the time they are capable of instruction, and let them not be delayed till they be of age to Communicat.

4. Let Persons grossly ignorant be debarred from the Communion; for the first and second time, let them be debarred, suppressing their names; for the third time, expressing their names; for the fourth time, bring them to publick repentance; all this is to be understood of those that profit nothing, and labours not for knowledge: But if they be profiting in any measure, or labouring that they may profit, their case is very considerable, they ought to have more forbearance.

2. Ecclesiastick Remedies against Prophanesse.

1. Let ignorant and scandalous Persons be put off, and kept off Kirk Sessions.

2. Let every Elder have a certain bounds assigned to him that he may visit the same every moneth at least, and report to the Session what scandals and abuses are therein, or what persons have entered without Testimonials.

3. Let all scandalous persons be suspended from the Lords Supper.

4. Let the Minister deal in private with them that are professing publick Repentance before the Elder of the bounds, thus to try the evidence of their Repentance.

5. Let these who have fallen in Fornication make publick profession of Repentance three several Sabbaths, who is guilty of relapse in Fornication six Sabbaths, who is guilty of relapse in Fornication, or hath once fallen in Adultery, 26. Sabbaths, and these sins to be confessed both in one viz. in Sackcloth, Quadrilapse in Fornication and relapse in Adultery, three quarters of a Year, Incest or Murder a Year, or 52. Sabbaths, in case the Magistrate do not his duty in punishing such crimes capitally; They that fall in Fornication or relapses therein, are first to confesse their Sin before the Session, and thereafter before the Congregation; They that are guilty of greater degrees of that Sin and of the other Sins mentioned in this Article, are to confess their Sin both before the Session & Presbyterie, and there to shew some signes of Repentance before they be brought to the Congregation.

6. Some are to be rebuked at the time of Catechising, who deserve more nor a privase reproof, and yet needs not to be brought to publick Repentance.

7. It will be a good remedie against Sabbath-breaking by Carriers and Travellers, That the Ministers where they dwell cause them to bring Testimonials from the place where they rested on these Lords dayes wherein they were from home.

8. Let all Persons who flit from one Paroch to another have sufficient Testimonials, This is to be extended to all Gentlemen and Persons of quality and all their followers, who come to reside with their Families at Edinburgh, or elswhere, and let the Minister from whom they flit, advertise the Minister to whom they flit, if (to his knowledge) they be lying under any scandal.

9. Let Ministers be free with Persons of quality for amendment of their faults, and (if need shall be) let them take help thereto of some of the Brethren of the Presbyterie.

10. Let the Presbyteries take special notice of Ministers who do converse frequently and familiarly with Malignants, and with scandalous and prophane Persons, especially such as belongs to other Paroches.

11. Let privie Censures of Presbyteries and Synods be performed with more Accuracie, Diligence and Zeal.

12. For better keeping of the Sabbath, let every Elder take notice of such as are within his bounds, how they keep the Kirk, how the time is spent before, betwixt, and after the time of publick Worship.

13. Let no Minister resort to any Excommunicate person without licence from the Presbyterie nisi in extremis, and let Ministers take special notice of such persons as haunt with Excommunicants, and processe them.

14. Frequent correspondence betwixt presbyteries is a good remedie.

15. At the visitation of each Congregation, let the Session Book be well visited, and for that effect, let it be delivered to two or three Brethren seven or eight dayes before the visitation, that their report of it may be in readinesse against the Day of Visitation.

The Assembly allows of all these Overtures and Remedies of the Sins of the Land; And Ordains all of them to be carefully and conscionably put in practise.

ACT FOR EXAMINING THE PARAPHRASE OF THE PSALMS AND OTHER SCRIPTURALL SONGS.

The Generall Assembly Appoints *Rouse* Paraphrase of the Psalms, with the corrections thereof now given in by the persons appointed by the last Assembly for that purpose, to be sent to Presbyteries, That they may carefully revise and examine the same, and thereafter send them with their corrections to the Commission of this Assembly to be appointed for publick affairs, Who are to have a care to cause reexamine the Animadversions of Presbyteries, and prepare a report to the next Generall Assembly; Intimating hereby, That if Presbyteries be negligent hereof the next General Assembly is to go on & take the same Paraphrase to their consideration without more delay: And the Assembly Recommends to Master *John Adamson* and Mr. *Thomas Crafurd* to revise the Labours of Mr. *Zachary Boyd* upon the other Scripturall Songs, and to prepare a report thereof to the said Commission for publick affairs, That after their examination, the same may be also reported to the next Generall Assembly.

OVERTURES CONCERNING PAPISTS, THEIR CHILDREN, AND EXCOMMUNICATE PERSONS.

The Generall Assembly considering the manifold inconveniences that follow upon the sending of the children of Noblemen and others of quality to Forraign Countries wherein Popery is professed, especially that thereby such children are in perill to be corrupted with Popery, and so corrupt these Families and Persons to which they belong, whereby that wicked root of damnable Idolatry, Errour and Heresie may again be occasioned to spring up and trouble many, and provoke the most High GOD to wrath, and to cause his Majestie leave this Land to strong delusions to believe lies; Therefore They Do in the name of GOD, Charge and Require all the Presbyteries of this Kingdom to observe and practice the Rules and Directions which are made in former Generall Assemblies for preventing of the said fearfull inconveniences, and namely the Overtures against Papists, non-Communicants, and Profaners of the Sabbath approven in the Generall Assembly held at St. Andrews in the year of God, 1642. and the Act anent children sent without the Kingdom made in the Generall Assembly at Edinburgh, Anno 1646. And that they use all diligence for putting in execution the Acts of Parliament and secret Councell made against Papists & Excommunicate Persons; And that they register their diligences thereanent in their Presbyterie Booke which are summarily to be recorded in the Synod Books from time to time, That the Generall Assembly may see how these laudable Acts are put in execution, which here are presented with some necessary additions in one view.

1. That every Presbyterie give a List of all Excommunicate Papists they know to be within their bounds to the Commissioners of the Generall Assembly, and of all Papists; yea of them also who professe to have renounced Popery, but yet have their children educated abroad, with the names of these children that are abroad, according to the fifth Overture of the Generall Assembly, 1642.

2. That every Presbyterie conveen at their first meeting all known Papists within their bounds, and such as having professed to renounce Popery have their children abroad, and cause them finde sufficient caution for bringing home within three moneths such of their children as are without the Kingdom; to be educated in Schools and Colledges at the Presbyteries sight if they be Minors; and to be wrought upon by gracious conference, & other means of instruction to be reclaimed from Popery if they be come to perfect age.

3. The Parents, Tutors or Frinds of Children and Minors shall, before they send them without the Kingdom, first acquaint the Presbyterie where they reside, that they may have their Testimoniall directed to the Presbyterie or Classe within the Kingdom or Dominion beyond Seas whither they intend to send their Children; And at the time of these Childrens return, that they report a Testimoniall from the Presbyterie or Synod where they lived without the Kingdom, to the Presbyterie who gave them a Testimonial at their going away, according to the Act anent Children sent without the Kingdom Anno 1646.

4. That all Presbyteries give the names of such Pædagogs as were abroad with the children of Noblemen within there bounds, and diligently enquire whether these Pædagogs do continue stedfast in the true Religion, and continue in their service, or whither these Pædagogs do either become corrupt in Religion, or (continuing constant) are removed from their charge and by whom they are removed, and that they signifie these things to the Generall Assembly from time to time or their Commissioners, That they may represent the same to the High Court of Parliament, Lords of secret Counsell or Committe of Estates, for such remedie as shall seem expedient to their Honours, for preventing of and purging the land from the plague of Idolatrie.

5. That such Parents, Tutors or Friends as either send away Children to forraign parts infected with Idolatry without such Testimonialls as aforesaid, or do not recall them who are already abroad within such time as is above prefixed, or do remove from them their Protestant Pædagogs (that they may the more easily be infected with Popery) be processed and in case of not amending these things, be Excommunicated.

6. That the names of such as are Excommunicated for these or any other causes, be sent in to the Generall Assembly from year to year, that (from thence) their names may be notified in all the Kingdom, and that the Acts of Parliament and secret Counsell may be put to execution against them, and all diligence used for that effect; and that by the effectuall dealing of the Generall Assembly, with the Parliament, Lords of secret Counsell, or Committee of Estates, their Lordships may Enact such further, just and severe civill Punishment on such Excommunicants for Terror to others, as shall be found necessary for purging this Covenanted Land from all Abominations.

Because persons addicted to Idolatry will use all means for their own hardening in their Superstitious and Idolatrous way, even within the Countrey; Therefore all known Papists, or persons suspect of Poperie upon probable grounds are to finde Caution before their Presbyteries, for their abstinence from Masse, and from the Company of all Jesuits, and Priests according to the second Overture against Papists, made Anno 1642. Also Presbyteries are to presse them to finde such Caution; And to observe what persons put their Sons or Daughters to such Families as are tainted with Popery within the Land, the same being a speciall mean to corrupt them with Idolatry, And to cause such Parents recall their Children, or else proceed with the Censures of the Kirk against them.

All which Overtures, Presbyteries are seriously required and Ordained to observe diligently with Certification, That they shall be severely censured, If they shall be found remisse or negligent in any of these points, which are so necessary for keeping of the Lords House and People unpoluted with Error, Idolatry, or Superstition.

AUG. 11. 1648 ANTEMERIDIEM, SESS. 39.

ACT FOR PROSECUTING THE TREATY FOR THE UNIFORMITY IN RELIGION IN THE KINGDOM OF ENGLAND.

The Generall Assembly, Taking to their consideration that the Treaty of Uniformity in Religion in all His Majesties Dominions is not yet perfected; Therefore, Renews the power and Commission granted by preceeding Assemblies for prosecuting that Treaty unto these Persons after-named viz. Mr Robert Douglas, Mr Samuel Rutherford, Mr Robert Baillie, Mr George Gillespie, Ministers. And John Earle of Cassils, John Lord Balmerinoch, and Sir. Arch. Johnston of Wariston Elders; Authorizing them with full power to prosecute the said Treaty of Uniformity with the Honourable Houses of the Parliament of England, and the Reverend Assembly of Divines there, or any Committees Appointed by them: And to do all and every thing which may advance, perfect, and bring that Treaty to an happie conclusion, conform to the Commissions given thereanent.

ACT RENEWING THE COMMISSION FOR THE PUBLICK AFFAIRS OF THIS KIRK.

The Generall Assembly Taking to their consideration, that in respect the great work of Uniformity in Religion in all his Majesties Dominions is not yet perfected (though by the Lords blessing there is a good progress made in the same) There is a necessity of renewing the Commissions granted formerly for prosecuting and perfecting that great Work; Do therefore Renew the Power and Commission granted for the Publick Affairs of the Kirk by the Generall Assemblies held at Saint Andrews, 1642. and at Edinburgh 1643. 1644. 1645. 1646. and 1647. unto the persons following viz Masters, John Lawder, Andrew Wood, David Calderwood, Robert Ker, John Mackghie, John Knox, John Sinclar, John Adamson, Robert Dowglas, George Gillespie, James Hamiltoun, Mungo Law, John Smith, Robert Lawrie, George Lesly, John Weir, Robert Eliot, Alexander Dickson, Patrick Fleeming, Thomas Vassie, Ephraim Melvil, Hew Kennedie, Kenneth Logie, Alexander Levistoun, George Bennet, David Weems, William Row, Robert Young, William Menzies, John Friebaine, John Givan, Harie Guthrie, Andrew Rind, David Auchterlony, Samuel Ousteen, Thomas Henderson, Charles Archibald, Andrew Lawder,

John Leviston, John Macklellan, Alexander Turnbull, William Fullerton, George Hutcheson, John Genell, Patrick Colvill, James Ferguson, Hew Peebles, John Hamiltoun, Alexander Dunlope, David Elphiston, David Dickson, Robert Baillie, Robert Ramsay, Patrick Gillespie, Patrick Sharpe, James Nasunth, John Home, Evan Camron, Robert Blair, Samuel Rutherfurd, David Forret, Robert Traill, Andrew Bennett, Walter Greg, John Macgill younger, John Moncreiff, Fredrick Carmichael, John Chalmers, John Duncan, Andrew Donaldson, Will Oliphant, George Simmer, Andrew Affleck, Arthur Granger, David Strachen, Andrew Cant, John Rex, John Paterson, Alexander Cant, John Young, John Seaton, David Lindsay at Bethelvie, Nothaniel Martine, John Annand, William Falconer, Joseph Brodie, Alexander Summer, William Chalmer, Gilbert Anderson, David Rosse, George Gray, Robert Knox, William Penman, James Guthrie, Thomas Donaldson, William Jameson, Thomas Wilkie, James Ker, John Knox, Andrew Dunkanson Ministers: Archibald Marques of Argyle, Alexander Earle of Eglintoun, John Earle of Cassils. William Earle of Lothian, Archibald Lord Angus, William Lord Borthwick, John Lord Torphichen, John Lord Balmerino, Robert Lord Burly, James Lord Couper, Lord Kilcudbright, Alexander Lord Elcho, Sir Archibald Johnstoun of Wariston. Sir John Hope of Craighall, Arthur Erskin of Scotskraig, Sir John Moncreiff of that Ilk, Boaton of Creigh, Sir John Wauchhope of Midrie, Sir Thomas Ruthven of Frieland, Sir George Maxwell of Netherpollock, Sir James Fraser of Brae, Sir James Hackact of Pitfirn, Sir William Carmichaell younger of that ilk, Walter Dundas younger of that ilk, Thomas Craig of Ricarton, Mr George Winrain of Liberton, Sir Alexander Ingils of Ingilston, Alexander Brodie of that ilk, Forbes of Eight, Will. More of Glanderston, John Ker of Lochtour, Alex Pringill of Whitbanck, Walter Scot of Whitstyid, John Crafurd of Crafurdland, Sir John Chisly of Carswell, Robert Monroe of Obsteall, Cornwall of Bonhard, George Dundas of Dudingston, Sir James Stewart of Kirkfield, Alexander Colvil of the Blair, Mr Alex. Petrson, Mr Robert Burnet younger, Mr Thomas Murray, George Potterfield, Mr James Campbell, James Hamilton, Lawrence Henderson, Mr Robert Barcclay, Mr William More, William Glendoning Doctor, Douglas, James Sword, Gideon Lack, Mr Dongall Campbell, John Besrall, John Brown, William Brown, Robert Brown, and William Russel, Elders: Giving unto them full Power and Commission, to do all and every thing for preservation of the Established Doctrine, Discipline, Worship and Government of this Kirk, against all who shall endeavour to introduce any thing contrary thereunto, and for prosecuting, advancing, perfecting & bringing the said Work of Uniformity in Religion in all His Majesties Dominions to a happy conclusion, conform to the former Commissions granted by proceeding Assemblies thereanent, And to that effect Appoints them, or any seventeen of them, whereof thirteen shall be Ministers to meet here in this City to morrow the 12. of this Moneth, And thereafter upon the last Wednesday of November, February, and May next, and upon any other day, and in any other place they shall think fit. Renewing also to the persons before named the power contained in the Act of the Assembly 1643. Intituled, A Reference to the Commission anent the Persons designed to repair to the Kingdom of England. And further, incase Delinquents have no constant residence in any one Presbyterie, or if Presbyteries be negligent or overawed, in these cases, The Assembly gives to the persons before named, such power of censuring complyers and persons disaffected to the Covenant according to the Acts of the Assembly, declaring alwayes and providing, that Ministers shall not be deposed, but in one of the quarterly meetings of this Commission, And further Authorises them as formerly with full power to make Supplications, Remonstrances, Declarations & Warnings to Indict Fasts & Thanksgivings as there shall be cause to Protest against all encroachments upon the Liberties of the Kirk, and to censure all such as interupt this Commission or any other Church Judicatory, or the execution of their Censures or of any other Sentences or Acts, issuing from them, And with full power to them to treat and determine in the matters referred unto them by this Assembly, as fully and freely as if the same were here fully expressed, and with as ample power as any Commission of any former Generall Assemblies hath had or been in use of before: Declaring also that all opposers of the authority of this Commission in matters intrusted to them shall be holden as opposers of the authority of the Generall Assembly, And this Commission in their whole proceedings are comptable to, and censurable by the next General Assembly.

AUGUST 11. 1643. POSTMERIDIEM, SESS. 40.

EXEMPTION OF MURRAY, ROSSE, AND CAITHNESSE FROM THE CONTRIBUTION GRANTED TO THE BOYES OF ARGYLE, WITH A RECOMMENDATION TO PRESBYTERIES, TO MAKE UP WHAT IS TAKEN OF THEM BY THAT EXEMPTION.

Concerning the overtture and desire of the Commissioners of the Presbyteries of Murray, Rosse, and Caithnesse for an exemption from that contribution of fourty shillings recommended for entertainment of the Irish boyes in Argyle; The Assembly having considered thereof, and of their offer in the the name of the said Presbyteries, if that exemption be granted, Do Approve their offer, And Therefore hereby Exoners the said Presbyteries of the said contribution of fourty shillings toward the entertainment of the boyes in Argyle, And Ordains for that exemption according to the offer of their said Commissioners, that each Presbyterie of the said Provinces entertaine one of the Irish language at Schooles, and if any be found already fit for Colledges, they shall maintain them at Philosophie, and so forward, untill they be fit for the Ministery: And Because by this exemption the contribution for the boyes in Argyle will be so much lessened. Therefore the Assembly Recommends to all other Presbyteries to think upon some way how by the charitable Supply that may be made up unto them.

ACT CONCERNING COLLECTION FOR THE POOR.

The Assembly Understanding that the collection for the poor in some Kirks in the Countrey, are taken in the time of Divine Service, which being, a very great and unseemly disturbance of Divine Worship Do therefore hereby Inhibit and discharge the same. And ordains that the Minister and Session appoint some other way and time for receiving the said Collections.

RECOMMENDATION FOR SECURING PROVISIONS TO

MINISTERS IN BURGHS.

In regard that the stipends of many Ministers in Burghs are not secured unto them and their successors; Therefore the Assembly Do seriously Recommend to the Honourable Commission of Parliament for planting of Kirks, to provide reall and valide security of competent and honest meanes to the present Ministers of Burghs and their successors; where they are not sufficiently provided or secured already; Ordaining Presbyteries to use all necessary diligence for prosecuting thereof before the said Commission for planting Kirks.

THE HUMBLE SUPPLICATION OF THE GENERALL ASSEM-BLY OF THE KIRK OF SCOTLAND, MET AT EDINBURG AU-GUST 12 UNTO THE KINGS MOST EXCELLENT MAJESTE.

Albeit your Majestie through the suggestions of evil men, may haply entertain hard thoughts of us and our Proceedings, yet the Searcher of hearts knowes, and our consciences bear record unto us, that we bear in our spirits these humble and duitifull respects to your Majestie, that loyall subjects owe to their native Soveraigne, and that it would be one of our greatest contentments upon earth, to see your Majestie reigning for the LORD, in Righteousnesse and Peace over these Nations: And therefore as we do bow our knees daily before the Throne of Grace on your behalf, and the behalf of your Posterity; So we finde our selves as heretofore, obliged faithfully and freely to warn your Majestie of your danger and dutie; Wishing, and hoping that the Lord will incline your Royall heart, from the sence of the evil which hath befallen You, through the slighting of former Warning, to be more attentive unto this. We are very sensible of your Majesties suffering, and low condition, and do not in the least measure approve but from our hearts abhorre any thing that hath been done to your Majesties Person, contrary to the common resolutions of both Kingdoms: Yet it shall be your Majesties wisdom, in this as in all that hath befallen you these years past, to read the righteous hand of the Lord, writing bitter things against you, as for all your Provocations, so especially for resisting his Work, and authorising by your Commissions the shedding of the blood of his People, for which it is high time to repent, that there be no more wrath against you and your Realms.

The Commission of the preceding Assembly, whose proceedings are unanimously approven by this Assembly, Having read your Majesties Letter of the date at Carisbrook Castle, December 27. And perused your Concessions, did finde some of these Concessions destructive to the Covenant, and all or them unsatisfactorie, and did therefore emit a Declaration concerning the same, least your Majesties Subjects in this Kingdom should have unawares imbarked themselves in an Engagement upon grounds·not consisting with the good of Religion, and the Solemn League and Covenant. For preventing whereof, they did also present most just and necessary desires unto the high and Honourable Court of Parliament of this Kingdom; which, if they had been granted, might have through the Blessing of God, either procured (upon Treaty) your Majesties re-establishment, and a solide Peace, or laid open the expedience and necessity of a lawfull War, and have united this Kingdom therein for the good of Religion, of your Majestie, and of your

Kingdoms. When the Parliament was pleased without satisfaction to any of these desires, to go on towards the determining of a War upon the grounds contained in their Declaration, As many of their own Members who have been faithfull in the Cause of GOD from the beginning, did dissent from their preceedings, so most of all the Presbyteries and Synods of this Kingdom, and the Committees of War in severall Shires did by humble Supplication represent to the Parliament, how unsatisfied they were in their consciences concerning the present Engagement: Notwithstanding of all which, the Engagement hath been carried on without clearing either of the lawfulnesse or necessity thereof. Therefore, We having now examined the same by the Rule of Gods Word, and having found it unlawfull, as we have warned the whole Kingdom of the danger thereof, So we hold it our Duty also to warne your Majestie as the Servants of the most High GOD, and in Name of the Lord Jesus Christ, who must Judge the quick and dead, Earnestly beseeching your Majestie that as ye would not draw new guilt upon your Majesties Throne, and make these Kingdoms again a field of Blood, you would be far from owning or having any hand in this so unlawfull an Engagement; Which as it hath already been the cause of so much sorrow and many sufferings to the People of God in this Land, who choose affliction rather then sin, So it tendeth to the undoing of the Covenant and Work of Reformation: As we do not oppose the restitution of your Majestie to the exercise of your Royall Power; So we must needs desire that that which is GODS be given unto Him in the first place, and that Religion may be secured before the setling of any humane interest; Being confident that this way is not only most for the Honour of GOD, but also for your Majesties Honor and Safety. And therefore as it was one of our Desires to the High and Honourable Court of Parliament that they would solicitie your Majestie for securing of Religion, and establishing the Solemn League and Covenant in all your Dominions, that your Majestie might know what they intend on your behalf was with a subordination to Religion; So we do now from our selves make this humble address unto your Majestie, intreating your Majestie as you tender Truth and Peace, you would be pleased to suffer your self to be possessed with right thoughts of the League and Covenant, and of the proceedings of your Majesties loyall Subjects in relation thereunto, and give your Royall assent for injoyning of it in all your Dominions. If your Majestie had been pleased to hearken to our Counsell heranent some years ago, the blood of many thousands, which now lyes upon your Majesties Throne, might have been spared, Popery, Prelacy, Idolatry, Superstition, Profanesse, Heresie, Error, Sects, and Schismes which are now grown to so great a height in England, might have been extirpate, and your Majestie sitting in Peace in your own House, Reigning over your Subjects with much mutuall contentment and confidence. And if your Majestie shall yet search out and repent of all your secret and open Sins, And after so many dear-bought experiences of the danger of evill Counsell, be now so wise as to avoid it, and to hearken to us speaking unto you in the Name of the Lord, We are confident by this means your Majestie may yet be restored, and a sure and firme peace procured. We take it as a great mercy, and as a door of hope, that God still inclines the hearts of all his Servants to pray for your Majestie; And we would not have your Majestie to look upon it as a light thing, that you have been preserved alive, when many thousands have by your means and procurement fallen on your right hand and on your left hand. God forbid that your Majestie should any longer dispise the word of exhortation, the riches of his goodnesse, forbearance and long suffering, not knowing that the goodnesse of God leads you unto Repentance; For if your Majestie do so, As we are afraid, all Counsels and Endeavours for your Majesties re-establishment shall be in vain and without successe, because of the Wrath of the Lord of Hosts, who brings down the mighty from his Throne, and scatters the proud in the imaginations of their hearts; So we shall mourn in secret for it, and for all the miseries that are like to come upon your Throne and your Dominions, and comfort our selves, in this, that we have delivered our own souls. But we desire to hope better things, and that your Majestie will humble your self under the mighty hand of God, and be inclined to hearken to the faithfull advise of his Servants, be willing to secure Religion, and imploy your Royall Power for advancing the Kingdom of the Son of God, which will turn as well to the Honour and Happinesse of your Majesties as to the Peace and Safety of your Subjects.

AUGUST. 12. 1648, SESS. ULT.

ACT DISCHARGING DUELS.

The Generall Assembly taking in consideration the many Duels and combats that have been fought, and Challenges that have been made, and carried, and received in this Land of late. And being sensible of the exceeding great offence that comes by so horrible and hainous a sin; which is a grosse preferring of the supposed credit of the Creature unto the Honour of the most High God, and an usurpation upon the office of the Magistrate by private mens taking of the Sword, And a High degree of murther both of body and soul, by shedding the blood of the one, and cutting of the other from time of repenting; And which doth ordinarily produce many wofull consequents, Therefore doth enact And Ordain that all Persons of whatsoever quality who shall either fight Duels, or make, or write, or receive, or with their knowledge carry Challenges, or go to the fields, either as Principals, or as Seconds to fight Duels and Combats, that they shall without respect of Persons be processed with the Censures of the Kirk and brought before the Congregation two severall Lords-dayes; In the first whereof they are sharply to be rebuked and convinced of the hainousnesse of their sin and offence, and on the next to make a solemn publick Confession thereof, and profession of their unfained Humiliation and Repentance for the same. And if the Person guilty of any of the former offences be an Elder or Deacon, he is to be removed from his office, and whatsoever person guilty of any of these offences, shall refuse to give obedience according to the tenour of this Act, shall be processed to Excommunication: Declaring always, that if any be killed at such Duels, the killer shall be proceeded against by the Kirk as other murtherers.

ACT CONCERNING DEPOSED MINISTERS.

The Assembly considering that divers Ministers deposed for Malignancy, and complying with the Enemies of this Kirk and Cause of God, may be suited by, and hope to get entry in some Congregation where a Minister deposed for Malignancy hath been, and may be supposed to have put on the people a stamp and impression of Malignancie, and being by the Act of the Generall Assembly in Anno 1645. Past all hope of being restored to the place out of the whilk he was cast: Now also Ordains and enacts that no Minister deposed for Malignancy and compliance foresaid (when it shall fall out that he be put in a capacity of admission to the Ministry) shall enter into the Congregation of any other Minister who also hath been deposed for Malignancy and complyance, as said is.

The Generall Assembly not having now time to consider the References of the preceeding Assemblies, and the most part of Presbyteries not having lent their opinions in Writ, Therefore do yet again Recommend to Presbyteries and Provinciall Assemblies to consider all matters referred by this or by any former Assemblies, and to send their opinions therein in writ to the next Generall Assembly.

The meeting of the next Generall Assembly is hereby Appointed to be at Edinburgh the first Wednesday of Iuly, 1649.

A. Ker.

THE GENERALL ASSEMBLY, HOLDEN AT EDINBURGH, JULY 7. 1649.

JULY 7. 1649. ANTEMERIDIEM, SESS 4.

APPROBATION OF THE PROCEEDINGS OF THE COMMISSIONERS OF THE GENERALL ASSEMBLY.

The Generall Assembly having heard the report of the Committe appointed for revising the proceedings of the Commissioners of the preceding Assembly; And finding thereby, that in all their proceedings they have been zealous, diligent and faithfull, in the discharge of the trust committed to them, do therefore unanimously Approve and Ratify the the whole proceedings, Acts and Conclusions of the said Commission; Appointing Mr *John Bell* Moderator *protempore*, to return them hearty thanks in the name the Assembly, for their great pains, travel and fidelity.

JULY 10. 1649. ANTEMERIDIEM, SESS. 6.

APPROBATION OF THE COMMISSIONERS SENT TO HIS MAJESTY.

The Generall Assembly having taken in serious consideration the Report of the Travels and proceedings of the Commissioners sent to his Majesty presented by them this day, Together with the Commission and Instructions which were given unto them; Do finde by the Report, that they have been very diligent and faithfull in the discharge of the Trust committed to then. And therefore doe unanimously Approve of their Carriage and return them hearty thanks for their great Pains and Travails in that Employment.

JULY 19. 1649 POSTMERIDIEM, SESS. 18.

ACT DISCHARGING PROMISCUOUS DANCING.

The Assembly finding the scandall and abuse that arises through promiscuous Dancing: Do therefore inhibite and discharge the same, and do referre the Censure thereof to the severall Presbyteries, recommending it to their care and diligence.

JULY 20. 1649. ANTEMERIDIEM, SESS. 19.

ACT CONCERNING THE RECEIVING OF ENGAGERS IN THE LATE UNLAWFULL WAR AGAINST ENGLAND, TO PUBLICK SATISFACTION, TOGETHER WITH THE DECLARATION AND ACKNOWLEDGEMENT TO BE SUBSCRIBED BY THEM.

The Generall Assembly considering what great offence against God, and Scandall to his People at home and abroad, hath arisen from the late unlawfull Engagement in War against England; whereby, contrary to the Law of God and of Nations, contrary to the Solemn League and Covenant, contrary to the Petitions of almost the whole Kingdom, contrary to the Declarations of the Judicatories of this Kirk, contrary to the Protestations of a considerable part of the Parliament, contrary to the frequent and clear Warnings of the Servants of God in his name, not only an Association in Counsels and Arms was made with Malignant Persons, who had formerly shewn their disaffection to the Covenant in and Cause, but are Invasion of the Neighbour Nation was prosecuted; from whence flowed the oppression of the Persons, Estates and consciences of many of the people of God in this Land, the shedding of the blood of some, the losse and dishonour of this Nation, and severall other Inconveniences: and considering that the Commissioners of the last Generall Assembly, have acquit themselves faithfully in ordaining to be suspended from the renewing of the Covenant, and from the Ordinance of the Lords Supper, such as are designed in their Acts of date the 6. of October & 4 of December last; referring the further consideration and censure of the Persons foresaid to this present Generall Assembly: Therefore the Generall Assembly, for removing of such Offences, and for prevention of the like in time coming, and for restoring of such as are truely humbled, do Declare and Appoint.

I. That all those who have been guilty and censured as aforesaid, and withall do not by their addresses to Kirk Judicatories testify their dislike thereof, and give evidences of their Repentance therefore, That these be processed and continuing obstinate, be excommunicated; But if withall they go on in premoving Malignant Designes, that they be forthwith Excommunicated: As also that all such persons guilty as aforesaid, who after Profession of their Repentance shall yet again hereafter relapse to the promoting any Malignant Designe, that these be likewise forth with excommunicated.

II. That all these who have been guilty and censured as aforesaid, and desire to testifie their Repentance, and to be admitted to the Covenant and Communion, shall besides any Confession in publick before the Congregation subscribe the Declaration herto sub-joyned, of their unfained detestation and renunciation of that Engagement, and all other Malignant courses contrary to the Covenant and Cause, Promising to keep themselves from such ways in time coming, and acknowledging that if they shall again fall into such defection thereafter, they may justly be accounted perfidious backsliders, and breakers of the Covenant and Oath of God, and proceeded against with the highest Censures of the Kirk.

III. That of these who have been guilty and censured as aforesaid, and desire now to testifie their Repentance, Whosoever were formerly joyned in Arms or Counsell with James Graham in his Rebellion, or who were Generall persons or

Colonels in the late unlawfull Engagement, Or who went to Ireland to bring over Forces for that effect, Or who have been eminently active in contriving of or seducing unto the said Engagement, or whosoever above the degree of a Leutenant Commanded these parties, that in promoving of the ends of the said Engagement shed blood within the Kingdom, either before that Army of Engagers went to England, or after their return, Or who above the degree foresaid Commanded in the late Rebellion in the North; That none of these be admitted or received to give satisfaction, but by the Generall Assembly or their Commissioners.

IV. That all the rest of these who have been guilty, or censured as aforesaid may be received by the Presbyteries where they reside.

V. That all who have been guilty as aforsaid, before their receiving to the Covenant, shall make a Solemn publick Acknowledgement in such matter, and before such Congregations as the Commission of the Generall Assembly or Presbyteries respectivè shall prescribe, according to the degree of their offence and scandall given.

VI. That none of the foresaid Persons be admitted, or received as Elders in any Judicatories of the Kirk, but according to the Act of the Generall Assembly of the last of August 1647. against complyers of the first Classe.

And because many have heretofore made shew and profession of their Repentance, who were not convinced of their guiltinesse nor humbled for the same, but did thereafter return with the dog to the vomit, and with the sow to the puddle, unto the mocking of God, and the exceeding great reproach and detriment of his Cause: Therefore, for the better determining the Truth and sincerity of the Repentance of those who desire to be admitted to the Covenant and Communion: It is appointed and Ordained that none of those persons who are debarred from the Covenant and Communion shall be admitted and received thereto, but such as after exact triall, shall be found for some competent time before or after the offer of their Repentance, according to the discretion of the respective Judicatories, to have in their ordinary conversatione given real Testimony of their dislike of the late unlawfull Engagement, and of the courses and wayes of Malignants, and of their sorrow for their accession to the same; & to live soberly, righteously & godly; & if any shall be found, who after the defeating of the Engagers have uttered any Malignant speeches, tending to the approbation of the late unlawful Engagement, or the blood-shed within the Kingdome for promoving of the ends of the said Engagement, or any other projects or practices within or without the Kingdome; prejudiciall to Religion and the Covenant, or tending to the reproach of the Ministry, or the civill Government of the Kingdom, or who have unnecessarily or ordinarily conversed with Malignant and disaffected persons, Or who have had hand in, or accession to, or compliance with or have any wayes countenanced or promoved any Malignant Design, prejudiciall to Religion and the Covenant; That these, notwithstanding their profession of Repentance be not suddenly received, but a competent time, according to the discretion of the Judicatory, be assigned to them for tryall of the evidence of their Repentance, according to the qualifications above mentioned. And the Generall Assembly Ordains Presbyteries to make intimation of this Act in the severall Kirks of their bounds so soon as they can, after the rising of the General Assembly, that none pretend ignorance; And that Presbyteries make accompt of their diligence in prosecuting of this Act to the Quarterly meetings of the Commission of this Assembly.

THE DECLARATION AND ACKNOWLEDGEMENT BEFORE MENTIONED.

I, after due consideration of the late Warre against the Kingdom of *England*; And having also considered the course pursued and promoted by the Earle of *Lanerk*, *George Monro* and their Adherents in and about *Stirling*, and by others in the late Rebellion in the North, against all which not only eminent Testimonies of Gods Wrath have been given in defeating of them, but they were in themselves sinfull breaches of Covenant, and preferring the interest of man unto God; I doe herefore in Gods sight professe, that I am convinced of the unlawfulnesse of all these ways, as contrary to the Word of God, and to the Solemn League and Covenant, not only in regard of the miscarriages of these that were imployed therein, but also in respect of the nature of these courses themselves; And therefore professing my unfained sorrow for my guiltinesse by my accession to the same, doe renounce and disclaim the foresaid Engagement and all the courses that were used for carrying on the same, either before or after the defeat of the Engagers, as contrary to the Word of GOD and Solemn League and Covenant, and destructive to Religion and the work of Reformation; And I doe promise in the power of the Lords strength, never again to own any of these or the like courses. And if hereafter at any time, I shall be found to promote any Malignant Design or course, that I shall justly be accompted a perfidious Covenant breaker and despiser of God, and be proceeded against with the highest Censures of the Kirk: Likeas I doe hereby promise to adhere to the Nationall Covenant of this Kingdome and to the Solemn League and Covenant betwixt the Kingdomes, and to be honest and zealous for promoving all the ends thereof, as I shall be called thereunto of God, and to flee all occasions and temptations that may lead me into any the like snares against the same.

JULY 24. 1649. POSTMERIDIEM. SESS. 23.

LETTER TO THE HIGH & HONOURABLE COURT OF PARLIAMENT.

The Generall Assembly, Humbly Sheweth,

That whereas we have seen & considered the Act of Parliament abolishing Patronages, and doe highly commend the piety and zeal of the Estates of Parliament in promoving so necessary a point of Reformation, The Generall Assembly do humbly supplicate, that beside the setling of the Ministers stipends, that the Tythes mentioned in the said Act, may be affected with the burthen of pious uses, within the respective Paroches, conform to a draught of an Act seen by the Commissioners of the late Generall Assembly before it pasted in Parliament, And that the foresaid Act, may be made effectuall for the setling of Ministers Stipends in Kirks erected, and necessary to be erected according to the Tenour of the Act of

Parliament, And for this effect, that your Lordships will hasten the sitting of the Commission for Plantation of Kirks, with all convenient diligence, and your Lordships Answer.

27. JULY, 1649. ANTEMERIDIEM. SESS. 27.

A SEASONABLE AND NECESSARY WARNING AND DECLARATION, CONCERNING PRESENT AND IMMINENT DANGERS, AND CONCERNING DUTIES RELATING THERETO, FROM THE GENERALL ASSEMBLY OF THIS KIRK, UNTO ALL THE MEMBERS THEREOF.

The Lord who chooses Jerusalem in a furnace of Affliction, hath been pleased since the beginning of the work of Reformation in this Land, to exercise his People with many trials; all that desired to keep a good conscience, were not long agoe under many heavy and sad pressures from the insolency and oppression of a prevailing party of dis-affected and Malignant men, who under a pretext of bringing the King to a condition of Honour, Freedom and Safety, did carry on an unlawfull Engagement against the Kingdom of England: and if the Lord had not been mercifull unto his people, they were like either to have been banished out of the Land, or to have been kept in a perpetuall bondage in their consciences, persons and estates: But he whose Messengers those men had mocked, and whose word they had despised, did bring them down suddenly in a day, and restored liberty and peace unto his people: A mercy and deliverance, which as it ought to be remembred with thankfulnesse and praise, so may it engage our hearts not to faint in troubles and straites that do yet abide us but to trust in the name of the Lord, who both can and will deliver us still out of all our afflictions.

Albeit, wee do now enjoy many rich and precious blessing wherin wee have reason to be comforted, and to rejoyce; yet it were to shut our own eyes if we should not see our selves involved in, and threatned with many and great dangers at home and from abroad, it is matter of exceeding great sorrow to think upon the ignorance and profanity, the impenitencie and security that abounds still in the Land, notwithstanding all the gracious dispensation of the Gospel, and means of grace in such purity and plenty, that none of the Nations round about us can boast of the like, and of all his sharp rods wherewith he hath afflicted us from year to year, and of all the mercies and deliverances wherewith he hath visited us, and of our late solemn confession of sinnes, and engagement unto duties, sealed with the renewing of the Covenant and the Oath of God; Which some men have so far already forgotten, as to return with the dogge to the vomit, and with the sow to the puddle: And many signes of inconstancy and levity do appear among all sorts and ranks of persons, who seem to want nothing but a sutable tentation to draw them away from their stedfastnesse; Our Army is not yet sufficiently purged, but there be still in it Malignant and scandalous men, whose fidelity and constancy, as it is much to be doubted, so is the wrath of the Lord to be feared, upon their proceedings and undertakings, without a speedy and effectuall remedy.

That prevailing party of Sectaries in England, who have broken the Covenant, and despised the Oath of God, corrupted the truth, subverted the fundamentall Government, and taken away the Kings life look upon us with an evill eye, as upon these who stand in the way of their monstruous and new fangled devices in Religion and Government; And though there were no cause to fear any thing from that party but the Gangrene and infection of those many damnable and abominable errours which have taken hold on them yet our vicinity unto and daily commerce with that Nation, may justly make us afraid that the Lord may give up many in this Land unto a spirit of delusion to beleeve lies, because they have not received the love of the truth.

Neither is the Malignant party so far broken and brought low, as that they have abandoned all hopes of carrying on their former designs against the Covenant and work of Reformation: Beside many of them in this Kingdom, who are as Foxes tied in chains, keeping their evill nature, and waiting an opportuny to break their cords, and again to prey upon the Lords people, there be standing Armies in Ireland, under the command of the Marquesse of Ormond, The Lord Inchqueen, the Lord of Airds, and George Munro, who forgetting all the horrible cruelty that was exercised by the Irish Rebels, upon many thousands of the English and Scottish Nations in that land, have entred into a Peace and Association with them, that they may the more easily carry on the old designes of the Popish, Prelaticall and Malignant party, And the Lord of Airds, and George Monro, have by treachery and oppression brought the Province of Ulster, and Garrisons therein, under their power and Command, and have redacted our country-men, and such as adhere unto the Covenant, and cause of God in that Province, unto many miseries and straits, and are like to banish the Ministers of the Gospell, and to overturn these faire beginnings of the work of God, which were unto many a branch of hope, that the Lord meant to make Ireland a pleasant land.

But which is more grievous unto us then all these, our King notwithstanding of the Lords hand against his Fathers opposition to the work of God, and of the many sad and dolefull consequences followed thereupon, in reference to Religion and his Sebjects, and to his person, and Government, doth hearken unto the councels of these who were Authors of these miseries to his Royall Father and his Kingdoms: By which it hath come to passe, that his Majesty hath hitherto refused to grant the just and necessary desires of this Kirk and Kingdom, which were tendred unto him from the Commissioners of both for securing of Religion, the Liberties of the Subject, his Majesties Government, and the Peace of the Kingdome; And it is much to be feared that those wicked Counsellours may so farre prevaile upon him in his tender yeers, as to engage him in a warre, for overturning (if it be possible) of the work of God, and bearing down all those in the three Kingdoms that adhere thereto: Which if he shall doe, cannot but bring great wrath from the Lord upon himselfe and his Throne, and must be the cause of many new, and great miseries, and calamities to these Lands.

It concerns a Nation thus sinfull and loaden with iniquity and involved in so many difficulties and dangers, by timous repentance and unfained humiliation to draw near to God, and to wrastle with him in Prayer and Supplication, that our sin may be pardoned, and our iniquity done away, and that he would establish the Land in the love of the truth and inable every one in their station to do their duty boldly and without fear, and in humble dependance upon the Lord, in whom alone is the salvation of his people; Every man ought with all faithfulnesse and diligence, to make use of all these means that are approven and allowed of God, for preserving and carrying on of his work, and for securing and guarding the Land against all enemies whatsomever, both upon the right hand and upon the left.

The Spirit of errour and delusion in our Neighbour Land, in the policy of Satan hath vailed it self in many, under the mask of holinesse and is in the righteous and wise dispensation of God, armed with power, and attended with successe: Therefore all the Inhabitants of this land would labour for more knowledge, and more love of the truth, without which they may easily be deceived, audled into tentation, and would learn to distinguish betwixt the shew and power of godlinesse. We know that there be many in England who be truly godly, and mourn with us for all the errours and abominations that are in that land, But it is without controversie, that that Spirit which hath acted in the Courses and Counsels of these, who have retarded and obstructed the work of God, dispised the Covenant, forced the Parliament, murthered the King, changed the civill Government, and established so vast a Toleration in Religion, cannot be the Spirit of Righteousnesse and Holinesse, because it teaches not men to live godly and righteously, but drawes them aside into errour and make them to bring forth the bitter fruits of impiety and iniquity and therefore ought to be avoyded. And not only are such of our Nation as travaile in our Neighbour-land, to take heed unto themselves that they receive not infection from such as are leavened with Errour, but these also who live at home, especially in those places where Sectaries, upon pretext of merchandise, and other civill imployments, ordinarily traffique and converse. Neither needs any man to be afraid of the power and successe of that party, Neither needs any man to be afraid of the power and successe of that party, they who have gadded about so much to change their way, shall ere long be ashamed; The Lord hath rejected their confidences, and they shall not prosper in them; How farre they may proceed in their Resolutions and Actings against this Kingdome, is in the hand of the most high; If the Lord shall suffer that party to invade this land, it may be the comfort and incouragement of all the inhabitints thereof, that not only hath that unlawfull engagement against the Kingdom of England been declared against, and condemned both by Kirk and State; but also that these men can pretend no quarrell against us, unlesse it be, that we have adhered unto the Solemn League and Covenant, from which they have so foully revolted and backslidden; and that we have borne testimony against Toleration, and their proceedings in reference to Religion and Government, and the taking away of the Kings life: And therefore we trust that in such a case none will be so farre deficient in their duty as not to defend themselves against such injust violence, and in the strength of the Lord to adhere unto their former principles, with much boldnes of spirit, and willingnesse of heart; In this certainly we shall have a good conscience and the Lord shall be with us.

We are not so, to have the one of our eyes upon the Sectaries, as not to hold the other upon the Malignants, they being an enemy more numerous, and no lesse subtile and powerfull nor the other, and at this time more dangerous unto us, not onely because experience hath proven that there is a greater aptitude and inclination in these of our Land, to complie with Malignants then Sectaries in that they carry on their wicked designes under a pretext of being for the King; But also because there be many of them in our own bowels, and for that they doe pretend to be for maintenance of the Kings Person and Authority, and (which is the matter of our grife) because the King ownes their principles and wayes; which if it be not taken heed unto, may prove a great snare, and dangerous tentation to many as side with them against the Lords people, and his cause. The constant tenour of the carriage of these in this land, who stand for the Cause of God; are undeniable arguments of their affection to Monarchy, and to that Royall Family and Line wich hath sweyed the Scepter of this Kingdom for many hundreds of yeers past. Albeit his Majestie who lately reigned, refused to harken to their just desires, yet did they with much patience and Moderation of mind, supplicate and solicite his Majesty for satisfaction in these things that concern Religion and the Covenant, and were still willing, that upon satisfaction given, he should be admitted to the exercise of his power; and whatsoever envie and malice objects to the contrary, were carefull to get assurance concerning the safety of His Majesties Person, when they brought their Army out of England; and when notwithstanding of that assurance, the prevailing party of Sectaries were acting for his life, did to the utmost of their power, endeavour by their Commissioners that there might have been no such proceeding, And when their desires and endeavours were not successfull, did protest and bear testimony against the same. And, as both Kirk and State had testified their tender respect to his Majesty who now reigns, by their Letters written to him whilst his Father was yet living, So no sooner did the Parliament heare of his Fathers death, but they did with all solemnity proclaim him King of these Kingdoms; And after they had acquainted his Majesty by Messages with their proceedings herein, Commissioners were sent both from State and Kirk instructed with power and Commission to expresse the affection of this Kingdome to Monarchy, and his Majesties Person and Goverment, together with their desires concerning the security of Religion, and the Peace of those Kingdoms. And albeit the desires of both which are now published to the world, with his Majesties answers thereto, are such as are most just and necessary; yet the Counsels of the malignant party had so great influence upon his Majesty, that his answers are not only not satisfactory, but short of that which was many times granted by his Royal Father, and cannot be acquiesced unto, unlesse we would abandon the League and Covenant, and betray Religion, and the cause of God.

We hold it the duty of all who live in this Land, to wrestle with God in the behalfe of the King, that he may be recovered out of the snare of evill Counsell, and brought to give satisfaction to the publick desires of Kirk and State; and in their places and stations to use all endeavours with himselfe and others for that effect, and to be willing, upon satisfaction given, to admit him to the exercise of his power, and cheerfully to obey him in all things according to the will of God, and the lawes of the Kingdom, and to do every thing that tends to the preservation of his Majesties Person, and just greatnesse and Authority, in the defence and preservation of the true Religion and Liberties of the Kingdomes.

But if his Majesty, or any having, or pretending power and Commission from him, shall invade this Kingdom, upon pretext of establishing him in the exercise of his Royal power, as it will be an high provocation against GOD to be accessory or assisting thereto, so will it be a necessary duty to resist and oppose the same, We know that men are so forgetfull of the oath of God, and ignorant of the interest of Jesus Christ and the Gospel, and doe so little tender that which concerns his Kingdom and the Privileges thereof, and do so much dote upon absolute and Arbitrary Government for gaining their own ends, and so much maligne the Instruments of the work of Reformation, that they would admit his Majesty to the exercise of his Royal power upon any termes whatsoever, though with never so much prejudice to Religion, and the Liberties of these Kingdomes, and would think it quarrell enough to make War upon all those who for consciences sake cannot condescend thereto. But We desire all these who fear the Lord, and mind to keep their Covenant impartially to consider these things which followes.

1. That as Magistrates and their power is ordained of God, so are they in the exercise thereof, not to walk according to their owne will, but according to the Law of equity and righteousnesse, as being the Ministers of GOD for the safety of his People; Therefore a boundles and illimitted power is to be acknowledged in no King nor Magistrate; Neither is Our King to be admitted to the exercise of his power as long as he refuses to walk in the Administration of the same according to this rule, and the established Laws of the Kingdom, that his Subjects may live under him a quiet and and peaceable life in all Godlinesse and honestie.

2. There is ane mutuall Obligation and Stipulation betwixt the King and his People; As both of them are tied to GOD, so each of them are tied one to another for the performance of mutuall and reciprocall duties: According to this, It is Satute and Ordained in the 8. Act of the 1. Parliament of King James the 6. That all Kings, Princes or Magistrates whatsoever, halding their place, which hereafter shall happen in any time to Raign and beare rale over this Realm, at the time of their Coronation and receipt of their Princely Authority, make their faithfull promise by Oath in the presence of the Eternall GOD that during the whole course of their lives, they shall serve the same Eternall GOD to the utmost of their power, according as he hath required in his most Holy Word contained in the Old and New Testament and according to the same Word, shall maintain the true Religion of Christ Jesus, the Preaching of His most Holy Word, and due and right ministration of His Sacraments now received and Preached within this Realm, and shall abolish and work against all false religion contrary to the same, And shall rale the peeple committed to their charge according to the Will and Command of GOD revealed in his Word and according to the laudable Laws and Constitutions received within this Realm, And shall procure to the utmost of their power to the Kirk of God and the whole Christian People, true and perfect peace in all time comming. And that Justice and Equity be keeped to all creatures without exception. Which Oath was sworn, first by King Iames the 6, and afterwards by King Charles at his Coronation, and is inferred in our Nationall Covenant, which was approven by the King who lately Reigned, As long therefore as his Majesty who now Reignes, refuses to hearken to the just and necessary desires of State and Kirk, propounded

to his Majesty for the Security of Religion, and safety of his People, and to engage and oblige himself, for the performance of his Duty to his People, It is consonant to Scripture and reason and the Laws of the Kingdom, that they should refuse to admit him to the exercise of his Government, untill he give satisfaction in these things.

3. In the League and Covenant which hath been so solemly sworne and renewed by this Kingdom, the Dutie of defending and preserving the Kings Majesties Person and Authority is joyned with, and subordinat unto the dutie of preserving and defending the true Religion and Liberties of the Kingdoms: And therefore his Majestie standing in opposition to the just and necessary publick desires concerning Religion and Liberties, it were a manifest Breach of Covenant, and a preferring of the Kings interest to the interest of Jesus Christ, to bring him to the exercise of his Royal power, which he, walking in a contrary way, and being compassed about with Malignant Counsels, cannot but employ unto the prejudice and ruin of both.

4. Was not an Arbitrary Government and unlimited power, the fountain of most of all the Corruptions both in Kirk and State? And was it not for restraint of this, and for their own just defence against Tyranny and injust violence, which ordinarily is the fruit and effect of such a power, that the Lords People did joyn in Covenant, and have been at the expense of so much blood, pains and treasure these yeers past? And if his Majestie should be admitted to the exercise of his Government before satisfaction given, were it not to put in his hand that Arbitrary Power, which we have upon just and necessary grounds been so long withstanding, and so to abandon our former Principles, and betrary our Cause?

5. The King being averse from the Work of Reformation and the instruments thereof, and compassed about with Malignant and disaffected men, whom he hearkens unto as his most faithfull Counsellers, and looks upon as his best and most Loyall Subjects, We leave it to all indifferent men to judge, whether his Majestie, being admitted to the exercise of his Power before satisfaction given, would not by such Counsells endeavour an overturning of the things which GOD hath wrought amongst us, and labour to draw publick administrations concerning Religion and the liberties of the Subject, unto that course and channall in which they did run under Prelacie, and before the Work of Reformation: Which we have the more cause to fear, because his Royall Father did so often declare, that he conceived himself bound to employ all the power that GOD should put in his hands to the utmost for these ends; and that he adheres as yet to his Fathers Principles, and walkes in his way, and hath made a Peace with the Irish Rebels, by which is granted unto them the full liberty of Popery.

6. It is no strange nor new thing for Kingdoms to preserve Religion of themselves from ruine, by putting restraint upon the exercise of the power and Government of those who have refused to grant those things that were necessary for the good of Religion, and the Peoples safety; There have bin many precedents of it in this and other nations of old, and of late. Upon these and other important considerations, It shall be the wisdom of every one who dwell in the Land, to take heed of such a temptation & snare, that they be not accessory to any such designes or endeavours, as they would not bring upon themselves, and upon their families,

the guilt of all the detriment that will undoubtedly follow thereupon to Religion and the Covenant, and of all the miseries and calamities that it will bring upon his Majesties Person and Throne, and upon these Kingdoms; Such a thing would in all appearance be the undermining and shaking—if not the overthrowing and destroying of the work of Reformation: And therefore whosoever attempt the same, oppose themselves to the Cause of GOD, and will at last dash against the Rock of the LORDS Power, which hath broken in pieces many high and lofty ones since the beginning of this work in these Kingdoms: And it is unto us a sure Word of Promise, That whosoever shall associate themselves, or take counsel together, or gird themselves against GOD and His Work, shall be broken in pieces.

It is not onely joyning in Arms with the Malignant partie, that all these who would keep their integritie hath need to beware of, but also subtil devices and designes, that are promoted by fair pretexts and perswasions to draw men to dispense at least with some part of these necessarie desires, that are propounded to his Majestie for securing of Religion, After many turnings and devises the foundation of the unlawful Engagement was at last laid by his Majesties Concessions in the year 1648. Wherein though many things seemed to be granted, yet that was denyed, without which Religion and the Union betwixt the Kingdoms could not have been secured: And it is probable, that such a way may be assayed again, and prosecuted with very much cunning and skill to deceive and insnare the simple. It doth therefore concerne all ranks and conditions of persons to be the more warie and circumspect, especially in that which concerns the National Covenant, and the Solemn League and Covenant, that before his Majestie be admitted to the exercise of his Royal Power, that by and aftour the Oath of Coronation, he shall assure and declare by his Solemn Oath under his hand and seal his allowance of the National Covenant, and of the Solemn League and Covenant, and obligation to prosecute the ends thereof in his Station and Calling, and that he shall for himself and his successours, consent and agree to Acts of Parliament, injoyning the Solemn League and Covenant, and fully Establishing Presbyterial Government, the Directory of Worship, the Confession of Faith and Catechisme, as they are approven by the General Assembly of this Kirk and Parliament of this Kingdom, in all his Majesties Dominions, and that he shall observe these in his own Practice and Familie, and that he shall never make opposition to any of these, nor endeavour any change thereof. Albeit the League and Covenant be despised by that prevailing party in England, and the Work of Uniformity, thorow the retardements and obstructions that have come in the way, be almost forgotten by these Kingdoms, yet the obligation of that Covenant is perpetual, and all the duties contained therein are constantly to be minded, and prosecute by every one of us and our posterity, according to their place and stations: And therefore we are no lesse zealously to endeavour, that his Majestie may Establish, and swear, and subscribe the same, then if it were unanimously regarded and stuck unto by all the Kingdom of England, for his Majestie swearing and subscribing the League and Covenant, will much contribute for the Security of Religion, his Majesties happinesse, and the Peace of his Kingdoms.

As it is incumbent to all, who live in this Kirk and Kingdom to be watchful and circumspect, so it concerns these of the High and Honourable Court of Parliament & their Committees, in a speciall way to see to their duty, & to be straight & resolute in the performance of the same; Their former proceedings is unto us a sufficient evidence and ground of hope, that they will not be wanting in any necessary testimony of dutie and Loyalty that they owe to the King, by using all just and seasonable endeavoures for obtaining satisfaction of his Majestie, that so he may be established upon his Thrones; And we trust, that upon the other hand, the sense of their obligations to God, and his Oath that is upon them, will make them constantly to adhere to their former principles resolutions, and desires concerning Religion and the Covenant, that real satisfaction may be had thereanent, before the King be put in the exercise of his power; And that they will carefully provide for the safety of the Kingdom, both in regard of the intestine dangers, and in regard of invasion from without; It is not long since they together with the rest of the Land, made solemn publick Confession of Compliance with Malignants, carnal confidence, following of self interests, and hearkening to the Counsels of flesh and blood, and did in a special way engage themselves to comply, and seek themselves and their own things no more, to abandon the counsels of their own hearts, and not to rely upon the Arm of flesh, and to purge Judicatories and Armies from Profane and scandalous persons; And God forbid that they should so soon forget, or neglect so necessary duties and fall again unto so great and grievous transgressions. We trust that they will seek the things of CHRIST, and not their own things, that they will hearken to His Word, and not walk in the imaginations of their own hearts, that they will relie upon the Arm of the LORD, and not upon the arm of flesh, that they will bewary and circumspect in discerning the dispositions and affections of those whom they put in trust, and that, seeing this Kingdom hath so much smarted, & been so often deceived by complyance with Malignants they will carefully avoid this snare, inregard of those who were upon the former unlawful Engagement & be tender in bringing in of such; And wee cannot but exhort them in the Name of the LORD, to take notice of the Oppression of the People and Commons in the Land, by the lawlesse exactions of Land-Lords, Collectours and Souldiers. We do not justifie the murmurings and grudgings of those, who, preferring the things of the world to the Gospel and things of Jesus Christ repine at necessary burthens, without which it is not possible that the Land can be secured from invasion without and insurrection within, or the Cause and People of GOD be defended from enemies: It is the duty of every one who hath taken the Covenant, willingly and with a cheerfull minde to bestow their means and their pains as they shall be called thereunto, in an orderly way: Yet should these to whom God hath committed the Government, take carre that they be not needlessely burthened, and that none grind their faces by oppression, not only by making of Lawes against the same, but by searching out of the cause of the poor, and by executing these Lawes timously upon these that oppresse them, that they may find real redresse of their just grievances and complaints, and be encouraged to bear those burthens which cannot be avoyded.

As the Parliament have begun, so we hope they will continue, to purge out all these from trust, that are not of known integrity and affection to the cause of God, and of a blamelesse and Christian conversation, and that they and the officers of the Army in their respective places, will seriously mind, and speedily and resolutely goe about the removing from the Army all malignant scandalous persons, and also the removing of Sectaries when any shall be found therein, that they may give real evidence that they did not deal deceitfully with God, in the day that they engaged themselves thereto.

Albeit we hope and pray that those who beare charge in our Army, will from the remembrance of the Lords goodnesse to them, and the honour that he hath put upon them, endeavour to carry themselves faithfully, and straightly, Yet it cannot be unseasonable to warn them to take heed of tentations, and to beware of snares that they be not drawn to indifference or neutrality in the cause of God, much lesse unto connivance at, or compliance with the courses and designes of malignants or Sectaries, but to stick closely by the same, and to be zealous against all the enemies and adversaries thereof: And it concerns souldiers to be content with their wages, and to doe violence to no man, but as they are called unto the defence of the cause and people of God, so to behave themselves in such a blamlesse and Christian way, that their carriage may be a testimony to his cause, and a comfort to his people; So shall our Armies prosper, and the Lord shall goe out with them.

But most of all it concerns the Ministers of the Gospel whom God hath called to give warning to his people to look to their duty; It is undeniably true, that many of the evils wherewith this Kirk and Kingdome hath been afflicted in our age, have come to passe because of the negligence of some, and corruptions of others of the Ministry; Whilest some fell asleep, and were carelesse, and others were covetous and ambitious, the evil man brought in Prelacy, and the Ceremonies, & had farre promoted the Service-Book, and the Book of Cannons; and the course of backsliding and revolting was carried on, untill it pleased God to stirre up the spirits of these few, who stood in the gap to oppose and resist the same, and to begin the work of Reformation in the Land; Since which time; the silence of some Ministers, and compliance of others, hath had great influence upon the backsliding of many amongst the people, who upon the discovery of the evill of their way, complain that they got not warning, or that if they were warned by some, others held their Peace, or did justifie them in the course of their backsliding; We can look upon such Ministers no otherwise then upon those that are guilty of the blood of the Lords people, and with whom the Lord will reckon for all the breach of Covenant, and defection that hath been in the Land. The Priests lips should preserve knowledge, and they should seek the law at his mouth, for he is the messenger of the Lord of Hosts; But such are departed out of the way, and hath caused many to stumble at the Law, therefore hath the Lord made them contemtible and base before all the people; acccording as they have not kept his wayes, but have been partiall in his law; because they have lost their savour, he hath cast out many of them as unsavoury salt: But such as have been faithfull, as he hath preserved from the violence and fury of men, so hath he verified his word in their mouths, both against his enemies, and concerning his people and his work; And makes them see, though not all their desires concerning the Gospel, and the work of God in the land yet very much of the fruit of their labour, by preserving the doctrine and all the ordinances of Jesus Christ in their purity, and adding in some measure thereto the power and life thereof. We doe therefore charge all the Ministers of the land, before God and the Lord Jesus Christ, who shall judge the quick and the dead at his appearing in his Kingdom, as in every thing to be ensamples of a good conversation, and to walk without offence, that the ministry be not blamed; So to take heed unto the flock over which the Holy Ghost hath made them overseers, to declare unto them all the Counsell of God, and to give them timous warning concerning every danger and duty, and to hold forth unto them the solid grounds of reall consolation, by which they may be encouraged and comforted in all their trials and afflictions; that they may be free of the blood of all men, and have this as a ground of rejoycing, even the testimony of their consciences, that in simplicity and godly purenesse, not with fleshly wisdome, but by the grace of God they have had their conversation in the world, and have exhorted and comforted and charged every one committed unto them as a Father doth his childrren. Especially, Ministers are to be careful to be much indiscovering the temptations, and pressing the duties of the times that these who are under their charge may know what to avoid, and what to embrace and pursue: If all the Watchmen in the Land shall give warning, and blow the Trumpet at once, it shall not be easie for enemies to prey upon the people of God. Wee know no cause why any whom God hath called to preach the Gospel, should be afraid to speak boldly in the Name of the Lord; since God hath given so manifest a testimony of his care and protection, in preserving them, these yeers past, who have striven to be faithfull to him who hath called them from all the fury and malice of haters of the work of God and of the Kingdom or of his Sonne Jesus Christ, who hath promised to be with his servants unto the end of the world.

Albeit the Land be involved in many difficulties, and compassed about with great and iminent dangers, yet there is hope and ground of consolation concerning this thing. The Lord is in the midst of us, and we are called by his name, our eares hear the joyfull sound of the Gospel, and and our eyes see our Teachers; We behold the arms of the Lord stretched out daily in working salvation for his people, and answering their desires upon their enemies by terrible things in righteousnesse; Although we be but few in number, yet the Lord of Hosts is with us, and in the power of his strenth we shall be able to prevaile. Although our land be filled with sin, yet we have not been forsaken of the Lord our God, but he hath alwayes had compassion upon us, and delivered us in all our distresses; Although some of understanding fall, it is but to try, and to purge and to make white even to the end, because it is yet for a time appointed; Although many cleave to us by flatteries, yet there be a remnant who keep their integrity, and the Lord shall doe good to these that be good, but such as turn aside to crooked wayes, shall be led forth with the workers of iniquity.

The Lords people in England and Ireland, who adhere to the cause and Covenant, may be perplexed, but shall not despair; they may be persecuted, but shall not be forsaken; they may be cast down, but shall not be destroyed: And although uniformity, and the work of Reformation in these lands, seem not only to be retarded, but almost pluckt up by the roots, and the foundation thereof razed; Yet the seed which the Lord hath sowen there, shall again take root downward, and bear fruit upward, The zeal of the Lord of Hosts shall performe this.

30. JULY 1649. ANTEMERIDIEM SESS. 30.

ACT CONCERNING CATECHISING.

The Generall Assembly taking to their serious Consideration the great darknesse and Ignorance, wherein a great part of this Kingdom lyeth, together with the late Solemn Engagement, to use all means for remedy thereof, doe ordaine every Minister with assistance of the Elders of their severall Kirk sessions to take course, that in every house where there is any who can read, there be at least one Copie of the Shorter and Larger Catechisme, Confession of Faith and Directorie for Familie worship. And doe renew the Act of the Assemblie August 30. 1639. for a day of weeklie Catechising, to be constantly observed in every Kirk, And that every Minister so Order their Catethetick Questions, as thereby the People, (who doe not conveen all at one time but by turns unto that exercise) may at every dyet have the chief heads of saving knowledge in a short view presented unto them, And the Assembly considering that notwithstanding of their former Act, these dyets of weekly Catechising are much slighted and neglected by many Ministers throughout this Kingdome, Doe therefore Appoint and Ordaine every Presbytery, to take triall of all the ministers within their bounds once at least in the halfe year, whither they be carefull to keep weekly dyets of Catechising; And if they shall finde any of their number negligent herein they shall admonish for the first fault, and if after such admonition they shall not amend, The Presbyterie for the second fault shall rebuke them sharply, and if after such rebuke they doe not yet amend, they shall be suspended.

4 AUG. 1649. ANTEMERIDIEM SESS. 40.

COMMISSION FOR PUBLICK AFFAIRES.

The Generall Assemblie Considering how necessary it is for preservation of Religion in this Kingdom, and prosecution of the work of uniformity in all his Majesties dominions, That the Commissions formerly granted to that effect be renewed: Therefore they doe renew the power and Commission granted for the Publick affairs of the Kirk by the Generall Assemblies held at Saint Andros 1642. and at Edinburgh, 1643, 1644, 1645, 1646, 1647. and 1648, unto the Persons following, viz. Masters Alex. Rollock, John Murray, Thomas Lundie, John Freebairne, Geo. Murray, Harie Livingston, William Macjore, Hew Henderson, Samuel Austine, Gavin Young, David Laing, William Maxwell, John Macleland, James Irving, Robert Ferguson, John Scot, Thomas Wylie, Hew. Eccles, John Bell, John Nevoy, William Gutherie, John Hammiltoun, Hew Peebles, Alex. Dunlope, Harie Semple, David Dickson, Patrick Gillespie, James Durham, Robert Baillie, William Hammiltoun, Francis Aird, James Nasmith, Richard Inglis, William Summervail, Evan Cameron, Robert Blair, Samuel Rutherfoord, James Wood, John Macgill Elder, Alex. Balfoure, William Row, John Moncriefe, Fredrick Carmichaell, Herie Wilke, William Oliphant, George Pitillo, John Robison, James Thomsone, William Rate,

Da. Campbell, Andro Cant, Io. Menzes, Andro Abercromby, Robert Sheyn, William Forbes, John Paterson, Duncan Forbes, Will. Chalmers, John Annand, Will. Falconer, Murdoch Mackenzie, Robert Jameson, Gilbert Marshell, Jo. Dallase, Wil. Smyth, Robert Hume, Tho. Suintoun, James Strateum, Jo. Douglass, James Guthrie, Tho. Donaldson, Will Jameson, John Livingstoun, John Scot, Andro. Dunkeson, John Dalzell, Arthur Forbes, James Fleming, James Robison, Hew Campbel, Robert Douglasse, Mungo Law, George Leslie, John Adamson, James Hammiltoun, John Smyth, Hew Mackell, Geo: Hutchison, Patrick Fleming, John Hay, Ephraim Melvill, Iohn Low, Gilbert Hall, George Bennet, Kenneth Logie, John Crafurd Ministers, Archbald Marquesse of Argyle, E. of Sutherland, Alex. E. of Eglintoun, John E. of Cassills, Wil. E. of Lothian, the Viscount of Arbuthnet, Da. L. Elcho Lo. Briehen, Rob. Lo. Burly, James Lo. Couper, Sir Archald Johnstoun of Waristoun Clerk Register, Sir Daniel Carmichael Thesaurer Depute, Sir John Hope of Craighall, Mr George Winraham of Libbertoun, Mr Alex. Person of Southhal, Alex. Brodie of that ilk, four of the ordinary Lords of the Session, Arthur Ersken of Scotscrage, Laird of Wauchtoun, Sir David Hume of Wedderburne, Laird of Edzell, Laird of Nidrie, Sir William Scot of Harden, Laird of Greenheid, Laird of Freeland, Laird of Cesnock, Sr. James Stewart of Kirk field, the Laird of Suintoun younger, Laird of Eight, Sir James Fraser, Sir Thomas Ker, Laird of Fernie, Sir Rob. Adair, Sheriff of Tiviotdail younger, Tutor of Pitsligo, Sir John Chiesly, Laird of Englistoun, Laird of Leslie younger, Laird of Dunbeth, La. of Wetertoun, Sir Jo. Smyth, Mr Alex. Colvill of Blair, Whitbank younger, La. of Grenock, Galloshiels younger, Buchchantie, Grachlaw, Cloberhil, Dalserf, Mr Robert Burnet younger, Mr Tho. Murray, James Eleis, David Kennedie, Alex Jaffray, James Sword, George Porterfield, Mr Rob. Barclay, Hew Kennedey, Will. Glendoning, Thomas Machirnie, Rob. Lockhart, Er James Campbel, John Carsane, John Boswel. D. Alex. Donglasse, Mr Alex. Skeen, William Broun Elders, Giving unto them full Power and Commission to do all and every thing for preservation of the Established Doctrine, Discipline, Worship and Government in this Kirk, against all who shall endeavour to introduce any thing contrarie thereunto; And for prosecuting, advancing, perfecting and bringing the works of uniformitie in Religion in all his Majesties dominions to a happy conclusion conform to the former Commissions granted by preceding Assemblies thereanent.

And to that effect appoints them or any nineteen of them whereof 13. shall be Ministers, to meet in this Citie to morrow the 7. of this instant, and thereafter upon the second Wednesday of Novemb. February and May next, and upon any other day, and in any other place they shall think fit: Giving also unto them full power, to send Commissioners to the Kingdom of England, for prosecuting the Treatie of Uniformitie as they shall find conveniencie, and to give Instructions and Commissions to that effect conform to former Commissiones granted thereanent: And Likewise in case delinquents have no constant residence in any one Presbyterie, or if Presbyteries be negligent or overawed, in these cases The Assembly gives to the persons before named power of censuring Compliers & persons disaffected to the Covenant, according to the Acts of the Assembly, Declaring alwayes and providing, that Ministers shall not be Deposed, but in one of the quarterlie meetings of this Commission; And further authorizes them as formerlie, with full power to make Supplications, Remonstrances; Declarations and Warnings, to Indict Fasts and Thanksgivings as there shal be cause, to protest against all encroachments upon the Liberties of the Kirk, and to Censure all such as Interrupt this Commission or any other Church Judicatorie, or the execution of their Censures, or of any of her sentences or Acts Issuing from them; And with full power to them to treat and Determine in the Matters referred unto them by this Assemblie, as fullie and freelie as if the same were here fully expressed, and with as ample power as anie Commission of anie former Generall Assemblies hath had or been in use of before: Declaring also that all opposers of the Authoritie of this Commission in matters intrusted to them, shall beholden as opposers of the Authoritie of the Generall Assemblie, and this Commission in their whole Proceedings are Comptable to, and Censurable by the next Generall Assemblie.

DIRECTORIE FOR ELECTION OF MINISTERS.

When any Place of the Ministrie in a congregation is vacant, it is Incumbent to the Presbyterie with all diligence to send one of their number to Preach to that Congregation who in his doctrine is to represent to them the necessitie of providing the place with a qualified pastor, and to exhort them to fervent prayer and supplication to the Lord that he would send them a Pastor according to his own heart: As also he is to signifie that the Presbyterie out of their care of that Flock will send unto them Preachers, whom they may hear, and if they have a desire to hear any other, they will endeavour to procure them an hearing of that person or persones upon the sute of the Elders to the Presbyterie.

2. Within some competent time thereafter, the Presbyterie is again to send one or more of their number to the said vacant Congregation, on a certain day appoynted before for that effect, who are to conveen and hear sermon the foresaid day, which being ended, and intimation being made by the Minister, that they are to goe about the Election of a pastor for that Congregation, the Session of the Congregation shall meet and proceed to the Election, the action being moderated by him that Preached, And if the people shall upon the intimation of the Person agreed upon by the Session acquiesce and consent to the said person, Then the matter being reported to the Presbyterie by Commissioners sent from the session, they are to proceed to the triall of the person thus Elected, And finding him qualified, to admit him to the Ministry in the said Congregation.

3. But if it happen that the Major part of the Congregation dissent from the person agreed upon by the Session, In that case the matter shall be brought unto the Presbyterie, who shall Judge of the same; And if they doe not find their Dissent to be grounded on Causlesse prejudices, they are to appoynt a new Election in manner above specified.

4. But if a lesser party of the Session or Congregation shew their dissent from the Election without exceptions relevant and verified to the Presbyterie, Notwithstanding thereof the Presbyterie shall go on to the trials and ordination of the person elected; Yet all possible diligence and tendernesse must be used to bring all parties to an harmonious agreement.

5. It is to be understood that no person under the Censure of the Kirk because

of any scandalous offence is to be admitted to have hand in the election of a Minister.

6. Where the Congregation is disaffected and Malignant, in that case the Presbyterie is to provide them with a Minister.

6. AUGUST, 1649. ANTEMERIDIEM, SESS. ULT.

A BROTHERLY EXHORTATION FROM THE GENERAL ASSEMBLY OF THE CHURCH OF SCOTLAND, TO THEIR BRETHREN IN ENGLAND.

The many and great obligations which lie upon us in reference to our Brethren in England, who hold fast their integrity, and adhere to the Solemn League and Covenant, together with the desire which we have to rectifie our Sympathie with them in their afflictions, and to preserve so far as in us lieth that fellowship and correspondence that hath been entertained betwixt the Church of Scotland and England these years past, do call upon us and constrain us not to be silent in this day of their trouble and distress.

Albeit the Lord (who hath his fire in Zion, and his furnace in Ierusalem) hath now for a long time past, afflicted these Kingdoms with many & sharp rods, and that his wrath seems not yet to be turned away, but his hand stretched out still; yet in all this, it becomes us who live in these lands to stop our mouthes, neither can any impute iniquity to the most High.

It is rather a wonder, that any mercy should be continued, and that England and Scotland are not cut off from being Nations, seeing the back-slidings and provocations of both has been so many and so grosse, Although the Solemn League and Covenant was sworne and subscribed by both, yet have many in both despised the Oath of GOD, as appears by the late unlawfull Engagement against the Kingdom of England, contrived and carried on by a prevailing party of Malignants in this Land, and by the proceedings of the Sectaries in England, in reference to Religion and Government.

We shall not insist upon what hath been the condition and carriage of the Lords People in this Land in reference to the late unlawfull Engagement: As we desire to magnifie the power and loveing kindenesse of the Lord, who enabled all the Judicatures of this Church, and a considerable part of the Parliament, and the body of the Land, to dissent from, and bear Testimony against the same, which made the House of Commons in their Letter directed to the last Generall Assembly or their Commissioners, to declare, that that Engagement could not be looked on as a Nationall breach, So we look upon it as a wonder of his Wisdom and Mercy, that he hath disposed and directed the same for the furtherance of his Work in our hand, and purging his House amongst us. All this cometh forth from the Lord of Hosts, who is wonderfull in Counsel and Excellent in Working. Neither was it the least part of the lords goodnesse to us, in that day of our strait that we were led in a plain path, and kept from complyance with Sectaries on the one hand, no less then with Malignants on the other. We have obtained this mercy to be steadfast to our old principles, in bearing free and faithfull Testimony against their proceedings, both in reference to Toleration and Government, and the taking away of the Kings life.

And as the danger and judgement which threatens the Authors and Abettors of these things, doth affect our Spirits with horrour, and maketh us desire that it may be given to them of God to repent: So we should conceive our selves void of Christian affection and compassion toward those in England, who suffer for the truth and Cause of God, if we were not very sensible of all their present troubles and calamities. It is no small grief to us, that the Gospel and Government of Jesus Christ are so despised in that Land that faithfull Preachers are persecuted and cryed down, that Toleration is established by pretext of Law, and maintained Military power, and that the Covenant is abolished and buried in oblivion. All which proceedings, cannot but be looked upon as directly contrary to the Oath of God lying upon us, and therefore cannot eschew his Wrath when he shall come in Judgement, to be a swift witnesse against those that swear falsly by his Name.

These things are the more grievous to us, because (beside many other wofull evils brought forth by them) they have interrupted the building of the Lords House in England; the foundation whereof was laid by Oath and Covenant with the most High God, and followed for some years with many Declarations and Protestations of Faithfull adhering thereto, and with great expense of blood and Treasure: Which things were to all the godly in these Nations a branch of hope, that the Lord would bring to perfection the Work of Uniformity (so far advanced in all the parts thereof) in these three Kingdoms.

But the great obstructions and sad interruptions that have been made therein, by the strange and unexpected practises of many now in place and power in England, are to all the welaffected in both Kingdoms, and in all the Churches abroad, the mater of their sorrow and humiliation. And if there be any place left for admonition, we Warn such as have forgotten the Covenant, and despised the Oath of God, and turned aside to lies and errour, to consider whence they are fallen, and to repent. Prosperity and success for a time are no warrantable evidences of a good Cause, nor sufficient guards against the wrath of God; It is no good use of the Lords mercy for such men under pretext of Liberty to make both themselves and others slaves to corruption, and to make all men both in Church and State like the fishes of the Sea, or the creeping things that have no ruler over them. Are these things according to the Word of God, and the pattern of the best Reformed Churches? Or is that the endeavour to bring the three Kingdoms to the nearest uniformity that may be in Doctrine, Worship, Government, and Discipline; Or is that the maintaining of the union betwixt the three Kingdomes, when the straitest bond thereof is utterly dissolved and quite taken away, and the fundamentall Government by King and Parliament wholly overturned; The just God who is of pure eyes beholds these things, and shall with no lesse fury and indignation break the horn of these men, then he hath broken the power, and brought down the pride of Malignants before them, if repentance prevent not.

Amidst these sors and griefes it is unto us matter of rejoycing, that there be many in England who mourn for all these abominations, and labour to keep their garments pure by refusing to comply with that course of backsliding, and by bearing testimony against the same. And we hope the expectation of such, shall not be disappointed, but that the Lord will open to them a doore for carrying on of his work, and making the lying spirit to passe out of that land.

And albeit many think no otherwise of the Covenant and work of Reformation, then as a mean to further their own ends; yet we are confident, that none who holds fast their integrity, have so learned Christ, but are carefull to make conscience of the oath of God lying on them; And we are sure (whatever be the base thoughts and expressions of backsliders from the Covenant) it wants not many to own it in those Kingdomes, who (being called thereto) would seale the same with their blood.

Although there were none in the one Kingdome who did adhere to the Covenant, yet thereby were not the other Kingdom nor any person in either of them absolved from the bond thereof, since in it we have not only sworne by the Lord, but also covenanted with him. It is not the failing of one or more that can absolve others from their duty or tye to him; Besides, the duties therein contained, being in themselves lawfull, and the grounds of our tye thereunto moral, though others do forget their duty, yet doth not their defection free us from that obligation which lyes upon us by the Covenant in our places and stations. And the Covenant being intended and entred into by these Kingdoms, as one of the best means of stedfastnesse, for guarding against declining times; It were strange to say that the back-sliding of any should absolve others from the tye thereof, especially seeing our engagement therein is not only nationall, but also personall, every one with uplifted hands swearing by himselfe, as it is evident by the tennor of the Covenant.

From these and other important reasons, it may appear that all these Kingdomes joyning together to abolish that oath by law, yet could they not dispense therewith; Much lesse can any one of them, or any part in either of them doe the same. The dispensing with oathes hath hitherto been abhorred as Antichristian, and never practised and avowed by any, but by that man of sin; therefore those who take the same upon them, as they joyn with him in his sin, so must they expect to partake of his plagues.

As we shall ever (God willing) be mindfull of our duty to the faithfull that adhere to the Covenant in England, having them alwayes in our hearts before the Lord, so we desire to be refreshed with their singlesse and boldnesse in the cause of God, according to their places. This is the time of their triall, and the houre of tentation among them; blessed shall they be who shall be found following the Lamb, and shall not be ashamed of his testimony. We know in such dark houres, many are drawne away with the multitude, whom the Lord will again purge and make white; And we doubt not but many such are in England, whom the bold clear preaching of Christ may reclaim; Much therefore lieth upon the Watch-men all this time, that their Trumpet may give a certain and distinct sound, warning and exhorting every one, as those that must give account; And blessed shall those servants be, who shall be found faithfull in their Lords house, distributing to his houshold what is meet for this season, and can say they are free of the blood of all men, having shewen them the whole Counsell of God, being in nothing terrified of the threats of their adversaries; And blessed & happy shall that people be, that walk in the light holden forth by them, and staye upon the Lord in this dark time, harkning to the voyce of his servants, & walking in the light of his word & not in the sparks of their owne kindlings, which will end in sorrow. How inexcusable will England be, having so foulie revolted against so many faire testimionies, which the Lord Christ hath entred as Protestations to preserve his right, in these ends of the earth long since given unto him for his possession, and of late confirmed by Solemne Covenant. Christs right to these Kingdomes is surer then that he should be pleaded out of it by pretended liberty of Conscience, and his begun possession is more precious to him, then to be satisfied with a dishonourable toleration. All that yet we have seen, doth not weaken our confidence of the Lords glorifying the house of his glory in these lands, and of his sonnes taking unto him his great power, and reigning in the beauty and power of his Ordinances in this Island. His name is wonderfull, and so also are his workes, we ought not therefore to square them according to our line, but leave them to him, who hath the government laid upon his shoulder, all whose wayes are judgement, & whose ruling these Kingdoms had never yet reason to decline. It is good for us to be stedfast in our duty, and therein quietly to wait and hope for the salvation of God. The word of promise is sure, (and hath an appointed time) that he that will come shall come and will not tarry. There is none hath cause to distrust the Lords word to his people; It hath often to our experience been tryed in the fire, and hath ever come forth with a more glorious lustre. Let not therefore these that suffer in England cast away their confidence, they are not the first who have needed patience after that they had done the Lords will. But let them strengthen the weak hands, and confirm the feeble knees, and say to the fearfull in heart, be strong, fear not, behold your God will come with vengeance, even God with a recompence, he will come and save you. Now the just shall live by faith, whereas these that draw back, or become lukewarm in the Lords work, his soul shall abhorre them, and he shall spue them out of his mouth, But we perswade our selves of better things of these our brethren in England, and prayeth that the God of Peace who brought again from the dead our Lord Jesus, that great Shepheard of the sheep, through the blood of the everlasting Covenant, may make them perfect in every good work to doe his will, working in them that which is well pleasing in his fight through Jesus Christ, to whom be Glory for ever. AMEN.

ACT FOR A COLLECTION FOR ENTERTAINING HIGHLAND BOYES AT SCHOOLES.

The Generall Assembly Considering that the contribution of fourty shillings for entertaining of Highland boyes at Schools, in respect of the penury and great indigence of those parts hath not taken the intended effect. Therefore in respect of the necessity and profitablenesse of so pious a work The Assembly in lieu of the said fourty shillings Do Appoint and Ordain that there be an extraordinary Collection at the Kirk doors for that use one Sabbath in the year: And to that effect, that a certain Sabbath yearly be appointed and designed whereupon that collection shall be gathered, intimation being made by the Minister the Sabbath before to prepare for such a collection, and the necessity and usefulnesse thereof being laid out to the people for that end. And if the collection in any little private Congregation shall be lesse then fourty shillings, The Session shall make up what wants of fourty shillings; And where the collection is more, it is hereby specially inhibited and discharged that any part thereof be retained or interverted to any other use whatsomever; and these Collections shall be sent to the persons formerly appointed to receive the fourty shillings, that they may see the right distribution and employment thereof; Recommending the Presbyteries see this punctually performed. And accompt thereof shall be craved at Synods and Generall Assemblies. It is alwayes to be remembred that the Congregations exeemed from the fourty shillings are also exeemed from this Collection.

COMMISSION FOR A CONFERENCE OF MINISTERS, LAWYERS AND PHYSITIANS, CONCERNING THE TRYAL AND PUNISHMENT OF WITCH-CRAFT, CHARMING AND CONSULTING.

The Generall Assembly Taking to their serious consideration the growth of the sins of Witchcraft, Charming and Consulting, notwithstanding the frequent Recommendations for restraining thereof; And remembring that the Generall Assembly 1647. did propose a good way for the tryal and punishment of these sinnes, by appointing conferences with some Ministers, Lawyers and Physitians in that matter which hath never yet taken effect; Therefore the Assembly doth appoint Masters, Robert Dowglas, Robert Blair, Mungo Law, James Hammilton, John Smith, Robert Traill, George Leslie, John Hamilton, Iohn Duncan, Samuel Rutherfoord, James Wood, Iohn Leviston, Iames Guthrie, Andro Cant, David Calderwood, Iohn Moncreiff, Frederick Carmichael, Iames Durhame, Patrick Gillespie, Robert Ker, Ephraim Melvil, Ministers, To consider seriously of that matter, and to consult and advise therein amongst themselves, As also with Sir Archibald Iohnston of Wariston, Clerk Register, Mr Thomas Nicolson his Majesties Advocate, Mr Alexander Peirson, one of the ordinary Lords of Session, Sir Lewes Stewart, Mr Alexander Colvil, and Mr Iames Robertson Iustice Deputes, Masters Rodger Mowit, John Gilmoir, and Iohn Nisbet, Laweers; and with Doctors Sibbald, Cunninghame, and Purves, Physitians severally or together as occasion shall offer; And the Assembly earnestly requests & confidently expects from their learned and Iudicious Lawyres and Physitians beforenamed, their best endeavours and concurrence with their brethren of the Ministrie for advise and counsell herein, and for conference in the said matter; And Ordaine the said brethren to make report of the result of their consultations and conferences from time to time as they make any considerable progresse to the Commission for publick affaires, And the said Commission shall make report to the next Generall Assembly.

RECOMMENDATION FOR MAINTENANCE FOR SCHOOL-MASTERS AND PRECENTERS.

The Generall Assembly do humbly Recommend to the Parliament or Committee for plantation of Churches, that whatever either in Paroches of Burghs or Landwart, was formerly given to the maintenance of these who were readers precentors in Congregations, and teachers of Schooles before the establishing of the

Directory for publick Worship, may not be in whole or in part alienat or taken away, but reserved for the maintenance of sufficient schoolmasters and precentors who are to be approven by the Presbyterie; And Presbyteries are hereby required to see that none of that maintenance given to the foresaid uses or in use to be payed thereunto before the establishing of the Directory of Worship, to be drawn away from the Church.

ACTS CONCERNING PERSONS TO BE ADMITTED BURSARS.

The Assembly doe hereby Ordaine That none be sent to Universities from Presbyteries, nor be admitted as Bursers of divinitie, but pious youths, and such as are known to be of Good expectation and approven abilities.

REFERENCE TO THE COMMISSION FOR PUBLICK AFFAIRES FOR RE-EXAMINING THE PARAPHRASE, OF THE PSALMES AND THE EMITTING THE SAME FOR PUBLICKE USE.

The General Assembly having taken some view of the new Paraphrase of the Psalmes in meeter with the corrections and animadversions thereupon sent from several Persons and Presbyteries, and finding that they cannot overtake the review and examination of the whole in this Assembly; Therefore now after so much time and so great paines about the correcting, and examining thereof from time to time some yeares bygone, that the worke may come now to some conclusion, They do ordain the Brethren appointed for perusing the same during the meeting of this Assembly, viz. Masters James Hammilton, Iohn Smith, Hew Mackall, Robert Traill, George Hutcheson, and Robert Lawrie, after the dissolving of this Assembly to goe on in that worke carefully, And to report their travels to the Commission of the Generall Assembly for publick affaires at ther meeting at Edinburgh in November; And the said Commission after perusall and re-examination thereof, is hereby authorised with full power to conclude and establish the Paraphrase, and to publish and emit the same for publick use.

LETTER TO THE KINGS MAJESTIE.

Most gracious Soveraigne,

Wee your Majesties most humble and Loyall Subjects, the Commissioners from all the Presbyteries in this your Majesties ancient Kingdome, and members of this present Nationall Assembly, Having expected to finde at our meeting, a gracious and Satisfactory returne to those humble representations made to your Majestie at the Hague, by the Commissioners of this Kirk, cannot but expresse our great sorrow and griefe, that your Majesties goodnes has been so far abused, As that not only the just and necessary desires presented by them to your Majestie, which so much concerne the glory of God, your owne honour and happinesse, the peace and safety of your Kingdomes, are utterly frustrated, as wee perceive by the paper delivered in answer to them; but also this Assembly hath not received so much as any signification by letter of your Majesties minde: Which princely condescension had not wont to be wanting in your Royall Father, to former Generall

Assemblyes, even in times of greatest distance.

Our witnesse is in heaven, and record on high, that wee are not conscious to our Selves of any undutifull thought or disloyall affection, that might have procured this at your Majesties hands; And that, as wee doe from our hearts abominate and detest that horrid fact of the Sectaryes against the life of your Royall Father our late Soveraigne, So it is the unfained and earnest desire of our soules, that the Ancient Monarchicall government of these Kingdoms, may be established and flourish in your Majesties person all the dayes of your life, and be continued in your royall Family which by divine providence hath without interruption raigned over us and our predecessors for so many Generations since the time that we were a Kingdom, And that there is nothing under the glory of God, and cause of our Lord Jesus Christ, for which wee doe more heartily solicit the throne of grace, Or would more readily expose unto hazard all that is deare to us in the world, then for this. And now though this very great discouragement might incline us to hold our peace at this time, Yet the tendernesse and uprightnesse of our affection and Love to your Majesties happinesse (which many waters cannot quench) together with the Conscience of our duty which Our Lord and Master has laid upon us, in this our place and station, constraineth us, yea, and your Majesties owne goodnesse and gracious disposition, whereof the late Commissioners have given us so Large a testimony, Doth much encourage us, to renew our addresses to your Majestie in this humble faithfull representation, both of the great and growing dangers to your Royall person and Throne, and of these duties, which the Lord of Lords and King of Kings, call for from you, as you would look to finde favour in his eyes, and to be delivered out of your deepe distresses.

Our hearts are filled with fears and troubles, in your Majesties behalf, when we look upon the sad calamities which have been already produced by such wayes and courses, as we perceive your Majestie is entred, and in danger to be further led away into, by the prevalency of evill Councell upon your tender age: Particalarly, Your refusing to give satisfaction to the just and necessary desires of the people of God, for advancing the work of Reformation of Religion, and establishing and securing the same in your Majesties Dominions, which is nothing else, but to oppose the Kingdome of the Sonne of God, by whom Kings doe raigne, and to refuse that he should raigne over you and your Kingdomes in his pure Ordinances of Church government and Worship; Your cleaving unto these men as your trustiest Counsellors, who, as they never had the glory of God, nor good of his people before their eyes, so now in all their wayes and Counsels, are seeking nothing but their owne interests, to the hazard of the utter subversion of your Throne, the ruine of your Royall Family, and the desolation of your Kingdomes; Your owning the practises, and intertaining the Person of that flagicious man, and most justly excommunicate Rebell, James Graham, who has exercised such horrid cruelty upon your best Subjects in this Kingdom, which cannot but bring upon your Throne, the guiltinesse of all the innocent blood shed by him and his Complices; and above all, that, which we cannot think upon without trembling of heart and horrour of spirit, Your setling of late such a Peace with the Irish Papists the Murderers of so many thousands of your Protestant Subjects, whereby not only they are owned as your good Loyall Subjects, but also there is granted unto them (contrary to the Standing Lawes of your Royall Progenitors, contrary to the commandment of the most high God, and to the high contempt and dishonor of his Majestie, and evident danger of the Protestant Religion) a full liberty of their abominable Idolatry; which cannot be otherwise judged, but a giving of your Royal power and strength unto the beast, and an accession to all that blood of your good Subjects, wherewith those Sonnes of Babell have made that Land to swim.

We do in all humility beseech your Majestie to consider & lay to heart what the mouth of the Lord of Hosts hath spoken of all the accompts of People, Nations, Kings, and Rulers against the Kingdom of his Son, that they imagine a vaine thing and that he that sitteth in heaven will have them in dirision and vex them in his sore displeasure. Consider, how he hath blasted and turned upside downe these yeares by past, all the devices and plots of those men that now beare the Swey in your Majesties Counsels: Consider, how the anger of God has been kindled, even against his dearest Saints, when they have joyned themselves to such men as he hateth and has cursed: Consider, how severely hee hath threatned and punished such Kings as have associate with Idolaters, and leaned unto their helps. Surely, great is the wrath of God, whereof you are in danger; And yet the Lord in the riches of his goodnesse, forbearance and long suffering, is waiting to be gracious to your Majestie; To day if ye will hear his voice, harden not your heart, but humble your self under the mighty hand of God, lamenting after him as, for the iniquities of your Fathers house, especially the opposition against the reformation of Religion and Cause of God, the permitting and practising Antichristian Idolatry in the Royall Family it self, and the shedding of so much blood of the people of God, so also, for your owne entering to walke in the like courses in the beginning of your raign. It is high time to fall downe before the Throne of grace, seeking to get your peace made with God through Jesus Christ whose blood is able to wash away all your sins, To walk no longer in the Councel of the ungodly, nor cleave to such as seeke their own things and not the things of Jesus Christ, nor the welfare of your Subjects and Government, but to set your eyes upon the faithfull in your dominions, that such may dwell with you, & be the men of your Councells, To serve the Lord in feare, and kisse the Sonne of God, by a sincere and cordiall contributing your Royall allowance and authority, for establishing in all your dominions the reformation of Religion, in Doctrine, Worship, and Government as it is now agreed upon according to the cleare & evident warrant of the word of God, by the Assembly of Divines at Westminster, and the Generall Assemblies of this Church; And also, laying aside that service book, which is so stuffed with Romish corruptions, And conforming your owne practise and the worship of God in your Royall Family, to that Gospell simplicity and purity which is holden forth from the word of God, in the Directory of worship, and not only to grant your Royall approbation to the Covenant of these three Kingdomes (without which, your people can never have from you sufficient security, either for Religion, or their just liberties) but also your selfe to joyne with your people therein as the greatest security under Heaven for your person and just greatness, and to cause all of them stand to it by your Royall Command, according to the practise of that gracious King Josiah, to whom, wee wish your Majestie in these your younger yeares, and this beginning of your raigne, to look as to an ensample and Kingly portract approven of God. These things if your Majestie do; As wee are well assured, that the hearts of all your good Subjects in these Kingdomes will be enlarged with all cheerfulnesse to imbrace your person, and submit unto your Royall Government, so wee darre promise in the Name of our Lord, that you shall finde favour with God, peace and joy unspeakable and full of glory to your Soule, and deliverance out of your sad afflictions and deep distresses in due time: But if your Majestie shall go on in refusing to hearken to wholesome Councels; We must for the discharge of our Conscience tell your Majestie in the humility and griefe of our hearts, that the Lords anger is not turned away, but his hand stretched out still against you and your Family. But we hope and shall with all earnestnesse and constancy pray for better things from, and to your Majestie: And whatsoever misconstruction (by the malice of those that desire not a right understanding and cordiall conjunction between your Majestie and this Kirk and Kingdome) may be put upon our declaration; Yet wee have the Lord to be our witnesse, that our purpose and intention therein is no other, but to warne and keepe the people of God committed to our care, that they runne not to any course which would bring upon themselves the guilt of highest perjury and breach of Covenant with God, and could not but prove most dangerous to your Majestie and your Government, and involve you in shedding the blood of those who are most desirous to preserve your Majesties Person, and just right in all your dominions. And now wee doe with all earnestnes beseech your Majestie, that you will follow the courses of truth and peace; And that when there is a doore opened for your Majestie to enter to your Royall Government over us, in peace, with the favour of God, and cordiall Love and imbracings of all your good Subjects, You will not suffer your selfe to be so farre abused and misled by the Councels of men, who delight in war, as to take away of violence and blood, which cannot but provoke the most high against your Majestie, and alienat from you the hearts of your best Subjects, who desire nothing more, than that your Majestie may have a long and happy raign over them, And that they may live under you, a peaceable and quiet life, in all Godlinesse and honesty.

Edinburgh 6 August, 1649.

Your Majesties most Loyal Subjects and humble servants the Ministers and Elders conveened in this Nationall Assembly of the Kirk of Scotland.

The Generall Assembly not having now time to consider the Reference of preceeding Assemblies, and the most part of Presbyteries not having sent their opinions in writ; Thefore do yet againe recommend to Presbyteries and Provinciall Assemblies to consider all matters referred by this or by any former Assemblies, And to send their opinions therein in writ to the next Generall Assembly.

The meeting of the next Generall Assembly is hereby appointed to be at Edinburgh, the second wednesday of July, 1650.

A. Ker

FINIS

THE PRINCIPAL ACTS OF THE GENERAL ASSEMBLY OF THE CHURCH OF SCOTLAND HOLDEN AT EDINBURGH THE 16TH DAY OF OCTOBER 1690.

EDINBURGH 16 OF OCTOBER 1690. POST MERIDIEM. SESS. 1.

I. THE MEETING OF THE GENERAL ASSEMBLY, AND THE RECORDING OF THEIR MAJESTIES COMMISSION, TO JOHN LORD CARMICHAEL, FOR REPRESENTING THEIR MAJESTIES THEREIN.

This day, being a day of Solemn Fasting and Humiliation, the General Assembly of the Ministers and Elders of this Church; did after Sermons (in the Forenoon by Mr. Gabriel Cunningham Moderator of the last General Meeting, and in the Afternoon by Mr. Patrick Sympson Moderator of the preceding General Meeting) Conveen in the Assembly-House at Edinburgh, according to the Indiction of an Act of the current Parliament, dated the 7 day of June last, and Directions given by the late General Meeting of the Ministers and Elders of this Church: And after Prayer, there was produced to them, by an Noble Lord John Lord Carmichael, Their Majesties Commission, for his being Their Majesties High Commissioner and Representative to this General Assembly, Dated at Kensingtoun the 10 day of October 1690. Which was with all due Respect publickly read: And Mr. Gabriel Cuningham, Moderator for the time, did in the Assemblies Name, Represent to his Grace, how Great a Mercy it was, to this Church and Kingdom, that Their Majesties had Countenanced this Assembly, with Their Authority, and Honoured it with a Representative of Their Royal Persons: And the Assemblies great Satisfaction, with Their Majesties choice of a person so well Qualified, and so Acceptable to this Assembly, to Represent Their Majesties therein. To whom His Grace was pleased to give this return, That it was his firm Resolution, in the Capacity, wherein Their Majesties had now put him, to lay out himself for their Majesties Service, and the good of the Church. The Assembly appointed the said Commission to be Recorded in Their Books, Ad futuram res Memoriam: The Tenour whereof follows.

GULIELMUS & MARIA, Dei Gratia, Magnæ Britannia, Francia & Hibernia, Rex & Regina, Fideique Defensores, Omnibus probis Hominibus, ad quos præsentes Literæ; Nostræ pervenerint, Salutem. Quandoquidem per actum, in secundâ Sessione Currentis hujus nostri Parliamenti, Expeditum, De stabiliendo Ecclesiæ Regimine, in antiquiori hoc nostro Scotiæ Regno; Primum Ecclesiæíllius Generalem Conventum, Edinburghi, Tertio die Jovis, Mensis Octobris Instantis, teneri Ordinavimus: Nosautem (Rebus magni Momenti alio vocantíbus) In dicto Conventu interesse nequimus: Abunde vero Cupidi, ut Idem Generalis Conventus, ad Religionem veram Reformatam melius firmandam, Pietatem & Sanctitatem Propagandam, Pacem itaque & Unitatem, in dictâ Ecclesiâ, & hoc nostro antiquiore Regno acquirendam; methodo debitâ & Regulari, Observetur: Cumque Testimoniis perplurimis & probatis, nobis abunde satisfactum sit, de Præclaris animi dotibus, & fide eximiâ, fidelisslimi & dilectissimi nostri Consiliarii. Joannis Domini Carmichael, quibus ad summæ fiduciæ Munus infra expressum, debite & exacte obeundum & excercendum, usque quaque est adaptatus: Noverítis igítur nos Nominasse & Constituisse, sicuti per hasce nostras Patentes Literas, Nominamus & Constituimus Eundem Joannem Dominum Carmichael, Supremum nostrum Commissionarium, quoad effectum intra expressum: Damus pariter & concedimus illi, sacram Nostram Personam & Authoritatem Regiam Repræsentandi, ac pro nobis præsentiam faciendi, locumque nostrum in subsequenti Generali Conventu, Tanquam Commissionario nostro, in hunc effectum specialiter Constitute, tenendi: Omniaque alia ad Imperium & Munus Commissionarii, pro Generali Ecclesiæ conventu peragendi, tam plene, adeoque libere, in quovis Respectu, quam Quilibet alius ejusdem Muneris & Characteris, fecerat, seu quovis tempore retroacto facere potuerat, atque adeo sicuti Nosmet ipsi personaliter præsentes Possemus. Plenissimam & amplissimam Nostram Potestatem & Commissionem. Quæquidem omnia & singula, a dicto Joanne Domino Carmichael, In hac nostra Commissione prolequendâ, legitime facienda, Nos firmiter approbamus, Rata habemus, & habituri sùmus. Omnibus & singulis insuper antedicti Conventus, & Ecclesiæ Pastoribus & Presbyteris, ac Cæterii quibuscumque hujus Nostri Regni Subditis, cujuscunque ordinis seu conditionis, ut eundem Joannem Dominum Carmichael, tanquam Supremum Nostrum Commissionarium, quoad effectum & modum supra mentionatum, agnoscant, Colant, & dicto ipsius audientes se præbeant, stricte Mandamus & Imperamus. Et denique hanc Nostram Commissionem, a die quo Magnum hujus Regni Nostri Sigillum, Presentibus est appensum, ac durante Primâ dicti Generalis Conventus Sessione, aut usque donec hæc Nostra Commissio per nos Revocetur, Continuare Declaravimus, ac per Præsentes Declaramus. In cujus rei Testimonium, Præsentibus Magnum Sigillum Nostrum appendi Mandavimus, Apud aulam Nostram de Kensingtoun, decimo die mensis Octobris, Anno Domini 1690. Regnique nostri, Anno secundo.

Per signaturam manu S.D.N. Regis supra Signatam.

(locus figilli appensi)

IN DORSO:

Sealed at Edinburgh the 16th of October 1690. Alex. Inglis.

Written to the Great Seal, and Registr at the 16 day of October 1690. Dun. Ronald Dpt.

EDINBURGH 17 OCTOBER 1690. ANTE MERIDIEM SESS. 2.

II. HIS MAJESTIES GRACIOUS LETTER TO THE ASSEMBLY.

This Session, His Majesties Gracious Letter Direct to this General Assembly, was publickly Read and Heard with great Respect; and appointed to be Recorded in the Books of the Assembly, The Tenour whereof follows.

William R.

Reverend, Trusty and Well Beloved,

Our Concern for the Good of Our Ancient Kingdom, hath been such, That We have left nothing undone, that might Contribute to the making of it Happy: And therefore having been informed, that Differences as to the Government of the Church have caused greatest Confusions in that Nation; We did willingly concurre with Our Parliament, in In-acting such a Frame of it, as was judged to be most agreeable to the Inclinations of Our Good Subjects: To which as We have had a particular Regard, in Countenanceing this Assembly, With Our Authority, and a Representative of Our Royall Person; So We expect, that Your Managment shall be such, as We shall have no reason, to Repent of what we have done. A Calm and Peaceable Procedure, will be no less pleasing to Us, than it becometh You. We never could be of the Mind, that Violence was suited to the advancing of True Religion; Nor do We intend, that Our Authority shall ever be a Tool, to the irregular Passions of any Party. Moderation is what Religion enjoynes, Neighbouring Churches expect from You, and We Recommend to You. And We assure You of Our constant Favour and Protection, in Your following of these Methods, which shall be for the real advantage of True Piety, and the Peace of Our Kingdoms. Given under our Royal Hand, At our Court at Kensingtoun, the 10 day of October 1690.

By His Majesties Command,

MELVIL.

Direct,

For the Reverend, Trusty and Wel-Beloved, Ministers and Elders, met in the General Assembly of the Church of Scotland. At Edinburgh.

EDINBURGH 18TH. OCTOBER 1690. POST MERIDIEM SESS. 4.

III. THE ASSEMBLIES ANSWER TO HIS MAJESTIES GRACIOUS LETTER.

May it please your Majesty,

Your Gracious Letter, Direct to the Ministers and Elders met here, in the General Assembly of the Church of Scotland was Read and Heard among Us, with all Joy and Thankfulness, that the Rising and Shining again of the Royal Favour, upon this long Afflicted and distressed Church, could possibly Inspire: For as Your Majesties Concern for the Good of this Your Ancient Kingdom, hath indeed been such, as nothing can impair the Happy State whereunto You have Restored it, save the want of the due sense and understanding of so great a Mercy; So We doe most heartily acknowledge, that through Your Majesties Care and Kindness, the Church of Christ therein, doth equally partake of the same Blessing. It was the sad Confusions, that differences as to the Government of the Church, had caused in this Nation, that according to Your Majesties first Declaration, for our Relief, moved our Gracious God, to Raise up and Prosper You, to Be our Glorious Deliverer, for Effectuating the Reestablishment that we now enjoy: So that we are perswaded, that it is not more Agreeable, to the Inclinations and Conscientious Perswasions of all within this Kingdom, who are best Affected to Your Majesties Person and Government, than it is acceptable to God, and will be Your Majesties perpetual Peace and Satisfaction. Nor are we less Sensible of the particular Regard, Your Majestie professeth towards us, on this occasion, in Countenancing this Assembly, with Your Authority, and a Representative of Your Royal Person; for which we most humbly acknowledge Your Gracious Favour; especially that it hath pleased Your Majesty, to fix Your Choice, upon a Person so well Qualified, and so acceptable to Us. And now, Great Sir, after so many and so great Mercies and Favours, Received from God and Your Majesty; We Hope we may with Confidence assure You, that our Managment shall be such, as Your Majesty hath so just Reason to expect, and shall never give you cause to Repent of what You have done for Us. The God of Love, the Prince of Peace, with all the Providences that have gone over Us, and Circumstances that We are under, as well as Your Majesties most obliging Pleasure, Require of Us a Calme and Peaceable Procedure, And if after the Violence for Conscience sake, that We have Suffered, and so much Detested, and these Grievious Abuses of Authority, in the late Reigns, Whereby through some Mens Irregular Passions, We have so sadly Smarted; We our selves, should Lapse into the same Errours, We should certainly prove the most Unjust towards God, Foolish towards our Selves, and Ungrate towards Your Majesty, of all Men on earth. Great Revolutions of this nature, must be attended, with Occasions of Complaint: And even the worst of Men, are Ready to cry out of Wrong, for their justest Deservings: But as Your Majesty Knows these things too well, to give us the least Apprehension of any impressions evil Report can make; So We assure Your Majesty, as in the Presence of God, and in expectation of his dreadfull Appearance, that We shall Study that Moderation, which Your Majesty Recommends, as being convinced, that it is the Duty that Religion enjoyns, and Neighbouring Churches doe most justly expect from Us: Desiring in all things, to Approve our selves unto God, as the true Disciples of Jesus Christ, who, though most Zealous, against all Corruptions in his Church, was most Gentle towards the Persons of Men: And to maintain as much as in us lyes, Peace and Concord with all the Reformed Churches: As likewise to comply in all obsequious Duty, with all that Your Majesty enjoynes, for the Real Advantage of true Piety, and the Peace or all Your Kingdoms. Heartily wishing, that God, who hath Graciously brought back Your Majesties Person, in Safety, from Your Late, no less Generous, than Dangerous Expedition, for his Cause and Truth, with joyfull Success; May still preserve Your Majesty, and Our most Gracious Queen; Granting You long Life, Health, and Prosperity, And may Establish Your Throne, and Bless Your Government, to the Glory of His Great Name, the Good of all his Churches, and the welfare of all Your People. Which shall ever be the earnest Prayer of,

May it please Your Majesty,
Your Majesties most Faithful,
most Obedient and most Humble Subjects.

Signed in our Presence, in our Name,
and at our Appointment, *By*
HU. KENNEDIE Moderator.

IV. APPOINTMENT OF A DIET, TO BE KEPT BY THE AS-SEMBLY FOR PRAYER.

The General Assembly Appoints Monday next, betwixt Eight and Twelve a Clock in the Forenoon, to be set a part for Prayer, by the Members of this Assembly: And Recommends to all the Members, to meet in the Assembly-House for that end, at Eight a Clock in the Morning.

EDINBURGH 25TH. OCTOBER 1690. ANTE MERIDI-EM. SESS. 9.

V. THE PROCEEDINGS OF THE ASSEMBLY, ANENT MR. THOMAS LINING AND OTHERS.

The General Assembly, having received a Report, from the Committee of Overtures, anent two Papers given in to the said Committee, and Subscribed by Mr. Thomas Lining, Mr. Alexander Shields and Mr. William Boyd, who had followed some Courses contrary to the Order of this Church; whereby, "The said Committee out of their ardent Desire of Union in the Church, Recommend to the Assembly, the Reading of the Shorter of these two Papers: In which the fore-named Persons Oblige themselves after the exhibiting of the larger Paper (which they offer, as they profess, for the Exoneration of their Consciences) and laying it down at the Assemblies feet, to be Disposed upon as the Assembly should think fit: That they shall in all required Submission, subject Themselves, their Lives and Doctrine, to the Cognizance of the Respective Judicatories of this Church, and equally to Oppose Schism and Defection, in any Capacity, that they should be capable of. But the said Committee, Judgeth, the Reading of the larger of the saids two Papers, in full Assembly, to be Inconvenient: In regard, That though there be several good Things in it, yet the same doth also contain, several Peremptory and gross Mistakes, Unseasonable and Impracticable Proposals, and Uncharitable and Injurious Reflections, tending rather to kindle Contentions, than to compose Divisions: Nevertheless, the said Committee, gives it as their Opinion, That the foresaid Offer of the above named Persons their Subjection and Obedience, to the Authority of this Church, in her Respective Judicatories, contained in the said Shorter Paper; should be Entertained and Accepted of, by the Assembly, and they Received into Communion with this Church, according to their several Capacities."

Likeas the above named persons, having Compeared, in presence of the Assembly, and Judicially Owned and Adhered unto their said Shorter Paper: And the Assembly having heard the above-written Report, of the Committee of Overtures concerning both the saids Papers; As also the said shorter Paper, Read in their Presence; The General Assembly, after mature Deliberation, did Unanimously, and without a contrary Vote, Approve the above written Report and Opinion of the Committee of Overtures, in the hail Heads thereof. Which being Intimate to the fore-named Persons, they Acquiesced thereto. Upon all which the following Act was made.

ACT ANENT MR. THOMAS LINING AND OTHERS.

Whereas Mr. Thomas Lining, Mr. Alexander Schields and Mr. William Boyd, have presented to this Assembly two Papers: One containing the Expressions of their Purpose and Promise, of being subject to the Authority of this Church, as formerly Constituted, and now Restored, in its several Judicatories: The other Offered for the Exoneration of their Consciences. Which Paper, containing their Submission and Subjection, did after the exhibition of the other to the Assembly, Become Binding upon them, according to the Promise therein made. Likeas, after that other and longer Paper had been Read, before the Committee of Overtures, It was exhibite to and received by the Assembly; together with the Reasons from the said Committee why it should not be Publickly read in full Assembly. Which Reasons being duely considered, and the said other Paper of Submission and Subjection publickly Read, and Judicially Owned by the forenamed Persons, in presence of the Assembly: The Assembly did conclude by one single Vote, that the foresaid longer Paper should not be Read: And that the above named Persons should be Received into the Fellowship of this Church, on the Terms of Submission and Subjection contained in the Shorter Paper: And after passing of the said Vote, and that they were gravely Admonished by the Moderator to walk Orderly in time coming, in Opposition to all Schisme and Division; It was declared to them, by the Moderator, in the Name of the Assembly, That the Assembly did receive them into the Fellowship of this Church, to enjoy the priviledges thereof, and Perform the Duties therein, whereof they are, or shall be found Capable. Whereupon, and at their desire, it was ordained that this Act should be made; and an Extract thereof given to them in good Form. Follows the Tenour of the said shorter Paper.

To the Moderator and Remanent Members of the General Assembly of the Church of Scotland.

Right Reverend and Honourable,

"With the greatest Earnestness of longing we have desired, and yet with a Patience perhaps to excess, we have waited, for an Opportunity, to bring our unhappy Differences (of which, all Parties concerned are weary) to a Happy and Holy close; And for this end to have access to apply our selves to a full and free General Assembly of this Church, invested with Authority and Power, in foro Divino & Humano, to Determine and Cognosce upon them. The want of which an Assembly constitute in that vigour, to which through the Mercy of God, This Venerable National Synod hath arrived, hath been the greatest let and impediment of our composing these Differences, in a way, wherein not only we, but all of the same Sentiments would acquiesce. Now having obtained this much longed, and long Prayed for priviledge; We cannot forbear any longer, humbly, to Accost and Address this Venerable Assembly, with a free and Ingenuous Representation of our Minds and Desires. The scope of which is, to Represent these things, which have been most stumbling to us, for the exoneration of our Consciences; and to declare our Design, after we have exhibited our Testimony against these Courses, which we understand to have been Corruptions and Defections in this Church, And laid it down at the Assemblies feet, to be disposed of, as their Wisdoms shall think fit: That we shall in all Required Submission, Subject our Selves, our Lives and Doctrine, to the Cognizance of the Judicatories of this Church, and shall equally oppose Schism and Defection, in any Capacity, that we shall be found Capable of. And here by these presents, we bind and oblige our selves Faithfully, to live in Union, Communion and intire Subjection, and due Obedience in the Lord, to the Authority of this Church in her Respective Judicatories: As witness our Hands at Edinburgh the 22 day of October 1690."

Thomas Lining.
Alexander Shields,
William Boyd.

EDINBURGH 28 OF OCTOBER 1690. ANTE MERIDIEM, SESS. 11.

VI. ACT ANENT MINISTERS THAT OBSERVE NOT THE PUBLICK ORDERS OF THE CHURCH.

The Assembly Recommends it to Presbyteries, to take Notice of all Ministers, within their Bounds, whether the late Conforming Incumbents, or others, who shall not observe Fasts and Thanksgivings, Indicted by the Church: Or who shall be found Guilty, of any other Irregular Carriage, in administrating the Sacraments in private, or Celebrating Clandestine Marriages, without due Proclamation of Bans: And to censure them accordingly.

EDINBURGH 29 OCTOBER 1690. ANTE MERIDIEM, SESS. 12.

VII. ACT APPROVING SEVERAL OVERTURES.

This day the Overtures following were Read in Presence of the Assembly.

Anent subscribing the Confession of Faith.

1. "For retaining soundness, and unity of Doctrine, It is judged necessary, that all Probationers Licensed to Preach, all Intrants into the Ministry, and all other Ministers and Elders Received into Communion with us, in Church Government, be obliged, to Subscribe their Approbation of the Confession of Faith, approven by former General Assemblies of this Church, and Ratified in the second Session

of the Current Parliament: And that this be Recommended to the Diligence of the several Presbyteries, and they appointed to Record their Diligence thereanent in their respective Registers."

Anent Papists.

2. "That it be Recommended to Presbyteries, to take special Notice, what Papists are in their Bounds, and that they take pains to Re-claim them, and to Advert how their Children are Educat: and if need be, to make Application to the Civil Authority concerning them."

Anent Celebration of Marriage.

3. "That the Celebration of Marriage, without due Proclamation of Bans, according to Order, three several Sabbaths in the respective Parishes, be discharged: And that it be recommended to Presbyteries, to Censure the Contraveeners."

Against profanation of the Sabbath.

4. "That it be recommended to Kirk-Sessions and Presbyteries, carefully to put in Execution, the Acts of former General Assemblies against Profanation of the Lords-day, and particularly by unnecessary Sailing and Travelling."

Anent Mercats on Saturdays and Mondays.

5. "That Application be made to the Parliament: for alerting all Mercats in Royal Burghs and other places, on Saturdays and Mondays."

The General Assembly after mature Deliberation, approves of these Overtures, and Recommends and Appoints accordingly: And ordains the same to be observed, and to have the Force and Strength of an Act and Ordinance of Assembly.

VIII. ACT APPROVING THE ASSOCIATIONS OF PRESBYTERIES.

The General Assembly, allows and approves of the Ministers of different Presbyteries, their Associating in Presbyteries; ay and while the Vacancies of the saids Presbyteries be filled: And declares them to have the Authority and Power of Presbyteries Respectively: And that notwithstanding, that according to the old Platform, the saids Ministers do reside in the Bounds of different Presbyteries.

EDINBURGH 31 OCTOBER 1690, ANTE MERIDIEM SESS. 15.

IX. ACT AGAINST MINISTERS REMOVING OUT OF THIS CHURCH.

The General Assembly does hereby appoint, that no Ministers, who have actual standing and absolute Relations, to any Charge in the Church of Scotland, shall remove out of the Kingdom, without the Consent of the Respective Judicatories of this Church.

X. ACT ANENT THE ADMINISTRATION OF THE SACRAMENTS.

The General Assembly considering, that the two Sacraments, that Christ hath appointed under the New Testament, viz. Baptism and the Lords Supper, are his Solemn Ordinances, and Seals of the Covenant of Grace (which is held forth in the Preaching of the Gospel). And that in the use of them, the Parties receiving them, are solemnly devoted and engaged to God, before Angels and men; and are solemnly received, as Members of the Church, and do entertain Communion with her: And that by the Authority of this Church in her former Assemblies. The private use of them hath been condemned: As also, that by allowing the private use of the same, in pretended Cases of Necessity; The Superstitious opinion is nourished, that they are necessary to Salvation, not only as commanded Duties, but as means, without which Salvation cannot be attained. Therefore, The Assembly hereby discharges, the Administration of the Lords Supper, to Sick Persons in their Houses, and all other use of the same, except in the publick Assemblies of the Church. And also doth discharge the Administration of Baptism in private, That is, in any place, or at any time, when the Congregation is not orderly called together, to wait on the Dispensing of the Word. And appoints that this be carefully observed, when and where ever the Lord giveth his people Peace, Liberty and Opportunity for their publick Assemblies. And ordains this present Act to be publickly Intimate in all the Churches.

EDINBURGH 11 NOVEMBER 1690. POST MERIDIEM SESS. 24.

XI. ACT APPROVING OVERTURES ANENT THE IRISH BIBLES, &C.

This day the Overtures following anent the Irish Bibles, New Testaments and Catechisms, were read in presence of the Assembly.

1. That a Letter of Thanks be written to these concerned, whether in this, or our Neighbour Nation, for their Care of, and Liberal Charity towards the Highlanders of this Kingdom, in their so Liberally Contributing, for the saids Irish Bibles, &c. And that Mr. David Blair be appointed to write the said Letter in the Name of this Assembly.

2. The whole Money so Charitably contributed, being expended, Therefore, and for making up of the same, and for Defraying of the necessary Charges of Transporting the saids Bibles, &c. to Scotland; It is thought most needful, that there be an advance of One thousand Pounds Scots, and that Their Majesties Privy Council be supplicat, for as much of some Vacant Stipends of Parishes, where the King is Patron, as will make up the said sum for the ends foresaid.

3. That it be Recommended to the Kirk Sessions, Heretors and others concerned in the Highlands, to see the Act of Parliament anent Erecting of Schools in every Parish, duely Execute, and the Fonds established by Law, for the same, made effectual.

4. That it be Recommended to the Agent for the Kirk, to Receive the foresaid sum, and to Deburse the same at the sight of Mr. John Law and Mr. David Blair, for the said use: And also to receive the Books above-mentioned, being three Thousand Bibles, one Thousand New Testaments, and three Thousand Catechisms, from London.

5. That the several Synods, who have Highland Parishes in their bounds, appoint one of their Number, to receive their proportion, of the saids Bibles, New Testaments, and Catechisms: And that in order thereto, the Ministers and Elders having Interest in the Highlands, present in this Assembly, shall meet and appoint some to receive these Bibles, &c. And proportion the number that each Parish shall have thereof.

6. That it be Recommended to the Ministers, concerned in the Highlands, to dispatch the whole Paraphrase of the Irish Psalms, to the Press. And if the Principal Copy can be Recovered, to expede the same; But that any other Copy they have, be Revised by the Synod of Argyle, and being approven by them; That the same be Printed.

The Assembly having considered these Overtures, they approve thereof, and Recommend and Appoint accordingly.

AT EDINBURGH, NOVEMBER 12. 1690. POST MERIDIEM. SESS. 25.

XII. ACT ANENT A SOLEMN NATIONAL FAST AND HUMILIATION, WITH THE CAUSES THEREOF.

The General Assembly, Having taken into their most serious Consideration, the late great and general Defection of this Church and Kingdom; Have though fit to Appoint a Day of Solemn Humiliation and Fasting, for Confession of Sins, and making Supplication to Our Gracious GOD, to Forgive and Remove the guilt thereof; In order whereunto, they have Ordained the Confession of Sins, and Causes of Fasting following, to be duely Intimate and Published; Recommending it most earnestly to all persons, both Ministers and Others, That every One of us may not only search and try our own Hearts and Wayes, and stir up Ourselves to seek the Lord; But also in our Stations, and as we have access, Deal with one another, in all Love and Tenderness, to prepare for so great and necessary a Duty, that we may find mercy in God's sight, and He may be graciously Reconciled to our Land in the Lord Jesus, and take delight to dwell among us.

Although our gracious God hath of late, for His own Name sake wrought great and wonderful things, for Britain and Ireland, and for this Church and Nation in particular; Yet the Inhabitants thereof have cause to remember their own evil wayes, and to loath themselves in their own sight for their Iniquities. Alas! Alas! We and our Fathers, our Princes, our Pastors, and People of all Ranks have sinned, and have been under great Transgression to this day: For though our gracious God shewed early kindness to this Land, in sending the Gospel among us, and afterward in our Reformation from Popish Superstition and Idolatry; and It had the Honour, beyond many Nations of being after our first Reformation, Solemnly devoted unto God, both Prince and People; yet we have dealt treacherously with the Lord, and been unstedfast in His Covenant, and have not walked suitably to our Mercies received from Him, nor obligations to Him. Through the mercy of God this Church had attained to a great purity of Doctrine, Worship and Government, but this was not accompanied with suitable personal Reformation, neither was our Fruit answerable to the pains taken on us by Word and Work; We had much Gospel-preaching, but too little Gospel-practice, too many went on in open wickedness, and some had but a form of Godliness, denying the power thereof: Many also who had the Grace of God in truth fell from their first love, and fell under sad languishings and decays; and when for our sins the Anger of the Lord had divided us, and we were brought under the feet of strangers, and many of our brethren killed, and others taken captive and sold as slaves; yet we sinned still, and after we were freed from the yoak of strangers, instead of returning to the Lord, and being led to Repentance by His Goodness, the Land made open Defection from the good ways of the Lord: Many behaved as if they had been delivered to work abomination, the flood-gates of Impiety were opened, and a deluge of wickednese did overspread the Land. Who can without grief and shame remember the shameful debauchery and drunkenness that then was? And this accompanied with horrid and hellish cursing and swearing, and followed with frequent Filthiness, Adulteries and other Abominations, and the Reprover was hated, and he that departed from Iniquity made himself a Reproach of Prey. And when by these, and such like corrupt practices, mens Consciences were debauched, they proceeded to sacrifice the Interest of the Lord Jesus Christ, and priviledges of his Church to the lusts and will of Men; The Supremacy was advanced in such a way, and to such an height, as never any Christian Church acknowledged; The Government of the Church was altered, and Prelacie (which hath been always grievous to this Nation) introduced, without the Churches consent, and contrary to the standing Acts of our National Assemblies, both which the present Parliament hath (blessed be God) lately found; And yet nevertheless, of the then standing Ministry of Scotland, many did suddenly and readily comply with that alteration of the Government, some out of Pride and Covetousness, or Man-pleasing, some through infirmity or weakness, or fear of Man, and want of Courage and Zeal for God; many faithful Ministers were thereupon cast out, and many Insufficient and Scandalous Men thrust in on their Charges, and many Families ruined, because they would not own them as their Pastors.

And alas! It is undenyable, there hath been under the late Prelacie, a great decay of Piety, so that it was enough to make a man be nicknam'd a Phanatick, if he did not run to the same excess of Riot with others.

And should it not be lamented, for it cannot be denied, that there hath been in some a dreadful Atheistical Boldness against God, some have disputed the Beeing of GOD, and His Providence, the Divine Authority of the Scriptures, the Life to come, and Immortality of the Soul, yes and scoffed at these things.

There hath been also an Horrid Prophanation of the Holy and Dreadful Name of GOD, by cursing and swearing: Ah! there hath been so much Swearing and

Forswearing amongst us, that no Nation under Heaven hath been more guilty in this than we; some by swearing rashly or ignorantly, some falsly, by breaking their Oaths. And imposing and taking ungodly unlawful Oaths and Bonds, whereby the Consciences of many have been polluted and seared, and many ruined and oppressed for refusing and not taking them.

There hath also been a great neglect of the worship of God, too much in publick, but especially in Families and in secret.

The wonted care of Religious sanctifying the Lord's Day is gone, and in many places the Sabbath hath been and is shamefully prophaned.

The Land also hath been, full of bloody Crimes, and Cities full of Violence, and much innocent Blood shed, so that Blood touched Blood, yea, Sodoms sins have abounded amongst us. Pride, fulness of Bread, Idleness, Vanities of Apparel, and shameful sensuality filled the Land.

And Alas! how great hath been the Cry of Oppression and Unrighteousness, Iniquity hath been established by a Law, there hath been a great perverting of Justice, by making and executing unrighteous Statutes and Acts, and sad persecutions of many for their Conscience towards God.

It is also matter of Lamentation, that under this great Defection, there hath been too general a fainting not only amongst Professours of the Gospel, but also amongst Ministers; yea, even amongst such, who in the main things did endeavour to maintain their Integrity, in not giving seasonable and necessary Testimony against the Defections and Evils of the Time, and keeping a due distance from them, and some on the other hand managed their Zeal with too little Discretion and Meekness.

It is also matter of Humiliation, that when Differences fell out amongst these, who did own Truth, and bear witness against the Course of Defection, they were not managed with due Charity and Love, but with too much heat and bitterness, injurious Reflections used against Pious and Worthy men on all hands, and scandalous Divisions occasioned, and the Success of the Gospel greatly obstructed thereby, and some dangerous Principles drunk in: And after all this, there were shameful advances towards Popery, the abomination of the Mass was set up in many places, and Popish Schools erected, and severals fell to Idolatry.

And though the Lord hath put a stop to the Course of Defection, and of his great mercy given us some reviving from our Bondage; yet we have sad cause to regrate and bemoan, that few have a due sense of our mercy, or walk answerable thereto; Few are turned to the Lord in truth, but the wicked go on to do wickedly; And there is found amongst us to this day, shameful ingratitude for our mercies, Horrid impenitency under our sins, yea, even among those, who stand most up for the defence of the Truth: And amongst many in our Armies, there is woful Prophanness and Debauchery. And though we profess to acknowledge, there can be no Pardon of Sins, no Peace and Reconciliation with God, but by the Blood of Jesus Christ; Yet few know Him, or see the Necessity and Excellency of the Knowledge of our Lord Jesus Christ; few see their need of him, or esteem, desire, or receive him as he is offered in the Gospel; few are acquainted with Faith in Jesus

Christ, and living by Faith in Him, as made of the Father unto us, wisdom, Righteousness, Sanctification and Redemption; And few walk as becometh the Gospel, and imitate our Holy Lord in Humility, Meekness, Self-denial, Heavenly mindedness, Zeal for GOD, and Charity towards Men: But as there is even untill now, a great contempt of the Gospel, a great Barrenness under it; So a deep Security under our sin and Danger, a great want of Piety toward God, and Love towards Men, with a woful Selfishness, every one seeking their own things, few the things of Christ, or the publick Good, or one anothers welfare: And finally, the most part more ready to Censure the sins of others, than to Repent of their own.

Our Iniquities are increased over our Heads, and our Trespasses are grown up unto the Heavens, they are many in number, and hainous in their nature, and grievously aggravated, as having been contrary to great Light and Love, under signal Mercies and Judgments, after Confession and Supplication, and notwithstanding of our Profession, Promises and solemn Vowing, and Covenanting with God to the contrary.

Have we not then sad cause of deep Sorrow and Humiliation? And may we not fear, if we do not repent, and turn from the evil of our wayes, and return to the Lord with all our hearts, that he return to do us evil, after He hath done us good, and be angry with us, until he hath consumed us?

Let us therefore humble our selves by fasting and Praying, let us search out our sins, and consider our wayes, and confess these, and other our sins, with Sorrow and Detestation; Let us Turn unto the Lord with fasting and weeping, and with mourning; Let us firmly resolve and sincerely Engage to amend our wayes and doings, and return unto the Lord our God, with all our hearts, and earnestly pray, that for the Blood of the Lamb of God, our sins may be forgiven, and our back slidings healed, and we may yet become a Righteous Nation, keeping the Truth, that Religion and Righteousness may flourish, and Love and Charity abound, and all the Lords People may be of one mind in the Lord: And in order to all these, that the word of the Lord may have free course, and be glorified, and that the Preaching of the Word, and Dispensing of the Sacraments, may be accompanied with the wonted Presence, Power and Blessing of the Spirit of the Lord, That the Lord would Preserve and bless our gracious King and Queen, William and Mary, and establish their Throne by Righteousness and Religion, and grant to these Nations, Peace and Truth together; And for that End, bless and prosper His Majesties Councils, and Forces by Sea and Land, and these of the Princes and States his Allies, for God and his Truth; That inferior Rulers may Rule in the fear of God and Judges be cloathed with Righteousness, and that many faithful Labourers may be sent out into the Lord's Vineyard, and they who are sent, may find mercy to be Faithful, and be blest with Success; That Families may be as little Churches of Christ, and that the Lord would pour out His Spirit on all Ranks of People, that they may be Holy in all manner of Conversation, and God may delight to dwell amongst us and to do us good.

And while we pray for our selves, let us not forget our Brethren in Foreign Churches, with whom, alas! we had too little Sympathy; Nay let us pray, that all the Ends of the Earth, may see the Salvation of God; And that he would bring His ancient people of the Jews to the Acknowledgment of Jesus Christ; And that he would hasten the Ruine of Romish Babylon and advance the Reformation in Christendome, and preserve and bless the Reformed Churches; That he would pitie His oppressed People, the French Protestants, and gather them out of all places, whither they have been scattered in the cloudy and dark day; And that He would be the Defence, Strength and Salvation of any of His People, who are in War or Danger by Infidel or Popish adversaries, in Europe or America: And in particular, that the Lord would be Gracious to Ireland, and sanctifie to His People there, both their distress and Deliverance, and perfect what concerneth them, that he would Convert the Natives there to the Truth, Reduce that Land to Peace; And appoint Salvation for Walls and Bulwarks to Brittain.

For all these Causes and Reasons, The General Assembly hath Appointed the Second Thursday of January next, to be Observed in all the Congregations of this Church and Nation, as a day of Solemn Fasting and Humiliation, and Prayer; Beseeching and Obtesting all, both Pastors and People, of all Ranks to be sincere and serious, in Humiliation and Supplication, and universal Reformation, as they would wish to find mercy of the Lord and have deserved wrath averted, and would obtain the Blessing of the Lord upon themselves and Posterity after them; And that the Lord may delight in us, and our Land may be as Married to Him. And Ordains all Ministers, either in Kirks or Meeting houses, to Read this present Act publickly from the Pulpit, a Sabbath or two before the said Day of Humiliation: and that the several Presbyteries take care, that it be carefully observed in their Respective bounds. And where, in regard of Vacancies, the Day hereby appointed, cannot be observed; The Assembly appoints the said Humiliation to be kept some other Day with the first convenient opportunity. And Appoints the Commission for Visitation, to apply to the Council for their Civil Sanction to the Observation thereof.

XIII. ACT ANENT SENTENCES PAST AGAINST MINISTERS FROM THE YEAR 1650. &C.

The General Assembly does hereby declare, all Sentences, past against any Ministers Hinc Inde, by any Church Judicatory, upon the Account of the late Differences among Presbyterians, from the Year 1650. Till the Re-introduction of Prelacy, to be of themselves void and null, to all Effects and Intents. And Siclike the General Assembly hereby Recommends, to the Respective Presbyteries, to take care, that such of these Ministers, as are not otherways disposed of by the Church, Return to the exercise of their Ministry, in their Respective Congregations. And also hereby Recommends to the Civil Magistrate, that the saids Ministers may have the Lega Maintainances and Stipends where they served.

EDINBURGH 13 OF NOVEMBER 1690. POST MERIDIEM. SESS. 26.

XIV. THE ASSEMBLIES LETTER TO HIS MAJESTY.

May it please Your Majesty.

The Happiness we have had by Your Majesties influence, as an Instrument in the Hand of God, towards us for good, and the Countenance You have given us in Holding this National Assembly of the Church of Scotland, Doth Encourage us to make Application again to Your Majesty; That as in our Answer to Your Gracious Letter direct to us in the Entrance of this Assembly, we Engaged to Your Majesty that in all things that should come before us, we would carry with that Calmnes and Moderation, which becometh the Ministers of the Gospel of Peace, and which Your Majesty did so effectually Recommend to us; So now in the Close of this our Assembly, we presume to acquaint Your Majesty, That through the good Hand of God upon us, we have in a great measure performed accordingly: Having applied our selves, mostly and especially, to what concerned this whole Church, and endeavoured by all means Ecclesiastical, and proper for us, to promote the Good thereof, together with the Quiet of the Kingdom, and Your Majesties Satisfaction and Contentment. And God hath been pleased to Bless our Endeavours, in our Receiving to the Unity and Order of this Church, some who had withdrawn, and now have joyned with us, and promised Subjection: And in providing for the Propagation of Religion, and the Knowledge of God, in the most Barbarous places of the Highlands, which may be the surest way of Reducing these people also unto Your Majesties Obedience: And especially in Regulating the Ministers of this Church, after so great Revolutions and Alterations: For we have according to the use and practice of this Church, ever since the first Reformation from Popery, appointed Visitations both for the Southern and Northern parts of this Kingdom, Consisting of the Gravest and most Experienced Ministers and Elders: To whom we have given Instructions about the late Conformists, that none of them shall be Removed from their Places, but such as are either Insufficient, or Scandalous, or Erroneous, or Supinely Negligent: And that these of them be admitted to Ministerial Communion with us, who upon due Trial, and in a Competent Time for that Trial, shall be found to be Orthodox in Doctrine, of Competent Abilities, of a Godly, Peaceable, and Loyal Conversation, and who shall be judged Faithfull to God and to the Government: And who shall likewayes Promise to own, Submit unto, and Concurre with it. We have also taken Care, that all persons, who shall be found to have received wrong, in any Inferior Judicatory of this Church, shall be duly Redressed: Other things which are not of so Universal a Concern, we have delayed till the next General Assembly. This Account Great SIR, we look upon our selves as Obliged to give unto Your Majesty, for that great Goodness, You have been pleased to express, in giving such Countenance to this Assembly, and in appointing such Commissioner to Represent Your Royal Person, who hath been in all his Conduct in this Affair, most acceptable unto us. That God may Bless Your Majesty, and our most Gracious Queen, with all Blessings, which concern both this Life, and the Life to come, is the earnest Prayer of.

May it please your Majesty,
Your Majesties most Faithful,
Most Humble and most Obedient,
Subjects and Servants.

Subscribed in Name, and at the Appointment of the General Assembly, by

HU. KENNEDIE. Moderator.

XV. INSTRUCTIONS TO THE COMMISSIONS FOR VISITA-TIONS ON THE SOUTH AND NORTH SIDES OF TAY.

The following Instructions to the Commission for Visitations on this side of Tay, were Read in presence of the Assembly.

"1. That there be appointed by the Assembly, a Delegate number of the most experienced Ministers and Elders. This number to be Forty Ministers, and Twenty Ruling Elders, fifteen of them to a Quorum, ten of these being alwayes Ministers; And that they at their first Session, Choose their Moderator and Clerk; And for the Sub-committe betwixt the Quarterly Meetings, nine to be the Quorum, six of these being alwayes Ministers."

"2. That the Work of this Commission for Visitations be, to take to their Cognizance all References, and Appeals, and other things, which being stated before this Assembly, shall by them be specially Referred to the said Commission, to determine the same."

"3. That the Commission give their Opinion to all Presbyteries and Synods, who shall apply to them for the same, in difficult Cases: and though Presbyteries shall not apply, yet if the Commission shall be informed of any Precipitant, or unwarrantable procedure of Presbyteries, in Processes, which may prove of ill Consequence to the Church, The Commission shall interpose their Advice, to such Presbyteries, to sift such procedure, till either the Synod, or next General Assembly take Cognizance of it; if the said Commission shall not find a present fit Expedient, to direct them, for bringing the matter sooner to a Right Conclusion."

"4. That in discussing References, Appeals and Bills, They take care to purge out all, who upon due Tryal shall be found to be Insufficient, supinely Negligent, Scandalous or Erroneous."

"5. That this Commission shall have Power of Visiting any Ministers within the Bounds of any Presbyteries, on this side of the Water of Tay, as they shall find need: And that this Power Reach Presbyterians as well as others."

"6. That they shall be Careful, that none shall be admitted by them to Ministerial Communion, or to a share of the Government; but such as upon due Tryal (for which the Commission is to take a competent time) shall be found to be Orthodox in their Doctrine, of Competent Abilities, having a Pious, Godly, Loyal and Peaceable Conversation, as becometh a Minister of the Gospel, of an Edifying Gift, and whom the Commission shall have ground to believe, will be True and Faithful to God and the Government, and diligent in their Ministerial Duties. And that all who shall be admitted to the Ministry, or shall be received to a share in the Government, shall be obliged to Own and Subscribe the Confession of Faith, and profess their Submission to, and willingness to Joyn and Concur with the Presbyterian Church-Government."

"7. That they be very Cautions of receiving Informations, against the late Conformists, and that they proceed in the matter of Censure, very Deliberatly, so as none may have just cause to complain of their Rigiditie: Yet so as to omit no means of Information. And that they shall not proceed to censure, but upon Relevant

Libels and sufficient Probation."

"8. That this Commission do not take on them, to meddle with any thing, not expressed in their Commission: And that it be declared, that this Commission is only given, Ad hunc effectum & pro præsenti Ecclesiæ statu."

"9. That this commission be in all their actings, Countable to, and Censurable by the next Ensuing General Assembly."

"10. That this commission continue till the first of November next: and in case the General Assembly Interveen; Then this Commission is to Terminate at the meetting of the said Assembly."

The General Assembly approves these Instructions, for the said Commission for Visitations on the South-side of Tay: And ordains the same also to serve for the Visitors that are to be appointed for the North.

XVI. COMMISSION FOR VISITATIONS ON THE SOUTH SIDE OF TAY.

The General Assembly Considering, that there are many Important and weighty Affairs, Processes, Appeals, and References, Tabled before this Assembly, which the Assembly could not overtake, for want of time to consider them naturely; Does therefore Nominate and Authorize a Commission of Ministers and Elders, for Visitation of the whole Presbyteries, on the South-side of Tay, viz. Mr. Hugh Kennedy, Mr. John Vetch, Mr. John Law, Mr. Gabriel Semple, Mr. Gilbert Rule, Mr. James Kirtoun, Mr. William Areskyne, Mr. William Weir, Mr. William Crichtoun, Mr. John Anderson of Perth, Mr. Alexander Pitcairn, Mr. Richard Howison, Mr. George Campbel, Mr. John Lawrie, Mr. Archibald Hamiltoun, Mr. Patrick Peacock, Mr. John Spalding, Mr. Michael Bruce, Mr. Gabriel Cuningham, Mr. Patrick Warner, Mr. Alexander Forbes, Mr. John Hutcheson, Mr. William Eccles, Mr. James Vetch, Mr. Patrick Simpson, Mr. Matthew Crawford, Mr. William Legat, Mr. Neil Gillies, Mr. Thomas Forrester, Mr. Andrew Mortoun, Mr. Robert Duncanson, Mr. John Bannatyne, Mr. William Ker, Mr. William Vilant, Mr. Robert Rule, Mr. James Frazer, Mr. George Meldrum at Kilnining, Mr. David Blair, Mr. Samuel Nairn, Mr. Edward Jamieson, Mr. James Rymer Ministers: and the Earl of Crawford, the Earl of Sutherland, the Viscount of Arburthnet, the Lord Halcraig, the Lord Aberuchil, the Laird of Cimistoun, Sir John Hall Provest of Edinburgh, Sir John Riddel, the Laird of Greenknows, Archibald Muir late Baylie of Edinburgh, James Mclurgh Dean of Gild, George Stirling Deacon Conveener, the Laird of Naughtoun, the Laird of Meggans, the Laird of Leuquhat, Sir Thomas Stewart, the Laird of Glanderstoun, the Laird of Lamingtoun, Provest Muir of Air, and the Laird of Grange Hamiltoun Ruling Elders: To meet for their first Diet at Edinburgh the fourteenth day of November Instant, Fifteen of them being a Quorum, whereof Ten are to be alwayes Ministers: And of their Sub-Committee in the Interval of their Quarterly Meetings, Nine to be a Quorum, Six of these being always Ministers, who only are to Rippen and prepare Matters for the Quarterly Meetings. And their next Quarterly Meeting to be at Edinburgh the Third Wednesday of January thereafter. And their next Quarterly Meeting to be on the Third Wednesday of April. And if afterwards the said Commission shall think fit, to appoint other Quarterly Meetings, they may do as they see Expedient With full Power to them and their Sub-Commission foresaid, to give Warrand for Citing Parties upon Fifteen free dayes. And the said Commission, being only appointed, Ad hunc effectum & pro prasentes Ecclesia Statu, Therefore, The Assembly Recommends particularly to the said Commission, to take Cognizance of, and finally determine in the particulars following, specially Committed and Referred to them, by this Assembly, viz. The Purging and Planting of the City and Presbytery of Edinburgh: The transportation of Mr. Robert Wyse to Hamiltoun: The Proces of the Heretors and People of Peebles: The Processes, of Mr. Thomas Wood at Dumbar, of Mr. Robert Spotswood at Abbotsrule, Mr. John Bowes at Abbotshail, Mr. Patrick Lyon at Kinghorm, Mr. Symon Compar at Dumfermling, Mr. William Crawford at Lady-Kirk, Mr. James Orr at Huttoun, Mr. Adam Peacock at Morbassie, Mr. Daniel Urquhart at Clackmannan, Mr. George Monro at Dollar, Mr. George Shaw at Logie, Mr. Alexander Ireland at Fossoway and Tilliboal, Mr. Robert Sharp at Muckart, Mr. James Grahame at Dumfermling, Mr. George Gray at Beath, Mr. John Monro at Stirling, and Mr. John Skinner at Bathkenner: The Petition of the Magistrates of Perth, and Reference anent Mr. John Anderson there: The Processes of Mr. William Alison at Kilboche, and Mr. James Cowper at Humbie: Some Reference of the Synod of Merse and Teviotdial to the Assembly, viz. One anent Doctor Canaries, and another anent Mr. Kirktoun and Mr. Jameson's returning to their Charges, or else to Dimit; And a third anent Mr. William Crawfurd Deposed, to procure him some Lively hood, because of his Age and Infirmity, and some others given in to the Clerk therewith from the said Synod: The Affair anent Mr. Duncan Campbel and the Parishes of Dinnoon and Kilmorn: The Process of Mr. Robert Glasford at Auchterderen: The Reference from the Presbyterie of Stirling, for advice anent Mr. Patrick Cowpar: The Petitions of Mr. William Hamiltoun and Mr. Hugh Nisbet: The Petition of Mr. Alexander Strang, anent his Clerks Fies. This Commission is also to Correspond with the State, anent Fasts and Thanksgivings, and their Causes, if the Occasions thereof fall out during the time of their sitting: Also to take the Monitory paper to consideration, and see what use is to be made of it: To consider what Acts of Assembly are fit to be Printed together, and order the same. To consider the form of process, being first Revised by the Lord Aberuchil and the Lord Halcraig. And to apply to the Privy Council for their Civil Sanction to the observation of the Fast. And this Commission is to walk in all things, according to the particular Instructions given unto them by this Assembly. And in all their Actings they shall be countable to and Censurable by the next General Assembly. And this Commission to Continue till the first of November next, or the diet, that shall be appointed for the next General Assembly.

XVII. COMMISSION FOR VISITATIONS ON THE NORTH SIDE OF TAY.

The General Assembly taking to their Consideration the necessity of Purging and Planting of the Churches on the North side of Tay, do by their Ecclesiastical Authority, Nominat, Appoint and Authorize their Reverend Brethren Mr. Hugh Kennedy, Mr. John Law, Mr. William Crichtoun, Mr. Edward Jamieson, Mr. Robert Rule, Mr. James Rymer, Mr. James Frazer, Mr. Alexander Forbes, Mr. John

Anderson at Perth, Mr. George Meldrum at Kitwining, Mr. Thomas Ramsay, Mr. Andrew Bowie, Mr. Robert Young, Mr. William Legat, and Mr. William Mackie, Ministers: And the Lord Viscount of Arbuthnet, the Laird of Meggins, the Laird of Naughtoun, the Laird of Leuquhat, and the Laird of Greenknows, Ruling Elders: To joyn with the Ministers and Elders in the North after-mentioned; Viz. Mr. John Stewart, Mr. James Urquhart, Mr. Alexander Dumbar, Mr. Alexander Frazer, Mr. Thomas Hogg, Mr. Hugh Henryson, Mr. William Mackay, Mr. Walter Dinnoon, Mr. George Meldrum of Glass, Mr. Arthur Mitchel, Mr. William Ramsay, Mr. Francis Melvil, and Mr. John Mculloch, Ministers: together With the Earle of Sutherland, the Laird of Brodie, the Laird of Grant, the Laird of Grange Dumbar, the Laird of Eight, the Laird of Culloden, the Laird of Darfolly, the Laird of Parkhay, Sir John Monro, Sir. George Monro, Sir Robert Gordon of Embo, David Frazer of Maine, Mr. John Campbel of Moy, Hector Monro of Drummond, Alexander Duff, and Robert Martyne of Burnbrae, Ruling Elders: To be a Commission for Visiting the whole Presbyteries on the North-side of the Water of Tay, In Planting Vacant Churches Constituting Elderships in Congregations, Trying & Purging out of Insufficient, Negligent, Scandalous and Erroneous Ministers, by due course of Ecclesiastical Process and Censures, according to the Particular Instructions, given them thereanent, and for that effect, to have their first Dyet of meeting, at Aberdeen, the Second Wednesday of March next, and thereafter to appoint the own Dyets and Places of meeting, as they see Expedient, with full Power to them, or their Quorum being seven Ministers and three Ruling Elders, to Issue out Warrants for Citing of Parties upon fifteen Free dayes, to Cognosce, Determine and finally decide, in planting of Vacant Churches, Constituting Elderships, and Trying and Purging out, all Insufficient, Negligent, Scandalous and Erroneous Ministers, conforme to the particular Instructions given them thereanent. They being alwayes Countable to, and Censurable by the next General Assembly of this Church: And this Commission to continue till the first of November next, or the Dyet that shall be appointed for the next General Assembly.

XVIII. COMMISSION FOR MR. GILBERT RULE AND MR. DAVID BLAIR, TO WAIT UPON HIS MAJESTY ANENT THE AFFAIRS OF THIS CHURCH.

The General Assembly judging it Expedient, to send two of their Number to London, to attend his Majesty, anent the Affairs of this Church; Does therefore Nominate and Appoint their Reverend Brethren, Mr. Gilbert Rule, one of the Ministers of the City of Edinburgh, and Principal of the Colledge thereof, and Mr. David Blair another of the Ministers of the said City; with all convenient speed to Repair to London, to attend His Majesty for the end foresaid: And Refers the Instructions to be given them, and what other things Concern their Journey, to the Commission for Visitations on the South side of Tay appointed by this Assembly.

This Assembly being Dissolved, and the next General Assembly appointed to be held at Edinburgh the first day of November next to come; the Members were dismissed with Prayer, Singing of the 133 Psalm, and pronouncing of the Blessing.

Collected, Visied and Extracted, from the Records of the said Assembly by Me

JOHN SPALDING Cls. Syn: National.

FINIS.

INDEX

INDEX OF THE UNPRINTED ACTS, &C. OF THE GENERAL ASSEMBLY, 1690.

Act Reviving the Overtures of the Assembly. 1649. Sess. 2. Anent the ordering of the Assembly House Ibid.

Act against Mr. John Mckenzie, declaring the Kirk of Karklistoun Vacant, with a Recommendation to the Presbytery of Linlithgow, to see the same planted. Ibid.

Overture anent planting of the North. Sess. 14.

Act appointing some Ministers to repair to Angus, with a Recommendation to the privy Council thereanent. Ibid.

Continuation of Mr. John Spalding, to be Clerk of this Assembly, till further Consideration. Sess. 15.

Act against Mr. John Park late Incumbent at Carriden, finding that he had fallen from his appeal, from the Presbytery of Linlithgow, by his non competeance Ibid.

Election of John Blair to be Agent for this Church. Sess. 16.

Remit Mr. Alexander Heriot at Dalkeith to the Synod of Loathian. Sess. 17.

Act Ratifiying the Sentence of deposition, past by the Presbytery of Stirling against Mr. James Forsyth Elder late Incumbent at St. Ninians, for Celebrating an Incestuous Marriage. Sess. 18.

Act in favours of Mr. James Couper Incumbent at Humbie Ibid.

Recommendation to the Commission of Parliament for Plantation of Kirks &c. in favours of the Synod of Argyl. Ibid.

Reference to the Commission to be appointed for Visitations on the South side of Tay, in favours of the Town of Perth, with an Approbation of the Presbytries procedure, in constituting a Kirk Session there. Ibid.

Recommendation to the Commission of Parliament for Plantation of Kirks. &c. In Favours of the Town of Drumfries. Ibid.

Election of George Mosman to be Printer to the Assemly, Sess. 21.

Recommendation to his Majesty, the Parliament, and Commission for plantation of Kirks &c. in favours, of the Laird and Lady Hoptoun for Erecting the Lead Mynes in a Parish. Ibid.

Recommendation to the Presbytery of Dambarten and Synod of Glasgow, in favours of Mr. Thomas Mitchell. Ibid.

Recommendation to the Commission for plantation of Kirks &c For Re-erecting the Kirk and Parish of New-Cumnock. Ibid.

Reference in favours of the Burgh and Parish of Stanrawer, and the Parishes of Anwith and Borgh, to the several Presbyteries, for applying to the Meetings in Ireland, to louse the Irish Ministers now serving in these Parishes to the end they may continue their setled Ministers. Sess. 22.

Reference to the Presbytery of Hamiltoun and Lanerk, in Favours of Mr. Samuel Mowat. Ibid.

Recommendation to the Commission for plantation of Kirks &c. For Re-erecting the Kirk of Robertoun. Ibid.

Act Impowering the Ministers and Elders in the North who are to joyn with the Visitation for that Countrey, to take Informations, and to cause Cite Parties and witnesses against the first Diet of the said Visitation. Sess. 24

Remit Mr. Forsyth Younger to the Presbytery of Stirling. Ibid.

The Opinion of the Assembly declining to meddle in the Petition of the Lord and Lady Crichtoun, as being a matter Civil, and so not comepetent to the Assembly. Ibid.

Reference in Favours of the Parish of Genluce to the Presbytery of the bounds, to apply for lousing some Irish Ministers, as in the case of the Burgh of Stranrawer., &c. Ibid.

The Opinion of the Assembly declining to meddle in a Petition of the Heretors of Collingtoun, as being a matter Civil and Incompetent to them. Sess. 25.

Recommendation in Favours of George Mosman anent some Books. Ibid.

Act appointing Mr. Gilbert Rule, to Writt an answer to some Pamphlets. Ibid.

Act for supplying the Charges of Ministers appointed for Visitations in the North. Ibid.

Act appointing some Ministers to Repair to the bounds of the Presbyteries of Lochmahan Middlebee, &c. Ibid.

Act declaring the Sentence of Deposition and Excommunication past by the late pretended Bishop of Dumblane, against Mr. William Spence to be void and Null. Ibid.

Letter from the Assembly to the Earle of Melvill Lord Secretary of State for Scotland. Sess. 26.

Act appointing some Ministers and Probationers to Repair to the North. Ibid.

Act appointing some Ministers to the like effect with the former. Ibid.

Committee for Revising the Acts of Assembly. Ibid.

Recommendation to the privy Council, for some Charity to Mr. William Cameron one of the late Conformists, Ibid.

Recommendation to the Presbytery of Edinburgh, and the Synod of Louthian and Fife, in Favours of Mary Aresyne. Ibid.

Act appointing the Synod Books to be sent in to the next General Assembly. Ibid.

FINIS.

AN INDEX OF THE PRINCIPAL UNPRINTED ACTS OF THE ASSEMBLY AT GLASGOW, 1638.

Act containing sundry protestations between the Commissioners Grace and the members of the Assembly.

Act of Election of Mr. Alexander Henderson to be Moderatour.

Act of Mr. Archibald Johnstoun his admission to be Clerk and his production of the Registers of the Kirk, which were preserved by Gods wonderful providence.

An act disallowing any private conference and constant Assessours to the Moderatour.

The Act Registrating his Majesties will given in by his Commissioner.

The Act bearing the Assemblies Protestation against the dissolution thereof.

Act anent the Presbitery of Auchterardors present seat at Aberuthven for a time.

Act anent the order of receiving the repentance of any penitent Prelate.

Act anent the admission of Mr. Archibald Johnstoun to be Advocate and Mr. Robert Dalgleish to be Agent for the Kirk.

Act anent the transporting of Mr. Alexander Henderson from Leuchars to Edinburgh.

Act containing a Commission to sit at Edinburgh December, 26.

Another Commission to sit at Jedburgh Ian, 22.

Another Commission to sit at Irwin Ian, 15.

Another Commission to sit at Dunde Feb, 5.

Another Commission to sit at Chantrie and Forres, March, 19.

Another Commission to sit at Kirkubright, Feb. 6.

A Commission for visitation of the Colledge of Aberdeen.

A Commission for visitation of the Colledge of Glasgow.

Act appointing the Commissioners to attend the Parliament, and the Articles which they are to represent in name of the Kirk to the Estates.

Act ordaining the Presbyteries to intimate in their several Pulpites the Assemblies explanation of Confession of Faith.

The Act against Episcopacy. The Act against the Five Articles.

The act against the Service Book. The Book of Cannons.

The Book of Ordination. The High Commission.

Act of Excommunication and deposition against some Prelates, and of deposition only against some of them.

Act ordaining all Presbyteries to keep a solemn thanksgiving in all Parishes, for Gods Blessing and good success to this Assembly, upon the first convenient

Sabbath.

Act warranding the Moderator and Clerk to give out summonds upon relevant complaints, against parties to compear before the next Assembly.

Act that none be chosen as Ruling Elders to sit in Presbyteries, Provincial, or General Assemblies, but those who subscribes the Covenant as it is now declared, and acknowledges the constitutions of this Assembly.

Act for representing to the Parliament the necessity of the standing of the Procurators place for the Kirk.

INDEX OF THE PRINCIPAL ACTS OF THE ASSEMBLY AT EDINBURGH, 1639, NOT PRINTED.

The Kings Majesties Commission to *John* Earle of *Traquair*.

Election of Master *David Dickson* Moderator.

The Kings Majesties Commissioners, and the Assemblies Declarations anent the Assembly of *Glasgow*.

Renounciation of Master *Alexander Lindsay* pretended Bishop of *Dunkeld*, of Episcopacy.

Commission for visitation of the University of *St. Andrews*.

Commission for visitation of the University of *Glasgow*.

Act reviving former Acts against going of Salt-pans on the Sabbath day.

Act for drawing up of a Catechisme.

Articles and overtures to be presented to the ensuing Parliament.

The report of the Committee appointed for examination of the Book called *The Kings Manifesto*, or *Declaration*.

The Covenant or Confession of Faith.

Act anent the adjoining of some Kirks in the Ile of *Boes* to the Presbytery of *Denune*.

Act adjoyning some Kirks in the Iles of *Coill* and *Tyrie*, to the Provincial of *Kilmoire*.

Commission for visitation of the Colledge of *Aberdeen*.

Commission to the Presbytery of *Edinburgh*.

INDEX OF THE PRINCIPAL ACTS OF THE ASSEMBLY AT ABERDENE, 1640, NOT PRINTED.

Election of Master Andrew Ramsay Moderator.

Act against Prophaning of the Sabbath.

INDEX OF THE PRINCIPAL ACTS OF THE ASSEMBLY HOLDEN AT ST. ANDREWS, AND EDINBURGH 1641. NOT PRINTED.

Reference to the Parliament anent the Kirks of Dunkeld.

Act anent Master David Calderwood.

Commission anent erecting of a Presbytery in Biggar.

Commission for visitation of Orknay and Zetland.

Act anent bringing of the Synod books to the Assemblies.

Reference from the Parliament anent a Band and a Paper called a Manifesto.

Act anent the deleting of the Earle of Traquairs Declaration out of the Books of secret Councel.

Report of Overtures made anent the Plantation of Kirks in the High-lands.

Commission for visitation of the University of St. Andrews.

Commission for visitation of the University of Glasgow.

Commission to attend the Parliament.

Reference to that Commission anent the Presbytery of Sky.

INDEX OF THE PRINCIPAL ACTS OF THE ASSEMBLY HOLDEN AT ST. ANDREWS, 27. JULY, 1642. NOT PRINTED.

His Majesties Commission granted to Charles Earle of Dumfermling.

Election of Master Robert Douglas Moderator.

Acceptation of the Commission from the Scottish Kirk at Camphire, granted to Master William Spong.

Act renewing the Commissions for Visitation of the Universities of St. Andrews, and Glasgow.

Act anent delivery of the Irish contribution to the receivers appointed by the secret Council.

Act anent Idolatrous monuments in Ruthwill.

Act anent the Books of the Presbyteries in our Army that went to England.

Act anent the planting of the Kirk of Kilwinning.

Commission anent the erecting of a Presbytery in Biggar.

Act repealing the Act of the Synod of Galloway concerning the tryal of Actual Ministers.

The Kings Declaration anent the gift of 500. Lib.

Act for sending of Expectants to Ireland, and for a Commission to be drawn up to some Ministers to go there.

Recommendation to the Marques of Argyle anent Patrick Egertie Priest, and all other Priests, or sayers of Masse in the North Iles, or within the bounds of his

Justiciarie.

Act anent the reponing of Master Gilbert Power.

Act for putting the Overtures anent maintaining of Bursars in every Presbytery in practice.

Report of the Commission for revising of some Synod Books, and the Assemblies approbation.

Act forgiving transumpts of the Covenant and Band.

Act for sending of General Acts of Assemblies to Synods.

Act anent James Murray.

Report of the Committee of reports of the proceedings of the Commissioners of the last Assembly appointed to attend the Parliament, with certain overtures of the Assemblies approbation thereof, with the double of the Signator of 500 lib sent to his Majesty.

Commission for visitation or Orknay and Zetand.

Reference to the Commission of this Assembly, anent the choice of any Minister to go to Ireland, in place of any of the six appointed by this Assembly to that effect, in case they or any of them be impeded by sickness or death.

Recommendation of the Iles, Anandail, Esadail, Liddedail, &c for want of Kirks and Schooles; of the Presbyteries of Lochmaben, and Nowhie, for want of a Civil Magistrate, to the Commission for Plantation of Kirks, and secret Councill, Respectivè.

Reference to the Commission of this Assembly for planting of the Kirks of Edinburgh.

Act anent Master Colvils invitation to St. Andrews.

Commission anent the planting of the Landwart Kirks of St. Andrews.

References and Overtures, and the Assemblies answer thereto.

Reference to the Commission of this Assembly anent Master James Fairlie.

Reference to the commission of this Assembly anent the planting of the Kirk of Dundie.

Overtures anent the Kirk of Camphire.

Recommendation to the Magistrates of Glasgow anent mundays market.

Act anent giving in to the Clerk the list of Expectants.

Act giving power and liberty to Sir. Archibald Johnstoun Procurator for the Kirk, and Clerk to the General Assembly, to adjoyne any to himself, or to depute in these Offices whom he shall think fit.

INDEX OF THE ACTS OF THE ASSEMBLY HOLDEN
AT EDINBURGH, 1643, NOT PRINTED.

The Kings Majesties Commission to Sir. Thomas Hope of Craighall Knight, His Majesties Advocate.

Election of Master Alexander Henderson, Moderatour.

Appointment of Master John Scot, who was sent from the Presbyterie in the Scottish Army in Ireland, to be present in the Assembly every session.

Questions propounded by the moderatour, to some brethren in the North, anent some Papists there, and their answers thereunto.

Commission for visitation of the University of St. Andrews.

Letters from Master William Spang, Minister of the Scot's Kirk at Camphire, with attestations of some Dutch Kirks, anent hanging of Pensils in Kirks, &c.

Act for Summar Excommunication of Adam Abercrombie.

Approbation of the deposition of Master John Forbes, With an ordinance for his Subscribing the Covenant.

Questions from the Presbytery of Hadingtoun, with the Assemblies resolution thereof, anent Sir John Seatan, and his Daughter.

Approbation of the advice of the Commissioners of the late Assembly at St. Andrews, for not Printing two Acts of the last Assembly held at Aberdene.

Approbation of the Lord Maitland his Faithful discharging the Commission given to him by the late Assembly at St. Andrews for repairing to the Kings Majesty and Parliament of England, &c.

Committee appointed to meet with the English Commissioners.

Power of Collectory to Master Robert Dalgliesh, of the annuity of 500. lib, Sterling granted by his Majesty to the Kirk.

Approbation of the Lord Marquesse of Argyle his apprehending Ronald Mackronald Priest.

Approbation of the Laird of Birtenboge, for apprehending John Robeson Priest.

Renounciation of the unlawful Band, conforme to the ordinance of the Assembly at Edinburgh, 1641.

Recommendation anent the captives in Argiers.

Approbation of Master Alexander Henderson his Faithful and wise carriage in discharging of the Commissions given to him by the Commissioners of the late Assembly, forgoing to his Majestie, &c.

Report of the Committee appointed to meet with the English Commissioners.

Report of the Committee appointed for trying the Presbytery of Auchterarder, the Assemblies approbation, admonition and publick rebuke of the several brethren of that Presbytery respectivè according to their behaviours. An Suspension of Master John Graham, With the ordinance for debarring the Ministers who are Commissioners of that Presbyterie from this Assembly.

Recommendation to the Synod of Perth for reconciling the differences amongst the brethren of that Presbytery.

Publick rebuke of Master Henry Futhie.

Recommendation of the desire of Sir John Crawford of Kilburnie Knight, to the Presbytery of Dumbartan.

Anent Doctour Howies papers.

Act anent the desire of the Letters sent from the Minister of the Scottish Kirk at Camphire.

Recommendation to him, to urge the subscribing of the Covenant.

Deposition of Master Andrew Logie.

Erection of a presbytery at Biggar, with a suspension of entry thereunto.

Reference of the matter betwixt the Parishoners of Closburn &c. and the Presbyterie of Penpont, to the Synod of Drumfreis.

Reference of the Petition of Dunscoir to the Commiss. Parl. for Plantation of Kirks.

Recommendation anent the Kirk of Carwhit, to the Presbytery of St. Andrews.

Remitt. anent Trastat and Drungey, to the Synod of Drumfriess.

Act anent Roger Lindsay of Maine his Excommunication, with a Recommendation to the Convention of Estates Concerning him.

Recommendation to the Convention of Estates, anent Persons Excommunicate.

Commission for visitation of Orkney, Zetland, &c.

Act anent the Kirk of Stracathro.

Recommendation anent Erecting a Kirk at Seatoun.

Reference to the Commission to be appointed by this Assembly, for the publick affairs of this Kirk, for providing the University of Aberdene with a Professour of Divinity.

Reference to the said Commiss. for providing a Professour of Divinity to the University of St. Andrews.

Committee appointed to conferre with the English Commissioners upon the papers presented by them to the Assembly upon the 15. of August.

Committee to conferre also with the Committee of the Convention of Estates thereanent.

Ordinance that Master Alexander Henderson, Master David Calderwood, and Master David Dickson, make some draught and forme of the Publick Directory for Worship.

Act for proceeding with Ecclesiastick Censures against the Murtherers of William Crichtoun.

Commission appointed to sit at Air for the particulars concerning the Parochiners of Stainiskirk, &c.

Tryal of the Synod Books.

Approbation of the Act of the last Assembly, concerning the power granted to Sir Archibald Johnstoun, Procurator for the Kirk, and Clerk to the Assembly.

Recommendation of the matter concerning a Collegue to the Minister of Drumfries, to the Commissioners of Parliament for Plantation of Kirks.

Recommendation to the Synod of Lewishsam to try the proceedings of the Presbytery of Peebles, in admission of Master John Hay to the Kirk of Peebles.

Reference of Master John Mackeinzie to the Commission of the General Assembly.

Act for proceeding against the Presbytery of Sky, for not keeping the Synod.

Recommendation to the Lord Marquess of Argyle, to move the ruling Elders in Argyle, to be more observant of Presbyteries and Synods.

Recommendation to the Lord Marquesse Argyle for planting Loquhaber.

Ordinance for supressing of Sub-Synods.

Ordinance for deleting an Act of the Synod of Murray.

Reference anent the order of Tryal of Synods, Presbyteries, and Kirks, with a recommendation for using the orders set down in the Assemblies 1638. and 1602. in the interim.

Commission for planting the Kirks of Edinburgh.

Remit to the Presbytery of St. Andrews, anent the Kirk of Largo.

Recommendation of Master James Fairlie, to the Commission of this Assembly.

Recommendation anent the Bill given in by William Janson Printer in Amsterdam.

Reference anent Master Robert Fleming to the Commission appointed to sit at Air.

Report and approbation of the proceedings of the Commission of visitation for the University of Glasgow.

Commission for Visitation of that Universitie.

Report of the Committee anent the distressed People in Ireland.

Recommendation to the Commissioners of the General Assembly, to sit at Edinburgh anent Expectants to go to Ireland.

Acts anent James Murray.

Recommendation of Master Robert Brown.

Commission to the Presbytery of Edinburgh, for his admission to the Earle of Irwines Regiment.

Report of the Committee anent the receiving and dispensing of his receipts of the annuitie of five hundred pounds sterling, &c. And approbation thereof.

Report of the Committee appointed to consider the References from the Commission of the late Assembly.

Act for Master Andrew Murray, Minister at Ebdie, his exercise of his calling of the Ministerie, and for rejecting honours, &c. Incompatible with that calling.

Recommendation of Master William Bennet Minister at Ancrum, to abstain from civil Courts and Meetings, &c.

Recommendation to the Commissioners of the Assembly for tryal if any Excommunicate Papists be in the Scottish Regiments in France, &c.

Recommendation of Master James Johnstoun.

Reference of Tillifrusbie to the Presbyterie of Edinburgh.

Recommendation anent Laird Gagies mortification.

Recommendation of Master Alexander Trotter.

Recommendation anent the dismembering some parts of the Paroch of Hadingtoun, to be a several Parochine.

INDEX OF THE ACTS OF THE ASSEMBLY HOLDEN AT EDINBURGH, 1644, NOT PRINTED.

Election of Master James Bonar Moderator. Sess. I.

Continuation of the decision in the question concerning the Commission from Crail, untill the appellation be discussed. Ib.

Appointment of Committees for Bills, Reports, &c, Sess. II.

A Letter from the Presbytery at the Armie concerning sending Ministers unto them. Ib.

A Letter from the Presbyterie in Ireland, Ib.

The Assemblies thankful resentment of the E. Louthians sufferings, Ib.

The desire of the Convention of Estates, to quicken the proceedings of the Assembly, and the Assemblies Resolutions thereinto. Sess. III.

Reference to the Commission to be appointed by the Assembly, for presenting Overtures, Acts, &c. to the Parliament. Ib.

Renovation of the Act of the preceeding Assembly, for planting the new Colledge of St. Andrews, Ib.

Ref. of Denmures Bill.

Ref. of Aytouns Bill.

Committee to consider some Overtures concerning Universities and Schooles. Sess. IV.

Commission granted to Mr. William Cockburn, & Mr. Hugh Mackel for the first 3. Moneths beginning the 1. of Aug. next; to Mr. George Dick, and Mr. John Dick, the next 3. Moneths, and to Mr. John Livingstoun, and Mrs. Thomas Wylie for the Last 3. Moneths, to repair to the North of Ireland, bearing the same power granted to the Persons appointed for that imployment by the preceeding Assembly. Ib.

Renovation of the Commission for sending Expectants to Ireland, Ib.

Recom. of Sir John Weemes of Bagie, his Bill. Ib.

Commission for visitation of Orkney, Zetland, Caithness, Sutherland and Rosse, to Masters William Falconer, and Murdo Mackeinzie, and Alexander Brodie of that Ilk.

Act for, M. George Halyburtouns going to the Army. Ib.

Report of the Lords of Exchequer their promise concerning payment of some of the arrears of the Annuitie of 500. Lib. Ib.

Act and Reference concerning Mr. James Wood, Ib.

Reference to the Commission of this Assembly concerning the Papers presented by my Lord Waristoun, which were directed to the Commissioners of the proceeding Assembly, Sess. V.

Ref. to the Commission for planting the New Colledge of Aberdeen. Ib.

Transportation of Mr. George Leslie to the Kirk of Leslie. Ib.

Act concerning the planting of the Kirk of Syres, Ib.

Ref. of the Countess of Kinnowles Bill to the Commission. Ib.

Act concerning Mr. Andrew Murray Minister at Ebdie, Ib.

Act and Ref. concerning the planting of the Kirk of Lamingtoun. Ib.

Ref. to the Commission of the Assembly concerning Overtures for Universities and Schooles, &c. Sess. VI.

Ref. to the said Commission for planting the Kirk of Aberdeen, Ib.

Indiction of a Fast, Ib.

Renovation of the appointment of the preceeding Assembly for framing a Directory for Worship, and for Tryal of Synods, Presbyteries, and Kirks, Ib.

Act for the Clerks subscribing the deliverance of the Committee of Bills for Charity to the distressed People of Ireland. Ib.

Ref. to the Commission for considering the formes and draughts of Commissions for Visitation of Universities. Ib.

Act recalling two Acts of Commission for Visitation of the University of S. Andrews. Ib.

Recom. to the said Commission concerning confirmation of Ministers Books in their Wives Testaments. Ib.

Recom. to the said Commission concerning Witches and Charmers. Ib.

Ref. to the Commission of Assembly of the desires and Overtures of Caithnes. Ib.

INDEX OF THE ACTS OF THIS ASSEMBLY HOLDEN AT EDINBURGH 1645. NOT PRINTED.

The Remonstrance sent to the Kings Majesty from the Commissioners of the preceding Assembly, concerning the Dyet and occasion of the meeting of this Assembly.

Election of Mr. Robert Douglas Moderator. Ib.

Report of Mr. Robert Baillie, and Mr. Geo. Gillespie, of the progress of the Treaty for Uniformity, Sess. 2.

Appointment of Committees for the Directory, and for Bills, Appeals, &c. Ib.

Ref. of the Petitions from Ireland to the Committee of Bills, Sess. 3.

Letter to Mr. James Martin for intimating the Deposition of Mr. William Barclay. Ib.

Acts appointing Mr. James Nasmith to attend the Lord Montgomeries Regiment; Mr. Arthur Granger, Lieutenant General Baillie his Regiment; and Mr. Thomas Wilkie to the Earl of Lothians Regiment. Ib.

Ref. of the Lord General's Letter to the Presbytery of Edinburgh. Ib.

Ref. of the Petition of Mr. James Hamilton's Wife to the Committee for the Directory. Ib.

Recommendation to the Parliament for Ministers losses, Sess. 4.

Committee concerning Bursars, Ib.

Committee to confer with the lord Ogilvie, Sess. 5.

Act ordaining the Presbytery of Hamiltoun to proceed against Mr. John Rae for refusing the Covenant. With an Ordinance for giving in to the Clerk the report of Mr. John Hamiltouns subscribing the Covenant, and of the Excommunication of D. Hamiltoun.

Act discharging the relaxation of Nash Gordoun, with a reference concerning the same to the Commissioners of this Assembly. Ibid.

Committee for examining the witnesses against Mr. John Robertson, and Mr. John Fife. Ib.

The Solemne League and Covenant of the three Kingdoms, (which is not here printed, because already printed by Ordinance of the Commission of Assembly 1643. and universally subscribed) with an Approbation of the Ordinances, and the diligence of the Commissioners of Assembly for receiving thereof, &c. Ib.

Committee concerning Col. Arcskines Regiment. Sess. 6.

Committee appointed to speak with Col. Munro, concerning Letters sent from the Officers of the Army of Ireland; Ib.

Committee for examining witnesses against Mr. James Oliphant. Ib.

Invitation of all who had scruples concerning the Directory, to address themselves to that Committee, with a reference to the said Committee concerning uniformity of practice of the Directory in this Kirk. Ib.

Committee to conferre with the young Laird of Drum. Ib.

Appointment of Mr. Hugh Henderson to Col. Stuarts Regiment. Sess. 7.

Committee for hearing Mr. James Wood, and the Commissioners from S. Andrews and Aberdene. Ib.

Recommendation of Barbara Meins Petition to the Parliament. Ib.

Recommendation to the Parliament concerning the Army in Ireland.

Invitation again of all that had scruples or doubts concerning the Directory, to address themselves to the Committee for resolution. Ib.

Recommendation to the Parliament of the Petition of the Hospital of Leith, Sess. 8.

Recommendation to the Parliament of the Petition of the Kirk Drummen. Ib.

Refer. of the Petition from the Northwest parts of Ireland to the Committee of Bills. Ib.

Recom. for a charitable supply to the people in and about Borrowstounness, visited with the plague. Ib.

Transportation of Mr. James Wood to S. Andrews. Ib.

Commission for Masters Alexander Blair Minister at Galstoun, Robert Hamiltoun Minister at Ballentrae, to go to Ireland for the first three Months, beginning the first day of July. Mr. Samuel Row Minister at Kirkmabrek, Mr. Alexander Levingstoun Minister at Carmichael for the next three Months, beginning the first day of October: and Mr. Henry Colwart Minister at Pasley, and Mr. Henry Semple Minister at Killcarne, beginning the first of January next. Sess. 9.

Act for Ministers to the Earl of Lanericks Regiment of Horse, Ib.

Sentence absolvitour of Mr. James Lichtoun. Ib.

Act for Ministers to the L. Balgonie and L. Kirkcudbrights Regiments. Ib.

Committee for Colon. Arcskines Regiment.

Committee for conferring with the Laird of Drums second Son, and their report. Sess. 10.

The Directory for publick Worship in the three Kingdoms. Ib.

Committee for presenting the Directory to the Parliament. Ib.

Act for planting the Kirk of Tarbes. Ib.

Committee appointed to assist the Petition given into the Parliament, for trying and executing some Witches. Sess. 11.

Committee appointed to visit young Drum. Ib.

Refer. to the Commission at Edinburgh, for planting the Kirk of Hamiltoun. Ib.

Exemption of Mr. Alexander Balnaves, from going to Kirkcudbrights Regiment. Ib.

Refer. to the Commission at Edinburgh, for planting the Kirk of Mauchline. Ib.

Committee appointed for considering the best means for planting the Kirk and new Colledge of Aberdene. Ib.

My Lord Angus, and the Laird of Lammingtouns submission to the Assembly, with the Assemblies determination, concerning the planting of the Kirk of Lammingtoun. Ib.

Recom. of Mr. Andrew Macghie to the Presbytery of Hadingtoun. Ib.

Recom. of Mr William Young to the Presbytery of Glasgow; Ib.

Recom. concerning the new Kirk of Carfarne to the Parliament. Ib.

Committee appointed to consider of the way for Printing Mr. Rob. Boyd of Trochrigs Works. Ib.

Ref. to the Commission at Edinburgh, for revising the Labours of a Brother, upon the continuation of the History of this Kirk, and thereafter to cause Print them with consent of the Author. Ib.

Approbation of the Report, concerning the injuries done to Mr. John Burne in London Derie, with a Recom. thereof to the Parliament, and a Letter to the Commissioners at London. Sess. 12.

Two Acts concerning James Murray. Ib.

Appointment of the Commissioners of Presbyteries, to give in a list of the Excommunicate persons within their bounds to the Clerk. Ib.

Committee for assisting the Petion. to the Parliament, for the necessities of the Army in Ireland. Ib.

Recom. of Mr. John Williamson to the Presbytery of St. Andrews. Ib.

Tryal of the Books of the Synods of Lothian, Dumfreit, Glasgow, Aberden, and Ross, which were only produced. Ib.

Admission of the Excuses for non production of the Books of Fife, Angus, and Perth. Ib.

Recom. of Sir James Hopes Petition to the Presbytery of Lanrick. Ib.

Recom. to the Parliament, concerning Suspensions against Ministers and Universities. Ib.

Recom. of Mr. Thomas Boyd to the Presbytery of Glasgow. Ib.

Recom. of Mr. John Bruce to the Parliament and Commission, for Plantation of Kirks. Ib.

Recom. of the Petition of the Synod of Galloway to the Parliament, concerning Tho. Mackee. Ib.

Recom. of the Petition of the Inhabitants of the Chanrie of Ross to the Parliament, and to the Commission for planting of Kirks. Ib.

Recom. of the Petition of Mr. Archbald Maccorquodill Student in S. Andrews, to D. Colvill Professor of Divinity there. Ib.

Recom. of the Petition of the Parochiners of Pasley to the Commis. of Parl. for planting of Kirks. Ib.

Recom. of Mr. Robert Torres to the Commission of Parliament, for Plantation of Kirks. Ib.

Recom. to the Parliament of the Petition of the Ministers upon the Borders, concerning the insolence of Moss Troopers. Ib.

Recom. of the Petition of the unprovided Ministers within the Provinces of Aberdene, Murray, and Ross to the Parliament, and Commission of Parliament for plantation of Kirks. Ib.

Recom. to the Parliament for changing the Fairs upon Mondays to some other day. Ib.

Ref. to the Presbytery of Lochmaben, for going on in the process against Mr. Geo. Bryde. With a Recom. to the E. Hartfell, to possess the Minister to the Kirk, and concerning Mr. Thomas Chambers Gleib. Ib.

Two Letters from the Commissioners at London. Sess. 13.

Act authorizing Mr. Alexander Henderson to assist the Commissioners of Parliament in the Treaty at Uxbridge, in matters concerning Religion. Ib.

Ref. of the Proposition concerning Excommunication to the Committee for the Directory. Ib.

Ref. of the Propositions concerning Government to the Committee for the Directory. Ib.

Deposition of Mr. George Halyburtoun. Ib.

Renovation of the Commission, for trying and censuring the Ryot at Stanikirk, Sess. 14.

Renovation of the Commission, for visiting the University of St. Andrews, Ib.

Renovation of the Commission, for visiting the University of Glasgow, Ib.

Indiction of a Fast. Ib.

Committee for presenting the Petition to the Parliament. Ib.

Act for a Minister to Preach to the Lord Uchiltrie in the Blackness.

Ordinance for Mr. James Campbell, his attending my Lord Coupers Regiment. Ib.

Invitation of any that had doubts concerning the Propositions of Government, &c. to come to the Committee for Resolution. Ib.

Ordinance for Mr. John Govans repairing to my Lord Kircudbrights Regiment. Ib.

Recom. to the Presbyteries of Linlithgow and Stirling, for a voluntar Contribution of Clothes to the Earl of Calenders Regiment. Ib.

Act for admitting Mr. James Livingstoun Minister to the Earl of Calenders Regiment. Ib.

Ordinance for Mr. John Hoomes attendance for the E. Lanricks Regiment of Foot. Ib.

Ref. to the Presbytery of Peebles, to consider Mr. Robert Scots Bill, and to appoint another of their number to Balgonies Regiment, in case his reasons be found good. Sess. 15.

Ref. Mr. Alexander Robertson to the Commission at Edinburgh, Ib.

Act concerning the admission of Mr. David Houstoun to the Kirk of Tyrie. Ib.

Deposition of Mr. John Grahame. Ib.

Recom. of the Petition concerning the Kirk of Logie Montrose to the Parliament, of their Commission for the plantation of Kirks. Ib.

Recom. of Mr. James Hamiltoun his relief to the Parliament. Sess. 16.

The Propositions of Government and Ordination. Ib.

Act concerning the Printing of Mr. Robert Boyds Commentar upon the Ephesians. Ib.

Act discharging the Printing or Reprinting of the said Commentary, and of the continuation of the History of the Kirk, and of Mr. David Dicksons short Explication of the Apostolical Epistles, without the consent of Mr. John Boyd, and of the Authors of the other works respectivè. With a Recommendation to the Parliament for their Authority to that effect. Ib.

Warrant for printing Mr. Robert Boyds Opuscula. Ib.

Recommendation of the Kirk of Calder to the Parliament. Ib.

Recommendation of the Petition of Mr. Alexander Trotter to the Commission of Parliament for plantation of Kirks. Ib.

Reference to the Commission at Edinburgh for petitioning the Parliament, That Commissions may be granted for Visitation of Hospitals in every Province. Ib.

Recommendation to the Synod of Aberdene, to crave account of the Laird of Drum his Bursers, and of any others in that Province. Ib.

Sentence absolvitour of Mr. James Oliphant, with a rebuke and admonition of the particulars proven. Ib.

Recommendation of Mr. John Weirs Wifes Bill to the Parliament. Ib.

Act giving Warrant to the Commissioners at London, to agree to the clause concerning Excommunication. Sess. 17.

Act concerning the Earl of Athols right of presenting to the Kirk of Blair in Athol. Ib.

Ref. to the said Commission, To present an Overture for restraining of printing without License. Ib.

Act appointing Mr. James Woods entry to S. Andrews To be the first Tuesday of June. Ib.

Ref. to the said Commission for presenting some Overtures to the Parliament for restraining the education of Youth in the Colledge of Doway, or any other corrupt Colledge. Ib.

Ref. of the Summonds against those that joyned with Montrose to the said Commission at Edinburgh, Ib.

Ref. to the said Commis. concerning Witches and Charmers, Ib.

Ref. to the said Commission, To revise the Paraphrase of the Psalms. Ib.

Ref. to the said Commis. concerning the transplanting of Mr. Jam. Nasmith. Ib.

Appointment of Mr. Robert Baillie, Mr. Geo. Gillespie, and the Lord Waristoun, To repair to England with all diligence. Ib.

Ref. of the Summonds against the Subscribers of the Declaration at Oxford to the said Commis. Ib.

Recom. of some distressed persons to the charity of Presbyteries and Synods.

INDEX OF THE ACTS OF THE GENERAL ASSEMBLY NOT PRINTED 1646.

Election of Mr. Robert Blair Moderator Sess. 1.

Committee for tryal of the Commissions questioned. Sess. 2.

Committee for References, Reports, and Appeals. Ib.

Committee for Bills and Overtures. Ib.

Committee for examining the proceeding of the Commissioners of the preceding Assembly. Ib.

Committee for revising the provincial Books. Ib.

Commission from Ireland for representing the condition of the Kirk there. Ib.

Letters from the Committee at Newcastle, the General, and the Commissioners at London. Ib.

Ref. concerning the printed Papers sent from the Commissioners at London to the Commis. Assem. Ib.

Thanks to Mr. David Calderwood, with a recommendation to him concerning the History of the Kirk. Ib.

Act concerning the charitable contribution for the distressed Brethren in Argyle. Ib.

Order for re-printing the Answer of the House of Lords to the City of Londons Remonstrance. Ib.

Ref. to the Commis. Assem. concerning absents from this Assembly. Sess. 3.

Report concerning the Kirks of Levingstoun and Slamanna approven. Ib.

Recom. sent by William Hume to the Earl of Wintoun, concerning the L. Semples education. Sess. 4.

Recom. to the province of Merss and Tivotdale, for abolishing Festival and Patron dayes in these bounds, and to report their diligence to the next Assembly. Ib.

Committee for the Querees from the Province of Merss. Ib.

Committee for the Petitions from Ireland. Ib.

Recom. for Mr. Alex. Case. Ib.

Committee to confer with Mr. James Kennedy. Ib.

Ref. to the Commis. Assem. for planting the South Kirk of Leith. Ib.

Recom. concerning the Spittle-Lands of Garvock to the Commission of Parliament for plantation of Kirks. Ib.

Act for the supply of Margaret Rind relict of Mr. Robert Lindsay Minister at Couper in Angus, murdered by the Rebels. Ib.

Ref. of the Petition from Doun and Antrim in Ireland, to the Commission of Assembly. Sess. 5.

Committee for the Petition of Robert Brysons relict. Ib.

Act for delating the Querees of Merss and Tiviotdale out of the Provincial Book. Ib.

Act concerning the Presb. of Kirkwall, and Mr. Ja. Morison their rebuke, with the reposition of the said Mr. James. Ib.

Report from the Earl of Wintoun, concerning the Lord Sempils education in Glasgow. Ib.

Letter from the Commissioners at London, with a Committee to consider the same. Sess. 6.

Ref. to that same Committee concerning Delinquents. Ib.

Concerning the relict of Mr. Rob. Lindsay. Ib.

Remit. concerning Michael Watson, Agnes Ritchie and Isabel Adam, to the Presbytery of Glasgow. Ib.

Rec. Ja. Bannerman to the Magistrate.

Recom. Mr. Robert Boyd for some supply to the Presbytery of Hamiltoun. Ib.

Ratif. of the Act made concerning the printing Mr. Boyd of Trochrigs Book, in favours of the Relick and Successors of Robert Bryson Printer. Ib.

Committee for the matter concerning the Kirk of Glenluce. Ib.

Recom. for Ministers to imploy their Talents in writing. Ib.

Act for Mr. John Hay at Peebles going to the Master of Testers Regiment. Sess.

7.

Recom. for conveening the Commission of Parl. for plantation of Kirks, and concerning the disorders in the Borders, to the Committee of Estates, Ib.

Recom. Glencorce, Tweedmore, Kailzie and Bath, to Commis. for planting Kirks. Ib.

Report of the answer of the Committee of Estates, to the particulars recommended to them. Ib.

Committee to consult upon the remedies of the disorders in the south borders. Ib.

Ordinance for Claude Hamiltouns relaxation. Ib.

Ref. Mr. Peter Inglis and his Tenents to the Commis. Assem. for publick affairs. Ib.

Refer. concerning idle and sturdy beggars, especially these called Gipsies, concerning concealers and destroyers of conception, adulterers, and incestuous persons to Commis. Assem. for presenting Overtures thereanent to Parliament. Ib.

Recom. of Arch. Douglas and Margaret Smith for charity. Ib.

Thanks to the E. of Bacleugh. Sess. 8.

Committee concerning the Earl of Seafort. Ib.

Recom. concerning the present election of the Magistrates and Counsel of Aberdeen to the Com. of Estates, Ib.

Ref. concerning the transportation of Mr. Rob Ker to Hadingtoun to the Presbytery and others adjoyned. Ib.

Ref. concerning the Kirk of Gordoun to the Commis. of Assem. Ib.

Warrant for examination of Mr. Ja. Daes as a witness in the matter concerning the Kirk of Gordoun. Ib.

Recom. Fothringhame Bigamist to the justice. Ib.

Commis. for visitation of the Universitie of St. Andrews. Sess. 9.

Commis. for visitation of the Universitie of Glasgow. Ib.

Commis. for visitation of the University of Aberdeene. Ib.

Committee for conference with Mr. James Kennedie excommunicate. Ib.

Recom. Mr. John Maccorne. Ib.

Ref. concerning Ministers to Ireland to the Commis. Assem. Ib.

Ref. concerning the Petitions of London-derry, Newtoun and Killeleauch, to the Commis. Assem. Ib.

Recom. of Mr. John Cunneson and Mr. Thomas Ireland. Ib.

Warrant for citing witnesses in the particulars of the Paper given in by Halyburton. Ib.

INDEX OF THE ACTS OF THE GENERAL ASSEMBLY HOLDEN AT EDINBURGH, 1647, NOT PRINTED.

Ref. to the Committee for Preaching, to appoint Ministers to the Army, with addition of others to that Committee, Ib.

Appointment of Mr. Robert Young for Lodevick Leslies Regiment. Sess. 6.

Committee for considering the dangers that are either from within or without this Kirk, and the best remedies for preventing the same, and to report. Ib.

Committee concerning John Wilkie and Master Tho. Ramsay, Ib.

Remitt. John Johnstouns desire of relaxation from Excommunication to the provincial of Drumfreis. Ib.

Committee for the vaking Stipends in Dunkeld, Ib.

Recom. Marjory Smith for charity, Ib.

Remitt. Mr. James Rosse a deposed Minister to Presbytery and Synod, Sess. 7.

Ref. Mr. James Nasmith to the Committee for appointing Ministers to the Army, Ib.

Committee for considering a Process in dependence before the Presbytery of Peebles, concerning a scandal upon the relick of umwhile Mark Hamiltoun, Ib.

Continuation of the Town of Edinburghs Bill for Mr. John Smith, till Saturday, Ib.

Advice and Ordinance for prosecuting the Process against Agnes Stewart, relick of Umwhile Mark Hamiltoun. Sess. 8.

Recom. of Mr. George Claghorne that he suffer no prejudice in his old Age, Ib.

Transportation of Mr. John Scot from Schottis to Glenluce, Sess. 9.

Act refusing Mr. Andrew Honymans transportation to Craill, Ib.

Transportation of Mr. James Hamiltoun from Dumfreis to Edinburgh, Ib.

Act concerning the planting of Eymonth Kirk upon the Submission of Earl Home and Wedderburne, Sess. 10.

Act concerning the tryal of Mr. William Home, Ib.

Transportation of Mr. John Smith from Bruntiland to Edinburgh, Ib.

Act for providing a Collegue to Mr. Thomas Wyllie. Ib.

Recom. Thom. Burnet to the Committee of Estates, Ib.

Recom. Mr. Martine Mackferson to the Committee of Estates, Ib.

Recom. Mr. Neill Mackinnan to the Committee of Estates. Ib.

Act concerning the Visitation of Kailzae and Lyne, Sess. 11.

Recom. Mr. John Houstouns Petition to the Commission for planting of Kirks, Ib.

Act for Excommunicating of William Forbes of Skelleier, his committing a late murther being sufficiently evidenced. Ib.

Transportation of Mr. Walter Comrie to Dunkeld. Ib.

Act for authorizing the Commissioners at London, to present the Declaration to the Parliament of England, City of London, and Synode of Divines, and to crave an answer to the Paper of the 25 December. Ib.

Act appointing some Brethren to present the Declaration for England to the Committee of Estates, and to crave their Lordships concurrance in the like desires. Ib.

Act continuing the Directions for Private and Family Worship, to be farther Considered and again read, with an Invitation to all that had any scruples to propone them to the Committee of dangers Ib.

Act for joyning the Committee for the Confession of Faith, to the Committee for dangers together to be one Committee, and their place of meeting to be the old Session-house, Ib.

Invitation of all that had any scruples or objections concerning any Article in the Confession, to propone the same to the Committee. Ib.

Report of the Committee touching the particulars in Mr. Gilberts Petition, with an appointment for drawing a Letter to those of the Scottish Nation in Poland, &c. Ib.

Appoint. for drawing a Letter to Lieutenant General David Lesly. Sess. 16.

Appoint. of Ministers for Ireland. Ib.

Letter to Major General Monro. Ib.

Continuation of the Directions for Worship, to be again read and considered upon Tuesday, and all invited to address themselves to the Committee who had doubts or objections. Ib.

Committee for thinking on Overtures for planting the Kirks in the Highlands, and advancing Piety and Learning there. Ib.

Recom. to the Ministers of Edinburgh for their assistance to Ministers before the Commission for planting of Kirks. Ib.

Committee to confer with the Lord Treasurer, concerning the Kings gift of Patronage of Lanerk, and to advise with the Committee for dangers upon the Kirks interest therein. Ib.

Recom. of the Petition of the Presbyteries of Deir, Ellon, and Turres, to the Commission for planting of Kirks, Ib.

Recom. Mr. Neil Mackinnan and Martin Mackferson, to be supported out of the vaking Stipends in the Sky, Ib.

Ref. to the Commission for publick affairs for the planting of Drumfreis. with a recommendation to the Treasurer for a presentation. Ib.

Recom. to the Commission of Estates, concerning the house of Dalgetie, Ib.

Act appointing Mr. Gabriel Maxwell for the Lieutenant General, Mr. James Nasmith for General Major Holburns Regiment, Mr George Pittillo for the General Artilleries Regiment. Mr. George Bonnet for the Troups of Horse with the General

Ref. to the Ministers of Edinburgh, to take course with the Monuments of Idolatry brought from the North, Ib.

Recom. of the petition for a Minister to Chanrie of Rosse to the Commis. for planting or Kirks, Ib.

Recom. Mr. Alexander Petrie, Ib.

Recom. Mr. Eleazar Gilbert, Ib.

Recom. Mr. William Douglas to the Committee of Estates, Ib.

Recom. Mr. George Sharpe to the Committee of Estates for reparation of his losses, Ib.

Ref. complyers in Murray to the Provincial, Ib.

Recom. to the Commission for planting of Kirks, concerning provisions to Ministers in the Presbytery of Kirkendbright, Sess. 25.

Act appointing conference with Earl Abercorne, until the last of March, Ib.

Recom. to the Synod of Murray of the petition of Badinoch, concerning Mr. John Dollar, Ib.

Recom. concerning the Minister of Corrie and Hutton, Ib.

Recom. to the Commission for planting of Kirks, concerning the adjoyning some lands to the Parish of Monswall. Ib.

Act for Printing the Directory for Church Government, to be examined by Presbyteries against the next Assembly, and for Printing the Catechism also when it shall be perfected, Ib.

Act concerning the contribution for the distressed people in Argyle, Ib.

Recom. to Committee for dangers, to consider of a Letter for the Scots in Poland, &c. Ib.

Ref. to the Committee appointed for tryal of proceedings of the Commission of Assembly, to consider of the process of Master John Rosse, and to report, Ib.

Act concerning the tryal of the payment of the contribution for distressed people of Argyle, Ib.

Act concerning Ja. Murray Sess. 26.

Act for collecting the contribution for the Province of Argyle, in these parts that have not yet contributed, and sending it to the receivers. Ib.

Recom. to the Synod of Glasgow, concerning a second Minister to Dumbarton, Ib.

Recom. to the Lords of Privy Council for punishing an injury done to a Presbytery about burying in a Kirk. Ib.

Act appointing a conference with some Divines, Lawyers, and Physitians, concerning witchcraft and charming, Ib.

Report of the tryal of the Synods Books with the Assemblies censure, Ib.

INDEX OF THE UNPRINTED ACTS OF THE GENERAL ASSEMBLY HELD AT EDINBURGH. 1648.

Paper from the Committee of Estates of the 24 July. Sess. 13.

Ref. of the said paper to the Committee for publick business to consider of an answer, and report their opinions, Ib.

Act concerning Patrick Lesly, Ib.

Appointment of a letter to Mr. Hew Henderson for setling in Dumfries according to the sentence of transportation, Ib.

Ref. for planting a Collegue in Air to the Commission for publick affairs, Ib.

Ref. of the remedies of the sins of the times to the Committee which was appointed for trial of the Commission of the preceeding Assembly, Ib.

Ref. Mr. Walter Comries transportation to the Committee of bills, and they to report, Ib.

Appointment that all bills, appeals, references, reports, &c. be given in before Wednesday next, Ib.

Paper from the Committee concerning Patrick Lesly, Sess. 14.

The Assemblies answer thereunto, Ib.

Ref. Patrick Lesly to a Committee for conference, Ib.

Suspens. Mr Harie Cockburn, Sess. 15.

Vote sustaining the summons concerning the transportation of Mr. John Levingstoun to Ancrum, Ib.

Recom. Mr. John Durie to the Earl of Hadingtoun, Sess. 16.

Ref. Mr. Samuel Douglas to the visitation of Dunse and Chirnside, Ib.

Ref. the dissent of the Brethren in the Provincial of Merse and Tiviotdale to the said visitation, Ib.

Ref. concerning Ministers to Ireland to the Commission to be appointed for publick affairs, Ib.

Advice concerning discipline to be used, with the Garisons and Regiments in Ireland, Ib.

Letter to General Major Monro, Ib.

Ref. for planting the Kirk of Bruntiland to the Commission to be appointed for publick affairs, Sess. 17.

Recom. concerning James Murrayes children, Ib.

Recom. to the Commission of Parliament for planting of Kirks the adjoyning Sutherland, Sutherlandhall, &c. to Lindean and making it a distinct Parish, Ib.

Recom. for keeping in the interim the Kirk of Galowsheils, Ib.

Recom. in favours of Mr. James Morison Minister at Erne and Randell, or his executors for the payment of a sum of money by the next Intrant, Ib.

Recom. for planting Kirks in Badinach to the Commission for planting of Kirks, Ib.

Recom. to the Commission for publick affairs to think upon and prosecute some wayes for planting a Ministry in Lochaber. Ib.

Recom. to Presbyteries to send a more particular information of the insolencies and miscarriages of the souldiers and the evidences thereof to the Commission for publick affairs, Ib.

Ref. to the Commit. of Bills to distribute the petitions for charity.

Recom. Mr. Robert Lindsayes relick and Children, Sess. 18.

Recom. Mr. Patrick Lindsayes children, Ib.

Paper from the Committee of Estates of the 28 of July, Ib.

Recom. to Presbyteries to supply the places of the Brethren sent in Commission to the General Assembly, or that attend the meetings of the Commission of the Assembly, Sess. 19.

Act for conference with E of Abercorne until first of March, Sess. 20.

Committee for considering the Hospitals, and to report their condition, Ib.

Commission for visiting, Rosse, Sutherland, Cathnes, Orknay, and Zetland, with a Reference concerning Mr. James Johnston, Ib.

Commission for visitation of Stirling, and Dunblane Presbyteries, with a Reference for the particular concerning Mr. Andrew Jaffray, Ib.

Ref. to the Commission for publick affairs for the trial of the Provincial Book of Argyle. Ib.

Act appointing the Clerk to print the Declaration with the first conveniency, and to send it to Presbyteries, Sess. 22.

Vote for removing the Commissioners in the Province of Galloway in the matter concerning Mr. John Levingstons transportation to Ancrum, Ib.

Declaration in favours of the Presbytery of Jedburgh, for preserving their right and Interest in planting Ancrum proprio Jure, Ib.

Transportation of Mr. John Leviston to Ancrum, Ib.

Order for some Brethrens presenting the Declaration to the Committee of Estates, Sess. 23.

Ref. to the Committee appointed for publick matters to consider of the materials and draught of a Petition to the Committee of Estates, Ib.

Ref. for planting Kirkcaldie to the Commission for publick affairs, Sess. 24.

Approbation of the manner and order of the calling and setling a Collegue in the Kirk of Culrosse, Ib.

Committee concerning Mr. James Row, Ib.

Committee for examining Witnesses upon the injury done to Mr. Robert Melvill, Ib.

Committee for examining a scandalous Pamphlet fastly put forth under the

INDEX OF THE UNPRINTED ACTS OF THE ASSEM-

BLY. 1649.

Election of Mr. Robert Douglas Moderator, Sess. 1.

Act concerning the Commission from Ireland, Ibid.

Committee for Refers and Appeals, Sess. 2.

Committee for Bills and Overtures, Ibid.

Committee for publick business, Ib.

Committee for tryall of the Synod Books, Ib.

Committee for the tryall of the proceedings of the Commissioners of the Generall Assembly, Ib.

Renovation of the Commission for visiting the University of Saint Andrews. Ib.

Recom. Gedeon Morise to the Committee of Estates. Ib.

Order for speaking the Earle of Abercorne for payment of the begone stipends of Kilpatrick, Ib.

Recom. business of Ireland to the Committee for publick business, Sess. 3.

Continuation of Generall Major Midleton to the 9 of July, Ib.

Committee for the Psalmes, Ib.

Ref. of the Protestation of Mr. James Morison to the Committee of Refers, Ib.

Act Concerning the papers comitted by the Parliament for correspondence, Sess. 4.

Continuation of particular References from the Commission of the General Assembly until the report thereof be brought in from the Committee of Refers, Ib.

Committee for considering the Earle of Egligtouns Bill concerning Mr. James Ferguson, Ib.

Comittee for conference with the Committee of dispatches, Ib.

Committee for conference with Mr. Walter Comrie to satisfie him in his transportation to Inneraray, Ib.

Continuation of the Lord Ogilvy to the 17 of that instant, Sess. 5.

Continuation of G. M. Midleton untill fryday next, Ib.

Letter to the Brethren of the Presbytrie of Carrickfergus, Ib.

Continuation of the Commission for visitation of the University of Glasgow, Ib.

Ratification of the act of the Presbytery of St. Andrews concerning the agreement betwixt the Laird of Anstruther and the Parochiners, Ib.

Act recommending to the Brethren to make out the descriptions of these parts of the Kingdom not yet described. Ib.

Remitt. Elizabeth Armestrange to the Province of Drumfries, Ib.

Ref. to the Commission for publick affaires concerning the providing a Collegue to the Minister of Air, Ses. 14.

Order for citing the witnesses in the matter of Mr. Thomas Ramsay elder, Ib.

Reposition of Mr. William Cowper to the office of Schoolmaster in Channerie, Ses. 15.

Approbation of the Deposition of Mr. James Lundie, Ib.

Act and Ref. concerning Mr. Walter Swinton, Ib.

Ref. Concerning Mr. Patrick Smith, and approbation of his suspension, Ib.

Act and Ref. concerning Mr. John Home for the farther tryall, Ib.

Approbation of the suspension concerning Mr. Ja. Edgar and Ref. concerning him, Ib.

Deposition of Mr. Andro Rollock, Ib.

Ref. Mr. William Sinclair to the visitation of Dunse, Ib.

Ref. concerning M. William Home, Ib.

Approbation of the diligence of the visiters of Dunse and Chirneside, Ib.

Committee to meet with the committee of Parliament for considering and revising the proceedings of the visitation of Saint Andrews, Ib.

Continuation of the business concerning Mr. James Durhames transportation till the morne, Ses. 16.

Recom. for incarcerating one delated for witchcraft, Sess. 17.

Committee for conference with the Lord Ogilby, Ib.

Recom. officers come from Ireland, Ib.

Committee for conference with the Earle of Galloway, Ib.

Recom. Helen Gordoun to the Parliament, Ib.

Answer to the Petition given in for the Earles of Damfermling and Lauderdalie. Ib.

Recom. of the Relick of umquhile Dr. Sharpe to the Parliament, Ib.

Ref. Mr. John Logie to the Synod, Ses. 18.

Committee for presenting overtures and desires to the Parliament, concerning the Moss troopers, Ib.

Committee for considering Mr. Alexander Smiths condition, Ib.

Ref. Liev. Col. Ker to his Presbyterie, Ib.

Ref. concerning Pitfoddells younger, Urquhart of Old Craig and Thomas Menzies to the visitation of Angus and Merns, Ib.

Ref. Sir John Weyme of Bogie to his Presbyterie, Ib.

Ref. Sir John Makenzie and Lieutenant Collonel David Weymes to their Presbyterie, Ib.

affaires, Ib.

Ref. and Recom. Mr. William Chalmers to the Synod of Aberdeen, concerning the supply of his necessities, Ib.

Declaration concerning the Act granted in favours of Mr. Richard Maitlands wife, Ib.

Ref. of the petition of the Earle of Sutherland in the name of the Presbyterie of Sutherland, Ib.

Recom. Mr. John Keyth to the Parliament, Ib.

Recom. for dividing the paroch of Ferne to the Commission for planting of Kirks, Ib.

Recom. the disjoyning of the lands of over and nether Dysert from Brichen to the Comission for planting of Kirks, Ib.

Causes of a publick fast, Ib.

Commission for considering the obstructions of pietie and the remedies for removing thereof, &c to report to the next Assembly, Ib.

Recom. to the parliament for punishing counterfeit Testimonials, Ib.

FINIS.

Lector House believes that a society develops through a two-fold approach of continuous learning and adaptation, which is derived from the study of classic literary works spread across the historic timeline of literature records. Therefore, we aim at reviving, repairing and redeveloping all those inaccessible or damaged but historically as well as culturally important literature across subjects so that the future generations may have an opportunity to study and learn from past works to embark upon a journey of creating a better future.

This book is a result of an effort made by Lector House towards making a contribution to the preservation and repair of original ancient works which might hold historical significance to the approach of continuous learning across subjects.

HAPPY READING & LEARNING!

LECTOR HOUSE LLP
E-MAIL: lectorpublishing@gmail.com